THE PRACTICE OF
CHINESE BUDDHISM

The East Asian Research Center at Harvard
University administers research projects
designed to further scholarly understanding
of China, Korea, Japan, and adjacent areas.

HOLMES WELCH

THE PRACTICE
OF CHINESE
BUDDHISM
1900-1950

HARVARD UNIVERSITY PRESS

CAMBRIDGE · MASSACHUSETTS

Distributed in Great Britain by Oxford University Press, London

Preparation of this volume has been aided by a grant from the Ford Foundation

Library of Congress Catalog Card Number 67-13256

SBN 674-69701-4

Printed in the United States of America

Preface

This book was begun in 1961. It was to cover Buddhism in Republican and Communist China, and it was to be finished in one year. Instead five years have passed and Communist China awaits not a second but a third volume.

Once I began work, it became clear that I had undertaken too much. Grateful for the patience of my sponsors, I felt an increasing urgency to finish the job. Therefore I decided that I would limit my scope and follow a certain order of priorities in collecting information.

First, in the present volume, which deals with Buddhist practice, I would avoid as far as possible any discussion of doctrine; and in the next volume, recounting the history of the Buddhist revival, I would avoid intellectual history and focus instead on events.

Second, I would avoid the details of ritual, liturgy, iconography, and architecture.

Third, I would avoid the historical development of any of the practices I described, since this was something that could be more efficiently investigated by professional Buddhologists.

Fourth, I would exclude altogether nuns and nunneries, which could be more effectively studied by a woman.

Fifth, I would also exclude the practice of Lamaism, either in Tibet and Mongolia or in China proper.

Sixth, I would deal only incidentally with Buddhism in Hong Kong, Taiwan, and among overseas Chinese.

In collecting material I was faced with the inadequacy of documentary sources, which simply did not offer full or precise information about the life of monks or the monastic system as actually followed in this century. The few published biographies of modern monks and recent monastic histories tended to be hagiographic and formalistic. The fullest information, perhaps, was to be found in monastic "codes of rules" (*kuei-yüeh*), which were like operation manuals, stuffed with details, but which had two drawbacks. First, they were written for those who were already familiar with the system, so that many of the terms used and practices referred to were not explained and could not be found even in the largest Buddhist dictionary. Second, they represented the way things were supposed to be done, not the way they were necessarily done in practice. I shall have more to say about this difference in a moment.

Oral sources, on the other hand, proved fruitful, though not always reliable. Soon after I set to work, I found that in Hong Kong, Taiwan, Singapore, Malaya, Burma, Thailand, and the Philippines there were refugee monks who had come from almost all parts of China and had held responsible positions in large monasteries there. Over a hundred were ready to tell me about Buddhism as they had practiced it themselves. Particularly with regard to the more elderly, it seemed to me that their testimony, if not collected, would soon become uncollectable; and as the years have passed and many of them have died, this has proved to be the case.

Perhaps half a dozen proved wholly reliable. They had long experience, good memory, and if they did not know the answer to a question, they said so. The others to a greater or lesser degree had the usual failings found in the witness box. Commonest, perhaps, was confusion. They were accustomed to answering questions about Buddhist doctrine but not about the monastic system. Although all their lives they may have been doing what I was asking them about, they had never given it much thought so that in formulating their answers they would often grope and contradict themselves. Some informants found it embarrassing to admit what they had forgotten or never knew, and they would guess at an answer or invent one. Others turned out to be compulsive exaggerators. Others had an axe to grind: their hearts were still in the factional struggles of the nineteen twenties and thirties.

These failings became clear as I asked the same questions about the same institutions of different people who had been connected with them. Correlation and cross checking were of the essence. Most of the oral information I have used comes from at least two informants independently, sometimes from four or five; or it is corroborated by a documentary source. If it comes from only one informant with no corroboration, this fact is flagged by the use of the singular—for example, "according to this monk . . ."—unless the information fits so perfectly with what is already known that I see no need to qualify it.

Ideally I would have posed every one of several thousand questions to every one of my hundred-odd informants. Time obviously made this impossible. I found the interview process to be time-consuming beyond belief. A single one-hour interview took ten to twenty hours to transcribe. This was partly because of the difficulty of Chinese patois and partly because of self-contradictions and anacolouthons. Most of my informants came from northern Kiangsu, Chekiang, and Hunan, where Mandarin is spoken with such a strong accent that many Chinese from other areas can only partly understand it. I had to take various precautions to see that I was accurate in recording what had been said, getting the help of Chinese friends where necessary.

As it finally turned out, about a third of the data that went into this book came solely from interviews; about a third came solely from documents; and the remainder from a consensus of both. Oral sources are seldom identified, since this was the condition on which they could be employed. Documentary sources are identified in footnotes, except where I placed more reliance on oral sources of the same information.

In documentary research I avoided Chinese materials that were of secondary value. The division of labor between Chinese and Western specialists on China is probably most efficient if each side mines the low-grade ore in its own language. In Western languages I have made an effort to read everything that might cast light. Often when I have encountered a question that could only be settled by further reading or more interviews, I have not taken the time unless the additional work promised to be brief and seemed essential to the topic. Otherwise I have left it to the future or to others. The alternative was to delay impracticably the completion of the book. I have remained very much aware of this "homework" left undone and have tried to draw attention to it in footnotes.

More and more interest is being shown these days in "oral history," of which this book is partly an example. It may not be amiss here in the Preface to share some personal impressions as to its usefulness and acceptability. After five years' work, it seems to me that to use interviews without documents involves the risk of faulty communication and errors of memory, especially when it comes to dates, names, numerals, and orthography. Because of the defects inherent in oral testimony (self-contradictions, anacolouthons, mispronunciations, and so on) it is possible—particularly if one depends on a single informant—to end up with the facts ludicrously garbled. On the other hand, dependence on documents without interviews involves the risk of finding out only how things should have been or had formerly been, rather than the way they actually were. I have sometimes been asked why I did not get my informants simply to write out the answers to my questions. I tried it, of course. Most of them were reluctant to do so. Those who were willing to do so gave little more than the bare events. The reader can see a good example in the Venerable T'aits'ang's autobiography at the end of Chapter X. Older Chinese writers tend to blur the facts with elegance of style and to idealize to a point that can be altogether misleading. For example, along with his autobiography, the Venerable T'ai-ts'ang provided me with a description of his monastery which, he said, stood in the midstream of the Yangtze River. Because so many boats were crossing to and fro, it could be easily reached by pilgrims. I seemed to recall that other informants had spoken of reaching it on foot; but how could I doubt the word of the abbot, who had lived there for thirty years? Yet when I rechecked, I found that other informants had indeed walked on dry land right up to the monastery's front gate. I asked for an explanation in my next letter. The abbot replied with some asperity that the river had silted up about 1870 and that during his residence there and for about fifty years earlier the monastery was accessible by road. But before then it had been in midstream just as he had said. "These are facts. I did not give you empty talk," he ended.

I have encountered many examples of this difference between ideal and reality, past and present, theory and practice (a difference that has suggested the title for this book). Tonsure, for the sake of the written record, could be considered to have taken place in Shantung, whereas actually it had taken place in Peking. The master could be one monk on the written record but another monk in fact. Congee could be called "tea." I have become exceedingly wary of accepting anything as fact unless it has been exposed to the give and take of interviews. Many of the most interesting facts, I have found, must be caught on the wing as they fly from the lips of the informant in surprise. It is not a method that appeals to everyone.

I remember being complimented by a university professor in Taiwan. "It is wonderful," he said, "that you go and ask the monks what they do. It shows great modesty." On another occasion I was puzzled by the meaning of certain technical terms. I found that the dictionary definition was at variance with the usage of my informants. I sought the advice of an eminent Chinese scholar. He recommended that I pay no attention to my informants. "Monks are ignorant," he said, "I don't believe people, I believe books." A few months later a Japanese Buddhologist, when I told him that much of my material was oral, shook his head sadly and said: "I am afraid that what you write may not be believed."

These anecdotes illustrate the problem of acceptability in a field where so little oral information has been gathered. Even if specialists concede its value, there is the problem of verification. When I claim to have been given facts that appear to be known only to an informant who has since died or who wishes to remain anonymous, I put myself in a sense beyond criticism. No one can disprove my claims, even when they contradict the established authorities in the field, as they often do. This puts me in a very odd position, and it is the reason I have taken such care in the transcription of interviews and kept such complete records—records which I am ready to show to those who have reason to see them.

Because so much of this book is the product of personal investigation, it has proved expedient to use the first person singular more often than is customary in academic writing, particularly where the alternative was an awkward phrase like "the present writer."

I owe a great debt to J. J. M. DeGroot, K. L. Reichelt, Lewis Hodous, W. E. Soothill, J. B. Pratt, John Blofeld, Kenneth Ch'en, Arthur Wright, and many other writers. Most of all I am indebted to Johannes Prip-Møller, who opened many of the trails that I have followed. His magnificent *Chinese Buddhist Monasteries* is the one book I would recommend to the reader almost without reservation.

During the first three years of research and writing I was generously supported by grants from the Joint Committee on Contemporary China, for which I here express my gratitude.

For assistance in the actual collection of material I am indebted to the following persons: Shui Chien T'ung, Ho P'eng, Matsumoto Shigeru, Wang Yeh-chien, Horst Pommerening, Mrs. John Quirk, and Mrs. Daisy Tao. For other kinds of help, particularly for suggestions and corrections, I am indebted to Zunvair Yue, Masatoshi Nagatomi, Dwight Perkins, L. Bianco, and Mr. and Mrs. S. C. Chiu. Mrs. Chiu (Ida Tong) typed much of the manuscript and assisted in other ways. Peter Muller compiled the glossary index.

The patron and foster father of this book is Professor John K. Fairbank, who urged me to apply for the grant from the Joint Committee on Contemporary China, and later a research position at Harvard, and who kept me moving onward with his encouragement and the best of advice. Although he has played no direct role in my work, I am also indebted to Professor F. W. Cleaves for the inspiration to try to make things—as he used to tell his classes—"crystal clear." If he had lived, I know that Professor Chang Hsin-pao would have helped me at many points, as he had before his death. Finally, I am indebted to my wife. She has acted not only as resident typist and editor, suggesting many improvements of substance and presentation, but has also been unfailingly willing to adjust her life and the lives of our children to the needs of the book.

HOLMES WELCH

Cambridge, Massachusetts
November 2, 1966

Acknowledgments

Permission has kindly been granted by Mrs. J. Prip-Møller to quote a number of passages from her late husband's book, *Chinese Buddhist Monasteries*, and to reproduce a number of photographs from his collection.

Permission has kindly been granted by Mr. John Blofeld to quote passages from his books *The Jewel in the Lotus* (London, 1948) and *The Wheel of Life* (London, 1959).

Permission has kindly been granted by Dr. D. Engel to reproduce photographs that he took in central China during the 1930's.

Contents

Contents

List of Illustrations

PART ONE

MONASTIC INSTITUTIONS

CHAPTER I

The People of the Monastery

C hinese Buddhism was above all a system of monastic life exemplifying a body of doctrine. What concerns us is the system. It was intended to create a model society that the whole world could copy. Thus it has the fascination of all utopias. The ideal is alluring, its realization is astonishing, and its failure is consoling.

What was particularly impressive about the Chinese monastic utopia was its size. It involved about half a million monks. Most of them fell so far short of the ideal that they could be said to exemplify its failure. They have earned a bad name that Chinese Buddhism does not deserve—nor do they really deserve it themselves in view of the needs of society. But what we shall consider in the first few chapters is the elite who, even in our day, approached the ideal.

The distinction between clerical elite and proletariat is based on statistical evidence. About 1930 there were, as just mentioned, approximately 500,000 monks in China living in about 100,000 temples.[1] Thus most temples were small, with an average of five monks each. These "small temples" or "hereditary temples" (*tzu-sun miao*),* as they were called, differed in operation and purpose from the "large

---

* Romanizations will follow each technical term both the first time it is used in the text and also in the glossary index, to which the reader may turn if, for example, he encounters "hereditary temple" hereafter and cannot recall its Chinese original.

public monasteries" (*shih-fang ts'ung-lin*), some of which had four or five hundred monks in permanent residence. Between the two there lay all gradations of size and character. The essential characteristic of the hereditary temple was private ownership. It belonged personally to a monk or group of monks, who operated it as they pleased. On the other hand, the public monastery was supposed to be the common property of the whole Buddhist sangha* and to be operated in accordance with a common monastic rule, even if it had only a dozen monks living on its premises. It housed the elite.

I have collected more or less detailed information on about one hundred large public monasteries with an average of about 130 monks apiece. I would assume that there were twice as many again on which I do not have such information, but that in these others the average number of resident monks was 50-75. If this assumption is correct, then China in the Republican period had about three hundred large public monasteries, with 20,000 to 25,000 monks, or less than 5 percent of the sangha.[2] As many as 95 percent were clerical proletariat living in hereditary temples. Needless to say, this division into elite and proletariat is oversimplified. A truer picture will take shape as we proceed.

It is stated in a monastic code of rules: "The more strictly the rules are applied, the more people there will be living in a monastery. The looser the rules, the fewer people."[3] This was partly because strictness attracted donations from the laity and partly because it would be impractical to have several hundred persons living together in disorder. Therefore this very small number of very large institutions served as exemplars for the whole Buddhist monastic system. We shall deal with them first, so that the reader may see the system at its best and most complicated; then it will be easier to describe the smaller and poorer variants that were, in practice, far more common.

The two most exemplary of all Chinese Buddhist monasteries were the Chiang-t'ien Ssu,[4] usually known as Chin Shan,** at Chen-chiang[5]

---

* Buddhist monks and nuns as a body. Translations of this and other Sanskrit terms that are now commonly used in English writing on Buddhism (like dharma, karma) may be found in the glossary index.

** *Ssu* means monastery; *shan* means mountain or monastery. For further details, see note 4.

1. A large monastery in central China: Ch'i-hsia Shan, near Nanking. Along the central axis (right to left) are the hall of guardian kings, great shrine-hall, and dharma hall; with operating departments on the side.

on the Yangtze between Nanking and Shanghai; and the Kao-min Ssu across the river in Yangchow not far away. "Chin Shan and Kao-min" is the phrase that one constantly hears when monks from any part of China are talking about the way things ought to be done. It happens that Chin Shan is the monastery on which I have been able to collect the most data myself, while the Kao-min's code of rules, which deal with every aspect of monastic life there during the Republican period, was reprinted on Taiwan in 1960.[6] Every monastery, however, had its idiosyncrasies and so the system described below will be a composite of Chin Shan, the Kao-min Ssu, and other large monasteries in central China, particularly Pao-hua and Ch'i-hsia Shan (Nanking), Chiao Shan (Chen-chiang), the T'ien-ning Ssu (Changchow), and the T'ien-t'ung Ssu (Ningpo), all of which were operated much the same way.[7]

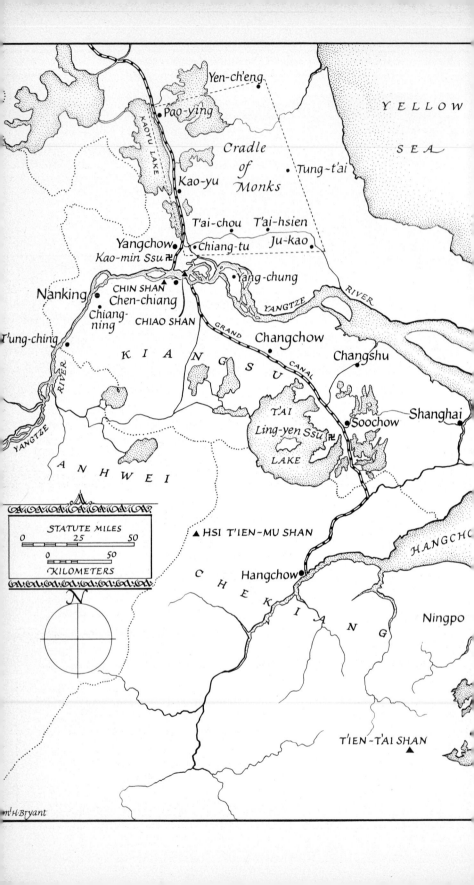

YELLOW

SEA

Yen-ch'eng

Pao-ying

KAOYU LAKE

Cradle
of
Monks

Kao-yu

Tung-t'ai

T'ai-chou   T'ai-hsien

Yangchow   Chiang-tu   Ju-kao

Kao-min Ssu

Yang-chung

Nanking

CHIN SHAN

Chen-chiang

RIVER

Chiang-
ning

CHIAO SHAN

YANGTZE

T'ung-ching

K   I   A   N   G   S   U

GRAND

CANAL

Changchow

Changshu

RIVER

YANGTZE

T'AI

Ling-yen Ssu

LAKE

Soochow

Shanghai

A   N   H   W   E   I

STATUTE MILES

0   25   50

0   50

KILOMETERS

N

▲ HSI T'IEN–MU SHAN

C   H   E   K   I   A   N   G

Hangchow

HANGCHO

Ningpo

T'IEN–T'AI SHAN   ▲

n' H·Bryant

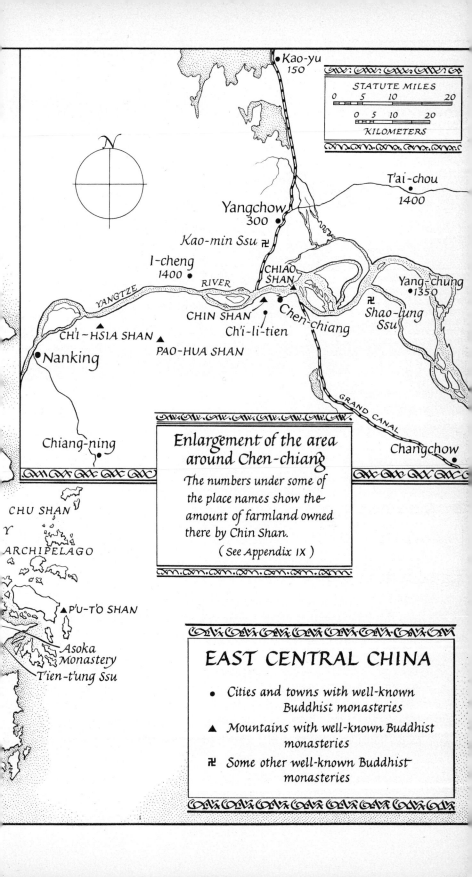

Kao-yu
150

STATUTE MILES
0   5   10   20

0 5   10   20
KILOMETERS

T'ai-chou
1400

N

Yangchow
300

Kao-min Ssu 卍

I-cheng
1400
YANGTZE   RIVER
CHIAO
SHAN
Yang-chung
1350

CHIN SHAN
Ch'i-li-tien
Chen-chiang
卍
Shao-lung
Ssu

CH'I-HSIA SHAN
PAO-HUA SHAN
Nanking

GRAND CANAL

Chiang-ning
Changchow

Enlargement of the area
around Chen-chiang
The numbers under some of
the place names show the
amount of farmland owned
there by Chin Shan.

(See Appendix IX)

CHU SHAN

ARCHIPELAGO

P'U-T'O SHAN

Asoka
Monastery
T'ien-t'ung Ssu

EAST CENTRAL CHINA

- • Cities and towns with well-known
  Buddhist monasteries
- ▲ Mountains with well-known Buddhist
  monasteries
- 卍 Some other well-known Buddhist
  monasteries

2. The great shrine-hall at Ch'i-hsia Shan was said to be large enough to hold a thousand persons. Over three hundred ordinands stand in front of it. This shows the scale of the buildings in Fig. 1.

THE FOUR DEPARTMENTS AND THEIR STAFFS

The center of such a monastery was usually its meditation hall. This was the flower which other departments served as stalk, leaves, and roots. The next chapter will be entirely devoted to it.

Whereas in the meditation hall one sought for enlightenment, the work of the three other departments was more prosaic. First, there was the guest department (*k'o-t'ang*), which was in charge of guests and of internal housekeeping. Second, there was the business office (*k'u-fang*), which collected the rents and bought the supplies that made housekeeping possible. Third, there was the sacristy (*i-po liao*), which served as the abbot's personal office and as such was often in charge of finances. In a large monastery with hundreds of resident monks, the four departments (*ssu-ta t'ang-k'ou*) were staffed by dozens of different officers. The personnel structure was almost as highly articulated as the central Chinese bureaucracy. Indeed, bureaucratic usage may have inspired certain monastic titles. The government had its *chih-fu, chih-chou,* and *chih-hsien* who "knew" (*chih*), that is, were in charge of the administrative divisions of *fu, chou,* and *hsien.*

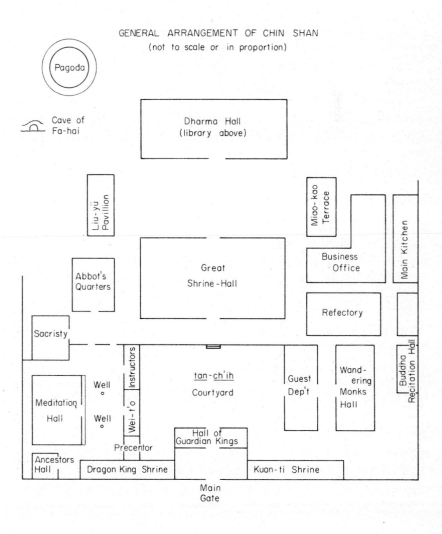

GENERAL ARRANGEMENT OF CHIN SHAN
(not to scale or in proportion)

Similarly, the monastery had its *chih-k'o* who was in charge of guests (*k'o*); its *chih-shan* who was in charge of the surrounding land on the mountain (*shan*); and its *chih-tsang* who theoretically assisted in the care of the sacred texts (*tsang*). Heaven and hell each had a bureaucracy that reflected the government of the empire: what could be more natural than for the monastery to have the same?

THE GUEST DEPARTMENT

People making their first visit to a monastery were received, to begin with, by the staff of the guest department. So be it with us. Let us attach ourselves to one of the guest prefects (*chih-k'o*)[8] and observe his work.

At a large monastery like Chin Shan he would be one of six or eight officers with the same title who served in daily rotation. If more work arose than the one on duty could handle, he would call for help from the next in order of rotation, often the next two or three, until each important party of guests had a prefect looking after it. There was also an order of precedence. The senior guest prefect (*ta chih-k'o*) had over-all responsibility. His assistants, known as the "second guest prefect" (*erh chih-k'o*), "third guest prefect" (*san chih-k'o*), and so on, worked under his instructions.

Their most obvious responsibility was to deal with guests. They dealt with the two main categories of guests—monks and laymen—in very different ways. Old China hands and those who have read their accounts of putting up at temples when traveling in the interior may be surprised to learn that laymen were not normally allowed to stay overnight at the model monasteries, which were very different from those in places of pilgrimage like Omei Shan. The latter fed and housed everyone—indeed, no other accommodations were available. But Chin Shan and like institutions offered lodging only to "special guests"—important donors or old friends or laymen who had ordered the performance of rites for the dead. Sightseers were welcome in the public part of the premises during the day and could be fed, perhaps, in the guest department, but they had to leave before evening. "Special guests," on the other hand, were given special attention—comfortable rooms, superior vegetarian food, and introductions to any resident scholar monks with whom they might wish to discuss Buddhist doctrine. In some monasteries their entertainment was the sole responsibility of a separate officer, the "visitors' prefect" (*chih-pin*).

Whereas among the laity only a privileged few could be put up at institutions like Chin Shan, any ordained monk could live there (*kua-tan*), free of charge, for as long as he liked. Indeed, no public monastery anywhere in China could refuse admission to a properly ordained monk in good standing. The problem was to determine whether he was such. Therefore when he came to apply for admission (*t'ao-tan*), the procedure was exactly prescribed. He left his bundle of effects (*i-tan*) on the right or left of the door of the guest department. If on the left, he stepped through the left side of the door left foot first, and sat on the bench against the right wall, from which he could keep an eye on his bundle while he waited; if on the right, then vice-versa. He was supposed to sit with his feet placed to form the Chinese character for "eight." If the guest prefect on duty was not in the room at the time, an usher (*chao-k'o*) would go and fetch him. As soon as he entered, the applicant would stand up, saluting with palms pressed together (*ho-chang*), and go over to prostrate himself three times before the buddha image[9] that stood at the back of the room, touching his head against the floor (*ting-li*) in the Buddhist equivalent of a kowtow. As he rose from the third prostration he would say: "A prostration to the guest prefect." Normally the latter would reply: "A bow will be enough" (*wen-hsün hao-le*). We might now reasonably expect to see the applicant bow to the guest prefect, but this is not the way it was done. With his back still turned to him, he would make a deep bow to the buddha image, or, if he had not been excused from it, he would prostrate himself before it for the fourth time.

Next he would return to his place on the bench for an oral examination. The guest prefect, sitting on the chair reserved for him just inside the door, would ask the applicant for his name, the name of the master who originally shaved his head, his place of ordination, his recent activities, and as many other questions as might be needed to remove any doubt that he was an ordained monk in good standing. If the guest prefect could not satisfy his doubts, either because the applicant's answers were inadequate or because the times were troubled and imposters common, he would ask to see his ordination certificate and

3. At the entrance to the guest department a wandering monk (right) answers the questions of the guest prefect. His bundle of effects can be seen outside the door. P'i-lu Ssu, Nanking.

possibly the bowl he had received from the monastery that ordained him. Usually, however, the guest prefect did *not* ask to see these items, nor did he either record the applicant's name or endorse his certificate.[10] He relied on personal appraisal and on the likelihood that an imposter would soon give himself away. This makes sense when we consider how easy it would be to go wrong on the details of etiquette —as easy as to go wrong passing oneself off as a Freemason at a Masonic lodge.[11] Because the ordination certificate was seldom examined, a visiting monk could preserve his incognito by giving a pseudonym. He might prefer to do this if he had come to have a rest after holding office in another monastery and feared that, as soon as his name was known, he would be urged to take office again. Although he could always refuse in such a case, it saved embarrassment not to be recognized at all. The use of a pseudonym was not considered dishonest. As we shall often see, the monastic vow against lying was elastically interpreted.

When the guest prefect finished his other questions, he would ask about the applicant's future plans. If the latter wished to spend only a night or two, he would say that he had come to "trouble the establishment" (*ta-jao ch'ang-chu*). If he hoped to stay for a longer period, he would say that he wished to "get on closer terms with the establishment" (*ch'in-chin ch'ang-chu*). In either case, provided his credentials were satisfactory, he had to be admitted (*liu-tan*). The guest prefect would give him as much of a lecture as he thought was necessary on the rules of the monastery or perhaps ask him to read the most pertinent of them. Finally he would escort him (*sung-tan*) to the accommodation that suited his status. If he was an eminent monk, he would be put in a superior guest room (*shang-k'o fang*). If he was a former officer or had some other connection with the monastery, he would be put up in a guest room (*k'o-tan*) that was superior but less deluxe. The great majority of visiting monks were escorted to the wandering monks hall (*yün-shui t'ang* or *shang-k'o t'ang*), which was a dormitory with a raised platform along the walls, on which many persons could sleep side by side.

There the new arrival would go through the same courtesies as in the guest department. He would leave his bundle outside, bow (or prostrate himself) before the buddha image as a salutation to the head of the wandering monks hall (*liao-yüan*), and finally escort the guest prefect to the door (*sung chih-k'o*) with palms pressed together. Courtesies completed, he was shown to an empty space on the sleeping platform in the east or west section of the dormitory, depending on his age (west for the older, east for the younger). There he was free to live as long as he liked, provided he complied with the rules. These required, among other things, that he attend morning and evening devotions every day, as well as all three meals in the refectory and three periods of meditation conducted by the head of the wandering monks hall. The layout was similar to that of the meditation hall proper, with an empty space in the center for circumambulation. The discipline, however, was not so strict.

Honored guests, lodged in their special quarters, were subject to none of these daily obligations. They had their meals served from the abbot's personal kitchen. Like lay visitors they were waited on by the ushers (*chao-k'o*), who performed all the menial tasks of the department: swept the floor and wiped the tables, carried baggage, served meals, and took care of the guest rooms. In some monasteries the ushers were monks; in others they were lay workmen, in which case they might be called "boys" (*ch'a-fang*).

We might wonder why the prospect of an easy life in the wandering monks hall, with adequate food and shelter, did not attract more monks than could be accommodated. But according to the abbot of Chin Shan the life there was not all that easy. The rules were so strict, in fact, that Chin Shan's wandering monks hall, which could hold more than a hundred persons, was seldom full. Here we see another correlation between the strictness of rules and material wealth. The richer the monastery was, the more necessary it became to discourage an excess of visitors. At the poorer monasteries they would be discouraged by magotty rice and leaking roofs. At the Kao-min Ssu they were discouraged by rules like the following:

> In the wandering monks hall of the T'ien-t'ung Ssu, speaking in a loud voice is not allowed, but one may whisper in a sheltered spot. Here, however [at the Kao-min Ssu], if two or three people seek out a quiet corner and talk in a low voice, they will immediately be expelled (*ts'ui-tan*). Visiting monks may not go outside the gates, nor intrude into the apartments of the monastery, nor wander about the [vegetable] garden or fields. Anyone detected will be severely punished and expelled. Daily devotions, meals, and chores are not to be missed, and those who break this rule even

once shall be immediately expelled. Personally drawn up by the head of the monastery, Lai-kuo, on the first of the ninth month, 1936.[12]

If these regulations were enforced (and according to an informant who served there three years, they were), one can understand why the Kao-min Ssu suffered no stampede of visitors from the more relaxed institutions that greatly outnumbered it. Few monasteries were so strict: most permitted visiting monks to leave the premises during the day with the approval of the head of the wandering monks hall so long as they returned in time for afternoon devotions. If the time ever came when there was no more space in the hall or not enough rice for additional visitors, a sign would be put up outside the guest department, reading "no vacancies" (chih-tan), but it was rare for this to happen.[13]

The wandering monks hall served two functions. It enabled a monk to travel up and down China at little expense, listening to eminent teachers wherever they might be found, and enrolling for meditation wherever it was best practiced. The monastery, for its part, had a "talent pool" within its walls that was being constantly renewed. A certain number of visiting monks who liked its atmosphere would decide to apply for office. At a few model monasteries like Chin Shan the prerequisite for office-holding was to enroll for at least one winter term in the meditation hall. At other monasteries this was not required: a visitor with enough talent and experience could take office directly.[14] But whether he was to take office directly or enroll for meditation, he normally had to wait until the beginning of the next semester, that is, the 16th of the first or seventh lunar month. Only then could he be given a permanent place; and only then was it obligatory to examine his ordination certificate and record his name in a personnel register (hao-pu) along with his age and other personal data. If he left the monastery and later returned, he would be looked up in the register and welcomed as a former resident. If, on the other hand, he had been expelled for violation of the rules, a note to that effect would be placed after his name, and he would forever afterward be refused admission.

There was no time limit on residence in the wandering monks hall.[15] No one could be forced to move into some other section, nor asked to leave the monastery unless he violated a rule. A few monks would continue living there for months or years. No further formalities were required. Semesters could come and go, but their names would never be entered in the register. Such an indefinite stay was called *kua hai-tan*. On the other hand, the great majority of monks were reluctant to eat a monastery's rice for month after month without taking part in its work. Some asked for a position. Others preferred to live up to their name—"cloud-water monks" (*yün-shui seng*)—which meant that they were as unattached as drifting clouds or running water. Particularly during the first part of their career, it was best to keep traveling, rubbing off superficialities with the hardships of the world. There was a saying that "if you have not traveled [to monasteries] in every quarter, you are like [the image of] a bodhisattva whose eyes have not been painted in." So, in fact, they stayed no more than a few days or a few weeks.

The right to stay in the wandering monks hall did not extend to "vagabonds" (*chiang-hu*) and "wild monks" (*yeh ho-shang*). These were disreputable types who may have once been properly ordained, but now lived by their wits—by fortune telling, for example, which was a prohibited livelihood—and broke many of their vows. If this included their dietary vows, they might be called "wine-and-meat monks" (*chiu-jou ho-shang*). They often appeared in Chinese novels and were conspicuous when they turned up in real life, so that they had a disproportionate effect on the popular picture of the sangha. This may be one reason why their admission was altogether forbidden by the Kao-min code of rules.[16] At some monasteries they were allowed to stay for a meal or, if they arrived late in the day, overnight. The guest prefect would size them up and say: "This establishment cannot let you stay for long. Please have a meal and then leave." The guest prefect also kept out lay beggars, who were usually refused even a meal. This may seem inconsistent with the Buddhist principle of compassion, but the latter was overridden by another principle, namely that the monks were supposed to be the receivers, not the givers of charity. Furthermore, as a practical matter, Chinese monasteries during the Republican period could not afford to start feeding and housing the beggars of China.

So much for guests. But guests were only one of the many responsibilities of the guest department. It was in charge of most of the tedious tasks of domestic housekeeping. It supervised the refectory,

4. A "wild monk" draws an audience. Central China.

the main kitchen, the vegetable garden, the grounds, the principal halls and shrine halls, the mill, the baths and latrines, and every other unit that lay outside the direct purview of the business office and sacristy. Some of these units had their own heads and operated more or less autonomously, but all came within the jurisdiction of the guest department, which therefore served as a kind of control center for the daily work of the monastery. Red wooden plaques, written up in washable ink by a secretary (*shu-chi*) and hung in the porch outside the departmental office, announced the scheduling of rites for the dead and who was to take part in them; lectures; chores; baths; festivals; personnel changes; and all other news that affected the life of the monks. Seeing to it that everything went off on schedule and that everyone attended who was required to was the responsibility of the proctor (*seng-chih*).

The proctor was one of the most important officers, not merely of the guest department but of the whole staff. He was empowered to enforce regulations throughout the premises, except in the meditation hall. He made sure that all the signals for activities were given on time. He watched over the refectory during meals to see that empty bowls were filled and that no one broke the silence. He patrolled the great shrine-hall during morning and afternoon devotions, and every procession of monks to and fro. If he saw someone walking out of line, he would shout at him. If he heard someone drawling the liturgy, he would come over and give him a blow on the cheek. On the other hand, when he encountered a more serious offender (guilty of quarreling, for instance), he would hale him before the guest prefect, who decided how large a fine he would have to pay or, as an alternative, how many blows he would receive with the incense board (*hsiang-pan*), a wooden, sword-shaped symbol of authority, wielded by the guest prefect himself.

The proctor also supervised bathing and the washing of clothes, which took place four times a month in the winter, but daily from the 1st of the sixth month to the 15th of the seventh and on any other days when he decided that it was necessitated by the hot weather. He was responsible for organizing manual labor or "chores" (*ch'u-p'o*). These were classified into four categories according to the number of monks required to participate. He would organize "chores for everyone" (*ch'u p'u-p'o*) with the abbot himself in charge when, for example, the rent grain had to be lugged back from the fields or unloaded from the monastery boats. If fewer hands were required, he would call on all units except the meditation hall. This might be for work like cutting brush or firewood on the slopes, tilling the vegetable garden, or helping the kitchen staff prepare a vegetarian feast. If still fewer hands were required, he would call on menial officers (*heng-tan*) and on the monks in the wandering monks hall. The most minor jobs he assigned to the latter alone.

The proctor had still other responsibilities. He oversaw the disposal of the dead and their property. He made sure that lamps were extinguished throughout the monastery when everyone went to bed at

5. View of the main kitchen at the Chao-ch'ing Ssu, Hangchow.

night and then again after dawn (since lamps were relit when the day's routine started at about 3:00 a.m.). He had to be everywhere and notice everything. One monk tells how he arrived at Chin Shan in 1937 and was admitted to the wandering monks hall. On his way to the refectory for his first meal he was spotted by the proctor who came over and told him that his silk gown and leather-soled shoes were contrary to the regulations (since animals had been killed to produce them). "You will either have to change into cotton or leave the monastery."

The largest of the units that came under the jurisdiction of the guest department was the main kitchen (*ta-liao*). It was often headed by a chef (*tien-tso*) under whom worked the monks in charge of food, water, and the fires.[17] The rice steward (*fan-t'ou*), for example, assisted by lay workmen, boiled rice and the various kinds of congee

6. The main cauldron for rice at the Chao-ch'ing Ssu, Hangchow. The sign above it reads: "Thousand monks cauldron; broadcast your seeds on the field of [future] happiness [by providing food for monks]."

7. The rice steward strikes the *huo-tien* (edge toward camera) to summon the monks to a meal. Pao-hua Shan.

in large cauldrons. Because he decided who was to receive the delicious deposits of crispy rice scraped from inside them, he was a popular person. He had other duties. About fifteen minutes before each meal was ready to serve, he gave the first of a series of "dinner calls," going from one department to the next and banging together two short split-bamboo sticks (*chiao-hsiang*). About five minutes before meal time he struck a series of blows on the huge wooden image of a fish that hung outside the refectory (*k'ai-pang*) and just before meal time either he or the vegetable steward struck another series on the *huo-tien,* a heart-shaped disc of bronze that hung near the fish. There was no excuse for being late to meals!

The work of the vegetable steward (*ts'ai-t'ou*) was to prepare the simple vegetarian dishes that were served with each meal and the more elaborate ones served on the first and fifteenth of the lunar month or when donated by a devout layman. The water steward

8. The tea steward has a bowl of rice as he watches the pot. Chao-ch'ing Ssu, Hangchow.

(*shui-t'ou*) provided cold water for the rest of the kitchen, while the tea steward (*ch'a-t'ou*) had to keep sufficient water on the boil to prepare tea as needed or to help out the rice steward if one of his cauldrons ran low. The stoker (*ta-huo*) was in charge of starting the fires, keeping them supplied with large quantities of firewood, and emptying the grates. Conflagration was a constant worry and his responsibility was a serious one.

In the refectory, meals were served by as many waiters (*hsing-t'ang*) as were necessary for the number of monks. They laid chopsticks and two bowls—one for rice or congee and one for a vegetable dish—before each monk's place on the long rows of narrow tables.[18] Following the signals on the wooden fish image and the *huo-tien* gong, they brought in the buckets of food and had the bowls filled by the time the monks had finished reciting grace. During the meal, under the proctor's supervision, they circulated through the refectory to give second helpings. After the meal was over, they washed up.

Closely associated with the kitchen was the mill, where the miller (*nien-t'ou*) assisted by lay workmen, hulled the monastery's grain and occasionally ground flour for dumplings. Not far off lay the vegetable garden, in charge of the head gardener (*yüan-t'ou*), usually with lay workmen doing most of the manual labor. Working either under the chef or sometimes under the direct control of the guest department was the sanitation steward (*ching-t'ou*), who took care of the latrines and of the bathing facilities. He had to keep the former clean, while in the latter he heated water for the weekly baths and tidied up after they were taken.

The main entrance gate had a gate-keeper (*men-t'ou*), while the woods and fields outside were looked after by a grounds prefect (*chih-shan*) and one or more grounds patrols (*hsün-shan*), whose duty it was to see that none of the vegetation was cut and removed by trespassers. Under their direction lay workmen brought firewood for the kitchen. If the grounds were extensive, there might be several such officers; in an urban monastery, none. For the buildings there was a night patrol (*yeh-hsün*), who struck the two series of signals that put the monastery to bed at night and awakened it in the morning, section by section, according to their duties. He was a different person from the night watchman (*k'an-keng, ta-keng*) who actually patrolled the monastery premises in the late hours, striking the watch.

9. The miller in the mill. Chiao Shan, Chen-chiang.

The last main category of personnel working under the guest department was composed of the officers who staffed the halls of worship. Every monastery, large or small, had a great shrine-hall (*ta-tien*), where morning and evening devotions and most of the major rites were held. There was also an ancestors hall (*tsu-t'ang*), where the soul tablets of former abbots were worshipped on the 1st and 15th of the lunar month; and separate installations for the tablets of other deserving monks and lay donors. There might be shrine-halls for one or more bodhisattvas as, for example, a Ti-tsang Tien where it was appropriate to perform masses for souls in hell, since Ti-tsang (Ksitigarbha) was the bodhisattva who had dedicated himself to their relief. There might be pagodas and pavilions, each with an altar, and there would be altars in the library (*tsang-ching lou*) and in the buddha recitation hall (*nien-fo t'ang*).

Every one of these altars was attended by a verger (*hsiang-teng*), whose duty it was to keep the oil lamps and the incense burning and to clean not only the images and vessels, but the entire room in which they stood. In the case of the great shrine-hall, there were two vergers, the senior holding the title of *tien-chu*. His office was an important one, not only because he cared for the place where most of the major rites were held, but also because so many lay worshippers (*hsiang-k'o*) came there to offer incense. Contact with them gave him an opportunity to make friends for the monastery and, in some cases, money for himself. For instance, he was allowed to pocket the fees paid by those who used the divination slips. He might also sell one worshipper the incense that another worshipper had left behind (rather than keeping it for the monastery's own use, as he was theoretically supposed to). Besides minor rites and housekeeping, he and his fellow verger often had the task of striking the great bell and drum which signalled the beginning and end of the day's work (after and before the signals of the night patrol). At about 3:45 a.m. a hundred and eight strokes were tolled on the bell; then the drum was sounded. In the evening at about 10:00 p.m. the order was reversed. At some monasteries there was a separate bellman (*chung-t'ou*) and a striker of the drum (*ku-t'ou*), who might live in the bell and drum towers that were more often found in north China than Kiangsu.

Still other duties devolved upon a verger depending on where he worked. If it was the wandering monks hall, for instance, he waited upon the monks who were staying there, brought them tea and hot water, basins to wash their clothing, and looked after personal effects in their absence. If it was the buddha recitation hall, he helped the head of it to care for its residents—mostly monks who felt too old or feeble for the rigors of meditation but who still wanted to take part in daily religious practice (see Chapter III).

All these many offices and activities came under the jurisdiction of the guest department, whose name, as the reader can see, is almost a misnomer. Where did it get the money and supplies for its housekeeping? That was the responsibility of the business office (*k'u-fang*).

THE BUSINESS OFFICE

The head of the business office was the prior (*chien-yüan*)[19] whose day-to-day authority in practical matters was second only to the abbot's. Under him worked several subpriors (*fu-ssu*) and under them, in turn, several clerks (*k'u-t'ou*), some of whom might have more specialized titles like "storekeeper" (*kuan-k'u*) and "work overseer" (*kuan-kung*). Down in each of the villages where the monastery had large holdings of farmland, there might be a village agent (*chuang-chu*). At all monasteries this chain of command was the same, but the function of offices varied. For example, clerks were always subordinate to subpriors, but whereas a subprior in one monastery might have control of the cash, in others it was controlled by the sacristy.

The village agent usually lived many miles from the monastery in a village whose tenants needed supervision. Although under the terms of their leases, they had to pay a fixed rental rather than a percentage of the crop,[20] nevertheless they often found it tempting to get the better of the landlord by adulterating their rent grain or by claiming that they were unable to deliver the specified quantity because of pests or drought or waterlogging. Therefore it was best to have a man on the spot who could keep the monastery informed about the real condition of the harvest. It was up to him to let the tenants know when they would be expected to deliver their rents. If the monastery loaned them agricultural equipment, he had to keep track of it, making sure that it was returned in good condition and repaired at the user's expense. If the monastery owned buildings in the village, their maintenance also came within his purview. Although his rank was not high, he was usually a responsible, older monk and he could exercise considerable power. If some tenant was a perennial troublemaker, the village agent could recommend a replacement to his superiors in the business office.[21]

When the harvest was in and the time came to deliver the grain rents, he was joined by subpriors and clerks who came down from the monastery with abacus and ledgers.[22] Grain was checked for moisture and adulteration, sunned and rewinnowed if these were found, and finally weighed and credited to each tenant's account in the ledger. The sacks were placed in a temporary storeroom that formed part of the village office (*chuang-fang*) in which the agent lived. They might be kept there for sale when prices reached a peak the following spring; or they might be shipped back to the monastery by boat or cart as soon as the collection of rents was over. If a village lay near enough so that the business office could exercise direct supervision or if the tenants of a distant village were loyal and dependable, the monastery might feel it unnecessary to station a village agent there, or it might entrust the work to a lay person who was usually called the "village foreman" (*chuang-t'ou*).[23]

Some tenants were anything but loyal and dependable. Even if they were in a position to pay their rent, they would refuse to do so. In that case the subpriors would go to the neighbors who had guaranteed the lease (all leases had guarantors) and ask them to reason with the tenants, and if that failed, the matter could always be taken to court. Or, since lawsuits led to ugly publicity, the subpriors might resort to more informal methods. The Kao-min Ssu, for example, instructed them to go to another neighborhood and hire two or three ruffians, who would hustle over to the house of the delinquent tenant and demand the rent, refusing to leave until it was paid. To underline the displeasure of the landlord, they would present a chit demanding immediately a small quantity of polished rice (as a penalty for being in arrears) and if this penalty were not paid, the ruffians would dismantle the tenant's front doors and tables and carry them away. But, as the code of rules reminds the subpriors, "this method is to be used only with people with whom no other method will work. For ruffians to carry off the front doors of those who are truly unable to pay up, would be detrimental to the conduct of the monastery officers, to the self-respect of the tenants, and to the mutual good feelings of the two sides."[24]

Between their trips down to the villages to collect the rents, the subpriors and clerks were kept busy in the monastery. In a large institution there were not only hundreds of monks to feed, but also a vast checkerboard of buildings to be maintained, each with its altar, incense, candles, its leaking roof and peeling walls. All this required a complicated inventory, and handling it was the main work of the clerks (*k'u-t'ou*). If there were lay workmen engaged in construction or repair, one of the clerks supervised them and kept their time sheet. He might have the special title of "work overseer" (*kuan-kung, p'o-*

t'ou). If the men he supervised were mainly engaged in cultivat-
ing nearby rice fields (for those nearby were often cultivated by the
monastery itself rather than rented out), then his title might be "fields
overseer" (*t'ien-t'ou*).

When outsiders came to see the business office—like the village
headman or grain buyers—the clerks would arrange for them to be
fed from its small kitchen and perhaps lodged for the night. In the
case of the more important visitors, they would personally serve them
tea and hot towels. Since there usually was no verger in the business
office, it was the clerks who had to keep its premises swept and the
altar lamps burning.

The subpriors (*fu-ssu*) were of higher rank. Assisted by one or more
secretaries (*shu-chi*), they kept the cash ledgers and oversaw the
work of the clerks. It was their responsibility to see to it that the
monastery did not run out of the "seven staples"—firewood, rice, oil,
salt, soy sauce, vinegar, and tea—as well as of candles and incense
and all other supplies. Monies received from the sale of rice or issued
with purchase orders passed through their hands and were entered
in their ledgers. In some monasteries (like the Kao-min Ssu) the ac-
counting section (*chang-fang*) was considered to be a separate unit
within the business office and had to be staffed by at least two persons, so that one could always check on the other and defalcation
would be discouraged.

Let us see what happened at Chin Shan and the Kao-min Ssu when
supplies were needed. If they could be bought out of petty cash, the
subprior would issue the money and send a chit for reimbursement to
the sacristy, which in these monasteries kept the main cash fund under its control. On the other hand, if the purchase was a large one,
the prior himself had to decide about it and get the sacristy's oral
approval. He then wrote out a purchase order in response to which
the sacristy issued the cash required. This transaction would be recorded by a subprior on the books of the business office. The monk
who actually took the cash to the supplier and came back with the
supplies was probably a clerk. He delivered them to the storekeeper
(*kuan-k'u*), who, before storing them, entered them in his inventory
book. At Chin Shan this was called the "oil and rice ledger" (*yu-mi
chang*). When the time came for the supplies to be used, a subprior
would send a chit to the storekeeper, who made a reverse entry be-

fore issuing them. The system was simple and businesslike, and was obviously designed to reduce the temptation to peculate or to show favoritism in the allocation of supplies.

At the head of the business office was the prior (*chien-yüan*). All of the activities described above were in his direct charge. If mistakes were made, it was up to him to notice and correct them. Actually his responsibility extended much further. Virtually the whole of the monastery was subject to his inspection and control. As one former prior explained it, he had to be "always alert, looking into everything, investigating everywhere." Not only his subordinates in the business office, but every officer of the monastery except those of higher rank were expected to consult him on difficult problems. The prior, in turn, could consult the provost or, on even weightier matters, the abbot.

The provost (*tu-chien*) was also one of the staff of the business office. Though his status there was the highest, he took little part in its day-to-day operation. Usually he was an older monk, who had had many years' experience as a prior himself. Thus he bore the same relation to the acting prior that the retired abbot bore to the abbot in office: an honored adviser. The provost did not have to wait to be consulted. He could take the initiative in inspecting and correcting. In particular, he would advise the abbot on the appointment of officers and, if any officer was not performing his duties satisfactorily, the provost could recommend his dismissal or, in case of a serious violation of rules, his expulsion (*ch'ien-tan*). The prior too had the privilege of making such a recommendation to the abbot, who had the final authority. Dismissal and expulsion were rare occurrences, more likely to take place for a breach of rules than for administrative bungling.

THE SACRISTY

The sacristy (*i-po liao*) was the personal office of the abbot (*fang-chang*). It was not a large unit, nor were its officers of high rank, yet they were closest to the seat of power. Chief among them were the sacristans (*i-po*). They acted as the abbot's private secretaries and immediate assistants. They were young monks, chosen for their quick mind and ability to deal with people. If visitors arrived whom the abbot did not wish to receive, it was up to a sacristan to make satisfactory excuses and act as the abbot's representative in dealing with whatever business had brought them. If the abbot was busy, it was a sacristan who lit the crematory pyre for a monk who died in the monastery. Sacristans oversaw precautions against fire and theft, posted letters, and performed various ceremonial duties. When a lay donor provided a vegetarian feast along with a gift of money, they might be responsible for distributing the latter among all the monks.

At many monasteries, including Chin Shan and the Kao-min Ssu, one of them—called the "financial sacristan" (*yin-ch'ien i-po*)—was also in effect the treasurer. The bulk of the money received by other departments was handed to him at the end of each day, along with a summary of the day's cash entries for transfer to the general ledger of the monastery (*ta-chang*). The abbot might deposit surplus cash in a "money shop" (*ch'ien-chuang*), or, in more recent years, in a Western-style bank. But it should be remembered that the bulk of current assets were not in the form of cash, but grain kept in the monastery's storerooms.

On the last day of the month there was what we might call a "meeting of the finance committee." The heads of the other departments foregathered with the abbot and the sacristan, read out their accounts for that month, and audited while the sacristan checked the figures against the general ledger. Petty cash remaining in each department was counted and compared with ledger totals. The accounts were then closed.

Another officer of the sacristy was the "baldachin sacristan" (*chuang-yen i-po*). He was in charge of the brocaded hangings (see Fig. 31), altar equipment, and rich vestments that were in daily use or required for special occasions. With the assistance of one or more "dispensers" (*t'ang-yao*), he made sure that these costly objects were taken out of the cupboards as needed and checked in again on their return, with the appropriate entry in a register. The dispensers are said to have gotten their title because it was they who used to prepare tisanes (*t'ang*) and medicines (*yao*) for the abbot when he was ill. In recent years, however, they staffed his private kitchen and dining room, and looked after the apartments where the most honored visitors were lodged as his personal guests. Many minor duties devolved upon them. They were the first line of defense against unwelcome callers, for whom they would take messages to and from the abbot, or summon the sacristan. They were responsible for checking the calendar (and checking it twice a day at the Kao-min Ssu!) to see if the anniversary of any former abbot of the monastery was due to fall on the morrow. If it was, they informed the abbot, who usually assigned a deputy to perform the necessary ritual. At the Kao-min Ssu the dispensary (*t'ang-yao liao*) included the central storeroom for tea, soy sauce, and the sort of dainties that were regularly offered to honored guests or to the body of monks on some special occasion. The dispensers were thus in charge of distributing these items to the different departments of the monastery.[25] This illustrates the principle that at some monasteries the greater the value of an object, the more closely it came under the abbot's personal control.

Lowest ranking in the sacristy was the acolyte (*shih-che*), who was seconded in rotation day by day from among the acolytes in the meditation hall. He helped the abbot on and off with his vestments, folded them up and put them away; held the incense tray for him during certain rituals; handed him the willow twig that he chewed after each meal to clean his teeth; carried his bag when he went out of the monastery; and in general acted as his body servant and runner. In some cases, this office was not filled in rotation, but permanently. The Venerable Hsü-yün, for example, had two acolytes who were his permanent personal attendants, not even subject to the semiannual reappointment that, as we shall see, was required for other offices of the monastery.[26]

VARIATIONS

This sort of variation in the personnel system was particularly common in the sacristy and business office. A certain officer might have one set of duties in this monastery and another set of duties in that monastery. Good examples are provided by the T'ien-ning Ssu in Changchow. There the clerks did not help with the collection of the rent in the villages, as they did at Chin Shan and Kao-min. Instead a weigher and a bookkeeper were seconded from the meditation hall or some other section. This may have been because of the size and complexity of landholdings—perhaps the largest of any monastery in China. An "east subprior," a "south subprior," and a "west subprior" were kept busy throughout the year administering the leases and mortgages in their respective quarters (the north, where there was less land, was included with the east). Only during the few weeks of rent collection did they need extra help in weighing and recording the grain. It was more efficient to borrow it from other sections.

Besides those "regional" subpriors, the T'ien-ning Ssu had both a general and a financial subprior (*tsung fu-ssu* and *yin-ch'ien fu-ssu*). The latter did the work that was done at Chin Shan and Kao-min by a sacristan. The abbot did not keep the monastic funds under his constant personal control; instead, it was the responsibility of the business office. If he himself wanted cash, he still had to go to the financial subprior to get it. According to one informant a similar system was in effect at both the Liu-yün Ssu and Fa-tsang Ssu in Shanghai.[27] This illustrates well how functions could vary from place to place, though departmental structure remained the same.

In some cases the functions remained the same, but the title varied. The proctor (*seng-chih*) was called *chih-chung* in monasteries of the Vinaya sect, but *chiu-ch'a* in those of the teaching sects.[28] The night patrol (*yeh-hsün*) might alternatively be entitled *chao-t'ou;* the miller (*nien-t'ou*) might be called *mo-t'ou;* and so on. There were also a number of specialized offices apparently preserved in only a few monasteries. At the Pao-kuang Ssu in Szechwan there was a supervisor of repairs (*chien-hsiu*) and a bath steward (*yü-t'ou*) who took care of the bathing facilities. A few offices appear to be wholly defunct. They are described in the "Pure Rules of *Pai-chang*," but their duties have been otherwise assimilated. A "taster" (*t'ieh-an*), for example, used to be charged with passing on the flavor of every dish before it was served and of standing in for the chef (*tien-tso*), who now passes on the flavor himself. Such variants are discussed in Appendix II, all of them, however, fitting into the scheme given above.

GROUPS OF PERSONNEL

Given an institution housing several hundred residents and visitors, dependent on land rents and donations, the monastic offices described above are what we might expect to find. They appear reasonable and necessary. But if, equipped with the information we have so far, we asked a monk about his place in the monastery, we might be unable to understand his answer. This is because there were ranks as well as offices, and in some cases ranks *were* offices. A monk might describe his position in terms of his office, or his rank, or one of the groups to which he belonged.

Let us first consider these groups. The lowest in status was not composed of monks at all, but of lay workmen (*kung-jen, tao-jen,* or *chai-kung*). We have already mentioned those who were to be found in the kitchen, the mill, the vegetable garden, the business office, and who at some monasteries acted as ushers (*chao-k'o*) in the guest department. There were also other kinds of workmen; tailors, barbers, and carpenters. Ch'i-hsia Shan, according to its former abbot, had about a hundred carpenters living on the premises during the period of the reconstruction that started in 1920 and continued for twenty years. It also had two or three barbers and three or four tailors. The latter increased to ten or twelve during the spring ordinations, since new robes had to be made for the new monks. At the T'ien-ning Ssu in Changchow (the largest monastery in China) there were perhaps fifteen tailors in continuous residence, while the total number of workmen needed for normal operation was approximately two hundred, so that their ratio to monks was about one to four. This is in line with figures from other large monasteries. Prip-Møller speaks of the poor living quarters allotted to the lay staff of the main kitchen at Pao-hua Shan.[29] This may not be typical. Hackmann recalls that at a small monastery in Chekiang, where he stayed five months, the kitchen workers were "all obviously in good spirits and quite content with their position in the universe . . . Perhaps the monastery servants, whose common dining room is in a part of the kitchen premises, have a far more comfortable time than the monks in the dining hall."[30]

The only workman of any monastery that I have been able to talk to was a tailor from the T'ien-ning Ssu in Changchow. He had spent twelve years learning his trade there, and said that he and his fellows were well treated, had decent quarters to live in, and got the same food as the monks. He was also proud of T'ien-ning's size and strictness and spoke with respect of the meditation and other religious work carried on there, although he himself took no part in it. Some lay workmen, because of the merit to be gained from serving the sangha, were willing to accept less than the standard wage; others depended on tips or fees for piecework.[31] All were fed by the monastery.

Among the ordained monks, those lower in the chain of command were called "menial officers." The Chinese term for this title, *heng-tan*,[32] is derived from the fact that their work was a kind of self-mortification (*k'u-heng*). All those who worked under the guest department, excepting only the guest prefects, secretaries, and the proctor, were "menial officers." This included the ushers, the kitchen staff, and the waiters, as well as the monks in charge of the mill, the vegetable garden, the library, the altars, and the wandering monks hall.

When I say that this group was lower in the chain of command, I do not mean that its members were looked down upon. Their rank, as we shall see in a moment, was relatively high. Whereas other offices were assigned, these were volunteered for. Monks volunteered because they felt that they had no vocation for the meditation hall or other such religious work and lacked the administrative qualifications for any of the higher offices. They were content to do the housekeeping without which the religious work could not be carried on, knowing that a share of the merit it generated would fall to them. There are stories that the bodhisattva Kuan-yin, in one incarnation, served as a rice-steward at the Kuo-ch'ing Ssu on Mount T'ien-t'ai and that the bodhisattva Samantabhadra was a waiter in the refectory of the Kuei-yüan Ssu, Wuhan. Once a monk to whom I was showing the plates in Prip-Møller's great work recognized the figure carrying a basket on page 22. "He was the stoker when I was a guest prefect at Chiao Shan. A real bodhisattva."

I asked what he meant. "That man was never greedy," he replied. "He wanted nothing for himself and was not in the least particular about his food and clothing. Yes, he was the incarnation of an arhat (*lo-han ti hsien-shen*)." There was a pause. "You do not have to do meditation, you know, in order to get enlightenment. All you need is an undivided mind (*i-hsin*). That fellow was illiterate. He spent the whole day in the kitchen, stoking the fires. In the evening, if he had time, he would come to the meditation hall. Many of the buildings at Chiao Shan had burned down. He planted melons in the vacant plots and used to give them away to people. He had no teeth.

A very interesting fellow: there were not many like him. A real bodhisattva."

This is typical, I believe, of the affection and respect that a menial officer could win from his colleagues.[33] Together with the merit arising from self-mortification in labor, it explains why there was never any lack of persons volunteering for even the most arduous of menial offices, that is, those in the kitchen. Monks went to the guest department and in the conventional phrase for the occasion, "asked for happiness" (ch'iu-fu). This meant that they were asking for a chance to earn the merit that would bring them happiness in this life or the next.

Although at most model monasteries the menial officers, like everyone else, were supposed to spend at least one semester in the meditation hall before they could take office, once in office their duties usually prevented them (as in the case of the stoker at Chiao Shan) from attending any but evening meditation. The kitchen staff was excused from morning devotions, since that was the time for getting the daily work of the kitchen underway and preparing breakfast. Attendance at afternoon devotions, on the other hand, was commonly expected.

At the other end of the scale from the menial officers were various leadership groups. In standard works on Chinese Buddhism we read, for example, of the "three principals" (san-kang), usually meaning the prior (chien-yüan), the precentor (wei-no),[34] and the rector (shou-tso). They were all important persons, but I have not heard of a situation that required their functioning as a group. There were also the "four great principal leaders" (ssu-ta kang-ling) and the "eight great officers" (pa-ta chih-shih), whose identity varies. One listing of the eight includes the provost, prior, guest prefects, proctor, precentor, subpriors, secretaries, and chef. In some parts of China the "eight great officers" might serve as a sort of cabinet, advising the abbot on such matters as the choice of his successor.

In the large public monasteries of Kiangsu, like Chin Shan and Kao-min, long-term power lay with another group altogether: the monks whose names were inscribed on the monastery's dharma scroll as its dharma disciples. The dharma scroll will be discussed in Chapter VI. Here let it suffice to say that it recorded transmission of the Buddhist truth from master to disciple, generation by generation, starting with the Buddha and ending with the disciples of today. Dharma disciples of a Kiangsu monastery had the privilege and the obligation to serve one by one as abbot. They transmitted the dharma collectively to the next generation of disciples, who also served as abbot one by one. In the Republican era it was common for the large Kiangsu monastery to have four or five such dharma disciples, who were, in effect, a self-perpetuating board of trustees that had nearly absolute control over the future of the monastery. What complicated the picture was that, at some monasteries, all the dharma disciples received the courtesy title of "prior."[35] At Chin Shan and the T'ien-ning Ssu there was normally only one prior who, as we have seen, was head of the business office. But at Ch'i-hsia Shan near Nanking and the Liu-yün Ssu in Shanghai, all the dharma disciples were priors. The senior prior (*cheng chien-yüan*) might serve as the head of the business office, that is, he would have the work as well as the title of a prior. The second prior might serve as the head of the guest department, that is, he would be the senior guest prefect. The third prior might be the head of the sacristry, that is, he was the senior sacristan. The fourth might be off heading a sub-temple, awaiting the time when he was needed.

RANKS

The prior who held the office of senior guest prefect would probably be an assistant instructor (*t'ang-chu*). This was his rank. Every officer in the monastery had a rank (*hsü-chih*). The hierarchy of ranks was parallel to the hierarchy of offices (*lieh-chih*), but comprised a separate set of titles. A monk's rank determined where he sat in the meditation hall, where he walked in processions, and where he stood in the great shrine-hall during religious observances. Rank was theoretically granted in token of accomplishments in religious practice, particularly meditation. In reality, it was granted as a concomitant of office. Thus promotion to the office of subprior also meant promotion to the rank of secretary. The latter was not the same as the office of secretary.

Generally speaking, only the monks in the wandering monks hall had no rank. The rank that they might have acquired in other monasteries was not recognized. If and when they enrolled in the meditation hall, they were assigned a rank by the precentor (*wei-no*). This meant that they knew their place in all gatherings and processions, and that if they someday took office, they could return to the meditation hall whenever they were free and understand how to conduct themselves without disturbing the good order of the hall. It was thus one reason why at most model monasteries no one could become an officer without first spending a semester in the meditation hall. In these monasteries rank was always acquired before office.

The reader may be relieved to learn that the list of ranks is relatively short. From the lowest to the highest it runs as follows:

    I.   Eastern ranks (*tung-hsü*)
        1. Verger (*hsiang-teng*)
        2. Acolyte (*shih-che*)
        3. Recorder (*chi-lu*)
        4. Thurifer (*shao-hsiang*)
        5. Deacon (*tsu-shih*)
    II. Western ranks (*hsi-hsü*)
        1. Water-bearer (*ssu-shui*)
        2. Contemplative (*ts'an-t'ou*)
        3. Canon prefect (*chih-tsang*)
        4. Librarian (*tsang-chu*)
        5. Secretary (*shu-chi*)
        6. Assistant instructor (*t'ang-chu*)
        7. Associate instructor (*hou-t'ang*)
        8. Senior instructor (*hsi-t'ang*)
        9. Rector (*shou-tso*)

It is difficult to find English equivalents that fit the duties of each rank, which in some cases were purely ceremonial while in other cases there were no duties at all. Some of the translations given above are arbitrary.

The reader may be curious about the division of ranks into east and west. This was metaphorical geography, based on the usage of the imperial court, where the emperor faced the main entrance door in the center of the south wall. At Chinese monasteries whether or not the main door of each hall opened to the south, we would find the western ranks on the left as we entered, and the eastern ranks on the right. Generally speaking, the monks in the west were older than those in the east. When the proctor at the Kao-min Ssu boxed the cheeks of an offender, he was supposed to strike more gently if the monk belonged to the west.[36] In the west one found most of the menial officers (*heng-tan*), and one also found the old hands at religious exercises (*lao-hsiu-hsing*) who were so subdued and dried up from years of meditation that they were nicknamed "the old papayas."

Division into two parties, east and west, was a feature of all gatherings and processions. West took precedence. The phrase "western party" (*hsi-tan*) is synonymous with "western ranks" (*hsi-hsü*). The head of the western party (*hsi-tan t'ou*) was the rector, while the "tail" of the eastern party (*tung-tan wei*) was the verger. This can be seen from the list given above.

Now let us consider what the ranks meant in practice. Aside from determining precedence, they entailed certain ceremonial duties. The verger dressed the altar, swept the floor, and, in the meditation hall, served the monks tea and supper in their seats. The acolytes took turns at waiting on the abbot in the sacristy. The recorders were theoretically supposed to make a summary of every sermon on the dharma (*shuo-fa*) by the abbot or one of the instructors. (In practice the summary might be prepared by someone else.) The thurifers had the duty of making nine full prostrations in offering incense before each dharma sermon. The deacons, so far as I have been able to learn, had no duties as such. Usually some of them held the office of succentor, which in itself involved many ceremonial duties, as we shall see.

In the west, the water-bearer worked with the verger. The contemplatives, canon prefects, and librarians appear to have had no regular duties. However, the monk who held the *office* of librarian and spent his time taking care of the books in the library would be chosen from among those who held this *rank*. Similarly, those who held the *office* of secretary and hence were termed "writing secretaries" (*shu-hsieh ti shu-chi*), since they kept accounts in the business office or wrote up announcements in the guest department, were chosen from among those who held the *rank* of secretary. Many of the other senior officers held this rank. It carried with it important privileges that were denied to those below.

The instructors, that is, the rector and the senior, associate, and assistant instructors, were charged with the work of teaching the monks how to meditate. They were collectively known as the "four great [ranks of] instructors" (*ssu-ta pan-shou*). Those actually engaged in teaching were considered to hold the office of "meditation hall instructor" (*ch'an-t'ang ti pan-shou*). Those who merely held instructor's *rank* and discharged some office outside the meditation hall were known as the "outer section instructors" (*wai-liao pan-shou*).

Ranks were permanent. If a thurifer returned to the monastery after an absence of twenty years, he was still a thurifer. He knew his place. Offices, on the other hand, were held for six months only: at the end of each semester every office-holder resigned. But what he was resigning was only his office and not his rank. He kept his rank until he was promoted to a higher one, either as a concomitant of higher office or by virtue of accomplishments or seniority.

This meant that when the "writing secretary" resigned his office at the end of the semester, he continued to hold the rank of secretary. The same applied to the librarian, vergers, and water-bearers, for all of whom rank and office coincided. It also applied to the meditation hall instructors who, after they resigned, either took some other office, still with instructor's rank (in which case they were "outer section instructors") or lived in retirement (in which case they were "idle instructors"—*hsien pan-shou*). In neither case did it mean that they were unable to give instruction in the meditation hall if they felt moved to do so. They had the privilege, but the regular obligation had ceased. They were always available to those who needed spiritual advice and encouragement.

THE APPOINTMENT OF PERSONNEL (*ch'ing-chih*)

The 16th of the first or seventh lunar month was the beginning of a new semester (*ch'i-t'ou*).[37] All the officers of the monastery except the abbot resigned (*t'ui-chih*) on the 8th, their resignations to take effect a week later. Those with the rank of secretary and above tendered their resignations orally to the abbot. Those with ranks lower than secretary tendered their resignations to the senior guest prefect

or to the precentor. The abbot, of course, had for several weeks past
been considering personnel changes and had consulted the senior
monks, particularly the retired abbots, the rector, and the provost. On
the 9th, having made up his mind, he would call in every officer of the
monastery with the rank of secretary or above and ask him either to
continue serving or take some other office—or, perhaps, to "enjoy a
well deserved rest," which usually meant that his work had been unsatisfactory. Among those appointed by the abbot on the 9th were
the senior guest prefect and the precentor.

On the 10th and 11th of the month, the senior guest prefect would
call on all officers with rank lower than secretary in all sections other
than the meditation hall and, just as the abbot had done, accept their
resignations or ask them to continue serving. In the meditation hall
the same was done by the precentor.

Before the senior guest prefect decided who should serve in the
various sections, he would get the approval of the section heads. Thus,
on clerks and village agents in the business office, he would consult
the provost and the prior. On sacristans and dispensers, he would consult the abbot. On the kitchen staff he would consult the chef. Tabulated, the system of appointments looks as follows:

ABBOT APPOINTS	RANK
Business office	
Provost (*tu-chien*)	Instructor
Prior (*chien-yüan*)	Instructor
Subpriors (*fu-ssu*)	Secretary
Secretaries (*shu-chi*)	Secretary
Guest department	
Guest prefects (*chih-k'o*)	Secretary
Proctor (*seng-chih*)	Secretary
Secretaries (*shu-chi*)	Secretary
Meditation hall	
Meditation hall instructors (*ch'an-t'ang ti pan-shou*)	Instructor
Precentor (*wei-no*)	Secretary
PRECENTOR APPOINTS	
Succentors (*yüeh-chung*)	Deacons, thurifers, recorders
Verger (*hsiang-teng*)	Verger
Water-bearer (*ssu-shui*)	Water-bearer

All other offices, from the clerks (*k'u-t'ou*) to the sanitation steward (*ching-t'ou*), were assigned by the senior guest prefect. But since most of them were menial offices, they were only assigned to those who first volunteered for them (*t'ao heng-tan*). There was, however, a "catch." Holding office was voluntary in the sense that a monk could avoid volunteering or refuse to serve when asked. He could plead poor health, lack of qualifications, a wish to devote his time to religious cultivation, or a commitment to go elsewhere. On the other hand, if a resident monk took no office for the ensuing term, he would have to enroll in the meditation hall or in the buddha recitation hall or leave the monastery. No one but a resident of the wandering monks hall was permitted to remain without a place (*tan*). Since there might not be a vacancy in the buddha recitation hall (at Chin Shan it only had room for twelve monks), the alternatives to taking office were either the rigors of meditation or leaving the monastery. This may have been one reason why most offices were easily filled. It was not the only reason, however. Refusing to serve where needed was looked upon rather as we look on "poor school spirit." If everyone refused, what would happen to the monastic system? Thus an associate instructor at the Kuan-tsung Ssu in Ningpo volunteered to serve as a mere chef because he was the only person who had the necessary experience in managing a kitchen.

There was one exception to the rule that resident monks had to have a place or leave the monastery. It did not apply to those who had retired after active service. Anyone who reached the rank of secretary or above was entitled to retire. The abbot would present him with an apartment (*liao-fang*) in which he would live for the rest of his days, obligated only to attend devotions, two daily meals, and three meditation periods. If he were venerable enough, he would even be excused from these. The system will be described at greater length in Chapter X, but what was most important about it was the incentive it gave a monk to continue serving at one monastery until he reached secretarial rank. After he reached it—after he became a proctor or a guest prefect, for instance—he had less incentive to continue, but all the monks I know did, in fact, continue.

On the 8th, as we have seen, everyone resigned; on the 9th the guest prefect and precentor were appointed; and on the 10th and 11th they in turn made appointments to all offices below the rank of secretary. It was usually not until the 12th that the new roster of personnel was made public. Early that morning a reception was held in the abbot's quarters (*fang-chang shih*) to which all monks with the rank of secretary or above were invited. After tea and refreshments had been served, the abbot announced his appointments, which, together with those of lower rank, were posted outside the guest department. Thus everyone in the monastery could find out who would be doing what for the next semester. After breakfast on the 16th of the month the new appointees assumed their duties; at noon they sat in the refectory according to their new rank; and that afternoon they might visit the apartments of their predecessors to pay their respects (*hsün-liao*). Many of them, however, had not yet been promoted to a new rank and still sat in their old seats. This requires explanation.

PROMOTION IN RANK

Only a few monks—mainly those promoted to the office of guest prefect, precentor, and proctor—were at the same time promoted in rank "automatically." The others had to wait until their superiors could observe the quality of their work. Between the 10th and the 20th of the following month the abbot called a "consultation on ranks" (*i-chih*), which was attended by the instructors, provost, prior, precentor, and senior guest prefect. When they gathered in the abbot's quarters, the three officers in charge of appointments would each table a slate of the promotions within his purview. The abbot proposed promotions to the rank of secretary or above; the guest prefect to ranks below secretary; while the precentor tabled a slate for all the monks enrolled in the meditation hall. Anyone present could object to any of the promotions proposed (although, needless to say, there were seldom objections to those proposed by the abbot). Silence indicated assent.

Let us take a concrete illustration. A monk, the Reverend N–n, arrives at Chin Shan in summer to enroll in the meditation hall. He has to wait until the beginning of the winter term, that is, the 16th of the seventh month. That morning a guest prefect escorts him to the hall along with the other "new boys" and gives the precentor a list of all their names. They are seated at the back, below the most junior acolytes. They have no rank at all. For about a month the precentor observes their work in meditation. Ten are qualified to become recorders. But there are already too many recorders staying on from the previous term. Therefore only five can get this rank. The rest must be satisfied to be acolytes, including the Reverend N–n. At the "consultation on ranks" in the eighth month, the precentor tables his slate, which also includes some promotions for the "old boys" in the hall. It is duly approved. The next morning after devotions all the monks of the monastery gather in the courtyard while the guest prefect, standing on the steps of the great shrine-hall, reads out the promotions in every department. Immediately afterward the names and ranks of all the monks enrolled in the meditation hall, both "new boys" and "old boys" alike, are pasted up on the wall over their seats. This is called "posting the places" (t'ieh-tan). Promotions in rank for monks outside the meditation hall are posted in the refectory or on the porch of the guest department, where the appointments to office had been posted a month earlier.

Six months pass. Reverend N–n, who enrolled in the meditation hall the year before, has had enough of its austerities and decides to leave it. He volunteers for the post of a dispenser in the sacristy. He is duly appointed and enters upon his duties on the 16th of the first month, that is, on the first day of the semester. But he remains an acolyte. He continues to walk, stand, and sit with the acolytes when he goes to the refectory and the great shrine-hall. Only after the consultation on ranks a month later is he promoted to the rank of recorder as recommended by the guest prefect. But two years later he has worked his way up to the office of senior sacristan and to the rank of deacon. In the first lunar month he is further promoted to guest prefect. This time his promotion in rank is "automatic." It does not have to wait for the consultation on ranks. On the 16th of the first month he becomes a guest prefect *with* the rank of secretary.

After every consultation on ranks the guest prefect entered all appointments to rank and office in the personnel register (hao-pu).[38] It included the name of every resident monk, followed usually by his style, native place, age, master, temple, and date of tonsure; the monastery where he had been ordained and his ordination age.[39] Often all this information was later copied into the "ten-thousand year book" that served as the continuous, year-to-year record of everything important at the monastery.[40]

THE PATTERN OF PROMOTION

At Chin Shan and other model monasteries each officer normally served until the end of the semester. In fact, it was customary to be reappointed for one or two semesters in the lower offices and two or more in the higher before getting promoted. Anyone could, however, lose his position at any time if he bungled his work or violated the monastic rules. He was then expected to "punish himself by leaving the monastery."[41] If he did not take the initiative in this, it would be taken, as we have seen, by the prior or provost or by the abbot himself. Naturally it meant a lesser loss of face to leave voluntarily than to be asked to leave.

Promotion usually followed a pattern. Except for those who had already achieved a high position in some other monastery (and such exceptions were rare), everyone had to begin at the bottom, usually as an acolyte in the meditation hall. There it was obligatory to spend at least one winter term, from the middle of the seventh month to the middle of the first. Many monks preferred to spend one to three years going up the ranks of the "rank and file" (ch'ing-chung).[42] They served successively as acolyte, recorder, and thurifer, meditating through most of the year nine to fifteen hours a day. A talented thurifer or even a recorder might be asked to accept the office of succentor (yüeh-chung). There were five to ten succentors, who took turns in assisting the precentor manage the meditation hall. Other monks left the hall earlier to become clerks, cooks, and so on, each with an appropriate rank.

It was common for a young "comer" to be rapidly promoted so that he skipped one or more ranks. Particularly common was promotion directly from deacon or thurifer to secretary,[43] skipping the three western ranks of contemplative, canon prefect, and librarian. These were usually held by menial officers and the "old hands at religious exercises."

As a concrete illustration, here is the personnel record of T'ai-ts'ang, the last abbot of Chin Shan. He was ordained there in 1917 and entered the meditation hall soon after ordination.

Personnel record of T'ai-ts'ang

Year	Semester	Office	Rank
1917	Second	Rank and file (*ch'ing-chung*)	Acolyte (*shih-che*)
1918	First	Dispenser (*t'ang-yao*)	Recorder (*chi-lu*)
1919	Second	Sacristan (*i-po*)	Thurifer (*shao-hsiang*)
1920	First	Senior sacristan (*t'ou-tan i-po*)	Deacon (*tsu-shih*)
1921	First	Guest prefect (*chih-k'o*)	Secretary (*shu-chi*)
1922	First	Left Chin Shan and spent two years studying Buddhist texts with different teachers; in 1924 returned to Chin Shan to attend an ordination.	
1924	First	Guest prefect	Secretary
1924	Second	Subprior (*fu-ssu*)	Secretary
1934	First	Prior (*chien-yüan*)	Assistant instructor (*hou-t'ang*)
later		Prior	Associate instructor (*hsi-t'ang*)
1945		Received dharma and became abbot (*fang-chang*)	Rector (*shou-tso*)

Note that T'ai-ts'ang's rise from acolyte to subprior took only seven years, whereas he spent ten years as a subprior and eleven years as a prior before becoming the abbot. This table is particularly interesting because it illustrates the wide evidence that the version of offices and ranks given in documentary sources is quite different from the actual practice in recent years.[44]

Let us test our understanding of the system. Suppose we are standing in the courtyard of Ch'i-hsia Shan (see Fig. 1) and see a middle-aged monk walking up the steps of the great shrine-hall. We ask some bystanders who it is.

"That is a prior," says one of our informants.

"That is the senior guest prefect," says the second.

"That is an associate instructor," says the third.

They will all be right, of course. As a dharma disciple and the future abbot of the monastery he has the title of "prior." His daily work is to manage the guest department. At meals and meditation he sits in the place to which he is entitled by his rank of associate instructor.

Now let us suppose that we question our informants about their own position.

"I am a secretary," says the first. But we know enough to ask him whether he holds the rank or office of secretary and, if it is the rank, whether he holds an office or lives in retirement in his private apartment.

"I am a librarian," says the second. We ask him whether he is actually in charge of the library or is enrolled in the meditation hall or works in the kitchen as a cook with librarian's rank.

"I am one of the rank and file," says the third. We ask him what he means by this ambiguous statement. Has he not yet received a rank or is he a menial officer?

The hierarchy of ranks and offices may sound not only complicated, but a deterrent to any monk's spiritual development, which required that he attend to his mind, not to promotion. It appears, however, that most monks took little interest in promotion and regarded ranks and offices as no more than necessary evils. They were necessary because religious exercises could best be carried out either entirely alone, as a hermit, or, if collectively, then at a large strict monastery, which required a strict and complex organization. Although there were certainly a few "organization men" in the sangha, office was more often regarded as a duty than a privilege. Many monks never held office at all, but spent their whole careers in the meditation hall or in the hall for reciting buddha's name or at small temples. I have talked to monks who did not even understand the meaning of "rank" and "office." Only the few who held responsible positions at large monasteries over a long period understood clearly what these terms meant in practice.

CHAPTER II

The Meditation Hall

The heart of Buddhism is enlightenment. The heart of the monastery was the meditation hall where enlightenment was sought. It could be sought elsewhere and we cannot say that a monastery without a meditation hall was not a Buddhist monastery. The traditional Chinese view has been that one could make progress toward enlightenment in many ways.

Dr. Suzuki and other writers on Ch'an (Zen) have told us how monks in the T'ang and Sung dynasties became enlightened. Usually after long years of preparation, the master would ask an enigmatic question or strike a blow on the face, and suddenly the disciple would find that he had crossed safely to the ineffable "farther shore." Some readers may have the impression that Ch'an (Zen) therefore depended on a close personal relationship between master and disciple. They may also have heard that, while Ch'an has survived in Japan, it died out long ago in China, choked by superstition and decay. After an inspection tour of Chinese Buddhism in 1934, Dr. Suzuki wrote: "Japanese Zen travellers . . . deplore the fact that there is no more Zen in China."[1] The facts are otherwise. At a small number of monasteries right up to the year 1949, hundreds of monks continued the strict practice of collective meditation under common masters. Ch'an Buddhism in China was destroyed, while still alive, by the land reforms of 1950. Meditation takes time, and time takes unearned income.

In the first chapter we examined the other departments of the monastery. Now we shall turn to the meditation hall, in particular to Chin Shan's, which was the most illustrious in China. Any Chinese

monk who had a serious interest in meditation would hope that someday he might enroll there. Many succeeded, and so it has not been
difficult to collect material on how its hall was operated. I have gotten
independent accounts from eight monks who enrolled between 1905
and 1944. The second of these eight was still at Chin Shan (as abbot)
in 1949, at which time, he said, the system was unchanged from what
it had been when he first entered the hall thirty-two years earlier. All
these informants spoke from memory, not from diaries or after consulting a code of rules. Hence it is impressive that their accounts were
in substantial agreement. Some readers may be skeptical about the
austerities that will be described below. I remember being told by a
Japanese Buddhist scholar that "ten hours of meditation a day is
simply impossible: perhaps the people you talked to were exaggerating." But then how would their exaggerations turn out to coincide?
Most of my informants had no contact with one another: they lived in
different temples, some in Hong Kong and some in Taiwan. I find it
simpler to accept their accounts as the truth.

THE LAYOUT OF THE HALL

Let us first see what the meditation hall looked like at Chin Shan
and other model monasteries. Then we shall follow its residents
through their daily routine. The details may prove tedious, particularly
for readers whose main interest is the spiritual content of meditation,
but some of these details have never been explained or recorded before. No Chinese meditation hall is left in operation anywhere in the
world. The monks who operated them are dying. So these are precious
details, however tedious. Without them it is impossible fully to understand the texts that may be studied now or in the future; and even the
spiritual content of meditation may be illuminated by what participants did with their bodies as well as by what they did with their
minds.

The meditation hall measured about sixty by a hundred feet. As
the reader can see from the floor plan opposite, on one side there
was a wide door or screen that folded upwards, almost like the garage
door of today. When it was down, a plaque was hung on it reading
"meditation underway" (*chih-ching*): this meant that no one could
enter and passers-by were well advised to tiptoe. At other times the

plaque was reversed, so that it read "recess" (*fang-ts'an*). Outside the doorway there was a porch that ran the length of the building. Below the porch was a large courtyard, with side doors that cut off the compound from outside noise. Across the courtyard was the Wei-t'o Tien, a shrine-hall with an image of Wei-t'o, the god who protected monasteries and the dharma. In all meditation centers there were two such shrines, one here and one opposite the central shrine-hall (*ta-tien*) where devotions were recited. Wei-t'o thus watched over the monks in their two most important activities. Another building that opened onto the courtyard was the ancestors hall (*tsu-t'ang*), with the tablets of earlier abbots. They too watched over the meditation. At Chin Shan

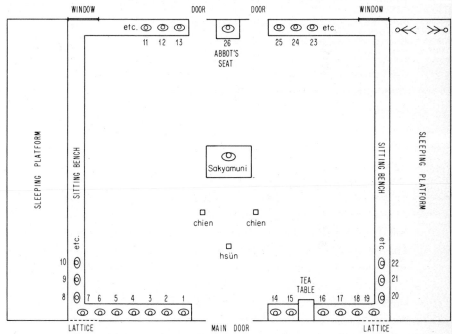

CHIN SHAN'S MEDITATION HALL

The numbers in this diagram refer to the seat numbers of the following: 1. Rector; 2. Senior instructor; 3-4. Associate instructors; 5-6. Assistant instructors; 7-12. Lower western ranks (secretaries, librarians, canon prefects, contemplatives), but when he is present the proctor sats at 7; 13. Water-bearer; 14. Meditation patrol (when not standing on the tile marked *hsün*); 15. Duty monk; 16. Precentor; 17. Duty succentor; 18-24. Succentors and eastern ranks (deacons, thurifers, acolytes), but when they are present a secretary and the head sacristan sit at 18 and 19, while within the ranks precedence is given to office holders when they are present; 25. Verger; 26. *Wei-mo k'an*—"the dais of Vimalakirti," that is, the abbot's seat.

the second story of the meditation hall contained the ordination platform—last used as such in 1924. Normally it provided sleeping quarters for any overflow of monks from downstairs.[2]

Thus this compound was the focus of monastic life where everything particularly sacred, including ordination and the ancestral rites, was performed. It was a world of its own, cut off as much as possible from the bustle of the "outer sections" (wai-liao), as all other parts of the monastery were called. At Chin Shan it even had its own wells.

The center of the meditation hall itself was occupied by a dais (fo-k'an), with an image of Bodhidharma, the First Patriarch of Ch'an Buddhism in China. Around the dais was a great expanse of tiled floor which was used for circumambulation. Circumambulation and sitting were the alternating phases of meditation: walk, sit, walk, sit, walk, sit. According to one source, this had only become the practice at the end of the Ming dynasty, its purpose being to overcome the drowsiness that often overcame the monks if they did nothing but sit.[3]

At either end of the hall along the opposite walls, the floor was raised in two steps. The lower step (ch'un-teng) was narrow. On it the monks sat in meditation under their name posters (see p. 43). Behind this was a much wider step (kuang-tan) where they slept side by side. During the day a curtain divided the "sitting bench" from the "sleeping platform," as we shall call these steps. This may have been in the interest of neatness, for at the back of the sleeping platform were clothes lockers and above them bamboo poles on which clothes could be hung and dried. Not all the monks slept on the platform. The precentor and instructors had individual apartments within the compound. But everyone else enrolled spent day and night in the hall.

The sitting bench, but not the sleeping platform, extended along the back wall, in the middle of which were two small "doors of convenience" (fang-pien men). In summer[4] they were opened to provide ventilation; the rest of the year they were kept closed. Between them was the abbot's seat (wei-mo k'an). Thus he sat below the lowest of the monks in east and west. "Low" meant near the back and "high" near the front of the hall.

The sitting bench also extended along the front wall on either side of the main door, but between the second and third seats to the right of the door it was interrupted by a "tea table" (ch'a-chi). This table was not used for tea, but as a place for certain ritual articles. More important, however, was what hung above it: a large bell, below

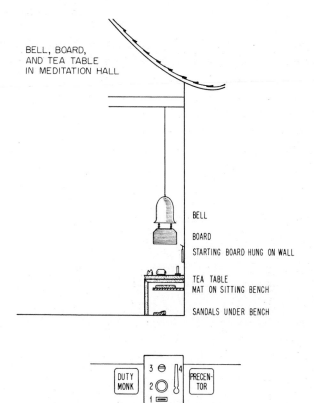

BELL, BOARD,
AND TEA TABLE
IN MEDITATION HALL

BELL

BOARD

STARTING BOARD HUNG ON WALL

TEA TABLE
MAT ON SITTING BENCH

SANDALS UNDER BENCH

DUTY MONK

3 ⊖ 4

2 ○

1 ▭

PRECEN-TOR

TEA TABLE

1. Tablet reading *ta-chung hui-ming tsai-ju i-jen,
ju jo pu-ku tsui-kuei ju-shen*

2. Incense burner

3. Wooden fish

4. Incense board used by precentor

which, suspended from the inside, there was a thick wooden board, perhaps two feet long and eighteen inches high (see diagram above). If the meditation hall was the heart of the monastery, this board was the heart of the meditation hall, for on it were struck the curious ringing thuds that signaled the beginning of the work. Nothing like it was found in any other hall and its shape was the emblem of the sect of the monastery.[5] In some monasteries the original board was preserved, dating perhaps to the Sung or Yüan dynasty, and literally perforated from centuries of striking.

Near the large bell and board (*chung-pan*) a smaller board was hung up on the wall. It was used for giving the signals that controlled

circumambulation. The use of signals, here and elsewhere, obviated
the need for words, so that mental concentration would be interrupted
as little as possible. Furthermore, Ch'an was proverbially the "wordless teaching." At one famous monastery (the T'ien-t'ung Ssu near
Ningpo) on the large sign that hung outside the meditation hall, the
character for "hall" was written without the usual element meaning
"mouth."

The ritual articles on the tea table under the bell and board were
as follows:

(1) A small "wooden fish" (*mu-yü*), the factotum among liturgical instruments. It was roundish with a slot into its hollow interior (see Fig. 11).

(2) An "incense board" (*hsiang-pan*) used by the precentor
(*wei-no*) to punish those who violated the discipline of the hall.
Like other incense boards, it was carried during circumambulation
as an emblem of authority (see Fig. 17).

(3) An incense burner in which sticks of incense were burned,
originally to measure the length of each period of meditation. Thus,
where monks sat for seven periods of meditation a day (as they
did at Chin Shan), one says in Chinese that they "sat seven sticks
of incense." As each stick burned down to its last two inches, it was
pulled out of the burner and a new stick was glued on to its lower
end with spit, but at an acute angle, so that when replaced in the
incense burner its upper end was like an inverted "V." By the time
the flame reached this joint, the spit had dried. A corresponding
stick of incense was kept burning before the image of Bodhidharma.
All this, however, was purely ceremonial. Since at least the beginning of the Republican era, the length of meditation periods has
been governed by a clock, placed on the same tea table.

(4) The final item was a small vertical tablet, inscribed as follows: "The spiritual life of everyone here is up to you as an individual; if you pay no heed, the sin (*tsui*) will be upon your own
head." It is hard to imagine a greater sin than disturbing the progress of others toward enlightenment.

On the left side of the tea table near the main door sat the duty
monk (*tang-chih-ti*)[6] who was drawn in rotation day by day from
among the rank and file. His duty was to strike the signals on the bell,
board, and wooden fish. To the right of the tea table sat the precentor,
who was in administrative charge of the meditation hall. The next
seat beyond him was occupied by the succentor-on-duty (*tang-chih
ti yüeh-chung*). He was the precentor's administrative assistant, who

struck signals on the hand-chime (*yin-ch'ing*). This corner of the room was therefore the command post, from which all activities in the hall could be observed and controlled. The military metaphor is not inappropriate. Monks often say that the discipline of meditation was like an army's. Every movement was exactly prescribed. From another point of view, because speech was avoided and movements were regulated by signals on the bell, board and wooden fish, we might compare meditation to the ballet.

The signals given in the meditation hall were part of a larger counterpoint that linked all the sections of the monastery. There were the bell and drum in the great shrine-hall, the gong outside the refectory, and a portable board carried by the night-patrol. Signals were sent back and forth like impulses in a nervous system. Every day there were three periods when, for an hour or two, one signal led continuously into another. For example, the striking of the bell in the meditation hall led into the striking of the bell in the shrine-hall, and this led into the striking of the large drum, with the first notes of each instrument falling between the last notes of the one before. Actually the counterpoint was far more complicated than this; many pages are devoted to it in Appendix III. It must have been fine to hear the instruments answering one another from different parts of the monastery compound, and have given the listening monk a feeling of good order and security. Of more practical importance, perhaps, was the fact that it told him exactly what was going on and where he was supposed to be.

THE DAY'S WORK°

Let us imagine that we are spending a day in the meditation hall early in the winter term, that is, in September. It is 3:00 o'clock in the morning. We hear the sound of footsteps crossing the courtyard. It is the night-patrol, come to awaken the monks with four strokes of his small portable board. He has already awakened some of the kitchen staff with three strokes half an hour earlier. Four strokes is the signal for everyone in the monastery to be up. The residents of the meditation hall rise from the sleeping platform, put away their bedding, go

° A more complete daily and annual chronology is given in Appendix III.

to the latrine, wash their faces at two large water basins out in the courtyard, and finally drink a mug of hot water, to which they add a pinch of salt. They have only slept five hours and the sun will not rise for two hours more. It is dark and cold. They put on their full-sleeved gowns (*hai-ch'ing*) and over this their robes (*chia-sa*). The clang of the large bell has led into the booming of the large drum and by the time the drum has ceased, they are ready to march in procession to the great shrine-hall (*shang-tien*). The western ranks, led by the rector, walk ahead of the eastern ranks, led by the suc-centors. Processions have a fixed order of precedence.[7]

In the great shrine-hall all the monks of the monastery except the kitchen staff have gathered to recite morning devotions (*tsao-k'o*).

10. Monks march in procession into the great shrine-hall for devotions. P'i-lu Ssu, Nanking.

11. The liturgical orchestra stands ready to begin devotions. The succentor (directly behind the precentor) holds the hand-chime and duty monks man the large wooden fish (right) and the drum and bell (left). P'i-lu Ssu, Nanking. (For a clearer picture of the hand-chime, see Fig. 39.)

Here too everyone has his place. The abbot stations himself at the back, to the left of the main door, while the proctor stands to the right of the door, from where he can see anything amiss throughout the hall. Up front, to the right of the Buddha image, we find the precentor. At first it might appear that his only responsibility is to strike the large bronze bowl (*ta-ch'ing*). In fact, he leads the chanting of liturgy just as in the meditation hall he leads the meditation. Behind him is the duty-succentor with the hand-chime as well as three duty monks who strike the wooden fish, the bell-and-drum, the cymbals (*ko-tzu*), and hand-gong (*tang-tzu*). Together these make up the liturgical orchestra.

The center of the hall is occupied by hundreds of monks, standing row on row. In general, the higher their rank, the closer they stand to the Buddha image. To the left are the western ranks, with instructors in the first row, and to the right are the eastern ranks, headed by the succentors. Residents of the meditation hall take precedence over those in the buddha recitation hall. At the very back, nearest the door, are the visitors staying in the wandering monks hall. No one may leave without the permission of the proctor and he is a fierce disciplinarian.

The liturgy in most Chinese monasteries was usually[8] as follows:

1) Surangama Mantra (*Leng-yen chou*)
2) *Heart Sutra* (*Hsin-ching*)
3) Gathas in Praise of the Buddhas (*Tsan-fo chi*)
4) Serpentining buddha's name (*jao-fo*)
5) Three Refuges (taking refuge in the Buddha, the dharma, and the sangha)
6) Hymn to Wei-t'o.

The first item, which amounts to about 80 percent of the morning liturgy, is meaningless to those who recite it. The words are a Sanskrit incantation transliterated into Chinese. Monks say that reciting it is effective in quieting and emptying the mind. It has another function, however. This mantra was first uttered by the Buddha to save his disciple Ananda from the wiles of a prostitute. She cast a spell over him one day as he was returning home with his alms-bowl. Under its influence he was about to violate his vow of chastity. The Buddha,

12. After offering incense the abbot prostrates himself to the Buddha image during devotions. P'i-lu Ssu, Nanking.

through his supernormal powers, saw the danger and uttered the Surangama Mantra, which he despatched through the bodhisattva Manjusri. It broke the spell and Ananda was saved. To recite it is, therefore, extremely efficacious in protecting oneself from sexual temptation. Since the latter is the greatest of all dangers to progress in religious cultivation, it is reasonable that prophylaxis should be the first step of the day.

The fourth item of the liturgy is recited in procession. The monks leave their places and wind about the shrine-hall, and then go down and wind about the courtyard in a serpentine course, all the while reciting "Homage to the buddha Amitabha." Hence it is called "serpentining the buddha['s name]" (*jao-fo*).[9] As the weather gets warmer, it is pleasant to get out in the fresh air, although they must go back inside to recite the concluding items.

At about 5:15 morning devotions are over and everyone returns to his own quarters (*hui-t'ang*). In the meditation hall the monks take up their positions cross-legged (*p'an-tso*) on the narrow bench for a period of "quiet sitting" (*ching-tso*).[10] They do not meditate, however, and whereas later in the day they would be struck for dozing, now they are expected to doze. They may even snore since now is the time "to get built up" (*yang-shen*) for the long day ahead of them. Some monks speak of this rest period with peculiar enthusiasm. It did more good, they say, than hours of ordinary sleep.

As they doze, they can hear the distant striking of the bamboo sticks that signals the approach of breakfast. They know that in the great shrine-hall the verger is offering a bowl of rice before the Buddha. About six o'clock, as the monastery resounds to the banging of the wooden fish image, they get ready to file over to the refectory (*kuo-t'ang*) and rejoin the rest of the monks for the day's first meal, which is termed "early congee" (*tsao-chou*), since it consists of congee and vegetables, particularly salted vegetables. Nothing is served to drink, though some of the dishes are semi-liquid.

In the refectory as in the great shrine-hall everyone has his place at the long narrow tables, east and west on opposite sides. The higher their rank, the nearer they sit to the center rear, where the abbot takes his place on a raised dais behind a low buddha image. The monks have to await the abbot's arrival and to rise in his honor. But they cannot then begin to eat the food that the waiters have been ladling

13. The wooden fish image (*pang*) outside the refectory, the sign on which reads "the hall of the five reflections" (*wu-kuan t'ang*). Chao-ch'ing Ssu, Hangchow.

out into their bowls. They have to watch it cool while they recite a short grace, the *Kung-yang chou,* after which an acolyte takes seven grains of rice from a bowl before the buddha image and places them on a low pillar in the courtyard. He snaps his fingers to notify the ghosts that they have not been forgotten. Ghosts are among the sentient beings whom the most orthodox follower of Ch'an (Zen) tries to assist—by feeding them, preaching to them, and transferring to their account the merit that is created by his religious exercises, in order that they may secure an earlier rebirth in the human plane or even in the Western Paradise. From the Ch'an point of view there is nothing superstitious about this concern for creatures in lower planes of existence. He would reject any distinction we might draw between a "pure" Ch'an Buddhism, as portrayed by Western-oriented writers,

14. A monk takes grains of rice to offer to the ghosts before a meal. Chiao Shan, Chen-chiang.

and a Ch'an that is corrupt because it concerns itself partly with the care and feeding of ghosts.

Only after the ghosts have been fed may the waiting monks start their breakfast. They eat quickly and carefully under the watchful eye of the proctor, who stands by the main door, from where he can see to it that food is fairly distributed. Anyone who wishes a second helping pushes his bowl forward on the table and points with chopsticks to show how full he wants it filled. The first helping can be left partly uneaten, but the second, since it is voluntary, has to be finished to the last grain.

15. Monks eating in the refectory under the watchful eye of the proctor, who stands by the door. The abbot sits on the central dais. P'i-lu Ssu, Nanking.

The proctor also sees to it that all the rules are strictly kept, particularly the rule of silence. (A lay informant recalled that as a boy he had been once permitted to watch the monks of the T'ien-ning Ssu at breakfast. None of them made a sound—something of a feat when eating congee—until a young monk audibly slurped. The proctor, wielding his stick, marched over, paused before him for a moment, and then hit his bare pate a resounding smack.)

While they eat, the monks are not merely silent, but supposed to be focusing their minds on the "five reflections" (*wu-kuan*), that is, on the debt they owe to those who provided the food, which they should eat as medicine, not with enjoyment. When they have finished, they recite a closing grace, the *Chieh-chai chi*. The proctor may make some announcements about the day's activities, after which they leave the hall in order of precedence and return to their respective quarters.[11]

This time there is to be no rest period for the residents of the meditation hall. They take off their robes and full-sleeved gowns, change into gowns with ordinary sleeves and into comfortable sandals,[12] then repair to the porch outside the hall to clean their teeth by chewing on green willow twigs (*yang-chih*) about the size of a pencil. Willow is considered to "lower the heat" (*hsia-huo*), that is, the blood that rises to the head from the rest of the body, particularly if one is constantly sitting cross-legged. Its twigs are used to clean the teeth after each of the meals taken in the refectory. The monk stands on the edge of the porch, holding a mug of cold water in one hand and a fresh twig in the other; chews, brushes, and rinses; and then spits into the courtyard drain.[13]

Next comes a visit to the latrines. The manner of excretion is exactly prescribed. When urinating (*hsiao-ching*) the monk has to stand about a foot away from the trough, lean forward against a bamboo rail for support, and in this discreet position undo and later do up his undergarments. Defecation (*ch'ou ta-chieh*) is full of taboos. The code of rules of the Kao-min Ssu prescribes that the lid must be lifted silently and then the monk must "snap the fingers of his right hand three times toward the opening of the pit. This is to avoid having the excrement dirty the heads of the hungry ghosts, thus incurring their revengeful wrath. It is terribly important." Certain kinds of hungry ghosts are apparently attracted by the smell of faeces. After snapping his fingers and seating himself, the monk must sit up straight and keep his legs covered with the corners of his underclothes. "He may not look this way or that, talk with people nearby, lean against the partition, or scratch his private parts"—and he must be quick about it, because others are waiting. When he is finished, the code of rules prescribes that he go to the water basin outside, dip in the two middle fingers of his right hand, wipe them on his left palm, and then run his hands quickly over the towel. He is specifically prohibited from putting his hands fully into the basin or wiping them hard.[14] According to informants from the Kao-min Ssu the reason for this is that with seventy or eighty monks hurrying to get back to the meditation hall, there is not time to change the towel and the water in the basin. They are only changed once a day and must not be dirtied by careless use. Some monks carry their own towels with them, although this, like the use of soap, is also forbidden by the rules.[15]

Now the monks are ready to begin the day's work. As they return one by one from the latrines, they join in the casual circumambulation that is already underway. The precentor enters and shouts "get moving!" They begin to walk rapidly almost with a swagger, swinging their left arm in and out and their right arm back and forth. In Chinese this is termed "running."[16] They run in several concentric circles, all moving clockwise. Nearest to the central altar are the rank and file; outside them are those with secretarial rank; and in the outermost circle walk the instructors and the precentor.[17] Even beyond them, however, skirting the meditation benches, is the disperser (san-hsiang). He has a four-foot bamboo rod, which he holds up perpendicular as he walks. Every few paces he arcs it down to tap the floor, almost like a knight dipping his sword. The taps are intended to remind the monks not to let their thoughts wander during circumambulation— which may be a rest for the joints, but not for the mind. Only opposite the buddha-image and the abbot's seat does he suspend his tapping, as a mark of respect to those who need no reminder.

At seven o'clock the board under the bell is struck three times. The monks go to their places on the sitting bench. To the left of the entrance door sit the instructors; to the right the precentor and his two aides (see diagram p. 49). Almost everyone sits in order of rank, so that the highest places in the west (except for the instructors) are occupied by secretaries and the lowest by contemplatives, while in the east the order runs from deacons through acolytes. Within each rank monks sit in order of seniority. Among the secretaries, for example, the monk who first attained this rank sits furthest "forward," except for the proctor (*seng-chih*) who, if he attends, is always in the corner next to the front wall. There are other exceptions, but they are minor.[18]

The system of precedence, while its details may seem tiresome, is extremely important in the meditation hall. Unless everyone knows his place, there will be jostling and confusion and perhaps even an exchange of words, thus breaking trains of thought. In a well-run hall the monk should be able to forget his body and let it be guided like an automaton by the bell and board. He sits erect on the narrow bench, his eyes fixed on a point no further than the third and no nearer than the second row of tiles on the floor. He tries to keep his spine perfectly straight and to control his respiration. Talking is forbidden. The silence must be absolute. If a monk in the east makes a sound, the precentor goes over and beats him then and there with his incense board—and beats him hard. If it is a monk in the west, the blows are administered by the senior instructor present. But the blows may not be struck with the sharp edge of the board, nor is boxing the cheeks allowed, as it is outside the hall.

Those who are new at meditation usually sit cross-legged with only one foot up (*tan-tso*). Even then it may be so painful that they cannot sleep at night. Some lose courage and flee the monastery (*t'ao-tan*). According to one informant, "the pain is cumulative. It hurts until the sweat pours from your body. Some people try to cheat by uncrossing both legs under cover of their gowns, but eventually the precentor will catch them at it and give them a beating. The loss of face is one reason why so many run away." How many? "About 30 percent in the first week or two of each semester."

Old hands, of course, are untroubled by leg cramps and sit with both feet up (*shuang-tso*). A few even learn to sleep in this posture and do not retire to the sleeping platform at night. But no one is allowed to sleep or even to doze during meditation. If they do, they are awakened by a meditation patrol (*hsün-hsiang*), who stands facing the altar, holding an incense board horizontally before him in two hands.[19] Whenever he spots anyone nodding, he makes a circuit of the hall until he stands before him and strikes him lightly with the

16. Monks sit in the meditation hall during summer. Each monk holds a piece of split bamboo to cool his hands. Chiao Shan, Chen-chiang.

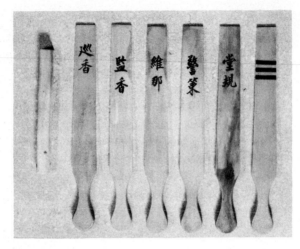

17. The different types of incense boards. Right to left: the abbot's board; the board for punishment in the meditation hall; the instructor's board; the precentor's board; the *chien-hsiang* board and the *hsün-hsiang* board (carried by meditation patrols). See Chapter II, note 36, and Appendix IV. These photos were posed in a small temple in Taipei.

18. The *hsün-hsiang* meditation patrol stands in front of the door while sitting is underway.

19. The *hsün-hsiang* meditation patrol makes a circuit holding the board next to his ear.

incense board on the upper part of the back. This is not a punishment but a reminder. If he strikes harshly or with the edge rather than the flat of the board, he is liable to be beaten himself by the precentor.[20] A high-ranking monk like an instructor is only touched on the knee.

The meditation patrol makes three to six regular circuits according to the length of each meditation period. On his first circuit he straightens out any sandals that are awry. It is not always easy for beginners to learn the art of seating themselves and then, without the use of hands, scuffing off their sandals so that these end up under the bench foursquare. As the meditation patrol makes his circuits, he holds the tip of the incense board above his right ear. He has the duty for only one period of meditation and then returns to his seat, to be replaced by the monk sitting next below him.

At eight o'clock the hand-chime is struck. This signifies the end of the "morning meditation period" (*tsao-pan hsiang*). The absolute silence is over, so that monks who have been waiting to clear their throats may cough in their sleeves or spit into a piece of toilet paper, which they slip under the cushion, to be disposed of on their next trip to the latrines. They all swing their legs down and wriggle into

20. The *chien-hsiang* meditation patrol makes a circuit carrying the board in front of him (see Appendix IV).

their sandals; then at a signal from the precentor they get up to circumambulate again. Thus begins the "fourth period" (*ssu-chih hsiang*).[21] Simultaneously a succentor lights a stick of incense and carries it over to the kitchen (*sung-hsiang*). This is to remind the kitchen staff that an hour later, when the stick will have burned down, they must be prepared to serve the noon meal. The daily routine of the whole monastery is geared to the meditation hall.

At nine o'clock, after their second cycle of running and sitting, the monks leave for the refectory to rejoin the rest of their brethren in eating "noon rice" (*wu-fan*), usually with *lo-han ts'ai,* a mixture of many different kinds of fresh vegetables. The rules are the same as at breakfast. When they return to the hall, they clean their teeth, visit the latrines, and begin circumambulating. After a few minutes of circumambulation, they go to their seats where, upon two strokes of the board, they drink the "two-stroke tea" (*erh pan-ch'a*). This is the first of three teas served to them in their seats during the course of the day. Tea and Ch'an have long been associated. Indeed the first tea plants are said to have grown from Bodhidharma's eyelashes, which he cut off to keep himself awake during meditation. It may be, however, that the "tea" is sometimes hot water.[22]

When the "two-stroke tea" has been drunk, three strokes are sounded on the board to signal the beginning of the "noon meditation period" (*wu-pan hsiang*). It is followed by the "fourth and sixth periods" (*ssu-liu chih-hsiang*)[23] so that the monks are steadily at work for about four hours, that is, until 2:00 p.m.

During the running that introduces the fourth period, there is an Explanation of how to meditate (*chiang k'ai-shih*).[24] It is always given by the abbot or one of the instructors present. Just as the precentor is in charge of the administration of the hall, the instructors are in charge of the mental training of those enrolled. They take turns. First the rector, then the senior, associate, and finally assistant instructors give Explanations one by one in order of seniority. If there are six instructors and if four Explanations are being given daily (as would be the case in September), then each of them speaks every other day, since the abbot usually takes a turn in the evening. According to one informant, junior instructors must attend when their seniors speak, but the reverse is forbidden. The master may not be taught by the disciple. Thus if the rector is giving an Explanation, all the instructors must be present, whereas if it is the turn of an assistant instructor, all except assistant instructors who are junior to him must leave.

Explanations invariably come in the middle of a period of running. The small board is struck as a signal to stop (*ta chan-pan*) and everyone takes the nearest seat to listen. The instructor speaks for a period that may last from a few minutes to half an hour. When he is finished, the small board is struck again to "start" the monks (*ta ts'ui-pan*), and they resume circumambulation.

So much for the mechanics of Explanations. Their content is up to the instructor. He speaks about whatever he has on his mind: perhaps some pointers on how to breathe or hold the spine, perhaps the "recorded sayings" (*yü-lu*) of earlier masters, or perhaps some passage in the Buddhist canon. "Recorded sayings" include the "public cases" (*kung-an;* Japanese *koan*) that have become familiar to Western students of Zen, as well as the *hua-t'ou* that often lie at the core of public cases. A "public case" is an anecdote of enlightenment,[25] in which some disciple exchanges cryptic questions and answers—and perhaps blows—with his master.

When I have asked Chinese monks about *hua-t'ou,* they have usually mentioned two:

1) Who is this reciting buddha's name?
2) Before my father and mother gave birth to me, what was my original face?

Both of these amount to asking "what am I?" Though monks were at liberty to shift to alternative *hua-t'ou,* either of their own choosing or suggested by the instructors, it was considered better not to shift often. To keep working on the same question was "like a rat gnawing at a coffin—if he keeps gnawing at the same spot, there will come a day when he gnaws his way through." There is a sign posted in many meditation halls: "See to your *hua-t'ou*" (*chao-ku hua-t'ou*). Even when circumambulating, monks are supposed to continue gnawing on it. (Hsü-yün, the leading exponent of Ch'an in modern China, warned that the question most widely used—"Who is this reciting buddha's name?"—must not be repeated mechanically. The "who" had to be gripped day and night, walking, sitting, going to the latrines. He made his remarks while giving a series of Explanations in Shanghai, not as the abbot or instructor, but as an eminent visiting monk. It was common to invite visitors to address the meditation hall or, as in this case, to lead a meditation week (*chu-ch'i*), even though they held no rank in the monastery. For readers who would like to see an example of Explanations, at least two English renderings of those by Hsü-yün are now available[26]).

In following the monks through their daily routine we have only gotten a little beyond noon. We shall try to deal with the rest of it more briefly. After the sixth period, which includes another Explanation, the residents of the meditation hall repair to the refectory at 2:00 p.m. for their third meal of the day, termed the "luncheon congee" (*tien-hsin chou*). Theravada countries like Thailand preserve the original Buddhist custom that no solid food may be eaten after noon, but this rule is not observed in China, where the evening activities and colder climate are considered to make seventeen hours of fasting impractical. In token, however, of the original custom the meals taken after noon are informal. Monks do not don their robes and at some monasteries they are even permitted to talk while eating.

After luncheon there is a short period for what we might call tutorials, but it is termed in Chinese "asking for an Explanation" (*ch'ing k'ai-shih*).[27] Any monk who wishes may put on his robe (*ta-i*), make three prostrations before the altar, and go to the apartment of an instructor or of the abbot to discuss his work. Since there are only about half a dozen instructors responsible for the hundred or more residents of the meditation hall, the individual can have no more than a few minutes with one of them every few days. He spreads his kneeling cloth, prostrates himself to the instructor, and respectfully states the difficulties he has been having. Perhaps he is troubled by a persistent cramp or a distracting thought or perhaps he has failed to understand an Explanation given in the hall. The instructor answers in accordance with the circumstances and the stage of development that the monk has reached. To gauge the latter he questions him. Here is an actual example of the questioning of a monk who was once a government official and has just started meditation.

"When you were in office, how did you protect the country and govern the people?"

The monk explains his methods of administration. Then he is asked: "Where did you get these methods?"

"From my mind."

"Where is your mind? Where is it after you die? You can't speak, you can't see, you lie there for three days and begin to stink. Where is it?"

The monk tries in vain to explain where his mind is and the instructor sends him back to the meditation hall to work on that as his *hua-t'ou.*

Monks can change instructors without embarrassment. It is not a fixed relationship. What the monk seeks is someone whose language he can understand and with whom he has an affinity from former lives (*yu-yüan*). He does not formally become the instructor's disciple.[28]

At 3:00 p.m., having finished with their tutorials or enjoyed a little free time, the monks go to the great shrine-hall for afternoon devotions (*shang wan-tien*). These are performed in the same way as morning devotions, but the liturgy is longer and includes different texts, like the short Pure Land sutra (*O-mi-t'o ching*), and an offering to the hungry ghosts (*Meng-shan shih-shih-i*). Several items from morning devotions are then repeated (the *Heart Sutra,* the gathas in praise of the buddhas, serpentining buddha['s name], and taking the Refuges). After the Pure Land Vow (*Ching-t'u wen*), a prayer is read to a group of guardian divinities, the Ch'ieh-lan, whose aid is invoked by reciting a short mantra, the *Ta-pei Chou.*[29] Among these guardian divinities is Kuan-kung, the hero of the *Romance of the Three Kingdoms,* who has been adopted by Buddhists and Taoists alike.

The longest item in the afternoon liturgy is the short Pure Land sutra. We should not be surprised to find Ch'an monks reciting the Pure Land sutra and serpentining buddha's name. The joint practice of Pure Land and Ch'an (*ch'an-ching shuang-hsiu*) is found in most Chinese Buddhist monasteries. We shall hear more about this in the closing chapter.

When the afternoon devotions are over and the monks return to the meditation hall a little after four o'clock, they have their second rest period of the day. The light is beginning to wane and the lamps have not yet been lit. They take off all their outer garments, climb up on the platform, and have a long sleep. It is not termed "sleep," but "let-

21. The monks kneel before the altar to recite the *Ching-t'u wen* during afternoon devotions. P'i-lu Ssu, Nanking.

ting go [of the work] to build up [the spirit] with rest" (*fang yang-hsi*). It lasts for two hours. Because it is immediately followed by the evening meditation period, the latter is called "*yang-hsi hsiang*."

This is the longest and the most important meditation period of the day. Officers whose work has kept them busy elsewhere in the morning and the afternoon, may now come to the meditation hall to join in. Since they have spent at least a term in the hall (or they could not be officers), each has a rank and accordingly goes to his place in east or west. If there is not enough room, matting (*chan-tzu*) is unrolled on the floor along the sides and back of the hall, so that up to a hundred extra persons can be seated. For circumambulation it is rolled up again. As at other times, residents of the wandering monks hall are not allowed to attend. They hold a period of evening meditation on their own. This exclusiveness is relaxed in the case of distinguished clerical visitors, who may be escorted to the hall by a guest prefect, while in monasteries less strict than Chin Shan the residents of the wandering monks hall and even lay visitors are sometimes allowed to take part.[30]

The evening period consists of the usual cycle of running and sitting. The sitting is the longest of the day, lasting about an hour and a half. When it ends at 8:00 p.m., the monks do not stir. A meal is served to them in their seats. It is called *ch'ih fang-ts'an* "eating [the meal served during] the recess." Big tubs of soft rice, soup and pickled vegetables, all wrapped up to keep them hot, are brought in by the verger and the water-bearer. Each monk pulls a thin slat part way out from under his cushion. The section that projects is held in place by his weight and serves as a tray for his bowls. For officers who come from outside, this may be the fifth meal of the day, since many of them have already had congee in their quarters at 5:00 p.m.[31] The food is tastier than what is served in the refectory and one can linger over it. "Eating the recess" takes half to three quarters of an hour.[32]

After the bowls have been removed, the second cycle of evening work begins. Circumambulation is particularly rapid. When the small board is struck, everyone stops and hears the longest Explanation of the day, almost invariably given by the abbot. It may last half an hour and is followed, as usual, by a shorter period of circumambulation. The final sitting is brief. At 10:00 p.m. work ends as the drum in the great shrine-hall begins to boom. Then the night patrol makes a circuit of the whole monastery striking his board twice. That is the sign for "lights out." Anyone found talking or with a lamp lit thereafter will be censured by the proctor.

In all the residents of the meditation hall have done seven periods of running and seven of sitting, a total of about nine hours' work. If we consider the four meals, three teas, two naps, and the alternation of sitting with running, this may not seem to be an unbearable program. But we have yet to hear about the period in autumn when the work reaches its peak.

The daily schedule varies throughout the year in accordance with the weather and the length of the day. During the five months from the 16th of the first lunar month to the 15th of the fifth, it is the schedule described above. For the next two weeks, the fourth and the sixth periods of morning meditation are replaced by what we might call choir practice. This is to prepare for the noon devotions that are added from the 1st of the sixth through the 15th of the seventh month, when the monks spend an hour each day chanting in the great shrine-hall. In these same six weeks the long meditation period in the evening is omitted. Instead, all the monks of the monastery recite buddha's name in the courtyard (*p'u-fo*). The weather is simply too hot for running and there are too many mosquitoes for sitting.[33]

Enrollment in the meditation hall for the entire summer term (the first six months of the lunar year) is generally much lower than for the winter term. Newcomers who have spent the winter term there are now qualified to take office and many of them do so. Old hands at meditation go back to their own hereditary temples to enjoy a respite. The summer is also the best time for pilgrimages to sacred mountains. As a result there may be only a handful of monks left in the hall.[34] Hence it is convenient to "redivide the platform" (*fen-tan*), that is, each person takes double the usual area for sleeping so that he can put up a mosquito net. But the number of monks is never allowed to fall below the level of the skeleton force necessary for orthodox meditation. There is always an instructor, a precentor, some succentors, and enough rank and file to serve as meditation patrols and duty monks.

MEDITATION WEEKS

With the start of the autumn semester (*ch'iu-ch'i*) on the 16th of the seventh month, which comes in our August or September, the work begins to accelerate. The monks return to the schedule described in the preceding pages. In the first month during circumambulation, the precentor talks about the forms and solemn etiquette (*wei-i*) of the meditation hall—how to sit, sleep, eat, dress, and so on. This is for the benefit of those who have never taken part before. Starting the 16th of the ninth month an extra cycle of running and sitting is added after 10:00 p.m. This is called "adding incense" (*chia-hsiang*). The purpose is to get everyone in training for the meditation weeks (*ch'an-ch'i*) that begin on the 15th of the tenth month, when the cold weather has come to stay. (Most Chinese monasteries held only one or two meditation weeks in the course of the year. Chin Shan and other model institutions usually held seven.) The abbot, the rector, or perhaps an eminent visiting monk takes over-all charge (*chu-ch'i*). The objective is to step up the schedule to the point where the mind, exhausted by lack of sleep and frustrated by work on the *hua-t'ou*, will make the jump to enlightenment.

During the forty-nine days of meditation weeks monks leave the hall only for meals and once a week to bathe. Instead of attending devotions twice daily, they use the time for additional cycles of running and sitting. They still have their nap from 4:00 to 6:00 p.m., but in the evening the number of cycles is stepped up from two to five, making a total of twelve cycles a day, lasting fifteen hours. At night they sleep two hours, from 1:00 to 3:00 a.m. It is true that the long eveing's work is interrupted by two extra Explanations, by "eating the recess" (in this case a twelve-ounce vegetable dumpling), by a later trip to the refectory for rice and vegetables cooked in sesame oil, and by an extra "recess" of fried vegetables eaten shortly before midnight. But it is still a frightening program of mental concentration.

To tighten the atmosphere certain alterations are made in the usual practices. Two meditation patrols stand guard instead of one. They are termed not *hsün-hsiang* but *chien-hsiang* since these are the words

inscribed on their incense boards. They make their circuits in opposite directions, so that each monk is doubly inspected.[35] When the
monks are circumambulating and they hear the stopping board, they
do not take the nearest seat to listen to the Explanation as at other
times of the year. They stand stock-still, feet apart, wherever they
happen to be, while the instructor continues to circumambulate as he
talks.

There are other peculiarities of circumambulation during these
seven weeks like, for example, shouting "up" (han "ch'i" tzu). This is
done two or three minutes before the end or break in a period of
circumambulation. While the monks walk in concentric circles around
the hall, the precentor shouts the single word "up" in a curious,
drawn-out note of rising pitch. He is answered by all the monks
carrying chien-hsiang incense boards,[36] who also shout in unison
"u-u-up!" This is the signal for the rank and file to rise up and struggle even harder against ignorance, error, and distraction, to grip their
question even more firmly. It is also a signal for a change of gait. The
monks abandon their fast, swaggering walk; they round their shoulders,
hunch down their heads, lean a little forward, and trot along with
loose joints as if they were fleeing marionettes. Indeed they are fleeing, for the precentor runs along between them beating them with
his incense board.[37] Again comes the long drawn-out shout of "up,"
this time from an instructor. Again it is echoed by all the chien-hsiang.
In some periods it is shouted three times, in others six, during the
last two or three minutes of circumambulation.[38]

The evening tenth period sees yet another departure from normal.
It begins about midnight. The monks have been at work since 4:00
a.m. Now, instead of walking in concentric circles, they move around
the hall as they please, "like stars filling the sky" (man-t'ien hsing).
This too ends with the shout of "up" and a hectic trot—just before the
abbot himself gives the final Explanation of the day. The climactic
pattern is obvious.

The only concession made to human frailty during meditation
weeks is that monks for whom the pain of long sitting becomes unendurable are allowed to get up from their places and stand by the
altar until the pain subsides. Otherwise the discipline is the same as
at other times.

When the meditation weeks are over, the monk in charge of them (*chu-ch'i*), usually chats with the participants to see what sort of achievements (*ch'eng-chiu*) they have made. Sometimes a formal examination is held. Meditation weeks were the high point of the religious year at great meditation centers like Chin Shan, Kao-min, T'ien-ning, T'ien-t'ung, and the Pao-kuang Ssu near Chengtu. Not only was formal enrollment higher in the winter term, but during these few weeks officers from the "outer sections" joined in far more than usual, especially in the evening, so that the hall became terribly crowded and there was scarcely elbow room between the seated monks who covered the floor. This too must have added to the tension.

VARIATIONS

At other than the model monasteries the work was not so rigorous. There might be none at all except for occasional meditation weeks in winter. Where there was a hall in regular operation (and this was probably at much less than half the large monasteries in China) there were normally three to six cycles of running and sitting each day, which would be increased during meditation weeks, but might not reach the twelve cycles a day at Chin Shan. The number of weeks depended on the wishes of the participants. If after the first week they wanted a second, it was so arranged. They did not necessarily sleep in the hall. Only the larger places had the necessary sleeping platform (*kuang-tan*). Discipline was relaxed in varying degrees. But there was everywhere, I believe, an awareness of the standards set at Chin Shan and the Kao-min Ssu.

Some large monasteries like T'ien-t'ung had separate halls for older and younger monks. In its western hall beginners were trained with maximum rigor: the system was the same as at Chin Shan. In its eastern hall old hands practiced meditation not collectively, but individually, each in his own cubicle, whenever they felt inclined.[39] They could come and go as they pleased (whereas in the western hall no one could be absent for even a period). The staff was there to serve them, not to supervise them. It consisted simply of a "hall manager" (*kuan-t'ang*), a verger, and a water-bearer. Many of those enrolled were retired menial officers. Indeed this was as much a place of retirement as a meditation hall.

I have collected little first-hand information about other variants from the norm that has been described.[40] However, there is an interesting account by the German architect, Ernst Boerschmann, of the meditation hall at the Fa-yü Ssu on the sacred island of P'u-t'o Shan. By the front wall, where we would expect to find a bench with places for the instructors, the precentor, and the duty monk, there was one chair for a single officer in charge. The bench ran only along the end walls and in front of it stood a series of high narrow tables, stacked with the books that the monks here were studying. Not only would the books never have been found in the meditation hall at Chin Shan, where Ch'an meant the study of a wordless doctrine, but the tables would have gotten in people's way when they left their seats to circumambulate. Yet this hall at the Fa-yü Ssu was called a *ch'an-t'ang* and some of the Ch'an tradition remained. Although Boerschmann does not give the daily schedule, he tells us that at fixed times the monks sat motionless with closed eyes "for hours."[41]

The contrast between the norm and variants is nicely illustrated by a pair of photographs published by Prip-Møller. The first was taken at the Pao-kuang Ssu in Szechwan and shows monks sitting as properly as at Chin Shan (it is the only such photograph, so far as I know, that has ever been printed). On the facing page we see the meditation hall at the Chao-ch'ing Ssu, Hangchow. As at the Fa-yü Ssu the monks sit behind tables piled high with books, like students in a classroom.[42] When I showed this to a monk from Chin Shan, he clucked disapprovingly and said that such a place did not deserve even to be called a meditation hall.

LEAVE

At model monasteries one could only enroll in the meditation hall at the beginning of a semester (the 16th of the first and seventh months) and thereafter one had to attend every period until the semester came to an end.[43] There were three exceptions to this rule. Monks were occasionally borrowed to assist at a plenary mass;[44] or were called out to take part in chores;[45] and, when the circumstances required it, they could apply to the precentor for leave (*hsiang-chia*). Leave would not be granted if they merely wished to go out and buy some minor necessity like ink or thread: a verger would be sent to buy it for them. It would be granted only for some important reason, like the death of parents. In addition, if a monk's clothes needed attention, he could apply for up to a day of "mending leave" (*kao feng-pu chia*); while if he fell ill he could apply for sick leave (*kao ping-chia*). In case of a minor illness, the precentor would excuse him from a certain number of meditation periods, but not from attending meals and devotions. He spent the day resting across the courtyard in the shrine-hall of Wei-t'o, the protector of monasteries. If he was seriously ill, he could move to the infirmary (*ju-i liao*), where a monk was appointed to care for the patients and bring them food, medicine, bedding, and so on—all in whatever form and quantities they desired (hence *ju-i*). A Chinese-style doctor might be called in. This and other medical expenses were borne by the monastery, not by the monk. Care of patients from the meditation hall was overseen by one of the succentors who paid sick calls several times a day. The Kao-min code of rules, with its usual severity, forbade reading and writing in the infirmary and prescribed that there, as in the meditation hall, a light was to be kept burning at night to discourage laxity.[46]

Illness was not necessarily regarded as a misfortune, and this was for more reasons than the prospect of the special treatment that monks got in the infirmary. The following is quoted from the *Pao-wang san-mei lun*:

> In your concern for your body, do not ask to avoid illness. If the body has no illnesses, then cravings and lust easily arise . . . Therefore the sages taught us to take the misery of illness as the best of medicines.[47]

Except when granted leave, every monk was obliged to abide by the full schedule of the meditation hall. It was work day and night: he was not even allowed to read the newspapers. If he could not put up with it and fled the monastery,[48] he could return after three days or more (there was no fixed limit) and either ask to be readmitted or collect his baggage. In both cases the precentor would upbraid him for his lack of resolution and urge him to think of his spiritual future (or, according to one informant, beat him). If the truant preferred therefore not to go back to the hall, he could ask the guest prefect to go and collect his luggage for him. Because of the loss of face involved, very few monks applied for readmission, but if they did, the request was granted.

The aspect of life in the meditation hall that may strike outsiders as most intolerable was not the long hours, but the confinement. At the Kao-min Ssu, for example, even if a monk was granted a leave of absence from meditation, he had to stay on the monastery premises. Only once annually were residents permitted to venture beyond the main gate. On New Year's Day, properly attired, they could step forth through the right side of the gate and later return through the left. This is what a former resident recalls. Some monks, of course, had to go out on monastery business and others presumably tried to use monastery business as an excuse. Private excursions were forbidden to all. The Kao-min code of rules threatened punishment and expulsion for anyone—even a visitor in the wandering monks hall—who, for his own private purposes, went to San-ch'a Ho or the Yangtze bridge.[49] These were places for shopping and amusement, which did not sort well with the spirit of the Kao-min Ssu.

THE FRUITS OF MEDITATION

Outsiders may find it hard to understand why anyone would be willing to put up with the hardship of the meditation hall. What were the fruits that justified it? Was any enlightenment achieved?

I have been largely unsuccessful in getting an answer to this question. For one thing, it has not pleased the venerable monks with whom I have raised it. To them it seemed inappropriate and in bad taste. Other people's spiritual accomplishments were their personal affair and, baldly put, none of my business. If I wanted to find out about spiritual accomplishments, I had better have some of my own. This was not because such things were esoteric or mysterious, but because they were private, like a man's intimate relations with his wife. So, after twenty pages of details on how meditation was conducted, I can offer scarcely a word (from my own informants at any rate) on what it achieved.

Is this perhaps because nothing was achieved? Were my informants simply too embarrassed to admit that the work of the meditation hall was, as a Christian missionary asserted, "merely external exercises, carried out in prescribed order"?[50] This is a possible explanation. But it does not seem adequate to account for the vigor with which these exercises were pursued nor for people's willingness to put up with such discomfort when they might have been happily lazing away in a small temple. If they found no rewards in meditation, why would they have enrolled for a second and third year, as many did? Furthermore, we do occasionally hear about the rewards. One informant told me that during meditation he had caught a glimpse of a peaceful, radiant world. Another said that one evening at Chin Shan, years ago, he felt as if he were sublimely floating (*p'iao-p'iao mang-mang-ti*). Later, during tutorials, the instructor asked him about his progress. My informant told him that he did not know, but it seemed to him that he had reached a different state of mind (*ching-chieh*). The instructor ordered him to get back to work as quickly as possible.

All this sounds unsatisfactorily bland. We hear a more pointed account through the ears of John Blofeld, who has sat longer in a Chinese meditation hall than any other Westerner I know of (although it was not at one of the model monasteries). He felt that for some of the monks with whom he sat the work was an ordeal, while others profited greatly. One of the latter described his sensations to Mr. Blofeld in the following terms:

I don't know how many of us younger monks here really understand the Preceptor [instructor]. I find his lectures far from clear. Still I have discovered for myself that if I just sit perfectly still, so still that I am conscious of the blood drumming in my ears and open my mind to—no, not to anything—just open up my mind; though nothing happens the first time or the second, one day I begin to feel some response. My heart seems to be talking to me, revealing secrets of which I have never so much as dreamt. Afterwards I am left in a state of marvelous happiness. A Light shines within me and about me and they are One. My heart seems to have seven doors which open one by one, the Light getting brighter and brighter all the time. And when the meditation period is over, I feel as if everything that happens to me is good; as if all of it is directed by the Light; as if, without thinking much, I do just what is best for me to do; as if I am being carried by a great stream just where it is best for me to go. Then, sooner or later, from habit I do something which brings me against the current of the stream; the Light fades and I am as before, but for a while I am lonely as when I first separated from my mother. I think this is because I have a heavy load of karma which drags me back and sets me against the stream again and again. What gives me hope is that, each time all this happens, the Light seems to stay with me a little longer.[51]

Even if we suppose that Mr. Blofeld's reporting has been affected partly by his own experiences and partly by what he thinks Ch'an ought to be, this quotation must still preserve something of what he was told.

We have also what purports to be a description of enlightenment—or something like it—in a monk's own words. It is found in the autobiography of the illustrious Hsü-yün. Hsü-yün arrived at the Kao-min Ssu in 1895 to take part in meditation weeks, but since he had fallen in the river on the way, he was gravely ill. "Awaiting death," he says, "I sat diligently in the meditation hall day and night."

My concentration became so pure that I did not know I had a body. After a little over twenty days, all my ailments were suddenly cured . . . From this point on all my thoughts suddenly ceased. My work began to progress (*kung-fu lo-t'ang*). Day and night were the same. When I moved, it was like flying. One night during the rest from meditation, I opened my eyes and suddenly there was a great radiance like broad daylight. I could see through everything, inside and out. Through the walls that separated us I could see the verger urinating. I could also see a monk from the Western ranks who was in the latrine. Further off I could see boats going up and down the river, and trees on its banks of every kind and color. At this point three boards were struck [about 2:30 a.m.]. The next day I asked the verger and the monk from the Western ranks, and it was just as I had seen it. Since I knew that this was simply a mental state (*ching*), I did not consider it anything strange. In the last month of the year, on the third night of the eighth week, during the recess after the sixth period, the attendants poured hot water according to the rule. It splashed on my hand. The tea cup fell to the ground and broke to bits with loud noise. Suddenly the roots of doubt were cut. In my whole life I had never felt such joy. It was like waking from a dream. I thought of the many decades of wandering since I became a monk. I thought of the hut by the Yellow River and how when that fellow asked me, I did not know what water was. At that moment, if I had kicked over Wen-chi's kettle and stove,[52] I wonder what he would have said. And now if I had not fallen into the water and gotten very ill, if I had not been through easy times and hard times that taught me lessons and changed my understanding, I might have almost missed my chance in this life and then how

could this day have ever come? For that reason I wrote the following gatha:

> A cup crashed to the floor
> The sound was clear and sharp
> The emptiness was shattered
> And the turbulent mind fell suddenly to rest.[53]

This reads almost like a classical description of enlightenment—a
"public case" (*kung-an*)—and although no term for enlightenment is
used,[54] it is regarded as such by some of his disciples.

A few of my informants were ready to affirm that not only Hsü-yün,
but Lai-kuo, Yeh-k'ai, and many famous monks of this century had
frequent enlightenments, large and small. But other informants refused to be drawn into any such evaluation. A leading disciple of
Hsü-yün, who followed him as abbot of the Nan-hua Ssu, was unwilling
to say what had happened—in terms of enlightenment—when the tea-
cup "crashed to the floor." He was even unwilling to make an evaluation of Hui-neng, the Sixth Patriarch. He admitted that Hui-neng had
attained a sudden enlightenment, but "we do not know what his spiritual accomplishments were. We have no right to say."

On the other hand, an old rector told me that he himself had often
seen cases of enlightenment. He could tell from the way people replied to questions during tutorials: they had answers to their *hua-t'ou*.
Perhaps he was just giving me the stock version of the way things
were supposed to happen. Other monks told me: "Only you yourself
can know whether you have been enlightened or not. It is like drinking water: only the person who drinks it can say whether it is warm."

When I quoted this back to the old rector, he commented: "They
just told you that because they had not achieved any enlightenment
themselves. Only if an instructor has achieved it himself can he tell
whether a disciple has achieved it."

"But *how* can he tell?" I asked.

"I cannot explain that to you. You would have to be enlightened
before you could understand it."

The abbot of Chin Shan took the opposite position. When I asked
whether he could detect enlightenment in the monks who came to him
for tutorials, he replied: "No, for I have never gotten paranormal
powers (*shen-t'ung*). If I had rooted out all erroneous ways of thinking (*wang-hsiang*), reached perfect concentration (*ting*) and attained

prajna (*hui*), then I would have had paranormal powers. Only with paranormal powers—telepathic powers (*t'a-hsin t'ung*)—could I have known whether a disciple was enlightened or not."[55]

Even as to methods it is difficult to get concrete information. In preparing this chapter I felt dissatisfied with the example of tutorials given on pp. 70-71. I wrote to a senior monk who had been most precise in explaining the daily routine of meditation. "Could you," I asked, "give me an example from your own experience of what happened during tutorials?" His reply was: "When students do not understand the profundities of the doctrine or the methods of the work of meditation, they ask some well-qualified older person to take pity on them, open the gate of expedient means, and explain the way things really are. I am afraid that this answer will not satisfy you, for which I am truly sorry. Please come and see me soon."

Probably the only way to penetrate this curtain of reticence and contradictions would be to enroll in a meditation hall oneself. This I have not had the opportunity to do. Of course, if I had, it might have made me as reticent as my informants. The inquisitive outsider seems to be caught on the horns of Lao-tzu's paradox: "Those who know do not speak, those who speak do not know."

While most informants discouraged personal questions and refused to give concrete examples, they were always willing to talk in general terms, that is, in terms of doctrine. It lies outside the scope of this book to discuss what Buddhist doctrine really is. I can only try to report what some Chinese Buddhists say it is. In the first place they make a distinction between enlightenment, nirvana, and buddhahood. *K'ai-wu*, the Chinese phrase commonly translated as "to attain enlightenment," actually means to attain a *degree* of enlightenment. There are large and small degrees (*k'ai ta-wu, k'ai hsiao-wu*). The word "degree" is appropriate here since monks compare enlightenment to a circle that must be filled sector by sector. This is done as the Buddhist proceeds along the "ten stages" (*shih-ti*, Sanskrit *bhumi*) of the bodhisattva career. Usually it takes many rebirths before one can become a fully enlightened or tenth-stage bodhisattva (*shih-ti p'u-sa*). The preliminary step is to resolve on bodhisattvahood (*fa p'u-sa hsin*), as is done by laymen and monks alike when they take the bodhisattva vows at ordination. Anyone who takes these vows becomes a "worldling bodhisattva" (*fan-fu p'u-sa*). Next, whether he is a monk or a layman, he must achieve a degree of enlightenment before he can be considered to have made any progress in following the bodhisattva path (*hsing p'u-sa tao*). He cannot get beyond its third stage, however, as a layman. No layman has ever become a buddha. Vimalakirti, for instance, the famous lay devotee who is believed to have come to China in the time of Sakyamuni himself, had entered the sangha in a previous incarnation. He was only apparently a layman: actually he was a buddha. Since some laymen would only believe in him if he took the form of a buddha (*hsien fo-hsiang*), at times he temporarily resumed it.

The seventh stage of the bodhisattva path is that of the arhat. Reaching it (*cheng lo-han kuo*) means reaching nirvana and being released from the cycle of birth and death. But the nirvana attained by the arhat is not equal to the nirvana of the tenth-stage bodhisattva. The latter's nirvana is accompanied by greater wisdom, which he dedicates to saving all sentient being, whereas the arhat is satisfied with his own salvation. Buddhas, in turn, reach a stage beyond the ten stages and achieve a "subtle enlightenment" (*miao-chüeh*) beyond the bodhisattva's. Although all living creatures have the buddha nature, none has become a buddha since the time of Sakyamuni and no one is going to become one until the appearance of Maitreya. Yet there is not the absolute difference between buddhas and bodhisattvas that we read about in Western books on Buddhism. I have read—and written—that buddhas are withdrawn in nirvana and take no active part in the saving of others, whereas bodhisattvas have postponed entering nirvana themselves until they can help all sentient beings to enter it before them. But according to the monks I have talked to, buddhas too exert themselves to save all sentient beings (*tu chung-sheng*). Furthermore, on their missions of salvation, all of them, like Vimalakirti, may take the form of bodhisattvas or of laymen. This blurring of distinction is not accepted by some of the lay Buddhists that I have talked to, particularly those who have read Western books about Buddhism. They believe that buddhas can only act through the bodhisattvas who are their agents, as Kuan-yin, for example, is the agent of Amitabha. There are also lay Buddhists who reject the concept of degrees of enlightenment. In Ch'an, they say, enlightenment is either sudden and complete or not at all. It has nothing to do with the ten stages and does not come by stages.

None of the monks I queried saw any contradiction between sudden and gradual enlightenment. These were different ways of looking at the same thing. As they put it, the sudden enlightenment of the Sixth Patriarch (who founded the "sudden" school) must have been the result of long training and self-cultivation in earlier lives.

In their view the objective was to move along the bodhisattva path as far as possible in each lifetime. The practice of meditation was one way of doing this. It could and should be combined with reciting buddha's name and the study of Buddhist doctrine, but the proportion devoted to each must vary with the individual. The point he reached in following the bodhisattva path depended on where he had started. If he had already covered a certain distance in previous lives, he had a head start, like the Sixth Patriarch. But with determination and hard work, even the retarded could make rapid achievements (*ch'eng-chiu*). The achievement especially hoped for by those who specialized in meditation was to break down erroneous ways of thinking (*wang-hsiang*), which prevented wisdom and were the root of birth and death. Release from birth and death, which was the fruit of arhatship —the seventh stage of the bodhisattva path—was the theoretical goal of the work of the meditation hall. Solving one's *hua-t'ou* was the method of reaching it.

But, in actual practice, release from birth and death was seldom expected, because ours is the last of the three eras that the Buddha predicted for the decay of the dharma. In the first five hundred years after he preached the doctrine, he said, it would be comparatively easy to achieve enlightenment. In the next five hundred years it would be more difficult. In the present era only a very small number of persons can, through their own efforts, become enlightened. The best that most people can do is to depend on the buddha of the West, Amitabha, through whose infinite mercy and merit they may be reborn in the Western Paradise which, as we shall see in the next chapter, also provides release from birth and death. Few monks expected that their efforts in meditation would take them very far along the bodhisattva path.

Why then were they willing to put up with the austerities of the meditation hall: leg cramps, mosquitoes, the exhaustion of meditation weeks, the confinement within the monastery, and most of all the inherent boredom of trying to think about the same thing for nine to fifteen hours a day? I have frankly asked my informants whether they did not get bored. Most of them have denied it. The *hua-t'ou* was effective, they said. A monk pursued it and concentrated all his energy upon it. He also learned to control his mind—to watch the stream of consciousness and, as soon as bad thoughts arose (greed, anger or stupidity), to dissolve them in the silent recitation of buddha's name. Thus busied with learning, how could he get bored? Furthermore, his character was improved. Bad habits were weeded out. Through meditation even the most active person gradually became peaceful and indifferent to the abuse of others.

When I asked the abbot of Chin Shan about the possibility of boredom, I got a franker answer. "If you did not have the mental equipment to cope with the work," he said, "then the meditation hall was worse than prison. So every year there were monks who fled. On the other hand, if your mind was really on your work, then there was nothing boring about it. Those who were doing well with meditation could hardly wait to get started each day."

I have mentioned the "old hands" who spent their whole lives moving from one famous meditation hall to another, utterly contented. K. L. Reichelt says that monks who achieved a sense of their buddha-nature "feel as if their seats have been changed to a flowery bed of the most brilliant and fragrant lotus. Personally I have met such persons. They long for the hour of meditation."[56] These were the "old papayas" or *lao-ts'an* referred to earlier, who got their nickname because they were dried up and so much less lively than the "naughty" young men in the eastern ranks. In 1952, even after the Communist victory, the Kao-min Ssu still had "twenty to thirty *lao-ts'an* who had not been out of the monastery for decades."[57]

On the other hand, one hears of monks who found it impossible to make any mental breakthrough (*hsiang-pu-k'ai*) either because they were "stupid" or because they could not stop thinking about their parents, wife, children, and the other things they had left behind. At first they would be unable to keep their minds on anything. Then they would begin to have hallucinations and "talk nonsense." At this point they were usually locked in a room and a Chinese doctor called to examine them. Some recovered; some died. According to one informant, fatalities were most common during meditation weeks and the bodies were not buried immediately. It was felt that their death must be retribution for sins committed in former lives,[58] so they were wrapped in their quilts and left to be disposed of when the meditation weeks were over.

Such casualties were regarded, I think, the way the Marine Corps regards casualties in boot-camp training: regrettable, but necessary. The eastern side of the meditation hall was the boot-camp of the large monastery. Anyone who could get through it had proved himself. He probably did not resent its rigors. If anything, he was proud of them, as were Chinese Buddhists at large. Senior monastic officers, who had been through these same rigors years before, regarded the graduate of the meditation hall as one of themselves. They felt that he must be a person of determination, or he would have fled; that he now understood the operation of the monastery's most important unit; and that he had deepened his knowledge of himself and of the dharma. Therefore he was qualified to hold office. They certainly did not assume that he had achieved any enlightenment during his months in the meditation hall. This was his own business.

An older monk told me once that the routine of the meditation hall was so intricate that it could not be mastered in less than "three winters and four summers." His own mastery was impressive. I noticed that when he performed even the simplest ritual, there was a withdrawn look in his eyes and a deliberateness in his manner that made him seem larger than he was, as if he were saying to himself: "These ritual movements are something precious that must be revered and preserved, and I am the vessel of preservation." Sometimes I wonder if the routine of the meditation hall did not have some of the same fascination and give some of the same satisfactions as the routine of the Masonic Lodge—ritual for the beauty of ritual, expertise for its own sake. We see this carried to an extreme in the Japanese tea ceremony, in which the means have become the end. Its Ch'an origin is not irrelevant.

Perhaps it is easier now to understand what made people willing to put up with the austerities of the meditation hall. Quite aside from the pursuit of enlightenment and the ineffable "joy of the dharma" that sometimes came to them, they were rewarded in other ways. They mastered an ancient ritual; they proved their power of endurance; they learned to discipline their minds; they began their career in the proper fashion; and they achieved a certain status. But no attempt to bring the meditation hall "down to earth" should be carried too far. The transcendental element was always there, commanding the respect of Buddhists and non-Buddhists alike, for it is really independent of Buddhist doctrine. As long as man exists, he will feel the need for an immediate, intuitive answer to the question "What am I?" The meditation hall provided one way of seeking it.

CHAPTER III

The Buddha Recitation Hall

According to the fundamental sutra of the Pure Land school, the *Sukhavati-vyuha,* there was once a monk, Dharmakara, who resolved that he would only become a buddha on the condition that his buddha realm had the following characteristics. It would be full of sweet smells, clouds of music, showers of jewels, and every other beauty and joy. All who were reborn there would be able to stay indefinitely and to attain their nirvana. Most important of all, anyone could be reborn there who called upon his name ten times, or even once only. After making this resolve, Dharmakara went on to become the buddha Amitabha (O-mi-t'o-fo). The realm that he had made a precondition of buddhahood was thereby created. It lay in the West and so was called the Western Paradise. Since it was without pain or sin, it was also called the Pure Land. Amitabha still presides over it, assisted by two bodhisattvas known in Chinese as Kuan-yin and Ta-shih-chih (Avalokitesvara and Mahasthamaprapta).[1]

The Pure Land lies outside this universe, outside the realm of the Buddha Sakyamuni, outside the vertical scheme of twenty-eight heavens, one above the other, where rebirth is just another incident in the mortal cycle, longer and pleasanter, but affording no permanent release. Rebirth in the Pure Land means release forever.

Since we are living in the age of the decay of the dharma, it is difficult, as mentioned in the last chapter, to reach nirvana here through our own efforts. Therefore most Buddhists in China prefer to get the help of Amitabha by reciting his name (*nien-fo*).² That is, they repeat the words "homage to the buddha Amitabha" (*na-mo O-mi-t'o-fo*) in the belief that if they do so wholeheartedly they will be reborn in the Western Paradise. "Wholeheartedly" means making their minds "whole and still" (*i-hsin pu-luan*), so that nothing is there but Amitabha. He is in their mouths (as they recite his name), in their ears (as they listen to the recitation), and in their minds (as they visualize him). This is called "perfect concentration in reciting buddha's name" (*nien-fo san-mei*). It corresponds to a degree of enlightenment achieved in the meditation hall. Achieving it does not necessarily mean that one goes to the Western Paradise when he dies, unless he dies at once. Otherwise it is possible to slide backwards.

Entry into the Western Paradise requires no enlightenment at all. It is not connected with any of the ten stages of the bodhisattva career. The devotee does not have to resolve on bodhisattvahood. On the other hand, his station in the Western Paradise depends very much on his accomplishments. There are nine grades (*chiu-p'in*). If he is born into the lowest grade, the petals of his lotus seat do not open for five hundred years, during which time he cannot see Amitabha and the wonderful sights around him. A high grade, on the other hand, is like a front seat in class: one can hear better what the teacher is saying and approach buddhahood more rapidly. Residents of the Western Paradise who are approaching buddhahood may choose to return to the world of men. They do not have to, since they have been permanently released from the cycle of birth and death, but they may decide to be reborn here in order to follow the bodhisattva ideal of compassionate help to all sentient beings.

Except for the first paragraph, the picture given above is based entirely on conversations with Chinese Buddhists of different sects.

LING-YEN SSU

To find the practice of the Pure Land school fully developed and at its model best, one had to go to the Ling-yen Ssu outside Soochow (not to be confused with the Ling-yin Ssu, Hangchow, nor with the Leng-yen Ssu, Yingkow). This monastery's preeminence was very recent. In the midnineteenth century the T'ai-p'ing rebels had burned it to the ground, leaving only a pagoda intact. At the beginning of the Republican period enough was rebuilt to house about a dozen persons. In the 1920's under the guidance of the Venerable Yin-kuang, its monks began to devote themselves entirely to reciting buddha's name. Lay donations flowed in and the size of the establishment rapidly increased. A new buddha recitation hall was built in 1933 with places for a hundred participants. Yin-kuang formulated a detailed code of rules to govern its operation, along with new codes for the other departments. A seminary was founded.[3] By the late 1940's there were 150 to 200 monks in permanent residence, supported by the income from rites for the dead and the rents from 500 acres of farmland that had been donated by enthusiastic devotees. This was not only one of the major monastery restorations of the Republican period, but also a new departure, in which Yin-kuang tried to bring the reciting of buddha's name to the same level of articulation and intensity as was found in the meditation hall.

LAYOUT

There were many differences between the two kinds of hall, but the key to them lay in the difference between trying to get enlightenment through one's own single-handed efforts (*tzu-li*) and humbly surrendering oneself to the compassion of an outside and greater power (*t'a-li*), that is, the power of Amitabha. The first led to severity, the second to gentleness. The hall for reciting buddha's name at the Ling-yen Ssu was a much gentler, milder place than the meditation hall at Chin Shan. One could see this as soon as one looked in the door. There was no sleeping platform: those enrolled slept in two adjoining dormitories, so that they were not confined day and night by the same four walls. The sitting bench extended not only around the room, but there was a section of it in the middle behind the altar. This was for laymen, whom Yin-kuang wanted to attract. Many came from Shanghai and other neighboring cities to join in the recitation. The whole system of enrollment was inclusive rather than exclusive. Whereas at Chin Shan wandering monks were only allowed to sit in the meditation hall as a special favor, at Ling-yen Shan they were welcomed, indeed expected, to attend all of the six recitation periods a day, unless they were as-

signed to monastery chores. They did not have to wait to enroll until
the beginning of the next semester. They could move their effects to
the recitation dormitory at any time, though once enrolled they had to
stay until the end of the semester, as at Chin Shan. All this meant
that the rise and fall in the number of participants could be considerable. By rolling down the long floor mats an extra hundred persons
could be accommodated, thereby doubling the capacity of the hall.

In the west the order of sitting was the same as at Chin Shan: instructors near the door, then secretaries, and then lower ranks. The
abbot, however, who sat at the back of the meditation hall, here sat
above the instructors just to the left of the door. To the right of the
door sat the duty monk. He struck signals on his wooden fish, but not
on the board and bell. The board under the bell—the emblem of Ch'an
—was missing. Otherwise the furnishings on and above the tea-table
were the same as in the meditation hall. Beyond the tea-table sat the
precentor and four succentors, and below them the rank and file. As
in the meditation hall there was a patrol against sleepiness, but instead
of an incense board he carried a strip of silk (*fan*) two or three feet
long, which he brushed lightly against the face of anyone who began
to nod. Hence he was called the *hsün-fan*. He made regular tours of
the room during the period of silent recitation.

On the central altar, instead of Sakyamuni or Bodhidharma, one
found the Three Holy Ones of the West: Amitabha, with Kuan-yin on
his left and Mahasthamaprapta on his right. Thus the reciter could
imagine that he was already in the Western Paradise, listening to their
instruction.

DAILY PROGRAM

The work was more varied than in the meditation hall. Instead of
alternate running and sitting, each "stick" of recitation consisted of
five phases.

1) After the usual trip to the latrine, the monks put on their robes
(the *chia-sa*), which were not worn in the meditation hall, and sat
awaiting the arrival of the precentor. When he entered, they got down
from the bench, stood in rows before the altar, east facing west, and
chanted either the Amitabha Sutra or the *Meng-shan shih-shih i*.[4]

22. In the buddha recitation hall the monks stand facing one another as chanting begins. P'i-lu Ssu, Nanking.

23. The monks serpentine buddha's name. P'i-lu Ssu, Nanking.

24. The Three Holy Ones of the West (left to right: Mahasthamaprapta, Amitabha, Kuan-yin) preside over silent recitation from the central altar of the hall.

25. The southeast corner of the hall during seated recitation. A succentor strikes the small bell and wooden fish, mounted on a rack in front of him. The duty monk sits next to the door, while the precentor sits on the other side of the table. Pi-lu Ssu, Nanking.

When they had finished chanting, they would begin to circumambu-late, reciting buddha's name. Because the pace was slow and unvary-ing, this was not called "running," but "circling" (*chuan*).[5] It was not done in concentric circles but in single file. If the line was too long, it moved in serpentine fashion among the kneeling mats. Whereas in the meditation hall no instruments were used to mark the pace, here a hand-chime and a small wooden fish were beaten to keep time.[6] Reci-tation was always begun by the precentor, who first chanted the words "Homage to Amitabha, the great compassionate buddha of the West-ern Paradise." Then other monks joined in: "Homage to the buddha Amitabha! Homage to the buddha Amitabha! Homage to the buddha Amitabha! . . ." It was sung slowly and sweetly to a melody that, as it was repeated numberless times, sounded not so much monotonous as otherworldly. Near the end it speeded up, the melody changed, and the word "Homage" was dropped so that the chant became an urgent "Amitabha! Amitabha! Amitabha! . . ." In all, this phase lasted half an hour. Every alternate period it was entirely devoted to circumambula-tion reciting buddha's name: the chanting of scriptures was omitted.

2) When the precentor gave the order, the monks returned to the narrow bench and recited buddha's name sitting cross-legged for fif-teen minutes. Time was kept on a small bell and wooden fish.

3) With three blows on the wooden fish, they "stopped and were silent" (*chih-ching*). This phrase was used in the meditation hall to denote the beginning of each period of sitting. At Ling-yen Shan, on the other hand, it meant the beginning of silent—as opposed to oral—recitation. For half an hour the seated monks recited buddha's name mentally without uttering a sound (*chin-kang ch'ih*). This was the time of greatest effort to make the mind "whole and still." Those who got sleepy were awakened by the patrol and anyone who did so too often was expected to leave his seat and prostrate himself before the images as a gesture of contrition.[7]

4) Still seated, they again recited buddha's name aloud for fifteen minutes, "breaking the silence" (*k'ai-ching*).[8]

5) They left their seats and chanted the formula for transfer of merit (*hui-hsiang*) standing in front of the central altar. In the last period of the day the formula was much longer, lasting for half an hour, to make up for which the first of the five phases was shortened and the fourth omitted.

This was the work of one period. It lasted an hour and a half. There were six periods a day: two in the morning, two in the afternoon, and two in the evening. These were fitted into a routine of the usual morning and afternoon devotions[9] and three rather than four meals. Whereas at Chin Shan solid food was taken twice after the middle of the day, here there was an effort to follow the strictest Vinaya tradition. Once the 11:00 o'clock lunch was over, many monks ate nothing until the next morning. The younger ones had a supper of congee, not in the refectory, but in the "medicinal food room" (*yao-shih so*), so-called because food taken there could be considered medicine. Neither tea nor *fang ts'an* was served to the monks sitting cross-legged in their places, though tea was available out back. The nine-hour working day was two hours longer than in the model meditation hall and there were only two free periods a day two days a month for shaving and bathing (versus three periods four days a month at Chin Shan). We might therefore say that the regime at the Ling-yen Ssu was the more arduous. On the other hand, there were many other ways in which it was milder.

All scolding and beating, either inside the recitation hall or outside it, were forbidden. There was no need to "knock people into enlightenment" because enlightenment was not being sought. When an instructor was giving an Explanation, his seniors did not have to leave the hall. It was considered that their absence would show contempt on the part of the master for the disciple (whereas in the meditation hall their presence was considered to show disrespect on the part of the disciple for the master). Explanations were optional, and might be given once or twice a day at the beginning of silent recitation if one of the instructors felt moved to speak. They did not necessarily speak in order of seniority as at Chin Shan. In the first period of the evening it was often the abbot. The subject matter did not include *hua-t'ou*. These enigmatic questions were never used in the recitation hall. Instead the instructor talked about the rules of the hall: "Today you recited poorly. Why? Your feet made too much noise while you were circling. You must do better." Or he talked about the sayings or achievements of earlier Pure Land masters,[10] or about a passage from the Buddhist canon.

Tutorials were also less formal. There was no fixed hour for monks to call on the instructors in their apartments and "ask for Explanation."

They simply went when they were free. This is understandable, since there would be less need for tutorials where the religious work was to focus the mind on Amitabha rather than to find the answer to a *hua-t'ou*. Especially during recitation weeks the instructor might be asked to attest to a disciple's work (*yin-cheng*). "Am I reciting buddha's name correctly?" the latter would ask. If the instructor answered that he was, it was the counterpart of the "transmission of the mind seal" (*hsin-hsin hsiang-yin*) in the Ch'an sect.[11] There was no written attestation, however, and no permanent relationship between master and disciple.

Seven recitation weeks (*ching-ch'i*) were held each winter at the Ling-yen Ssu, with two "sticks" added each day, making a total of twelve hours of recitation. During these weeks Explanations were heard sitting (not standing stock-still as in the meditation hall). The recitation patrol was joined by a *chien-hsiang* of secretarial rank, who carried an incense board with which he prodded sleepers on the shoulder, but there was no beating or shouting "up."

One of the most important features of recitation was the transfer of merit (*hui-hsiang*). A brief formula was recited after each period so that the merit generated thereby would be credited to three accounts. First, it was transferred to the benefit of others, so that they too might go to the Western Paradise (*hui-tzu hsiang-t'a*). Second, it was transferred to one's own credit in the Western Paradise so that one might have a higher position there (*hui-yin hsiang-kuo*). Third, it was transferred to one's credit in the absolute (*hui-shih hsiang-li*). The last apparently meant "May this meritorious work of mine in the phenomenal world accrue to be in the noumenal world of nirvana"—an idea that I do not altogether understand.[12]

The formula for transfer of merit was recited not only in the recitation hall, but in the library above it. There the rites for the dead were performed that were the chief source of income for the Ling-yen Ssu, aside from its 500 acres of farmland. Laymen paid the equivalent of U.S. $40 a day to have a paper soul tablet written up and then to have seven monks from the recitation hall go upstairs twice daily; at noon to make an offering and in the evening to transfer the merit they had accumulated by reciting buddha's name.[13] Thereby the deceased could hope for an early and better rebirth. There were also permanent soul tablets kept in the hall of rebirth (*wang-sheng t'ang*) that lay behind the recitation hall. Offerings were made before them on the 1st and 15th of the lunar month. Whereas at other monasteries such tablets were bought for a fixed capital sum, at Ling-yen Shan the amount was "left to the conscience of the layman."

I do not know of another recitation hall like this one. Most were smaller and all appeared to have been more simply operated. They usually were in charge of an assistant instructor or a hall manager, assisted by a verger. The rank and file sat simply in order of their seniority in the hall, not in order of rank. Enrollment was informal: at some places they could more or less come and go as they pleased. Normally at least three "sticks" were recited each day, while in the course of the year there might be one recitation week. Nonetheless, somewhat as those who conducted meditation anywhere in China looked to Chin Shan as their model, those who recited buddha's name looked to the Ling-yen Ssu.

It would be interesting to learn what inspired the system introduced there by Yin-kuang (1861-1940). He had spent his late twenties at a monastery north of Peking—the Tzu-fu Ssu on Hung-lo Shan—which had become a center of Pure Land practice about a century earlier. Although we do not know how the practice was carried on there, Yin-kuang took part in it.[14] In 1893, on a visit to Peking, he happened to meet a most remarkable monk, Hua-wen, who had been in the midst of a promising official career when he renounced the world. He was now the abbot of the Fa-yü Ssu on the sacred island of P'u-t'o Shan, far to the south. This monastery had been largely destroyed by fire in 1880 and Hua-wen, with the help of his excellent connections, was engaged in rebuilding it on a lavish scale.[15] He invited Yin-kuang to join him. Yin-kuang accepted and lived in an apartment next to the library there for most of the next two or three decades. Since he continued to specialize in Pure Land, presumably he joined in the work of the buddha recitation hall, which, like its counterpart at Hung-lo Shan, must have to some extent inspired the system he was later to establish at the Ling-yen Ssu in Soochow.

FA-YÜ SSU

Boerschmann visited the Fa-yü Ssu in January 1908. He published floor plans and a physical description of its buddha recitation hall, together with just enough details on the practice there to make us wish for more.[16]

The hall was on the second floor, with dormitories on either side. Instead of a sitting bench along the walls, there were only desks, at which the monks pored over the scriptures. To recite buddha's name they went downstairs to the ancestors hall (*tsu-t'ang*) that lay directly beneath. But here too there was no sitting bench. They recited sitting on cushions that lay in rows across the floor, as in a shrine-hall.[17]

These monks were the elite of the monastery. Their enrollment was limited to twenty-four (although monks from other departments occasionally joined in). When a vacancy occurred, it was filled from the wandering monks hall and the meditation hall by competitive examination (*Prüfung*). Only the most pious, able, and learned monks—usually of advanced age—could qualify. While they enjoyed the privilege of a clothing allowance of $20 a year (Chinese currency), they were also subject to a stricter discipline than their colleagues. Unless they had obtained sick-leave, they had to attend all formal meals in the refectory and every period of devotions in the shrine-hall. They were not permitted to leave the monastery except in the fourth and sixth month, and even then only with the abbot's permission. Because of their learning and discipline, they were, as Boerschmann puts it, "the trunk, the backbone of the monastery."

In token of their primacy, their work was conducted as close as possible to the ancestral tablets and to the abbot, whose quarters adjoined. Their rules and regimen were the most arduous and they apparently took precedence in seating and processions. All this was the reverse of Chin Shan, where primacy was given to the meditation hall.[18] But both monasteries had both kinds of hall and therefore exemplified the joint practice of Ch'an and Pure Land, the two schools being regarded not as alternatives, but as complementary. More will be said about this in Chapter XII.

It is too late to learn how many monasteries in China had halls for meditation, for reciting buddha's name, or for both practices; and, where a monastery had halls for both, which of them was given primacy. However, it seems likely that there were more institutions like Chin Shan than like the Fa-yü Ssu, whose location made it exceptional. The island on which it stood was sacred to Kuan-yin, the bodhisattva particularly associated with Pure Land. Probably at a majority of Chinese monasteries, as at Chin Shan, the buddha recitation hall was a place of relative relaxation—even of retirement—for monks who had had enough of Ch'an beatings and enigmas, and who wished only to visualize ever more clearly the Western Paradise to which they hoped to go. As old age came upon them, they wanted to see Amitabha seated on his lotus throne, his hand beckoning, and to feel that they were being drawn to his very lap.

Monks who could make their minds whole and still in such a vision could visit the Western Paradise while still alive. Some succeeded in doing so and reported that it was ten thousand times more wonderful than the wonderful description in the *Sukhavati-vyuha*. Some were said to have breath like sandalwood incense. Some knew beforehand the hour of their death. But, as in the meditation hall, no one talked about his achievements. I have been told that many monks reached the state of perfect concentration at Ling-yen Ssu, but I have not met anyone who would acknowledge having done so himself. Nevertheless, there was a sure way of knowing whether a person had succeeded in going to the Western Paradise. For a few hours after death every corpse was believed to have a warm spot. If it was on the top of the head, it meant that the deceased had joined Amitabha. This happened, as it turned out, to two of the informants for this book.

OTHER HALLS

There were halls for other kinds of specialized practice besides meditation and reciting buddha's name. This seems an appropriate point to give a couple of examples.

The Liu-yün Ssu in Shanghai had a "scripture perusal chamber" (*yüeh-ching lou*), where about thirty elderly monks spent their time reading Buddhist scriptures. "They did not necessarily study them," said my informant. "They simply read them.[19] There was no way of telling whether they thoroughly understood them or not."

"Did any of them ever lecture on the scriptures?" I asked.

"No," he replied at once, "they would not have been qualified for that."

It was considered a serious practice in China to turn the thousands of pages of the Tripitaka, glancing at each. Apparently this is what was done by some of the monks in the scriptural perusal chamber. They were "old hands at religious cultivation" who lived there, two or three to a cubicle, under the supervision of a hall manager. The altar and many of their personal needs were attended to by a verger and a water-boy. Since the refectory lay just downstairs, it was a convenient place for elderly monks to live. To get to their books they went across the courtyard to the library which was installed on the second floor of the buddha recitation hall.

The T'ien-ning Ssu in Changchow was a much larger and stricter monastery. One of its many sections was a "scripture chamber" (*ching-lou*) which served a very different purpose from the scripture perusal chamber just described. It was designed not for the "old hands," but for the young and inexperienced, who had just been ordained and could not qualify for any other hall or office. They had no rank. The layout was similar to a meditation hall. There were sleeping platforms at either end of the room (which was as large as the refectory that lay downstairs) and a central altar. The floor, however, instead of being left open for circumambulation, was taken up by four or five long tables with sitting benches beside them. The residents of the hall sat cross-legged on the benches and chanted the *Diamond Sutra*, which lay in front of them on the tables. This was the only sutra that they chanted and they did so twice after breakfast, twice after lunch, and twice after supper. After supper they were alternatively entitled to go to the meditation hall and take part in the evening period.

There was only one permanent officer in the hall—a hall manager. He slept in an adjoining room, whereas the young monks in his charge spent the night on the sleeping platform, where there was space for about forty of them. The verger, water-bearer, and duty monk served in rotation from among the rank and file. To start a period of recitation the hall manager struck the large chime and during recitation time was beaten by the duty monk on a wooden fish. Every month each of the rank and file received an allowance of 600 cash—equivalent to about 20¢ (Chinese currency). Certificates for "so many recitations of the *Diamond Sutra*" were sold to laymen, who burned them in order to make the merit therefrom available to deceased relatives. It was a custom in Changchow to burn such certificates on New Year's and on anniversaries of the dead.

I do not know of any other Chinese monastery that had a section

specially devoted to chanting a single text. The abbot said that it had
been set up in the last years of the Ch'ing dynasty in order to cope
with popular demand.[20] (Apparently Changchow people had a particularly high regard for the efficacy of the *Diamond Sutra*.) But perhaps
other kinds of specialized halls could be found here and there. Certainly religious practice was not limited to Ch'an meditation and
reciting buddha's name.

CHAPTER IV

Observance of the Rules

The monastic system was based on three textual layers. The oldest was the Vinaya, that is, the section of the Buddhist canon that dealt with discipline. It included the Pratimoksa—two hundred and fifty prohibitions to be observed in daily life. Even more important for Chinese monks were the fifty-eight prohibitions of the *Sutra of Brahma's Net*.[1] These were only two items of the immense Vinaya literature.

The second textual layer dealt with the monastery as an organization. Here the basic work was the *Pai-chang ch'ing-kuei*, that is, the pure rules composed by Pai-chang, a Ch'an monk who died in 814 C.E. His real name was Ta-chih Huai-hai; Pai-chang was only the name of the mountain he lived on. Therefore, "Pai-chang" came to mean either the man, the mountain, the book, or the rules therein. The book was only one of several such compilations made from the T'ang through the Ming dynasties.

In the third layer was the code of rules of the individual monastery (*kuei-yüeh*). It spelled out how Pai-chang was to be applied from day to day in that monastery's particular circumstances.

THE ROLE OF NORMATIVE TEXTS

Thus the life of the monks was governed by a corpus comparable in size to statute law. As with statute law, the question arises: how closely was it followed? We know that much of it was ignored. The

Pratimoksa, for example, includes vows not to handle gold, silver, or copper; to bathe no more than twice a month; to ordain no one under twenty; and so on. These vows were accepted by Chinese monks but regularly violated.

As to the *Pure Rules of Pai-chang*, toward the end of the last century the Dutch Sinologist, J. J. M. DeGroot, wrote that they "still now rule over the church with an absolute authority."[2] H. Hackmann, after visiting more than a hundred monasteries in eleven provinces during the years 1902-1903 and living in some for weeks at a time, wrote that he "soon noticed the great authority which the above-named work enjoyed everywhere. There is practically no feature of [Buddhism] as a monastic institution which is not thrown light upon by this book."[3] Hackmann hoped to translate it but its length and difficulty must have discouraged him.

In conversation with monks who had held high office in Chinese monasteries, I repeatedly asked how often they consulted Pai-chang. Did his book gather dust on the shelf or was it used from day to day? The gist of their answers was that everyone knew its contents so well that there was seldom any need to refer to it, but when a perplexing problem arose that could be solved in no other way, Pai-chang was the final authority. In any case, they said, public monasteries would never tolerate a major departure from his Pure Rules. Interesting light on their importance is cast by the *Hua-pei tsung-chiao nien-chien* (North China yearbook of religion) for 1941, compiled at the instance of the Japanese occupation authorities. It lists the monasteries of the northern provinces and then proceeds to describe their system of operation. Many paragraphs are simply lifted from Pai-chang without attribution.[4] The reader might think he was being told how things actually worked in 1941, whereas in fact he is reading how they were supposed to work in earlier centuries. This saved the editors time, no doubt, but it also suggests that they considered Pai-chang's rules to be nearly as valid in 1941 as they were in the ninth century.

The ninth-century text of Pai-chang has been lost. The earliest edition available was published in 1336 under an imperial decree of the Yüan dynasty, repeated by the Ming, which ordered all the monks of the empire to follow Pai-chang's rules. This text is familiar to scholars since it is included in the Taisho Tripitaka (vol. 48, no. 2025). But the text that was in common use at Chinese monasteries during the Republican period was first published in 1823 as *Pai-chang ts'ung-lin ch'ing-kuei cheng-i chi* (Pai-chang's pure rules for large monasteries with explanatory notes). The compiler, I-jun Yüan-hung, admitted that it differed from earlier editions, and we should probably read it as a guide to the Ch'ing monastic system rather than to that of earlier dynasties.[5]

The monastic system was always in the process of slight but steady change. Furthermore, Pai-chang's Pure Rules, voluminous though they were, spoke to general practice rather than particular circumstances. They had more to say about ritual than administration. Hence there developed the third textual layer. Any monastery that was large and important enough compiled a code of rules (*kuei-yüeh*), usually divided into sections, one for the meditation hall, another for the guest department, another for the business office, and so on. Every department had a copy on hand for reference. Violation of the code could bring swift punishment or expulsion. New rules were issued by the abbot as required (for an example, see p. 14). Some of the contents, however, were simply copied from Pai-chang. This is the case, for example, with the basic regulations of the guest department and the business office in the codes of both Chin Shan and the Kao-min Ssu. But many of the detailed regulations, especially of the meditation hall, are not to be found in Pai-chang. They are the codification of the practice at a particular monastery.

The only code that appears to have been individually published is that of the Kao-min Ssu.[6] Others have been widely copied by hand. For example, I have photographed manuscripts of the Chiao Shan and Chin Shan codes. The latter was transcribed about 1948 from another manuscript copy kept at the guest department of the Nan-hua Ssu in northern Kwangtung. It was common for a monastery that had not compiled its own code of rules to rely on Chin Shan or the Kao-min Ssu. The abbot of Chin Shan recalled that several outsiders hand-copied its code during his years there.

The codes of different monasteries showed different emphases. Chiao Shan's, for example, omits the long section on the business office found in Kao-min's. Instead there is a more detailed treatment of ritual observances. Kao-min's code is extraordinarily harsh. One can

almost feel the displeasure of the abbot as he dashed off a rule against
some abuse that had just come to his attention. It is also extraordinarily frank, not just about the bodily functions but also when it calls
for the hiring of ruffians to intimidate tenants who have been delinquent in paying their rents (see p. 27). In reading it one feels close
to reality. In the Chin Shan code, on the other hand, some of the material appears to be made up of conventional archaisms, far removed
from modern practice (for examples, see Appendix II, pp. 421-422).

I have not had an opportunity to make a close study of these documents or to investigate their history. According to several of the monks
queried, the codes in modern use were compiled largely in the last
two centuries. We know that at least five were compiled during the
Republican period.[7] But all of them are subject to the original question: how closely were they carried out in practice? For example, the
rules for the latrine and the washroom at the Kao-min Ssu (see pp.
62-63) were followed quite closely according to informants from that
monastery, but these were only a few among thousands of rules.
What is needed is a systematic comparison of actual practice with
all three layers of regulatory texts. That lies beyond the scope of this
book, which can do no more than furnish material for it. To that end
there is offered below a number of minor practical details, as recalled
by my informants, about the monastery calendar, meals, clothing,
personal hygiene, sexual activity, punishment for violation of the
rules, and heterodox practices.

THE MONASTERY CALENDAR

The principal divisions of the monastery calendar have already been
referred to:

Summer term or semester (*hsia-ch'i*)—16th of first lunar month
through 15th of seventh lunar month.

Winter term or semester (*tung-ch'i*)—16th of seventh lunar month
through 15th of first lunar month.

Of the thirty-five to forty events in the calendar, the most important
were: the anniversary of the Buddha's birth on the 8th of the fourth
month; Kuan-yin's birth, enlightenment, and death on the 19th of the

second, sixth, and ninth months; and the Festival of Hungry Ghosts on the 15th of the seventh month.

These celebrations were usually attended by large numbers of lay people, particularly in urban areas. On the morning of the 8th of the fourth month, for example, they came to watch the bathing of the Buddha (yü-fo). After hymns and offerings the monks poured spoonfuls of water over a tiny image of the infant Sakyamuni, standing in a low basin of water. Sometimes each of the visitors was allowed to pour a spoonful too (see Fig. 60), and afterwards they would have a vegetarian feast. It was a popular day for the release of living creatures, so that pet shops did a brisk business.[8] This is typical of the major festivals. Minor ones, like the birthdays of Amitabha or of Wei-t'o, the guardian of monasteries, were usually celebrated by the monks alone, no laymen attending, with an offering before the appropriate image or tablet. At many smaller monasteries the minor anniversaries were ignored, and some of those listed in the large breviary[9] would seem to be out of place in any Buddhist temple, since they include, for example, the birthdays of the principal Taoist divinity, the Jade Emperor, and even of the Taoist "pope." But I have never heard of these being celebrated.

A very special occasion was the Ullambana, or Hungry Ghosts Festival, which was held for seven days ending the 15th of the seventh month for the purpose of providing food and instruction for hungry ghosts from all quarters. Since no one could be sure of the rebirth allotted to his deceased relatives, lay people took part with enthusiasm. At New Year, on the other hand, they came to the temples not so much for religious purposes as to enjoy an outing and to consult the bamboo divination slips. The monks themselves held a midnight service, and in the first two days of the first month the monastery routine was suspended while they went about in groups paying reverence to all the altars of the monastery. There might also be visits to brethren in neighboring institutions with which they were connected. But according to one informant the New Year was not an occasion for monks to be particularly happy. It merely reminded them of the passage of another twelve months during which they might not have made as much spiritual progress as they hoped.

A different kind of event in the calendar was the "summer retreat" (an-chü). This is a conspicuous feature of monastic practice in

Theravada countries, where the monks keep to their temples for the three months of the Indian rainy season. In China, however, the summer retreat was generally ignored. Monks were aware that it was supposed to run from the 15th of the fourth month to the 15th of the seventh and some might choose to observe it as individuals, but in most institutions life continued much as usual. Lay worshippers were not discouraged from coming to the temple. Wandering monks could arrive, stay on, or depart. Officers went abroad on their business. In the meditation hall leave could be obtained on the usual grounds. On the other hand, at many monasteries during this period it was customary to expound the sutras. The abbot, or perhaps some eminent dharma master called in from outside, would lecture for a couple of hours a day.[10] This meant that although summer retreat was no longer a period of immobilization, as it had been originally, it was still a time for study.

At a few Vinaya centers the original rules were better preserved. At Pao-hua Shan entry or exit during the summer retreat was only permitted to wandering monks. Others could not leave the monastery —not even officers going on monastery business. Each day, in addition to the lectures on the sutras, there were two periods of meditation in the classrooms, three periods of circumambulation in the courtyard, and five periods of devotions in the great shrine-hall, with all the monks dressed in their outer robes. "In the hot summer weather we sweated profusely," a former resident recalled. "There was no rest in twenty-four hours. It was really miserable."

Another custom preserved at Pao-hua Shan was reciting the Pratimoksa vows twice a month throughout the year. The Sanskrit term for this is uposatha, which became *pu-sa* in Chinese. Pao-hua Shan had an uposatha hall (*pu-sa t'ang*) and there on the evening of the 1st and 15th of every lunar month, the monks recited all 250 of the vows together.[11] At most Chinese monasteries, including Chin Shan, there were no uposatha days, although these are universal in Theravada countries. The only liturgical change on the 1st and 15th of the month was the addition of certain items to morning and afternoon devotions. Morning devotions, for example, concluded with a prayer for the long life of the president of the Chinese Republic (before 1912, of the emperor).[12]

MEALS

In Theravada countries like Burma and Thailand great stress is laid on the rule that no solid food may be eaten after noon. Chinese Buddhists recognized the rule and ascribed it to the resentment that would be felt by hungry ghosts, who go abroad after noon, should they see the monks taking nourishment. The Chinese maintained, however, that because the work of the monastery continued into the evening, monks could not do without an evening meal. Supper was eaten in most Chinese monasteries, although there were usually a few monks who preferred to follow the rule strictly and eat nothing solid later than 12:00.[13] They were free to do so, but according to one informant they were still expected to come to the refectory along with everyone else unless their age or status excused them.

At Chin Shan the monks of the "outer sections" (wai-liao)—that is, all but those in the meditation hall—ate a supper of congee not in the refectory but in their own quarters. They fetched it from the small kitchen attached to the business office.[14] At the T'ien-ning Ssu, on the other hand, rice was served at 6:00 p.m. in the refectory. It was an informal occasion since food after noon was regarded as medicine. As at luncheon congee, the abbot did not attend; there was no grace before and after; and monks could leave the table as soon as they were finished. But talking was still forbidden and the proctor stood watch to enforce the rules.

The Nan-hua Ssu in northern Kwangtung came closest, perhaps, to observing the original Buddhist rule. Indeed, a couple of informants ordained there stated that nothing solid was eaten after noon by anyone in the monastery. Two former abbots had more precise information. It was quite true, they said, that ordinands ate nothing after noon and that no meal was served to the monks in the refectory. But as elsewhere any resident monk who attended the evening meditation period enjoyed two bowls of fang-ts'an (see p. 73). Even if he did not attend the evening period, he could still go to the kitchen and get a little something to take back and eat in his apartment. This was termed "expedient eating" (fang-pien ch'ih), since it was not done openly; in the abbot's words: "the rules of the establishment forbade anyone eating after noon."

Presumably the reason that ordinands had to fast was because they had just taken or were about to take the vows that enjoined it. We might therefore expect that at the greatest ordination center, Pao-hua Shan, fasting would be strictest of all. So it was in writing and speaking, for only "hot water" was consumed after 12:00 a.m. But if anyone examined the "hot water" with his own eyes, it turned out to be congee.[15] Furthermore, this was merely what the ordinands ate in the refectory. All the permanent residents "cooked small pots" (*shao hsiao-kuo*). Every apartment and hall had its own stove, on which its residents prepared an evening meal with vegetables that they bought with their own money from shops outside the main gate. The establishment provided them with faggots and rice.

In China the stress was not on the hours of eating but on the nature of the food. Meat, fish, eggs, dairy products, vegetables of the onion family, and all intoxicating beverages were forbidden or customarily avoided. The Buddha himself said that the monks might eat meat and fish so long as they had no reason to think that the animals had been killed expressly to feed them. In Theravada countries such food may be consumed along with whatever else is placed in the begging bowl, on the principle that monks should not be particular about their food. In China, however, the monks did not normally go out to beg. Their meals were prepared at the monastery from foodstuffs that had been grown, bought, or collected as rent. Under these circumstances it would have been difficult to maintain that the eating of meat was unintentional. Furthermore, dietary abstinence was an ancient Chinese tradition that antedated the arrival of Buddhism.[16] The Chinese have always had a deep-seated feeling that if a person gave up something desirable, he would be repaid for it by acquiring magical potency or, in the case of Buddhists, transferable merit. Therefore monks who abstained from meat were able to perform rites for the dead with greater effectiveness. If lay people knew that meat was being eaten at a certain monastery, it was less likely to receive their patronage. This accounts for the complaints by foreign travelers in China that monks would not allow them even to pass the night at their temples because of the fear that meat might be smuggled in and eaten on the premises.[17] After the last war when the mayor of Tsingtao asked the abbot of the Chan-shan Ssu if he might serve beer at a party he was giving there for the commanding American general, his request was refused.

But some places were much less scrupulous. We also read of foreigners who were regaled with meat and wine when they stayed at temples—and even toasted by the monks.[18] According to one informant, small temples in the Shantung countryside permitted the consumption of meat and even wine because it was the local custom, and if the monks had abstained, they would have been regarded as odd. In 1963 the obituary for an American Buddhist monk in Malaya, composed by a Chinese monk, contained the following statement:

> As to his partaking of meat we are sure that charitable-minded admirers of the American monk were never disturbed by qualms of conscience when out of love and hospitality they placed delicious mutton curry or tender roasted chickens before their esteemed guest.

At model monasteries like Chin Shan, on the other hand, there was simply no question of violating the dietary rules. The daily fare consisted of rice, congee, beancurd, turnips, and mixed vegetables, the best known of the latter being *lo-han ts'ai,* said to be so-called because it consisted of eighteen kinds of vegetables and there are eighteen lohans. On the 1st, 8th, 15th and 23rd of the lunar month somewhat better dishes were added, such as mushrooms, noodles, or Chinese vermicelli. The same happened whenever a lay patron furnished a vegetarian feast (*she-chai*), which was one of the principal ways to gain merit.

CLOTHING

Animal products were avoided in dress as they were in diet. There was a prohibition on the use of silk or leather that is not observed in Theravada countries.[19] Whereas in Theravada countries the color of monk's clothing was saffron, in China yellow of any shade, even so dark that we would call it brown, was considered a mark of superior status. Most monks felt that they were only entitled to grey or black, and grey was perhaps the most widely worn.[20]

The three main categories of garment, aside from underclothes and footwear, were as follows. The most informal was the *ch'ang-shan* (also known as the *ch'ang-kua* or *ta-kua*), a long gown worn for most of the monastic work. There was a shorter version (*tuan-kua*) suited to manual labor. At formal meals and all performance of ritual, the monks put on a gown that had much fuller sleeves than the *ch'ang-shan*, hanging down perhaps eighteen inches from the wrist. This was called the *hai-ch'ing* or *ch'ang-p'ao* or *ta-p'ao*. It might be worn alone, as at meals in summer time, but for all the important ritual it was worn under the third and most formal category of garment, the *chia-sa* (Sanskrit *kasaya*) or robe (*i*). This covered only the left shoulder, so that if there had been no *hai-ch'ing* under it, the right shoulder would have been bare as it is in some Theravada sects. Chinese monks say that to have the left shoulder covered symbolizes the fact that the wearer is still in search of buddhahood, while to have the right shoulder bare means that he is trying to save all sentient beings.

The status of a monk could be discerned from the colors and pattern of his robe. If seams divided it into five strips, it was called a *wu-i* and was worn by novices, nuns, and lay devotees. If it had seven strips, it was a *ch'i-i* and could be worn only by fully ordained monks (see Fig. 65). Everything with a more elaborate pattern was known as a patriarch's robe (*tsu-i*)[21] and belonged to high rank. The abbot, for example, normally wore a red robe in twenty-five strips (*hung-i*). For great ritual occasions, like an ordination, a plenary mass, or a transmission of dharma he put on a *ch'ien-fo i* (thousand-buddha robe), a *lo-han i* (arhat's robe), or a *wan-tzu i* (ten-thousand-character robe), all magnificently embroidered. A robe with dragon embroidery (*lung-i*) owned by one old Kiangsu abbot that I know cost him nearly US $200. All monks' garments had the same distinctive feature: a y neck formed by one side crossing over the other, leaving the throat bare like a Western bathrobe. If one saw a man in China with this kind of a collar, the chances were that he was a monk.

Aside from the seven-strip robes that they received when they were ordained, monks were normally expected to buy their own clothes with money that they earned from Buddhist services or were given by lay supporters. At model monasteries, however, there was usually provision for those who could not afford to do so. At Chin Shan, the T'ien-ning Ssu, and elsewhere, there was a store of "merit clothing" (*kung-te i*) that had been donated by laymen as a meritorious act. It could be loaned to any monks who needed it, but principally to those enrolled in the meditation hall.

HEALTH AND HYGIENE

We have already touched on questions of personal hygiene in earlier chapters. Here only a few words need to be added on the subject of shaving and bathing. Residents of the meditation hall in public monasteries had their heads and faces shaved only twice a month, usually on the 14th and 29th or 30th. This meant that by the end of every two weeks they were covered with long stubble. As one informant said, "You laymen have to look pretty, but we didn't." For monks outside the meditation hall, shaving could be done when convenient and was spread over the month so that the barbers did not have more work than they could cope with on any one day. In small temples the monks might shave one another.

Some shaved more than twice a month. Some did not shave at all; this was the mark of the ascetic (*t'ou-t'o,* Sanskrit *dhuta*) and the most famous example of recent times was the Venerable Hsü-yün, who had long hair and a wispy beard.

Baths were taken four days a month, usually on the 8th, 14th, 23rd, and 29th or 30th, and on the same days or on the days preceding, the monks washed their own clothes so that they could change into clean ones after bathing. All this took place daily rather than weekly from the 1st of the sixth month to the 15th of the seventh, or at any other time when the proctor determined that the hot weather made it advisable. He was in general charge of bathing, which was done group by group under his supervision. The first group was composed of ex-abbots, officers, and others of high rank. They went into the bath-house, took off their clothes, and washed in a hot pool. They did not sit on the bottom, but along the rim with their feet in a foot or so of water and cleaned themselves as best they could with a washcloth. They were forbidden to splash, to use soap,[22] or to wash their private parts. After the first group had left the bathhouse, the second entered, composed of residents of the meditation hall; then the third, composed of the other resident monks; and finally those who lived in the wandering monks hall.[23] The water was not changed from group to group, since it took hours to heat. It had a rich dark hue by the time the last of the three or four hundred monks had finished his ablutions.

A brief description of the infirmary was given in Chapter II (on p. 79). There is disagreement as to how often its facilities were needed. Some informants have told me that there was very little illness at the monasteries they lived in. According to others, life was so rigorous that many monks fell ill, particularly of tuberculosis. This was said to be the case at Kuan-tsung Ssu in Ningpo, a city where the monks apparently could find no medical facilities for treating TB and simply had to wait for death to come. One informant contracted the disease at the seminary of the Kuang-chi Ssu in Peking but recovered after two years of rest in his native Shantung. K. L. Reichelt states that "Chin Shan was one of the most notorious places for developing tuberculosis," and describes in ripe detail how the monks in its meditation hall used to spit on the unswept floor.[24]

The abbot of Chin Shan, while he denied both the spitting and the prevalence of TB (of which there had been only one or two cases, he said, in the thirty years he lived there), admitted that hygiene at even the best monasteries "left much to be desired." Some monks were personally very dirty, he said. Various fevers were common in winter and dysentery was common in summer. The infirmary was really no place for the infirm (*ju-i liao shih-tsai pu ju-i*). He wanted to introduce improvements, but they had been vetoed by the retired abbot.

SEXUAL ACTIVITY

Monks were forbidden by their vows to have any form of sexual outlet. If detected, it meant a beating and expulsion for the monk and discredit for the monastery. Continence was just as important as vegetarianism if the support of lay patrons was to be retained. It is not a subject, therefore, on which frankness can be expected. The few monks that I have come to know well enough to ask about it have said that sexual activity in any form was rare in large public monasteries. Small temples were another matter: there all kinds of abuse could and probably often did occur. But it is difficult to separate rumor from fact. A sensational illustration is the case of the

Venerable Miao-lien, a monk from Ku Shan, Fukien, who built its large branch temple in Penang, the Chi-le Ssu. Such was the scale of building and the respect he won among local Buddhists that in 1904 he was summoned to Peking, where he received a set of the Tripitaka and an imperial patent from the Kuang-hsü Emperor. But already rumors had begun to circulate "of orgies and secret underground tunnels used for vicious purposes." As the years passed, the rumors intensified until one night early in 1907 Miao-lien cut off the whole of his genitalia with a large vegetable chopper. The illustrious Dr. Wu Lien-teh, then a young man just beginning his medical career, was called to treat him. As soon as the wound had healed, Miao-lien returned to Ku-shan, where he was given a new office. He died, however, before the summer was out.[25]

Dr. Wu, who had already established a "cordial friendship" with the "devoted and sensitive-minded artist-abbot," interpreted his act as an heroic protest against baseless rumors that had been spread by persons in charge of existing temples who were jealous of the success of the Chi-le Ssu and resented the resulting decrease in their own patronage.[26] Arguing for this interpretation is Miao-lien's age (he was sixty-three at the time) and the proverbial popularity of rumors among the Chinese, with whom it is never safe to assume that where there is smoke, there is fire. But how can we be perfectly sure that Miao-lien had not, in fact, been involved in orgies and that his self-castration was not an act of penance rather than protest?

One informant said: "If a monk sees a beautiful woman and says he does not like her, he is telling a lie. I don't believe him. He is still a human being and a human being is an animal that has desires. So in monasteries there are no women to be seen. But if a monk does see a beautiful woman, he can suppress the train of thought that arises by reflecting: 'I must not think about her. I am a person who has left lay life. I want to become a buddha. If I think about her, I will not become a buddha. I have accepted the prohibitions of ordination and I must keep them. Otherwise I shall become a cow or a horse in my next life.'"

Another monk said that women were demons and the cause of all the troubles in the world. If there were no women, everyone would be a bodhisattva. Although admitting that sex was chief among desires, he too considered that it could be successfully suppressed.

When meditating, for example, a monk could use his *hua-t'ou* or recite buddha's name to dissolve licentious thoughts. It was easier for him than for a layman. His life was one of discomfort and deprivation. He was often ill, and this was beneficial because it reminded him of the approach of death and the need for religious diligence. Once he reached middle age, sexual desire dropped off anyway.

Both these informants said that homosexuality was very rare. It was "a low taste" (*hsia-liu*). As one of them put it, "What is the point of men with men?" The laymen who have stayed at public monasteries also say that it was rare. John Blofeld writes the following about the nine months he lived at the Hua-t'ing Ssu near Kunming:

> I came to know a great deal about my immediate companions without discovering traces of sexuality of any sort. Rules, tradition and spiritual aspirations apart, the diet alone was enough to reduce physical desire to a minimum; but my impression is that even the least sincere monks, the refugees from conscription and so on, were quite uninterested in homosexual attachments.[27]

The only dissent I have heard came from a monk who had returned to lay life and therefore had no stake in maintaining the reputation of the sangha. He began by saying that he had seen a great deal of homosexuality, but, when pressed for details, he explained that what he meant was emotional attachments. An older monk often became so fond of a younger one that he was resentful if anyone else was nice to him. There would be a lot of gossip about it. But there was no way of knowing whether such a relationship was physically consummated. If it was and if the monastery authorities found out, both offenders were beaten and expelled, but he had never been in a monastery where this had taken place. It was commoner, he said, for monks to consort with women. In Shanghai they used to go to the brothels. His own master's master had another man's wife living in his small temple as his mistress.

We have already noted that several of the monastic rules were designed to reduce sexual stimuli to a minimum. Monks seldom undressed completely (they slept in their underclothes) and they were supposed to cover their private parts when dressing and undressing before their bath. A light was kept burning in the meditation hall and other dormitories to discourage "laxity."[28] The person in charge would come in after the monks had retired to make sure that everything was in order. The diet was free of foods that were believed to "heat" the blood. Lay patrons were allowed to bring their wives when they came to stay, but they seldom did so and in any case the wives were lodged in separate chambers. Nuns were never allowed to stay in public monasteries, except during ordination and in Kwangtung province. In either case, they too were lodged in separate quarters.

Some observers maintain that sexuality is less insistent for Chinese than for Westerners, and that, if deprived of sexual outlet, they do not suffer as much discomfort as people of a culture where sex is looked on as a problem. Given their diet and beliefs, it seems likely that the monks of China were able to adjust themselves more easily to continence than their counterparts in Europe.

PUNISHMENT

The Kao-min Ssu code of rules is veritably punctuated with the phrase ". . . and offenders will be punished." Punishment took many forms and varied from monastery to monastery. Usually it was allotted and administered by the guest prefect. The proctor could punish minor infractions with a blow on the cheek, then and there, and offenses committed in the meditation hall were dealt with by the precentor, but all serious offenders were haled before the guest prefect, who imposed a fine or administered a certain number of strokes with the incense board inscribed "pure rules" as the monk kneeled contritely before him. Fines of $2 to $10 (Chinese currency) were imposed for lighter offenses. If the offender did not have the money to pay, he would be beaten. Income from fines was often allocated to provide special vegetarian dishes for the main body of monks (*kung-chung*).

The heaviest penalty of all—expulsion from the monastery (*ch'ien-tan*)—was normally the prerogative of the abbot alone. A monk could be expelled for one serious offense (like embezzlement) or three ordinary offenses (like fighting). I have asked my informants if they could recall an instance of expulsion. None were able to. This may simply have been because they did not wish to get involved in a discussion of the offense that led to it.

At some monasteries, especially where the emphasis was on study of doctrine or reciting buddha's name rather than on meditation, the penalties were milder. The offender might be ordered to prostrate himself three times to the buddha image in a spirit of repentance. If he owed an apology to another monk, he would have to make three prostrations to him as well. The mildest penalty was chanting a sutra, which could be done at his own convenience. As one monk from such a monastery said, "This was a better method because prostration meant a loss of self-respect." Beating was avoided. If the offender did not have enough money to pay the fine for a serious offense, then he would simply offer a greater number of prostrations. At the Pure Land center of Ling-yen Shan he could decide for himself how much he ought to pay, just as those who went to sleep while reciting buddha's name could decide for themselves whether they should do prostrations before the buddha dais. The Venerable Yin-kuang believed that as much as possible should be voluntary. The Ling-yen Ssu also used a form of punishment that appears to have fallen into disuse elsewhere. It was termed "kneeling the incense" (*kuei-hsiang*). Offenders would be told: "Unless you want to leave the monastery, you will have to repent (*ch'iu ch'an-hui*). Go and kneel before the altar for the length of time it takes a stick of incense to burn down" (*kuei i-chih hsiang*). People who saw them kneeling there in the guest department (or the recitation hall) would be told what their offense had been, so that part of the penalty was loss of face. One "stick" lasted about an hour and was normally the maximum. For light offenses they would have to kneel ten minutes.

It could be argued that every rule is evidence of its own violation. It would only go onto the books to correct an existing abuse. This seems reasonable, although it gives us no measure of the frequency of the different kinds of abuses. One hears most often about disorderliness, fighting, and minor peculation. There is a saying that the sangha was a group in which "dragons and snakes co-mingled."[29] That is, the very worst as well as the very best type of people were to be found even in reputable public monasteries. It was commoner, however, to find the worst type in small temples or out on the streets preying on the gullible. But no matter how badly they appeared to behave, it was not wise to jump to conclusions. Monks who broke the pure rules might be bodhisattvas in disguise. There is a story of a pious woman who made a pilgrimage to the island of P'u-t'o Shan. By the roadside there she saw four monks playing mahjong. This made a very poor impression on her, but she continued her round of P'u-t'o's monasteries. Sailing back, when she was in mid-passage, she spied the same four monks sitting on a water-borne kneeling cloth and still playing mahjong. Then she realized that they were bodhisattvas who had taken this form in order to get closer to the people who needed salvation. Kuan-yin, the patron bodhisattva of P'u-t'o Shan, could take any of thirty-two different forms (*hsien-shen*) to save those who had been trapped in a life of drinking, gambling, and crime. Wen-shu, the patron bodhisattva of Wu-t'ai Shan, made a vow that he would take the same form as every pilgrim who visited his mountain.[30] Therefore one might find the most advanced spiritual beings among thieves and gangsters.

HETERODOX PRACTICES

Certain practices that were forbidden to the sangha as a livelihood could be dabbled in as an avocation: for example, medicine, divination, astrology, and the "reading" of faces. Although these practices were not considered so heterodox as communicating with spirits (in which no self-respecting Buddhist monk would engage), still they could not be carried on for gain.[31] This was precisely what was done by "vagabond monks," sometimes with a conscious charlatanism that brought discredit on the whole sangha. Hence they were refused admission at the better monasteries. Yet even at the better monasteries, when lay worshippers came to learn their fortune from the bamboo divination slips (see p. 212), the verger who did the interpreting was allowed to pocket a small tip. "He was poor and needed cash," said the abbot of Ch'i-hsia Shan. "Of course," he went on, "divination by bamboo slips was useless, since it did not change the future of the worshipper, which was determined by the karma of his deeds. Nonetheless, it appealed to weak people. Although we did not encourage it, we had to tolerate it as a popular custom. There was scarcely a monastery or temple, large or small, that did not have a tube of bamboo slips in one of its shrine-halls."

Otherwise it was exceptional for money to change hands. The reputable monk might become quite annoyed if he was treated like a commercial fortune teller. One of my informants, I remember, was an old ascetic who let his hair grow long and lived alone. At the end of our second interview he told me to take down my trousers. A little puzzled, I did so, and he proceeded to feel the calves of my legs and my abdomen, and asked me to stick out my tongue. This examination enabled him to say that I would live to be eighty-eight, but, in the meantime, would fall ill at forty-four, forty-nine, fifty-nine, and sixty-four. From the shape of my skull he deduced that I was clever, and from the tuft between my eyebrows that I was was petty (*hsin-liang hsiao*), while my hands revealed that I had no talent for making money—all too true. He gave me this information as a kindness and became really indignant when I tried to make an offering to his temple.

Geomancy (*feng-shui*) was another form of nonprofit divination carried on by men as eminent as the Venerable Hsü-yün. On one occasion he told a group of monks who were planning to erect a temple on Chung-nan Shan: "To the North it faces the White Tiger and the Evening Star. There is no mountain behind it to lean on. It does not seem to me a good place." His view was confirmed when the temple failed. He attributed the failure of another temple to the rock that stood to the right of the main entrance "so that the White Tiger was not propitious." When he decided to restore this temple, he had the rock moved.[32]

In 1947 a prominent Kiangsu monk paid a visit to Chin Shan, where his elder brother, the Venerable T'ai-ts'ang, was abbot. He told T'ai-ts'ang that a disastrous fire would soon take place there. Asked how he knew, he said he had been making a special study of geomancy, and according to its principles there was no doubt that a fire would destroy most of Chin Shan the following year. T'ai-ts'ang reflected that this was his own brother, who would certainly not be trying to cheat him, and so he wondered what to do. After talking the matter over with Shuang-t'ing, the retired abbot, he bought some fire-fighting equipment, including a pump and fire hose. Later Shuang-t'ing suggested that they should obtain another professional opinion. T'ai-ts'ang agreed, for he "did not understand this sort of thing." So Shuang-t'ing wrote to Shanghai for the help of a very famous geomancer, Mr. Jung Pai-yün, who came to Chin Shan, looked the situation over, and announced that there would be no fire. Nonetheless, on the third day of Ch'ing-ming the next year (April 1948), when T'ai-ts'ang went to the Ch'i-li Tien to sweep the graves of his ancestral masters, fire broke out in the great shrine-hall from unknown causes. Within two hours a large part of the monastery had burned to the ground.[33]

The practice of medicine appears to have been exceptional in recent decades. Not clerical, but lay physicians (more often Chinese-trained than Western-trained) were called in to care for ailing monks and to dispense remedies in the clinics that some monasteries established for the poor. I have found almost no trace of the tradition of monastic medicine brought over from India by monks like An Shih-kao and Fo-t'u-teng.[34] Yet there was one monk during the Republican period who, although his techniques sound unconventional, engaged in medical practice of a sort. This was the "Living Buddha of Chin Shan," an eccentric whose real name was Miao-shan and who had been given his sobriquet because the local laity were disappointed by the Mongolian Living Buddha, Chang-chia. When the latter had visited their city in 1919, they saw nothing remarkable about him and said that if anyone was looking for a *real* living buddha, their own Miao-shan was obviously it. Many tales are told of his remarkable powers, psychic as well as medical. The latter are what concern us here.

In 1923 T'ai-ts'ang, who was then serving at Chin Shan as guest prefect, went home for the first time in years and found that his mother was afflicted with an exceedingly painful stomach ailment. When he returned to the monastery, he and his younger brother (the same one who was later to study geomancy) asked the Living Buddha for his help. The latter's reaction was characteristic. He pressed his hands together in a salute to the void and cried: "Ah Buddha! The Buddha's mother is ill. Amitabha!" After a moment's pause he added "Never mind. Little brother, you go and get a basin of wisdom soup."[35] They asked what he meant. He explained that this was the water left in the pool after all four hundred of Chin Shan's monks had taken their weekly bath. When they brought him a basin of this exceedingly ropy fluid, still warm from the bathers, he told them to place it on the altar, light incense, and join him in reciting buddha's name. He then proceeded to recite the names of buddhas that they had never heard of in their whole lives. A little diffidently they pointed out that the water was rather murky and "stiff" and that their mother, who was a very clean person, might not care to drink it. "No matter," said the Living Buddha, "bring me some alum." When he dropped it in, the water cleared. They left it on the altar and the next year, when relatives came to visit, had them take it home. Their mother drank a little every day and recited the name of Kuan-yin. Her pains ceased and from that time on until she died seventeen years later, they never recurred.[36]

Another interesting cure was given to the daughter of Mr. Wu Lan-pin, a prominent citizen of Chen-chiang. He was very rich. He had passed the provincial examinations under the Ch'ing dynasty, qualified as both a lawyer and a doctor, and headed the "Institute of Hygiene" (apparently some sort of medical center). He was, however, rather an aggressive, unpleasant person, at whose hands many of his neighbors had suffered. He felt a special loathing for Buddhism and the sangha. One by one his children and his grandchildren died, and yet he refused to see that all this was due to the bad karma that his actions had created. At last only a favorite daughter remained. Her eyes began to redden and swell and they grew worse in spite of the medicines he gave her. When she pleaded with him to summon the Living Buddha of Chin Shan, her father refused to listen to such "damned nonsense." Finally, despite all his medical expertise, she went completely blind. Only then did he give way. The Living Buddha arrived at their house, took one look at young Miss Wu, and said: "Ah! You are my mother, I am your son, and I have come to save you." Whereupon he spat into the palm of his hand and rubbed the spit all around her eyes, then blew into them twice, saying: "It's all right now, it's all right." The effect on her father standing nearby—the head of the Institute of Hygiene—may be imagined. But when her eyesight was immediately restored and the inflammation and swelling subsided, "his anger changed into indescribable joy." He and the whole family became firm admirers of the Living Buddha of Chin Shan.[37]

This happened in 1919. But even in 1964 faith healing was not a lost art. When my wife was troubled with sciatica a friendly monk suggested that I rub her back and recite the Six Character Mantra.

This would let the spirit of all the buddhas enter her body through my fingers. Unfortunately at the time I could not find this mantra in my breviary.[38]

It was stated earlier that no self-respecting monk would engage in the heterodox practice of communicating with spirits. This, at any rate, is what my informants maintained. Repeated inquiry failed to uncover a single case where a reputable member of the sangha had gone into a trance to communicate with the spirits of the dead (except in the Esoteric School) or used the planchette (*fu-chi*), a kind of two-handled stick with which characters were written on a tray of shallow sand. Perhaps the sangha avoided such practices because they were so popular in the syncretistic sects that the Ch'ing government had harshly proscribed and persecuted. This did not mean, however, that Chinese monks regarded them as fraudulent or ineffective. In 1918, when the planchette had become the "rage" in Peking, the great T'ien-t'ai monk, Ti-hsien, came there to deliver a series of lectures on the sutras. Presently he received a message from a group of laymen to the effect that a City God who often communicated with them had said that he was attending Ti-hsien's lecture series, but that there were certain points that he could not understand. Would Ti-hsien kindly come over and have a chat with him? Some of Ti-hsien's followers were opposed, because they regarded the practice as heterodox. He went nevertheless. The City God was terribly polite to him and explained (through the planchette) that he took a great many ghosts with him to listen to the lectures and guard the lecture hall. Ti-hsien's exposition, he said, had been so effective that many of the ghosts had been saved, but others, who had too heavy a burden of bad karma to expiate, were asking what could be done for them. Ti-hsien explained that on the 15th of every seventh month his own monastery, the Kuan-tsung Ssu in Ningpo seven hundred miles away, celebrated the Ullambana festival by performing a *fang yen-k'ou* to feed and save all hungry ghosts (see p. 185). "I don't know," he said, "whether the effect of the ceremony can reach as far as Peking." The City God gratefully assured him that it could. Next, the heroic divinity Kuan-ti arrived on the scene, but chose to speak through the City God because he was afraid that his spirit-force was so great that the medium would be unable to hold the writing stick. He exchanged courtesies with Ti-hsien and said that in the future wherever the latter might be lecturing on the sutras, he, Kuan Ti, would always be there to give protection. A transcript of this supernatural conversation was published and greatly improved the prestige of Buddhism throughout religious circles in Peking.[39]

VARIATION IN THE CHARACTER OF MONASTERIES

A fact that should never be lost sight of in discussing Chinese Buddhism is that the character of monasteries varied. Not only was there a difference between those publicly and privately controlled, between elite and proletariat, but there were also regional differences. During the Republican period the model institutions lay almost without exception in central China. In the rest of the country there was widespread decay. One feature of the Buddhist revival was the restoration of decayed monasteries in the south and the establishment of new ones in the north. These consciously took as their model the religious centers of the lower Yangtze valley. Meditation was modeled on Chin Shan; buddha recitation on Ling-yen Shan; ordination on Pao-hua Shan. Monks were invited from these and other central Chinese monasteries to serve as officers. They trained a new generation of monks, some of whom eventually came to Hong Kong, where they are among the most highly respected members of the sangha. (I remember attending a plenary mass in Hong Kong where northern monks were performing at one altar and Cantonese monks at another. The dignity and meticulousness of the northerners offered a contrast to the Cantonese, who even as they chanted were smoking cigarettes, yawning, and scratching themselves.)

Invitations to monks in central China came not just from monasteries that were established or restored but also from those that were prosperous. Wherever the need was felt for prestige or a tightening of the administration, a new abbot or prior might be invited from Kiangsu and Chekiang, particularly from Chin Shan. Even foreigners became aware that Chin Shan was the place where "all the abbots of the larger monasteries go through their severe course of meditation and asceticism."[40] A lay informant who spent several years at Omei Shan in Szechwan said that temples there would "snap up" any monk who had done two or three years in Chin Shan's meditation hall, and make him abbot—even though his talents were inferior. To a lesser degree the same sort of prestige accrued from service in any of the famous monasteries of Kiangsu and Chekiang. Nan-yüeh in Hunan and Chiu-hua Shan in Anhwei also enjoyed good reputations. Two Szechwan institutions, the Pao-kuang Ssu and Wen-shu Yüan in Chengtu were considered to be exemplary by some informants, but scorned by others as "free hotels." Peking got very low marks from everyone. Though it had many monasteries and numerous monks, it was mainly at a few, little-known temples that the dharma was considered to flourish.

According to one informant, monasteries in the outlying provinces tended to be old-fashioned and preserved practices that had become obsolete in central China. Uposatha days, observance of the summer retreat, formal begging with bowls, gifts of money for traveling monks, archaic monastic offices—such things seem to have been found more often at some ordinary monasteries in Hunan and Szechwan,[41] whereas in Kiangsu and Chekiang they were to be found in Vinaya centers or not at all.

Nor was the monastic system in central China adopted *in toto* by the new monasteries that took it as a model. At the Chan-shan Ssu in Tsingtao, for example, little emphasis was given to semesters. Officers could resign and take office at any time, not merely on the 15th of the first and seventh month. A former proctor there told me that he had no responsibility for chores, bathing, and cremations, all of which were the duties of his counterpart in Kiangsu. Discipline was so mild that he did not shout at offenders and, as for blows, he had never struck anyone during his whole time in office. If he noticed a monk talking in the refectory, he would walk over and say in a low voice "Please don't talk." At Chin Shan the same offender would have been beaten or fined. One reason for these differences, he said, was that the Chan-shan Ssu specialized in teaching the doctrine, not in meditation. Such differences illustrate the danger of overgeneralizing from the system at the model meditation centers that has been described in the foregoing chapters.

Not every model was model in every respect. At the Kao-min Ssu, otherwise so strict, monks were sometimes appointed to office who had never spent a term in the meditation hall. A few were appointed who had never even been ordained! This would have been unthinkable at Chin Shan, T'ien-t'ung, or T'ien-ning. My information comes from a monk who was himself so appointed. Two years before his ordination he became acolyte and personal attendant to the abbot, Lai-kuo.[42] According to the rules, as a novice he should not even have been allowed to pass the night in the monastery. After a year he was made clerk in the business office, although he was still unordained and had not spent a term in the meditation hall. Yet the Kao-min Ssu, more than any other monastery, was insistent on the purity of Ch'an practice. It performed no rites for the dead, held no ordinations, had no seminary or hall for reciting buddha's name, and even expunged the name of Amitabha from its liturgy.

In general, observance of the rules was in inverse proportion to contact with the populace. Urban monasteries usually had to depend for their income on performing rites for the dead, so that not only were the monks distracted by the pleasures of the city around them, but they simply did not have time for religious cultivation. On the other hand, at the distant places of pilgrimage like Omei Shan, they had to spend much of their day acting as hotel keepers, and a little of the dust of the world was brushed off on them by every traveler. Strict observance of the spirit as well as of the letter of the rules could most often be found at monasteries that had their own landed income and hence did not depend on mortuary rites; that were not an object of pilgrimage and did not welcome lay people to dine or spend the night; and that were so large that the only alternative to strictness was total disorder.

CHAPTER V

Hereditary and Branch Temples

If there was variation in the character of the large public monasteries (*shih-fang ts'ung-lin*), which housed most of the elite—perhaps 5 percent of the sangha—there was even more variation among hereditary temples (*tzu-sun miao*), which were far commoner. When the Chinese layman had business to do with monks, he usually did not go to a public monastery, since the nearest might be miles away, but to the hereditary temple that was probably "just around the corner." He went there to order rites for the dead, to pray for divine assistance, and to tell his fortune with the bamboo slips. He also went there if he wanted to become a monk himself or to have one of his children become a monk. In China hereditary temples were the only channel through which it was normally possible to enter the sangha. Since they were privately owned, usually by a "family" of monks, the sangha could not treat them as its common property. Visiting monks could expect to be put up for only three days.

The "family" that owned the hereditary temple was composed of several generations of masters and disciples, all of them "heirs" (*tzu-sun*). The literal meaning of this term is "sons and grandsons," but normally there was no blood relationship between any of the individuals involved. It was not like the present system in Japan where priests marry and a temple is usually passed down by the father to his son by blood. In China all these relationships were based on tonsure. When a monk shaved the head of a layman, the latter thereby became a novice (*sha-mi*), an heir of the monk's temple, and the monk's adopted son, termed in Chinese "tonsure disciple" (*t'i-t'ou ti-tzu*). Two tonsure disciples of the same generation in the same family were considered "brothers" or "cousins" (*shih hsiung-ti*). They had an obligation to keep up the worship of their "ancestors." For example, when their master died, they performed rites to secure him a better rebirth, made regular offerings to his soul tablets, and swept his grave at Ch'ing Ming. This will be explained more fully in Chapter IX. It is worth noting here, however, that the system appears to have been unique to Chinese Buddhism. In other religions disciples are aware of their lineage, that is, the succession of masters that connects them with some great teacher in the past; in Christian monasticism the monks of a monastery are often thought of as members of a family (the very word "abbot" means "father" in Aramaic); and in some Hindu orders the disciples of the same master refer to one another as *gurubhai* (an exact equivalent of *shih hsiung-ti*). But only in Chinese Buddhism have family institutions been so substantially translated from secular to monastic life—which is testimony, no doubt, to the strength of familism in the Chinese way of thinking. Even in traditional law the master and his disciples were considered a family.

Most hereditary temples could also be called "small temples" (*hsiao-miao*), even though they had a large number of residents or extensive land holdings. I remember meeting a monk in Singapore who impressed me by his aristocratic features and courtly manner and by the fact that he wore a silk gown. He told me that he came from a small temple in eastern Kiangsu. At the age of sixteen he had his head shaved there and after three years of training went to be ordained at Pao-hua Shan. His master believed that monks should receive higher education, so that they might know more about the world in which they were going to preach the dharma. Although his own education was cut short by illness, his "younger brother" (*shih-ti*) graduated from Tsinghua University and became abbot of a large monastery in Peking. Soon afterwards their master decided to retire. The only other brother was busy in Ningpo and so my informant was made the temple's new head monk (*chu-ch'ih*) or manager (*tang-chia*).[1] There was no question of his brothers returning some day to claim a share of his inheritance or authority. The temple was fully and irrevocably his. He took two disciples himself, after getting his master's approval. The four of them continued to live there until the Communists executed his master in 1948 and he fled to Hong Kong.

His master was executed on the grounds that he was a landlord. That would be hard to deny. The temple had 140 acres of paddy, yielding rents of 67 tons of unhusked rice a year, enough to feed two hundred persons. There was very little income from performing services for the dead because with only a hundred families in the village such services were seldom required. On the other hand, expenses were low because the temple's lay workmen were willing to work for a reduced salary, or in some cases for none at all, in order to earn the merit of serving the sangha.

Part of what my informant modestly described as their "substantial surplus" was used to beautify the premises. Part was given to the needy families of the village. Part went to pay tuition fees at Tsinghua University. Part was used to buy more land. It was out of surplus income that the large holdings had been bought by successive generations of masters. With ten workmen to wait upon them, fine buildings to live in, and few demands on their time, the four monks of this small temple were able to lead a life of luxury and leisure. Not only were they seldom called on to perform services for the dead, but, as at most small temples, there was no regular program of meditation or reciting buddha's name. There were few visitors and little administrative work, as there would have been in a large public monastery. There were not even morning and afternoon devotions. At hereditary temples these were usually recited only on uposatha days, twice a month, and daily during the last month of the lunar year. The reader may wonder how the monks spent their time. According to my informant they spent much of it in study, and I must say that he seemed to be a most cultivated person.

He said that there were many small temples as rich as his in Kiangsu. I have not heard of another where so large an income was enjoyed by so few monks.[2] But most small temples had the same atmosphere of relaxed informality. There was no proctor to shout at a person or beat him if he broke the rules. In fact, small temples seldom if ever had any code of rules that governed their activities like the codes of Chin Shan or Kao-min. Furthermore, the monastic vows were more lightly regarded. There was the saying:

When I sleep, may it be in a public
        monastery
It is impossible to practice the religion
        at small temples.

One hears far more stories about monks at these institutions enjoying meat, wine, and women. But leisure rather than immorality was their universal characteristic. Monks could go to bed and get up when they pleased and eat what they felt like. The latter was particularly appreciated by elderly monks, who might suffer from a poor digestion or bad teeth. The elderly were also happy not to recite devotions; many of them were short of breath. But some were men of learning and virtue, well qualified to teach and train the novices who lived with them.

Unordained novices could not be trained at public monasteries. They were not even supposed to spend a night there. As we noted earlier, the guest prefect would not admit them. This rule was enforced at some of the model monasteries, but less rigorously elsewhere. Informants have mentioned several cases where a novice, accompanied by his master, was allowed to stay in a wandering monks hall. At the Kuang-hsiao Ssu, Kiangsu, and the Kuan-tsung Ssu near Ningpo, novices were regularly enrolled in the seminary, on the grounds that they were students rather than visiting or resident monks. It was felt that since their heads had not been shaved on the premises, the key principle was not in danger.

The danger was that nepotism based on tonsure would vitiate the public character of a monastery. Hereditary temples were handed from generation to generation of heirs in a "tonsure family." Any public monastery that permitted tonsure relationships to flourish might end up being handed from generation to generation in the same way and thereby become hereditary too. This was one reason for the rules against shaving heads, against training novices, and against even letting them spend the night. Another reason was that the presence of untrained novices in a public monastery impaired the good order of processions, meals, and ritual. Where hundreds of monks were involved, every one of them had to know his part well.

Statistics indicate that monasteries and temples with monks in residence had, on the average, five monks apiece (see Appendix I). This average must reflect the existence of a large number of temples having only one apiece, as well as a small number having dozens. There was probably a dip in the graph between one and five. This is because casual donations at a small temple were seldom enough to support more than one person, while to perform rites for the dead at least five persons were required to man the liturgical instruments. It might be possible for a temple with two or three monks to call in two or three more from the neighborhood, but it was more reliable to have a full complement in residence.

The residents of the typical small temple would usually include a "grandfather master" (*shih-kung*) who might have already handed the burdens of management to one of his disciples. If so, the latter was the head of the temple, either for life or until he too chose to retire. Some of his brothers had probably gone off to enroll in a meditation hall or take office at public monasteries. They could return at any time, but in practice many of them became involved in separate careers and might acquire their own small temples. The brothers who remained at home, including the manager, would have taken disciples themselves, and this third generation, some of them already ordained and some of them novices in training, would usually comprise the majority of residents.

In any case the total number of residents was small. Hence they kept house *ad hoc*. There was no hierarchy of officers serving by semester. The only office was that of the manager. If he told a monk to entertain a party of guests, it did not make this monk—in any formal sense—a guest prefect, and the next time a different monk might be asked to do the job.

Usually the buildings and land were registered in the temple's name, but the rights of ownership were to be exercised by the manager as an individual. Although he had to follow his master's wishes in handling it (if his master were on hand to express his wishes), it was much easier for him to sell institutional property than it was for the abbot of a public monastery. Thus an unscrupulous person could usually make more money as head of a small temple.

In some cases the rights of ownership were not exercised by the manager, but by a group of laymen who had built the temple and then endowed it or supported it from year to year. Such a lay family, clan, or village was known as the "mountain owner" (*shan-chu*) and, in fact, the property might be registered in their name. Whether it was or not, the rights they exercised were unknown in other Buddhist institutions. They could decide, for example, who was to be the manager and insist on the expulsion of monks that they did not care for. They could ask to be served a vegetarian feast from time to time. They had to be addressed respectfully as "uncle" or "elder brother" by the monks who lived there. What they principally expected of the monks was the regular worship of the family or clan tablets that were hung in the halls of rebirth and longevity. In other cases such a temple's *raison d'être* was to provide security and comfort for some member of a rich family who had decided to become a monk or nun. According to one source, lay ownership was especially common in south China.[3] In the country as a whole, it seems to have been exceptional. Most temples were established with funds collected from various lay supporters, who retained no control over them once they were built.

Sometimes the building site might come from a large monastery as a token of gratitude to a monk who had served it well. The Ch'i-hsia Ssu near Nanking, for example, had over the years provided the land for about ten hermitages scattered about its slopes.[4] All of them were independent of its authority but not of its generosity. They received annual gifts of rice and oil. The siteland still belonged to the Ch'i-hsia Ssu. If any hermitage became the scene of gross offenses against the monastic rules, then the abbot of Ch'i-hsia could consult with "the elders of neighboring monasteries" (*chu-shan chang-lao*) since joint action was necessary to expel the offenders. According to the abbot, this happened rarely if ever.

BRANCH TEMPLES

Such independent institutions as these hermitages must be distinguished from the "branch temples" (*fen-yüan*) or "sub-temples" (*hsia-yüan*) that might also lie on the slopes of the mountain, but were more often to be found in the neighboring village or city or sometimes much farther away. Branch temples were wholly subordinate to their parent monasteries. Chin Shan had two branches, for example. One of them was about three miles off with only a couple of monks in residence. The other was at a distance of about twenty-five miles, with seven or eight monks. Chin Shan owned and controlled them both, though it had no control over the three hereditary temples situated on its own hillock.

At each of Chin Shan's two branches the abbot appointed a manager (*tang-chia*). There were no other officers. The manager did all the day-to-day administration and consulted the abbot only on exceptional matters. He did not have the title of manager with respect to Chin Shan, but only with respect to the branch temple. He did hold senior rank, however,[5] and he was loyal to the traditions of Chin Shan, seeing to it that its rules were enforced. No novices could have their heads shaved or undergo training. Although devotions were not recited daily, all the monastic vows were strictly observed. Actually there was little problem of discipline, since most of the residents were quiet, elderly monks who had been given places there by Chin Shan because they were not strong enough to endure its rigorous schedule. They had not reached the secretarial rank that would have entitled them to a private apartment and did not have a small temple they wanted to return to. Many had been menial officers working in the kitchen. In the branch no work was required of them (there were lay workmen), but they had a general responsibility for looking after the graves of the ancestral abbots of Chin Shan, whose ashes were buried on the premises. Thus these two small temples combined the role of home for the aged with cemetery custodianship.

Wandering monks were not allowed to stay there (*kua-tan*) except by special permission of the manager. One reason was that the supply of rice was only sufficient for the regular residents. The smaller of the two branches was wholly subsidized by the parent monastery, while the larger one had a little income of its own, derived from 120 acres of forest and from a few fields. When this proved insufficient, it received a subsidy too.

The term "sub-temple" (*hsia-yüan*) was used particularly for the office of the village agent (see p. 27) and for the resthouses often erected at convenient points along the way if the road up to the monastery was a long one. The term "branch temple" (*fen-yüan*) was applied to the buildings maintained by many a large monastery in a metropolis like Shanghai or Nanking, where officers could stay when they went to the city on business or to preach. In between their visits, the resident manager served as the monastery's representative, not only to arrange for the purchase of supplies and sale of produce but also to keep in contact with the lay disciples and supporters who had soul tablets at the parent monastery or customarily asked it to perform Buddhist services. If some building or restoration project was under way for which extra financial support was required, the manager could let this fact be known. The urban branch, like the others, could also serve as a place for rest or retirement. Jo-shun, the abbot of the Ch'i-hsia Ssu near Nanking, built a branch temple in Hong Kong as the place to which he could, and did, retire to spend his last years.

Although a branch or sub-temple was wholly owned by its parent monastery, the title to its land and buildings might be registered in its own name. This was the case for the larger of Chin Shan's two branches, the Shao-lung Ssu. Its deeds were made out to "Shao-lung Ssu," not to Chin Shan. But they were kept at Chin Shan so that there could never be any question as to who the real owner was.

Some branch temples were built overseas to spread the dharma there and to raise money among overseas Chinese. An outstanding example is the Chi-le Sse at Ayer Itam in Penang, which is said to be the largest Buddhist temple in Malaya. It was established in 1891 as a branch of the Yung-ch'üan Ssu at Ku Shan near Foochow. Its successive heads were appointed by the abbots of Ku Shan from among the leading monks there, or in some cases the abbots concurrently headed it themselves. But, perhaps because it lay in a foreign country, it appears to have been loosely controlled. Its head monks were termed *chu-ch'ih* instead of the more usual *tang-chia* (see note 1). I have been told that the second head did not send in the regular financial reports that were expected of him. He was criticized for this when he returned to Ku Shan, but because he had had great success in raising money to expand the premises, he was allowed to continue in office.

At this point the reader might find it useful to see a tabulation of the differences between the public monastery, the branch, and the hereditary temple.

Public Monastery	Branch Temple	Hereditary Temple
Named-*ssu*[6]	Named *ssu, an, ching-she, yüan, mao-p'eng,* etc.	Named, *ssu, an, ching-she, yüan, mao-p'eng,* etc.
20 to 1,000 ordained monks	1 to 20 ordained monks	1 to 30 monks and novices
Less accessible to populace	More accessible	Most accessible
Property of whole sangha	Property of parent monastery	Property of tonsure family
Headed by: *fang-chang,* who was chosen by consultation and could not be tonsure disciple of predecessor	Headed by: *tang-chia,* who was chosen by *fang-chang* of parent monastery	Headed by: *tang-chia* or *chu-ch'ih,* who was chosen by predecessor from among tonsure disciples
He served 1-2 terms of three years	He had no set term	He served until he died or retired
Unlimited stay for wandering monks	No stay, or limit of three days	Limit of three days
Devotions twice a day	Devotions two days a month	Devotions two days a month[7]
Code of rules	Code of rules	No code of rules
"48 offices and ranks"	No offices and ranks	No offices and ranks
Office held by semester	No semesters	No semesters
No shaving of heads	No shaving of heads	Specialized in shaving of heads
No training of novices	No training of novices	Specialized in training of novices
Held ordinations	No ordinations	No ordinations
Many operated seminaries for ordained monks	No seminaries	No seminaries
Income from 1) land, 2) performing rites for dead	Subsidized by parent monastery	Income from 1) performing rites for dead, 2) donations

This table oversimplifies the facts in order to show what was typical. Not every institution conformed to type.

HYBRID INSTITUTIONS

Both in the city and the countryside many temples were public in certain respects, but hereditary in others. They might have forty or fifty monks and a large complement of officers who served by the semester. Visiting monks could stay as long as they wished. Perhaps there was a regular program of meditation or buddha recitation. On the other hand, as in the hereditary temple, the heads of novices were shaved and they were trained for ordination. Control was closely held within a single tonsure family. The abbot and the higher officers were all related to one another by ties of tonsure. Such institutions were usually called "hereditary public monasteries" (*tzu-sun shih-fang ts'ung-lin*).

A few monks deny that there was such a thing as an "hereditary public monastery." What they mean is that they disapprove of the term and the anomalous practice that it represented. There is no doubt that such things existed, and were, indeed, probably far commoner than the orthodox, purely public institutions. But because they were smaller and less elite, few of their former residents can be found abroad today. Indeed, I have had to depend in each case on a single informant, so that the resulting information is unsatisfactory. Therefore I have decided to relegate it to an appendix (Appendix V). The example that will be offered here is not a perfect hybrid, not half and half, but weighted more toward the public than the hereditary. Nonetheless it commends itself to our attention by the number of good informants available and by the fact that it played an important role in modern Chinese Buddhism. I refer to the Yung-ch'üan Ssu on Ku Shan near Foochow. This famous monastery, built in the tenth century, was the largest in Fukien province. Foreigners as well as Chinese often went there for an outing. They would take a boat down the Min River estuary and then go by sedan chair up the 1500-foot ascent. Since it was the parent monastery of the Chi-le Ssu in Penang (see p. 136), overseas Chinese from Penang and other points in Malaya came to be ordained there as did many Buddhists from Taiwan. An ordination was held every spring.[8] During the Republican period there were three to four hundred monks in residence. The produce of its farmland was usually enough to feed them, and supplementary income came from rites for the dead and donations by visitors. Photographs taken of Ku Shan in 1929 show its vast complex of buildings in an excellent state of repair.[9] It had a meditation hall where three periods were held daily, stepped up to twelve periods in meditation weeks. But the atmosphere was not strict. There was no formal enrollment and monks could enter and leave the hall as they pleased. "Compared to Chin Shan," said a former resident, "it was pretty sloppy (ma-ma hu-hu)."

Besides the meditation hall there was a large library and a scriptural press with thousands of printing blocks. Those who cared to could immerse themselves in the study of the sutras. If they were in the wandering monks hall, they could stay for as long as they liked (kua hai-tan). The three-day limit found in hereditary temples did not apply. Nor was control of the monastery closely held. According to my informants, the new abbot never inherited his post as a tonsure disciple of his predecessor[10] and high officers were not heirs of a single tonsure family. Yet despite these eminently public characteristics, Ku Shan was called "half public, half hereditary."[11] This was because it permitted the shaving and training of novices. It also permitted the sale of monastic titles. In some ways it had become less like a monastery than a cooperative apartment house.

These innovations went back to the abbotship of the Venerable Miao-lien (died 1907). Once upon a time, when the need for money arose, he decided to raise it by selling the titles of "rector" and "guest prefect" to any monk who was willing to put up a sizable lump sum. Along with the title the purchaser acquired the right to a private apartment of his own, where he could live until the end of his days, eating the monastery's rice free of charge. He was not obliged to assume any duties, or even to attend devotions in the great shrine-hall. His time was his own. More than that, he had the privilege of taking disciples. To shave their heads he would withdraw to the Ho-shui Yen, a small sub-temple perhaps half a mile off.[12] Thus he complied with the rule against tonsure in a public monastery. Ho-shui Yen belonged to Ku Shan, but it was not within its walls. Afterwards he would bring them back to live in his apartment and undergo training for their ordination, which they would also receive at Ku Shan. If they were less than sixteen years old when the next ordination was held, they would wait until a later one.

In the ordination records no reference would be made to the fact that their heads had been shaved in the Ho-shui Yen. Instead, every document would show that tonsure had taken place at the master's hereditary temple, which the disciple might never have set foot in. This was called "borrowing a name," a very common procedure in Chinese Buddhism. After they had been ordained, some disciples would enter the meditation hall for a year or two. Later they might go elsewhere to engage in training and study (*ts'an-hsüeh*); or perhaps hold office at Ku Shan itself.

The privilege of taking disciples was not restricted to those who had purchased a title. Except for the rank and file, all residents of Ku Shan could do so, nor were they required to seek the abbot's permission first. Taking disciples was their personal affair. Since they were not all members of a single tonsure family, as they would have been at a purely hereditary temple, there was no filial obligation to consult the senior family members.

According to an informant who held office there 1926-1928, Ku Shan then had sixty to seventy titular rectors and eighty to ninety titular guest prefects. The former had paid $100 each for their title, the latter $50-60 (Chinese currency). Considering the fact that they could count on board and lodging for life, it was quite a bargain! They were understandingly indignant when the Venerable Hsü-yün, chosen abbot in 1929, cancelled their sinecures without compensation. Hsü-yün also put a stop to the tonsure and training of novices. Ku Shan was thereby restored to the state of a purely public monastery.[13]

Its unregenerate state may have flouted the rules, but it produced (perhaps by chance) two of the most eminent monks in modern China. Hsü-yün, who reformed it, was himself one of its products. He had been tonsured and ordained at Ku Shan under Miao-lien, supposedly in 1858-1859.[14] Yüan-ying, who headed the Chinese Buddhist Association and served as abbot of many famous monasteries, was tonsured and ordained there about 1897.[15]

I do not know how many other monasteries had this particular variety of hybrid system. According to one informant "the bad practice of selling monastic titles did not exist outside Fukien province." But certainly the shift from public to hereditary was an omnipresent threat in Chinese monasticism. Impersonal, public control was always being infiltrated by elements of nepotistic, hereditary control. Mention has been made of the abbatial acolytes of the Kao-min Ssu (p. 128). They were not only the acolytes of the abbot, but also his tonsure disciples, and he had shaved their heads within the very walls of that strictest of public monasteries. Nominally he was considered to have done so at his own hereditary temple, and appearances were further preserved by avoiding hereditary terms of address (they always called him "abbot," never "master"[16]). But it was still a sorry departure from the traditions of the Kao-min Ssu. How had it come about?

Many, many years earlier, when Lai-kuo was first abbot, a tenant farmer asked him to shave his head. Lai-kuo refused, saying that such a thing was impermissible at a public monastery. That night the tenant kneeled until dawn outside the abbot's quarters. Lai-kuo still refused. But the retired abbot intervened. He was impressed by the tenant's piety and told Lai-kuo to shave his head in spite of the rule. The retired abbot could not be disobeyed, and so the rule was broken. From that time on there was no basis for refusing others who made the same request. Often Lai-kuo had as many as ten unordained novices, all his own tonsure disciples, serving in the sacristy and other parts of the monastery.[17] A shift toward the hereditary had begun. In one sense, it had been under way for a long time, for at all the large Kiangsu monasteries the abbotship was closely held within a dharma—not a tonsure—family. This will be explained in the next chapter.

CHAPTER VI

The Abbot

The early monastic communities in India were not monasteries, but avasas. The avasa was a loose collection of monks living within fixed boundaries, sometimes within an enclosure. They carried on their religious exercises individually. There was neither collective worship nor collective meditation. The only regular collective act occurred twice a month on uposatha days when all the residents of the avasa were obliged to recite the Pratimoksa rules together and confess their offenses. Irregularly they gathered to ordain, to receive the distribution of robes, and to decide any question affecting the welfare of the community. However, as the monastic system grew, the avasa came to include a communal bath, latrine, storeroom, kitchen, refectory, and so on. Laymen endowed it with land to supply food. A staff of monastic officers arose to manage the various sections. There was still no single officer in over-all charge; there was no abbot.[1] Every important decision from the appointment of officers to the distribution of a monk's personal effects after he died, was made at a meeting of all the ordained monks who resided in the community. Any one of them could introduce a motion. If all the rest were silent, it meant that the motion had carried. If there was discussion, it usually led to unanimity. But if a difference of opinion could not be resolved, a vote was taken, sometimes with wooden tallies.

Dr. Sukumar Dutt favors the theory that this direct democracy was derived from the customs of North Indian tribes who "were conversant with free institutions like voting, meeting, popular tribunals, and collective legislation."[2] In any case complete and direct democracy was consistent with the Buddha's injunction that his disciples should depend on no one but themselves in the search for truth, and in his refusal to appoint a successor as head of the sangha.

This anti-authoritarian tradition of Buddhism in India was conveyed to China. There too no single monk headed the sangha. There was nothing equivalent to pontiff, cardinal, or bishop. The highest ecclesiastical officer was the abbot,[3] and although this in itself was a step away from the direct democracy of early Buddhism, much of the democratic spirit was preserved. At public monasteries in China all important decisions were supposed to be reached by consultation.

CONSULTATION

Theoretically each monastery was autonomous. Not only was there no higher ecclesiastical authority, but the sangha as a whole claimed to be outside the jurisdiction of the State and all its representatives, from the district magistrate to the emperor himself. This claim was only partly honored. Monks were exempt from taxation, conscription, and the corvee, but the legal codes of successive dynasties restricted many of their activities, such as taking disciples, ordination, building temples, and preaching in public places. The government also appointed a hierarchy of monks to adjudicate violations of discipline and to act as intermediaries between the sangha and the State. However, during the late Ch'ing dynasty these monastic officials played a largely nominal role and the restrictive laws in the code were usually ignored unless their violation affected public order, in which case the magistrate could apply their full penalty. Under the Republic a new set of restrictive laws was passed, but they were even more sporadically applied than under the Ch'ing. The intermediary role of monastic officials was assumed by the Buddhist associations, which turned out to have little more effective authority.

In practice the autonomy of monastic institutions was almost complete. Yet because of the concept that every public monastery belonged to the whole sangha, the abbot consulted other abbots whenever an important or delicate problem arose. Such a problem, for example, would be a dispute about the choice of his successor or the expulsion of a monk who denied having broken the monastic rules. Generally speaking, whenever the abbot foresaw the possibility that he or his associates might be accused of prejudice or self-interest, he preferred to secure the approval of the elders of neighboring monasteries (*chu-shan chang-lao*). This might be done by going to call on them individually; or they might be invited to meet at the monastery. In that case their deliberations were not governed by any parliamentary rules of procedure, nor was a vote necessarily taken. The purpose was to determine the "sense of the meeting."

THE AUTHORITY OF THE ABBOT

Consultation was considered equally desirable within the monastery. To the casual observer the abbot's authority might seem to be unlimited. As we saw in Chapter I, he appointed all the senior officers and conferred all the higher ranks. He could dismiss any officer for incompetence or reward him for meritorious service by giving him a private apartment to retire to. It was he alone who had the right to sentence a monk to expulsion for breaking the rules—and he could promulgate new rules. The monastery's income was spent as he decided. Every important problem was referred to him for decision. Yet he would seldom decide an important problem without consulting his predecessors (the retired abbots), the senior officers, and, if the problem was sufficiently important, the elders of neighboring monasteries.

There was usually at least one former abbot in residence. If he liked power, he could retain so much of it that his successor was little more than a figurehead and his own role was like that of the late Dowager Empress. But even if he wanted to divest himself of all the cares of office, he would be consulted on important questions as if he were the grandfather in a large Chinese family. Indeed, the manner in which decisions were reached within the monastery shows as much the influence of the Chinese family system, with its deference to collective age and wisdom, as the tradition of direct democracy brought over from India.

At Chin Shan, for example, there were three apartments for retired abbots (*t'ui-chü liao*), but when the last abbot held office, only one of them was occupied and the occupant was his immediate prede-

26. The abbot sits in his bedroom. P'i-lu Ssu, Nanking.

cessor. "According to the ancient rule," he told me, "it was not obligatory for the abbot to consult his predecessor, but I always got his
approval for important decisions because he was of the senior generation (*ch'ien-pei*). I would also consult the other officers. I had no
desire to be autocratic."

If monastic property was involved, consultation became obligatory.
No permanent property of the establishment (*ch'ang-chu wu*),
whether it was an acre of farmland or a set of the Tripitaka, could
be alienated without the consent of the senior officers. Once a month
and at the end of the year, all the accounts, including the abbot's,
were read off by the persons in charge of them and collectively approved when the senior officers met. Personal use of public funds,
whether by the abbot or anyone else, was thus closely guarded
against.

This severely limited the perquisites that the abbot enjoyed. At the
T'ien-ning Ssu, for example, he had to pay out of his own pocket for
any candles issued to him above the established quota of eight ounces
a month. There is a story of one Chinese abbot long ago who went to
the business office and asked for some ginger. The clerk, Yang-ch'i by
name, told him that ginger was for equal distribution to everyone and
not just for the abbot. This anecdote gave rise to saying that "Yang-
ch'i's ginger stays hot ten thousand years." The fact remains, however,
that at many monasteries the abbot's quarters were spacious, even
luxurious, and that some of his meals were prepared in his own private kitchen, particularly when he was entertaining visitors. He often
received an extra share of fees from rites for the dead and it was to
him more than to anyone else in the monastery that lay devotees made
personal donations.[4] In the Buddhist world, at least, he enjoyed lofty
status. When he retired, he was assured of a comfortable apartment,
probably larger than average, and when he died, his tablet was placed
in the ancestors hall where the offerings were the most punctilious.

We might therefore suppose that the post of abbot was sought after.
In fact, it was usually not. This was because the better the monastery
and, therefore, generally speaking, the larger the abbot's perquisites,
the more onerous were his duties. His first duty was "to lead the monks
in religious exercises" (*ling-chung hsiu-hsing*). Before dawn he was
waiting for them in the shrine hall to take part in morning devotions.

He was expected to preside over the two main daily meals in the refectory. Most onerous of all, the rules required that he attend four or
more meditation periods a day: the morning period, the noon period
and all the evening periods (see Appendix III). At least once (in the
evening fourth period) he gave an Explanation. During the early afternoon he was supposed to be available for tutorials (*ch'ing k'ai-shih*).
On every important ceremonial occasion he was expected to preach
the dharma. During the summer retreat it was often he who lectured
on the sutras. In addition he had the administrative responsibilities
already described. No wonder that many monks, when they were
asked to take over a large monastery, stole off at night and that others
died in office.[5]

The apportionment of the abbot's time between religious exercises
and administration varied from monastery to monastery and from man

27. The abbot kneels before his private altar. P'i-lu Ssu, Nanking.

to man. He could, if he wished, delegate nearly all the daily administrative work to his subordinates. At the T'ien-ning Ssu, for example, the sacristan (*i-po*) entertained important visitors and made arrangements with them for Buddhist services. Money and accounts, elsewhere kept under the abbot's close supervision, were handled entirely by the business office. The seminary was in charge of a specialist in teaching. The abbot was therefore free to devote most of his time to leading the monks in religious exercises. He attended not just the four obligatory periods, but *all* periods in the meditation hall. At night he did not leave the hall until the precentor had completed his inspection. Only for the most serious reason would he take time off during the day, and in that case, he had to ask for leave like anyone else. For

28. The abbot preaches the dharma in the dharma hall. He holds the crooked stick (*shuo-fa kan*) that is an emblem of his authority to preach. P'i-lu Ssu, Nanking.

example, if he was unable to attend morning devotions, he would send a sacristan to ask the proctor for "shrine-hall leave" (*tien-chia*) or "sick leave" (*ping-chia*). If an important lay patron invited him for lunch, he asked for "street leave" (*chieh-chia*). It should be pointed out, of course, that when an abbot "asked for leave," there was no question of it being denied. He was simply informing the sections concerned that they should carry on without him. This could be important, since the monks in the refectory, for example, could not begin eating before he arrived.

There may have been a tendency on the part of my informants to exaggerate the hardships that they underwent in office, partly in order to correct the popular idea that they reveled in luxury and power. The abbot at Chin Shan told me that he only missed an obligatory period in the meditation hall if he had to entertain important visitors. Other business was taken care of by his subordinates. But a monk who sat in the hall during his abbotship stated that visitors and other business kept him away more than half the time. Informants from the Kao-min Ssu say that the illustrious Lai-kuo during his early years as abbot, when he was still young (the dates mentioned were 1919-1931), regularly attended the four obligatory periods, but that when he passed the age of fifty or sixty, he did not have enough strength to do this and still fulfill his administrative obligations.

If the abbot was to be absent from the monastery for more than a few hours, he might leave it in charge of a deputy abbot (*tai-li fang-chang, hu-li fang-chang*), who was usually the rector. Alternatively, he might prefer to leave religious responsibilities to the rector and administrative responsibilities to the provost, without naming any single deputy over-all. Sometimes an abbot was elected who had to spend most of his time elsewhere (see p. 172), and in that case the deputy abbot he appointed was a good deal more than a deputy.

The abbot was important not because he exercised absolute authority, but precisely because he had to rule without it. Therefore the only monks qualified to hold this office were those who would be able to win the voluntary support of senior officers and the respect of the rank and file. They also had to have a following among the laity. Lay donations and, in times of trouble, lay protection were important to the monastery. But the reverse was also true: the monastery was important to laymen. This was because, unlike its counterparts in the

West, it also served as the parish church. Laymen came to attend rites for the dead, to receive religious instruction, and to take the Five Vows. The abbot presided not only over monastic life, but also over pastoral care. His influence on the laity as well as the sangha could be immense. During the past half century a small number of eminent abbots lectured tirelessly on the sutras to growing audiences; administered the Three Refuges to thousands of lay disciples; and collected enough donations not only to revive old monasteries and build new ones, but also to start schools, orphanages, and clinics.

On the other hand, an unsuitable person in the position of abbot could be disastrous. If he was merely weak and incompetent, the senior monks could guide him. But if he combined unscrupulousness with administrative ability, he could gradually get rid of the "old guard," fill the top posts and ranks with his own henchmen, and milk the monastery for his personal profit. Discipline would suffer and lay support would drop off. If he and his clique retained control for several generations, the monastery might fall into ruins. The choice of abbot was therefore the single most important event in the administration of Chinese monasteries.

QUALIFICATIONS

To be chosen as abbot a monk needed more than the charismatic qualities of leadership that would enable him to govern by consent and to attract donations from the laity. He had to have five specific qualifications. The first was administrative experience. Preferably he had held office in all four sections of the monastic establishment: sacristy, business office, guest department, and meditation hall. Next, he was expected to be expert in the Vinaya and faultless in his observance of the rules and etiquette of monastic life. After all, it was he who set the example. Third, he should have a thorough grounding in Buddhist texts and doctrine and the ability to teach them, as well as a general literary competence. If he made mistakes in writing characters or could not pick his way through the pitfalls of classical Chinese, he might make the monastery a laughing stock. Fourth, it was desirable—though by no means necessary—that he be well connected. If he was on good terms with eminent monks, they could be persuaded to come to the monastery and share his burdens. If he had already attracted lay followers who were very rich or very powerful, there would be obvious advantages.[6] Last and most important of all, he had to be willing to serve. The monk who was best qualified in other respects was usually an older man who wanted to devote his remaining years to the religious exercises that would prepare him for death. He had no interest in status and a positive distaste for the tiresome administrative details of monastic housekeeping. If he knew his Buddhist texts, he wanted to devote all his time to teaching them. For him the abbotship was nothing but a burden, an unwelcome duty, to be accepted only because the welfare of the sangha required it. This has been particularly true in the last fifty years, when so many monasteries have been threatened with confiscation of their property by an unfriendly government or with destruction in the course of civil wars and the Japanese invasion.

Thus the qualifications on the basis of which an abbot was chosen were mutually exclusive. It was very hard to find the right man. Most of my informants, in fact, looked upon the post the way the full professor looks on being chairman of the department. As the abbot of the T'ien-ning Ssu remarked: "The higher type of person (*kao-shang ti jen*) did not want to be abbot. He wanted to practice religious cultivation (*hsiu-ch'ih*)." The result was that the candidate chosen did not always fulfill all the five qualifications listed above. At Chin Shan, for example, neither Tz'u-pen nor Jung-t'ung (see p. 159) had ever served in the "outer sections." They had served only as instructors in the meditation hall. Their *forte* was religious cultivation. T'ai-ts'ang, on the other hand, had never held any office in the meditation hall. His work had been almost entirely in the business office, and his *forte* was administration.

SELECTING ABBOTS BY CONSULTATION

It was possible for an abbot when he was retiring to consult no one at all, to pick his successor single-handedly, and to install him in the presence of witnesses on the appointed day. But usually the residents of the monastery would look askance at such an autocratic procedure. They might refuse to accept their new head, and, if he did not resign, take the case to court and have him replaced with someone they had chosen in the usual way, that is, through consultation and compromise.

Most of the features of the monastic system in China discussed so far have been clearcut. This has made it easier to explain. It is very difficult to explain how abbots were elected, particularly to readers who may be accustomed to think that an election is only fair if it follows some form of parliamentary rules. It is tempting to make a comparison with the Quakers, whose "sense of the meeting" seems equally hard to define. But it is my impression that the Quakers are more insistent on unanimity than Chinese Buddhist monks, and are willing to spend more time on the persuasion of those who dissent.

The manner of choosing abbots varied with the province and the type of monastery. It was a question of precedent and local custom. Here we are not discussing small hereditary temples, where control passed from tonsure master to tonsure disciple, but institutions large enough to have an abbot, that is, a *fang-chang*. Generally—very generally—speaking, the system worked as follows. The abbot was supposed to serve at least one term of three years (the same as the district magistrate). When he decided to retire, he would talk over the choice of his successor with the retired abbots, with the rector, and with the other instructors and senior officers. Perhaps he took them aside one by one before he called any general meeting. He might be "pushing" his own candidate; or he might be at a loss to think of any candidate who was both qualified and willing to serve. Once he and his associates agreed on someone, they might talk it over with the elders of neighboring monasteries; or they might not. It would depend on how sure they were of the wisdom of their choice. They would be more likely to seek outside counsel if they could not find any suitable candidate at all. Candidates could either be monks then in residence or living elsewhere. The only restriction (in public monasteries, at any rate) was that none of them could be a tonsure disciple of the abbot who was retiring. They might not be told that they were being considered for office, lest they steal away at night as soon as they heard the news, in order to avoid unwelcome responsibility.

During this process of consultation, it was not uncommon to canvass the lay patrons of the monastery, particularly if their patronage was essential. In theory, they had no say whatever in the conduct of internal affairs; in practice, they might exercise considerable influence.

Opinions might be sought from the local gentry and possibly even from friendly officials.[7] The latter, however, were not consulted officially, nor was any formal approval sought from groups like the Buddhist Association.[8]

No one among those consulted, inside or outside the monastery, had an absolute power of veto, but if they expressed a cogent objection, it would be taken into account. If they were important enough to the monastery, even their personal dislikes would be considered.

In many institutions this was all there was to the process of choosing an abbot. The candidate who received the general approval of those consulted was notified and, if he accepted, he was installed on the first auspicious day.[9] Alternatively, according to one or two informants he might first go through a period of apprenticeship, perhaps for as long as a year. It was also possible for the abbot to make up his mind privately about his successor, train him, and only then begin to secure the approval of his colleagues.

If the process of consultation failed—if, that is, it resulted in a deadlock or if no suitable person could be found who was willing to serve—then a vote was held with all resident monks taking part. If the vote resulted in a tie, then lots were drawn. But at some monasteries it was customary to hold a vote in any case. There the role of the abbot and elders was merely to nominate one or two of the candidates. Additional candidates could be nominated from the floor. At still other monasteries there was the same system of nominations from the floor, but no ballot. Instead the selection was entirely by lot.

SELECTION BY LOT

This was done notably at the T'ien-t'ung Ssu near Ningpo. The details of the procedure there were said to be as follows. First the senior officers would decide on one or more candidates through consultation. Then they would call a meeting of all the monks of the monastery. If they had chosen only one candidate and if, when his name was announced at the meeting, no one nominated a rival candidate, that was the end of it. Silence indicated assent just as it did in Buddhist India. But usually the elders nominated several candidates (two or three, for instance) and more nominations came from the floor. Any resident had the right to propose a name, including even the menial officers and the rank and file. If serious objections were voiced to a nominee, or if the nominee was present and expressed his unwillingness to serve, his name would be withdrawn. Finally, when a slate had been agreed on, all the names would be written on slips of paper and placed in a metal tube before the image of Wei-t'o, the guardian of monasteries. Incense would be lit and all present would recite "Homage to the bodhisattva Wei-t'o, who protects the dharma." Then, as they looked on, ready to detect any sign of fraud, a senior officer appointed by the abbot would shake the metal tube and pick out one slip with a pair of chopsticks. It would be recorded and re- placed and then he would shake the tube again and make a second drawing. This was repeated until the same name was drawn out three times in a row. That was the name of the abbot to be. He could not refuse to serve because it was Wei-t'o who had chosen him. Although many of the candidates nominated by the senior officers were out- siders, living at some other monastery, care was taken not to nominate anyone unless he was free to serve. According to my informants, when the successful candidate got the news of his election, he invariably accepted.

The nomination of outsiders was *prima facie* evidence that the elec- tion was genuinely public (*shih-fang*) and had not been "cooked up" by a controlling clique within the monastery. Hence T'ien-t'ung was regarded as a model for election by lot. A good reputation was also enjoyed by the Ying-chiang Ssu in Anking. Elsewhere there was con- siderable variation in method. At Ting-hu Shan in Kwangtung Prov- ince, for example, divining blocks were used. These were quarter-discs of wood with one side flat and one side rounded. If two of them were dropped so that the round side of one and the flat side of the other landed upward, then it signified divine approval.[10] A senior officer of Ting-hu Shan would propose the name of a candidate and then throw the blocks repeatedly over his back. The candidate who got the largest number of auspicious throws—preferably ten in a row—was elected (if I understood my informant correctly).

At the P'u-chi Ssu in Hunan (see Appendix V), not only was the abbot chosen by lot, but the senior officers were chosen with him. On the slips were written titles rather than names. They were drawn by the candidates themselves and the person who got the slip marked "prior" became the prior. It was not necessary to draw three times in a row: once was enough. The P'u-chi Ssu was an hereditary temple. Any heir sponsored by three others was eligible to draw (although, of course, he could be excluded if cogent objections were voiced to his candidacy).

As usual, my sample is large enough to show the range of different practices, but not their relative incidence. In certain provinces one or another practice predominated, as in the case of Kiangsu and Hunan, which will be discussed below. Elsewhere, according to my informants, abbots were usually chosen by consultation alone. It was rare to ballot or draw lots. At almost every monastery, however, the incoming abbot was the dharma disciple of his predecessor.

TRANSMISSION OF THE DHARMA

Dharma transmission is a complicated practice the details of which I have described in a long article.[11] There is no point in repeating them here. What I shall try to do, therefore, is to explain the main principles (which are looser than I once thought) and to give fresh illustrations of them.

The word "dharma" has many meanings. Among other things it means the norms of righteous conduct; the laws that govern the universe; the components into which all phenomena can be analyzed. Hence it means Buddhist doctrine or truth. To transmit the dharma means to transmit an understanding of the truth. The first transmission is said to have taken place on Vulture Peak when the Buddha was given a flower and asked to preach the dharma. He simply held out the flower. One of his disciples, Mahakasyapa, smiled. The Buddha then said: "I am the owner of the eye of the wonderful dharma, which is Nirvana, the mind, the mystery of reality and non-reality, and the gate of transcendental truth. I now hand it [the eye] over to Mahakasyapa."[12] Later he handed him his robe and begging bowl. This incident, perhaps invented by the Chinese, became the model for a special relationship between master and disciple, in which an understanding of the dharma was wordlessly transmitted from one to the other "by a direct imprint of mind on mind." The Chinese eventually worked out a genealogy tracing the transmission, generation by generation, from Mahakasyapa to Bodhidharma. Bodhidharma arrived from India in the sixth century C.E. and became the first Chinese patriarch, that is, the first patriarch of the Ch'an sect of Chinese Buddhism. Within five generations after Bodhidharma the lineage began to branch out. Instead of acknowledging only one disciple, Ch'an masters began to transmit the dharma to several. Thus sub-sects arose within Ch'an. The sixth patriarch, Hui-neng (638-713), was apparently the last to receive his master's robe as a token of the fact that he had received the dharma. At some later time, perhaps only within the last three centuries, the custom arose of getting a written attestation instead. This was called a "dharma scroll" (*fa-chüan*). The text of the typical scroll began with the story of how the Buddha held up a flower at Vulture Peak and Mahakasyapa smiled. It then traced the line of descent, giving the name of every successive Chinese master. Starting with the founder of the sub-sect to which they belonged, every name was assigned a generation number. For example, the Venerable I-hsüan of Mount Lin-chi was the founder of the Lin-chi sect and so this section of a Lin-chi scroll reads: "The first generation was the meditation master Lin-chi I-hsüan. The second generation was the meditation master Kuang-chi Ts'un-chiang. The third generation . . ." and so on. The scroll ends with a statement like the following: "Master so-and-so transmitted to me and I am transmitting to you as the fiftieth generation in the orthodox Lin-chi line and as the eighty-ninth generation tracing back to the Buddha Sakyamuni."

What was being transmitted here was an understanding of the dharma. The scroll purported to prove that the understanding was orthodox, since it came ultimately from the Buddha himself. Therefore the person who owned the scroll was qualified to teach. The abbot of a monastery was above all a teacher. So it made good sense for a retiring abbot to transmit the dharma to his successor as a seal of the transfer of authority. In effect, what was being transmitted was the authority to teach.

The ceremony usually was held in the dharma hall (*fa-t'ang*) immediately after the new abbot took office. It completed the proceedings of investiture. Sometimes, however, the retiring abbot transmitted the dharma to his successor *before* the investiture or even before his successor had been selected. Also, as we shall see in Chapter X, the dharma was often transmitted from monk to monk without any refer-

ence to the abbotship of the monastery, but simply as a private transaction to signify approval or cement a personal connection. An abbot
who had taken a dharma disciple on this private basis might later
decide that no one else was better qualified to succeed to the abbotship. If his colleagues agreed, the succession was so arranged. In such
a case there was no need to transmit the dharma to the disciple a
second time. Indeed at some monasteries, if an appointee had privately
received the dharma from any previous abbot, there was no need for
him to receive it again. He had the "seal" already.

Transmission of the dharma as a seal of office was the practice at
most Chinese monasteries, unless the dharma and the abbotship were
connected in other ways—ways that we shall now examine.

THE KIANGSU SYSTEM

In Kiangsu the dharma scroll, instead of being a mere seal of office,
determined the succession of abbots. Dharma relationships, instead of
being a matter of courtesy, outweighed tonsure relationships in establishing loyalties and, indeed, in shaping a monk's career. The peculiarities of the system may partly explain why during the Republican
period monastic Buddhism was stronger in Kiangsu than in any other
Chinese province—unless, as some of the reformers would assert, it
was strong there in spite of the dharma system, not because of it.

The first peculiarity was collective transmission. Whereas elsewhere
one master transmitted to one disciple at a time, in Kiangsu several
masters transmitted collectively to several disciples. All the masters
served successively as abbot at a certain monastery and then all the
disciples would serve as abbot there too. What had been transmitted
was thought of as the dharma *of that monastery*. Receiving it gave a
right and also an obligation to serve as abbot. This was the second
peculiarity of the system. It provided for dependable transfer of responsibility. An aging monk would not have to hang on in office because he could find no one who was willing to succeed him.

The reader may find the system easier to understand from an illustration. Let it be Chin Shan, which, as in other respects, was the model
that others followed. Here is the genealogy of dharma transmission at
Chin Shan in this century.

44th generation
1. Tz'u-pen Yin-kuan
2. Ch'ing-ch'üan Yin-k'ai
3. Mei-ts'un Yin-hsiu
4. Tsung-yang Yin-leng
5. Jung-t'ung Yin-ch'e

45th generation
1. Ching-kuan Wei-tao
2. Yin-ping Wei-i
3. Shuang-t'ing Wei-kuang
4. name cancelled
5. Jo-shun Wei-te

46th generation
1. T'ai-ts'ang Hsin-jan
2. Miao-hua Hsin-
3. P'u-hsiu Hsin-
4. Hai-ting Hsin-
5. Yung-ch'ing Hsin-

The 44th generation received the dharma about 1890 and they began to serve one by one as abbot after the last member of the 43rd generation had completed his term. In 1910 they decided to transmit themselves. That year they took as their disciples the five monks next listed, who were then given important positions. Since they were slated to be abbots, they had to become familiar with the various departments. In 1912, for example, when Ch'ing-ch'üan of the 44th generation headed the monastery, Yin-ping of the 45th was prior in charge of the business office and Shuang-t'ing was guest prefect in charge of the guest department.[13] About 1915 Ch'ing-ch'üan decided to retire. Mei-ts'un, however, was in Hangchow, where he had been invited to head the Hai-ch'ao Ssu. For the time being he was unavailable. The abbotship should therefore have passed to Tsung-yang, since he was the brother next in line. But because Tsung-yang had taken part in politics and worn lay dress, the rest of the "dharma family" refused to agree to this. Denied office, Tsung-yang shut himself up for three years and in 1919 left Chin Shan to restore the Ch'i-hsia Ssu, a famous monastery near Nanking that had been destroyed in the Taiping rebellion. The abbotship of Chin Shan passed to the next in line, Jung-t'ung. Later Mei-ts'un returned and took over from him. This exhausted the 44th generation.

The 45th generation then began to serve, first Ching-kuan, then Yin-ping, and finally Shuang-t'ing. There had been a fourth brother who should have succeeded Shuang-t'ing, but he had shown himself to be incompetent and his dharma was tacitly cancelled.[14] He left Chin Shan, presumably because of chagrin. The fifth brother, Jo-shun, had gone off to help Tsung-yang restore the Ch'i-hsia Ssu. Therefore in 1945, all the rest having died, Shuang-t'ing alone transmitted to five disciples and resigned immediately afterwards. T'ai-ts'ang succeeded him. If it had not been for the Communist victory in 1949, the other members of the 46th generation would be serving in turn and probably by now would have transmitted to a 47th generation.

By transmitting the dharma to a slate of future abbots years ahead of time, a monastery provided for orderly succession. The earlier the transmission, the less worry about the future. If on the other hand it was delayed until the last member of the generation was ready to retire, there was the risk that he might die suddenly before doing so. Yet last-minute transmission seems to have been fairly common.

In the article referred to earlier, I stated that for dharma disciples of a Kiangsu monastery, "just as the right to become abbot was inalienable, so the obligation to do so was inescapable." This was, indeed, what I had been told by several informants, but the abbots of Chin Shan and the T'ien-ning Ssu later made it clear to me that the system was much more flexible than this. If the dharma disciple was considered to be incompetent or guilty of violations of the Vinaya, the matter was discussed by all members of the "family" and perhaps with the elders in the neighboring monasteries. They would decide whether he was too old or too young, or did not have the confidence of the monks, or would not be able to keep peace among them, or was incompetent for any other reason. If so, they could either pass over him or summarily cancel his dharma and his status as a disciple. Sometimes a very young man would be passed over, but given the post when he had attained greater maturity. Unless his dharma was cancelled, he could expect to get it eventually.

Conversely, any disciple could refuse to serve and some did. Two famous examples are Yüeh-hsia and Ying-tz'u, who received the dharma of the T'ien-ning Ssu in 1906. When their turn came, both refused to serve as abbot on the grounds that they wanted to devote their time entirely to spreading the doctrine. Often a disciple, like Mei-

ts'un in the 44th generation at Chin Shan, would be temporarily committed elsewhere, so that he served his term out of sequence. Sometimes a dharma disciple would simply go off, without leaving an
address. If he could not be found or if, when found, he was unwilling
to serve, the next younger brother took his place. If there were no
younger brothers and if the next generation was not mature enough
to serve, the dharma could be transmitted again by the older brothers
remaining.

These were all exceptional circumstances, however. The usual thing
was for members of the "dharma family" to serve as abbot in order of
their seniority. They were rather like a self-perpetuating board of
trustees, charged with the welfare of the monastery. Like a lay family,
or like the heirs of an hereditary monastery, they tended to act as a
body. When the time came to transmit the dharma, it was common
for every member of the "family" to be consulted unless he was unavailable or had shown no interest in "family" matters. The practice
varied from place to place. At Chin Shan and the Ch'i-hsia Ssu consultation appears to have been particularly conscientious. If a brother
was absent, he was consulted by letter. At the T'ien-ning Ssu, on the
other hand, no attempt was made to get the approval of brothers who
had gone elsewhere. As the abbot put it, "only those in residence had
proprietary rights (*chu-ch'üan*) over the monastery." Proprietary rights
also involved filial obligations, like sweeping "ancestral" graves at
Ch'ing-ming.

As we have just seen in the case of Chin Shan, once a monk received
the dharma, he was considered to be on trial and in training for the
post of abbot. If there were five brothers, they were like five heirs
apparent. At some monasteries it was the custom to recognize their
special status by giving them the title of prior (*chien-yüan*). Their
actual duties, however, might belong to other offices. As we saw in
the first chapter (see pp. 35-36), one of them might act as the senior
guest prefect in charge of the guest department, another as the sacristan, while a third might hold the office as well as the title of prior.
This was the practice at Ch'i-hsia Shan and also the Liu-yün Ssu in
Shanghai. It was not the practice at Chin Shan and the T'ien-ning Ssu.
There only one monk held the title of prior and he was the real prior;
that is, the acting head of the business office. In 1945, for example,
when T'ai-ts'ang became abbot of Chin Shan as the senior brother of

29. At Ch'ing-ming, offerings are laid out before the grave of a former abbot of Ch'i-hsia Shan near its branch temple in Hong Kong.

30. The former abbot's dharma disciple and successor as abbot filially sweeps the grave.

the 46th generation, the second brother became prior; the third became associate instructor in the meditation hall; the fourth became senior guest prefect; and the fifth became a subprior under the second brother in the business office. Almost the same situation existed then at the T'ien-ning Ssu, except that one brother headed the seminary and another was studying at a university in Nanking. At neither monastery was the word "prior" in use as a courtesy title—nor was the actual prior necessarily a dharma disciple. At the T'ien-ning Ssu that office was long held by a monk who absolutely refused to receive the dharma—"and he never made a mistake of even a penny."

The ceremony for transmission of the dharma was simple, but solemn. After breakfast on the appointed day, the brothers of the transmitting generation would take their seats on a raised platform in the dharma hall (*fa-t'ang*). Wearing patriarch's robes (*tsu-i*), they sat in order of seniority, that is, 4 – 2 – 1 – 3 – 5 (if their back was to the bottom of the page, left being senior to the right in China). A venerable instructor would usher in the disciples-to-be, also wearing patriarch's robes, and have them take their places before the platform. They too stood in order of their seniority, which had been decided ahead of time on the basis of their competence and maturity. It was an important decision, since the senior brother or *ta fa-shih*, would probably become abbot fairly soon. After the disciples had fully opened their kneeling cloths and made nine full prostrations, touching their heads to the floor, they remained there kneeling while the eldest brother of the transmitting generation gave a short address[15] on the significance of the ceremony. He then read out the dharma scroll including the names of ancestral masters generation by generation from Bodhidharma to his youngest brother. When he had finished, the disciples would make one more full prostration and rise. This concluded the ceremony, for which the technical term was *shou-chi*.

At Chin Shan all this was witnessed by other members of the dharma family and the elders of neighboring monasteries. Ordinary officers and monks were excluded. It was a purely "family" matter and even the elders would have been excluded if it were not thought desirable to have outside witnesses. At the Ch'i-hsia Ssu, on the other hand, all resident monks could attend and invitations were even sent out to the local gentry. The T'ien-ning Ssu exemplified the opposite extreme, for it practiced "secret transmission" (*mi-shou*), modeled on the transmission from the fifth to the sixth patriarch. No one at all was present except the participants.

Another and much more important variation was in the giving of scrolls. Most monasteries, including some of the most famous (like T'ien-ning, Hai-ch'ao, Liu-yün), gave every disciple his own dharma scroll, copied out from a scroll belonging to someone in the previous generation. Chin Shan and the Ch'i-hsia Ssu, on the other hand, gave their disciples nothing at all. Unlike other monasteries, they had only a "general scroll" (*tsung-ti fa-chüan*), which was permanent monastic property. It was kept by the abbot and sheets were apparently pasted onto it as new generations were added. If the disciple wished to make a copy of it, he was at liberty to do so, but according to my informants this seldom happened.

It must have happened, however, on at least a few occasions, because the Chin Shan dharma was borrowed for use by other monasteries, not only by Ch'i-hsia Shan, but also by the T'ien-ning Ssu and the Hai-ch'ao Ssu, and later the dharma of these two was carried over to the Hsing-fu Ssu in Ch'ang-shu and the Liu-yün Ssu in Shanghai. This is confirmed by the fact that the dharma names given to disciples of all these monasteries have the same generation characters as at Chin Shan.[16] In some cases we know the history of the "branching." Venerable Ta-hsiao carried the Chin Shan dharma to the T'ien-ning Ssu during the Ch'ien-lung period. Venerable Yüeh-hsia carried the T'ien-ning dharma to the Hsing-fu Ssu in 1917. Indeed, any monk who had received the dharma of one monastery could carry it over to another, whether it was a new institution that he was founding or an old one that needed restoration or a better lineage.

If another monastery had a good lineage already, he could accept its dharma too when he took over as abbot. There was nothing to prevent a monk from becoming the dharma disciple of successive monasteries, one here, one there. It did not matter if they were of different sects. Sect, in this respect, was a matter of genealogy. Well-known monks who served as abbot of one monastery after another had many dharma scrolls. Usually they were all of the Lin-chi sect, since this was by far the most widespread, but sometimes they had Ts'ao-tung scrolls as well. There was competition among leading monasteries to get bright young men to become their disciples and therefore have some assurance of their services in the future. The talent of the Venerable Lai-kuo, for example, was recognized at an early age and both Chin Shan and the Kao-min Ssu asked him to accept their dharma. He chose Kao-min's and remained there forty years.

Most of the information given above on the Kiangsu system came directly from informants who took part in it. It may not be amiss to end with a published memoir that is certainly as frank as anything I have gotten by word of mouth. It concerns the Liu-yün Ssu in Shanghai. The fourth generation there had five brothers: Ta-i, Ch'an-ting, Te-hao, Chao-kao, and a Korean monk. They transmitted to Ts'ung-shan, Ta-pei, and Chih-k'uan, and the memoir begins when the last —Chih-k'uan—was abbot.

> In the spring of 1944, Ta-pei, the former abbot of the Liu-yün Ssu, had retired as abbot of the T'ien-t'ung Ssu and was living quietly at the Kuan-yin Ssu, Shih-hui Ch'iao, Shanghai, to avoid being bothered by the Japanese. One morning at nine o'clock he came to the Chieh-yin Ssu. I had been one of his students . . . He said that the then abbot of the Liu-yün Ssu, Chih-k'uan, was ready to retire. They wanted to transmit the dharma to four disciples and had decided on Hsin-yüan, Hsiu-chen, Ting-yao, and myself. Reverend Ta-pei wanted me to accept. "This is a friendly act that we three dharma brothers have resolved on. You four come from the Liu-yün Ssu. How can you refuse?" he said. He first asked the four of us to be assistant instructors (*t'ang-chu*), and then a day would be chosen to "transmit the dharma." A few days later a time was fixed to hold a simple ceremony for dharma transmission in the dharma hall. The three retired abbots—Ts'ung-shan, Ta-pei and Chih-k'uan—mounted the dais and handed dharma scrolls to us four. In actuality this kind of "dharma transmission" has become a formality in the Ch'an sect. It is a million miles away from the dharma transmission by the direct imprint of mind on mind. This kind of dharma transmission is simply a traditional formality of genealogical succession. Afterwards abbot Chih-k'uan again picked a day for the senior dharma brother to take office as head of the Liu-yün Ssu and for Hsiu-chen, the next brother, to take office as prior. Ting-yao and I separately took responsibility for the sub-temples as titular priors [of the parent monastery].[17]

THE HUNAN SYSTEM

In respect to the selection of abbots, monasteries in Hunan—and probably in Szechwan and several other provinces—were divided into three categories: public (*shih-fang*), dharma-type (*fa-men*), and hereditary (*tzu-sun*). At a public monastery any monk could hold any office. At a dharma-type monastery only its dharma disciples could serve as abbot or as a senior officer. At an hereditary monastery this was restricted to heirs, that is, to monks whose heads had been shaved there.

At all three kinds of monasteries the procedure for choosing an abbot consisted of consultation, ballot, and drawing lots, but the franchise varied. When the abbot of a public monastery, for example, decided to retire, he would hold a caucus with the senior officers. They would try to pick a candidate who was already resident, but if none of the residents were qualified, they would look abroad. Their candidate's name would then be presented to a plenary meeting of all the monks of the monastery, including even those in the wandering monks hall. Unless other nominations were made, this candidate became the new abbot. Other nominations could only be made by officers, but when the election was held, everyone present could vote. We have not yet seen how voting was done in a Chinese monastery, and the details of the practice in Hunan, though not necessarily typical, may be of interest.

First, two examiners, two callers, and two recorders were nominated from the floor; they could be proposed by anyone and, unless there was opposition, this meant that they served. Then paper ballots were distributed, bearing the names of the rival candidates. Everyone placed a circle after the name of the candidate he favored, but did not sign his name. The ballots were collected and checked by the examiners, read out by the callers, and listed by the recorders. If the result was a tie or if a candidate refused to serve, then lots were drawn before Wei-t'o's image as described above (p. 155). All this sounds as if it had been inspired by Robert's *Rules of Order,* but conceivably its roots lie in India.[18]

At large hereditary temples a ballot was somewhat less likely to occur because the principal qualification for the abbotship was seniority in the tonsure lineage. A large hereditary temple might have hundreds of heirs (tonsure disciples). They were divided into "houses" (*fang*). These were not buildings but genealogical divisions. They had no function in the daily life of the monastery. If, for example, the founding monk had four disciples, then there were four houses, which continued until a new subdivision occurred. Seniority was by gen-

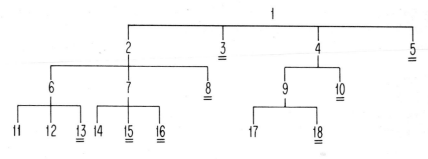

Order of seniority

eration. The most junior member of one generation was senior to the most senior member of the next as illustrated by the chart. Some heirs died without having taken disciples, while some moved away permanently, forfeiting their places in the lineage (both indicated by double underlining on the chart). If nevertheless the lineage fanned out so that it became unwieldy, limitations might be placed on shaving the heads of more disciples. At a meeting of the whole "family" it would be decided that no one should take more than one disciple; or perhaps different quotas would be assigned.

Normally, however, the lineage was of a manageable size. When the abbot wanted to retire, he would decide which monk with the necessary competence stood next in line. Sometimes he consulted the senior officers. He seldom if ever consulted lay patrons or the elders of neighboring monasteries. This seems to have been very much of a "family matter." On the other hand, even if he reached his decision single-handedly, he could not flout the rules of seniority. He was not free to pick any heir that he happened to like. However, it was not always clear who was senior and stood next in line. If an heir had left the monastery temporarily, had he forfeited his place? When did leave of absence become a change of domicile? Competence to serve was also, of course, very much of an arguable question.

After the abbot had picked a candidate, he presented his name to a meeting of all the resident heirs,[19] any one of whom could nominate a rival candidate (and this gave senior officers their chance if they had not already been consulted). If there was no rival nominee, the abbot's candidate was considered elected. Otherwise a ballot was held exactly as at public monasteries, except that only heirs could elect and be elected. A tie was resolved by drawing lots.

The system at dharma-type monasteries in Hunan was the same as at hereditary monasteries, with the sole difference that the franchise was restricted to dharma disciples rather than heirs. In contrast to Kiangsu, the dharma was widely held and individually transmitted. That is, any disciple of a dharma-type monastery could transmit its dharma to anyone he chose.[20] There was neither consultation nor collective transmittal, although as a matter of courtesy he was supposed to get the approval of his own dharma master or, if the latter was not available, of his dharma brothers. Therefore the number of dharma disciples was very large. For example, the abbot of the Chu-sheng Ssu on Nan-yüeh used to transmit the dharma to all members of the graduating class of the seminary there—about sixty persons in 1944. Naturally most of them made their career elsewhere, but some stayed on. There were openings for them at the Chu-sheng Ssu, because at this type of monastery in Hunan all senior officers had to be dharma disciples, just as at hereditary monasteries they all had to be heirs.[21] The order of seniority was also the same as at hereditary monasteries: "houses" were arranged by generation. When an abbot resigned, he chose as his successor the monk standing next in line with the necessary competence. Because the dharma tradition was slightly more "public" than the tonsure tradition, he was more likely to consult his colleagues; and at the plenary meeting held to approve the nomination, other names were more likely to be proposed. In the latter case, a ballot was held at which all dharma disciples (but no one else) could vote.

Hunan appears to have differed from other provinces in that these three categories of monastery are said to have been mutually exclusive. At public and hereditary temples, the dharma was not transmitted at all—not even as a seal of office (or so my informants said) —and at public and dharma-type monasteries the abbot could never be succeeded by his own tonsure disciple. The largest monasteries in the province seem to have belonged to the dharma type: examples are the Chu-sheng Ssu on Nan-yüeh and the Jen-jui Ssu and Fo-kuo Ssu at Heng-yang.

KUEI-YÜAN SSU

The Kuei-yüan Ssu in Hanyang, Hupeh, was rare among Chinese monasteries in that it dispensed altogether with consultation and left the choice of abbot directly and entirely to the bodhisattva Wei-t'o. It was unique (so far as I know) in that every monk ordained there was offered its dharma. An ordination was held each winter and immediately afterwards many of the hundreds of ordinees became dharma disciples, each receiving a dharma scroll and having his name entered in a dharma register (*chieh-fa pu*). When an abbot's three-year term was up, all the names in this register would be copied onto slips and placed in a tube before Wei-t'o's image. The abbot himself did the drawing. The first name to be drawn three times in a row became his successor. If this individual had gone elsewhere (as he usually had), he would be traced and brought back. Even if he were young or incompetent, he still served. Competence, as if by magic, appeared with investiture. One informant, who visited the Kuei-yüan Ssu in 1947, found that the abbot was only eighteen years old. Another recalled that in the early 1930's the choice fell on a monk who was then serving as a stoker (*ta-huo*) at the Ling-yin Ssu in Hangchow. He was so stupid that he had the nickname "Big Stoop," but as soon as he took office, people found that he was able to preach the dharma and do everything else expected of an abbot. "It was the bodhisattva who helped him," as my informant explained.

If the elections at the Kuei-yüan Ssu were rigged, why would anyone like "Big Stoop" have been elected? But if they were honest, how could anyone at all have been elected? With hundreds of slips in the tube, if all were properly shuffled each time, how could the same slip be drawn three times in a row? Mathematically speaking, the chances were infinitesimal. Yet this is what always happened according to all the monks I have talked to about it. One informant was present at another monastery, the Yün-men Ssu in Kwangtung, when a new abbot was selected by lot there in 1952. The Venerable Hsü-yün, who was retiring, had written from Peking and ordered that each of the seventy to eighty permanent residents be given a lot. The drawing continued for two days while they all stood on the porch of the Wei-t'o Tien and watched. On the third day at about 3:00 p.m. one name came out three times in a row. Who was it? It was Fo-yüan, to whom Hsü-yün had transmitted the dharma the year before and who was the ablest of all the candidates. Indeed, if he had not been chosen, "things would never have worked."

"That was a little odd," I said to this informant, "and very much of a coincidence. How was it that the man with the best qualifications was chosen?"

He laughed a little nervously, I thought, at the word "coincidence" and replied: "The choice was made by Wei-t'o."

In 1930 the abbot of the P'u-chi Ssu in Hunan (see p. 155), was chosen by lot from among fifty-four candidates. Because he had been ordained only three months before, he demurred. A second drawing was held, this time among seventy-eight candidates. Again he drew the slip. In 1935, when his term had ended, he drew the abbot's slip a third time. Truly a remarkable coincidence!

SELECTION OF THE WORTHY

Except for the case in which the abbot of an hereditary temple, without consulting any of his colleagues, handed his office to his tonsure disciple, it was possible to call any of the methods discussed above "a selection of the worthy" (hsüan-hsien). But reform-minded monks, who disapprove of most of the usual methods, assert that only one monastery in China practiced "selection of the worthy" or, to be more explicit, "public selection of the worthy" (shih-fang hsüan-hsien), and that was the T'ien-t'ung Ssu near Ningpo (see pp. 154-155). At T'ien-t'ung the scope of consultation was broad and usually included the elders of neighboring monasteries. Outsiders were usually among the candidates and lots were usually drawn. The successful candidate was never the tonsure disciple of the retiring abbot, nor did he receive the dharma from him. Everything was public and nothing was private.

Most monks give the term hsüan-hsien a much broader meaning. To them it means any selection of abbots in which consultation or balloting or lots played any sort of a role. For example, at a Kiangsu monastery when the dharma was transmitted to a new generation, the consultation involved was considered to make this a "selection of the worthy." Indeed I have even heard the term applied to the procedure at hereditary temples in Hunan, where, although the abbot was succeeded by his own tonsure disciple, consultation and balloting played a role in deciding *which* tonsure disciple it was to be. To suggest that any tonsure disciple could be "worthy" aroused the indignation of the reformers. In their view not even a dharma disciple could be "worthy." We shall soon see a sample of their indignation.

TERM IN OFFICE

Prip-Møller states that the abbot's "tenure of office is limited to three years and re-election is not supposed to take place."[22] I have never heard of a monastery that had such a rule. It is true that the usual term was three years, but tenure was not limited to this. The abbot could serve as many terms as he cared to or he could resign at any time, provided a successor was available. In a few monasteries (like Kuan-tsung and T'ien-t'ung) the customary term is said to have been not three years, but five. In some places there was a theoretical limit of two terms (according to some informants); or three terms (according to others). I have been given different information on all these questions, but there was one point everyone agreed on: a capable abbot was welcome to serve as long as he wished. Usually he wished to retire as soon as possible, but he might go on serving until he had completed some construction project that he had undertaken. The limitations to his tenure were practical. Was he doing a good job? Could a successor be found? If he was doing a poor job, either his conscience would prompt him to resign voluntarily (although resigning before the end of three years involved a certain loss of face) or he would be asked to resign or he would be impeached. On the other hand, if no qualified successor could be found, he was expected to go on serving indefinitely. Sometimes he grew desperate.

An example of this desperation is provided by the Venerable Ch'an-ting, an eminent monk who had served successively as abbot of the Liu-yün Ssu in Shanghai, the Kuan-tsung Ssu in Ningpo, and the T'ien-t'ung Ssu nearby. In about 1931, on his retirement from T'ien-t'ung,[23] he was invited to go to Liaoning to become the first abbot of a large new monastery, the Leng-yen Ssu, that had been founded there partly under his inspiration. At the end of his three-year term, he decided to return to Shanghai, but no one suitable successor could be found to take his place. He served another term or two. Then he insisted that a successor be found, whether suitable or not. But as it turned out, the new abbot was hopelessly unsuitable. He could not keep the monastery going and Ch'an-ting had to resume office. He began to feel desperate, to the point where his health was affected. He got chronic dysentery, and after a year he was so ill that he could not get up from his bed. By now it was 1944. The war and the Japanese occupation were adding to the burdens of office. He wrote letters to three old colleagues, imploring them to come to his rescue. But, as one of them told me, "I had no interest in taking over the Leng-yen Ssu. It was useless from the point of view of religious cultivation." But he went anyway. Three days after he arrived, Ch'an-ting was out of bed, eating normally, and after three weeks, my informant took over as abbot. It was another two years before Ch'an-ting returned to Shanghai. It had not been homesickness that had made a wreck of him, but the treadmill of abbotship.[24]

CONCURRENT SERVICE

The difficulties of finding men qualified to serve meant that there was often intense competition to secure those who were. In 1935, for example, Yüan-ying completed a five-year stint as abbot of the T'ien-t'ung Ssu.[25] No less than six monasteries then asked him to come and be their head. He finally accepted Ku Shan because it was his "old home" (he had been tonsured and ordained there). But earlier on, in 1928-1930, Yüan-ying had concurrently headed the Ch'ung-sheng Ssu and Fa-hai Ssu in Foochow and the Ch'i-t'a Ssu in Ningpo, while most of the time he had actually resided at a small temple he owned in Shanghai, where he was president of the Chinese Buddhist Association. Usually concurrent service meant that one or more monasteries were left in the hands of a deputy abbot. Ku Shan was left in the hands of a deputy abbot in 1948, when Yüan-ying was elected again. Hsü-yün left deputies in charge of the Nan-hua Ssu and the

Liu-jung Ssu, while he himself lived at the Yün-men Ssu, during much of the period that he headed these monasteries.[26]

The reason that abbots had to serve in several places concurrently or long beyond their time for retirement was not only the shortage of good men, but also because—let it be emphasized again—the best men did not want to be abbots at all. What they wanted was to practice religious cultivation (*hsiu-ch'ih*). The Kiangsu system was probably designed to counteract this reluctance. Once a monk had accepted the dharma of a monastery, he usually felt a certain obligation to serve as abbot—not, as we have seen, an absolute obligation, but strong enough so that he was likely to be ready when needed to fill the vacant seat. The system would appear to have given greater stability to the monastic administration. But this was not the way it was always looked at.

CRITICISM OF DHARMA ABBOTSHIP

Several of the most eminent monks of the Republican period were opposed to any connection between the dharma and the abbotship. Hsü-yün refused to receive or transmit the monastery dharma as abbot of Ku Shan and later as abbot of the Nan-hua Ssu, the Liu-jung Ssu, and other monasteries. T'ai-hsü did the same at Nan P'u-t'o, as did T'an-hsü wherever he held office. One informant, who was an associate of Hsü-yün, has told me that in his own view transmitting the abbotship along with the dharma led to malpractices. Private interests came to take precedence over public interests. Sometimes even money changed hands. These objections are stated eloquently by T'an-hsü. Toward the end of his autobiography we find a section entitled "Transmitting the dharma without transmitting the abbotship,"[27] which is translated below.

> I consider that the system of public selection of the worthy should be practiced everywhere and that it is impermissible for a public institution to be privately handed from person to person on the basis of personal feelings. As to the system of transmitting the dharma, the masters of former times did so by an imprint of mind on mind: everyone who achieved enlightenment got an attestation of the fact in the form of such an imprint. Only then could they have confidence in their own enlightenment. The ancestral master

Bodhidharma, for example, was the twenty-eighth patriarch in India and the first in China. In India from the Buddha Sakaymuni to Bodhidharma, transmission was always by the imprint of mind on mind. In China from Bodhidharma to the Sixth Patriarch, the Venerable Hui-neng, it was also by the imprint of mind on mind, but in addition the robe and bowl were transmitted from person to person as a token of trust. Before the Sixth Patriarch, although a great many enlightened disciples handed on the dharma and transmitted the robe and bowl, they had to wait for the right person, and the robe and bowl were transmitted to only one disciple. After the Sixth Patriarch, because more people developed the good roots of faith, the robe and bowl became an object of dispute so that only the dharma could be transmitted and not the robe and bowl. But today dharma transmission is taken lightly and people consider that it is not worth treating as anything important.

Actually, however, transmitting the dharma is a difficult business. One must have clarity of perception to be able to recognize the right person among all the masses of humanity. If you do not know the right person and give the dharma to anyone who comes along, it will probably become a butt for jokes. There is no need to discuss those who really know their own mind, see their own nature, and transmit by an imprint of mind on mind. What I am going to talk about is this modern business of transmitting from generation to generation with dharma scrolls. This is something that deserves serious reflection. At present the system in a majority of large monasteries (ts'ung-lin) is for the post of abbot to be transmitted along with the dharma (scroll).[28] There are three or perhaps five dharma disciples (fledgling abbots) who, having received the dharma, become the future heads of the monastery. If one of them is carelessly chosen, it can lead to many irregularities. I have been pondering this for decades, and I believe that private transmission of dharma and abbotship is one of the main reasons why large monasteries throughout the country have gone into a decline and have been unable to keep going over the long term. Furthermore, it is a defect in our religious practice. Nearly all the persons who head monasteries and temples (lao ho-shang, fa ho-shang),[29] in order to have someone succeed them and also because they want to get hold of people with talent while they are available, transmit the dharma well ahead of time to several disciples who become the heirs apparent[30] that we have today. When the time comes for the abbot to retire, one of these heirs apparent takes the post right over. Of course no one can object to transmitting the Buddha's dharma and discharging monastic business. However, in this case there are a great many defects.

The first is that for persons who transmit the dharma favoritism displaces objective choice. Originally the Buddhist clergy advocated the idea of kinsmen in the dharma, making the dharma the basis for kinship. But the result has been that certain abbots, when they transmitted the dharma, have done so for the sake of personal feelings, which they have made the basis for kinship rather than finding it in the dharma. Such connections arising from personal feelings are built either on the concept of common locality and ancestry or on the concept of friendship between neighboring temples. This has been the foundation for an imperceptible change to secret consultation with private benefits in view, and for the formation of this and that clique and sect.

The second defect is as follows. When an abbot transmits the dharma, he may not have a clear understanding of the people [to whom he transmits]. Frequently his senior disciple and the other disciples each transmit to four or five disciples of their own. Naturally, in terms of spreading Buddhism, this is something that should be done. But later on, because every disciple has a dharma scroll in his hands, he thinks that he is legally a fledgling abbot and that the abbotship is his duty and right. On the one hand, the old abbot has transmitted both the dharma and the post; on the other hand, the new abbots have received both the dharma and the [right to the] post. Therefore when the time comes for the post to change hands, you want to seize it, he wants to seize it, with the result that there are disputes among the disciples and between the disciples and the abbot—to the point where they go to court and fight like wolves. Some slip into office surreptitiously and some get kicked out summarily, so that it becomes a great joke and the religion is disgraced. But these two defects may be said to be slight in comparison to the third and greatest defect.

When an abbot is going to transmit the dharma to the next generation, he employs three criteria. 1) He wants to pick young men who are not as old as he is. 2) Their virtue, prestige, and qualifications must all be less than his own. 3) In every matter they must follow his directions. Generally this is what the criteria for dharma transmission come down to with extremely few exceptions. The abbot of the senior generation transmits this way, the next generation does so too, and so does the third. With this sort of transmission, each generation is a falling off from the one before. This has meant that religious establishments of every school have lost their religious traditions before the dharma has been transmitted too many times. Look at the great number of large monasteries throughout the country which originally were public in character, with a bell and board, but which through repeated transmissions have become hereditary temples. Although there is still a dharma scroll for transmission downwards, it is simply master transmitting to disciple[31]—nothing but a formality. A very large temple may only have two or three people living in it and no outsider can call them to question. On the contrary, if there are any monks of real virtue, advanced in years and religious accomplishments, they will certainly be left "out in the cold." No one will take any notice of them. Either they are in charge of some place of their own or they practice religious cultivation as hermits. At the same time, because of the dharma lineages of the various schools, although they see that many establishments are on the decline, they are prevented from saying anything. For a great many years now the gradual decline of famous old monasteries has been brought about under the influence of this kind of transmitting the dharma and abbotship together. At present there are only a very few large monasteries in the country that really do not transmit the dharma, and that practice the system of public selection of the worthy. These places can keep going over the long term. Everywhere else it is a different matter.

T'an-hsü, the author of this reproof, did not make a profession of reform like T'ai-hsü. On the contrary, he was a conservative, widely respected, for whom the purpose of reform was to preserve the best in Buddhism, not to innovate. Nonetheless, we should remember that he spent most of his life trying to revive Buddhism in North China, where many monasteries were in the state of decay that he mentions. He apparently had little opportunity to observe the successful operation of the dharma system at the large monasteries in Kiangsu—monasteries that hardly fit his description of having "two or three people in residence." He had few links with Kiangsu abbots and it may be that when he visited there, he was treated as an outsider, so that even though he found monasteries obviously flourishing, he resented the monopoly of the power by a small group of local monks. It is also possible to see here a Buddhist echo of the widening movement against familism and filial piety.

Whether or not T'an-hsü is right in attributing the decline of monasteries in the north and south to transmission of the abbotship along with the dharma, he is certainly right in saying that this practice was widespread and that it represented a shift from public to hereditary, or at any rate, a narrowing of the circle of authority. It was another step in the progress of Buddhism away from the Indian Buddhist ideal of universal, direct democracy and toward the Chinese ideal of the family as the model for all social organizations. But the analogy of monastic life to family life should not be pushed too far. It is true that the Kiangsu abbot looked upon his predecessors as ancestors, oversaw the regular offerings to their tablets, and went to sweep their graves at Ch'ing-ming; and that in all parts of China neighboring institutions had "family connections" based on tonsure and dharma. But I have the impression that none of this went quite as deep as the analogues in natural family life. I think that in China Buddhism retained much of its original insistence on the equality and independence of monks. Chinese social forms were adopted within the monastic system to make it more familiar, more livable and easier to administer, but they did not alter the essential loneliness of the monastic life.

CHAPTER VII

Rites for the Dead

Buddhist doctrine, let it be said again, lies outside the scope of this book and the competence of its author, but we have again reached the point where a word about doctrine is needed to introduce the discussion of practice. No one can understand the rites for the dead without first understanding what was believed to happen to a man after he died. The difficulty is that there were many inconsistencies in the two systems of belief, one of Buddhist and one of Chinese origin, that enjoyed many centuries of easy coexistence in China.

It is sometimes said that at the hands of the Chinese, Buddhism degenerated largely into ancestor worship—as though in its original form it had paid no heed to ancestors. But this was not the case. In the ancient India of the Aryans, the son was required to make periodic offerings to his father, who like all his ancestors had gone to dwell forever in Pitrloka, "the realm of the fathers," under the protection of the benevolent deity, Yama. Descendants who made ancestral offerings in the right way could expect to be rewarded with riches, children, and long life.

The theory of rebirth, of which there is no trace in the Vedas, had not yet been formulated. It was mentioned in the Brahmanas, developed in the Upanishads, and by the time of the Buddha it was generally accepted. It affirmed that after death every man became a *preta* (literally a departed person) and remained in this intermediate state until his funeral rites were completed, whereupon he was "born again here as a worm or as a moth or as a bird or as a tiger or as a lion or as a fish or as a boar or as a man or as some other being in these states, according to his karma, according to his knowledge."[1] The son hoped, of course, that his father had been reborn in heaven, in which case filial offerings would prolong his sojourn there. This gave the son an additional reason for making them.

This system was preserved by the Buddhists when they adopted the theory of rebirth, which they changed and articulated. One of the changes was to systematize possible reincarnations into five and later into six "paths" or planes of existence: gods, men, asuras, animals, pretas, and creatures in hell. All of the last four paths were punishment: only those reborn as gods or men had enjoyed at the time of their death a net balance of good karma.

Yama, who in Vedic times had presided over the happy realm of the fathers, was transformed by the Buddhists into the lord of hell and the superintendent of punishment there. Pretas, who had previously been persons in the intermediate state between rebirths, were now considered to be in a separate path, only one level higher than hell. The sufferings of anyone reborn as a preta were appropriate to his evil deeds: the former slanderer was reborn with an ulcerated mouth exuding a foul smell. The former backbiter was doomed to keep eating the flesh of his own back. The man who had killed another with a slingshot blow on the head was battered by 60,000 iron arrows on his own head three times a day. Most pretas also suffered the tortures of Tantalus. When they were thirsty and went to the river, it turned to blood. When they sought refuge from the heat in a shady place, it became like a furnace. The variety of their deformities and frustration is painted with alarming detail in the *Petavatthu,* an early Buddhist collection of preta stories.

The devout Buddhist layman in India had no way of knowing which of his ancestors had become pretas after death. But he could relieve any that had by providing them with food. The Buddha is quoted as saying "the pretas subsist on food that they obtain in the pretaloka or that is offered to them by their friends, associates, relatives, and blood relations. If a preta for whose sake the offering is made does not perchance come to receive and enjoy it, then another preta who is expecting such an offering profits by it."[2] This carried on the much earlier Vedic tradition of offerings to ancestors in the "realm of the fathers." But as the preta theory later evolved, such offerings came to be regarded as unreliable, or at any rate as much less reliable than offerings to the sangha. This was because the preta to whom food, drink, or clothing was offered might have no way of accepting it. If his evil deeds weighed heavily upon him, food would turn to pus and water to fire. He could only be helped by transfer of merit, in particular the merit that arose from donating a feast or a building to pure monks. Such merit could be transferred to his account, alleviate his sufferings, and perhaps release him from the pretaloka for a better rebirth.[3] The stated purpose of the *Petavatthu* was "to establish the superior merit of making gifts to the Buddhist Holy Order and their efficacy as a means of releasing the pretas from their state of woe."[4]

The word "preta" was and is ambiguous. Anyone who had died could be called a "preta," which never lost its original sense of "the departed." Thus the Buddha said that parents normally desired to have children in the expectation that children would make offerings to them when they (the parents) became pretas.[5] Everyone was due to become a preta in this sense, and even today in Ceylon the dead can be so termed. So the practice of offerings to pretas has been filled with ambiguity and uncertainties from the earliest times. When such offerings were made by a Buddhist in ancient India, he was caring for his departed ancestors wherever they were. Perhaps they were pretas in the sense that they were in an intermediate state between rebirths. Perhaps they were pretas in the sense that they had already been reborn in the pretaloka and were suffering for their evil deeds. To cover either contingency he would not only offer them food and drink, but also make gifts to the sangha and dedicate the merit therefrom to relieve and release them.

CHINESE CONCEPTS OF THE AFTERLIFE

Before the introduction of Buddhism the Chinese had only hazy notions of what happened to the individual after death. Their cosmology had not six planes, but three: heaven, the human world, and the subterranean. Like the early Aryans, they believed that death was permanent: there was no such thing as rebirth. After death the various elements of the personality dispersed in several directions. The heavy, animal element (*p'o*) stayed close to the corpse and gradually sank down to the Yellow Springs. The lighter element (*hun,* which I shall translate as "soul") stayed close to the tablet, that is, a wooden plaque perhaps eighteen inches high and three inches wide, inscribed with the name of the deceased and certain other particulars. Here the soul would take up residence, feed on the offerings made by filial descendants, and receive their reports of family news. If a man had been particularly virtuous in life, his soul would take up residence in heaven, from which it could return to the tablet whenever necessary. All the deceased, but particularly those in heaven, had the power to help their descendants. They helped if offerings were dutiful, whereas if offerings ceased, they became "orphaned souls" (*ku-hun*), much to be pitied, and perhaps to be feared. Particularly an object of fear was the vengeful ghost (*li-kuei*), that is, the ghost of a man who had been unjustly executed or killed before his time—as in war, accident, or plague—or who had been improperly buried. He might take his revenge indiscriminately on all who crossed his path. The welfare of the family and the community depended, therefore, on the care of the spirits of the dead.

The impact of Buddhism upon people with such a belief is easy to imagine. Previously the worst worry had been that one's late parents might be hungry and irritable. Now the possibility arose that they had been condemned to the fires and indignities of hell, or were wandering about the earth as pretas, not merely hungry for offerings, but unable to eat them because their throats were as small as the eye of a needle and everything put in the mouth turned to pus or blood. The thought was almost too horrible to be entertained by a filial child, but what if it were true? Buddhism introduced these fears just as China was falling into the turmoil of the Six Dynasties, when many Chinese must have been wondering whether the troubles of the family and the State were not due to some shortcoming in the service of the ancestors.

Buddhist ideas of the afterlife did not displace indigenous ideas but complemented and fused with them. Pretas, for example, were strikingly similar to orphaned souls. They were forever wandering through the world, waiting to be fed, "behind the boundary wall of the old homestead, where crossroads meet, even by doorposts."[6] Whereas in India they had not been considered dangerous (because they were too preoccupied with their own suffering), the Chinese imputed to them the potentiality of the orphaned soul for taking revenge on those who had failed to nourish it. Rather naturally it was the preta's tantalizing hunger that most impressed the Chinese, who gave them the name of "hungry ghosts" (*e-kuei*).

Some Chinese realized that hungry ghosts had fallen into their lamentable state because of their own misdeeds, whereas the orphaned souls were the victims of neglect. But the two categories became confused, just as the realm of the hungry ghosts became confused with hell.[7] According to the *Petavatthu* their realm was separate and distinct. In China it became hell itself or an antechamber thereof, from which they issued forth to wander, particularly in the evening and in the middle of the seventh month. High-born pretas were considered actually to hold office in hell, working as jailors and executioners for Yama (Yen-lo), its terrible judge and king.

As early as the fourth century C.E. the Chinese began to accept the idea that it took forty-nine days to be assigned a new life in one of the six paths.[8] But this did not bring them to abandon the practice of offering food to the dead for years and even for generations after they had died. Like the Aryans, the Chinese preserved the cult of ancestors as though rebirth had never been heard of.

Their approach, while it might seem to be inconsistent, was actually that of a prudent man dealing with the unknown. There was no way to be sure which version of the afterlife was correct. On the chance that it was the Chinese version, the filial son made regular offerings at his father's tablet, reported all important family news, and thanked him for help received. On the chance that it was the Buddhist version, he had rites performed immediately after his father died to help him toward a better rebirth in forty-nine days. But suppose these rites were unsuccessful; suppose that despite them his father had been reborn as a hungry ghost or in hell. Once again there was no way to be sure. On the chance that the worst had transpired, the duty of the son was to have *more* Buddhist rites performed to secure a second and better rebirth for his father at the earliest possible moment, and to relieve his sufferings in the meantime. It would have been unfilial to suppose that his father had deserved to be reborn as a hungry ghost, but it would have been even more unfilial to neglect the appropriate measures if he were one.

This desire to do everything possible for the deceased, so that no matter who was right—Confucians, Buddhists, or Taoists—he would get maximum protection, fostered the development of an extraordinarily rich assortment of posthumous rites in China. Their history lies outside our purview, but they eventually became the most conspicuous feature of Chinese Buddhism. The general term for them today is "delivering the souls of the dead" (*ch'ao-tu wang-hun*).

Deliverance is considered possible in three ways. First, monks perform rites that cancel out the bad karma of the dead by transferring to their account the good karma accumulated by bodhisattvas and by the monks themselves. Second, they instruct the dead in the dharma in order to dispel the ignorance that may be holding them back from a more favorable rebirth. Third, in the case of hungry ghosts, since their sufferings make it difficult for them to focus their attention on the dharma, monks begin by alleviating their hunger with food. This food has a dual character. While from a compassionate Buddhist point of view it relieves their suffering, from the traditional Chinese point of view it reduces the danger of their becoming angry. Since the anger of ghosts is apt to be indiscriminate, the whole community is benefitted.[9]

Most rites for the dead in China are supposed to be universal rather than exclusive. Their object is to feed, instruct, and deliver as many hungry ghosts as possible, and sometimes to do the same for souls being tortured in hell. The merit arising therefrom is transferred to the account of the particular dead person for whose benefit the ceremony is being held and whose soul tablet is usually on the altar. If he happens to be a hungry ghost himself, he is doubly benefitted, but the merit transferred reaches him wherever he is, in whatever path of existence. This provides a rationale for performing rites long after the forty-ninth day. Even if he has already been reborn as a child in a neighboring city, he still receives the merit arising from the rites: the net balance of his karma is improved. Therefore to hold such rites for a person a year or two after he has died does not imply that he is a hungry ghost. What a thought!

Many Chinese, including even many devout Buddhists, have not bothered to put their ideas about the afterlife into such logical order. I recall, for example, meeting a very well-educated mainlander at the gate of a Buddhist temple in Taiwan where he had paid to have his family tablets installed for the Festival of the Hungry Ghosts. He had never heard that rebirth occurred after forty-nine days. In general, he said, he was unfamiliar with the theories that underlay offerings to the dead. Yet he was on his way to make those offerings and gave me an expert's lecture on the different kinds of hell money, some of which he was buying. Like him, many Chinese seem to regard the whole gamut of Buddhist services as simply one form of filial piety. They may become very angry if anyone suggests that they are offering incense, rice, and fruit at the altar because they think their parents have been reborn on a lower plane. Their parents are, of course, *ling-ming*—virtuous spirits who reside in heaven and descend to their tablets to receive filial offerings and reverent reports of family news. Why then do they pay the monks to recite sutras? Because it is a customary form of filial commemoration, they say. No one can be called "superstitious" for engaging in filial commemoration.

ANNIVERSARY RITES

There were two varieties of rites for the dead: elaborate ceremonies performed on some anniversary* of death and routine offerings made before the tablet on the 1st and 15th of every lunar month. We shall deal first with the special rites, among which the most picturesque was "the release of the burning mouths" (*fang yen-k'ou*). This was a Tantric ritual lasting about five hours and always held in the evening when it was easier for hungry ghosts to go abroad. The presiding monks wore red and golden hats in the shape of a five pointed crown.[10] Before them was a collection of magical instruments—mirrors, scepters, spoons, and so on. The monks assisting them—usually six to eighteen[11]—were equipped with *dorjes* and *dorje* bells (which sounded, when rung together, rather like a team of reindeer). In the first half of the ceremony the celebrants invoked the help of the Three Jewels. In the second half they broke through the gates of hell, where,

---

* Here and below, for want of the right word in English, I apply "anniversary" to rites that took place from one day to one year after death.

31. A "release of burning mouths" is performed by three presiding monks and eight assistants. Note the brocaded altar hangings (*chuang-yen*) with auspicious phrases. Taiwan.

32. One of the presiding monks, wearing a Vairocana hat, gives the mudra (magic hand gesture) which disperses those demons who attach themselves to sacrificial vessels and consume the food intended for the ghosts of the deceased. Taiwan.

with their instruments and magic gestures, they opened the throats of the sufferers and fed them sweet dew, that is, water made holy by reciting a mantra over it. They purged away their sins, administered the Three Refuges, and caused them to take the bodhisattva resolve. Finally they preached the dharma to them. If all this was properly done, the ghosts could be immediately reborn as men or even in the Western Paradise.[12]

The merit arising therefrom accrued to the deceased persons whose relatives were paying for the ceremony—and who, of course, might also have been among those directly benefitted. *Fang yen-k'ou* were not only performed for the benefit of particular persons, but as a community service on the 15th of every seventh lunar month, the Festival of Hungry Ghosts, when most of the populace joined in various kinds of observances on behalf of the dead.

33. A mother and her children offer incense and prostrate themselves at the temporary altar of rebirth set up for a Festival of Hungry Ghosts. The wall is covered with paper soul tablets of the deceased, while the more expensive wooden frame tablets are set up below. The deceased will receive the merit transferred after the "release of burning mouths" being performed for the festival. On the floor lie bags of paper ingots, waiting to be dispatched to them by fire. Taiwan.

Less picturesque but no less beneficial was the reciting of a penance (*pai-ch'an*), which drew on the inexhaustible store of merit of buddhas and bodhisattvas to cancel the bad karma that the deceased had accumulated. There were many varieties of penance, some extremely curious in origin. Consider, for example, the Water Penance (*Shui-ch'an*). It is said to have been composed by a T'ang dynasty monk named Chih-hsüan. Early in his career he showed some kindness to a foreign bhiksu who had fallen ill in the Chinese capital. In gratitude the latter, before departing, told him that if he were ever in trouble he should seek him out in Szechwan. Later Chih-hsüan won great renown. He was given the title of "national teacher," and the emperor himself used to come to hear him preach. Before long a boil developed on his knee that had the semblance of a human face. There were eyes, nose, and a mouth, which could talk. He found this intolerable, so he went to Szechwan and sought out the foreigner, who was living in a mountain temple there. When he had explained his problem, the foreigner told him to bathe in a spring at the foot of the mountain, the waters of which had the remarkable quality of washing away the karma of injustice. He was about to begin washing when the boil asked him to stop. It explained that the two of them had been mortal enemies hundreds of years before during the Han dynasty. It had been unable to take revenge for the injuries it had then received because the monk had been a monk, leading a pure life, for the last ten reincarnations. Now that the emperor's patronage had turned his thoughts to fame and profit, revenge was possible. Despite this plea Chih-hsüan washed in the spring, whereupon the boil disappeared, along with the temple. He built a new one there and wrote the *Water Penance*. Most of it is an exposition of the doctrine of karma, but each section begins with a hymn in which the author refers to his own peculiar experience.

These were not the only kinds of mortuary rites. If monks simply recited buddha's name, it was considered to give rise to merit. Therefore, after someone died, they might be asked to recite buddha's name for a week (*fo-ch'i*) and then transfer the resulting merit to his account. They might also be asked to chant sutras, which not only gave rise to merit, but constituted a form of instruction. The soul of the deceased would be summoned to his tablet (and attracted by offerings) to hear the *Ksitigarbha Sutra* or the *Diamond Sutra* or the

Amitabha Sutra. The latter was particularly effective in turning his mind toward the Western Paradise, where it was hoped he would be reborn.

All the rites described above were called "Buddhist services" (*fo-shih* or *ching-ch'an*).[13] They would be performed according to a schedule that varied with the wealth and piety of the bereaved and with the customs of the region. If a family could afford it they were performed day and night: otherwise on the third, fifth and seventh days after death and on several of the seven "sevenths" during the first forty-nine days.

For example, on the first seventh a text like the *Surangama* or *Lotus Sutra* might be chanted to instruct the soul of the deceased. On the third seventh the monks would offer a penance or recite buddha's name during the day, while in the evening they performed a *fang yen-k'ou.* In Peking it was the practice on the fifth seventh to burn a paper boat, piloted by Kuan Yin, but in south China this might have already been done two weeks earlier.[14]

34. A paper boat with Kuan-yin at the tiller is ready to ferry to the Western Paradise all the souls who are saved by the "release of burning mouths," a paper performance of which, presided over by Ti-tsang, is going on inside the cabin. Hong Kong.

In central China the ordinary family might be able to do no more than to ask the monks to the house the first night. They would chant a short text, like the *Amitabha Sutra,* and then circumambulate around the corpse, reciting buddha's name and keeping time with a hand chime and small wooden fish. They would recite for an hour, then rest for an hour, and so alternately recite and rest until dawn. This meant that the family did not have to keep the vigil themselves. Usually the corpse had not been encoffined and, as one monk told me, in summer there was often a bad smell.

Once the forty-nine days were over and the permanent wooden tablet was installed on the family altar, services continued to be performed on certain anniversaries, particularly the hundredth day after death and the first and third years. Beyond three years, which was the traditional period of mourning, rites were seldom held.[15]

The larger the number of monks participating in Buddhist services, the greater was the amount of merit available for transfer, assuming, of course, that they had lived by the rules and kept up their religious practice. The number might be five, seven, twelve, twenty-four, forty-eight, a hundred and eight, or a thousand. Since the soul could come to its tablet regardless of where the corpse was lying, the services could either be performed in the monastery or at home. Poor families might not have the space to set up an altar and accommodate the monks. Rich ones sometimes turned part of their houses into a temple for the occasion. It depended on the circumstances and the region.[16]

The *tour de force* among rites for the dead was the "plenary mass" (*shui-lu fa-hui*), common in central China, rare in Peking. It was very large, very long, and very expensive. Lasting seven days and nights, it included different kinds of services at seven different altars, often going on simultaneously: recitation of buddha's name, chanting of various sutras, offering of penances, and the release of burning mouths. Each had to be performed by the number of monks prescribed in the missal, while all the monks in the monastery turned out to march in the serpentine processions reciting buddha's name (*p'u-fo*).

The purpose of the plenary mass was to save all the souls of the dead on land and sea (hence the term *shui-lu*), but as usual the merit arising therefrom was credited to the account of the deceased relatives of the family that was paying for it. They paid a great deal. For example, at Chin Shan the price was $1,200 (Chinese currency). At least sixty monks took part, drawn from those living in retirement, from the meditation hall, from the hall for reciting buddha's name and, if there were still not enough hands, from the wandering monks hall. Except for the precentor, most officers were too busy to assist. Up to ten plenary masses, lasting seventy days in all, were performed each year at Chin Shan, usually during the second and third, eighth, and ninth lunar months, but never during meditation weeks. After the Japanese occupation there were none at all, reportedly because no one could afford it. Yet Chin Shan's charges were not exorbitant. Whereas at small temples a reduction in price could sometimes be negotiated, large monasteries charged up to $5,000 (Chinese currency) and might be unwilling to bargain.[17] In Hong Kong during recent years plenary masses have been held at several of the larger temples and the charge has run to the equivalent of US $3,000—a charge so high that sometimes it has been shared by a syndicate of several families.

Although as much as half the charge represented profit for the monastery, there were heavy expenses to meet: paying for the monks who were called in to take part (the fee, *tan-ch'ien*, for each monk ran from fifty cents to one Chinese dollar a day); serving everyone three vegetarian feasts; and preparing elaborate paper figures. Among these were the celestial horses that were burned to notify the Jade Emperor (a Taoist divinity who reigned over the Buddhist heaven of desire) that he should descend and partake of the feast and release the hungry ghosts from hell so that they could partake too.

Other paper figures were burned by the lay donors of the mass. As during many such rites they set fire to paper houses, servants, and even automobiles so that their late relatives might have use of them. It may be hard to see what use a Cadillac would be in hell, and, of course, once a man was condemned in the courts of hell, he would find it of very little use. But even the worthiest citizen had to go through these courts, which lay a considerable distance apart, and his son naturally wanted him to be as comfortable as possible. Therefore he also provided his father with money for incidental expenses, like gifts for infernal officials. Like so many officials, those in hell were venal. There was a good chance that the deceased could buy his way out, or at any rate get his torturers to "loosen the screws" a little.

35. Paper offerings to be burned on the third or fifth seventh: a partly assembled automobile (with its wheels stacked in the foreground). Hong Kong.

36. A paper house, duplicating the house of the deceased. Note servants on the balcony. Hong Kong.

Thus during almost any Buddhist mortuary rite, while the monks chanting in the shrine-hall were engaged in the lofty task of transferring the merit of compassionate bodhisattvas to the account of the deceased, his relatives were out in the courtyard helping him in a more practical way. Every temple courtyard had a kind of incinerator where paper offerings could be burned and thereby translated to the

37. Busy courtyard with the smoke of paper offerings rising from the incinerator. Probably Ching-an Ssu, Shanghai.

38. A hell bank note of the kind burned by the package in the incinerator. Hong Kong.

nether world. Into it lay people tossed banknotes, coins, and ingots,
all of paper. The banknotes were usually in high denominations and
issued by the Bank of Hell.[18] The coins were disks of silver cardboard
sometimes imprinted with the head of President Yüan Shih-k'ai (like
real silver dollars); or sheets of yellow paper impressed with the
shapes of copper cash, each with a hole in the middle. But it was the
ingots that really counted. There were both gold and silver ingots
made of paper tinfoil in the appropriate color. If one visited a temple
before a Buddhist service, one usually saw female relatives of the
deceased—or women hired by the temple—sitting around a table fold-
ing sheets of tinfoil into little hats—the shape of the heavier ingots in
traditional China.[19] Even one such ingot, representing fifty ounces of
gold or silver, ought to have been persuasive in dealing with infernal
officials, but their rapacity was presumably greater than officials on
earth and so thousands of ingots were folded for every large rite. To
make sure they reached their destination they were placed in roomy
paper bags (*pao-fu p'i*), yellow for those who had died within three
years, red for those who had died earlier. Sometimes one whole corner
of the temple workroom would be stacked to the ceiling with them.
On each bag there would be written with a brush the name of the
deceased and his native place as well as the name of the sender. It

was important that the sender be identified so that he would be given credit by the recipient.

Not all the paper burned by laymen was so mercenary. One of their favorite offerings, for example, was the Mantra of Rebirth (*Wang-sheng chou*). It was printed on a single sheet in Chinese and Sanskrit, then folded up like a fan, and tossed into the incinerator in large quantities. Also burned were sheets of paper imprinted with pictures of scissors and bolts of cloth, which were intended to represent clothing. It was the thought that counted.

None of these things were usually bought from the temple, but rather from a paper shop, which sold them in packages of fifty or a hundred. (When I have bought such packages, they have usually been short a few sheets. Not all rapacity is confined to hell!) Monks might write the addresses on the bags of ingots, but otherwise they took little part in the dispatch of paper offerings. Their attitude was at least tolerant and many believed in the practice. I remember one monk telling me that when he forgot to address some bags of ingots during a Buddhist service several years ago, the ghost appeared to the family of the deceased in a dream and complained that his remittance had failed to arrive. Such stories were widely regarded as everyday confirmation of everyday facts. Quaint as they may sound to some readers, they were prompted (like all the practices described in this chapter) by the most universal human feelings: fear of death and love and fear of parents.

Rites for the dead were sometimes referred to collectively as "white services" (*pai-shih*), since white was the color of mourning in China. Rites for the living were called "red services" (*hung-shih*). The living, too, could benefit from each offering of a penance, since it washed away their bad karma and so "annulled disasters" (*hsiao-tsai*). Thus in order to bring rain monks recited the "Penance of Three Thousand Buddhas," so-called because it was meant to obtain the transfer of enough merit from past, present, and future buddhas to cancel out the bad karma that was causing the drought.[20] Appropriate penances could also be recited to bring an end to illness, haunting, or war. Even for the red services performed on birthdays or on the opening of a temple, it was appropriate to recite a penance, since it averted dangers as yet unseen. Perhaps the most universal feature of red services was

39. A procession of monks sprinkles holy water with willow twigs before performing rites to bring rain. The first monk carries a hand-chime. Hong Kong.

the worship of the buddha of medicine, Bhaisajyaguru (*Yao-shih fo*), who presides in the East just as Amitabha presides in the West. When I have attended the birthday of a leading monk or layman, we circumambulated reciting "Homage to Yao-shih Fo who annuls disasters and lengthens the life span," after which came a hymn to the incense (*hsiang-tsan*) and a vegetarian feast.

If services were being performed for a man who had died at a great age, the atmosphere was naturally less mournful than if he had died before his time. Sometimes, according to one informant, it was more like a red than a white service, since the family felt that thanksgiving was in order for the blessings their late relative had enjoyed. In Peking on such occasions the monks might even be asked to sing popular songs, which added a certain piquancy to the festive mood.

ATTITUDES TOWARD RITES FOR THE DEAD

Foreign writers on Chinese Buddhism have portrayed the sangha as divided into two camps: those who performed Buddhist services with the enthusiasm of greed or superstitious ignorance; and those who did so as a disagreeable necessity because they depended on it for livelihood. Prip-Møller remarks: "To the more spiritually-minded monks, masses like these, full as they are of superstition and exorcism, are an abhorrence, but for the monasteries and temples they provide a splendid source of income, which they cannot afford to do without."[21] R. F. Fitch states that: "Intelligent priests will most seriously attack this practice in private conversation, but one has not heard of any who had the courage of their conviction so as to try to break the practice."[22] One Kiangsu monk estimated to me that twenty percent of the sangha are skeptical about the efficacy of rites for the dead. They consider that our next rebirth is inexorably determined by the good and bad karma we have accumulated. The rest of the sangha, he said, feel that while the future is largely up to each individual, he can be assisted by the transfer of merit, particularly within the first forty-nine days after death when his case is, so to speak, still open.

It is true that in recent decades, at least, the better monasteries have refused to send their monks to people's houses or to hold the smaller rites (like penances) within their own walls except for the most important patrons. A few monasteries have refused to hold any Buddhist services at all. The code of rules for the Kao-min Ssu states that it is a "*ts'ung-lin* whose perpetual work is meditation and religious study. No major or minor Buddhist services whatever will be accepted."[23] According to an informant who spent several years there, this rule had been observed since Lai-kuo took office as abbot early in the Republican period. For an important lay patron or a resident monk who had died, Lai-kuo would arrange a plenary recitation of buddha's name (*p'u-fo*), but rather than reciting the name of the buddha Amitabha, the monks would recite the name of Sakyamuni. In no case would the Kao-min Ssu perform plenary masses, penances, or "release of the burning mouths."

A few other monasteries are reported to have had the same rule, as for example the Chu-sheng Ssu on Nan-yüeh and the Jen-jui Ssu in Heng-yang (both of Hunan). The reason usually given was that rites for the dead would have disturbed the peaceful routine of the monastery and impaired the single-minded devotion to religious exercises. But there is a possibility that the prohibition was a relatively new phenomenon, inspired by the winds of reform. Already in 1912 some conservative monks were coming to feel that the commercialization of such rites reflected poorly on the sangha. There was also a tendency to look down on those monks who spent their time going out to perform them in people's homes. They were popularly referred to as "monks on call" (*ying-fu seng*) in contrast to those who spent their time in the monastery on meditation and study (the *hsiu-hsing seng*). The "call monks" formed the majority of the clerical proletariat. Their ignorance of texts and doctrine did not impair their usefulness in the eyes of the populace, but in Buddhist circles it tended to attach a certain stigma to rites for the dead.[24]

This did not necessarily mean that the clerical elite were skeptical of the efficacy of these rites. At Chin Shan a plenary mass was held every year[25] in which only unpaid volunteers took part. Hence it was called a "volunteer plenary mass" (*fa-hsin shui-lu*). Any resident of the monastery had the right to install two paper tablets in the Pure Land Altar for the seven days it lasted. One of the tablets would be for laymen (usually his parents) and the other for a monk (usually his tonsure master). There was no charge for this. All expenses were paid by the establishment: incense, candles, paper figures, and three missal feasts. There were always sixty to seventy monks who were willing to put in an exhausting week without compensation, and *all* the resident monks took the opportunity to put up tablets. If they had considered the rites ineffective would they have done so?

THE COMMERCIALIZATION OF RITES

The issue was not the effectiveness of rites, but their commercialization. This was exemplified at some of the large urban monasteries that did not have income from land and hence had no choice but to give priority to Buddhist services, which at some of them became "big business." For a first-hand and perhaps somewhat embittered description of this we shall hear from a monk who spent a year at the Fa-tsang Ssu in Shanghai. This temple was housed in a new building in the French concession, looking from the outside like any other house in the block. When he was living there in 1938, it had over a hundred monks in residence. Here is what he told me about it.

That was a place that really made money conducting Buddhist services. From morning to night, from the beginning of the year to the end, there were plenary masses. I was one of the ordinary monks. During the day I recited a penance—one penance took the whole day—and in the evening a *fang yen-k'ou*. There was no time to rest. If you wanted to rest, you had to ask for leave, and this was very hard to get. If, for example, you said that you were sick, you would be told that since you could not recite penances, you should go to the buddha recitation hall and recite buddha's name. There it was possible to sleep—and still get your 25¢ a day [Chinese currency]. Laymen were willing to pay for this because the merit generated could be transferred to the deceased, just as in the case of a penance. Regardless of the type of work performed, the monastery charged one dollar per monk per day for daytime work, of which the monk got 25¢; for an evening's work the monastery charged $2, of which each celebrant at the lower table got 40¢, while the three who presided got 80¢. So in the course of twenty-four hours the ordinary monk could make 65¢. But at that time 65¢ was a reasonable amount of money. We made a little more when we went out to perform services in people's homes—walking around the corpse on the first night, for example. They had to pay $1.50 per monk per night for this, out of which we got 50¢ apiece. Except when we were in people's homes, the monastery provided our food. We were not paid directly, but given bamboo slips each day. We kept these until the end of the half month, and then got a lump-sum in accordance with the slips we had accumulated.

If one was willing to stay there for many years and put up with the misery of the work, one could become an officer of the monastery and really make money. The abbot, the retired abbot, the manager, the guest prefect, the precentor, the proctor, and other high officers would each get a bamboo slip for each of the services performed in a given day, so that if ten groups of monks performed services, the abbot would get ten slips, whereas the monks participating would only get one apiece. The monastery used to cheat its patrons. They were laymen and did not understand. There should have been ten or twenty monks performing at each service, but because business was so good, there were not enough to go around and they would be divided into small groups—as few as three or four monks. Another way in which patrons were cheated was by pretending that the monks in the great shrine-hall were reciting a penance for only one family of worshippers. If the Wang family came they would be shown the monks reciting there and told that it was for the Wangs, and if the Chang family came they would be shown the same monks and told that it was for the Changs. When the monks left the shrine-hall to transfer merit in front of the tablet of the departed, they would do it first before the Wang tablet and then before the Chang tablet, each in its own hall for the occasion. The monastery used to make an enormous amount of money.

Ordinarily one could not leave the premises—except to perform Buddhist services at people's homes. It was like living in a prison. There was a meditation hall, but it was not a real one; it was just used for Buddhist services. There was no meditation. Life was harder physically at the Fa-tsang Ssu than it was at Chin Shan, but one made more money. It was like being in business.

The monk who told me this belonged to the rank and file. He never served as an officer. His account reveals the same attitude toward the "higher-ups" that one finds among enlisted men in the army. Though most of what he said was confirmed, certain important details were contradicted by another informant who spent a year in the Fa-tsang Ssu at about the same time (1938-1939). Because he was well connected, he was given an apartment to live in and the rank of thurifer. He denied categorically that every high officer received one credit for each Buddhist service held, whether he attended or not. "That way officers would have made a *terrible* lot of money," he said. "How could the establishment have paid them?" What actually happened, he went on, was that one credit for each service was given to all the officers *collectively*. At the end of the month the total was divided up among them in equal shares as a solatium. Thus if there were ten officers and fifteen services a day, each officer received one and a half credits. "That other monk you were talking to remembered it wrong. He didn't know about it because he was never an officer himself."

According to this second informant the Fa-tsang Ssu was one of the three strictest monasteries in Shanghai. True, its work was almost entirely performing Buddhist services, but how else could it have survived? It had no land. The situation was different at the Liu-yün Ssu, where he had held office for many years. The Liu-yün Ssu received enough grain rent from farmland south of Shanghai to feed its residents four months of the year. Therefore it was able to operate a meditation hall where thirty to a hundred monks followed the same rules and schedule as at Chin Shan. They normally took no part in rites for the dead, which were manned by other residents in much the same way as at the Fa-tsang Ssu.[26]

During his years as visitors' prefect[27] this informant had often had the duty of dealing with the public, taking their orders for Buddhist services, keeping them company while these were under way, and collecting payment afterwards. He said that a typical conversation with a donor (*t'an-yüeh*) might run as follows:

Donor: "My father's sixtieth birthday is on the 18th and I would like to have a service performed."
Visitors' Prefect: "Would you like us to perform a one-day Longevity Penance or to recite the Longevity Sutra[28] for a day?"
Donor: "I'd like you to recite the Longevity Sutra."
Prefect: "How many monks (*shih-fu*) do you want to ask?"
Donor: "What is the minimum?"
Prefect: "With us here the minimum is seven."
Donor: "What is the maximum?"
Prefect: "That's as you like—108, for example."
Donor: "This time I am afraid I cannot afford to ask too many."
Prefect: "Twenty-four, then, or twelve?"
Donor: "With twenty-four, how much would I have to give?"
Prefect: "The monks are now getting 40¢ apiece."
Donor: "Per day?"
Prefect: "That's what the monks get; our temple takes one dollar in all."
Donor: "All right, make it twelve monks. Then we will want to eat a vegetarian meal (*ch'ih-chai*)."

Prefect: "Do you want to have superior dishes or ordinary ones?"
Donor: "I want superior ones."
Prefect: "Preparing them on your behalf would be $12 per table."
Donor: "There would be thirty of us, which would be three tables.
  Let me see, the total would be about $50."
Prefect (perfunctorily): "Amitabha!"

When arrangements were being made for services and a feast at a large urban monastery, monks did not feel the same reluctance to talk in terms of fixed tariffs as when they were entertaining pilgrims in a country monastery or a place of pilgrimage. But in the latter, too, Buddhist services might be an important element of the monastic economy. According to one monk, they were the largest single source of revenue for the Pure Land center at Ling-yen Shan[29] near Soochow, although the rents from its 500 acres of farmland must also have been considerable. At P'u-t'o Shan, the sacred island off the Chekiang coast, they were "the main income," yielding an estimated two million Chinese dollars a year to the many temples there, which sometimes could not keep up with the demand.[30]

INCOME FROM TABLETS AND URNS

As we noted at the beginning of this chapter, it was the traditional Chinese belief that a filial son was obliged to make offerings of food before his parents' tablets and report all family news, while according to Buddhist belief he was obliged to provide food, instruction, and the transfer of merit to assist them toward a better rebirth. The former obligation he usually carried out himself in the family shrine at home. The latter obligation was one that he seldom had either the time or the competence to undertake. Therefore he would purchase the right to place additional tablets for his parents in a monastery where the monks would act for him in perpetuity. On the 1st and 15th of the lunar month, and on Ch'ing-ming, the Festival of Hungry Ghosts, and the Winter Solstice (or, in some temples, every day of the year), they would make an offering, recite an appropriate text like the *Amitabha Sutra,* and transfer the resulting merit to the account of the deceased. The offering provided nourishment and the recitation an opportunity to hear the dharma. Since a soul could travel great distances instantaneously, there was no reason why it should not have several residences, at each of which it could enjoy the care of the monks, receive the merit generated, and thereby qualify sooner for a favorable rebirth. I know a layman who had one set of tablets for his parents at the Nan-hua Ssu in Kwangtung province (as well as their ashes in a columbarium), a second set at the Kao-min Ssu in Kiangsu, and a third at home.[31] The first cost him $100 and the second $200 (Chinese currency). Elsewhere the price went up to $400–500. The payment was always in a lump sum, which could be used by the monastery to purchase income-producing property. The tablets were green or dark blue and were usually installed in a "hall of rebirth" (*wang-sheng t'ang*).[32] The largest and most costly were placed in the center and had elaborately carved frames with paintings or photographs of the deceased. The least expensive arrangement was merely to have the name of the deceased added to a collective tablet at the cost of about $50.

Some monasteries also had a "hall of longevity" (*yen-shou t'ang*)[33] where one found another kind of tablet, painted red and put up during a person's lifetime. Here prayers were recited and merit transferred in the morning of the same days that services were performed in the hall of rebirth after noon. The objective was to lengthen the life of the persons whose names the tablets bore. They were commonly erected by filial sons for their parents. Just as Amitabha, who confers rebirth in the Western Paradise, presided over the hall of rebirth, so Bhaisajyaguru (Yao-shih), the buddha of healing and of longevity, presided here. Although prayers were said (like the *Yao-shih kuan-ting chen-yen*), no offerings were made, since, after all, these people were still alive.

Sometimes the tablets in the hall of longevity were convertible. They would be painted green, but covered with a strip of red paper on which there would be a text like: "Seat of long life and emoluments for devotee so-and-so (husband) and so-and-so (wife), patrons of this temple, on whom may Buddha's radiance shine." When they died, it was a simple matter to move the tablet to the hall of rebirth and lift off the paper, exposing the usual text for the dead: "The lotus seat of rebirth for so-and-so and so-and-so, deceased father and mother, followers of the Pure Land." No additional payment had to be made for this conversion. Tablets were not always placed in the halls of longevity and rebirth. They might be at opposite sides of the hall of merit (*kung-te t'ang*) or the ancestors hall (*tsu-t'ang*), which respectively housed the tablets of worthy monks and of abbots. In small temples they could be found in the principal shrine-hall, those for the dead in the west and those for the living in the east. Small temples probably depended more on income from tablets than the large ones. They did not have the space or personnel to perform such profitable services as the plenary mass. Furthermore it is my impression that the size of the hall of rebirth was not in ratio to the size of the institution. Large halls with many tablets were probably as common in small temples as in large, and provided a higher proportion of the lower income needed to support the few resident monks.

I have heard of a monastery in Manchuria that operated a profitable cemetery, although my informant admitted that this was exceptional. A more common source of income, although not as common as the hall of rebirth, was the colombarium (*p'u-t'ung t'a*),[34] where ashes from the crematory were stored in urns (*ku-hui t'an*). In some cases this too was arranged by lump-sum payment, while in others there was an annual charge. One small temple in Wuhan, for example, had a colombarium with two thousand urns, for each of which it received the equivalent of US $1.60 a year. They provided its largest single source of income. When relatives came to do reverence on the birthdays of the deceased, many of them would pay a little extra to have a short service read while they offered incense and prostrated themselves. On these occasions the urn itself played the role of the tablet. The name would be pasted up on it and it would be placed on the altar of Ti-tsang inside the colombarium. In this particular temple there were no permanent wooden tablets in the hall of rebirth, but only the temporary paper plaques put up for Buddhist services.

The Lung-ch'üan Ssu in Peking offered a different kind of service. Many people who died in the capital came from other parts of the country, to which their bodies had to be shipped back for burial. It was customary not to inaugurate shipment until an auspicious day, which might not come for months or years. The Lung-ch'üan Ssu was ready to store the coffins in the meantime, each in its own room, for $3 a month (Chinese currency). Long rows of coffin warehouses lay between the monastery and the exemplary orphanage it ran, which will be described in the next volume—and which the coffins may have helped to support.

A word of caution is needed, perhaps, at the end of this discussion of rites for the dead as a source of income for Buddhist monks. There is danger of losing sight of the substance of the work in analyzing its financial context—just as there is when discussing medical practice as the source of income for physicians. From a Chinese Buddhist point of view, even the most perfunctory rites, performed by the most commercially minded monks, probably gave some relief to creatures suffering in the lower paths of existence, no less than the physician who is more interested in fees than healing may still heal. Rites for the dead were essentially compassionate, regardless of the money that changed hands in connection with them. Such, at least, was the orthodox, conservative viewpoint.

CHAPTER VIII

The Economy of Monasteries

Rites for the dead were the principal source of income for the most numerous category of Chinese Buddhist institutions, that is, the small hereditary temples that dotted the town and countryside. But these small temples also received a steady flow of donations, and a few of them owned land. The relative economic importance of rites, donations, and land varied with the category, size, and locale of the institution. A large public monastery that was located at a center of pilgrimage might depend mostly on donations and own no land at all. A large public monastery elsewhere might discourage pilgrims, depend mostly on land, and even have a rule against rites for the dead. But it would still receive donations, which were, in one form or another, a universal phenomenon.

DONATIONS FROM BEGGING

In a Buddhist context the word "begging" may suggest a brightly robed line of monks making their way through the early mist to the nearest village. They carry their begging bowls, which the villagers will reverently fill with cooked food to be taken back to the monastery as the fare for that day. This is the custom in Theravada countries like Burma and Thailand. But in China begging has never had the same *cachet* of sanctity as in civilizations of Hindu origin. The Chinese tend to look on beggars simply as men who are not being supported by their relatives, presumably for some good reason, and who therefore deserve only the most cursory support from the rest of the community. Most of my informants, in and out of the sangha, said that they had never seen or heard of Chinese monks begging for their food in any form.

Nonetheless begging did exist. It was localized or specialized, but the instances of it deserve attention, if only as exceptions to the rule. For example, a banker who was brought up in a country district of Chekiang told me that during his teens (that is, about 1900) he often saw monks begging from house to house for uncooked rice. Such a monk would come to the door and stand there, ringing a hand-chime with his right hand and holding a staff in his left. His begging bowl would hang at his chest from a kind of shoulder strap. Into it the householder would put a little uncooked rice, and the monk without a word would move on to the next house. An informant brought up in Nan-k'ang, Kiangsi, said that he sometimes saw the same thing as a boy there in the late 1920's. Prip-Møller, writing in the 1930's, says that "each winter monks go out once in groups with their bowls, taking with them a very large bowl. They go to all the shops in town and beg for rice with which they fill the big bowl. The custom is now seldom practiced, but is still to be found in the big monasteries of the Lower Yangtze valley."[1] I have inquired about this from several monks connected with big Kiangsu monasteries, who said they had never heard of the practice.

In all these cases the rice was uncooked. From a second Chekiangese, however, I have heard of the house-to-house collection of cooked food before Buddhist festivals. It had to be of good quality and freshly prepared. The monks would take it back to the monastery to be eaten by all the residents together. Money, however, was collected along with the food, and the collection was restricted to festivals. So here we still do not have the same daily collection of cooked food—and food only—as in Theravada countries.

Begging for money and commodities was commoner in China than begging for food. About a century ago in Foochow foreigners used to see a procession of monks march slowly through the streets, sometimes silent, sometimes chanting. As they went by, shopkeepers and pedestrians would make donations of cash, rice, or oil, which attendant workmen carried back to the monastery for use over the ensuing months.[2] I have been unable to find any informant who remembered such collective begging in eastern China, but I have been given an instance from Szechwan. The Chin-shan Ssu (which had no connection with the Chin-shan Ssu in Kiangsu, mentioned so often above), was a large monastery in eastern Szechwan with a surplus of landed income (see p. 239). Once a year in the 1920's and 1930's, after the winter ordination, its monks would go begging in the neighboring town of K'ai-chiang. Three or four hundred of them would walk in a single file through the streets, each carrying his bowl and chanting "Homage to the buddha Bhaisajyaguru, who annuls disasters and lengthens the life-span" (the commonest chant for the welfare of the living). At their head walked the precentor carrying an incense board as the symbol of his authority in the meditation hall. Behind him came a liturgical orchestra of five monks striking the hand-chime, wooden-fish, cymbals, hand-gong, and drum. Because of the length of the procession, their accompaniment was inaudible to those who walked further back. So there had to be another orchestra for each section of thirty to thirty-five monks, like extra locomotives on a long freight train. The sections would chant one by one, giving the others a chance to catch their breath. At the end of the procession came the abbot wearing his patriarch's robe of splendid brocade. Just ahead of him walked two acolytes while just behind him walked a layman holding a ceremonial canopy (*pao-kai*). Obviously the whole population of the town turned out to enjoy the show, and many made donations of money, rice, incense, medicine, dainties, or even such humble necessities as needles. Heavy or bulky gifts were accepted by the twenty to thirty lay workmen from the monastery who followed the procession. Buddhism was looked on with favor in K'ai-chiang and a rich layman might give as much as a picul of rice. But the size of the gifts mattered little to the monks. They had enough of everything anyway and made their begging procession simply to give the laity a chance for "sowing good roots" (*chung shan-ken*) or, as we might say, for character-building. This account of the procession comes from a monk who spent seven years at the Chin-shan Ssu and annually took part in it.

Since it closely resembles the processions observed in Foochow a century earlier, we might take it to be an instance of ancient customs surviving longer in Szechwan than in the area of the treaty ports. But Prip-Møller quotes the rule of a famous Szechwan monastery, the Pao-kuang Ssu in Chengtu, that "whoever goes out to beg for alms, thus obscuring the law of retribution, will not be allowed to live in the monastery."[3] Different institutions in Szechwan seem to have had different rules. In central China, at least, no form of begging was practiced at the best public monasteries. The two instances from Chekiang mentioned above involved monks from local small temples. It was also such monks who used to make house-to-house collections of money in urban areas. One of them would come to the door, strike his hand-chime, and chant a sutra, hoping to attract attention. Most families put a few cents in his hand, but there were a few who disapproved of this kind of beggar and would post a sign at their gate: "No gifts to Buddhist and Taoist monks (seng-tao wu-yüan)." According to one informant, such mendicants were still common in Peking during the 1920's, but, he said, the times changed and as the people of the city grew poorer, "dogs and beggars decreased." The custom has not entirely died out, however. I have seen Buddhist monks collecting money in middle-class apartment houses in Hong Kong.

FUND RAISING

Solicitation for some special purpose (hua-yüan) was looked on differently from begging with the bowl (t'o-po). The person who was asked to contribute toward the construction or repair of a monastery building knew that his money was going into something visible and permanent. Merit would continue to accrue to him so long as the building was in use. It would be an ornament to the community. His name would be listed among the donors on a commemorative tablet, along with the amount of money he gave. So he would hardly look upon the solicitor as a beggar.

During the Republican period well-known monks from famous monasteries often made trips to distant parts of the country, where, after proper introduction to rich Buddhist laymen, they would solicit funds for a special purpose. In the 1920's, for instance, the abbot of the Kuan-tsung Ssu in Ningpo wanted money for the purchase of a Tripitaka. He traveled north to Peking and there collected the necessary $5,000 (Chinese currency),* among others from Premier Tuan

---

* From here on, unless otherwise specified, all figures will be in terms of Chinese currency, that is, Chinese silver dollars (ta-yang). The official exchange rate, which varied widely and was not an accurate indicator of purchasing power, fluctuated between 54¢ and 22¢ (U.S. currency) in the years 1925-1934.

Ch'i-jui.[4] In 1931 the Kao-min Ssu in Yangchow had plans for a new pagoda. One of its monks went all the way to Mukden, where he had considerable success soliciting among the local Buddhists.[5]

Monasteries did not always have to take the initiative in fund-raising. Shryock tells of such a case in Anking, Anhwei. A rich citizen of that town was visited in a dream by the goddess Kuan-yin. She warned him not to sail on a certain river steamer as he had been planning. He changed his plans and, in the event, the steamer was rammed by a gunboat with a loss of hundreds of lives. Moved by gratitude, he gave several thousand dollars to the Ying-chiang Ssu for the repair of its pagoda.[6]

Some institutions depended on donors not for a special project, but for current expenses. The Ching-lien Ssu, for example, a temple in Peking, had three lay patrons who took turns in meeting its entire budget during the 1930's. The Kao-min Ssu, although it was a model public monastery, received only enough grain rents to feed its monks nine months out of twelve and, as noted earlier, it performed no rites for the dead. To meet the resulting deficit, rich laymen in Nanking and Shanghai regularly made donations (*pu-shih*). The Chan-shan Ssu in Tsingtao was often visited by the lay Buddhists who had helped to establish it and while they were there, many of them would ask if there was enough rice in the storeroom. If there was not, they would send up a few bags themselves or, if more was needed, pass the word along to their fellow devotees. It was a precarious livelihood, for the Chan-shan Ssu had no income-producing land at all, and aside from donations, depended entirely on tablets and rites for the dead.

Particularly at urban or newly founded institutions which had no endowments, it was important to cultivate lay support. This might be done in all sorts of ways. One was to hold lectures on the sutras that laymen might attend. A more traditional attraction was the temple fair or theatrical show. Outside some temples in Peking and Shanghai hundreds of booths were set up once a year (or oftener). Many of those who came to shop for a bargain would also go into the temple to make an offering. According to one source, Buddhist nunneries in Peking used to put on plays "to amuse the gods." Actors would be hired, a mat-shed theater erected, and the nuns would wait on the spectators. Profits helped defray the nunneries' current budgets.[7] At one Shanghai temple, it was possible for the devotee to have his own buddha image installed in a room set aside for the purpose and regularly worshipped. The verger offered incense twice a day for a fee of several dollars a month plus the cost of the incense. The devotee might continue to worship similar images retained at home, thus presumably getting "double credit" from the divinities for whom he was providing so well.

DONATIONS FROM VISITORS

Even where a temple made no effort to attract patronage, there was always a trickle of coin falling into the donations box or the palm of the attendant. At a public monastery or large temple, the attendant would be the verger. At a smaller place he was probably the monk who owned it or a layman he had appointed. It was the attendant's job to look after the worshippers, among whom women usually out-numbered men. One of the first thoughts of a Chinese woman when she was worried about an unfaithful husband, a sick child, or any other of life's problems, was to visit the nearest or most appropriate temple. This might be a Buddhist institution, though other kinds of temples were often more numerous. Possibly she brought some fruit along to place on the altar. In any case, she offered incense, sticking three sticks into the incense burner. Then she knelt before the divinity whose help she needed (Kuan-yin, for instance, in case of a sick child), her lips moving in silent explanation of her problem and prayer for its solution. After praying she might leave at once, but she was more likely to try to find out whether her prayers would be answered and what the future promised her in general. This she could do by "asking the slips" (*ch'iu-ch'ien*). Still kneeling before the altar, she would deliberately shake a large cylinder of numbered bamboo slips, holding it over on its side, almost horizontal, so that several of them would begin to work their way out. Finally one would drop to the floor. Now she would have to confirm it. She would cast divining blocks, which were like a wooden kidney split down the middle, each half having a flat and a round side. Only if they landed one with the flat side down and the other with the round side down did it mean that she had, most probably, drawn the correct bamboo slip.[8] She would note its number and go over to a little booth at one side of the shrine-hall, where the verger gave her a piece of paper with the same number. On this paper her fortune was printed, but in such oracular and flowery Chinese that she would be able to make nothing of it— even if she were literate. There would usually be an explanation printed below, but this too she might find obscure, and so most people would ask the verger to interpret it all. Whether he interpreted it or not, he was given something for the use of the slips—usually the equivalent of a few cents. Not only serious worshippers, but casual visitors might have their fortune told or drop a coin in the donations box.

At the busiest and smallest of small temples (which had only one mouth to feed), donations and bamboo slips might provide an adequate living. The larger the temple, the smaller the role played by such casual income in the over-all economy. At the more orthodox public monasteries there was seldom a donations box in front of the main altar, where it would have introduced a jarring, commercial note. It was to be found, if at all, on one of the side altars or in a subsidiary shrine-hall like that of the four guardian kings.

DONATIONS FROM PILGRIMS

At the great centers of pilgrimage, donations came in other forms and reached a different order of magnitude. Many of them were received in connection with food and lodging furnished by the monastery. At P'u-t'o Shan, for example, where there was little arable land, this was probably as large a source of income as rites for the dead. Pilgrims came by the thousand to worship its patron deity, Kuan-yin. Since there were no hotels, all of them ate and lived in the temples there. In return they gave as much money as they felt able to. Some Westerners in China during the late Ch'ing dynasty have written how they were charged a fixed tariff or had to haggle over the amount that they would pay for lodging.[9] This was probably the result of their attitude or the circumstances. In recent decades at most centers of pilgrimage the payment was entirely at the pleasure of the visitor.[10] The rich were expected to pay more and the poor less, but then the rich were given sumptuous treatment while the ordinary pilgrims were lodged in a dormitory. When the payment was accepted, it was recorded in a donations book,[11] often in the pilgrim's own hand.

Although the provision of food and lodging yielded a profit to the monastery, there is some danger of seeing in it more commercialization than there really was. From the monastery's point of view, it was a duty to care for pilgrims. From the pilgrim's point of view, he was not merely paying his hotel bill, but supporting the sangha. He wanted to feel that he had gained merit from his long journey. If he only paid enough to reimburse the monastery for what he had received, where was the merit? Therefore most pilgrims were ready to be

40. Crowds of pilgrims arrive at the quay on P'u-t'o Shan. Note the waiting chair men. Chekiang.

generous. On the same principle they liked to drop a coin into the donations box in one or more of the shrine-halls, and to give a few cents to get a memento of the monastery, such as its seal imprinted on a scroll or even on their clothing. They did not buy anything, however. The monastery was not a shop. Incense, for example, they either brought along themselves or purchased from the lay vendors who usually had their stalls outside the main gate.[12]

41. A vendor (behind the monk) spreads his wares on the terrace of the dharma hall of a large monastery, possibly the T'ien-t'ung Ssu.

At centers of pilgrimage—or at any large monastery—the rich worshipper who wanted to gain merit on a large scale could make a contribution of cash or rice either "to thank the establishment" (*hsieh ch'ang-chu*) or to furnish a vegetarian feast (*she-chai* or *ta-chai*). The latter meant that superior dishes were served at his expense to all the monks of the monastery, and sometimes to pilgrims as well, who ate in a separate dining room. The merit arising therefrom would usually be transferred to the account of a deceased relative of the donor. There were three grades of feasts: to serve the best grade to several hundred monks (inviting in those from neighboring monasteries) might cost many hundreds of dollars, some of which was clear profit to the establishment. This was called a "thousand-monks feast" (*ch'ien-seng chai*), although of course there were not necessarily a thousand monks present. Donors of a vegetarian feast would arrange for a small gift to be laid at the place of each monk (*chai-ch'en*). Usually it was a gift of money (up to $1 or $2), but sometimes clothing and other necessities were provided as well. One special reason for hoping to gain merit by providing a vegetarian feast was the belief that some of those who ate it might be arhats. Feeding arhats, of course, would give rise to very great merit indeed.

CULTIVATION OF LAND BY MONKS

If a monastery owned land, some of its income was in the form of grain rents, while some was in the form of produce raised by the monks themselves. The ratio between these two kinds of income is an important question, since only after settling it can one appraise the changes in the monastic economy that have taken place since 1950.

Buddhists in the "new China" are forever quoting Pai-chang's rule for the large monastery: "Every day that you do not work, you shall not eat." Not only they, but others take this as evidence that after Pai-chang's reforms in the T'ang dynasty Buddhist monks became self-supporting and raised their own food, working in the fields like the farmers around them. If this were not the case, why would Pai-chang have been castigated by his contemporaries for violating the Vinaya on the grounds that farming involved the killing of insects and field animals?[13]

This might seem to be an historical question that lies outside our purview, but there are assertions that even in this century monks have worked in the fields. Prip-Møller states that "the smaller and nearer part [of a monastery's land] may be tilled by the monks themselves, whilst the larger and more distant lots are as a rule sublet to tenant farmers who pay an annual rent to the owner, mostly in kind."[14] C. K. Yang quotes a statement that the twenty-four Buddhist monks of Ting *hsien* in Hopei, "farmed on the temple land in normal times, while occasionally they went on calls to mourning families to conduct services for the dead."[15] On the other hand there is good evidence that farm work by monks has long been exceptional. One of the justifications for a Ch'ing dynasty ban on building Buddhist temples was that Buddhist and Taoist monks "do not till the land and do not engage in trade, but dress and eat off the people."[16] This ban was imposed in 1654. Still more ancient evidence is a phrase in the "five reflections," which monks are enjoined to keep in mind as they eat their meals (see p. 62). The first of the five is: "Let me reckon how much merit [I have] and ponder from whence this [food] comes." This means, according to my informants, that the diner should reflect how others have toiled in the fields to produce what he is eating and that he should dedicate to their account some of the merit he has accumulated through religious exercises. There should be an exchange of merit for food.

When I have asked Chinese Buddhist monks themselves about working in the fields, their answers have been unanimous: they never did. They reject the idea that Pai-chang intended them to grow all their own food. In their view his intention was simply that all monks should be ready to do manual labor when it was required of them. Furthermore, the intensive program of the meditation hall, which they also trace back to Pai-chang, made full-time farm work impossible for those who were enrolled in it.[17] It was equally impossible for those who were busy with the administration of a large establishment. Most of the menial officers were committed to eight or ten hours a day in the kitchen. Only if the whole monastic system had been changed (as it was after 1950), could the monks have raised everything they ate.

There may be a way of reconciling the conflicting evidence. Almost every rural monastery had a vegetable garden (*ts'ai-yüan*) which lay nearby. If there were hundreds of monks in residence, it had to be very large and, by foreigners at least, might be thought of as a "field" (*t'ien*). At the larger institutions it was cultivated by lay workmen under the supervision of the head gardener (*yüan-t'ou*), who did not necessarily put his hand to the hoe himself. But the poorer the monastery, the fewer workmen it could afford to employ and the more of the manual labor had to be done by the gardener.

At the smallest of the small temples like the *mao-p'eng* the recluse to whom it belonged would spend a good part of his time in his plot of turnips and greens. Though Chinese monks themselves distinguish sharply between the raising of grain in fields and the raising of vegetables in a garden, outsiders might easily confuse the two activities. Then, too, there was the practice of monastery chores (*ch'u-p'o*). As many monks as were needed would be assigned to manual labor whenever and wherever it was required (pp. 18-19). This included cultivation and harvesting of vegetables, but in an emergency (of weather, for instance) it might also include cultivation and harvesting in the fields that were normally worked only by the tenants. If the crop was in danger, the monastery stood to lose its share. However, even in an emergency the monks could only lend a hand on fields that lay nearby. As we are about to see, in many cases the bulk of the land lay dozens of miles away, and it would have been impractical for the monks to go there. Then there were some institutions that regularly cultivated nearby fields with hired labor. This was the case at Ch'i-hsia Shan, at Chin Shan, and at Ku Shan near Foochow. It could well give rise to statements that monks farmed their own land. In fact, however, only one or two monks were involved in such cultivation and all they did was to supervise the labor of others.[18] So, while we cannot say that there were no monks in China who raised what they ate before 1950, it was certainly exceptional. In almost all cases where monasteries owned farmland, they leased it out and lived on the rents.

LAND RENTS

In China as one moved from province to province, or even from township to township, the form of land tenure changed, the system of rent collection changed, the taxes changed, the weights changed. I have collected materials to draw reasonably full economic portraits of four landowning monasteries, three of them in Kiangsu. But even for those in Kiangsu the differences outweigh the similarities, so that generalization about the monastic economy in this one province (let alone the remainder of China) is dangerous. One can say little more than that these and a few other rich monasteries each owned hundreds of acres in widely scattered plots that were cultivated by tenants who paid a fixed quantity of rice in winter and of wheat or barley in spring.

It is easier to generalize about economic trends. During the Republican period the imbalance between land and population increased. Population growth had passed the point where more hands meant proportionately higher production. The old ways to supplement a declining income (through handicrafts and cottage industries) were being undermined by cheap foreign goods and urban industrialization. Intermittent civil warfare from 1911 onwards not only damaged crops and tools, but imposed higher taxes on a lower income—lower because hostilities interfered with transport from farm to market, if not with production itself. This depressed the value of land in some areas, while in other areas land values were bid up by new urban capital seeking a secondary outlet in the countryside.

The discontent that was therefore growing among the peasantry was fanned and exploited by various groups who hoped to use it as the motive power of political change. Landlords, especially Buddhist monasteries (because of the antireligious movement that was launched in 1922), found it increasingly difficult to collect their rents. This difficulty rose a step in 1926, as the Communists moved into the countryside, and another step in 1937, when the Japanese occupied the urban centers, but left much of the countryside in the hands of guerrillas. Thereafter, even more than before, the further land lay from the city, the more difficult the landlord found it to collect his rents and transport them safely to the market or warehouse. His income varied not only with the time, but with the place.

Even for a given time and place we have little in the way of hard facts. Not one of the monks that I interviewed was able to bring ledger books along with him when he left China. The best memory is liable to anachronisms and confusion when it recalls thirty years of constant change. I have had to be satisfied with approximations. Yet, paradoxically enough, these may be more reliable than what I would have obtained if I had gone to the China mainland in the Republican period to investigate monasteries as "going concerns." At that time, I suspect, no outsider would have been given frank information about monastic finances. Even now, when it all lies in the past, I have sometimes been treated like a "revenooer" from Peking. A former abbot of the T'ien-ning Ssu, for example, began our interview by asking me how much I was being paid a month to study Buddhist monasteries. I replied rather lamely that "we foreigners do not like to talk about our income much." Later in the conversation I asked about his monastery's landholdings. His answer was that since I refused to talk about my pay, he would refuse to talk about their land.

Some people say that the T'ien-ning Ssu had ten thousand acres. A layman who was brought up about fifteen miles away had an impression that it owned half the county. The question was finally settled by the abbot who headed the monastery before the Japanese occupation and was the dharma master of the abbot just mentioned. He told me that, in fact, it owned only about 1,300 acres. This would still give it the largest landed income of all the Chinese Buddhist monasteries I know about.[19] Since it also carried on the most varied and intricate financial operations, it deserves our attention on several counts. But it seems appropriate that our first example of the monastic economy should be Chin Shan, so that we may complete the picture of that model monastery whose other aspects have already been described at such length. We shall then discuss Ch'i-hsia Shan (since it had some characteristics of a place of pilgrimage) and finally give a brief account of one monastery outside Kiangsu province, the Chin-shan Ssu in Szechwan. All this will involve a wealth of detail, but where generalization is difficult, it seems best to use the "case method." The non-specialist reader may find that one case is enough and prefer to skip from p. 228 to the end of the chapter.

CHIN SHAN

The Chin-shan Ssu in Kiangsu (that is, the Chiang-t'ien Ssu at Chin Shan in Chen-chiang, usually referred to in this book as "Chin Shan") offered Chinese Buddhists a model of religious practice largely on the basis of its land rents. Though it did not own as much acreage as the T'ien-ning Ssu, its holdings were still considerable—some 4,800 *mou* (hereafter we shall use the Chinese unit because, although usually equivalent to about a sixth of an acre, it varied from place to place). Only about two percent of these 4,800 *mou* lay in the monastery's home district of Chen-chiang. Indeed the best land was the farthest away. This was the 1,400 *mou* in T ai-chou[20] which was perhaps one hundred kilometers' journey by the inland waterways. The leaseholds there were large. Averaging about 35 *mou*, the tenants were able to make a good living, and Chin Shan had excellent relations with them. They paid their rents readily and in grain of such good quality that the monks seldom had to have it run through the winnowing machine again before weighing it (whereas in other areas tenants would try to build up the weight with impurities). The monastery, for its part, provided each of them with a large, ox-driven water pump and paid for its maintenance and repair. But all other tools, here as elsewhere, were owned by the tenants.

In T'ai-chou, the village office was left locked between seasons. No monk had to be stationed there as village agent. It was looked after by two of the tenants who lived on either side of it and were loyal and dependable. Every spring and autumn the prior would send his staff to collect the rents, not only for Chin Shan, but on behalf of two associated monasteries that also had land in the area. The rents they collected would be stored there in the village office until prices reached their peak in March or April, then sold.[21]

There was quite a different situation in Yang-chung, about 40 kilometers from the monastery. There Chin Shan had almost as much land (1,350 *mou*), but it was in smaller lots (3-10 *mou* per tenant). These were too small either for the landlord to provide water pumps or for the tenants to make a decent living. (The average farm household in Kiangsu worked 17 *mou*.)[22] Since the Yang-chung tenants were very poor, they were also very troublesome, repeatedly balking at paying the rents agreed to, and in 1928 refusing to pay them altogether. Because they were so troublesome (in 1913 they had even burned the village office to the ground), a monk was kept stationed there as village agent, whose duty it was to guard the monastery's property and to expedite the shipment of its grain.

The tenants to the northwest in Yangchow were also troublesome, but since the holdings amounted to only 300 *mou* and could quickly be reached by river steamer, there was only a lay "village foreman" rather than a monk. The same was true in I-cheng, equally accessible, where Chin Shan had 1,400 *mou*.[23] The tenants there were cooperative and the monastery provided them with pumps.

Except for the land in Yang-chung, which was a grant from the Ch'ing government, all these holdings had been gradually purchased out of surplus income. Most of the choice acreage in T'ai-chou, for example, had been bought during the last years of the nineteenth century. In the 1930's purchases were still being made there, usually at a price of over one hundred silver dollars a *mou*, on which there was a transfer tax of about ten percent. With a disposable income worth $20,000 a year, it is not difficult to see how Chin Shan, already rich, grew richer.

Although it held no mortgages, much of its land (the 1,400 *mou* in I-cheng, for instance) was under "perpetual lease" (*yung-tsu*). This meant that the monastery only had the "right of ownership," not the "right of cultivation." In other words, legally it could force tenants to pay their rent, but not to vacate the property. Tenants, for their part, could sell the right of cultivation to new tenants without getting Chin Shan's permission—despite the fact that Chin Shan was the registered owner. The reader who is interested in the details of this system will find them in Appendix VII.

Rental agreements in all cases were in the form of a written pledge, that bore a date, but no term.[24] It ran until one of the two parties wished to cancel it. In such a pledge, the tenant accepted the lease of so many *mou* of land and agreed to pay a rent of so many *tan*[25] of paddy (unhusked rice) and so many *tan* of wheat or barley. In T'ai-chou the total production per *mou* ran about three *tan* of paddy in a good year, of which the monastery took one *tan*. In other words, the rent there was about a third of the crop. But it was not calculated as such. Chin Shan had no share cropping leases anywhere.[26] Hence a tenant could not lower his rent by falsifying his production figure. If he had leased ten *mou* for ten *tan*, he had to deliver the ten *tan*. If he defaulted, the monastery was usually protected in one of two ways. Either it had gotten a deposit on the rent (*ya-tsu*) or it could look to the persons who had signed the rental agreement as guarantors. If they too defaulted, it could call on the *hsien* government to enforce collection. The agreement usually contained a clause in which the tenant asked that in case of waterlogging or drought, the monastery inspect the fields, but since the monastery did not sign the agreement, it was under no obligation to do so. On the other hand, its interest was obviously in maintaining good relations wherever possible. If most of the tenants in an area complained that natural disasters had made the original rental excessive, the monastery would investigate and try to make a fair adjustment.

By these methods Chin Shan in an ideal year collected about 4,000 *tan* of paddy from the autumn harvest. The T'ai-chou paddy was kept there and sold, as we have noted; most of the rents from other areas were shipped back to the monastery to be consumed by its 300-400 residents. Shipment was made on Chin Shan's two boats, propelled by oar or sail as the wind allowed. There was also a summer harvest of wheat (*hsiao-mai*) and barley (*ta-mai*). About 700 *tan* of barley were collected and sold in T'ai-chou, while 450 *tan* of wheat were dispatched to the monastery from I-cheng and elsewhere. Perhaps a third of the latter was used to make bread (*man-t'ou*), noodles, and dumplings, while all the rest was sold. The proceeds from the sale of barley and wheat were enough to cover the taxes (*t'ien-fu*) that Chin Shan had to pay on its land. These varied from district to district. They were twice as high in I-cheng as in T'ai-chou though T'ai-chou yielded a higher income. Other monasteries too (the T'ien-ning Ssu, for example) operated on the rule-of-thumb that secondary production should normally cover the land tax.[27]

In a poor year rents might drop to 2,000 *tan* of rice and in a disastrous year (like 1928) Chin Shan demanded no rents at all in some areas. But this did not mean that its residents went hungry. There were normally 4,000-5,000 *tan* of grain in the storerooms at the monastery—enough to feed them all for three years. Even at the end of the troubled 1940's Chin Shan still had in store some 3,000 *tan* of unhusked rice and 1,000 *tan* of wheat. Every year these would be taken out and dried in the sun. The oldest paddy (perhaps four or five years old) was consumed as cooked rice, while the new crop was used for making congee, which was better for its fresh aroma.

Grain rents were not the only income Chin Shan received from its land. Across a small creek it had 3,000 *mou* of brushland (*ts'ao-ti*), on which grew a kind of reed (*lu-ch'ai*) that made excellent firewood. It was harvested on shares by lay workmen under the supervision of the business office. The monastery's share was stored, some to be used in the kitchen as fuel and some to be sold in summer when the prices were high.

Chin Shan received only negligible income from donations. There were several restaurants outside the gate and it was to these that most of the casual visitors would go for a meal after seeing the sights of the monastery. They were not allowed to spend the night. There was no donations box in the great shrine-hall. Coppers given to the verger were considered his own income. The post was considered particularly onerous and was usually assigned to a monk who needed the money. As to revenue from rites for the dead, between 1924 and 1937 ten plenary masses used to be held each year. The charge was $1,200, which included installation and "perpetual care" of tablets in the *shui-lu t'ang* (there was no *wang-sheng t'ang*).[28] It was also possible to have tablets installed there for a simple lump-sum payment of $100, without any plenary mass. But very few laymen did this. Sometimes years would go by without its happening.

While my informants were able to work out a fairly complete reconstruction of monastic revenues, they threw up their hands when it came to disbursements. The abbot of Chin Shan, for instance, who furnished most of the income figures given above, could recall only a few scattered figures on the expense side of the ledger. This may be partly because for twenty years (1924-1945) he was mainly in charge of administering the landholdings, first as a subprior and then as the prior. His concern was the debit not the credit side of the ledger.

The largest block of cash income, he said, was received in early spring from the sale of grain in T'ai-chou. Some of it was spent at once on supplies (especially those needed for maintenance and repair). Some of it went to pay the land tax. The rest was deposited with money shops (*ch'ien-chuang*) in neighboring Chen-chiang. Chin Shan had no traffic with public banks controlled by the government. It preferred the customary way of doing things. Money shops paid interest of one-half percent[29] per month and, despite occasional failures, were fairly reliable.

The money so deposited was kept to buy land whenever a good bargain came on the market and to meet any unusual expenses. Most of the day-to-day expenses were met by sale of wheat. Of the 450 *tan* of wheat received in rent, about 300 *tan* were surplus and could be sold in small batches as cash was needed through the year. Presumably

42. The roofs of Chin Shan, seen from the pagoda—enough to keep a crew of ten tilers busy throughout the year. Chen-chiang.

a portion of the other income, like the profits on plenary masses, was also used as cash to meet current expenses. Cash was used by the business office to buy commodities like oil, salt, incense, tea, candles, matches, kerosene, and toilet paper, among which the first two items were the most expensive. (Chin Shan used annually 140 *tan* of oil.) But the largest expenditures were on maintenance and repair. A crew of ten carpenters and ten tilers were kept working through the year except at the times for sowing and harvesting, when they were allowed to return home. Each of them was paid 20 cents a day—yes, admitted the abbot, a very low wage (it would have been $1.00 a day in Shanghai), but the monastery fed and housed them. All these figures, of course, held good only prior to 1937, when serious inflation began.

Chin Shan suffered greatly not only from the inflation, but also from the civil unrest that came when the Japanese occupied Kiangsu. This was because it depended so much on its land, as the reader may see from the following figures:

Estimated income of Chin Shan in a good year
before 1937

Sale of 1,500 *tan* of paddy @ 4	$ 6,000
Sale of 700 *tan* of barley @ 4	2,800
Sale of 300 *tan* of wheat @ 7	2,100
Sale of surplus firewood, cut on shares	2,000
Profit on ten plenary masses	5,000
Miscellaneous income	300
	$18,200[30]

These figures indicate that two thirds of Chin Shan's cash income came from its land. But land provided an even higher proportion of its real income, since this would include the value of the 1,500 *tan* of paddy consumed at the monastery and of a similar 150 *tan* of wheat. With these counted in, nearly four fifths of its real income came from its land, and most of the land lay at a distance.

This meant that its economy was particularly vulnerable. As civil unrest grew, rents became difficult to collect and even more difficult to transport, and the unrest had begun long before the Japanese occupation. We have already mentioned the trouble that started at Yang-chung in 1928. That was a bad year in many areas. (There was a drought in T'ai-chou and a plague of locusts in I-cheng.) But the harvest in Yang-chung was passable. Nonetheless the tenants there refused to pay their rents. They claimed that the land belonged to them and so did its produce. After they had withheld three crops over a two-year period—the autumn rice crop, the summer wheat crop, and a second rice crop—Chin Shan complained to the provincial government. The government set up an *ad hoc* Tenancy Arbitration Committee chaired by Ho Yü-shu, head of the provincial Bureau of Agriculture and Mines. Though it included no one representing Chin Shan, it quickly decided that the rents should be collected and sent in a company of troops to do so. They demanded payment; the tenants still refused. So after a brief skirmish the troops arrested a hundred or more of them and held them until the grain was handed over to the monastery. This was embarrassing for the monks, who regarded it as a "barbarous way of handling the matter." In their view the tenants were certainly troublesome, but that was because they were poor—and because they had been stirred up by Communist instigators.

But it was not only Communist instigators that caused trouble like this. It was the popularity of new ideas being espoused, theoretically, by the government itself. As Fei Hsiao-t'ung wrote in 1938:

> Recently the situation has been changing. The economic depression in the rural district has made rent a heavy burden on the peasant and the income derived from the rent much more vulnerable for the landlord. The peasants are more susceptible to new ideas . . . "Those who till the land should have the land" is a principle laid down by the late Dr. Sun Yat-sen and accepted, at least theoretically, by the present government. A more extreme view is spreading among the Communists and other Left groups . . . Peasants unable to pay rent now feel justified in neglecting to do so, and those who are able to pay will wait and see if they are compelled to do so.[31]

This corresponds perfectly with the information furnished by the officers of landowning monasteries. New difficulties were added in 1937. The Japanese occupation forces controlled only the urban centers. The countryside fell increasingly into the hands of bandits and rival guerrilla bands. Bandits seized grain in shipment, and guerrillas imposed "taxes." Nationalist guerrillas would collect the land tax in a district and then Communist guerrillas would collect it again. By about 1940 the taxes imposed on Chin Shan's land in T'ai-chou (its choicest 1,400 *mou*) began to exceed the rents. For that reason the monastery suspended rent collection there and let the tax-collectors settle directly with the tenants. This cut off its largest source of cash income.

Grain rent from other areas, which was usually consumed at the monastery, also dropped off, although not so much as it would have if most of Chin Shan's holdings had not lain close to the principal waterways, which were secured by the Japanese. Only in Yangchow were there collection difficulties. Income from the sale of firewood held up well, since the brushland adjoined the monastery. But income from rites for the dead ceased altogether. From 1937 to 1945 not one plenary mass was said at Chin Shan. Laymen either did not have the money or were afraid to make the trip to the monastery because of bandits and guerrillas on the roads. The total income dropped to subsistence level. After victory in 1945, it partially recovered, but four years later came the Communists and land reform.

CH'I-HSIA SHAN

Ch'i-hsia Shan was the monastery restored by Tsung-yang in 1919 (see p. 159). Although it ordained one or two hundred monks every spring, it had no meditation hall. The atmosphere was not so strict and old-fashioned as at Chin Shan. Both monasteries lay on the main railway line between Nanking and Shanghai, but Ch'i-hsia Shan was a much shorter walk from the station. Furthermore, it offered more "sights"—interesting caves and carvings, and a pagoda connected with the Sui Emperor Wen-ti. For all these reasons, it attracted a much larger number of casual visitors than Chin Shan, although it was a much smaller monastery (see Plate 4).

It had lost its farmland as well as its buildings in the T'ai-p'ing rebellion. The deeds had been burned along with everything else. How could it prove ownership? So new landholdings had to be gradually acquired in the thirty years after it was restored in 1919. About half the acquisitions were made in the first decade and the other half in the second and third. Some were donated: most were purchased out of surplus income. In about 1939, for example, parcels totaling 262 *mou* were presented by a nun, Hsiu-hui. Ch'i-hsia Shan was trying to start its seminary then and needed additional rents to do so. Hsiu-hui had been a rich laywoman who built and endowed a small temple for herself with a great deal of land. Since she had more than she needed and Ch'i-hsia Shan less, she donated some of her surplus to promote monastic education.

Besides the 1,400 *mou* that it owned outright, the monastery held a perpetual lease on 420 *mou* near Chiang-ning. This land had belonged to Ch'i-hsia Shan before the T'ai-p'ing rebellion. When the monastery was destroyed, the monks scattered and no one came to collect the rents. The peasants continued to cultivate it, but "the land was without a master." This continued for several decades until the Education Bureau of the Chiang-ning district took over the rents and ownership to support the new school system. After the monastery was restored in 1919, it applied to recover the land. The local authorities, of course, refused. But it kept trying and finally, with the help of Lin Hsiang, the head of the Supreme Court,[32] it won a compromise. The Chiang-ning Education Bureau agreed to lease the land in perpetuity to Ch'i-hsia Shan for a rent of $300-400 a year. The monastery, in turn, received the usual rents from the tenants, which were worth $1,500-1,600 a year. Thus in a good year it made a clear profit of $1,200, but in a very bad year it would have to pay the Education Bureau out of its own pocket. This shows what a monastery could do, even in un-friendly times, if it had the right connections.

Ch'i-hsia Shan's 1,400 *mou* were mostly in very small, scattered parcels.[33] This made it both troublesome to collect the rents and not worthwhile to maintain any village offices. Fortunately two thirds of the land lay within three miles of the monastery. The tenants delivered the grain to its door. On the other hand, 266 *mou* lay outside the south gate of Nanking about fifteen miles away and 271 *mou* lay in T'ung-ching, 25 miles up the Yangtze River beyond Nanking. Here the absence of village offices where grain could be collected and stored resulted in a very different collection system from Chin Shan. The officers sent out to collect would try to sell the grain back to the tenants. If the tenants would not buy, then local dealers were ap-proached. One way or another it was disposed of on the spot and only cash was brought back to the monastery. Much less cash was received this way than if Ch'i-hsia Shan had stored the grain until prices reached their peak in spring, but it was spared the expense and trouble of maintaining village offices, which, according to the abbot, were only worthwhile if one had 700-800 *mou* concentrated in one area.

The system of land tenure also differed from Chin Shan—a remark-able fact in view of their proximity. In the area where the Ch'i-hsia Ssu had its land, only a little to the west of Chin Shan's, "tillage rights" could not be bought and sold separately from the "rights of ownership." The landlord owned both surface and subsoil. He could expel a tenant for failure to pay the rent. A fixed quantity of rent was specified in leases, but it was apparently a little higher than for Chin Shan: 125 *chin* to the *mou*. On the other hand, abatement in a bad year seems to have been more liberal. When monastery and tenant disagreed on the percentage of abatement, the village head (*ts'un-chang*) would arbitrate. He would suggest a cut of 20, 30, or 40 percent, and reason with both sides in favor of it. Usually both sides accepted. ("It was always the landlord," the abbot said with a sigh, "who came out with the short end of the stick"—although I suppose that if I had interviewed tenants rather than officers of the monastery, I would have heard the opposite complaint.) Ch'i-hsia Shan never took any of its tenants to court because none of them ever flatly refused to pay his rent as did Chin Shan's tenants in Yang-chung.

Also unlike Chin Shan, it used to make mortgage loans. It loaned up to 50 percent of the market value of the piece of land. The borrower paid interest in the form of either cash or grain. For example, on the security of five *mou*, worth $500, a farmer would borrow $250 and pay interest of five *tan* of paddy per year. The interest rate was thus the same as the rent: one *tan* per *mou* equivalent to about 8 percent a year.[34] If the borrower could not pay back the principal when it was due (usually after three years), he would either renew the loan or offer to sell the land to the monastery. The monastery would have to pay the difference between market value and what it had already advanced. Thus in the example we have just mentioned, it would pay the borrower $250.

Why make this additional payment? The loan was in default. Why not foreclose the mortgage and get title for nothing, as would any self-respecting oppressor of widows and orphans in the United States? Because, I was told, in China it could not be done that way. There was no right of foreclosure (in these areas of Kiangsu province, at least). The borrower had to receive full value for his property. The "hitch" was that the value had not been specified in the loan agreement. So, when the time came, the debtor and creditor had to work it out on the basis of fairness and that indefinable thing called *kan-ch'ing*—"feelings" (a sense, that is, of what each side owed the other on the basis of favors exchanged in the past, or as we might say, "being human about it"). Fuzzy and improbable as this sounds, it fits in with the rest of the system, where so little was done by the letter of the law and so much by custom and compromise.[35]

Unfortunately the former abbot of Ch'i-hsia Shan could not recall and would not estimate the income that it received in the form of interest. Other forms, however, he was quite ready to give figures on. In a good year, he said, the total grain rents received amounted to about 1,200 *tan* of paddy, of which about 870 *tan* were required to feed the two hundred residents of the monastery. The remaining 330 were sold. From the summer harvest of wheat and barley about 100 *tan* were sold. In a poor year production per *mou* might be halved, and rents would drop proportionately. The monastery would then have to reduce its reconstruction program and perhaps buy rice with cash it received from other sources. It did not have large stores of grain like Chin Shan.

In a good year the surplus paddy could be sold for about $1,300 and the wheat and barley for about $400. Much larger revenues were based on side-line production. Brushwood (*mao-ts'ao*) from extensive holdings of hillside land (*shan-ti*) was sold on shares. The farmers who came to cut it would give perhaps a half to the monastery, which thereby avoided the trouble of close supervision of their work. Some of this brushwood was used in the monastery kitchen and kiln. The rest was converted to charcoal and sold. The kiln produced bricks, tiles, and lime, of which part was sold and part was utilized in rebuilding the monastery. Over twenty lay workmen were employed in side-line production. They were given their rice and a small share of the materials they produced, but no cash. Wages in cash as well as in rice were paid to the hundred carpenters, masons, and tilers who worked at Ch'i-hsia Shan for almost twenty years, restoring the monastery to the size and splendor it had had before the T'ai-p'ing rebellion. A good portion of their cash wages could be met from the sale of the side-line products, which brought in $5,000 a year. Another $5,000 worth of these materials was used at the monastery, more than half of whose real income went into rebuilding.

Ch'i-hsia Shan, as we have already noted, was a popular place for an outing, particularly in the pleasant weather of spring and autumn. Many visitors stopped for a meal, sometimes dozens in a day, sometimes hundreds. They were not presented with a bill, but usually volunteered to pay about twice as much as the meal would have cost in a restaurant. Since most of what they ate was produced in the monastery fields and garden, their donations were largely clear profit and amounted to about $3,000 a year. Donations on a larger scale were made by Buddhist lay devotees for a variety of meritorious purposes: to provide a vegetarian feast, "to show reverence to the monks," "to thank the establishment," and so on. They totaled perhaps $2,000 and reached their peak during the spring ordination, when lay people who had ordered plenary masses were staying at the monastery. Three or four plenary masses were recited during the thirty-odd days of the ordination ceremonies. The charge for each was $2,000, of which about $800 were paid to the celebrants as their fees (*tan-ch'ien*) and $200 went for paper figures, incense, and the like. Thus in terms of attracting revenue ordination played the same role as the birthday of the patron deity at a famous center of pilgrimage.[36] Buddhist services other than plenary masses, of which only a very few were held in the course of the year, brought in $1,000 or so. About the same sum was received as lump-sum payments for new soul tablets in the hall of rebirth. Finally there were the coins dropped by visitors in various donations boxes. They were opened once a month and usually found to contain $80-120.

Estimated income of Ch'i-hsia Shan in
a good year before 1937

Income from property

Sale of 330 *tan* @ $4	$1,320	
Sale of 100 *tan* barley and wheat @ $4	400	
Sale of brushwood, charcoal, bricks, tiles, lime	5,000	
Interest on mortgages (arbitrary figure)	880	
Profit on land leased from Education Bureau	1,200	
Total		$ 8,800

Income from laity

Donations by patrons of restaurant	$3,000	
Donations by Buddhist devotees	2,000	
Profit on three plenary masses	3,000	
Profit on other Buddhist services	1,000	
Payment for soul tablets	1,000	
Donations boxes	1,200	
Total		$11,200
Grand Total		$20,000

In giving these figures, I have tried to make the best of frequent self-contradictions—or what appeared to be self-contradictions—in the abbot's testimony. Not too much reliance should be placed on any one entry in the table just provided. Income from laity amounted to over 50 percent of cash income, but considering the value of products consumed at the monastery, including $4,000 worth of grain, it amounted to under 40 percent of real income. Like Chin Shan, Ch'i-hsia Shan did not depend so much on lay support as on its own fields, garden, and workshops. In a way, it was more self-sufficient than Chin Shan, since it produced not only its own food, but a large part of the building materials that were needed to maintain and expand its plant. Nor was it so seriously affected by the Japanese occupation. Lay support did drop off: there were fewer visitors and no plenary masses. But most of its landholdings were nearby and none were in guerrilla areas like T'ai-chou. Its landed income scarcely declined at all.

T'IEN-NING SSU

Of all the monasteries I know of, the one that was most severely affected by civil unrest and foreign invasion was the one that had the most to lose: the T'ien-ning Ssu in Changchow. This monastery with its 800 monks and 8,000 *mou* was the largest monastic establishment in Republican China; or at any rate it is commonly described as such[37] and I have heard of none larger. It had been destroyed in the T'ai-p'ing rebellion and was gradually rebuilt on its present scale in the last decades of the Ch'ing dynasty. Much of the credit goes to Yeh-k'ai, its illustrious abbot and meditation master, and to an overseer who served under him. This overseer, Kao-lang, is said to have saved every copper —even letting new buildings lie unfinished—in order to have money to buy more land.

Except for its size the T'ien-ning Ssu had little to attract visitors. There was nothing remarkable in its scenery, art, or architecture except, perhaps, for its hall of five hundred lohans. It lay in flat country on the outskirts of Changchow, a large city on the same Nanking-Shanghai railway line that ran past Chin Shan and Ch'i-hsia Shan. Just in front of the main gate was a landing on one of the inland waterways that form a network over that part of Kiangsu. Grain rents could be easily unloaded from the monastery boats.

Besides its meditation hall, which was considered one of the four best in China, the T'ien-ning Ssu had sections not found in other monasteries, as may be seen from the following list (in which the figures probably represent peak rather than average enrollment).

1. Meditation hall with 130 monks
2. Hall for reciting buddha's name with 35 monks
3. Scripture chamber (*ching-lou*) with 50 monks (see p. 103)
4. Seminary (*fo-hsüeh yüan*) with 150 monks
5. Hall for monks who were blind or otherwise disabled (*an-le t'ang*) with 45 monks
6. Sanatorium (*yen-shou t'ang*, separate from the infirmary or *ju-i liao*) with 20 monks, including outsiders in need of long-term treatment
7. Halls for the aged (*tung-t'a yüan, hsi-t'a yüan*) with 60 monks over 60 years old
8. Wandering monks hall (*yün-shui t'ang*) with 60 monks

Add to these about 100 officers and perhaps 150 monks living in retirement and we reach the figure of 800, besides which there were 200 lay workmen to be fed and housed—a total of a thousand souls.

Grain rents were sufficient to feed them and still leave 5,000 *tan* of paddy for sale and 1,000 *tan* of wheat to pay the taxes. All of T'ien-ning's 8,000 *mou* lay in the adjacent *hsien*, but none of it close to the monastery. Rents were collected by weight, not by volume as elsewhere. They averaged 130 *chin* to the *mou* (1 *tan* 3 *tou*); less on land purchased at an early date and more on land purchased later. Rents were collected more rigidly than at Chin Shan and Ch'i-hsia Shan. The business office paid no attention to complaints of flood or drought. If a tenant wanted his rent reduced, he could apply to the *hsien* authorities. It was for them to decide whether there should be an abatement in a bad year. Unless they ordered otherwise, the T'ien-ning Ssu went out to collect the amount of grain specified in the lease —and no nonsense about it! It furnished its tenants no tools and did not concern itself with their houses, water supply, and so on. If tenants refused to pay, it would ask for help from the heads of townships, districts, or villages (*hsiang-chang, ch'ü-chang, li-chang*). Under their persuasion about 70 percent of the delinquents would deliver the grain they owed. About 30 percent would not. Some tenants had not paid their rent for years or for decades. Some had never paid it. The T'ien-ning Ssu did not like to take them to court. For one thing, a monastery was supposed to be a compassionate organization. For another thing, the courts favored the poor and would seldom rule against them (according to the abbot). All the monastery could do was try to evict the bad tenants and lease the land to good ones. In many cases it succeeded, partly because the leases were not "perpetual" as in I-cheng to the west and Changshu to the east.

Whereas other monasteries sold their surplus grain to dealers as unhusked paddy, the T'ien-ning Ssu sold it as polished rice to individual customers. Only what the latter could not absorb went to dealers. Its customers were the patrons of the monastery (*hu-fa*) in Changchow, who liked to buy its rice because it was very dry and very clean. So annually these families would order what they needed for the year (usually 30 to 50 *tan*) and then send a chit whenever they wanted to draw on the order. It would be freshly milled by the monastery's workmen. This meant more work and more equipment, but a higher price.

Not only rent grain was sold at retail this way, but interest grain too. The reader may recall that Ch'i-hsia Shan loaned money on mortgages and received grain as interest. The T'ien-ning Ssu did the same, but on a much larger scale. Its income from loans equaled its income from land. In all, borrowers paid interest of 5,000 *tan* a year. About half of this was called *kan-tsu* ("quasi-rent") and was received on loans made before 1912. About half was called *huo-t'ien* ("live fields") and was received on loans made after 1912. The reader who is interested in the details will find them in Appendix VIII. With a few exceptions, these loans were made only to tenants, secured by land they owned apart from the land they rented from the monastery. Because the monastery was sensitive to the accusation of usury, it was satisfied with a low rate (15-16 percent per annum for the *kan-tsu*). Many of the loans had been outstanding since the nineteenth century. Delinquent interest was more difficult to collect than delinquent rent. This was because, unlike the tenant, the mortgagor could not be forced off his land so that it could be rented to someone else. Though the monastery held the deed, the mortgagor still had the title. In some cases the local authorities refused to apply pressure. If so, the monastery would take whatever it could get in principal and interest, and write off the rest.

Besides its operations as landowner and money lender, the T'ien-ning Ssu was in the grain business. It loaned, bought, and sold paddy and rice. Loans of paddy were short-term and restricted to tenants.

If a tenant borrowed two *tan* of paddy this year, he would have to pay back two *tan* four *tou* next year (which meant interest of 20 percent per annum); or he could pay off the loan in polished rice or soybeans or some other product to the equivalent value. When a tenant lacked a market, the monastery was ready to provide one. It would buy his paddy after the harvest (about October 23-November 7) for the going price, perhaps $3 a *tan,* and store it until prices reached their peak in spring, perhaps $4-5 a *tan.* Then it would be milled and sold to the monastery's customers.[38] Loans and dealings in paddy each brought in a net income of about $5,000 a year. Such business operations were permitted by the Vinaya rules so long as they were carried out not for personal gain, but for the advancement of the dharma.[39]

Rites for the dead brought in another $10,000 a year. There was no set charge for performing them. The charge varied with the circumstances and the donor. Often it was paid in oil or in rice. For a plenary mass a donor might be expected to give 100-300 *tan* of rice, worth $1,000-3,000. This is comparable to the fees at other monasteries. I received the impression that minor rites for the dead ("releasing the burning mouths" and penance services) were performed more readily at the T'ien-ning Ssu than at Ch'i-hsia or Chin Shan. If so, it might have been because of the monastery's constant need to augment its sources of income. Despite its vast holdings of paddy fields, it had no brush or hill land. It had to buy its firewood, which cost about $3,000 a year. Since there was no side-line production, it also had to buy its building materials. The expense of maintaining a monastery that housed a thousand persons was enormous. Aside from maintenance there were the usual staples to be bought. Making beancurd alone required 30,000 catties of soybeans. There was a payroll to be met. All the teachers at the primary school it ran and some of the teachers at its seminary were laymen on salaries.

To meet these expenses, the only sources of income were land and rites for the dead. Ordinary donations were negligible, since there were few casual visitors. Not only did the monastery have little to attract them, but it made no effort to entertain them. Time spent on their entertainment meant less time for its proper activities. The T'ien-ning Ssu did not look to others for support, perhaps because support on the scale required for such a huge establishment would never have been forthcoming. It supported itself.

The abbot recalled that until 1937 its cash income ran from sixty to seventy thousand silver dollars a year, and in the course of successive conversations, he broke it down in different ways. His final breakdown, which is the basis of the figures given above, was as follows:

Land rents	$20,000
Interest on loans of money	20,000
Interest on loans of paddy	5,000
Dealings in paddy	5,000
Buddhist services	10,000
	$60,000

These figures are even more approximate, I think, than those given by the abbots of Chin Shan and the Ch'i-hsia Ssu. One reason is that T'ien-ning's economy was more in a state of flux and different phases tended to run together in the abbot's memory. There was a point beyond which persistent questioning became offensive. What is clear is that at an early date the senior monks grew skeptical about investment in land. The times were too unsettled. Too many unfriendly ideas were in the air. Proposals that the government confiscate all monastic landholdings had been broached repeatedly, starting in 1898. The T'ien-ning Ssu was already a large landholder. Why make it even more of a target for confiscation? In 1927 after the Northern Expedition, said the abbot, Communists began to infiltrate the rural areas where its land lay. They made propaganda and urged the tenants not to pay their rents. "People's attitude became bad." Furthermore, lay Buddhist patrons no longer had the same influence with the new government.[40] The monastery therefore began cutting down on land purchases and new mortgage loans. After 1931 it made no purchases or loans at all, except where the land involved filled a gap among the plots it had already. It directed its efforts instead toward recovering principal on loans in default. Whatever principal could be recovered was spent partly for upkeep and current expenses and partly invested as working capital to finance its dealings in paddy. No money was deposited in banks. Paddy was safer.

The consequences of Japanese occupation were even more serious for the T'ien-ning Ssu than for Chin Shan. Income from rites for the dead dropped off. Paper money had already ceased to be convertible into silver and now inflation began.[41] At the same time landed income

—the usual safeguard against inflation—declined. The monastery's grain rents had to be brought by boat through narrow inland waterways over distances of up to thirty kilometers. The landholdings were not so scattered as Chin Shan's, but none lay in secure areas accessible by secure routes. Bandits and guerrillas started to seize shipments. Because of the administrative vacuum in the countryside, the Communists, whose operations had once been clandestine, now came out in the open. About 1941, monks sent out to collect the rents began to be attacked. A subprior, a weigher, and a bookkeeper were murdered. The total of the rents collected had been dropping at the rate of perhaps 5 percent a year. Now it dropped more sharply. Rents ceased to be enough to feed the monastery.

Some of the workmen were dismissed and monks worked in their places (on the vegetable garden, for instance). A far more important step, however, was taken by the former abbot, who had retired in 1938. In 1941 he went to Shanghai, leased a building in the French concession, and set up a sub-temple, the Chuang-yen Ssu, in order to earn additional income, especially from the rich Changchow families who had moved to Shanghai "for the duration." Forty-eight monks transferred to it. They performed penance services, "fed the burning mouths," and chanted sutras. Assisted by thirty lay workmen, they served an average of forty tables of vegetarian food a day. At ten persons per table, this meant four hundred "customers." All the profits were remitted to the parent monastery in Changchow, so that it would have money to buy rice. The establishment of the sub-temple showed resourcefulness. Since lay patrons could no longer come to the monastery to have services performed, the services were brought to them. Beating a wooden fish for a dollar a day was not in T'ien-ning's best tradition, but it was better than closing down the seminary or the meditation hall.

Victory in 1945 did not restore order in the countryside around Changchow. Communist influence remained. Tenants still had a "bad attitude," refused to pay their rents, and nothing could be done about it. Income from land stayed low while the price of goods continued to rise. But even now the monastery did not take the ultimate step of stopping the admission of monks (*chih-tan*). It simply did its best to find new sources of income. It had friends at three different banks who allowed it to overdraw up to $60,000 without security. It would use the overdraft to buy more paddy at a low price in autumn, eat some of it, and sell the rest at a high enough price in spring to repay the loans.[42] A deficit could usually be made up out of the profits from the sub-temple. By such expedients the T'ien-ning Ssu stumbled along until the Communist victory in 1949.

The trend over the preceding decades is clear. Land rents and interest grain declined from a surplus worth perhaps $40,000 a year to the point where they did not cover consumption. Income from dealings in paddy grew from probably less than $5,000 a year to a much larger figure. In one conversation the abbot said that they amounted to $20,000. The monastery had to depend more and more on its activities as a trader. This was not a welcome change. As the abbot said, "being in business—buying and selling—is a thing that the clergy ought not to do." But most of the monks at the T'ien-ning Ssu took no part in the commercial activities that fed them. In the inner parts of the monastery, behind high walls, they were enabled to continue their religious work as usual.

CHIN-SHAN SSU

Our last example of the monastic economy is classically simple. The Chin-shan Ssu in K'ai-chiang, Szechwan, stood on a steep mountain shaped like the character *chin* (hence its name). Around it stretched a rich valley and in this valley were some 6,000 *mou* of the monastery's farmland, mostly acquired by its founder, Te-an, in the Ming dynasty. The abbot could stand on the terrace and survey his domain —none of which lay far from the base of the mountain.

The lease arrangements were quite different from those in Kiangsu. The whole rice harvest went to the monastery except for a quantity large enough to feed the tenant and his family through the year. But the tenant kept the winter harvest of miscellaneous grains for his own use. According to custom, all crops sowed after the sixth month were his. Since the average plot was large, his share of the paddy was presumably a small one,[43] yet he was assured of his livelihood. The system seems to have worked well. My sole informant on the Chin-shan Ssu, who lived there from 1927 to 1933, serving as a subprior in the last two years, had never heard of a tenant refusing to pay his rent.

Under this system the landlord had more of a stake in the crop. In case of natural disaster it was the landlord's share, not the tenant's, that dropped. Therefore if the harvest was threatened by wind or rain or any other agricultural emergency which the tenants had not hands enough to cope with, the business office of the monastery would dispatch as many monks as were needed to help. Once the harvest was in, the monks would stream down from the mountain and carry the bags of grain back up to the storeroom. What could not be eaten was sold.

It was from this monastery that monks used to make an annual begging procession through the streets of the neighboring town (see p. 209). But income from donations was small. There were no forms of side-line production, no mortgage loans, no dealings in paddy, and no rites for the dead. The monastery lived almost entirely on its grain rents, which were more than sufficient to maintain its two or three hundred residents. The surplus was used to buy more land.

CONCLUSIONS

The four monasteries discussed above were very rich. My informants have attributed comparable endowments to only seven others.[44] But there must have been many more. The chances are that any monastery with over 200 monks and not in a metropolis or a center of pilgrimage had better than 1,000 *mou* of farmland. I have heard of at least twenty such monasteries.

The richest were financially independent of the laity. They did not need income from rites for the dead. Yet most of them were ready to perform these rites, partly because it was customary and compassionate, and partly in order to cultivate the friendship of the influential laymen who ordered them. No matter how rich a monastery was, it needed friends to whom it could turn for protection from hostile officials. In fact, the richer it was, the more it needed them.

In contrast to this small group of heavily endowed institutions, most public monasteries in China depended more or less directly on lay support. They had some landed income, but seldom enough to maintain the number of monks they had in residence. Willy-nilly they had to depend on performing rites for the dead, caring for tablets, and attracting pious donations. We have already had occasion to note that the Kao-min Ssu in Yangchow received only enough grain rents to feed its monks for nine months of the year and depended on donors for the rest of its budget. The grain rents of the Nan P'u-t'o Ssu in Amoy were enough for only *three* months. Otherwise it depended 40 percent on Buddhist services and the installation of soul tablets, and 60 percent on pious donations from lay supporters. Overseas Chinese were particularly generous when they visited this, the most famous monastery of their home city. Another case in point is the Ling-yin Ssu near Hangchow. It had almost no farmland but enjoyed a very large income from services and donations. Visitors from Hangchow gave rice, which the monastery would send workmen to collect, while devotees from farther off gave money. Two smaller monasteries in Hangchow are said to have gotten financial support from the local Buddhist Association, and this happened elsewhere too.[45]

Large monasteries on "famous mountains" and other centers of pilgrimage depended, as we have seen, on donations received from laymen who stayed or ate there. Large monasteries in a metropolis (like Shanghai and Nanking) sometimes had a good income not only from rites, but from urban real estate. Others (especially in Peking) were at a low ebb and had to support themselves in part by letting out their empty rooms.

Smaller, hereditary temples whether in city or countryside were far more dependent than the larger institutions on rites for the dead. Many were simply in the funeral business. Of course there were exceptions like the very small, very rich hereditary temple in Kiangsu described in Chapter V (pp. 130-131).

Regardless of size or location, there were few sources of income other than rites, donations, and land. The T'ien-ning Ssu was exceptional. I have yet to hear of any institution, large or small, that functioned as a pawnbroker like Buddhist monasteries during the T'ang and Sung dynasties, or made money by auction sales, lotteries, or mutual financing associations.[46]

The two most important conclusions to be drawn from the facts at hand are: 1) The economic status of a majority of large Buddhist institutions deteriorated in the first half of this century and 2) they came to depend more than ever on lay support. The Ch'ing dynasty had protected their property. Under the Republic what protection the government gave was local and sporadic. Vacant buildings were often confiscated by the authorities and monastic rights to land ownership or rent were violated by peasants against whom the monks had little recourse. In particular, the Japanese occupation and the Communist infiltration of the countryside dealt harsh, sudden blows to landowning monasteries. But even without the Japanese and the Communists, the tide was running against them. Repeated moves toward government confiscation of all monastic property failed only because Buddhism had friends in high enough places to block an idea that was popular with the bureaucracy as a whole. Would they have been able to block it forever? Even if they had, the monasteries faced the threat of land reform. Sun Yat-sen's ideal of "land to the tiller" was being slowly implemented and it made no distinction between a lay landlord whose rents brought luxury to a few, and a monastic landlord whose rents made it possible for hundreds of people to practice religious austerities. Legislation passed in 1930 protected the tenant against eviction for nonpayment of rent (he could not be evicted unless he was two years in arrears) and it limited rent to 37.5 percent of the crop. Even when the lease expired, he could not be evicted unless the landlord was ready to operate the land himself (impractical for a far-off monastery). If the landlord wanted to sell, the tenant had preemptive rights. Since this law was never widely enforced, it had less effect on monasteries than the unrest in the countryside, though it did make land a less attractive investment. In 1942 the earlier law was revised to provide for redistribution of land. The government would purchase it for cash and bonds and sell it to the tenants on an installment plan.[47] Implementation was delayed by the civil war, but it probably would have come eventually. So even if there had been no Communist victory in 1949, it seems likely that the large monasteries would have been left holding paper instead of land, and faced with the choice of going into business like the T'ien-ning Ssu or reducing their activities, closing down their meditation halls, abridging their retirement system, and becoming essentially places for entertainment and funerals.

At the very time that monastic Buddhism was losing its economic base, lay Buddhism was burgeoning. Increasing support from lay devotees in metropolitan areas became available just when it was needed to make up for the decline of landed income. This was one reason for the turning outward of the sangha, the spread of public lectures, charitable activities, and associations of the sangha, just as these were reasons for the burgeoning of lay Buddhism. As monks had to devote more and more time to outside activities, they had less and less time to give to religious cultivation for its own sake.

PART TWO

THE INDIVIDUAL
BUDDHIST

CHAPTER IX

Entering the Sangha

The Chinese term *ch'u-chia* is derived from the Sanskrit *pravrajya*, "going forth." It means "to leave the home," "to renounce lay life." Since the word *chia* means "family" as well as "home," there is also the idea of renouncing the family. In a civilization that was based on family relationships, it is hard to imagine a greater offense to public decency, as the enemies of Buddhism were always ready to point out. Yet what really happened was that a new family was acquired as the old was renounced. A Chinese could only "leave the home" by accepting a monk as his master. That monk became his "father." Fellow disciples became his "brothers." Not only were all the kinship terms borrowed from lay life, but family institutions and attitudes were borrowed too. A disciple often inherited his "father's" temple and was expected to look after his grave and soul tablet like a filial son.

All this was based on tonsure. That is, the master-disciple relationship was established when a monk shaved the head of a layman, who thereby entered the sangha. In Theravada Buddhism no one entered the sangha until he received his first ordination, that is, until he took the ten vows of the novice. But in Chinese Buddhism tonsure entailed no vows and was clearly distinguished from ordination, which usually came years later in his career.

MOTIVATION

In view of the strength of familism, what would lead a Chinese to renounce his family? What were the motives for becoming a monk? This is a question on which, according to C. K. Yang, there is no statistical data.[1] Even if there were such data, it would be suspect because motivation is always so difficult to establish. I remember being told by an eminent abbot that he had renounced his family when he was nineteen years old because the middle school he had been attending closed down after the Republican revolution. He spoke of his disappointment to a relative who happened to be a devout Buddhist.

"Why don't you become a monk?" the relative suggested.

"All right," said the young man in an offhand way.

"Do you really mean it?" said the other.

The young man reflected that to give such an offhand answer was disrespectful and so he paused for a long time to reconsider. Finally he said: "I really do, I really do."

Finding that this explanation was rather unsatisfactory, I mentioned it to a Buddhist friend, who told me not to accept things at their face value. Perhaps the real reason, he suggested, had been disappointment in love. How could an eminent dharma master, now in his seventies, talk about a boyhood love affair? I should not expect a frank reply to such a question. Furthermore, even when a monk intended to be frank, perhaps he himself did not understand the true nature of his motivation.

This comment seems quite valid. Although I have collected many case histories on reasons for taking the robe, I have reservations about them. This is not merely because motives are hard to establish, but also because of the nature of my sample. Four fifths of the informants had held high office in mainland monasteries and most of them had had the foresight and initiative to flee the Communist persecution of Buddhism in which they, as office-holders, would have suffered the most. In other words, they were an elite. This could partly explain— but only partly—why their motives for entering the sangha were not the ones commonly ascribed to monks by most of the Western authorities who have addressed themselves to the problem so far. According to these authorities, monks were usually sold into their vocation as children by impoverished parents or joined as adults in order to get an easy life. Huc, for example, states that the Buddhist priesthood "is compelled to recruit itself in a singular manner. The Bonze who is attached to a pagoda buys, for a few sapecks, the child of some indigent family, shaves his head, and makes a disciple of him, or rather a servant." Later, as Huc explains, the disciple becomes his heir and procures his own disciple in a similar way. "In this manner is perpetuated a race of Bonzes."[2]

Hackmann states: "The monastic communities are mainly recruited from the ranks of children who are designated for this life by their parents in early youth and are brought to the monastery. Only comparatively few monasteries have any important influx of grown men. Not infrequently the children destined for the monastic life by their parents are given in exchange for a money indemnification . . . In cases which were personally known to me, twenty-five Mexican dollars were paid for a child, of which the value at that time was about forty shillings. A similar statement is given in Milne's *Life in China,* p. 132."[3]

J. B. Pratt, who was a less biased observer than either of the missionaries just quoted, believed that the religious motive for taking the robe was rare. "The very great majority of Buddhist monks were either put into the order by their parents or chose the religious life as an easy and sure way of getting a living."[4]

One can hear the same generalization from the lips of many Chinese —and one can also hear it about Buddhist monks in Theravada countries. But we are seldom told on how large a sample it was based, or how the sample was selected, or how well acquainted the observers were with the people whose motives they were judging. John Blofeld, however, was better acquainted than most, since he spent some seven months living and working with thirty to forty monks from different parts of China in a meditation hall near Kunming. He writes the following:

> When I grew to know my companions better, I found that they fell loosely into several categories. Besides the pious ones self-dedicated for the love of a contemplative life and thirsty for nirvana's peace, there were many who had drifted into the life—vowed by their parents upon condition of mother or father recovering from some illness, or driven to seek refuge from conscription (which in Chiang Kaishek's China often spelled death from malnutrition and disease long before the soldiers received their first weapons or came within a hundred miles of the enemy). Yet others were lazy fellows

who preferred pleasant quarters, an assured supply of bad food and the dignity of monkhood to having to contend with natural calamities and predatory soldiers for their livelihood. In fact the hundred or so monks there included almost every type of human being except, of course, the riotous, swashbuckling, adventurous and physically heroic types, all of whom would have found the timeless calm unendurable.[5]

I have asked a few of the monks I know to comment on such generalizations. One said that it was rare for children to be sold or pledged to the monastery. It might happen when a child fell ill to the point where his life was in danger and his parents promised that if he recovered he would become a monk. But more than half, according to this informant, entered the sangha in their twenties and between a quarter and a third in middle age. Some did so because they felt that the world had nothing to offer and could not be depended on and others (particularly older persons) did so in order to practice religious cultivation (*hsiu-ch'ih*). A second informant, after giving a similar explanation, added that many people entered the sangha under the pressure of circumstances. For example, a man might be short of money or have broken the law or have troubles at home. For such a man the sangha was the only way out. Although the ordination of criminals was theoretically prohibited, it did happen in practice.

This sort of testimony from the monks themselves is doubtless based on broad personal knowledge, but it leaves us unsatisfied. We would like to have quantitative data. While there may be almost none that bears directly on the motivation of monks, it does exist on their age and place of origin. The sample is small (only a few monasteries), but it is large enough to cast the most serious doubt on generalizations like those of Huc and Hackmann.

As we shall presently see, large ordaining monasteries gave each ordinee a certificate, a bowl, a robe, and several books, among which was a *t'ung-chieh lu* or "record of those ordained at the same time." I translate this as "ordination yearbook" because it resembled so closely the "class yearbook" that we receive when we graduate from school. It listed the names of all the officiants and ordinees along with certain details of their personal history. Although hundreds of thousands were printed (since there were hundreds of thousands ordained), I have looked in vain for them in libraries and bookshops and when I ad-

vertised for them in Buddhist journals, offering a very high price, I
received but one reply. The reason is that most monks left their yearbooks behind when they fled the Mainland and those who managed
to bring them, preserve them as treasured momentoes. Worst of all
from the investigator's point of view, when monks die, the yearbook
is usually cremated along with the body.

I have gone into these details because some readers who never have
heard of this bibliographical *rara avis* may wonder if it really exists.
But I can assure them that I have in my possession an original copy of
one ordination yearbook and photographic copies of nine more. They
are: Ku Shan (1916, 1926, and 1932); Nan-hua Ssu (1949); Pao-hua
Shan (1916, 1940); Ch'i-hsia Ssu (1929, 1933, and 1941); Lung-hua Ssu
(1947). At the last three monasteries the following data are given for
each ordinee: dharma name, style, place of origin, name of tonsure
master, and name and location of temple where tonsure took place.
The yearbooks of Ku Shan and the Nan-hua Ssu, however, give in
addition the lay surname, the age at tonsure, and the age at ordination
(see Fig. 49). What is particularly relevant to the study of motivation
is the age at tonsure, since this was normally the age at which the
ordinee first embarked on a monastic career. In the four ordinations at
Ku Shan and the Nan-hua Ssu, the vows were administered to a total
of three hundred monks. Twenty-three of them, eight percent, had
received the tonsure under sixteen years of age. The highest incidence
of tonsure came between the ages of twenty and thirty, as the following figures show.[6]

Ku Shan, Yung-ch'üan Ssu: 1916 Ordination

Age	Number of monks in this age range at tonsure	Number of monks in this age range at ordination
0-9	1	0
10-15	3	0
16-19	5	0
20-29	27	33
30-39	17	14
40-49	13	18
50-59	7	9
60-69	5	4
70-79	1	1

1926 Ordination

Age	Number of monks in this age range at tonsure	Number of monks in this age range at ordination
0-9	1	0
10-15	3	0
16-19	10	6
20-29	26	24
30-39	14	23
40-49	15	11
50-59	8	12
60-69	1	2
70-79	1	1

1932 Ordination

Age	Number of monks in this age range at tonsure	Number of monks in this age range at ordination
0-9	1	0
10-15	3	2
16-19	6	6
20-29	20	22
30-39	13	13
40-49	3	3
50-59	1	1
60-69	2	2

Nan-hua Ssu: 1949 Ordination

Age	Number of monks in this age range at tonsure	Number of monks in this age range at ordination
0-9	1	0
10-15	10	0
16-19	11	7
20-29	33	25
30-39	13	28
40-49	10	16
50-59	10	8
60-69	5	7
70-79	0	2

Is there any way of reconciling these figures with the assertion that most monks were sold to the temple in childhood? There seem to be three possibilities. One is that children lived at the temple for many years before receiving their tonsure. They were purchased at five, let us say, and received their tonsure at twenty-five. I have never heard of such a case and cannot imagine one. Usually the tonsure was given as soon as a boy reached ten (the minimum age for novices), if not before. The master had every reason for wanting to make his disciple feel committed to the monastic career at an early date. The second possibility is that the ordination yearbooks were falsified. Monks, that is, who received the tonsure at ten, may have recorded it as twenty. But there seems to be no conceivable reason for doing so. It is not like the falsification of the name of the small temple where tonsure took place. This, as we shall see, was a common abuse, done in order to make the records comply with the rules. But so long as a boy had reached ten years of age at tonsure, the rules had been complied with. Finally there is the possibility that Ku Shan and Nan-hua Ssu were exceptional. Perhaps Fukien and Kwangtung were particularly strict in this one respect (for they were certainly not strict in others). But though most of the Ku Shan ordinees were from Fukien, those at the Nan-hua Ssu came from eighteen provinces (only fifteen percent came from Kwangtung). The figures in these tables are therefore difficult to explain away.

Child monks caught the attention of Western observers. There was no such thing in the West and when they were seen in temples or on the streets or in photographs, they were not forgotten. Their number probably tended to be inflated in the memory. This could perhaps account for the widespread impression that most monks took the robe in their childhood. In conflict with both the observers and the ordination yearbooks, however, there are the data that I collected myself. Of the fifty-three monks whose tonsure age I have recorded in the course of interviews, only nineteen or 36 percent were shaved at the age of twenty or over. Almost half were shaved at thirteen through nineteen. The figures are as follows:

Under ten	4	16 through 19	7
10 through 12	6	20 through 29	12
13 through 15	18	30 and over	6

43. Child monks in north China.

This shows the incidence of tonsure reaching its peak in the mid-teens, which fits in neither with the sale of young children to the temple as reported by Western observers, nor with tonsure in maturity as indicated by the ordination yearbooks. The former may be treated skeptically, but the latter is evidence for which some sort of reconciliation must be attempted. Recalling the nature of my sample, I wonder if there may not be a correlation between holding high office, as did most of my informants, and entering the sangha at an early age. My informants themselves say that this was the case, and there is confirmation from an unexpected quarter. The nineteenth-century missionary, Reverend George Smith, after expatiating on the degradation of the sangha, adds: "The better order of priests were almost invariably those who in childhood had been dedicated to the priesthood."[7] Reverend J. H. Gray was told by an abbot in Canton that "the priests who had been brought up from boyhood were the best."[8] It would appear that the *most* monks joined in maturity, but the *best* monks—or most of the best—joined in their teens.

The yearbooks of Pao-hua and Ch'i-hsia Shan and the Lung-hua Ssu do not give us the age of ordinees, but they provide intriguing information about their place of origin. Seventy-five percent of all the Kiangsu ordinands at Pao-hua Shan came from one small area in the northern part of the province. Sixty-nine percent at Ch'i-hsia Shan came from the same small area, while for the Lung-hua Ssu the corresponding figure was sixty-five percent. The area in question was a rough parallelogram, one hundred kilometers on a side, having at its four corners the districts Pao-ying, Chiang-tu, Ju-kao, and Yen-ch'eng.[9] It covered nine thousand square kilometers or only one twelfth of the province. Why should one twelfth of the province with no large centers of population produce something like three quarters of its monks?[10]

When I have put this question to non-Buddhist Chinese friends, they have had a ready answer. Northern Kiangsu was poor. Its residents became monks to escape poverty. In Shanghai, they said, most of the lower castes—the barbers, the rickshaw coolies, and the boys in massage parlors—came from northern Kiangsu. So did the monks. The soil there was low-lying, saline near the sea, and water-logged inland, where it was often flooded by the Huai River. As one person told me, "those who lived in northern Kiangsu looked on the southern part of the province as paradise." This sounds reasonable enough and it would seem to argue that even if monks were not sold to the monastery in childhood, they were driven into it by poverty when they grew older.

But the monks who actually come from the parallelogram denied that it was poverty stricken. They said that it had much good land, none of which was saline, since it lay far from the coast.[11] The explanation they gave for the high percentage of monks was that "it was the custom there" to take the robe. Let me quote from some of their rather rambling statements.

> When I was young it seemed to me that a monk's life was very peaceful (ch'ing-ching). I was interested in becoming that kind of a person. I admired the monastic life. Naturally I was too young to understand anything about Buddhism, but I had a very good impression of entering the monkhood (ch'u-chia). A layman's life was full of hardships and troubles, while after one became a monk, life was more peaceful and more secure. My family were prosperous farmers (hsiao-k'ang chih chia) and I was able to go to school, but I still felt this way. Also in my part of the countryside, people re-

spected monks—except for those who did not keep the rules or who behaved contemptibly. So long as a monk kept the rules, he did not have to have great learning or do great things in order to get the people's respect. My father's eldest sister became a nun. She had a small temple. Ordinary people's houses were not as good as temples. Temples were bigger and more impressive. When my mother went to worship, we would go along and play. We liked to play there. We liked the surroundings. It was peaceful. The monks were very good to children. Some children wanted to become monks; others did not. If they wanted to, it was not in order to escape hardship at home, but because they liked the monks and wished to get closer to them. This was because of their "mind-roots" (*hsin-ken*), because of an affinity from previous lives. They had had intercourse with monks in their previous lives and so a seed had been sowed because of which they wanted to take the robe themselves in this life. The parents did not object. If the family had three or four sons, it was customary for one to become a monk. I was the youngest in my family, but it was not necessarily always the youngest who did so.

Another monk from the same district told me that he had taken the robe for three reasons. First he had often been sick as a child. When he was about seven or eight years old, he became so ill that his breathing and pulse stopped, as if he were dead. His mother, who was a devout Buddhist, went to a temple and made a vow that if he got well, he would become a monk. From then on she encouraged him to do so. Secondly the environment was Buddhist. His mother often used to take him to temples.

The buildings were so much bigger and better laid out than at home and so were the furnishings. The monks were terribly kind to me, gave me fruit to eat, and I could play there. There was also a teacher in my private school, who was a devout Buddhist and showed great respect to the monks, with whom he had frequent intercourse. This example given by my teacher made a deep impression on me. Finally, there was a belief in my area that it was advantageous to one's ancestors if one became a monk. There was a saying: "when a son takes the robe, his ancestors for nine generations go to heaven (*i-tzu ch'u-chia chiu-tsu sheng-t'ien*)." This belief had a great influence on the people there so that they considered it a good thing when a boy took the robe. In my case it was discussed with all my relatives first, and they approved. I was the youngest of three brothers. No one else in the family had become a monk. We were not rich, but better off than the average family. We had sixty to seventy *mou* of farmland. By the time I took the robe, my father had died.

A third monk from the north Kiangsu parallelogram stated that he had become a monk 1) in order to have a peaceful life; 2) because his elder brother had done so; and 3) because it was considered a good thing in northern Kiangsu—people there respected monks.

This customary popular respect for monks and monasteries is the thread that runs through most of the explanations that I have been given by monks from this area. It suggests that monkhood was correlated less with poverty than with attitudes. There may be a certain parallel in the number of Massachusetts Irish who have entered the priesthood. Poverty has been one factor, no doubt, but probably a more important and pervasive reason has been that it was an approved career. I imagine that when a north Kiangsu father said that his boy was now in the meditation hall at Chin Shan, there were the same nods of approval from his neighbors as when a proud father in the South End of Boston announces that "my boy has gone to the seminary in Rome." The soil of north Kiangsu was soaked in Buddhism. Here had been the earliest Buddhist community mentioned in Chinese historical records; the first Buddha image; the earliest temple. So when monks cite the customs of the area, history supports them.[12]

There is another fact that argues against the "poverty theory" and that is the rate of literacy. On the basis of inadequate samples, it appears to have been higher among monks than is generally supposed.[13] No nation-wide survey has ever been conducted, but the Communists did at least three local studies during their first three years in power. A survey in Ningpo April 18-27, 1950, showed that 35 percent of the 470 monks and nuns of that municipality were completely illiterate; 62 percent had done primary school; and 3 percent had done middle school.[14] A survey made in 1952 at the Asoka Monastery's Agricultural Producers Cooperative showed that 10 percent of the 132 monks were illiterate. The rest ranged from persons with one year of primary school to those who had graduated from upper middle school.[15] The Asoka Monastery is in the Ningpo area and its monks were probably included in the 1950 survey mentioned first. One reason for the difference in illiteracy rates (10 percent versus 35 percent) is probably that the figure for the whole area included 210 nuns, who, like most Chinese women, had had less opportunity for education than their male counterparts. The third survey was made in 1953 at Omei Shan, where 60 out of its 292 monks and nuns were illiterate, that is, a little over 20 percent.[16] Twenty-eight nuns were included, so that assuming all of them to have been illiterate, male illiteracy was 11 percent.

Of course these figures are scarcely adequate as a basis for generalizing about the whole Chinese sangha. But they support the generalization that I have heard both from monks and Buddhist laymen, who say that anything above primary school education was rare in the sangha but that illiteracy was even rarer. If that is the case, then the sangha was certainly an elite compared with the Chinese population as a whole, which had an illiteracy rate of perhaps 80 percent.[17] The question is whether the present level of monastic literacy was reached during the Republican period or goes back into the Ch'ing dynasty. Something on the order of 7,500 monks graduated from the seminaries established during the Republican period, that is, perhaps 2 percent of all the monks in China. Hence seminaries cannot have brought about any substantial change in the percentage of illiteracy. We might also ask: were better educated persons attracted to the sangha between 1912 and 1950? Yes, but there do not seem to have been enough of them to change the literacy rate substantially. It would appear that there were about as many monks who could read and write at the beginning of the Republican period as at the end of it.

On the other hand, what if most of them had learned to read and write *after* they entered the sangha? Then literacy would have no bearing on their class origin. But most of my informants had had their heads shaved at an age when primary school should have been completed and, in fact, they had completed it. The monks listed in the ordination yearbooks had had their heads shaved at an even higher age. On the whole, it seems likely that during this century the majority of the sangha has not come from a background so poor that it excluded education.[18]

THIRTY-NINE CASES

In the course of interviewing, I had an opportunity to find out in only twenty-eight cases why monks had taken the robe. With the rest, either priority had to go to other questions or I did not feel that our relationship was such that I could expect a frank answer. To these twenty-eight I have added eleven more cases from documentary sources, making a total of thirty-nine.

Usually my informants gave more than one reason. We have just seen examples of this in the case of monks from northern Kiangsu. For purposes of tabulation I have chosen the reason that they said was most important or that seemed to me so. Either way, the choice may have been subjective.

Thirteen of the thirty-nine monks took the robe to escape from the secular world. For instance, one had failed his civil service examinations. Another had become disgusted by the corruption he found in government service. Another was a deserter from the army. Another found himself jobless and futureless in middle age. Another had a father who had failed his civil service examinations and did not want his son to go through the same frustrating experience. Two were disappointed in love.[19]

Six of the thirty-nine had fallen ill as children or their parents had fallen ill. An example is the monk from northern Kiangsu whose breathing stopped when he was eight years old. Sometimes a child would be given to the monastery to effect a cure while the illness was still under way; sometimes only after recovery in order to redeem a vow made earlier.

Another six of the thirty-nine became monks because they had lost one or both their parents and had no one else to support or to care for them.

Still another six gave as their main reason a liking for monks and the monastic atmosphere. They used to be taken as children to the monastery for outings or to play there while their mother made offerings. They were impressed by the size and the splendor of the buildings, and attracted by the peacefulness of the life. The monks would play with them, often giving them little presents. (Monks have a real fondness for children, perhaps because their paternal instinct, being frustrated, is all the stronger. I shall never forget the sight of the old abbot of Chin Shan, in his august seventies, scampering down the street after a woman who had a baby on her back, in order to give it a playful smack.)

Four out of the thirty-nine became monks because they were interested in Buddhist doctrine and wanted to devote themselves wholly to its study and practice.

Two were persuaded by relatives (one brother and one uncle) who had already joined the sangha.

One took the robe because his parents hated him, and one because he wanted to obtain supernatural powers. Not a single monk among the thirty-nine was sold to the temple as a child by his parents.

These reasons may be tabulated as follows:

Reason	Number of persons	Nearest percentage
1. Escape from the world	13	33
2. Illness	6	15
3. Orphaned	6	15
4. Persuaded by relatives	2	5
5. Liked monastic atmosphere	6	15
6. Interested in Buddhism	4	10
7. Other reasons	2	5

These figures might be summarized by saying that 25 percent became monks because they felt attracted toward Buddhism or its institutions and 75 percent for nonreligious reasons.[20] On the other hand, the largest single category—those who wanted to escape from the secular world—was not as unreligiously motivated as it might appear. The Buddha himself took the path to enlightenment because his illusions about the world were shattered. He began to see the First Noble Truth, that life was inseparable from suffering, disease, old age, and death. This was why he too "left home." Escape appears an unworthy act to our Western society preoccupied with meeting challenges, but there could scarcely be a more appropriate motivation for a Buddhist monk. It meant that like the Buddha he had begun to learn the First Noble Truth.

If we add the "escapists" and orphans to those who felt attracted to Buddhism or to its institutions, we find that the percentages in our small sample are reversed; nearly 75 percent entered the sangha for appropriate reasons. Less than 25 percent enter involuntarily or under persuasion, and without any lesson in the First Noble Truth—although some, at least, could have gotten the lesson from illness.

Tabulations, even based on a large sample, can only be simplistic. They need to be brought to life by case histories that do justice to the complexity of human motives. Let us consider the detailed explanations given by some of my informants—one or two in each of the six categories. The largest category—the "escapists"—will be considered last, since it is the most interesting.

Illness (Case 1). A monk born in Chen-chiang in 1881 had eye trouble as a child. The abbot of an hereditary temple there was supposed to be good at opthalmology, so his parents gave him to the temple when he was nine years old. As it turned out, his eye trouble was not cured until many years later in Shanghai. But he was not unhappy or lonely in the monastery. "It was much bigger than home and there were lots of places to play." He never tried to go back to his parents. As he said himself, how could he have found his way?

Illness (Case 2). A Fukienese monk born in 1892 came from a Buddhist family. His father was a vegetarian who had taken the Three Refuges. When he was nineteen, his mother fell ill and so he too took the Refuges and prayed to the Buddha for her recovery. Although she did recover, her illness had showed him the impermanence of human life. He wished to become a monk and practice religious cultivation, but his mother would not permit it. He had to wait until her death six years later before he was able to take the robe.

Orphaned. A monk born in Szechwan in 1900 was six years old when his father died and thirteen years old when his mother died. There was no one left to take care of him, and so his grandmother sent him to an hereditary temple on Omei Shan that same year. There he had his head shaved at the age of fifteen.

Persuaded by relatives. A monk born in Honan in 1928 said that he was persuaded by his mother's elder brother, who was the head of an hereditary temple. He came to their house once, saw the boy, and urged him to become a monk when he was older. Later the boy went and lived at the temple for a time, heard his uncle preach the dharma and chant sutras, and "came to have faith." He told this to his uncle, who urged him to go at once to Peking and be ordained.

Liked monasteries (Case 1). A monk from Yangchow, born in 1928, whose account resembled that of the north Kiangsu monks already quoted, told me that "children like to become monks. They see that things are very nice at the temple. The first time I went, the old abbot gave me candy. I was just a child. I thought that things were very good at the temple, so I left lay life. I did not know anything about Buddhism.

I only knew that this was what I wanted to do. My parents urged me several times to come home, but I was unwilling to." This monk was the youngest of four sons. He said that in this area if any family— even a *rich* family—had three or four sons, the father would present one to an hereditary temple. His own second brother had also become a monk.[21] The family had a house with a tiled roof and over thirty *mou* of their own farmland. He had started primary school at the age of eight and had already learned by heart the *San-tzu ching, Pai-chia hsing, Ch'ien-tzu wen,* and so forth.

Liked monasteries (Case 2). The following explanation was given by a monk born in 1928 in a small country town in Kiangsi. "I became a monk because my father was a Buddhist. He had taken the Three Refuges and was a vegetarian. My eldest brother also believed in the Buddha but he did not become a monk. Neither did any of my uncles. I am the only monk in the family. Different people leave lay life for different karmic causes (*yin-yüan*). Some do it because they are disillusioned with the world; others because they get a good start in Buddhist studies early in life. In my case the first reason was because from the age of five or six I could not eat any nonvegetarian food.[22] If I ate lard or duck or eggs, I felt like throwing up. The second reason was that I found monks terribly congenial, as if we had an affinity from past lives. My [future] master's master and his disciples were always coming to the house and often spent the night there when I was a child. The custom in China was that children slept with their father and mother or, when they were older, the boys slept with their father and the girls with their mother. But when the monks came to spend the night my father did not seem so close to me anymore and I used to go and sleep with them. It made me so happy to sleep together with them —it was this affinity from former lives. As soon as I saw monks' robes, I was happy. When they did their worship, I would go and worship with them. We had a Buddha shrine in our house and when the monks came, they used to worship there morning and evening, recite sutras, and burn incense. I could not recite sutras, but I would stand in back and listen and enjoy it tremendously. So my father said to me: 'You're destined to be a monk. You don't eat nonvegetarian food. You get along with the monks so well and are so happy to be with them during worship. You're destined to be a monk.' That was the way it was, and I got my chance when I was fourteen."

At this point I suggested to the informant that his father had urged him to become a monk. He replied almost indignantly: "No, I wanted it myself. It was of my own volition. Let me tell you. Ordinarily a child had to go to school and could not go to the temple whenever he felt like it. But when I was fourteen, in the second month on Kuan-yin's birthday, school had not yet started and my father took me along to the temple so that I could have a look. There were many monks, dressed in their robes, performing the Ta-pei Ch'an. They were striking their instruments. It was a fine sight. Since my father was a lay devotee, he put on a long gown and joined in. I stayed beside him and felt that it was very interesting. I was very happy. After the ceremony was over my father sat down with the monks for a chat. Since they were the disciples of my [future] master's master, they were my father's brother-disciples.[23] My father said: 'This boy likes to worship. He does not like to eat nonvegetarian food. He is very happy when he is together with monks because, I think, he is destined to be a monk.' My master's master said: 'Why not let him become one now? The younger the better. Once they've grown up it does not work. Ask him if he would like to.' So my father asked me: 'Do you want to become a monk?' I said: 'Good! Good!' So that was the way it was done. I renounced lay life at once. I was very happy and so was my father. After I did this, I did not feel homesick. All day the only thing I knew was worshipping and listening to the sutras."

Interested in Buddhism (Case 1). An eminent monk, born in Liao-ning in 1884, did not take the robe until 1932. Starting in his twenties, however, he had been active in a lay Buddhist club that often held lectures and discussions not only about Buddhism, but also about filial piety and the Confucian five relationships. In the early 1920's he was the chief promoter of a large new monastery in Yingkow. Only in his forties did he decide that he had to pursue Buddhism whole-heartedly and become a monk. His career was similar to that of his illustrious colleague, T'an-hsü, who also renounced his family in middle age after years of study of the dharma.

Interested in Buddhism (Case 2). The reasons why T'an-hsü became a monk are given in his autobiography with frank and curious detail. To begin with, from birth until the age of two or three, he had never learned to say "mama" or "dada." The only words he would pronounce were "eat vegetarian food" (*ch'ih-chai*)—words that no one had taught him. When he was five or six, his mother dreamt that she saw him wearing a robe and chanting the sutras with a group of monks. She therefore believed that he was destined to become a monk himself. Nonetheless, when he was seventeen, she arranged for his marriage. He too felt he was destined to be a monk (although he was not sure whether he should be a Taoist or a Buddhist monk), but he still proceeded to raise a large family. In 1904, at the age of thirty, he moved to Yingkow in Liaoning province. There he joined the Buddhist club and began for the first time to study the dharma. As the years passed, he became still more inclined toward a monastic career. In 1914 he thought about it in the following terms.

"From youth onwards I had known that it was my destiny to become a monk, but the opportunity to do so had never come . . . When I was running my pharmacy in Yingkow, I read the *Surangama Sutra* every day and found it full of meaning. I felt that the usual explanation of things was false and superficial and that only the Buddha's explanation got to the final truth . . . I thought: what is the reason why people have lost their old virtues and the times have reached such a state of demoralization? Isn't it because they do not understand the truth? If everyone understood the truth as stated in the sutras—discard the little self and realize the greater self—how could the ills of the world have gotten to this stage? So my idea was to get the *Surangama Sutra* into circulation and make everyone understand the truth and reach happiness. Otherwise there would be no limit to human misery . . ."

But it was not until 1917, at the age of forty-three, that he made the final decision to become a monk and set out from Yingkow to Tientsin. He did not tell his clerk in the pharmacy that he was leaving, nor did he inform his wife and children. He simply left. Thirty-five years later he could still recall his thoughts as he walked along the road. "Earlier on (I thought to myself) because my parents were there and I had no brothers, I had been reluctant to renounce family life. Later I got tied down with a wife and involved with worldly pursuits—terribly involved—so that I still could not become a monk. Thinking of that made me very unhappy. Again I thought: what if I were now to die, wouldn't it come down to the same thing? Suppose they believed that I had died from some sudden attack of illness; that would give me the chance to become a monk and pursue my studies, and if later on I returned and brought salvation to my wife—well, in that case, why shouldn't I renounce everything now? So, as I walked along the road, despite my unhappiness, I used this thought of death to pretend that it was my soul, after dying, that was marching forward.

"I went on thinking: today I have one daughter, who is already married, and five sons. The eldest son is only fourteen and the youngest has just learned to walk. There will be no one to support them. In these thirty or forty years of hectic activity, I have not saved any money at all, and they are entirely dependent on my little pharmacy. Now that I have left, there is no one to look after the pharmacy and it will certainly fail, so that my whole family will go hungry and become homeless vagrants. What is to be done? But (I thought) there are already so many homeless vagrants in the world. Am I willing to let other people's wives and children be homeless vagrants, but not my own? Again I thought: if, after I have become a monk, I am traveling about the country on pilgrimage, and I happen to see one of my children there by the roadside begging, would I pay any attention to him or not?—Ach! there are already so many children in the world who are begging. Am I willing to let other people's children beg, but not my own? This is not worth thinking seriously about. But my wife, after I have left without a word, is certainly going to have difficulties providing for five children. If she decides to marry someone else, won't I find this hard to take? . . . But (I thought) though she is mine in this life, whose was she in her last life, and whose will she be in her next? This too is something that it is not worth worrying about. If I let my own life be tied down by my wife, it will not end with this life, but life after life will be lost. That way, not only will I be unable to secure salvation for my wife, but I will not even be able to secure it for myself. But if I can carry out my purpose and become a monk, deepen my knowledge of the Buddhist canon, and achieve true religious cultivation, then in the future if I happen to see them, I can urge them to recite buddha's name and practice cultivation so that they will be released from birth and death—will not this be best for all concerned?"

When he reached Tientsin, the monk who he had hoped would shave his head was skeptical about his motivation. T'an-hsü protested that he was not like some other people who wanted to enter the sangha when they were in the throes of trouble and then changed their minds a few days later. "I have already studied the Buddhist sutras for many years," he explained. "Although as a layman I did not have a really good livelihood, still with that little pharmacy I did not make out too badly, especially since medical work has a certain status in society. So it is not a question of livelihood; my goal in becoming a monk is certainly not to get clothing, food, or shelter, nor is it to escape from reality. My goal is this: although I have already spent seven or eight years studying the Buddhist sutras, I still do not understand where the real essence of the dharma lies, and after I have renounced lay life and been ordained, I want to go about the country and pursue my studies under famous masters so that in the future, when I have the opportunity, I can spread the dharma and bring the Buddhist sutras into general circulation and get everyone to know them. Otherwise the world will go steadily downwards, men's desires will grow ever more unbridled, and there will be no way at all to save them from disaster."[24]

With this desire to save the world through Buddhism, T'an-hsü renounced lay life and went on to become one of the most influential monks in modern China. It sounds like a most noble, rational, and, from a Western viewpoint, exemplary motive. And yet, we cannot but ask, would he have acted as he did if he had not felt that he was "destined to become a monk"? Was his motivation as rational as it appears? How much was it affected, for example, by what happened to him just after he was married, at which time, according to his autobiography, he died in an epidemic and went down to hell to be judged by Yen-lo—a proceeding that he recounts in detail. Yen-lo, the King of Hell, told him that his life was over because of the burden of his sins. T'an-hsü protested that he had recited the *Kao-wang Kuan-shih-yin ching* a thousand times—and was not this supposed to lengthen one's life? Yen-lo admitted that it was, but pointed out that if he had not recited it, he would have died five years earlier. Finally T'an-hsü offered to recite the *Diamond Sutra* (which he had never read, but merely heard fellow villagers speak of) ten times a day. Grudgingly Yen-lo agreed that in that case he would be permitted to revive, and sent two ghosts to escort him back to his corpse. Experiences like this could not fail to have played a role in the development of his sense of a monastic vocation. Was this therefore less real?

Escape from the world (Case 1). An informant born in Kiangsu in 1929 was the eldest of three brothers. The reason he became a monk, he said, was because he had seen the cruelties of war as a child. When the Japanese attacked Shanghai in 1937, his family had fled, taking the train back to their old home near Yangchow. But after passing

Wusih, the train was bombed by Japanese planes and they had to go on by boat in the waterways, but the boat too was bombed and set on fire and many were killed. They got to Yangchow only to be bombed again. Later the Japanese occupied this area and came constantly to the village to requisition grain and to rape Chinese women. There was an epidemic, in which many people died. Toward the end of the war there came a division of family property among the members of his father's generation. Some were dissatisfied with their share. There were unseemly quarrels. For a long time, like other people in the area, this informant had been going to the Kao-min Ssu on festival days and for Buddhist rites. Once when he was there, a monk said to him: "Why do you get so upset about property? Why not renounce lay life?" His parents approved and so he did.

Escape from the world (Case 2). This concerns the monk described in Appendix V as "supreme among masters of confusion." His reasons for entering the sangha were as confusing as everything else that he told me. Originally he had been a successful businessman operating three inns in southern Hunan. One day he happened to meet a physiognomist who insisted on reading his face free of charge. The reading was extremely pessimistic: namely that his was the face of a person who was destined to go to prison. This frightened him, so at the suggestion of his brother-in-law he began to recite sutras everyday in a local Taoist temple. Some of them were Taoist sutras, but some were Buddhist. He also began to do good works. In 1929, when he was thirty-four years old, his wife and all his three children died in an epidemic. He decided to become a monk. After studying various religions, including Christianity, he decided that Buddhism was the best. In becoming a monk, he said, he proved the physiognomist to have been right, since monastic life and prison life were similarly shut in.

Escape from the world (Case 3). There is an even greater element of the supernatural in our final example, which involves a monk born in Manchuria about 1915. His father, who was an elected public official, had fallen ill with a pulmonary disorder when the boy was ten or twelve years old and remained bed-ridden for many years. Though he was a Buddhist, he still ate a chicken every day, no doubt on doctor's orders. Once when he wanted to cross the room to prostrate himself before the image of Amitabha, he found that he could not move because hens were tugging with their beaks at a string tied around his waist. This gave him a bad turn and he became a complete vegetarian.

On another occasion he dreamed that he saw a huge black man writing a number on his (the dreamer's) forehead. The number showed he still had some years to live. The chief physician of the Manchurian railway, a Japanese, was called in to examine him and said that there was no known cure and the only thing to do was to worship. The son had by then grown older and come under the influence of the May Fourth movement. "I considered that all religion was superstitious. But here was a great doctor, with the best scientific training, telling me to worship. Surely religion could not be unscientific. I asked a Buddhist abbot who was a friend of my father what I ought to do. He said that I should join the Buddhist association and I did so. I began to go and listen to monks lecturing on the sutras. What they had to say was not superstition, but very subtle and wonderful (*ao-miao*). Once I went to Dairen where I was having the monks recite the *Ta-pei chou* for five days. On the last day my father was sitting on the sofa at home in Antung when he saw an old woman come in the door. She told him that he had killed someone in Heilungkiang, who in revenge wanted to drag him down to hell. But if he had Buddhist services performed for his enemy, he would go directly to the Western Paradise. My father protested that he had not injured anybody in Heilungkiang and the old woman vanished into thin air." Despite this sinister episode, the old man lived on for several years more.

His son took the Three Refuges at the age of twenty-four and the Five Vows at the age of twenty-six. Only when his father died a year later did he decide to become a monk. "I did not want to give birth to a son who might have to go through the same thing as I had. But first I had to see if I could endure the hardship of monastic life. I spent two weeks at a monastery at Harbin and then at another one in Peking, still as a lay devotee. My mother was very much against my becoming a monk, but I did so anyway three years after my father died."

These last two accounts illustrate, I think, the labyrinth of motivation through which many Chinese entered the sangha and the difficulty of generalizing about it. The difficulty seems insuperable. In the first place no two psychologists are likely to agree on how such accounts should be interpreted; in the second place we obviously need hundreds of accounts rather than dozens before we have enough data to interpret. The opportunity to collect a representative sample has gone forever. The only conclusion that can now be reached is that the commonly accepted conclusions are unsubstantiated. There is not enough evidence to say that a majority of monks were either sold to a temple by impoverished parents or took the robe in maturity just to get an easy life. Most of what little evidence there is argues for a much more complex and varied motivation.

What is more to the point is that after people entered the sangha, their motivation changed. Many who had just been trying negatively to get away from things in the secular world, came to feel a positive vocation for the transcendental. Even those who entered for the worst motives sometimes came to have the best motives for remaining. Missionaries used to call the sangha a refuge for criminals. Yet, as one missionary admitted, at least it gave criminals a better chance to start new lives than in prison, and many did so. "Some of these bad characters are in an amazing way changed by the monastic life. They repent and become new men who with intense fervor concentrate on meditation and worship. I have several times had a chance to verify this."[25] The monastery, which served society as orphanage and home for the aged, also served it as a successful house of correction.

TONSURE

According to the Buddhist rule, no one was supposed to enter the sangha without his parents' consent. In the case of a disciple who had not yet reached majority, there was also the practical danger that his parents might hail the master before a magistrate on a charge of abduction. Therefore some masters would only shave the head of a minor if they had his parents' consent in writing. I heard of a case in Yangchow where this was insisted on even though the applicant had reached the age of seventeen. In other cases, where the master knew the family well, he was satisfied with their verbal authorization.

The actual ceremony of tonsure was a simple one, although no description of it, so far as I know, can be found in Western sources. The master would call in as many of the existing disciples as possible, of every generation, so that they could bear witness to the adoption of their new brother. Friends and relatives of the latter would also be invited. After they had all assembled in the shrine hall, the master

44. Tonsure. Taiwan.

a. The disciple,
wearing a business suit,
enters behind his master.

b. He offers incense
at the main altar.

c. He kneels at the
side altar.

d. He makes a last kowtow
to his parents.

e. His master sprinkles
him with holy water.

f. He offers his
master a razor.

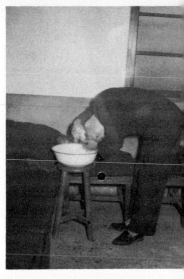

g. He shampoos his own head.

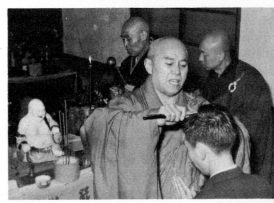

h. His master shaves off the hair on the sides of his head.

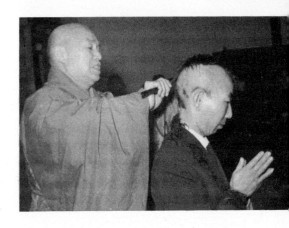

i. His master shaves off the last tuft.

j. The barber finishes the job.

k. The disciple stands before the altar.

l. He offers incense.

m. The tonsure family
and friends.

clad in a patriarch's robe and the candidate clad in lay clothes would enter and prostrate themselves to the Buddha image in tandem. When each had offered incense, they would repair to a low side-altar—almost a table—on which there stood an image of Maitreya, the smiling Buddha of the future. To the kneeling candidate the master, sitting behind the table, read a short sermon, in which he described how Sakyamuni stole out of his palace at night, cut off his hair, and renounced lay life. He warned the candidate that after he too had renounced lay life, he would not be able to show reverence to his ruler or to his parents; and suggested that he might wish to make them one last salute. Accordingly the disciple kowtowed facing north to the ruler and facing south to his parents. Then facing the main altar he made nine prostrations to the Three Jewels: the Buddha, dharma, and the sangha. Thus he said farewell to the past and greeted the future.

When he returned to the side-altar, the master sprinkled his head with holy water and handed him a razor. Offering it back, the candidate said: "I, your disciple, N-n, today beg Your Reverence to be the Teacher (*Acarya*) who shaves my hair . . . I wish to renounce lay life as your dependent." The master instructed him to shampoo his head and, after he had done so, began to shave it.

When the sides were bare, the master said: "Only the hair on the top of your head remains. You must consider carefully whether you can forget your personal concerns, enter the Way, and conscientiously practice the religion. A little hair is left, so that I can still let you go home as a layman. It is not too late. Therefore I ask you today before all those present, whether you can really make up your mind to renounce lay life so that you will never regret and withdraw?"

The disciple answered: "I have made up my mind to renounce lay life and I will never regret or withdraw."

Three times the question was asked and answered. Finally the master said: "Inasmuch as you have made up your mind to renounce lay life so that you will never regret and withdraw, now the hair on the top of your head goes under the knife, cutting you off forever from all your ties, in order that you may cultivate holy conduct in the sangha, and your happiness and wisdom may gradually increase." With these words the master cut off some of his remaining hair and handed him over to a barber, who shaved him completely. When he had changed into a monk's gown (*hai-ch'ing*), he knew from the rustle of the full sleeves and the draft on his scalp that he had really started his new life. Often he had a happy smile as for the first time, he prostrated himself to the Buddha, offered incense, and joined the other monks in the chant that ended the ceremony. After the last stroke of the hand-chime, the spectators pressed forward to offer congratulations.

That was all there was to it. The disciple received no document attesting to his renunciation of lay life or to his relationship with his master. Though he was now called a "novice" (Chinese *sha-mi*, Sanskrit *sramanera*), he had not yet taken the novice's ordination. Though he had to keep the ten prohibitions (*shoŭ-chieh*), he had not yet accepted the ten prohibitions (*shòu-chieh*).[26] Yet from that day on he practiced chastity, ate vegetarian food, abstained from wine, wore monastic dress, and in all other respects, began learning how to live as a monk. If he found it not to his taste—if he had regrets after all— he could still return to lay life without embarrassment. Despite the high seriousness of the ceremony of tonsure, his status was informal.

A few novices, however, did obtain the formal status of novice through ordination either by their tonsure master or at an ordaining monastery. But this was a separate ceremony and an embellishment rather than an essential part of their initiation. At Pao-hua Shan, for instance, a few unordained tonsured novices would come each year and go through the first part of the triple ordination. That is, they would take the sramanera's vows (*sha-mi chieh*). They would then watch the bhiksu and bodhisattva vows being administered, and when those who took the latter got twelve scars burned on their heads, the novices would get three, after which they would go home to continue their training. Only when they reached the minimum age for the full ordination would they return to take their novice's vows again, this time followed by the vows of the bhiksu and bodhisattva (see p. 291).

The minimum age for full ordination was twenty according to the Vinaya rule, but the rule was not always observed, even at model monasteries. At Pao-hua Shan, for example, if an applicant was tall and looked mature, he could by fully ordained at sixteen. This was termed "expedient ordination" (*fang-pien chieh*). One of my informants was fully ordained when he was only eleven years old at the T'ien-t'ung Ssu, which in other respects was the model monastery of Chekiang province.[27] But such cases were exceptional. The great majority of my informants remained in the bosom of the tonsure family until they were close to twenty.

THE TONSURE FAMILY

As was stated earlier, through tonsure a monk entered a "family." The head of the "family" was his "father-master" (*shih-fu*) or his "grandfather-master" (*shih-kung*). The rest of the family included members of various generations, who were called "older-brother-masters" and "younger-brother-masters" (*shih-hsiung, shih-ti*), "uncle masters" (*shih-po, shih-shu*), "nephew-disciples" (*t'u-chih*), "grandson-disciples" (*t'u-sun*), and so on. Before any of these terms the word "tonsure" (*t'i-tu*) could be prefixed to show that this, rather than ordination or transmission of the dharma, was the basis of the kinship in question.

The tonsure family was a private organism within the public body of the sangha. Just as there was supposed to be a clear distinction between public and the private in lay life, so monks attempted to keep the "family matters" of the private temple separate from the public operation of large monasteries. This was one reason for the rule that disciples could have their heads shaved and receive their training *only* at private hereditary temples. As we noted in Chapter V, if a large public monastery allowed tonsure families to take root there, the selection of abbots and officers would come to depend increasingly on kinship and less and less on qualifications to serve. If office became hereditary, there would be danger that office-holders would use monastic property for personal advantage. In any case, the large public monastery was not suited for the training of novices. Its hundreds of residents had to move from hall to hall and to take their places without jostling and confusion. They had to understand the complicated system of signals on bells, boards, and gongs. The strict atmosphere would have been vitiated by the presence of persons who did not know the rules of dressing, eating, washing, and so on. Therefore, just as the lay family was responsible for teaching its children how to act in public, the monastic family was responsible for training its novices how to live in the public monastery.

This is the way it was supposed to be, but in practice the rules were sometimes violated, as for instance at Ku Shan (see p. 139). Even within the rules, the monks living in public monasteries could keep in close contact with their hereditary temples, which they sometimes concurrently headed, thus wearing "two hats." If they wanted to take a disciple, they usually went back to the temple to shave his head, and left him there to be trained by a tonsure brother or some other member of the "family." But if it lay far off, they might not bother to return. I know of one monk who tonsured his disciple in the great shrine-hall of the Ta-pei Yüan, a reputable public monastery in Tientsin, of which he was the abbot. He found it inconvenient to return to his own hereditary temple hundreds of miles away in Shantung. So he shaved the disciple's head on the basis that *nominally* the act was taking place at the hereditary temple which, as it turned out, the disciple was never to visit in his whole life. Another monk I know, whose head was shaved in a Shanghai barbershop, was *nominally* considered to have received the tonsure in an hereditary temple in Liaoning province which, again, lay hundreds of miles away and he was never to see. In each case it was considered that the master had administered tonsure not in his capacity as officer of a public monastery, but solely in his capacity as the head of an hereditary temple.

Sometimes the very identity of the master was nominal. The hereditary temple was usually headed by a monk of the senior generation in the tonsure family, who remained in office until the infirmities of old age impelled him to retire. His own disciples, the second generation, were often abroad, studying or serving as officers of large public monasteries. When a promising applicant came to the temple and asked for tonsure, the second generation might already contain an appropriate number of disciples. The applicant would be accepted, therefore, as a disciple of the third generation. The senior monk would decide, like any head of the family, which member of the second generation should become the nominal master. Sometimes the latter would return home to shave the disciple's head. More often, perhaps, it would be done on his behalf by the senior monk, who, although he was nominally the "grandfather," then trained the disciple and acted *in loco parentis* until he was ready for ordination. Thus the actual master-disciple relationship was between persons separated by two generations. This kind of nominalism was institutionalized at some large hereditary temples, like the Chin-shan Ssu in Szechwan (see p. 239). There, while it was possible for a monk to take his own disciple after getting permission from his master, it was more often the master who made the choice for him and, even if he was present in the temple, he left the care and training of the disciple entirely in his master's hands.

In Kiangsu province and perhaps elsewhere it was common to acknowledge several monks as tonsure masters; not as father and grandfather, but all as fathers. Thus in the ordination yearbooks of Pao-hua and Ch'i-hsia Shan (but not in those of Ku-shan and the Nan-hua Ssu), we find many ordinees who list two or three monks as their masters. Sometimes this was purely nominal. If there was a good friend of the "family" who had always taken a kindly interest in the ordinee, his name might be listed beside the master's name in the ordination yearbook. It was rather like the courtesy title of "uncle." But there were cases where the plurality of the masters was more than nominal. In the 1930's a certain monk in Kiangsu instructed his three disciples to act in common when they came to take disciples themselves. The eldest of the three was abbot of a famous monastery in Soochow; the middle brother lived in one of their hereditary temples; while the youngest lived in another. My informant became a disciple of the youngest, who shaved his head. Later he went to stay with the middle brother. When he was ordained at Pao-hua Shan, he listed all three as his masters. Their names are printed in the ordination yearbook according to seniority (3-1-2), with the eldest brother in the center, although he was the person with whom the ordinee had had the least contact. But this was not like the collective transmission of the dharma where all the masters sat together on the dais to transmit to all the disciples kneeling before them. Only one master had shaved one disciple's head and he was the same master who had primary responsibility for his training.

Another kind of nominalism is illustrated by a case from Liaoning. In 1926 a Buddhist layman there took the Three Refuges with a monk who died shortly thereafter. In 1929 the layman decided to become a monk himself, but he wanted to be loyal to his late Refuges master. Therefore he asked the latter's elder brother to administer tonsure as his proxy. Thus he became the disciple of a master who was already dead. There were doubtless other varieties of nominalism. The statement that "my tonsure master was so-and-so" should never be taken at face value.

Tonsure was not the only basis for religious kinship. The elders who presided at a monk's ordination were considered his "ordination masters" (*chieh shih-fu*) and his fellow ordinees were his "ordination brothers" (*chieh hsiung-ti*). Later in his career, he might enter into a series of master-disciple relationships with those from whom he received the dharma. Each time he did so, he acquired a new set of dharma relatives. But, except where the dharma involved the right to an abbotship, both ordination and dharma types of kinship were largely nominal.

TONSURE AND DHARMA NAMES

When a layman renounced lay life, he gave up his lay names. From that day on he used the surname Shih, which is the first syllable of Sakyamuni (written *shih-chia-mou-ni* in Chinese). This signified that he was now "a son of the Buddha" (*fo-tzu*). His master chose two personal names for him by which he would thereafter be known. The first was a tonsure name (*t'i-tu ming*) that could be used by members of the same tonsure family who stood senior to him.[28] It always had two characters, one of which (more often the first than the second) was taken from a gatha or religious poem that was used character by character to name monks generation by generation. That is, all members of one generation had the same character embodied in their respective names, just as in the case of dharma disciples (see p. 159). Many of these name gathas are printed at the end of the large breviary (*Ch'an-men jih-sung*) and from them one can trace the ancestry of most Chinese monks. Once I met in Singapore a monk whose tonsure name was Sheng-shou, and whose master's tonsure name had been Jen-kung. I looked through the end of the breviary for the words *jen* and *sheng* in sequence. On p. 4b I found the verse "*Neng-jen sheng-kuo,*" meaning, perhaps, "ability and human-kindness [an epithet of the Buddha] are the fruits of sainthood." This monk's disciples, if he took any, must therefore be named *Kuo*-this or *Kuo*-that, since *kuo* was the next character after *sheng* in the gatha, just as his tonsure grandfather would have to have been *Neng*-this or *Neng*-that, since *neng* was the character that came before. This verse was part of a gatha in thirty-two characters that could be traced back through antecedent gathas to one spoken by I-hsüan of Mt. Lin-chi, a famous monk of the T'ang dynasty. This meant that my friend in Singapore was a member of the Lin-chi sect. If his name had been taken from a Ts'ao-tung gatha, then he would have been a member of the Ts'ao-tung sect. I am speaking of sect in respect to tonsure only, not in respect to the transmission of the dharma. Though a monk could receive the dharma many times, he could receive the tonsure only once, and in this respect belong to only one sect.

When the characters of each gatha had been exhausted in the course of generations, they could be used all over again, starting from the first. Alternatively, as in the case of the Singapore monk, a continuation (*hsü-p'ai*) could be written by the disciple whose name incorporated the last character. Sometimes a disciple of an intermediate generation would write a continuation that started with the generation character of his own name. This, in effect, created a new sub-sect.

Beside the tonsure name the master also gave his disciple a style (*tzu*).[29] This was the name by which he would be known to outsiders and to his equals or juniors in his tonsure family. In some provinces (like Fukien and Szechwan) the style might also incorporate a generation character taken from a gatha. In central China it usually did not. But even in central China many a master liked to use the same generation character in the styles of all his disciples in order to show that they were brothers. It was not taken from a gatha, but chosen arbitrarily. A few masters would use one such character to style some of their disciples and then shift to another.[30] Some monks, on the other hand, gave every disciple an entirely different style with no character in common. It was a matter of personal preference. They might also incorporate one character from the original lay name or choose characters that had some deep significance. For example, the Venerable Hsü-yün gave a disciple the name Miao-yün and the style Shao-men. The two second characters taken together made Yün-men, the name of the monastery that Hsü-yün hoped this particular disciple would help him restore.

It was possible to have more than one style. Hsü-yün himself, for example, was originally styled Yen-ch'e, and had adopted "Hsü-yün" because he wanted to live incognito and obtain some privacy.[31] During the Second World War, one of my informants found that the food ration was inadequate and adopted another name in order to get a second ID card and thereby a second ration book. He was not in the least embarrassed when he told me about it.

Sometimes the usage of name and style was reversed. One of my informants made a mistake in filling out the various forms when he enrolled at a seminary after ordination. He put down his name instead of his style and everyone there started to call him by it. Since he did not feel it was worth making a fuss about it, to this day he is so known. The same is true for several other informants, and in the Ku Shan ordination yearbooks names are used instead of styles in half a dozen cases. Therefore it does not appear that the restriction on their use was a very powerful one.

Sometimes it became necessary for a monk to change his style because it included a tabooed character. This happened only if, when he received the dharma, the dharma name of an ancestral master within three generations contained one of the characters in his own style. For example, Cheng-lien, who became abbot of the T'ien-ning Ssu in 1931, had originally been given the style Chen-lien by the master who shaved his head. But when he came to receive the dharma of the T'ien-ning Ssu as a brother of the 43rd generation, he found that the brothers of the 40th generation—that is, his "great grandfathers" —had used the generation character *chen,* which was therefore taboo (*hui-tzu*). Accordingly he changed his style from Chen-lien to Cheng-lien—from "Truth Lotus" to "Proof Lotus," the two sounds being homophonous for many Kiangsu residents. This practice is an additional element in the almost perfect parallel between blood kinship and religious kinship, although here too the latter was more elastic than the former since the taboo was often ignored.[32]

The monastic name system is important to understand because it reveals the nature of sects in Chinese Buddhism. Belonging to a sect did not necessarily have any doctrinal significance. It could be purely a matter of lineage. Almost all Chinese Buddhist monks belonged either to the Lin-chi or Ts'ao-tung sect in respect to tonsure.[33] Only in respect to transmission of the dharma were some of them T'ien-t'ai or Hsien-shou. None could belong to the Pure Land sect, since there were no Pure Land name gathas. Yet Pure Land was the sect whose doctrines almost all Chinese monks followed in their religious practice. More will be said about these anomalies (so different from sects in Japan and the West) in the final chapter.[34]

TRAINING IN THE HEREDITARY TEMPLE

After a novice had received the tonsure and his religious names, he began to train for ordination. According to custom the training period was supposed to be a minimum of three years. In practice it might be as little as three months or even three days. But most masters took pride in sending up candidates for ordination who were trained well enough to do credit to their temples. The great majority of my informants, as well as the monks whose dates are given in the ordination yearbooks, were trained one or two years, and most of the exceptions were those who had to wait even longer in order to reach the minimum age for being ordained.

During these one or two years the master cared for the disciple like a father for his son. He clothed him, gave him pocket money, and showed him how to live as a monk—how to dress, eat, and walk; how to prostrate himself and recite devotions; how to handle the liturgical instruments; how to order his life by the signals on the bell, drum, and board until it became second nature to him. One informant said that it had taken him only three months to memorize the texts of morning and afternoon devotions, but a year to learn how to chant them. By the end of the year he had also mastered the basic points of etiquette, such as always stepping across the left-hand side of the threshold with the left foot first. At a well-run hereditary temple the novices— commonly referred to as "little monks" (hsiao ho-shang)—were kept as busy as the pupils in a well-run boarding school. Here is a composite of several accounts.

The schedule began at 5:00 a.m. when they took part in morning devotions just as they would if they were living at a large public monastery, except that those who had not yet memorized the liturgy were allowed to use a breviary. After breakfast they did housework— cleaned the altar, swept the floors, and washed their own clothes and their master's. Then they went to the schoolroom to hear the master explain a text, after which they memorized it and recited it back. Sometimes they also practiced chanting (ch'ang-tsan). In the early afternoon they wrote out the text they had learned that morning, or at many temples they might have done this before lunch, so that their time was now their own. Sometimes they were sent out to do some work of merit, like collecting paper in the streets if it had writing on it (in China the written word was reverently burned to prevent it from being trampled on). Afternoon devotions were held at 4:00 p.m. and supper at 6:00 p.m., after which the novices would "worship buddha" (*pai-fo*) in the shrine-hall, alternately prostrating themselves and reciting "homage to Amitabha" or "homage to Kuan-shih Yin." At some temples this lasted an hour. At others, where it lasted only half an hour, it was followed by meditation. According to one informant, this was taught to beginners in the following way. Ten sticks of incense were laid side-by-side and then cut transversely at a fifteen-degree angle, so that twenty sticks of varying lengths resulted. The beginner sat in lotus position, holding the shortest stick in his hands. He would fix his eye on its glowing end in order to clear his mind of all extraneous thought. The smoke, according to this informant, did not hurt his eyes, since the incense used had no bamboo core. Day by day he worked up from the shortest stick to the longest, thus gradually increasing the period of concentration. As he recalled, "it was a wonderful feeling, as if a great weight, like a heavy coat, had been lifted off my body. This was the joy of the dharma (*fa-le*)." He was then fourteen years old.

Such was the daily life of a group of novices—perhaps eight or ten of them—in a well-run hereditary temple that had adequate income and a sufficient number of resident monks. But if the temple was poor and shorthanded, its two or three novices spent their time quite differently. They did all the work that would elsewhere be done by servants: not only sweeping, but cooking, gardening, and cleaning the latrines. As soon as possible they were taught how to recite penances and "release the burning mouths" so that they could help out when an order was received to perform a Buddhist service. Quite often there were only three or four ordained monks in residence, so that two or three novices would be required to bring the number of performers up to the minimum of five. The master, of course, pocketed their fees. Thus the poor temple was like the poor lay family where the father treated his children as useful chattels. Only a modicum of religious education was given.

Though my informants knew about such temples, none of those queried had been trained in one. During their novitiate none of them had gone out to take part in Buddhist services. Their time had been

entirely devoted to training and study. The only exception was a monk
who seems to have been exposed to a different system of novitiate altogether. He was not a very reliable informant,[35] but his account is
at least worth recording. He said that he had renounced lay life (*ch'u-
chia*) in the fourth month of 1944 at a small temple between Chengtu
and Omei Shan, but that this did not make him a member of the clergy
(*ch'u-chia jen*). His head had not been shaved and he had not been
given a religious name. For about a year, wearing lay clothes, he
simply did manual work about the temple, cooking and sweeping. He
was the only disciple there. In 1945 his master decided that he was fit
to become a monk. He gave him a name, allowed him to wear the
full-sleeved monk's gown, but still did not shave his head. Finally, at
the end of 1946, he took him to the Fu-hu Ssu, a large hereditary temple at Omei Shan. There the young man met twenty other novices,
who had also spent two or three years in various small temples and
had been brought to the Fu-hu Ssu by their masters who, like his
own, were all its heirs. The Fu-hu gatha was the basis for all their
names. From the 5th to the 8th of the twelfth lunar month the novices
went about the monastery prostrating themselves to all the members
of its tonsure family. On the 8th their heads were shaved before Wei-
t'o's image in a collective ceremony, each master shaving his own
disciples (some masters had more than one). Many laymen attended
and presented clothing and other necessities to the newly tonsured.
The latter had now become heirs of the Fu-hu Ssu themselves and
their names were so registered. After the ceremony was over, they
returned to their respective small temples to train further for ordination, which in the case of my informant took place the next year in
Kunming.

This system added two more stages to the process of entering the
sangha: first a period as a lay servant and then a period as an un-
tonsured novice.[36] Tonsure was deferred to the point usually reserved
for ordination, and ordination was deferred to a still later point. The
master benefitted by having a houseboy to whom he paid no wages.
The novice benefitted by learning humility through manual labor—if
he needed the lesson. Looking through my records, I find one other
monk who entered a temple on Omei Shan at the age of thirteen but
did not receive the tonsure there until he was fifteen. I did not have

the wit to ask him whether the system was the same, and he died soon after our interview.

In every Chinese system of novitiate there was the same advantage. Candidates were given an opportunity to find out what it meant to be a monk before they took their vows. Although for most of them tonsure was a blind step in the dark, made without any knowledge of Buddhism or monastic life, this was no longer true when they went for ordination. That may be one reason why so few Chinese monks voluntarily returned to lay life.

ORDINATION

Ordination was termed in Chinese "to accept the prohibitions" (*shou-chieh*), that is, to take a series of vows most of which were in the negative.[37] These vows, if kept, made it impossible to carry out various civic duties, especially military service. Recognizing this, successive Chinese dynasties exempted monks from conscription, corvee labor, and taxes. In return the sangha had the duty of creating merit for the benefit of the emperor and the commonwealth. The government was always concerned lest the special privileges it gave the sangha might be abused. Unscrupulous persons might take the robe not in order to lead pure lives creating merit, but simply to evade conscription and taxes. This would have weakened the State financially and militarily. Hence laws were formulated to limit the number of persons entering the sangha. Certain monasteries received imperial authorization to ordain at certain intervals. An unauthorized ordination was to be punished by eighty strokes of the stick. In most cases the interval was three years; in some it was as little as three months. If an authorized monastery wished to hold an extra ordination or if an unauthorized monastery wanted to hold any ordination at all, the law required it to apply to the district magistrate.

In practice the law was often ignored. Many small institutions that lay in remote but peaceful countryside ordained without any authorization whatsoever (this according to monks who remember the last decades of the Ch'ing dynasty). But if they lay near the city or in countryside menaced by bandits, they were likely to apply for authori-

zation, and even those that were permanently authorized to ordain
might send a notice to the magistrate. This was for two reasons. In
bandit-ridden countryside they hoped the magistrate would send
soldiers to secure the road leading up to the monastery. Near the city,
on the other hand, as one of my informants put it, "ordination involved
large numbers of people, bad ones as well as good ones. There was a
problem of public order." If any trouble developed, the monastery
wanted to have put the magistrate on notice, if not to have his men
already there to deal with it.

In 1911 central government control over ordination came to an end.
But the monasteries' need for security did not. Furthermore, laws went
into effect in some urban areas that required a permit to hold public
gatherings. This may explain, for example, why the Ching-tz'u Ssu,
Hangchow, in 1929 applied for an authorization to ordain from the
Hangchow Municipal Government, which issued it through the Public
Security Office.[38] Chiao Shan, on the other hand, which held ordinations all through the Republic period, never applied for a permit to do
so or gave a notice thereof. It lay securely on an island in the middle
of the Yangtze.

Although imperial authorizations to ordain lost their legal force with
the fall of the Empire, their practical effect continued. This was because Chinese monks, if they were serious about their career, wanted
to be ordained properly. Properly performed, the rites were long and
complicated and involved a large number of ordinands. Only monasteries with decades of experience and many buildings could perform
them. These were for the most part the monasteries that had been
imperially authorized to do so. Even after 1911, Chinese monks continued to flock to them for ordination.

The most famous among them was the Lung-ch'ang Ssu at Pao-hua
Shan, between Nanking and Chen-chiang. Every region had one or
two monasteries where it was considered particularly desirable to be
ordained, but the prestige of Pao-hua Shan was nationwide. J. Prip-
Møller stayed there during the entire spring ordination in 1930,
making careful notes and photographs.[39] K. L. Reichelt witnessed
ordinations both there and elsewhere in Kiangsu,[40] while J. J. M. De
Groot witnessed them at Ku Shan in Fukien and obtained a copy of
the ritual formulae employed.[41] Unfortunately, the accounts of these
three eminent investigators are inconsistent both with one another

and with the testimony of my informants, half a dozen of whom were ordained at Pao-hua Shan, and one of whom spent four years there as an ordination instructor (*yin-li shih*) and later three years as the catechist (*chiao-shou*), one of the trio of officers in over-all charge of ordinations.

According to these informants, proceedings were divided into two periods. During the first period, known as the "hall of sojourn" (*chi-t'ang*), ordinands arrived at the monastery, some of them weeks ahead of time, and lived as guests in the wandering monks' hall with no other duties than to register and to attend morning and evening devotions. In registering, they gave various details of personal history, including the name of their master and the year of tonsure. From this the officers of Pao-hua Shan could gauge how long and how well they had been trained and assign them to a group of ordinands of the same level. Each group had its own hall into which its members would move at the beginning of the second period.[42]

The beginning of the second period was called "division into classes" (*fen-t'ang*). No more ordinands were admitted, registration closed, and classwork began (*k'ai-t'ang*). The classes were known collectively as the "hall of ordinands" (*hsin-chieh t'ang*), which meant both a period of time and a place. As a period of time it lasted through the final day of ordination. As a place, it meant each of the halls in which classes (*t'ang-k'ou*) met. There were six of them, known as "first hall, second hall, third hall (*i-t'ang, erh-t'ang, san-t'ang*). . . ." Each hall—each class —had sixty to seventy persons. It was arranged like a meditation hall, with sleeping platforms along the sides. There were separate classes for monks, nuns, and lay brothers and sisters (bhikshus, bhikshunis, upasakas, and upasikas). Usually there were at least three classes for bhikshus alone.

During the first two weeks, those who were becoming monks and nuns—the clerical ordinands—studied how to eat, how to dress, how to lie when sleeping, how to make their beds, how to pack their belongings for a journey, how to stand and walk, how to enter the great shrine-hall, how to make a prostration to the buddha image, how to receive guests, how to hand over the duty (as a duty monk in the meditation hall, for example), and so on. Most of them had already learned much of this from their tonsure master while being trained in their small temple. But Pao-hua Shan put a high polish on the perfec-

45. An instructor inspects the ordinands. Pao-hua Shan.

tion of their deportment. Like Eton or Groton or, perhaps more appropriately, like Sandhurst or West Point, it left its mark. As my informant put it, "these things were taught properly only at Pao-hua Shan. Other places were slipshod about it. One had to live in Pao-hua Shan for ten years before he knew all this well enough to teach it."

The truth appears to be, however, that most of the instructors did not have this much experience and had, in fact, been studying at Pao-hua Shan for only two or three years. Four of them, known collectively as *yin-li shih*, were assigned to each class. The senior was the *k'ai-t'ang shih*, the second was the *p'ei-t'ang shih*, and the others were the "third master" and "fourth master" (*san shih-fu, ssu shih-fu*).[43] The ordinands also chose two of their own number as their representatives, who, since they walked first and last in processions, were called the "head novice" (*sha-mi t'ou*) and "tail novice" (*sha-mi wei*). They were chosen on the basis of their good looks, ability, and financial resources—the latter because they were expected to donate money for a vegetarian feast for all the monks in the monastery. If they did not have enough money of their own, their masters were usually happy to provide it, since they shared in their disciples' "glory."

Besides deportment the ordinands during these first two weeks studied certain texts, in particular the fifty-three gathas and mantras. These were sentences that a monk was supposed to recite mentally on various occasions each day (when getting out of bed, drinking water, hearing the large bell, and so on). After deportment and texts had been mastered, there came a night of repentance and purification during which all the ordinands—lay as well as clerical—prostrated themselves in the great shrine-hall. On the following day the first ordination was held. The head novice and tail novice would go in to make obeisance and, as deputies for their fellows, to ask the three masters (*san-shih*) and seven honored witnesses (*tsun-cheng*) to come forth and administer the vows. The three masters consisted of the ordaining abbot (*te-chieh ho-shang*), who was usually the retired abbot of the monastery and was considered to represent the Buddha; the confessor (*chieh-mo*) who sat on his left representing Manjusri; and the catechist (*chiao-shou*), who sat on his right representing Maitreya. At Pao-hua Shan the three masters and seven witnesses were all permanent residents. Elsewhere some of them were invited from other monasteries.

After the masters and witnesses had seated themselves on the porch
of the great shrine-hall, the clerical ordinands kneeled in the courtyard, recited the Three Refuges, and accepted the Ten Vows of the
sramanera. When they withdrew, the lay ordinands came forward,
recited the Three Refuges, and accepted the Five Vows of the upasaka.[44] The first part of the triple ordination concluded as each of the
sramaneras received his robes and bowl. The former consisted of the
five-part robe worn by novices and the seven-part robe worn by
bhiksus. Although they were not yet bhiksus, they filed over to the
refectory that noon, wearing their seven-part robes and carrying their
bowls just like the permanent residents.

Training for the next part began at once. Clerical ordinands now
had to learn a great deal of liturgy, particularly the 250 vows of the
Pratimoksa. After about two weeks of further study there was a second

46. Ordinands kneel as their representatives petition the ordination masters to come forth and administer the vows. Pao-hua Shan.

47. The ordination masters at Ch'i-hsia Shan, 1933. Ch'ing-ch'üan, the retired abbot of Chin Shan (center), presides, with the confessor on his left and the catechist on his right. Jo-shun, the incumbent abbot of Ch'i-hsia Shan, is on the right rear.

night of penance, followed by ritual bathing and cleansing. Whereas the other parts of the ordination could be witnessed by outsiders, these vows were administered on the secluded ordination platform (*chieh-t'ai*) and all outsiders were barred. Prip-Møller, one of the few foreigners who has witnessed it, writes: "That which was seen here is probably the most solemn ceremony within the Buddhist ritual, conducted in a spirit of devotion on the part of all the participants which is so wholehearted as to be seldom seen in the temples."[45] After accepting the 250 vows collectively, the ordinees went up to the platform in groups of three. Each group was termed an "altar" (*t'an*) and given a number. In the ordination yearbook we find all the ordinees listed under "first altar," "second altar," and so on. Starting in the early afternoon and continuing until well after midnight, the three ordination masters sat on the platform, examined each group, and accepted them as bhiksus. It must have been a real ordeal for the ordination abbot, since he was usually an old man. On the occasion witnessed by

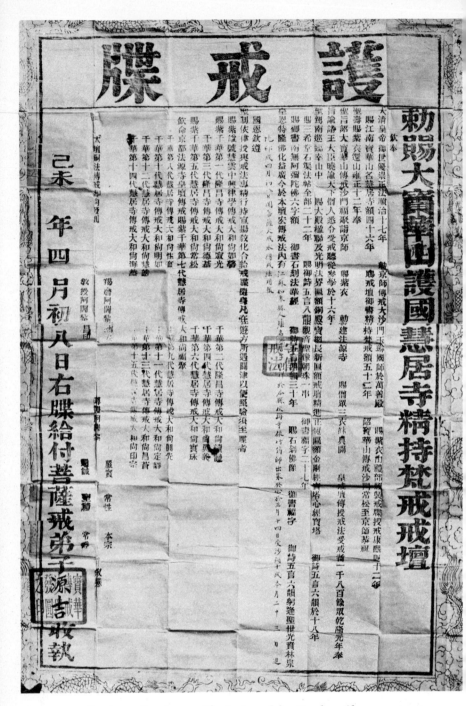

48. An ordination certificate issued by Pao-hua Shan, 1919.

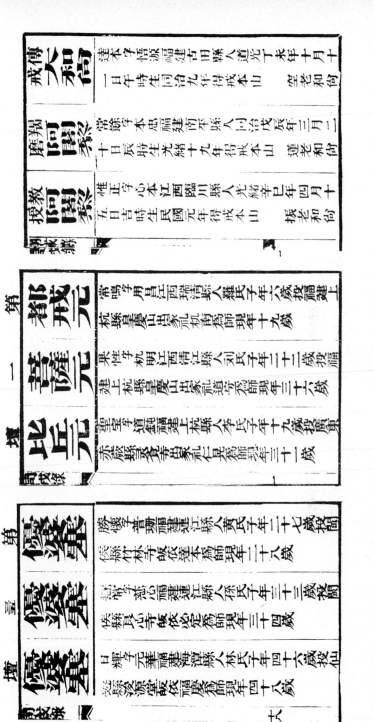

49. Pages from the Ku Shan ordination yearbook for 1926. Right to left are the initial pages of 1) section on officiating personnel, 2) section on monks ordained, and 3) section on lay ordinees.

Prip-Møller he let his place be taken later in the evening by his disciple, the abbot then in office.

The clerical ordinands thus became full-fledged members of the sangha according to the original Indian Buddhist practice, but according to Mahayana practice in China they still had another set of vows to take a week or so later. These were the fifty-eight vows of the *Fan-wang ching*,[46] which imposed a higher stratum of discipline and a commitment to lead all sentient beings into nirvana before attaining it themselves. Hence they were called the "Bodhisattva Vows." The clerical and lay ordinands recited the Bodhisattva Vows in a single ceremony with each group withdrawing while the other recited, but both groups kneeling together before and after. On the day before, heads had been burned in a manner to be described below. On the afternoon following, ordination certificates and yearbooks were handed out to everyone, while the monks received as well copies of the Pratimoksa, *Fan-wang ching*, and *P'i-ni jih-yung* (Daily Vinaya observances). The ordination abbot gave a valedictory address, with which the "ordinands' hall" was closed and the ordination came to an end.[47]

LENGTH OF ORDINATION

Now that we have a general idea of the proceedings, we can address ourselves to certain significant details. First of all, it is important (for reasons that will become apparent below) to know how long ordinations lasted, not only at Pao-hua Shan, but elsewhere. If we ask a monk about this, the chances are that he will answer "fifty-three days." This was the traditional period of the "ordinands' hall" from the division into classes through the day of the bodhisattva vows. The former catechist from Pao-hua Shan stated that in former times ordinations there used to last fifty-three days, starting the 15th of the second month and ending the 8th of the fourth. However, since at least as early as 1924, when he had been ordained, they had lasted only thirty-seven or thirty-eight days, starting the 1st of the third month and ending, as before, on the 8th of the fourth. This was the Buddha's birthday, the most important festival of the year, and it was the customary date for the end of the spring ordination at most Chinese monasteries.[48]

According to the catechist the period from the division into classes to the novice's ordination—that is, the preparatory training period—usually lasted two weeks. This is confirmed by the only documentary source I have seen that includes the date of the division into classes.[49] All other documents, including ordination certificates, simply give the dates of the vows themselves. In general, therefore, the longest period we know about is the interval between the novices' vows and the Bodhisattva Vows. Let us call it the "ordination interval" (including the two days on which the vows were taken).[50] In examples from Kiangsu supplied by Prip-Møller the ordination interval was about three weeks; in examples from Hupei it dropped to two weeks; and for Szechwan and Shansi it was one week only. At Ku Shan in 1916 it was four days, while in 1930 at a small monastery in Hunan it was just three days.[51] Such regional differences are extremely significant. As Prip-Møller remarks:

> These dates indicate that which is also confirmed in other ways,—that there is a tendency in the big monasteries of the lower Yangtze Valley districts to try to give the candidates for ordination as good a training as possible under the circumstances, in this case by making the time of preparation between the three parts of the ordination as long as possible, while in other parts of the country, even big monasteries such as Pao-kuang Ssu, which is one of the most famous ordination places in China, seem to follow the practice of the shorter intervals.[52]

The length of ordination gives us a rough numerical gauge of the seriousness with which masters and ordinands alike regarded a monastic career. No one who zipped through his vows in three days could take the same pride in his vocation as a monk who had undergone five or six exhausting weeks at Pao-hua Shan. Quite aside from the perfection of deportment that Pao-hua Shan instilled, it left unforgettable memories. The severity of the instructors, who beat the ordinands, young and old, with green willow switches; the hours of kneeling in a huge darkened hall; the solemnity of the proceedings and the eminence of those who oversaw them—all these produced, I suspect, a kind of trauma that was analogous to the trauma of the meditation hall.

What proportion of the Chinese sangha was affected by such solemn and lengthy ordinations? Pao-hua Shan itself ordained twice a year, once in the spring and again in the winter. The winter ordination

usually ended just before the New Year. Because of the cold weather
it was attended by only a few lay ordinands, hundreds of whom might
come in the spring. But winter and spring alike, according to the former
catechist, about three hundred monks were ordained—six hundred in
the course of a year.[53]

There were reported to have been approximately 90,000 monks in
Kiangsu.[54] Let us suppose that they spent an average of forty years in
the sangha (most, as we have seen, were ordained soon after twenty
and, in the cases I know about, lived to be sixty or seventy). On this
basis an intake of about 2,250 monks a year would maintain the
monastic population of the province. Pao-hua Shan alone ordained six
hundred. Ch'i-hsia Shan ordained between seventy-five and a hundred
and fifty, and other reputable Kiangsu monasteries ordained at least
three hundred more.[55] Even allowing for the outsiders who came to
Kiangsu for ordination and then returned home, it seems likely that
nearly half the monks in the province had been properly launched on
their career. This was probably one reason why Buddhism in Kiangsu
was flourishing.

PLENARY MASSES

It might seem as if the two hundred resident monks at Pao-hua Shan
would have had enough to do playing host and teacher to five hundred
ordinands. It certainly kept them very busy. But what made them
even busier was the custom of holding a series of plenary masses
while the ordination was under way. This was done in order to defray
the extra expense to which the monastery was being put. Ordinands
paid only a small fee: two to five dollars for monks, twice as much
for nuns, and three times as much for lay people.[56] This was not even
enough to cover the cost of feeding them.[57]

Each mass lasted seven days, sometimes falling between ordinations,
which was more convenient, sometimes overlapping. Prip-Møller includes photographs that show a mass under way in a corner of the main
courtyard at the same time that the ordinands were taking their
Bodhisattva Vows.[58] According to the former catechist the reason lay
people liked to have plenary masses performed during the ordination
ceremonies was that the monks were then particularly pure and, in

50. A serpentine procession, including ordinands, winds through the main courtyard during a plenary mass as workmen complete Kuan-yin's boat to be burned. Pao-hua Shan.

terms of merit, had a high "positive charge." Before the rites began the entire monastery was purified by sprinkling with holy water (*sa-ching*) and during the rites the participants constantly purified themselves through penance. Ordinands did not take part in the more intricate ritual of the mass, but they were on hand to "swell a procession" whenever large numbers were desirable. Some sixty ordained monks were usually required to conduct a plenary mass, and more hands were needed to house and feed the lay patrons who were paying for it. Although not many masses were performed during the winter ordination (because patrons preferred to wait for the warm spring weather), in spring there were usually enough to occupy the entire period from division into classes through the Buddha's birthday. What a relief his birthday must have been for the exhausted staff of the monastery!

MOXA

Sometimes I have been asked how to tell a Chinese Buddhist monk. The answer is: look at his head. Unless he has let his hair grow, you should be able to see on his scalp several lines of small, round, white scars. Termed "incense scars" (*hsiang-pa*), they were burned into his scalp by moxa at the end of his ordination. I have not myself investigated the history of this practice, which may postdate the Sung dynasty.[59] According to one of my informants, when government control over the issuance of ordination certificates was suspended by the Yung-cheng Emperor (1723-1736), monks were required to burn scars as a substitute means of identification. According to another informant, the practice began as an offering to the Buddha comparable to the burning of fingers that we shall discuss in the next chapter. Whatever its origin, it was nearly universal for the Chinese sangha in this century. The exception was Kwangtung province. There, in monasteries like Ting-hu Shan, the inside of the left forearm was burned instead of the pate.[60]

J. B. Pratt writes that a monk could choose to have three, nine, twelve, or eighteen scars "according to his zeal and courage."[61] At Pao-hua Shan, however, there was no such option. Those who took the bhiksu ordination received twelve scars, no more, no less. People taking the laymen's vows received nine scars. Novices received three. While the practice is said to have been similar throughout Kiangsu, in some monasteries elsewhere the number did vary. If nine was set as the minimum in a certain year by the ordination masters, an ordinee might still have another three burned as an expression of piety.

Usually (as at Pao-hua Shan) the burning took place the day before the bodhisattva ordination. At some monasteries it came just afterwards. In either case it was not done late in the day for reasons that Prip-Møller makes clear. His whole description of moxa is worth quoting.

> The novice wraps his praying rug tightly around his neck, holding in his hands before him a small red parcel given to him at the preceding ceremony. This parcel contains twelve to fourteen small black cones about 1 cm high, AI-JUNG Moxa Punk made from the Artemisia Chinensis, AI. In front of him stands one of the leading monks who has smeared some plant wax made from the dried pulp,

KUEI-YUAN, of the Lungan fruit, LUNG YEN, on the thumb of his left hand. Taking the combustible cones from the little red parcel tendered him, he touches the bottom of them with wax and places them one by one on the scalp in the places indicated by the small ink rings. This done, he takes a paper spill and quickly lights all the twelve cones. He himself and perhaps an assistant standing behind the kneeling novice now press their hands firmly around the latter's head, keeping it fixed as if in a vice. On account of the pain the novice will be sure to make some involuntary movements and as the cones thereby may tip over and brand scars in the wrong places, this procedure, as well as that of wrapping the rug around the neck, is necessary. During these preparations, as well as during the lighting and burning of the cones, the novice and the assisting monks continuously reiterate the prayer to Sakyamuni or to O Mi T'o Fo: NAN MO PEN SHIH SHIH CHIA MOU NI FO I Take My Refuge In Thee, Thou Original Master, Sakyamuni—or Amitabha. As the twelve small glowing points grow nearer and nearer the scalp, one can almost measure the degree of pain felt, by the cadence of the prayer, which in the mouth of the novice is repeated quicker and quicker and in a voice which grows more and more pitched until it ends, as is often the case when the fire reaches the skin, in a cry of pain. The burning itself lasts about a minute or so. The author has seen people going through this ordeal without flinching, but has also seen old men and boys throwing their arms around the knees of the leader as if they were all of the same juvenile years. It was interesting to note that while this occurred among the men, I did not see a single nun or lay-sister, who did not take the branding, whether of three or twelve marks, without a sound or quiver.

The acute pain felt at the moment is, however, not the only unpleasant result of the branding. In addition hereto comes the dangerous possibility of lasting injuries to the eye-sight and system, almost certain to come if preventive measures are not taken. The branding causes a temporary blood-poisoning followed by a sleepiness which is almost irresistible. If the novice gives way to this overpowering drowsiness and lies down to sleep, fatal effects such as impaired eye-sight or blindness, swollen heads, etc., will be the inevitable result. To assist the novices in their fight against this, it is decreed that on this day they are allowed to go wherever they please in the whole monastery, men and women, visiting guest halls, private halls, the abbot's quarters, etc., thus by a natural feeling of curiosity being helped to keep awake. The branding was done about nine o'clock in the morning at Hui Chü Ssu and at a similar hour at Ku Lin Ssu, Nanking, and during the whole day the novices were seen wandering all over the grounds, peeping in and looking around rooms

which on ordinary days would be absolutely taboo to them. At nine
o'clock in the evening an order was given by the abbot that vigilance
was to be kept until twelve o'clock at night. Not until then was it
considered safe to let the tired wanderers seek their well earned
and much-longed-for rest.[62]

The former catechist from Pao-hua Shan said that they were supposed to eat a lot of melons that day (at the Nan-hua Ssu, it was water
chestnuts) in order to "reduce the heat" (*t'ui-huo*). Another informant,
however, denied that there was danger of blindness. Only if a monk
had concealed his sins during the catechism—if, for example, he
killed a man, but kept silent when the question was raised (since a
murderer was disqualified from ordination)—then the ghost of the
murdered man might cause him to faint or even to die after his head
had been burned.

HINAYANA TENDENCIES

It was a custom rather than a regulation of the Chinese sangha that
monks should go to a large public monastery to be ordained. It could
also be done at an hereditary temple. Some hereditary temples held
regular ordinations (every winter, for example, at the Chin-shan Ssu
in Szechwan). Monks thus received their tonsure, their training, and
their ordination at one place. There was also a conscious effort on the
part of at least one eminent monk in China to revive the ordination
practice of early Indian Buddhism. Tz'u-chou, who died in 1957, was
considered second only to Hung-i (who died in 1931) as an authority
on the Vinaya. He was head of a temple in Peking, the An-yang Ching-
she, which often had a hundred student monks in residence. It was
"public" (*shih-fang*) in that pilgrim monks could stay there indefinitely.
Tz'u-chou made a specialty of lecturing on the *Avatamsaka Sutra*,
which he went through from beginning to end in three years. But his
most interesting specialty was to give the novices' ordination at the
time of tonsure, as is the custom in Theravada countries, and then to
delay the bhiksu and bodhisattva ordinations until the novice was
completely trained and had reached the minimum age of twenty that
is specified in the Vinaya. These higher vows too he gave himself in
his own temple rather than sending his disciples to an ordination

center. One of my informants had had his head shaved originally in Honan and then gone to Peking to be ordained at the Kuang-chi Ssu. He was only sixteen years old at the time, but he received all three ordinations. This was in 1944. Subsequently he went and studied the Vinaya at the An-yang Ching-she. When Tz'u-chou found out that he had received the two higher ordinations under the minimum age of twenty, he withdrew them. He then trained the young man four years and, when he reached the age of twenty, gave him the vows again.

Such conscious archaism was, so far as I know, a new phenomenon of the Republican period. It may have resulted from the increasing contact with Buddhists in Southeast Asia—contact that was limited, however, to only a few monks, so that most of the sangha was little affected.

CHAPTER X

The Monastic Career

Monks probably enjoyed more freedom than any other members of traditional Chinese society. Once ordained, all normal obligations ceased to exist for them. They owed nothing either to their parents or to the State.[1] While it is true that obligations to the natural family were often replaced by obligations to the religious family, this was optional. The monk could, if he wished, be as free as the cloud to which he was often compared. He was even free of the necessity to support himself, since if he could put up with the austerities of a public monastery, it would house, feed, and clothe him for as long as he cared to stay.

There were many different ways in which he could spend his time. Although they might be thought of as phases of his career, they did not come in any fixed order or last for a set period. Indeed, the only "career" in the usual sense of the word lay in monastic administration. A monk could start out as an acolyte and, after serving for many years in the sacristy, guest department, and business office, he might end up as abbot of a large monastery.

The majority of Chinese monks spent most of their time in small temples. Since the average small temple had neither land nor generous patrons, its residents had to support themselves by beating a wooden fish for a dollar a day. It was usually an easy life, or if it was not easy, it was profitable. Some monks were content to make it their career. Others only stayed at it long enough to earn the money for their next pilgrimage.

A few small temples, as we saw in Chapter V, because they had income from land or patrons, did not depend on rites for the dead. Their residents were free to devote themselves to scholarly pursuits. The owner might be an eminent monk who used the premises as a school for his disciples from which he went forth on lecture tours. Such a temple was often called a "hermitage" (*ching-she*).[2]

The real hermitage was the "thatched hut" (*mao-p'eng*), usually built with the hermit's own hands in some remote spot where he would not be interrupted in study and religious exercises. The life of the hermit had roots in China that go back at least five hundred years before the introduction of Buddhism.

Still other kinds of life were to be found in the great public monasteries like Chin Shan and the Kao-min Ssu. Sitting on the western side of the meditation hall were the *lao hsiu-hsing*, the "old papayas," who spent their days in the yogic pleasures to which they had become addicted. Out in the kitchen and service area were the menial officers who eschewed both the difficulties of meditation and the cares of higher office, preferring to cook rice and boil water, perhaps for a few semesters or perhaps until they died. Other monks, after beginning to work up the administrative ladder turned instead to study and teaching, which they could pursue at the public monastery under a retirement system that will be described below.

Let it be emphasized that these different kinds of life were alternating rather than alternative. A monk might wander about China for a few years, then save up a little money from performing rites for the dead, then live as a hermit, then take office for a while at a large monastery, and then begin to wander again. In theory, on the other hand, there was a proper sequence. The first five years after ordination were supposed to be spent in study of the monastic rules. There was a saying: "Until the fifth summer specialize in perfecting yourself in the Vinaya. Only after the fifth summer may you listen to the doctrine and take part in meditation." Study of the monastic rules could best be carried on in a Vinaya center like Pao-hua Shan. This was because the average tonsure master was unqualified to instruct his disciples in the finer points. As one informant said: "If you just went back to live in your hereditary temple after ordination, you had no hope of learning the rules well." In practice, however, very few monks spent the first five years in a Vinaya center. The unambitious (probably in a majority) returned instead to their hereditary temples to earn a living by the wooden fish. Those who were more serious about their vocation entered a meditation hall or took up the life of a wandering monk.

WANDERER AND PILGRIM

Wandering was a most important phase in a monk's career. In the first place the hardship that it entailed wore away his attachment to comfort and security. Even in the Republican period he had to travel much of the time on foot, either because he did not have the money for a ticket or because there was no public transportation along his route. If he was going to a country monastery, the last few miles of his journey were almost sure to be on foot, since such monasteries lay back in the hills. All his possessions were in a bundle (*i-tan*) that he carried on his back. It was wrapped in a special way, and tied to it was a yellow "incense bag" (*hsiang-tai*) embroidered on each corner with the characters of the four elements (symbolizing the four quarters of the land) and in the center with the character "buddha." In his hand he carried a pilgrim's shovel (*fang-pien ch'an*), which he could use to bury the bodies of men or animals that he found along the road, and which also served as a weapon of self-defense. It was not always easy to find lodging. Public monasteries, which offered hospitality to any ordained monk, were few and far between and they would not admit him if he was accompanied by an unordained novice.[3] He might not have the money for an inn, and in any case the rules did not allow him to spend more than two nights under the same roof as laymen.[4] Small, hereditary temples would give him three nights' lodging if they chose to do so, but they did not always so choose. In 1902, for example, when Hsü-yün was on his way back to Yünnan from a pilgrimage to Omei Shan, he fell in a river and reached the next town toward evening, soaking wet. He found that the inns there would not take in monks and that the one monk in town was equally inhospitable. Finally this inhospitable monk agreed to let Hsü-yün and his companion spend the night outdoors near his temple under a platform which was normally used for giving theatrical performances. They wanted to light a fire and gave him money for straw, but what he brought them was wet straw that would not burn. "We put up with it and sat waiting for sunrise."[5]

But wandering monks had a higher purpose than "roughing it." The usual expression for wandering was *ts'an-fang,* which may be translated as "traveling to every quarter of the country." But the word *ts'an* also suggests *ts'an-hsüeh,*[6] "to engage in training and in study," not only of books, but of meditation (*ts'an-ch'an*) and all other religious exercises. Wandering monks wanted to study and to practice religious exercises under the best possible guidance. Wherever they found such guidance, they would interrupt their travels to enroll for a term in the meditation hall (usually the winter term, when the brisk weather favored the work) or to hear a course of lectures on the Tripitaka (usually in summer). This was in accordance with the adage "in winter meditation, in summer study" (*tung-ch'an, hsia-hsüeh*). In the course of many years of wandering a monk would hope to have sat in the best meditation halls and studied the important texts under the leading authorities on each. Among the eminent masters with whom he came in contact, there might be one with whom he felt a special affinity (*yu-yüan*) and whose follower he became (*ch'in-chin*).

When the wandering monk arrived at a monastery where he had no friends or connections, he would be lodged in the wandering monks hall (see p. 13). There he might find many kinds of people—not only Buddhist monks from different regions of China, some virtuous, some rascally, but also Taoist priests and Tibetan lamas (only nuns were absolutely excluded). Thus the wandering monks hall was an interesting place to be, a place where he had lots of time to gossip and interesting people to gossip with—all part of his education. When he felt that he had exhausted its possibilities, he simply gave notice of his impending departure to the head of the hall and left. No permission to leave was required, and no record was made of his visit.

If, on the other hand, a visitor arrived who had some connection with the monastery, he would not be lodged in the wandering monks hall, but given superior accommodations and exempted from the normal requirement to attend devotions and meditation. In some cases he might even be presented with a courtesy rank. In 1947 one of my informants, when he was guest prefect of a Hunan monastery, had been particularly kind to a visiting monk from Kwangtung. The next year he went to Kwangtung himself and stayed at the latter's monastery. Their positions were now reversed, for his friend was guest prefect there, and, to repay the kindness he had received, arranged that the Hunanese monk should be given the rank of junior instructor as well as an apartment to live in. Some monasteries (Ku Shan, for example) are said to have had dozens of honorary rank-holders, some on the basis of courtesy, and some out of the desire to cement a useful connection.

It was the hope of devout Chinese monks to visit all the "four famous mountains," each sacred to a bodhisattva, as tabulated below:

Mountain*	Province	Bodhisattva	
		Sanskrit	Chinese
Omei	Szechwan	Samantabhadra	P'u-hsien
Wu-t'ai	Shansi	Manjusri	Wen-shu
P'u-t'o	Chekiang	Avalokitesvara	Kuan-yin
Chiu-hua	Anhwei	Ksitigarbha	Ti-tsang

The bodhisattvas of these mountains were believed to take the form of men and show themselves to devout pilgrims who came to worship them. For example, one of my informants, together with the party of lay pilgrims whom he was leading to the island of P'u-t'o Shan, spied an old monk sitting in a cave by the beach. When they looked again his appearance had changed, and finally he disappeared. This was seen clearly by all but one of the party, and they knew that they had been vouchsafed a glimpse of Kuan-yin. Similarly, when Hsü-yün made a pilgrimage to Wu-t'ai Shan in 1882, he was helped out of difficulties along the way by a beggar, who gave his name as Wen-chi. Later Hsü-yün realized that it had been an avatar of Wen-shu, Wu-t'ai's presiding bodhisattva.

The purpose of Hsü-yün's pilgrimage deserves notice. He wanted to get Wen-shu's intercession on behalf of his deceased parents "so that they would be delivered from suffering and reborn in the Pure Land as soon as possible." Hence he made a prostration, touching his head to the ground, every three steps along the road from P'u-t'o Shan to W'u-t'ai Shan, a thousand miles as the crow flies. It took him two years.[7] This sort of penance was known as "burning the prostration incense" (shao pai-hsiang), although, in fact, no incense was neces-

---

* P'u-t'o Shan is an island. The others are mountains.

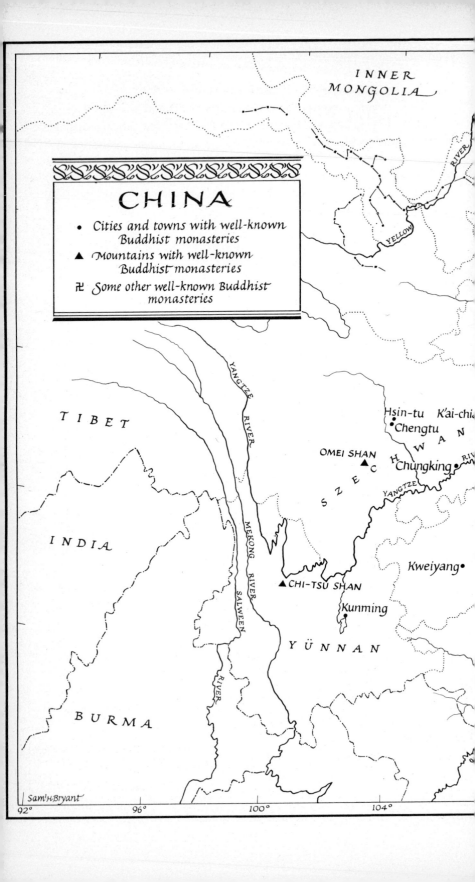

INNER MONGOLIA

YELLOW RIVER

CHINA

- • Cities and towns with well-known Buddhist monasteries
- ▲ Mountains with well-known Buddhist monasteries
- 卍 Some other well-known Buddhist monasteries

TIBET

YANGTZE RIVER

Hsin-tu K'ai-chi

• Chengtu

OMEI SHAN ▲

S Z E C H W A N

Chungking • RI

YANGTZE

INDIA

MEKONG RIVER

SALWEEN

▲ CHI-TSU SHAN

Kunming

Kweiyang •

Y Ü N N A N

RIVER

BURMA

Sam'l H Bryant

92°   96°   100°   104°

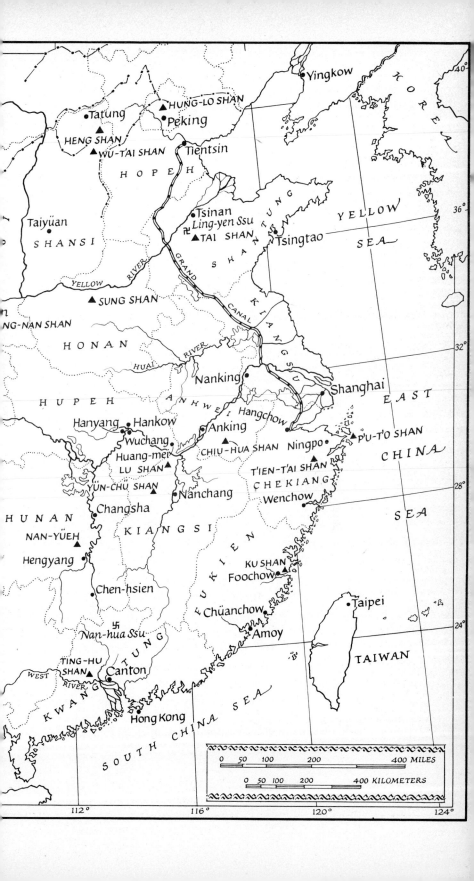

sarily burned. On a less heroic scale than Hsü-yün's, the practice was fairly common. Another of my informants joined a group of pilgrims who journeyed to P'u-t'o Shan from Shanghai in 1941. He and the other six monks in the party prostrated themselves every three steps, while their lay companions did so every nine steps. With each step they recited the words "Homage to the great compassionate bodhisattva, Kuan-shih Yin." In this wise they made the circuit of all the temples and shrines as was the practice at sacred mountains. If nightfall caught them on the road, they would leave a stone to mark the place and then return the next day to resume their prostrations where they had left off. It took them a month to complete the circuit of the island, which is only three or four miles long.

Whereas the ordinary Buddhist institution offered no mementos, centers of pilgrimage like P'u-t'o Shan were exceptional. There the visitor could have the seals of every monastery imprinted on the border of his ordination certificate, and, if he wished, on his yellow pilgrim's bag as well. Some monks considered this in poor taste and preferred to carry a small album (almost like an autograph book) in which the seals could be imprinted page by page. In any form they were tokens of a meritorious journey that would be treasured until death.

STUDENT AND LECTURER

As the wandering monk traveled up and down China, he did not always find that it was "in winter meditation, in summer study." At some monasteries lectures on a sacred text might be held in any season of the year, while at others they were never held at all. They were never held at Chin Shan, for example, because they conflicted with its Ch'an tradition of a wordless teaching. But at many, if not most monasteries they were customarily held during the summer retreat[8] from the 15th of the fourth month to the 15th of the seventh. They would be delivered by the abbot if he felt competent to do so. If not, a specialist would be invited from the outside.

The program varied from monastery to monastery. It might be limited to a single two-hour lecture delivered in the middle of the day. The noon periods in the meditation hall would be cancelled so that the monks enrolled there could attend. At other monasteries, which placed less emphasis on meditation and more on teaching, there would be a round-the-clock program of lectures and study that turned the premises virtually into a school. According to one monk, this had been an established form of religious instruction since the Six Dynasties. He had often taken part himself in such instruction, first as a student and later as a lecturer, in the years between 1918 and 1950.

First, he said, the monastery would get a commitment from some eminent dharma master to deliver the course, probably on a sutra in which he specialized. Once he had accepted, handbills (*pao-tan*) would be printed on yellow paper, pasted up at the main gate, and sent to other monasteries in the area to be pasted up not only at their gates but in the streets of neighboring cities and towns. If the lectures were to be in T'ai-hsien, for example, handbills might be sent as far away as Chen-chiang (75 kilometers), but not to Nanking or Shanghai (140 and 175 kilometers). The text of such a handbill would read something like this:

> From the nth day of the nth month dharma master So-and-so has been reverently invited to expound the complete text of the *Lotus Sutra*. All good and devout laymen and laywomen will then be welcome to attend at their pleasure and to listen reverently to the principles of the dharma. Those members of the sangha who decide to attend and take part in the study[9] are asked to come to the monastery ahead of time in order to enroll and take up temporary residence (*pao-ming chin-tan*).
>
> > Nth day, such-and-such monastery's
> > head monk So-and-so.

Monks who saw this notice and decided to attend would immediately pack their bags and take to the road. The monastery where the lectures were to be delivered might lie in the mountains several days' journey away. They would try to get there ahead of time.

Once it began, the daily program of lectures and study consisted of four parts.

1) The principal lecture (*ta-tso*). This was delivered with impressive and exacting ceremony, so that it was ritual no less than instruction. Shortly before 2:00 p.m. all the monks who had enrolled would gather in the lecture hall, which could be any room in the monastery

that fitted their number, but was usually the dharma hall (*fa-t'ang*). They would be formally dressed in their robes of gray or brown (*ch'i-i*). At exactly 2:00 the principal lecturer would enter, dressed in a red robe, and be escorted slowly down the hall between the ranks. Before a low altar he offered incense and prostrated himself to the Buddha. Then he mounted a raised platform behind and above the altar, where he settled himself on a very wide seat (of a sort known to curio buyers as a "monk's chair"). He sat there cross-legged, motionless, as if in meditation, while his audience chanted the "incense hymn" (*hsiang-tsan*), all standing with palms pressed together. Only when the hymn was over (and it took fifteen to twenty minutes) did his lecture begin. He would read a sentence or two from the sutra, which lay open on the low table before him, and then give an exegesis. In the case of a pithy text like the *Heart Sutra,* he might spend one or two hours on a single phrase. If the text were longer, he read more and explained less. He might employ a lively informal delivery; or he might be one of those who preferred to sit with eyes half closed, motionless except for their fingers running continuously over their beads, and to speak in a curious singsong. When two hours were up, he would transfer merit, close the book, descend from the dais, and leave the hall. The audience would enjoy a rest period of about an hour.

2) The side lecture (*p'ien-tso*). The principal lecturer (*ta-tso fa-shih*) usually brought with him a group of his pupils. There might be as many as eight or ten. Each day he would appoint one of them in rotation to serve as side lecturer (*p'ien-tso fa-shih*). At about 5:00 p.m. a signal was struck and everyone reassembled in the lecture hall. The side lecturer entered, went through the same ritual, and lectured on the same section of the text as the principal lecturer. The only difference was that he and his audience wore full sleeved gowns (*hai-ch'ing*), not robes, since this now was a form of drill (*hsüeh-hsi*), not an original lecture by a dharma master.

3) Study (*yen-chiu*). After eating supper the audience would again return to the lecture hall, bringing with them copies of the text and commentaries. They would ask all eight or ten of the side-lecturers to join them. "We worked by lamplight," said my informant. "It used to be bean oil or kerosene. We would study the commentaries. When we found something we could not understand, we would ask one of the side-lecturers or one of the older monks in the audience. There were

usually two or three older monks who had been attending lectures for years and understood much more than we did. So in this study period, which lasted about one hour, we carried on mutual study."

4) The minor lecture (*hsiao-tso*). The next morning after breakfast, at about 9:00 a.m., everyone would gather in the lecture hall, refreshed by a night's sleep, to go over the same section of text a fourth time. The principal lecturer, sitting up on the platform, would choose by lot a student monk in the audience, drawing his name from a tube of bamboo slips. The student would do exactly as the side-lecturer had done the day before.

A lecture series of this kind in a rural monastery was attended almost solely by monks. Lay visitors might attend for a few days, but they seldom if ever stayed for the entire course. Nuns could seldom attend because they were not permitted to stay under the same roof. But if the monastery lay in the city the composition of the audience would be quite different. All four categories—monks, nuns, male and female devotees—might attend in force. Many of the lay devotees, when the lecture series came to an end, might take the Refuges with the monk who had given it. For example, after Hsü-yün lectured at the Kuei-hua Ssu in Kunming in 1904, over 3,000 persons took the Refuges with him. In 1905 after he lectured on the *Lotus Sutra* in Penang, there were only a few hundred who did so, but the total in Malaya that year was over 10,000.[10]

There have been many other famous lecturers who traveled up and down China in the last century to spread the dharma. In 1892, Yüeh-hsia assisted Fa-jen lecture on the *Lankavatara Sutra* at the Kuei-yüan Ssu in Hupeh. In 1897 he visited many provinces lecturing himself. In 1911 he was doing so in Hupeh again. Three years later he expounded the *Surangama Sutra* in Peking; two years later in Hangchow. Then he went to Ch'ing Shan to expound the *Lotus Sutra*.[11] Another eminent monk, Tao-chieh, lectured at the T'ien-t'ung Ssu in 1906 and again in the spring of 1907, the first year on the *Lotus Sutra*, the next year on the *Surangama Sutra*.[12] The practice continued—indeed expanded—during the Republican period. Two of the leading lecturers were Ti-hsien and Ying-tz'u. A disciple of Ying-tz'u has told me that every winter in the 1930's they went to the T'ien-t'ung Ssu, where they took part in meditation weeks, while every spring they went somewhere to lecture, usually on the *Avatamsaka Sutra*.

Besides the texts already mentioned, others that were commonly expounded included the *Heart Sutra*, the *Diamond Sutra*, the *Yüan-chüeh ching* (Taisho 842), and the *Vimalakirtinirdesa Sutra*. Most monks used the "great seat style" (*ta-tso i-shih*), in which the ceremony and the red robe were invariable, although there was not necessarily the complete program of side lectures, small lectures, and study.[13] During the Republican period, however, a new style was introduced. The lecturer wore an ordinary monk's robe; he spoke in an ordinary voice, writing often on a blackboard; and he stood while his audience sat.

The "great seat style" was preferred by those who felt that the sutras deserved special reverence and should not be treated "like a common textbook." The new style was preferred by those who felt that the sutras should be mastered more rapidly, which the use of the blackboard facilitated. The Chinese language has so many dialects and homophones that without a blackboard, technical terms cannot be easily understood.

Lectures have played an important role in Chinese Buddhism from the earliest days. Probably one of the reasons why Buddhism succeeded in China was that it included the very Chinese institution of having disciples study a canonical text under the guidance of a master who used it to shape their character. There was a certain parallel to Confucius and Mencius in the monks who even in this century traveled from place to place, a few followers at their side, lecturing on the sutras.

DHARMA DISCIPLE

Some of the pupils who followed an eminent lecturer from place to place as his assistants and understudies might eventually receive the dharma from him, that is, be given dharma scrolls that formally acknowledged them as his dharma disciples. But this was not a relationship limited to lecturer and understudies. Any monk who had received the dharma himself could transmit it to any other monk he chose. In theory, at least, he was transmitting the same wordless understanding which Mahakasyapa had received from the Buddha on Vulture Peak and which had been handed down through eighty or ninety generations.

We saw in Chapter VI how the dharma was transmitted in connection with the post of abbot. What we have here is a quite different type of dharma transmission that had nothing to do with abbotship. It was private rather than institutional, individual rather than collective. A single master transmitted to a single disciple: later he might transmit to another. Or perhaps he transmitted to several disciples at the same time. None of these disciples, however, was supposed to receive this sort of private dharma from a second master, since that would have been disloyal to the first. He could, however, receive additional dharmas from every monastery that asked him to serve as abbot. *That* kind of relationship was institutional and did not conflict with the private relationship that we are discussing.

For private transmission the master did not necessarily get the approval of his own master and he seldom got the approval of his dharma brothers if he had any. There was little "family spirit" and no collective action. Perhaps this was partly because there was no collective property involved. Often, indeed, little more was involved than the master's desire to present a token of friendship or make a courteous gesture or acquire politically useful connections. During the 1950's, for example, a well known abbot in Taiwan wrote to a monk in Rangoon who was an agent of the Nationalist government there, and asked him to suggest the name of another Chinese monk in Burma to whom he, the abbot, could transmit the dharma. His colleague in Rangoon suggested the name of a sturdy, half-illiterate soul who had fled across the border from Yünnan before the Communist advance in 1950 and was staunchly pro-Nationalist. Without ever having met him and, indeed, without even finding out whether he would accept the dharma, the abbot sent him a dharma scroll. This was intended to bring him into the group of the abbot's supporters.

I have heard of no other instance of such flagrant abuse of the tradition started by the Buddha when he held up a flower at Vulture Peak. More often the act was precisely what the Chinese call it: "transmission of the dharma for the sake of spreading the dharma" (*hung-fa ti ch'uan-fa*). Thus Ying-tz'u, the eminent lecturer, transmitted the dharma to one of his pupils on the eve of the latter's return to Malaya, so that he might have greater authority in preaching the doctrine there.

Originally Ying-tz'u had toyed with the idea of transmitting the dharma of the Avatamsaka sect, since he specialized in lecturing on the *Avatamsaka Sutra*. But in the end what he transmitted was simply the Lin-chi dharma (of the Ch'an sect) which he had received himself from T'ien-ning Ssu.[14] This had been an institutional dharma as he had received it, but it became a private dharma as he transmitted it. That is, it conferred no rights whatever to the abbotship of the T'ien-ning Ssu. But (and here is the "catch") it could become an institutional dharma again if his disciple used it to found or restore a monastery. All future abbots of that monastery would then be his dharma descendants.

Ti-hsien, when he wished to spread the doctrine of the T'ien-t'ai sect, transmitted its dharma to ten disciples, whom he sent forth in the "ten directions." In a few years they were preaching T'ien-t'ai and taking disciples themselves all the way from Manchuria to Hong Kong.[15] Even when private transmission did not serve such a specifically missionary goal, at least there was supposed to be an affinity between master and disciple. For example, at Ku Shan before Hsü-yün reformed it, many of the officers transmitted their private dharma to their private disciples—monks whose heads they had shaved at Ku Shan, then trained there, and later ordained there—a mere gesture, but a gesture between two people who were by then extremely close. Elsewhere too, it was not uncommon for a person to become successively the Refuges, tonsure, and dharma disciple of the same monk: "there was an affinity between them from former lives (*yu-yüan*)," as one informant explained it. Thus a dharma scroll could mean more than mere intellectual understanding, or it might mean less than the most superficial acquaintance. In a way it was like an M.A., which at some universities requires two years' work, whereas at others it can be obtained by paying £5 a few years after graduation. Therefore some who were offered scrolls refused, while some who accepted them were unworthy.

Generally speaking, T'ien-t'ai and Hua-yen scrolls were not connected with the abbotship of monasteries.[16] There was more often such a connection in the case of Ch'an scrolls (Lin-chi and Ts'ao-tung). As to the Pure Land school, presumably because it was based on faith rather than understanding, there was no dharma transmission at all.

PROSELYTIZER

Every Chinese monk felt committed to follow the path of the compassionate bodhisattva by helping all other sentient beings towards
salvation. Creatures condemned to the two lowest planes of existence
could be helped by rites for the dead, which were discussed in Chapter VII. Animals and humans could be helped by conversion, that is,
by getting them to take Refuge in the Three Jewels: the Buddha, the
dharma, and the sangha. This made them "sons of the Buddha" (*fo-
tzu*), gave them "good roots," and increased their chances for a better
rebirth. The latter was particularly important in the case of animals,
since if they could be reborn as men, they would be able to benefit
more from hearing the dharma preached. Even as animals, however,
they were not without understanding. The proof of this is that, when
they received the Refuges, some would respond. Turtles, for example,
often bowed three times, to show that their buddha nature had been
aroused. In 1909, when the Venerable Hsü-yün was traveling in Yünnan, he was having a chat with a high official. Suddenly a cow came
over to where they were sitting and knelt before him, with tears
streaming from both eyes. It belonged to a cattle butcher, who soon
appeared on the scene. Hsü-yün said to the cow: "If you want to
escape from life, you must take Refuge in the Three Jewels." The cow
nodded its head and Hsü-yün recited the Three Refuges on its behalf.
When it got up, it was as quiet and docile as a human being. Hsü-yün
tried to offer compensation to the cattle butcher, but the latter would
not accept it. He was so overcome by the miracle he witnessed that
he renounced his trade, took the Refuges himself, and became a
vegetarian.[17]

One monk I know administers the Three Refuges to every cow he
meets. He takes just as lively an interest in human converts. When
he was visiting the United States, I took him to see the Concord Battle-
ground. While admiring the spot where the famous shot was fired, he
noticed two Concord boys, ten or twelve years old. Though he was
unable to speak English, he made friends with them and before I knew
it he was stroking the head of each and saying "Take refuge in the
Buddha, take refuge in the dharma, take refuge in the sangha." Then
he got each of them to repeat in Chinese "Homage to the buddha

Amitabha." He went away happy. "Who knows?" he said. "The good roots have been established. They may go to Harvard someday and study Buddhism."

HERMIT AND ASCETIC

Hermits were to be found on almost every sacred mountain in China, living in caves and huts. Reichelt states that they spent their days reciting sacred texts "in fanatical ecstasy.[18] Prip-Møller supplies a photograph of a cave where the character *fo* (buddha) was carved into the stone floor, allegedly by years of tracing with a hermit's fingertip.[19] We read in Hsü-yün's autobiography about the period early in 1902 when he was living alone in a "thatched hut" that he had knocked together on Chung-nan Shan, a famous Buddhist mountain in Shensi. Since water was scarce, he had been melting snow to drink and eating wild herbs. He frequently exchanged visits with other hermits on the mountain. One day in the twelfth month he put some taros on to boil and sat waiting for them to be done. Without being aware of it, he entered samadhi. At New Year's his neighbors were surprised that he had not been over for a long time and went to convey New Year's greetings. Around his hut the ground was covered with tiger tracks and not a human footprint. They went in to look and found him in samadhi. When they brought his meditation to an end with a note on the *ch'ing,* they asked: "Have you eaten?" He answered: "Not yet. The taros in the pot must be cooked by now." When they looked they found that there was over an inch of mold and the taros were frozen hard as a rock. Fu-ch'eng (one of his neighbors) said: "You have been wholly in trance for half a month."[20]

The hermit usually had a more substantial diet than taros and melted snow. He might have supporters in the city who sent him an occasional bag of rice; or he might depend on a nearby monastery or on the charity of pilgrims. To take advantage of the pilgrim traffic, he sometimes built his "thatched hut" close to the main path up the mountain. Even if he was away from the path, he would still be welcome to partake when a rich pilgrim donated a vegetarian feast to the monks of the monastery, and he too would receive a little money as a feast gift (*chai-ch'en*).[21] No matter where he lived, he probably had a vegetable garden, where he spent a few hours a day with a hoe, raising his own greens. He cooked for himself, swept and cleaned (though cleaning was not always his forte), and foraged on the mountain slopes for faggots. Thus he was busied with self-sufficiency as well as religious exercises. Also, unless he had chosen a really inaccessible spot (as some preferred), he could expect to spend part of each day talking to visitors. Lay devotees came to partake of his wisdom and sanctity. Scholars and officials came to enjoy the sense of vicarious escapism that contact with him afforded. Although he was fully Buddhist, he exemplified the ancient Taoist tradition of love of nature and of uncompromising individualism. Often the place he had chosen for his cave was spectacularly beautiful.

The only hermit that I have met lived near a pagoda that he had turned into one of the most successful tourist attractions in the New Territories of Hong Kong. He had let his hair grow long (like the monk in the photograph opposite). He had such an aversion to the amenities that whenever I asked him to write words out for me on a fresh 4 x 6 filing card, he would refuse and extract the leaf of an old calendar from a pile of rubbish. Rubbish filled the whole house he lived in, although he was extremely rich (from speculation in real estate). He was the monk who told me to take down my trousers so that he could tell my fortune. Yet he was a famous lecturer on the sutras. Despite his 80-odd years, he had a kind of free-wheeling vigor —almost rascality—that made him perfectly delightful.

Because his hair was long and he eschewed the amenities, he was called an "ascetic" (t'ou-t'o heng, Sanskrit dhuta). Prip-Møller furnishes a fine photograph of the cave lived in by such an ascetic. His bed was made of several granite blocks, up-ended and covered with layers of rags. It was too short to lie on, so that he never slept prone, but always in a sitting position. He had let the hair on his head grow down to his shoulders. He was supported by devotees in Shanghai who regarded him as a saint. A hundred and eight of them had made him a robe of a hundred and eight patches, the patches symbolizing poverty.[22]

It was common for hermits in their huts and caves to practice various kinds of self-mortification. The same practices were also to be found at large public monasteries. The life of the meditation hall was in itself a kind of self-mortification, as was the work of the menial officer (heng-tan), who spent his day toiling in the heat of the kitchen.

51. A long-haired ascetic in a patched gown. Central China.

But there were other, more specialized practices that we shall now consider in the order of their severity.

1) Striking the bell for the sake of the nether world (*ta yu-ming chung*). A monk would vow that for a certain number of months or years he would strike one of the large bells of a monastery or temple for a certain number of hours a day. If it was to be for twenty-four hours a day, he moved into the belfry, where he would sleep and have his meals. A string would be run from his cot to the bell-clapper and every five or ten minutes throughout the night he would wake up and give it a tug. Even in the early hours of the morning the deep tones would fly out over distant hills and villages and penetrate even to hell, reminding all creatures to take refuge in the dharma. During the day, at least, it was common for such a monk to recite a sacred verse between the notes.

2) Sealed confinement (*pi-kuan, tso-kuan*). This meant staying within the confines of one room, usually for a term of three years, and devoting oneself to religious exercises, perhaps studying a particular text or reciting buddha's name.[23] The confinement was inaugurated with a certain flourish. Friends and lay supporters would be invited to attend and some eminent monk would read a solemn declaration of how the period of confinement was to be spent. Farewells would be said, the ascetic monk would enter his solitary abode, the door would be locked, and two boards would be nailed over the doorway like an "X", inscribed with the date and particulars. Thus he was sealed in—in a sense. Usually he had large, airy windows as well as a wicket into the corridor through which he could receive his food and chat with visitors—even courteously handing them oranges, as one monk did to me. I found a little bell on the sill of the wicket, which I banged to summon him. He gave me not only oranges, but a copy of his book on Pure Land doctrine. He was not scheduled to be confined for three years, but for however long it took him to make a thorough study of the *Avatamsaka Sutra*. I remember him well, partly because he was such a civilized person, and partly because of the attractiveness of his little *mao-p'eng*—in his case, a "thatched hut" in fact as well as in name—which he had built on a mountaintop with his own hands. He was not a hermit, however, because two devout laywomen lived there taking care of him. Sometimes the operation would be financed by a rich devotee, who thereby shared in merit created.

It would be unjust to belittle the hardship of sealed confinement. However comfortable the quarters might be, it meant putting up with a much longer period within four walls than I would have cared to—three years in the case of two other such monks I have visited.

52 In the ceremony inaugurating sealed confinement the abbot (center) watches as strips of paper are tacked up over the door The superscription reads *"prajna* (wisdom) confinement" and the strips give the date and the formula: "Homage to the celestial bodhisattva Wei-t'o, protector of the dharma." Taiwan.

53. Same.

3) Vows of silence and facing the wall (*pi-yü, pi-kuan*). Although none of the Chinese informants I queried were able to recall having encountered either of these practices, at least three instances of the former and one of the latter were casually observed by Westerners. Lewis Hodous, for example, saw a monk at Ku Shan who had kept a vow of silence for fourteen years.[24] This was presumably early in the Republican period. In the middle of the nineteenth century, the Reverend Joseph Edkins saw a monk who was engaged in silently facing the wall like Bodhidharma. He had been at it for six or seven years and had vowed to continue for the rest of his life. It was part of his discipline not to change his clothes and not to shave his face or cut his hair, though he *combed* his hair and washed his face. Edkins states that "he could read, but never took book in hand. His only employment was to mutter the prayers of his religion in a low voice. We wrote on a piece of paper a sentence 'Your vow not to speak is of no benefit to you.' He looked at the paper, read it, and gave a faint smile. He refused to write any reply . . . Soon after we saw him, he was found sitting on his board in the sunshine, dead."[25]

4) Writing with blood (*hsüeh-shu*). This meant that a part of one's body was being offered to the Buddha. It was inspired by the 44th article of the *Fan-wang ching:* to use one's own bone as a pen, one's skin as paper, and one's blood as ink. In recent years, at any rate, monks have been content with the last only. They obtained the blood by cutting their tongue or fingertips and then mixed it with water. They might use it to sketch a sacred image or copy out a whole sutra. The practice appears to have been fairly common in the Republican period.

5) Burning scars (*shao-pa*). Some monks decorated their chest with a rosary of one hundred and eight "beads," or a Buddhist swastika, or the character *fo* (Buddha). Prip-Møller prints a photograph of a *fo* and rosary together, freshly burned on the chest of a monk from Peking. Another monk, who had just had a rosary branded on his back, was unwilling to let it be photographed by Prip-Møller, who says that it "reached from his hips to between his shoulder blades and represented at that stage almost one big wound."[26] Usually the burning was done with sticks of incense while the subject recited homage to the buddha or bodhisattva whose aid he was seeking. One of my own

informants whose forearm was covered with scars, three in a row, told me that each row had taken about five minutes to burn.[27]

6) Burning fingers (*jan-chih*). This offered a larger fraction of the body to the Buddha and argued a higher level of religious enthusiasm. Another of my informants, who had burned off the two outer fingers of each hand, was very proud of it and eager to tell me how it had been done. He said that twenty or thirty monks has assisted him. Two of them wound a string around one of his fingers just inside the inner joint, then pulled it tight from each side with the whole weight of their bodies. This cut off both nerve impulses and blood supply. His hand was then placed, back down, in a basin of mud and salt. The two upper joints of the finger to be sacrificed stuck up above the surface of the mud, but the rest of his hand was flat at the bottom of the basin, protected from heat. Pine resin and sandalwood, apparently in a sort of amalgam, were then applied to the finger (Prip-Møller says wrapped around it).[28] They burned with a fierce flame, consuming flesh and bone.[29] As they burned, all the monks, including the owner of the finger, would recite the *Ch'an-hui wen*. The whole ceremony took about twenty minutes.

This informant burned one finger a year for four years in succession. He did so at the Asoka Monastery (Yü-wang Ssu) near Ningpo. Interestingly enough, that was the monastery where the illustrious Chich'an and Hsü-yün, as well as another of my informants, also had their fingers burned. In the case of Hsü-yün the motivation was more than a desire to offer part of his body to the Buddha. "From the time of my birth," he states, "I had had no mother [she had died bearing him]. I had only seen her portrait when I was at home. Every time I thought of her my heart broke. Once formerly I had taken a vow to go to the Asoka Monastery, pay reverence to the sarira relic, and burn off a finger as an offering to the Buddha and secure salvation for my mother." He reached the monastery in 1897 and worshipped the relic with such abandon (making more than three thousand prostrations a day) that he became ill in the eleventh month and was moved to the infirmary. Since he did not respond to medical treatment, the rector wanted to postpone the burning. Hsü-yün wept and said: "Who can escape birth and death? I want to repay my mother. I have taken a vow to burn off my finger. If I stop because of illness, what is the use of living? I would rather die." The prior agreed to help him go through with it on schedule. Early on the morning of the 17th of the twelfth month, "many people took turns in helping me up into the great shrine-hall to prostrate myself before the Buddha and go through various ritual and liturgy. The assembled monks recited the *Ch'an-hui wen,* while with my whole mind I recited buddha's name to secure release (*ch'ao-tu*) for my mother. At first I felt pain. But my mind gradually clarified until finally wisdom and awakening shone through. When the recitation reached the words *fa-chieh tsang-shen O-mi-t'o-fo* I got goose flesh over my whole body. The burning of my finger was now completed. I got up on my own and made a prostration before the Buddha. There was no need for people to support me. At that point I did not even know that I had been ill. I walked about thanking everyone and returned to the infirmary. People were surprised. On the same day I moved out of the infirmary and I spent the next day soaking in salt water. The flow of blood stopped. In a few days the skin and flesh were completely healed. Gradually I began making prostrations again. I passed the New Year at the Asoka Monastery."[30]

Accounts like this raise some doubt as to the justice of Professor Wing-tsit Chan's statement that "in China asceticism is not taken seriously."[31]

7) Self-immolation by fire (*fen-shen*). If we accept the account of a British physician, Dr. D. J. MacGowan, this practice was much commoner in nineteenth century China than it had been earlier. He cites one case in 1878, two in 1888, and one in 1889, all in the area of Wenchow where he was stationed. He was told that on T'ien-t'ai Shan three or four hermits burned themselves alive each year. Since in the whole of China, only twenty-five cases of self-immolation appear to have been recorded from the fifth through the tenth century and the practice is generally believed to have died out thereafter,[32] MacGowan's figures are hard to credit.

He did not witness any immolation himself. He simply interviewed those who had. They said that the candidate had usually prepared himself by weeks of fasting and ablution, "purification being promoted by Gum Sandarac." A little booth was built just large enough to hold him, seated in lotus position. Around it were piled pine-kindling, shavings, and resin, on which sulphur and camphor might be sprinkled. Small packets of gunpowder might be fastened under his armpits and about his clothing, apparently to accelerate his departure. He would light the pyre himself. In some cases the door of the booth would shut him off from the view of the large audience that had gathered. In other cases there would be apertures so that his behavior could be observed. He sat quietly, palms pressed together, and recited buddha's name "until he was concealed by flame and smoke."[33]

The motives for self-immolation in the cases described by Mac-Gowan appear to have been complex. It was thought to create an enormous fund of merit, in which the whole district shared. Brisk trade and plentiful harvests could be expected to follow and the laymen who shared most directly in this merit—by reciting sutras as the flames crackled—could look forward to rebirth in the Western Paradise. Hence in the weeks before the event the sponsoring temple enjoyed a sharp increase in donations and the monk who was purifying himself was worshipped like a Living Buddha.

The original basis for sacrifice by fire, whether of all or part of the body, is in the Lotus Sutra. It recounts how the bodhisattva Bhaisajyaraja (Yao-wang p'u-sa), in a former reincarnation, grateful for having obtained an advanced form of religious ecstasy, ate sweet-smelling substances, resin and oil for twelve years. Then he bathed his body in oil and set fire to it as an offering to the Buddha and to the doctrine of the Lotus Sutra. "Well done," shouted the enlightened onlookers, "well done, young man of good family, that is the real heroism which the Bodhisattvas Mahasattvas should develop; that is the real worship of the Tathagata, the real worship of the law . . . Sacrificing one's own body, young man of good family, is the most distinguished, the chiefest, the best, the very best, the most sublime worship of the law." After his body had burned for twelve thousand years, this young man of good family disappeared. He reappeared to oversee the funeral of his teacher and to pay homage to his relics by burning off his arm, a task that took seventy-two thousand years. The text comments: "The young man or young lady of good family, striving in the Bodhisattva vehicle toward the goal and longing for supreme, perfect enlightenment, who at the Tathagata-shrines shall burn a great toe, a finger, a toe, or a whole limb, such a young man or young lady of good family, I assure thee, shall produce far more pious merit, far more than results from giving up a kingdom, sons, daughters, and wives, the whole triple world with its woods, oceans, mountains, springs, streams, tanks, wells, and gardens."[34]

This quaint allegory was probably not intended to be taken literally, nor does it appear to have been so taken in India, where there is no record of Buddhist self-immolation. It was apparently not until the *Lotus Sutra* got into the hands of the sensible, this-worldly Chinese that the example of Bhaisjyaraja began to be followed.

When I have asked my informants about self-immolation, they have spoken of the practice with respect, although most of them claimed never to have seen it done themselves or even to have heard of it being done in China during the past century. This is odd, because there were at least six cases during the Republican period alone, five of which were publicized in Buddhist books and periodicals. The motive was usually to imitate Bhaisajyaraja in offering the body to the Buddha for the salvation of all sentient beings. None of these six cases involved a public festival like those described by MacGowan in the late Ch'ing dynasty. Each monk made his preparations in secret and set himself on fire alone.[35]

The last case is perhaps the most interesting because it was a forerunner of the self-immolations in Vietnam. On May 16th, 1948 a monk named Kuo-shun, who lived in a solitary hut near Harbin, apparently decided to protest against the treatment of Buddhism by the Chinese Communists. "Monks were being persecuted on a large scale, images were being destroyed, sutras were being burned." Therefore he got three and a half catties of soybean oil and poured it over a hundred catties of sawdust piled in front of the altar. He seated himself in lotus position on the pile, lit it, and was consumed by fire. The next day the neighbors came over, attracted by the smoke. They found that his heart was still unconsumed, which greatly astonished them (as it was later to astonish the followers of Quang Duc). The news reached Hong Kong by letter and was published in the *Wah Kiu Yat Po* of October 22, 1950.[36] Kuo-shun's sacrifice attracted little attention, partly because he burned himself alone rather than in a city square and partly because Peking gave less freedom to foreign correspondents than did the Diem regime.

Chinese monks distinguish clearly between self-immolation as a protest in defense of Buddhism and self-immolation as a pious offering to the Buddha. Both kinds, they believe, require spiritual development to the point of egolessness (*wu-wo*).

To outsiders either kind may seem incomprehensible. Yet it has proved as contagious for some of us as it is incomprehensible for most of us. During the events in South Vietnam in the summer of 1963, I noted in haphazardly reading the newspapers that a young man in France "suffering from nervous depression" soaked himself in gasoline and set himself ablaze; a Buddhist nun in Korea tried to do the same (to protest discrimination against married monks); and an eighty-two-year-old Buddhist devotee burned himself to death with kerosene in Taiwan for no apparent reason. In 1965 there were four cases in the United States alone, all inspired by events in Vietnam.[37]

Therefore it is no longer possible to think of self-immolation by Chinese monks as something that makes them wholly alien to ourselves. Yet in many cases, the real motivation, which obviously can be different from the stated motivation, remains obscure. Has it been the "death wish" of Western psychoanalysis, or the ancient hope that, like other burnt offerings, the body would be translated by fire to heaven and eternal life? In the case of Kuo-shun and the Vietnamese monks, has it been love of their religion or hatred of those who were harming it? These questions can be asked, but there seems to be no way of answering them, and even to ask them is to belittle what may have been superhuman faith and courage.

WAGE EARNER AND ENTREPRENEUR

The percentage of the sangha involved in even the mildest of the ascetic practices described above was probably very small. Most monks were content with the hardship of being monks—deprived of sex, wine, meat, family ties, and personal wealth. Of course, their deprivation was not as complete as it might sound. Instead of chicken from the barnyard, they had chicken made of bean curd. Instead of a natural family, they had the tonsure or dharma family. Instead of personal wealth, they had their share of the communal property of the sangha.

But they were not altogether without personal wealth. They could not afford to be. China was never such a Buddhist country that monks were excused from paying their way. It was not customary for a *dayaka* to accompany the monk (as in Theravada countries) so that he did not have to handle money. That is why monks in Theravada countries have been able to abide by the Vinaya rule against handling money, whereas in China they have not.

Theoretically the Chinese monk needed no money at all. He could live free of charge in a public monastery for as long as he liked. If he was enrolled in the meditation hall, he was loaned all the clothing he needed. But what if he wanted to write a letter—where was he to get paper, brush, and ink? Or if he decided to move on to another public monastery, who would pay the ferryman along the way? Suppose he took office as a clerk. If at the end of his term a physical inventory revealed that there were fewer candles in the storeroom than there should have been according to the inventory records, he would be asked to pay the difference.[38] Suppose he wanted to spread the dharma. He needed money not only to facilitate travel, but to purchase a temple that could serve him as a base, both for giving lectures and for training disciples. Even if he had no such lofty vocation, he felt the natural human need for a place to retire to in his old age. If there was no room for him in the temple where his head had been shaved, and if he did not expect to earn the privilege of retirement at a public monastery, then his problem could best be solved by buying a small temple of his own. Some monks, therefore, wanted to accumulate capital, while others (whose future was secure or who gave no thought to the future) were satisfied with just enough to cover current expenses. The latter amounted to very little. Before 1937 the cloth for a couple of gowns (ch'ang-kua) cost about a dollar, and tailoring them would run a dollar more. Shoes, robes, and underclothes were equally reasonable. Paper, brush, ink, needles, thread, money for a train or boat ride, money to pay an occasional fine for breaking a minor rule—the total might not exceed $10-15 a year.

Even at a large public monastery this much money could be earned performing Buddhist services. At Chin Shan, for example, each participant in a plenary mass received a dollar a day for seven days. If he took part in only two of the ten of the plenary masses usually held there each year, he would earn $14. In addition to that he had the feast gifts (chai-ch'en) distributed to all the monks during vegetarian feasts. But if he was anxious to accumulate money on a larger scale—as capital in order to buy a temple of his own—it was advisable for him to go to a monastery like the Fa-tsang Ssu in Shanghai where by working hard he could earn $120 to $150 a year. There he had the added advantage of being paid monthly, whereas at the model monasteries he did not receive his fees until the end of each semester. If he left before the semester was over, he forfeited what was due him (an arrangement that must have discouraged sudden departures inconvenient for the administration).[39]

According to my informants, fees from Buddhist services were the principal source of income for the average monk. But at a few monasteries all the residents received an unearned allowance—something that many informants had never heard of, or, if they had heard of it, had never seen. Discussion of this practice is complicated by the fact that fees for performing Buddhist services were usually called *tan-ch'ien* or *tan-yin,* while the term for an unearned allowance was also *tan-ch'ien,* abbreviated from *i-tan ch'ien* or "clothes money."[40]

An unearned allowance was generally provided when earning power was restricted. At the Chin-shan Ssu in Szechwan, for example, no Buddhist services were performed at all. Its residents therefore received an allowance of $3 apiece on the 13th of every first and seventh month. At Ch'i-hsia Shan, as I understand it, no allowance was given before 1937, when fees from services were still adequate, but an allowance began to be given in later years as economic deterioration reduced the demand for elaborate rites for the dead. Chin Shan did not provide for its monks this way, and they felt the pinch. After 1937 the younger monks enrolled in its meditation hall had to go back from time to time for a stint in their hereditary temples, where they could save up a little money performing Buddhist services, and then return to Chin Shan for another semester of meditation. The older monks, who could not leave because they had to carry on in office, would get their hereditary temples to send them remittances. As officers they received an unearned allowance of $2 a semester, but this was not enough to cover even minimal personal expenses. The T'ien-ning Ssu gave 600 cash a month to monks enrolled in several of its halls (for example, the buddha recitation hall and the hall for disabled monks). This was partly because they were not eligible for the loan of clothing. The monks in the meditation hall, who *were* eligible, received no monthly sum.

Officers were usually better off than the rank and file. Although they were often too busy to take part in Buddhist services, at some monasteries they received the same fees as if they had. There were also other sources of income. A verger, for example, was permitted to pocket the donations of those who came to worship in the shrine-hall that he was in charge of. With a little initiative he could augment his income. For example, one of my informants secured the post of a senior verger at Chin Shan about 1938. "Lots of Japanese soldiers came to the monastery," he said. "Although the Japanese army was harsh towards Buddhists, many of the soldiers still believed in Buddhism. The verger and I would bring a small tray with 'contributions' (*hsiang-ch'ien*) written on it and bow to the soldiers very politely. Some of them angrily refused, some would be very polite and put in a dollar. These contributions we kept for ourselves. The abbot and prior did not object. We were menial officers (*heng-tan*). Also, we could use the money that we collected to make contributions for the general welfare. That is, every so often we would pay for an extra dish to be eaten by all the monks in the monastery during one of the regular meals. Then we had another idea. We wrote the following on slips of paper: 'Homage to the Amitabha Buddha! Here in this ancient monastery, the Chiang-t'ien Ssu, Chen-chiang, the illustrious Fa-hai practiced religious cultivation.' The people who came were like children. They all wanted to buy them at ten cents apiece. We could not keep up with the demand, so we had to print a second ten thousand. Many Japanese bought them, in order that someday they would be able to show them to people at home, and say 'Once when I was fighting in China, I went to Chin Shan.' We made quite a lot of money this way."

I asked the abbot of Chin Shan, who had been the prior in 1938, if he remembered the activities of this enterprising verger. He answered with some asperity that he did not and if he had known anything about them at the time he would have put a stop to them, for such profiteering was contrary to Chin Shan's rules and tradition.

The officers of the guest department had a more orthodox source of income. When a layman was paying for a Buddhist service, it was only common courtesy to hand a red envelope (*hung-pao*) to the monks who had helped arrange it. The money therein was termed an "incense gift" (*hsiang-i*). Any such gift received by the guest department was usually shared equally by all its officers.

The business office could also have its "perks." The only instance given me came from the T'ien-ning Ssu, but probably there were parallels at other monasteries. The business office of the T'ien-ning Ssu was responsible for the milling of immense quantities of rice each year (see p. 236). One of the by-products was bran (*hsi-k'ang*), which was sold as pig fodder at 200 cash per *tou*. Another was chaff (*hui-k'ang*) which was sold as fertilizer. The proceeds did not go to the establishment, but were divided up in equal shares among all the officers of the business office—about a dozen persons.

For the higher ranking monks the most important category of personal income was "fruit gifts" (*kuo-i*).[41] These came from lay admirers who were grateful for their instruction or wanted to share in the merit they were accumulating. Although other monks too received "fruit gifts"—even the lowliest acolyte might get them from lay people who were connected with him or felt sorry for him—in the case of a high officer they could add up to a really sizable sum, as the following story shows. About 1936 the prior of Ch'i-hsia Shan was informed by his good friend, the abbot of the Ling-yin Ssu in Hangchow, that two small temples nearby were in bad straits. Their former head had borrowed $5,000, defaulted, and disappeared. Anyone who would pay off the debt could take them over. This the prior did, using $5,000 from the "fruit gifts" he had accumulated since his ordination seventeen years before. From that time on (and even after 1939, when he became the abbot of Ch'i-hsia Shan) he made frequent trips to Hangchow, spending several months a year there in all. On the one hand this gave him a rest from his duties at Ch'i-hsia (where a prior took his place) and on the other hand it enabled him to exercise close supervision over his two temples. He kept them staffed with about a dozen monks who specialized in reciting buddha's name which, he said, Hangchow people particularly liked. Presumably it yielded him a good income, although I did not feel it tactful to ask about this.

Another informant spoke quite frankly about the income he derived from the ownership of small temples. In 1939 he was staying at a large monastery in Shanghai. One night a monk who was a friend of his dreamed that if he (the friend) went to the gambling quarter, he would win a lot of money. He did go and did win. With it he proposed that the two of them should start a temple. They bought quarters near a funeral parlor on Yen-p'ing Road and fitted them up with an altar. They hired servants and persuaded seven or eight monks to live there and help with the performance of Buddhist services. The venture was soon a financial success. The next year, however, the funeral parlor closed down, so that the demand for services slacked off and it began to be necessary to draw on savings in order to keep going. About this time my informant was approached by the cook of another small temple. After a good deal of hemming and hawing, it became clear that he had been sent as a middleman by the temple owner, who wanted to sell it.

"Will you take it over?" said the cook finally.

"I haven't any money," my informant replied.

"If you will take it over," continued the cook, "no money is necessary. If you were anyone else, you would not get it for $5,000. But you and the abbot are from the same area and he'll only be at peace in his mind about it if he hands it over to you. If someone wanted to buy it, he simply wouldn't sell." He paused. "On the other hand, if he does hand it over to you, there are still conditions to be met. He wants to transmit the dharma to you."

"Oh? What other conditions?"

"He also has some debts that he wants to pay back by installment. If you will make an offering to help him and to show your respect, then he will be able to retire. Won't that be an excellent arrangement?"

For a while my informant continued to hesitate for lack of money, but finally he agreed and became head of the second temple. The first was sold to someone else.

This sort of trading in places of worship was probably commoner in the commercial atmosphere of Shanghai than elsewhere. My informant seemed devout and sincere, and probably looked on the commercialization of urban Buddhism as just one more ugly fact of life, for which he saw no remedy. It was ugliest of all when an avaricious monk took over an hereditary temple that had previously been operated for the benefit of an entire tonsure family—or a public monastery that had been operated for the benefit of the entire sangha—and milked it for his own private profit, even selling off its permanent property. Laws were passed to prevent this, but they were difficult to enforce and there were occasional lawsuits. Naturally one heard more about such "operators" than about the honest abbots who outnumbered them.

A few monks were rich to begin with. Usually they had been middle-aged businessmen or officials who had not distributed their wealth to their heirs when they took the robe. Although they would have found it difficult to provide themselves with private comforts if residing at a strict public monastery, they could live as comfortably as they liked in their own small temple, and often did so. This also happened when the daughter of a rich family, after some personal disappointment, decided to withdraw from the world. A temple would be specially built and endowed for her, and she would live there with two or three nuns as her companions.

DISROBING AND RE-ORDINATION

In Theravada countries it is common for monks to disrobe and return to lay life. Some go in and out of the sangha several times, although this is considered to indicate a vacillating temperament. But in China, according to my informants, return to lay life (*huan-su*) under normal circumstances was rare. I have heard of only a handful of cases before 1950. Three were monks involved in the 1911 Republican revolution. Seven had gone abroad to study Theravada Buddhism in Ceylon. One embezzled monastic funds in Hong Kong. Several were converted to Christianity by Dr. K. L. Reichelt. The closest thing to a common factor appears to be foreign influence.

There was no legal impediment to disrobing in China, but according to the Buddhist custom it was desirable to renounce the ordination vows in front of one of the masters who had administered them, or, if he was not available, before some other respected senior monk. But the master would only permit renunciation of the vows for a good cause—if, for instance, all the monk's brothers had died and he alone was left to perpetuate the family. Those who could not point to such a cause, but were determined to disrobe anyway, did so without permission.

If a monk changed his mind a second time, it was still possible to be re-ordained, though I only heard of one such case. What was fairly common, however, was to be re-ordained without having disrobed at all. This was done with motives that may remind us of the husband and wife in the West who take the marriage vows again in order to gain a sense of re-dedication; or because they believe there was some flaw in the original ceremony. Re-ordination was called *pu-chieh*, which means to strengthen the vows or to make up for a deficiency in

them. One of my informants, for example, had originally been ordained in Hunan at the age of eight. When he realized that this was
a flagrant breach of the rules, which even at their most lenient did
not permit ordination under sixteen, he waited until he reached eighteen and then went to be re-ordained in another monastery. It is interesting that a few days after he had given me this information, he
asked me to delete it from my notes. It would be more "proper," he
said, to refer to the second ordination only. Another informant, also
from Hunan, had been old enough (thirty-four) when he was ordained, but the rites had lasted only three days. So fourteen years
later, in 1944, he went to the Nan-hua Ssu to have the rites performed
at their full length under the aegis of the eminent Hsü-yün. The yearbook for a later ordination at Nan-hua Ssu (1949) shows that thirty-
two out of the ninety-three ordinees had received the tonsure more
than six years earlier (fourteen of them more than ten years earlier).
Only one of these thirty-two was under twenty at the time (cf. p.
252). It therefore seems likely that a third of the ordainees were
taking their vows for a second time. One of them certainly was, for
he has told me so. He explained that his motive was to benefit from
the saintly influence of Hsü-yün. Later he went to Rangoon and took
his vows still again, but on this occasion according to the Theravada
formulary. Another informant was re-ordained first by the eminent
Ti-hsien and later by Ti-hsien's disciple, T'an-hsü. It would seem that
after ordination under the master, little could be gained from ordination under the disciple, but this informant explained simply that he
found it salutary to repeat the prohibitions and renew his commitment to them.

Each time a monk was re-ordained he received a robe and bowl,
and a certificate that bore no allusion to earlier ordinations. He did
not necessarily have all the scars on his head burned again. If he had
fewer scars than required, more would be burned to bring the number
up to par.[42]

OLD AGE AND RETIREMENT

Longevity has always had a special value for the Chinese. It is appropriate that Hsü-yün, who was considered the most eminent monk

in modern China, should also have been considered the oldest.[43] In the Confucian tradition of filial piety, old age was something almost to be worshipped. In the Taoist tradition it was proof of progress in the pursuit of immortality and hence of the absolute. Buddhism incorporated both traditions. An abbot who reached his eightieth birthday had by that very fact given evidence of his sanctity. This was one reason for birthday ordinations like the "time of the lohans" (see Chapter IX, note 50).

The ordinary Chinese monk lived out his old age in a small temple. Some, however, preferred to utilize the retirement program of a large public monastery. It could be a very liberal program—more so than in any modern welfare state. At Chin Shan, for example, every monk who attained the rank of secretary (shu-chi) was entitled to ask the abbot to present him with a private apartment (sung i-ko liao-fang) and if one were available, he would probably get it. He might be only forty years old, but there he could live for the rest of his life without holding office. His obligations were to take part in the three major periods of meditation a day (see Appendix III, p. 428); to attend morning and evening devotions; and to go to the refectory for breakfast congee and noon rice. He was expected to help out when necessary in the performance of plenary masses. As he grew old and infirm, however, these obligations gradually weakened, and he lived more and more as he pleased.

The retirement privileges were not lost if he went elsewhere, perhaps to study, perhaps on a pilgrimage. When he returned, whether it was after a year, three years, or even five years, his right to an apartment was still unimpaired. Departure (kao-chia) and return (hsiao-chia) were entered in the "ten-thousand-year book" (wan-nien pu). Chin Shan had twenty or thirty apartments, built over the years. Some were grouped together in a building called the "longevity hall" (yen-shou t'ang).[44]

Other monasteries were more elastic than Chin Shan. They might present apartments to monks who had merely reached the rank of thurifer, having, for example, served a couple of terms as succentor in the meditation hall. But whereas the ex-secretary could come and go as he pleased and still retain his right to an apartment, the ex-thurifer was denied this privilege. When he returned from a leave of absence, he had to spend another term in the meditation hall before he could retire again.

54. An aged monk studies the sutras in the hall of rebirth of a small temple. Central China.

This was the practice at the T'ien-ning Ssu, in Changchow.[45] There the right to retire was only a nominal one. A monk might have reached secretarial rank, but unless he had done good work in office, he would not be given an apartment, even though one was available; nor would he get it if the abbot had doubts about his character, since once he had the right to live permanently at the T'ien-ning Ssu, he might take leave of absence, go off, misbehave, and bring discredit on the monastery. Therefore when some officers asked for apartments, they were flatly refused. Refusal was the equivalent to censure. In their mortification they would usually leave at once—which was precisely what they were meant to do.

At the T'ien-ning Ssu those who benefited least from the retirement program were the instructors in the meditation hall. It was difficult to find qualified instructors (*pan-shou*) and when the abbot felt that a monk had talent in this direction, he expected him to take office. If he refused, he had to leave the monastery. If he accepted, he had to spend many years in the meditation hall, attending every period, accompanying the rank and file to the refectory and the shrine-hall, and giving Explanations and tutorials. The day might come when he demanded the right to retire to a private apartment. He would argue that he had long since passed secretarial rank and complain of age and fatigue. But unless the establishment decided he was really old and weary and had done many years of good work as an instructor, the privilege of retirement would be denied. Under such circumstances, some instructors would leave the T'ien-ning Ssu to start temples of their own; and if their temples failed, they might return to become instructors again. But no one, until the abbot decided that he had earned the privilege, could move from instructor's quarters (*pan-shou liao*) to an apartment for the retired (*hsien liao-fang*).

Once they had done so, however, they led a happy life, whether at T'ien-ning or elsewhere. Prip-Møller writes the following about two monks who occupied a pair of buildings at the back of Pao-hua Shan. The Wen-shu Tien and the P'u-hsien Tien, he says,

> now provide quarters for a couple of elderly retired monks, who may live here as free and as detached from the daily life and work of the monastery as they choose . . . Downstairs the monk has his small stove, his supply of fuel, vegetables, etc., which all come from the K'u Fang [business office]. Opposite the entrance is a recess in the wall, where a small altar is arranged, carrying candlesticks, incense burner, and an image of O Mi T'o Fo. Here are also chairs and a table, where the old master of the house may sit and eat and chat with visitors, who have come from one of the other small halls up here or whom he does not care to take upstairs. In the heavy wall of the outer gable, a brick built stair leads to the monk's more private room on the first floor, where he has his bed, his writing desk near the window, his wide meditation seat used in his privately

conducted meditation hours, and a box or two containing his clothes and other belongings. On the table stands a small image of O Mi To Fo. Above, on the wall, are two photographs of himself taken on his pilgrimages throughout the land. Beside them are a few color prints, rather naïve in design and color, issued by a big Indian Buddhist association and showing scenes from Sakyamuni's life, his entering Nirvana, etc. In front of the recess in the gable wall, where a small window hole lets in a little fresh air, he has set a wooden door, locked with a modern padlock. In here is his small supply of such delicacies as do not belong to the regular menu of the monastery, but which he and his like can have from the K'u Fang for the asking, or which may be bought in town next time someone goes there on an errand.[46]

Such elderly monks were available even in retirement to counsel young pilgrims and contemplatives on their spiritual development. If they had held high rank, they were also consulted by the abbot and other office-holders on the affairs of the monastery, like benevolent grandfathers in a large Chinese family.

What happened to the menial officers—the humble rice steward and stoker? At Chin Shan few of them reached a rank high enough to qualify for retirement there. Most of them returned to their small temples. If they had none to return to, they might be offered a place in one of Chin Shan's branches (see p. 135). Otherwise they might retire to a hall for the aged, like the one at the T'ien-ning Ssu, open to monks over sixty (see p. 234). Hackmann describes such a hall at T'ien-t'ung. It had its own shrine, kitchen, and common room. It embraced a large number of apartments with small courtyards in front. Here too monks had to be over sixty to enroll and were excused from devotions and all other duties. "Most of them were smiling happily at the spring sun and seemed to feel that they were in safe haven."[47]

It would be interesting to know what proportion of the monks in large monasteries were living in retirement and to what extent, therefore, the monasteries were centers for individual study and meditation. This is a question on which I have failed to collect enough data. Inasmuch as not age but rank was what qualified people to retire, their ratio to those in active service may have been quite high at institutions with enough food and space.[48]

It would also be interesting to know how many monks in China at any given moment were engaged in what phase of the monastic career. Again, I have not collected enough data. But as a guess I would say that there were dozens of lecturers, hundreds of instructors in meditation, thousands of hermits, thousands of administrators, thousands of monks in retirement, tens of thousands of wandering monks on pilgrimage or attending meditation or listening to lectures, and hundreds of thousands of monks earning their living in small temples.

DEATH AND FUNERAL ARRANGEMENTS

It was the hope of the monk, as of the layman, to die "at home" surrounded by his "family" of brothers and disciples. If so, it was they who arranged for the mortuary rites and for the disposition of his effects. If a monk fell ill at a public monastery with none of his "family" at hand, the guest department would obtain medical treatment and have a penance recited to assist his recovery. If death came, it made all necessary arrangements. At the Kao-min Ssu, for example, the proctor would at once sequester any personal effects, examine the corpse, and get four monks to recite buddha's name around it. After seven hours he would have the infirmary attendants wash it, shave the head and beard, and dress it in underclothes and full-sleeved gown, all half worn out. It was not dressed in a robe (*chia-sa*).[49] The kneeling cloth (*chü*) was then placed on the bottom of a wooden or wicker box (*k'an-tzu*) just large enough to hold the corpse seated in lotus position.[50] In case *rigor mortis* had begun, hot water was used to soften the joints and arrange the limbs. Once arranged, *rigor mortis* held them in place. If necessary a crossboard was nailed inside to keep the head upright.

Before the box was closed, an instructor (*pan-shou*) would preach the dharma to the spirit of the deceased, who was considered to be still clinging to his mortal remains. The instructor would urge him to let go of life and secure the great deliverance. He would point out that whatever was born had to die and urge him to go now to the Western Paradise. Finally he would close and seal the box. On the third day (or on the second in hot weather) cremation took place.[51] A procession escorted the coffin to the crematorium. Before it was placed inside, the dharma was preached again. The proctor lit the fire. Afterwards the ashes were placed in the monastery columbarium (*p'u-*

t'ung t'a) and the dharma might be preached for the third time.[52] Sometimes the ashes were stored on shelves according to rank in individual urns; and sometimes they were thrown loose or in little red bags into a common cavity.[53] Ashes of an abbot, on the other hand, were usually deposited in a grave built especially to receive them.

So much for burial. Rites of deliverance were another matter. In the nineteenth century a Christian missionary who was visiting P'u-t'o Shan asked a monk there whether, when a member of the sangha died, a large number of his colleagues performed masses for his soul. The reply (according to the missionary) was: "Oh! If he leaves six or eight pounds sterling they will, but if he dies without money, he has no funeral."[54] My informants say otherwise. If a monk died in a small temple, as most monks did, he would be as solicitously provided for by his disciples as the father of a family in lay life. If he died at a large public monastery where he served in a high office, his associates made sure that his obsequies were duly performed, regardless of his personal wealth. That is, his soul tablet would be placed on an altar in the great shrine-hall with offerings of fruit, rice, and vegetarian dishes. All the monks of the monastery would recite the Maitreya Penance, the Maitreya Hymn, and the name of Amitabha. The merit created thereby would serve to speed the deceased to the Western Paradise. Following the service an inventory of his personal effects was published by the guest department and they were then divided up among the needy menial officers. This too created merit for his benefit.

In other cases only the friends of the deceased would perform services on his behalf and then divide his effects among themselves. If he had no friends and had not held high office—if he were, for example, a visitor in the wandering monks hall—his effects would be publicly sold and the proceeds used to pay for a service.[55] Or if he had been well-to-do, he might have given death-bed instructions for his funeral and the disposition of his property.[56] Total neglect was rare.[57]

After forty-nine days the soul tablet was moved to a hall where regular offerings were made before it on the 1st and 15th of every lunar month. At Chin Shan the tablet of an abbot was set up in the ancestors hall (*tsu-t'ang*); the tablet of a high ranking officer or important donor in the hall of merit (*kung-te t'ang*); the tablet of a menial officer in the hall of service (*kung-heng t'ang*); and the tablets of other monks in the nirvana hall (*nieh-p'an t'ang*).[58]

OMENS AND MEAT BODIES

According to my informants there was scriptural authority for believing that a man's next rebirth could be foretold from the circumstances of his death, in particular by finding what part of his body cooled last. If it was the top of his head, he would be reborn in the Western Paradise. If it was the area around his eyes, he would be reborn in one of the twenty-eight heavens (see p. 89). If it was in the lower part of his chest, he would be reborn as a man; if in his belly, as a hungry ghost; if in his knees, as an animal; and if in his feet, the poor fellow was on his way to hell. These were not the only omens (*yü-chao*). As one informant told me, "a great monk dies peacefully whereas, when an ordinary person dies, there are urine and faeces, he weeps and yells—aiya, it is an ugly sight. The great monk can be peaceful because he knows that life is illusory, that his pain is illusory, and so he can keep control of himself, just as an ordinary person may realize in a dream that it is a dream."

I was living in Hong Kong when the Venerable Ting-hsi died there of cancer in 1962. One of his disciples told me that on the evening before he died, a neighboring farmer saw a ball of white light come from his room and shoot over to the grave he had built for himself. This showed that "a great monk would be returning to the West." Despite the nature of his illness he gave no sign of pain. Shortly before he died, he sat up and recited buddha's name and told the people around him not to be sad. Then he composed a gatha. Eighteen hours after he died, his body was still soft, as if he were simply asleep. There was no *rigor mortis*. "His lips were still red, whereas in the case of ordinary people, they would be white. The palm of one of his hands was red—something that you find in one person out of a thousand or more. All this was because he had practiced Buddhist cultivation. He had recited buddha's name with complete single-mindedness, and even before his death he had entered into another realm."

Outsiders must respect these marks of a noble death, although they are entitled to wonder how many have been supplied by hagiographers and how many represent efforts by the dying man, who may have read the "Lives of Eminent Monks," to conform to tradition. The picture of the disciples feeling around for the "hot spot" on the corpse of their master may be unedifying, but at least they were motivated by loyalty and pride. There were, however, more macabre possibilities in the treatment of the dead, which recall the Roman Catholic concern for the minutiae of putrefaction.[59]

In China just as in the West nonputrefaction has been taken as evidence of sanctity. Mummified monks have been set up for worship like images or ancestor tablets. They are called "meat bodies" (*joushen*).[60] Many are said to be several hundred years old. The oldest (and most famous) is that of the Sixth Patriarch of the Ch'an sect, who died in 713 C.E. It was kept at the Nan-hua Ssu, Kwangtung, along with the meat bodies of two later abbots.[61] But not all were antiques. Prip-Møller saw one at Chiu-hua Shan that dated from 1900. He states that meat bodies were "found frequently in central China and may be almost said to abound in Szechwan."[62] Usually they were gilded. Sometimes the lobes of the ears were lengthened and a dot was placed between the eyebrows. Golden skin, long lobes, and the *urna* dot were among the thirty-two sacred marks of a buddha. The implication was therefore that in his lifetime the monk whose corpse the visitor saw before him had attained buddhahood. Sometimes a notice was placed alongside pointing out that nonputrefaction was proof of this and inviting the visitor to contribute money so that his progeny would "continue for countless ages to be distinguished scholars and enjoy glory and riches."[63]

I know of at least one case in recent years. This was Tz'u-hang, a monk who was much revered and had many disciples. During his lifetime he indulged in a whim that seems to have been popular at the time: he had his photograph taken in the pose of Maitreya. Maitreya is the buddha-to-be who will lead mankind toward enlightenment in his next incarnation. In one of his previous incarnations, which is believed to have taken place during the Sung dynasty, he appeared as Pu-tai, a wild, happy monk who carried presents for children in a cloth bag (*pu-tai*). He was enormously fat and it is his image that we call the Laughing Buddha. The frontispiece in the biography of Tz'u-hang shows him sitting like the Laughing Buddha, great stomach hanging over the folds of his robe, breasts sagging, and a happy smile on his face that the caption compares to Maitreya's.[64] (T'ai-hsü had an almost identical photograph taken in 1935.)[65]

Before Tz'u-hang died, he left instructions for his corpse not to be cremated, but to be kept in a jar for three years. If at the end of that period it was well preserved, he expressed the hope that it might be gilded and kept. His instructions were not, however, followed. When three years had passed, certain senior monks reminded his followers that the climate in Taiwan was very hot, that Tz'u-hang had been very fat, and that he had been stricken only four hours before his death (so that there had been no chance for illness to reduce his obesity). They considered it improbable that his body was intact. The plans for exhumation were therefore shelved. The next year the same view prevailed. However, on the fifth anniversary of his death (May 11, 1959), a large group of his followers insisted on holding a vote. Some of them had been having dreams in which Tz'u-hang asked them why his instructions had not been followed. The vote was held and 162 out of 220 ballots were marked "exhume." Accordingly, eight days later a group of monks and nuns opened his grave in the dead of the night.

They found "a miracle. . . . On the entire body there was not one place that had rotted. It is said that in the past on the mainland some meat-body bodhisattvas had toes missing or fingers missing, but Tz'u-hang's meat-body was all there." They were overjoyed and hired a sculptor to make the face more lifelike (with clay modelling) as well as another specialist to lacquer the whole body and apply gold leaf. (The photographs made just after exhumation, showing the twisted face and shrunken body, with the remains of the stomach draped grotesquely over the knees, were so horrible that they were never reprinted.)[66] The repairs proved successful and today the reader who goes to Taiwan may see the "Diamond Undecaying Body" of Tz'u-hang being worshipped on a high altar in a handsome temple built to house him. Kindly Taiwanese nuns accept a small stream of donations from the devout and the curious.

Tz'u-hang's example may have impressed Ting-hsi, the venerable monk whose death from cancer was described above. A week before he died, he suddenly summoned into his bedroom all the disciples who were reciting buddha's name outside the door. He told them that his end was near. His testamentary instructions were first that they must not tell people to come and perform rites to save his soul (ch'ao-

tu). "This is not a good thing," he said. Second, they must not cremate his body, but bury it in a jar. If it had not decayed after three years, they were to leave it as it was. If it had decayed, they were to burn it. His disciples knew what he meant. They did not make public his order for exhumation (since they did not want to risk a loss of face three years later).[67] They simply placed his corpse in a large earthenware jar, seated in lotus position. It was large enough so that his chest and head projected above the rim. A second jar was placed upside down on top of it and sealed with putty. According to my informant, no artificial means of preservation were employed. It was to be opened in 1965. If his disciples found no serious decay, the body would be gilded and placed on an altar. I have seen no news of the outcome, which presumably was unsatisfactory.

It is odd that Ting-hsi should have forbidden rites of salvation, which are considered by Buddhists of modern outlook to be "superstitious," and yet make himself a candidate for enshrinement as a meat body, which, if not superstitious, is at least old-fashioned. Indeed, the whole concept of the meat body would seem to exemplify the antithesis of the doctrine of impermanence and to violate the spirit in which the bhiksus of Buddhist India were urged to sojourn in cemeteries, drawing lessons in impermanence from the decomposition of corpses—a fairly repellent custom in itself.

The same objections may be made to the cult of relics, another feature that Buddhism and Roman Catholicism have in common. Hsü-yün, it is pleasant to report, was cremated, but there was a veritable scramble to get sariras (*she-li*) and strands of his hair (which had been cut before cremation). Sariras are crystalline morsels believed to be left in the ashes of any saintly monk. Some modern biographies include photographs of sariras in neat piles, graded by size and color, like gravel for road building. Worship of a sarira gives rise to special merit (and hence to an increase in donations for the temple that owns them). It may have been for this reason that one of Hsü-yün's former disciples was so eager to get hold of his sariras that he told a lie: he wrote asking for them on the basis that he was authorized to do so as the representative of all the Buddhists in Hong Kong, who had, alas! given him no such authority. As in other religions, the saintly and the sordid seem to be inextricable. "Dragons and snakes co-mingle."

THE ACHIEVEMENTS OF THE MONASTIC LIFE

In the last chapter we considered the reasons why monks entered the sangha. But reasons do not necessarily correspond with results, nor purposes with achievements. What were the results and achievements of the monastic life? How did the monks feel about it "forty years on"?

Sometimes, in conversation with those who appeared to have achieved little, I have asked them whether they would still take the robe if they were living their lives over again. Their reply has almost always been in the affirmative. Yet there must have been others who, having entered the sangha only because they had to, never came to believe in what they were doing, and for whom the deprivations of monastic life led either to misery or hypocrisy. There is no way of knowing how many such "rice monks" there were. It is clear, however, that many who entered the sangha for extraneous reasons *did* come to believe in what they were doing and adopted the same goals as the most devout and eminent monks.

These goals were described in Chapters II and III (pp. 84-87, 89-90). The monk found them easier to pursue than he would have as a layman because he had freed himself from major attachments: family, job, and duties to the State. He was therefore able to devote himself unreservedly to a life of religious exercises. His negative karma could gradually be washed away through penance and mortification, while he accumulated positive karma through the salvation of others. In the meditation hall by his own efforts he could inch forward toward enlightenment. In the hall for reciting buddha's name he could prepare to be swept upwards by the firm hand of Amitabha. Daily, as he recited the *Heart Sutra,* he was reminded that the world he had renounced was empty of permanence and meaning. As he recited the *Amitabha Sutra* he affirmed the existence of a supernal world towards which his course now lay. It did not matter if he recited these sutras inattentively. Incantation could penetrate where discourse was barred. Thus the closing words of the *Heart Sutra,* which he chanted in the evening as well as before dawn, told him that the ultimate wisdom (*prajnaparamita*) was an incantation, a mantra, and this mantra ran:

> Gone, gone, gone beyond, altogether beyond,
> Awakening, fulfilled!

The monk who was preparing to "go beyond" could, by his pure life in the monastery, keep closely on the bodhisattva path. At each stage of this path he achieved certain fruits (*cheng-kuo*). These were, for example, seeing past, present, and future lives; clairvoyance; being able to tell what stage had been reached by others; immunity to wild beasts; and so on. Release from birth and death—the most important achievement—was the fruit of the seventh stage, the stage of the lohan (arhat).

The lohan's release, however, had a very large drawback. As soon as anyone achieved it, he was expected to return to the world of men to save others. If he refused to return, he was sure to be upbraided by Sakyamuni when he saw him face to face (a privilege of lohans). Sakyamuni upbraided all nonreturners, just as he upbraided the Hinayanists when he was here in the world, saying that they were spoiling the seed by scorching the sprout, that is, were selfishly concerned only with their own spiritual development.[68] The person who was treading the bodhisattva path could not look forward to final release until all sentient beings had been released before him.

That may have been one reason why most monks, although they were formally committed to the bodhisattva path, dwelt more on the hope of rebirth in the Western Paradise. It conferred a release from birth and death that seemed preferable to the lohan's release because Amitabha did not scold the nonreturners. All who were reborn in his paradise were at liberty to stay forever.

Thus the goals that monks came to pursue as they settled into the monastic career were optional and alternative. If they achieved samadhi in the meditation hall, or saw an episode from former lives, they were encouraged by these fruits of progress along the bodhisattva path. If they were granted a vision of the Western Paradise, it gave them reason to hope they would be reborn there. If they understood the profundities of a sacred text, it confirmed the validity of these goals. The common factor was otherworldliness: all the goals of the monastic career lay beyond the senses.

It is difficult to appraise success in the pursuit of such goals. As indicated in Chapter II, monks are reluctant to talk about their own spiritual achievements or even about the achievements of others. Except where omens at the time of death were made public, we have no way of knowing how many of them were considered to have reached the goal of rebirth in the Western Paradise—if in fact, that was their goal, and this too we cannot be sure of. We are thrown back, therefore, on appraising their achievements not by their own criteria, but by ours. We ask what they *objectively* achieved.

Some monks in the last half century achieved a great deal. They had such personal charisma and talent in spreading the doctrine that their disciples numbered tens of thousands of persons, to many of whose lives they brought meaning. With such a following, they were able to raise money for the restoration of ancient monasteries and the building of new ones. Hsü-yün, for example, restored the Hua-t'ing Ssu and Chu-sheng Ssu in Yünnan; Ku Shan in Fukien; the Nan-hua Ssu and Yün-men Ssu in Kwangtung; Yün-chü Shan in Kiangsi; and half a dozen smaller institutions. T'an-hsü founded the Chi-le Ssu in Harbin; the Po-jo Ssu in Changchun; the Leng-yen Ssu in Ying-k'ou; the Ta-pei Yüan in Tientsin; and the Chan-shan Ssu in Tsingtao. Tsung-yang, besides restoring the Ch'i-hsia Ssu near Nanking, reprinted the entire Chinese Tripitaka. Ti-hsien revived the tradition of the T'ien-t'ai School and Yin-kuang brought Pure Land practice to the same level of articulation as Ch'an. These were large accomplishments.

I have myself had several meetings with the second of the monks just named, T'an-hsü, who died in Hong Kong at almost ninety during the summer of 1963. Although he was very feeble, he had an immense and benign warmth, faith, and sense of humor. His smile made one want to follow him like a pied piper wherever he might lead. If he was a fair sample of China's long line of eminent monks, they achieved a lot simply as human beings and the world is poorer for the extinction of their line. Their lives may seem unutterably dreary to outsiders who cannot accept Buddhist premises about karma and rebirth and who have never experienced the "joy of the dharma" in meditation. But it is my impression that it was not dreary for them. The very privations that make their lives seem dreary assured them that they were moving toward their goals.

55-58. Retired abbots in many moods:

55. Fu-jen, abbot of the Nan-hua Ssu, the monastery of the Sixth Patriarch (p. 83 *et passim*). Hong Kong.

56. Ming-ch'ang, abbot of Ch'i-hsia Shan (pp. 228-233) indulges in a little badinage with Ming-kuan, abbot of the Liu-jung Ssu, Canton. Hong Kong.

57. Chih-kuang, abbot of Chiao Shan (p. 5 *et passim*). Taiwan.

58. T'ai-ts'ang, abbot of Chin Shan. Taiwan.

T'AI-TS'ANG

The first eight chapters of this book, since they dealt with the organization of Chinese Buddhism, may have led the reader to believe that most Chinese monks—or the best Chinese monks—were "organization men" who spent their lives working their way up the ladder of posts at large public monasteries. I hope that any such impression has now been corrected and that justice has been done to the freedom and variety of the monastic career. The variety could best be illustrated by tracing the steps of a monk like Hsü-yün: his decades of pilgrimage up and down China, to Tibet, India and Southeast Asia; his years as a menial officer, as a hermit, as a scholar, as a teacher, as an abbot, and as an eminent monk. But the interested reader can read Hsü-yün's autobiography in English,[69] and there are biographical sketches of other Chinese monks as well.[70] What he will not find in print is material on the "organization men." They may not have been typical, but they exemplified the side of monastic life that is our particular concern. It is therefore appropriate to take one of them for

our illustration of the monastic career. The following is the autobiography of T'ai-ts'ang, the last abbot of Chin Shan, as dictated to his
disciple, Wu-i, and later amplified.

"T'ai-ts'ang was born on the morning of the 16th day of the eighth
month in the twentieth year of Kuang-hsü [September 15, 1894].[71] He
was a native of Ju-kao *hsien*, Kiangsu. His family surname was Chang,
his father being Chang Pao-t'ien, while his mother's maiden name was
Chou. His forebears had been literate farmers.

"From the age of eight to twelve, he attended a private school. Then
the Ch'ing government abolished the examination system and set up
public schools. In 1906, when he was thirteen years old, he entered
one of these. In 1910, after passing the entrance examination, he enrolled in the old-style middle school of Tung-t'ai *hsien*. In 1911 he
placed fourth in the winter term examinations. In 1912, because of the
basic political changes that came with the introduction of the Republic, the Tung-t'ai *hsien* middle school closed down for lack of
funds. He missed a year of study. Since he could not go on with his
education, he decided to seek the truth in religion.[72] So on March 19,
1913, he left lay life under the Venerable Hai-ch'eng of the Bodhi
Meditation Institute (P'u-t'i Ch'an-yüan), commonly known as the
Bodhi Center, outside the east gate of the Ju-kao county seat.

"First he learned the liturgy of morning and evening devotions and
the rules and ritual for novices. The next year he studied the *Lotus
Sutra* until he could recite the whole of it by heart. In 1915 Venerable
Hai-ch'eng asked a holder of the first degree (*hsiu-ts'ai*) to come and
teach him the Four Books and the Five Classics and the "Appreciation
of Ancient Literature" (*Ku-wen kuan-chih*). After two years of intensive work, he had a good foundation in Chinese letters.

"In 1917 the Venerable Hai-ch'eng told him to go to the Chiang-
t'ien Ssu at Chin Shan and ask for the full ordination. When it was
over he stayed on there to study the Vinaya and afterwards enrolled
in the meditation hall to study the practice of meditation. He was
asked to take the rank of acolyte (*shih-che*). That year eight meditation weeks were held. T'ai-ts'ang worked on the *hua-t'ou* "Who is this
reciting the buddha's name?" and just when he was making progress
(*te-li*), the weeks came to an end. That was disappointing, but there
was nothing to be done about it. In the years that followed he was

busy in other parts of the monastery and was only able to go to the meditation hall in his spare time for occasional periods. He was never able to recapture that first experience.

"In the first month of 1918 he asked to be given the office of dispenser with the rank of recorder. After serving three semesters he was promoted to the office of sacristan with the rank of thurifer, beginning in the seventh month of 1919. For the term that began with the first month of 1920, he was promoted to the office of senior sacristan with the rank of deacon, in which capacity he was in charge of all the income and expense accounts of the entire monastery. In the first month of 1921 he was promoted to the office of guest prefect with the rank of secretary. He resigned from this office as of the first month of 1922 and left Chin Shan to pursue his study of the doctrine. First he attached himself to the Reverend Hui-hsi and the Reverend K'o-fa at the T'ien-ning Ssu in Yangchow [not Changchow], under whom he studied the T'ang dynasty translation of the *Avatamsaka Sutra* and the doctrines of the Avatamsaka School. He listened to Hui-hsi, who was a Szechwanese, for about three months. Then in the autumn of 1922 he enrolled in the Anhwei Buddhist School at the Ying-chiang Ssu in Anking, where under Reverend Ch'ang-hsing he studied the fivefold Avatamsaka doctrine, the *Treatise on the Awakening of Faith*, and the Sung dynasty translation of the *Lankavatara Sutra*. He spent two years there and left without completing the course. While there he listened to lectures on the *Shen-mi Ching* by the Reverend Shao-san, and to lectures on the *Surangama Sutra* by the Reverend Tu-wu. Along with Hui-t'ing and Te-i he gave the side lectures on the latter. (Hui-t'ing later died as abbot of the Ch'ao-an Ssu in Chenchiang; Te-i became the abbot of Lung-ch'ih Shan and died in a Shanghai hospital.)

"In winter 1923 at the Ting-hui Ssu in Ju-kao he heard Ti-hsien lecture on the meaning of the *Amitabha Sutra*. In 1924 an ordination was held at Chin Shan. Accordingly he brought his leave of absence to an end, returned, and took the position of guest prefect. The ordination that year at Chin Shan was unprecedentedly large. Over six hundred bhiksus were ordained and three hundred bhiksunis. At the beginning of the semester in July 1924, he entered the business office as a subprior. In the spring of 1926 he left the business office at Chin Shan to go to the Chin-ling Ssu in Nanking and listen to the

Reverend Mo-ch'en lecture on the *Lotus Sutra* [returning soon after-wards]. In the first month of 1934, at the beginning of the semester, he was promoted to the position of prior with the rank of associate instructor and later rector. On May 22, 1945, he received the dharma of Chin Shan along with four others, and on the same day he suc-ceeded the Venerable Shuang-t'ing as the head of the monastery.

"On March 22, 1949, Wei-fang was to take office as the head of the Jade Buddha Monastery (Yü-fo Ssu) in Shanghai. A day ahead of time T'ai-ts'ang went to Shanghai from Chin Shan to congratulate him. At that time people were in an indescribable state of consterna-tion [because of the Communists]. So on April 23rd T'ai-ts'ang fled from Shanghai, sailing on the *Szechwan* and reaching Hong Kong on the 27th.

"His senior dharma cousins, Ming-ch'ang and Ta-pen, as well as Chih-lin, his senior ordination brother, had already arrived. They and many others went to the pier to greet him. Ming-ch'ang and Ta-pen accompanied him to the Tz'u-hang Ching-yüan in Shatin, where he spent the night. Next day he went to the Lu-yeh Yüan in Tsuen Wan to take part in the seven-day celebration of Buddha's birthday.

"By the eighth month the Mainland had fallen completely to the Communists. T'ai-ts'ang stayed on at the Lu-yeh Yüan. At the end of 1951 he sailed on the *Szechwan* to reach the protection of his mother country [in Taiwan], where he has lived ever since.

"These are the main events in T'ai-ts'ang's life."

Such was the rather dry, formal account that he gave of himself. I would like to try to bring it to life so that the reader who has never met such a monk can sense his human qualities.

T'ai-ts'ang was tall, massive, and alert—a little like a bear, and sometimes as gruff. But when he was amused or happy, he was capa-ble of a boyish smile and a gaiety that belied his seventy years. One of his most deep-seated traits was loyalty. Once he said of another Kiangsu abbot: "He is loyal and solid." It was the highest compliment he could pay. Usually he avoided discussion of personalities. Many Chinese monks (many Buddhists everywhere, I am sorry to say) are wont to criticize one another: "So-and-so does not understand Bud-dihism. His knowledge is superficial, etc., etc." No such words ever passed T'ai-ts'ang's lips in my presence. Even where it was clear that he must have had a low opinion of a monk, he kept it to himself. Above all he was loyal to Chin Shan. During his three decades there he returned to his small temple in Ju-kao but once a year and, after his parents died, once every two or three years. It was only at the end of months of interviews that I was able to get him to talk frankly about anything that might be used by unfriendly persons to discredit his old monastery. His loyalty to Chin Shan was tempered by other loyalties. A former colleague once brought him a silk robe from Hong Kong as a gift. He admitted that silk could never have been worn at Chin Shan, but he wore it. How could he show ingratitude to a friend? Otherwise he was punctilious. When someone kowtowed to him, he kowtowed in return—down on his old knees, head knocking on the floor—none of your half-hearted half-bows. It hurt to see how much less punctilious some of the younger monks in Taiwan were toward him, interrupting him and contradicting him as if he were a "back number."

In many ways I suppose he was a "back number." He had a prejudice against the simplified characters that have long been used by most Chinese when writing informally, and he always expressed wonderment at how fast I wrote in English. He addressed himself to every ideogram as a task that deserved as much time as would be necessary to make it solid and correct. He much preferred a brush to a fountain pen. Once he was sent a wristwatch by a colleague in Hong Kong. He kept it in his pocket. I showed him how convenient it was to have it strapped on his wrist, but the next day it was back in his pocket. That, he said, was where he was used to having his watch. He disliked photography partly, I suspect, because he disapproved of the vulgar hoopla of Buddhist get-togethers with everyone's picture in the papers the next day. I used to watch him at the get-togethers that he had not been able to avoid. He could manage a pleasant smile for the cameraman's first shot. Then his face would set and with each click of the shutter his lower lip would protrude a little further until by the end he was scowling in Churchillian defiance at the whole procedure. The same stubborn set of the lower lip often appeared when he listened to views that he disapproved of. I have been told that as an administrator, he was just, but unbending. It is altogether in character that he never resigned as abbot of Chin Shan. He simply failed to return. Since the Communists had taken over, that was that.

Despite his old-fashioned outlook, he had a lively interest in almost everything in the larger world outside Chinese Buddhism. He would ask intelligent questions about American politics, universities, religion, international events, and my own personal history. He used to store away what I told him and introduce it into our conversation days or weeks later. Once I was astonished to hear him list the parts of speech in English which he learned when studying fifty years before: "Adjective," he said with a grin, "verb, noun, pronoun, adverb, interjection."

His mind was quick. Whereas many of my informants had difficulty grasping a question because they had never been asked about the monastic system before, T'ai-ts'ang often understood a question before it was out of my mouth. In answering he perfectly exemplified the Confucian ideal of wisdom: "To know what one knows and to know what one does not know." When he did not know something, he wanted there to be no mistake about it. On many topics where he might have been expected to have at least hearsay information (like conditions at neighboring monasteries), he would say: "I don't know about that. I never went there."

"Not going there" appears to have been his settled inclination. I remember being surprised one day when we crossed the street to call on an old colleague of his and found that T'ai-ts'ang had not been to see him for six months. Even stranger was the fact that during the entire period of construction of a new temple that was being built for him a few miles away, he never went to see it—until I took him. He had given the responsibility to a disciple, and that was that.

As head of the most illustrious meditation center in China, one might have expected T'ai-ts'ang to be a man of spiritual accomplishments. If he had them, he categorically denied it. All he could do, he said, was to teach the doctrine. He had achieved nothing in personal experience to offer his students. He had never attained any enlightenment nor could he tell whether anyone else had. After he said this, I had an opportunity to inquire about his work in the meditation hall from monks who were enrolled there when he was abbot. They told me that his Explanations were "run of the mill. He had a clumsy tongue and did not like talking. But this did not matter because in the meditation hall one was not supposed to say very much. If you did, people would know that the contents were not your own." Perhaps it was because of his "clumsy tongue" or because of his shyness that in his whole career he took only two tonsure disciples and "very few" Refuges disciples, although many laymen would like to have taken the Refuges with the abbot of Chin Shan, if only because of the prestige it would have given them.

However poor his spiritual accomplishments, there is no question about his devotion to the role of teacher. When he spoke of this monk or that who had been at Chin Shan, it reminded me of the headmaster of a boarding school speaking of his "old boys." He remembered what years they were there, their ranks in the meditation hall, and where they went afterwards. At our last meeting he said to me (as he had said several times before) that if I was going to start a Buddhist monastery in America, he would come to help me. He wanted no money: all he wanted was to set up a proper meditation hall and make sure it was properly operated. "I am seventy now," he added. "That means there are still ten years in which I can do it."

The last time I saw T'ai-ts'ang, he did not know that I had arrived in Taiwan. His small temple was silent and deserted except for the attendant who let me in the gate and said: "He is in the shrine-hall upstairs. You can go up." I went up quietly and found the old man sitting at the east end of the altar in the fading light of a winter afternoon. There was a book before him, which he was reading intently. I noticed that it was T'an-hsü's commentary on the *Lotus Sutra*. Even at seventy he had not given up his study of the dharma. When I spoke to him, he turned in surprise and smiled at me, but I noticed that before he got up to greet me, he carefully folded over one corner of the page, so that he would not lose his place. He intended to go on studying.

CHAPTER XI

The Lay Buddhist

irst of all, we have to decide what a lay Buddhist is. If we were preparing a census questionnaire for use in China, how would we phrase the entry on religion? This is not a hypothetical problem. The director of the 1961 census in Hong Kong was unable to solve it and therefore no entry on religion was included. Suppose we asked: "Do you believe in the Buddha (*hsin-fo*)?" In that case most of the rural population of China would answer in the affirmative, because to them *fo* (buddha) and *p'u-sa* (bodhisattva) are terms that can be loosely applied to all divinities, Buddhist, Taoist, and even Christian. If we asked: "Do you go to worship at Buddhist temples?" almost all would answer that they did, although they might add that they worshipped at other temples too. It would not help to inquire whether they called in Buddhist monks to perform rites for the dead, since this was done even in strict Confucian families that would normally have no traffic with the sangha. On the other hand, if we said "Are you a Buddhist (*fo-chiao t'u*)?" we would find that instead of some claiming to be Buddhists who were not, there would be some claiming not to be Buddhists who were. This is partly because the term "Buddhist" has a little stronger connotation in Chinese than it does in English[1] and, partly because, as Gamble discovered, "a man will usually claim that [Confucianism] is his religion, even though he believes in others as well."[2]

There are two questions, however, to which the answer would be revealing: "Have you taken refuge in the Three Jewels (*kuei-i san pao*)?" and "Have you taken the Five Vows (*shou wu-chieh*)?" All who answered either of these questions affirmatively would be likely to have a clear idea of Buddhism as a distinct religion and to have decided that they belonged to this religion rather than to any other. They would acknowledge that they were "Buddhists (*fo-chiao t'u*)," since they had become the disciples (*t'u*) of the Buddhist monk with whom they took the Refuges.

If they had taken the Five Vows, they would also say that they were *yu-p'o-sai* (male) or *yu-p'o-i* (female), terms transliterated from the Sanskrit *upasaka* and *upasika*. Bhiksus and bhiksunis,[3] upasakas and upasikas, are the four groups (*ssu-chung*) that make up the Buddhist community. A somewhat broader term is "devotee" (*chü-shih*), literally "a person who resides [at home]."[4] "Devotees" include not only devout laymen who have taken the Refuges or Five Vows, but those who are merely scholars and friends of Buddhism. Indeed it can be loosely applied as a title of courtesy to anyone who has any interest in Buddhism whatever. But it would not be applied to the peasant woman who offers incense to Kuan-yin in hopes of bearing a son. This would be because, although she might be more devout than most devotees, she does not distinguish the Buddhist religion from any other. She has no affiliation with it. Such a woman, like the Confucian official who has a Buddhist service performed for his parents, might best be called an "occasional Buddhist." In the sections that follow, there will be an effort to keep the reader clearly informed as to what category of lay person is under discussion.

First let us consider the formal steps by which affiliation with Buddhism was celebrated. The first step, taking the Refuges, meant that the lay person declared his faith in the Buddha, the dharma, and the sangha. The second step, taking the Five Vows, meant that he promised not to kill, steal, lie, drink alcoholic beverages, or commit any immoral sexual act. The third step, taking the Bodhisattva Vows, meant that he was committed to follow the bodhisattva path in helping and saving all other creatures. These three steps could either be separated over the years, or be taken close together in a brief period.

TAKING THE REFUGES

When the Refuges were administered by a monk to a layman, the effect was to make the layman the monk's disciple, that is, his Refuges disciple (*kuei-i ti-tzu*) and hence formally a Buddhist (*fo-chiao t'u*). Taking the Refuges might be compared to baptism and confirmation together. A monk did not become the Refuges disciple of another monk, nor a layman of a layman.[5]

The layman prostrated himself as he recited the Refuges and received a religious name from the monk exactly as he would if he were entering the sangha. The name included a character, which was the same as the one received by his master's tonsure disciples. The latter, therefore, could be considered his "brothers."[6] Unlike tonsure, however, the Refuges could be taken over and oven again with different masters or with the same master. Like most master-disciple relationships, it was not exclusive.

These features were universal. Others varied. Usually, for example, the disciple repeated with his own lips the formula: "I take refuge in the Buddha, I take refuge in the dharma, I take refuge in the sangha." Sometimes, however, he stood in silent assent while the master pronounced the formula on his behalf. This was the procedure, for example, when the Venerable Yüeh-hsi administered the Refuges to a crowd of four hundred persons gathered in the park of the Seventy-two Martyrs in Canton before the Second World War. Afterwards they filed past and he gave each a slip of paper with their religious names. He did not give out certificates, however. This may have been because he was old-fashioned or because of the size of the crowd. Certificates became increasingly common during the Republican period, perhaps as a countermeasure to the baptismal certificates handed out by the Christian missionaries. Termed *san-kuei cheng-shu, kuei-i cheng,* or *kuei-i tieh*, they stated that "So-and-so of such-and-such a place has this day taken the Refuges under Reverend So-and-so," whose signature was affixed below. Usually the text of the certificate admonished the disciple to do nothing evil, but good to all, and in particular, to forsake other religions. For example, one certificate lists the following prohibitions: "If you take refuge in the Buddha, you may no longer take refuge in other religions, whether they deal with Heaven or demons, for they do not provide escape from the cycle of birth and death. If you take refuge in the dharma, you may no longer accept the scriptures of other religions, for their principles do not reflect the true reality. If you take refuge in the sangha, you may not become the disciple of a master who belongs to another, heterodox religion, because that would be the blind leading the blind." I have never seen a Refuges certificate from the Ch'ing period and I do not know whether they were marked by the same sort of exclusivism.

Usually the Refuges were administered to a group, but it could just as well be done individually. One of my lay informants went to get them from the Venerable Yin-kuang. He found the great Pure Land monk in sealed confinement, and the ceremony was performed through the wicket (see p. 321). Yin-kuang recited the formulae and my informant repeated them after him. Next came a short Explanation (*chiang k'ai-shih*), and finally he was handed his Refuges certificate. Another informant, who was unable to go to Yin-kuang to take the Refuges in person, applied by letter. He soon received a certificate, already filled out, together with instructions on what to do with it. He was to place it in front of the Buddha image at home, make three prostrations, recite the formulae, and then make three more prostrations. Having done this, he could consider himself Yin-kuang's disciple. Later he took the Refuges with Hsü-yün in exactly the same way, except that a monk he knew acted as his sponsor, asking for the favor by letter and presumably assuring Hsü-yün that he was a worthy applicant.

Most masters felt little concern for worthiness. What concerned them was the opportunity to make another convert. One monk told me with pride that he had administered the Refuges to over two hundred persons. In most cases, he admitted, it had been in the form of "expedient Refuges (*fang-pien kuei-i*)," that is, with a simplified version of the ceremony. I was present when he made such a convert. A young woman had come to the monastery for an outing. She got into conversation with my informant, who soon suggested that she ought to take the Refuges. She seemed reluctant, so he gave her a five-minute sketch of the Buddha's life. To clinch his argument he pointed out that Buddhism was not superstitious and was being studied by foreign scholars like this American who was listening to them. Perhaps out of politeness she appeared to find the last argument irresistible. We were standing at the time some distance from the monastery buildings. He had her recite the formulae "I take refuge . . ." and bow to the south after each sentence. (I asked why to the south and was properly reminded that the Buddha nature was everywhere.) Then he gave her a little talk on her future conduct. She was not to worship Ma-tsu or any other popular divinity (*shen*) and she was to try to eat a little less meat and to avoid killing animals at home. Finally he took her name and address so that he could send her the Refuges certificate.

Such a "conversion" should not be laughed off. A seed was planted: perhaps it grew. But it is certainly fair to say that this first step in the lay Buddhist career was not necessarily an important one. While some devotees only took it after a long study of Buddhist doctrine, for other disciples it made their "occasional Buddhism" only a little less occasional. Their master might write to them from time to time asking for money. They were usually glad to send it, since it made them feel that some of the merit he was accumulating by his pure life would be transferred to them. If he were a great abbot, like Hsü-yün, even the indifferent Buddhist would take pride in the connection he had established by becoming his disciple. But pride too can start people along the path to enlightenment.

LAY ORDINATION

If the Three Refuges were an initiation, the Five Vows were an ordination. They were usually administered in a monastery as part of an ordination of monks. The ceremony was elaborate and solemn, and at the end of it a lay "ordination certificate" was conferred.[7] Serious obligations resulted. The devotee who took the vow against killing could not, for instance, hunt or fish. So seriously were the vows looked upon, in fact, that not all five were necessarily taken. When one or two were taken, it was called a "minor ordination (*shao-fen chieh*)." When three or four were taken, it was called a "major ordination (*to-fen chieh*)." When all five were taken, it was called a "plenary ordination (*man-chieh*)." In the printing of some lay ordination certificates, a space was left before the word *fen*, which could be filled in to show

which of these three categories the holder belonged to. A businessman, for example, might be reluctant to take the vows against lying
and stealing, since this would interfere with the conduct of his business.
A person who felt unable to forego the pleasures of the "flower house"
would omit the vow against sexual license. Almost everyone, however, included the first vow: not to take the life of any sentient being.
It may be argued with some force that if the Five Vows were a mere
form, there would not have been such scrupulousness in taking them.

An increasing number of male devotees took the Five Vows outside
monasteries during the Republican period. T'ai-hsü, for example, administered them to four hundred members of the Right Faith Buddhist
Society in Hankow in 1929.[8] The ceremony was held at the Society's
headquarters. Those being ordained first recited the Three Refuges
(many of them for the first time) and then, kneeling, responded to
T'ai-hsü's catechism. "Can you accept the prohibition against killing
living creatures?" he asked the assembly. All those who were prepared
to undertake this answered "I can," and prostrated themselves. Even
some of those who were *not* undertaking it prostrated themselves, although there would have been no embarrassment if they had simply
remained on their knees (or so my informant said). After the other
vows had been administered, everyone received a certificate bearing
his religious name as well as his surname, domicile, age, and so on—
data taken from a form that they had filled out ahead of time.

More typical instances are provided by an informant who took the
Three Refuges and the Five Vows under the Venerable Hsü-yün on
two occasions several years apart. The first time was in Chungking
during the war. A great crowd had gathered, perhaps four to five
thousand persons. They were packed together so close that it was
impossible to kneel or even to bow as they accepted the vows, which
were relayed to them by monks standing in different parts of the field
where they were assembled. According to my informant, another
crowd of the same size took the vows on the following day and again
on the day thereafter. "Ten to twenty thousand people became disciples of Hsü-yün in those three days," he said. This caused a delay in
the delivery of their ordination certificates, which they came back to
collect a week later.

Perhaps because he felt that this sort of mass ceremony was too
casual, my informant took the Five Vows under Hsü-yün again, this

59. Lay women, dressed in five-strip robes, prepare to receive the lay ordination, while beyond them stand those being ordained as monks and nuns. Pao-hua Shan.

time at the Nan-hua Ssu, Kwangtung, in 1949. The procedure was largely the same as at other large monasteries. The lay ordinees arrived at the beginning of a regular ordination of monks and nuns, and took the Three Refuges and the Five Vows on the same day that the novices took the Ten Vows.[9] Many stayed on while the novices went through the second part of the triple ordination, and then took the Bodhisattva Vows during the third part. The night before they performed the same penance as the monks and nuns[10] and during the actual ordination they left the hall only when the latter recited the articles of the *Fan-wang ching*. Whereas the monks and the nuns were burned on the scalp, the lay ordinees were burned on the inner side of the forearm—three scars or more.[11] They too received ordination certificates (with a different text) and their names were printed at the end of the ordination yearbook (see Fig. 49).

There was no fixed charge for all this. Most of the lay ordinees made whatever donation they felt they ought to, considering the fact that they had been living in the monastery for a couple of months. The rich might give the equivalent of one or two hundred silver dollars.

Some devotees who took the Three Refuges did not go on to take the Five Vows. Some who took the Five Vows did not go on to take the Bodhisattva Vows. The relationship between those three principal steps in the lay Buddhist career is controversial. Several lay informants have insisted that the Three Refuges were never taken alone, but always in conjunction with the Five Vows. Other informants had themselves taken the Three Refuges alone. It was common to do so in a local hereditary temple under one of its heirs, and then after a few years had passed, to go to a large monastery and take the Five Vows in a group organized by one's master.[12]

I have found similar disagreement as to whether a majority of lay people who took the Five Vows did or did not go on to take the Bodhisattva Vows.[13] On the whole, it seems that they usually did if they went to a monastery for ordination, although there was no obligation to do so. If, however, they went to a secular place of ordination (like a lay Buddhist association) the Bodhisattva Vows were usually omitted.[14]

In general the monastery ordinations were far more impressive. The layman who kneeled for a few minutes one morning in an auditorium cannot have felt so fully initiated as the layman who had spent two months in a secluded monastery, studying with the monks-to-be, drilling with them in the courtyard, taking part in the same night-long vigils, and undergoing the fiery pain of moxa. Furthermore, they emerged feeling a connection with the ordaining establishment. One devotee described himself as an "heir" (*tzu-sun*) of the monastery where he had been ordained. He was speaking loosely, of course, because he had acquired no proprietary rights whatsoever. On the other hand, he had undoubtedly become an "ordination disciple" of that monastery as much as any of the monks ordained there at the same time. Ordination disciples could—like Refuges disciples—be approached for support if it was needed.

OBSERVANCE OF THE LAY VOWS

The Bodhisattva Vows formalized the lay resolve to follow the bodhisattva path and to help all living creatures. Taken word for word, they did not appear to add a great deal to the Five Vows already accepted. Most of my informants, however, maintained that they added the obligation to be a vegetarian (*ch'ih ch'ang-su*). The first of the Five Vows, they said, meant simply to avoid killing animals oneself or eating an animal that had been killed on one's account, while the Bodhisattva Vows forbade contributing in any way to the use of animal products.

Other informants, on the whole better qualified, took a different view. They maintained that the first of the Five Vows carried with it the clear obligation to become a vegetarian. They were quite indignant at the idea that this obligation arose only from the Bodhisattva Vows. There was a similar difference of opinion about sexual abstinence. All informants agreed that the third of the Five Vows (against illicit sexual activity, *hsieh-yin*) prohibited visits to a brothel or even intercourse with one's wife in an improper place at an improper time or with the use of instruments ("improper" meaning, for example, in the living room during the afternoon, which, I was told, has been in vogue among those of modern outlook). But some informants said that a devotee who had taken the Five Vows was required to put away his concubines. Others said that he was merely prohibited from taking additional concubines. Still others maintained that these restrictions did not begin until he had taken the Bodhisattva Vows. One upasaka I know, who had not taken the latter, avoided intercourse with his wife when its purpose was to satisfy sexual desire. He only had relations to beget children and, he said, children begotten without sexual desire were always superior. I have heard of devotees (though my informants were not among them) who avoided sex and animal food on holy days like the festivals of Kuan-yin and the 1st and 15th of the lunar month. There was obviously a wide variety of interpretation and practice.

Breaking the vows (*fan-chieh*) was distinguished from suspending or "opening" them (*k'ai-chieh*). In the treatment of some illnesses, for example, the doctor would prescribe eggs or wine. In that case the upasaka could consume prohibited foods with a clear conscience. Nor did his conscience trouble him if he violated the vows he had *not* taken. It was up to each individual how far he wanted to go in abstinence and how much merit he wanted to accumulate. As one devotee remarked: "There is nothing embarrassing in being unprepared to give up sexual immorality. The embarrassing thing would be to take the vow and then not to carry it out."

Some lay people practiced abstinence without any formal ordination. One informant, for example, had been afflicted with eye trouble since she was a child. It was suggested that she promise to become a nun if the affliction were healed. When her grandfather vetoed this proposal, she and her two sisters promised instead "to eat an eyesight maigre feast" (*ch'ih yen-kuang chai*) on the twentieth of every month for the rest of their lives. Her eyes did improve and so every twentieth they ate vegetarian food, dedicating the merit arising therefrom to repay the merit transferred by the bodhisattva to bring about the cure.

FALSE ORDINATION

The lay ordination must be clearly distinguished from the novice's (*sha-mi*) ordination, which was received only by monks. In China, unlike some Theravada countries, it was not the custom for laymen to be ordained as novices in their teens and to spend at least one summer retreat living in a monastery. There was, however, a kind of a false ordination employed to protect children from disease. If the parents were worried about the health of a child, either because he was sickly or because all his brothers had died, they might take him to a monk, who for a fee would ordain him as a novice. His head was shaved and he might be given a necklace of red silk (yarn) to wear about his neck.[15] He was then returned home and brought up like any other child except that in some families his head might be kept shaven and he would be referred to as "little monk." When the danger was considered over, perhaps at the age of twelve, another ceremony would be held, either at the temple or at home. The child would stand with a low bench behind him, facing his "master." The bench was meant to represent the walls of the monastery. The "master" would scold him furiously for having eaten meat, broken the Ten Vows, and failed in study and devotion. Finally he would pretend to beat him, perhaps with a bundle of chopsticks. This was the signal for the child to flee, jumping *over* the bench. Thereby he was symbolically expelled from the monastery and the sangha. He would discard his necklace of yarn and let his hair grow long.

The underlying thought was presumably that a child who had taken the novice's vows would enjoy divine protection. (In some cases it was part of the ceremony that he should worship Kuan-yin and be entrusted to her care, thereafter returning every holy day to offer incense to her.) A different explanation is given by several Western writers, who maintain that this sort of ordination was given a boy "in order that the evil spirits may think that he is of no consequence— in fact worthless to his parents—and thus pass him uninjured."[16] Probably the rationale varied with the region and circumstances.

TEMPLE WORSHIP

One monk told me that most worshippers came to ask the gods for some selfish personal advantage—success in business, the birth of a son, better education for their children, or promotion in office. Such motives were not bad, he said, but childish. Buddhas and bodhisattvas could do little to overcome anyone's innate deficiencies and bad karma. The proper motive in worship was the desire to save all sentient beings and become a buddha. But not one in a hundred worshippers were thus motivated, he said.

The commonest time to visit temples was on festival days, particularly on the anniversaries of the divinities worshipped there, for example, Kuan-yin's birthday in a temple to Kuan-yin. This was partly because the Chinese enjoyed the festival atmosphere, with large crowds and lots of noisy excitement, with vendors, fortune tellers, and often a temple fair. It was also partly because if they were to make an offering to Kuan-yin or pay their respects, it was only proper to do so on her birthday, just as they would in the case of a human being. Often, besides the offering, they performed certain ritual acts. An

60. During the Buddha's birthday celebration in a small temple, a lay devotee pours a spoonful of water over the miniature image of the newborn Sakyamuni. Hong Kong.

example was "bathing the Buddha" (*yü-fo*) on his birthday, the 8th of the fourth month (see p. 109). Many worshippers also took the opportunity to consult the bamboo divination slips (see p. 212).

According to several of my informants, more women than men came to worship at such festivals in South China, especially in Kwangtung province, whereas further north men outnumbered women. The explanation, they said, was that women in South China did manual labor and had a much harder life, so that more of them came to ask for divine assistance. I can think of other reasons. In the urban middle class, precisely because women did *not* do manual labor, they had time for temple worship, whereas their husbands were unable to leave work during the latter part of the morning when most of the festival rites were held. This would apply particularly in the Treaty Port areas because of Western business hours. In the north, on the other hand, since it was closer to the old capital, the laws of the Ch'ing dynasty had greater residual effect. These laws prohibited women from worshipping at Buddhist monasteries or temples, and even from entering their premises.[17] Therefore more male than female devotees came to worship. This is reflected in the fact that twice as many male as female devotees are listed in the northern provinces, but less than half as many in central and southern China.[18]

In rural areas, on the other hand, what determined temple attendance was the cycle of cultivation. Peasant worshippers of either sex were freest to come in February and March, the slack season on the farm.

Not all the people who came to the temple on festival days were worshippers. Many were "occasional Buddhists." During the universal festivals like New Year's or Ch'ing Ming, occasional Buddhists were in the great majority, and they came mainly to "have a good time" (*wan*). Few of them knelt before the altar, unless it was to tell their fortunes with the bamboo slips. Some temples near large cities served as places of entertainment through the year. A layman brought up in Chen-chiang recalled that the Chao-yin and Chu-lin Ssu nearby had suites where rich people could entertain their friends. Some of the monks there were accomplished *literateurs* and would help "make the party" by eating, chatting, and capping verses with the guests. Thus there was no necessary correlation between temple patronage and the number of serious devotees in an area.

All this may seem strange to readers accustomed to the purposes of churchgoing in the Christian West, that is, to attend Sunday services and to receive the sacraments of baptism, confirmation, marriage, and confession. But these purposes would seem equally strange to Chinese Buddhists. Confession was completely unknown to them. Devotees who were troubled by some personal problem might conceivably go to seek the advice of the monks with whom they were on particularly close terms, but usually they went to them only for instruction in doctrine or religious practice. Absolution (if it can be called that) was not achieved through confession by the sinner, but usually through the recital of a penance on his behalf by the monks. He might feel quite reluctant to divulge to any of them the reason he was having the penance recited. Baptism and confirmation had an analogue, perhaps, in taking the Three Refuges and the Five Vows. Yet there were many differences, particularly in the lesser rigidity of commitment (see pp. 361-362). As to marriage, monks seldom took any part in it, although it was perfectly possible for the father of the bride, if he were a Buddhist devotee, to order a "red service" performed for the occasion. Most important of all, there was nothing like Sunday church attendance. Any devotee who knew the liturgy could stand in the back row and join the monks in morning and afternoon devotions, but very few did so in practice. Thus, while the monastery served also as a parish church for Chinese Buddhists, its role was not comparable to that of the parish church in the West.

This was part of an over-all difference in the nature of religion. The basic religious question in China, I think, was not how man saw himself in relation to God, but how he saw himself in relation to all the events that overtook him. He was part of a continuum of the human, the natural, and the supernatural. There was no dividing line between gods and men, monks and magicians, the sacred and the secular. It would be as true to say that the Chinese were a highly religious people as to say that they were a secular, practical people. In their case it amounted to the same thing.

LAY PILGRIMAGES

The Chinese term for pilgrimage was "journeying to a mountain and offering incense" (*ch'ao-shan chin-hsiang*—often abbreviated to *ch'ao-shan*). The journey might be long or short. City dwellers often spent a night at a monastery on some mountain nearby, perhaps to join in seasonal rites. For example, it used to be customary for female devotees to go to T'ien-t'ai Shan on the birthday of Kuan-ti (the 13th of the fifth month) and pray that while sleeping they would have a significant dream. If they had one and its import was favorable, they would burn incense the next day and recite prayers of gratitude. When Timothy Richard visited T'ien-t'ai Shan in 1895, he found the road crowded with women on their way to spend the night for this purpose.[19]

C. B. Day offers a good description of a party of pilgrims that he followed about the temples near Hangchow during the Ch'ing Ming festival. They were peasants who had come by boat from a town forty-five miles up the river. Arriving in the early morning, they visited every shrine, cave, and monastery in the hills by the West Lake and returned to their boat only at dusk. Day surmised that "their friends in the home village will, on their return, listen with awe to their tales of the wonders of Hangchow's magnificent temples, and secretly form the resolution to go themselves the following spring."[20]

Longer pilgrimages were made only for special purposes and to special places. One such purpose was to "redeem a vow" (*huan-yüan*). That is, the pilgrim had encountered difficulties—perhaps someone in the family was ill, or perhaps he was worried about business losses or a bad harvest—and he had gone to a temple and vowed that if the difficulties were resolved, he would make a pilgrimage to such-and-such a mountain and perhaps perform such-and-such a penance (if he felt that some former wrongdoing was the cause of his difficulties).[21] According to D. C. Graham, pilgrims on their way to Omei Shan would usually say they were going there so that "our family may prosper, that we may be protected from disease and calamities, that our crops may be good, that we may grow wealthier, and that we may have many children."[22] But there were also more general purposes in making a pilgrimage, as C. B. Day suggests. The Chinese, though normally sedentary, were not immune to the lure of distant, almost legendary places, visiting which was an accomplishment they could be proud of.

61. A pilgrim on her way to the T'ien-t'ung Ssu near Ningpo.

62. Pilgrims entering the outer gate of the T'ien-t'ung Ssu.

Chief among these places were the "four famous mountains" (see p. 307), as well as T'ien-t'ai Shan in Chekiang, the birthplace of the T'ien-t'ai sect; and Nan-yüeh (Heng Shan) in Hunan province, which was one of the Five Peaks that had been originally sacred to Taoism and Confucianism but had gradually become half-Buddhist and half-Taoist. Each of these mountains had dozens of monasteries and temples. They all lay several days or several weeks journey from the nearest large city and attracted pilgrims from thousands of miles away. Overseas Chinese from Singapore, for example, could be found at Wu-t'ai Shan near the Mongolian border. Usually pilgrims traveled to such distant places in groups for mutual protection and assistance and to lower the cost of the journey. Richer pilgrims could afford to travel in smaller groups, accompanied by servants and bodyguards, for protection against bandits, or, if they had to travel singly, they might wear their poorest, dirtiest clothes or a monk's robe, in hopes that the bandits would find them uninteresting. Larger pilgrim groups would be formed months in advance, partly to allow their members to accumulate the necessary travel money (handled much as in a Christmas Club) and partly so that those in charge could arrange by letter for accommodations and transport. This was important when the size of a group reached one or two hundred persons. Many a monastery at Omei or Wu-t'ai Shan could put up a group of two hundred persons in their guest halls, but if several such groups arrived on the same day, some would have to sleep in the courtyard. This was particularly true during the festival period (usually the birthday of the mountain's presiding divinity) when pilgrims preferred to come.

Many pilgrim groups carried identifying banners. For example, at Omei Shan (which was sacred to the bodhisattva Samantabhadra), such a banner might read "The Hong Kong Samantabhadra Society" (*Hsiang-kang p'u-hsien hui*), or simply the "Hong Kong Incense Society" (*Hsiang-kang hsiang-hui*). Migot gives the following impression of his visit to Omei Shan in 1947. "All along the sacred path I met large numbers of pilgrims, often grouped by villages, under a common banner. They were not tourists but real devotees, and I was struck by their seriousness. They moved forward at a regular pace without idling, without talking, although the Chinese love to hang about and chat. Walking in Indian file, gowns hitched up above the knee, bent under poor bundles of clothes, shod in straw sandals, carrying slung across the back the thermos and umbrella from which the traveling Chinese is inseparable, they left out not one shrine and not one pagoda, passing from statue to statue, prostrating themselves and lighting before each of them a stick of incense."[23]

The same sights could be seen at every great Buddhist mountain. The round of shrines and temples could take two days or two months. It depended not only on the size of the mountain, but on the thoroughness with which the pilgrims performed their devotions. Many carried yellow pilgrims' bags like those carried by monks. The layman's, however, instead of being embroidered with characters for the four elements, might bear the text: "Journey to a mountain to offer incense."[24]

Wherever pilgrims spent the night, males and females were lodged in separate halls. Not even husband and wife would sleep together. Monasteries served them only vegetarian food. On the whole of P'u-t'o Shan no animal could be killed and woe to the visitor who was caught with a tin of corned beef! Because Westerners so often tried to evade these dietary rules, they were sometimes refused permission to stay. This was not merely because of the scruples of their hosts, but because of the possibility of losing the patronage of Chinese pilgrims if the monastery's reputation for purity was compromised.

There was no fixed tariff for room and board. What pilgrims gave depended partly on how much merit they wanted to acquire and partly on the accommodations received. The poorer pilgrims slept in a dormitory,[25] whereas a rich family might have a whole suite to itself. Hackman describes such a suite at the T'ien-t'ung Ssu. It had two bedrooms, with four beds in each; a large reception room between them, clean and attractively arranged, with heavy chairs and tables, scrolls of calligraphy on the walls, and a quiet courtyard outside.[26] The countryside around the T'ien-t'ung Ssu was among the loveliest in eastern China. No wonder foreigners liked to vacation there!

Pilgrims usually made arrangements for their stay with one of the guest prefects. He was the monk with whom they had the most contact. In at least one case, however, the guest prefect in charge of lay visitors was himself a layman. According to an informant connected with the Nan-hua Ssu, lay visitors there in the 1940's were taken care of by a devotee who had the title of *chih-pin,* wore lay clothes, and lived permanently at the monastery. I have not heard of such a thing anywhere else on the Chinese mainland.[27] In general, except for the lay "temple owners" in south China and the occasional donor who was consulted on the choice of an abbot, laymen played no role whatever in the internal administration of monasteries.[28]

Most of the model monasteries of Kiangsu and Chekiang did not welcome pilgrims overnight. At Chin Shan, Kao-min, and the T'ienning Ssu and also further north at the Leng-yen and Chan-shan Ssu, lay visitors were only given lodging for some special reason as, for example, because they were having a plenary mass said or were actual or potential benefactors of the monastery. It was felt that large numbers of lay people in residence would vitiate the religious atmosphere, and therefore few of the better monasteries were located on the sacred mountains. There were, of course, differences in atmosphere even there. It was considered relatively strict at P'u-t'o Shan and relatively loose at Omei Shan. T'ien-t'ai Shan was the strictest of all and pilgrim traffic the lightest.

If the traffic was light enough, the religious atmosphere was unimpaired. There were many monasteries on lesser mountains where pilgrims came in small numbers with serious intent and where religious exercises, while perhaps not as formidable as at Chin Shan, were still the main preoccupation of the resident monks. Even in places like Omei Shan, once the pilgrim season was over, silence returned and it became propitious for meditation and study. Perhaps only in centers of pilgrimage that were a one-day excursion from a large city like Hangchow or Peking could little peace be counted on from one end of the year to the other.

SPREADING THE DHARMA

No less meritorious than pilgrimage was to spread the dharma either in print or through the spoken word. Most of the scriptural publication in China over the past century has been subsidized by lay donors. Sometimes a single rich devotee paid for a very large printing project (like the entire Tripitaka), but more often many donors gave a few dollars apiece to defray the cost of one volume. When such literature was distributed, the price was kept low or it was given out free. I have collected several shelves of books that were pressed on me by kindly Buddhists who were unconcerned by my protests that I would not have time to read them. It would be better, of course, if I could read them, but there was merit in the mere transfer of ownership: merit for the person who received as well as for the person who gave. The printed word had *mana* for the Chinese; witness the societies for collecting any waste paper that had writing on it. The spoken word was analogous. There was merit to be gained by merely being present at a lecture on the sutras. As one lecturer told me, perhaps half of those who attended did not understand what he was saying. It was better if they did, but even if they did not, he said, they gained some merit. This was because they subconsciously absorbed the sacred words and when they heard them next, perhaps in some future life, they would understand them that much better. Even the most illiterate members of the audience could appreciate the elevated style and catch some of the grandiose images.

Far greater merit, of course, accrued to the devotee who arranged for lectures—who invited an eminent monk, made him the necessary offering, and paid for the rent of the hall. During the Republican period some lay devotees took a special interest in spreading the dharma among their subordinates. For example, during the early 1920's the superintendent of rolling stock on the Shanghai-Nanking Railway had Buddhist tracts distributed at his own expense among the employees of his department and urged them to attend monthly lectures that he arranged for them on the Buddhist canon.[29] It also became common for laymen to expound the sutras themselves. When J. B. Pratt was in Peking in 1924, the only regularly scheduled lectures that he was able to discover were being given three times a week by one layman to other laymen at the Kuang-chi Ssu, a large monastery which still had many resident monks.[30] "The morning that I visited it," he writes, "there were in the audience thirty-six men and twelve women. Each was provided with a copy of the sutra that was being explained and followed with evident interest the words of the lecturer."[31]

Well-educated devotees, apart from attending lectures, studied Buddist texts on their own. They were quite ready to cope with the specialized vocabulary. Textual difficulty, if anything, attracted them. If they needed elucidation, they could seek out an eminent monk in a nearby monastery. Such persons, when they recited the sutras as a devotional exercise, understood what they were reciting. They were intelligently devout.

There was another class of Buddhists, however, who might be called the "pure intellectuals." They were embarrassed by devotions, usually despised monks, and maintained that all forms of religious practice were "superstitious." For them Buddhism was a philosophy, not a religion, and they found satisfaction in its abstruseness. They regarded themselves (quite correctly) as members of a small elite who understood texts like the *Ch'eng wei-shih lun*. More will be said about them in the next volume.

MERITORIOUS PRACTICES

The ordinary layman's desire to acquire merit toward some specific personal end like the healing of disease, the birth of a son, or promotion in the civil service, gave rise to a wide range of practices. Some of them were quite businesslike. It was possible, for example, to contract for the recitation of buddha's name. "The worshipper proposes a certain number of repetitions as the price he will pay for a desired mercy, and then throws down the [divining] blocks. If they fall in such a way as to mean No, he tries again, offering a larger figure, and so continues until he and the Fo or the P'u-sa have struck a bargain."[32]

Merit could be acquired by charity, both in its old forms and new. For example, a layman in Peking promised that in return for divine help on a personal problem he would maintain five rest houses on the road up to a temple northwest of the city. He got the divine help he asked for, built the rest houses, and during the 1930's pilgrims could stay in them overnight at no charge and get free vegetarian meals. Even the repair of their shoes was free.[33]

Modern forms of charity did not appear on a large scale before 1912. Soon thereafter Buddhists began to organize orphanages, schools, and relief work. During the 1921 famine a Buddhist Relief Association was established to assist the five drought-stricken provinces in North China. It collected enough money to send them 5,500,000 catties of food, 46,000 catties of seed, and 22,700 pieces of clothing, which it distributed through eighteen relief stations. Since laymen outnumbered monks on its board of directors by five to one, we may assume that it was mainly a lay effort.[34] Of course 5,500,000 catties of food was a trifling quantity vis-à-vis the population's need, but it was a large quantity to come from Buddhist devotees. One of my informants, a retired provincial governor, spent twenty-three years (1926-1949) organizing relief drives. He called them "dharma meetings" (*fa-hui*), as, for example, the "flood-relief dharma meeting."[35] A group of lay sponsors would form such a "meeting," raise money, spend it on the designated relief, and then dissolve. Sometimes they sponsored Buddhist services so that victims of the disaster might receive not only material but also supernatural assistance.

It can be argued that the proliferation of such modern forms of charity during the Republican period was stimulated by the Christian missionaries, whose schools and orphanages reminded Buddhists of their own compassionate principles. But one practice, at least, had no Christian analogue whatever: the release of living creatures (*fang-sheng*). This was an ancient and attractive Chinese Buddhist custom that struck the visitor as soon as he approached almost any large monastery. Near the main gate there would be a "pool for the release of living creatures" (*fang-sheng ch'ih*), into which the pious could drop the live fish that they had rescued from the fishmonger. Out behind the monastery there would be stables for the care of cows, pigs, and other livestock similarly rescued. Males and females were kept separate—lest they indulge in sexual intercourse. Predatory fish might also be kept in a pond of their own—lest they commit murder, which would have an even more adverse effect on their next rebirth. At some monasteries anyone who brought livestock was required to contribute to its keep during its lifetime. That was reasonable enough, for otherwise the monks might have been eaten out of house and home. Nor could produce from released animals be used. Eggs, for instance, were buried, as were the animals themselves when they died.[36] In the case of pigs a few monasteries solved the fodder problem by keeping them in a sty outside of the main gate where the public could feed them directly.[37] Some pigs became enormously fat and their contrast to the human population made a poor impression on the Christian missionaries.

The animals that it was most convenient to release were those that could take care of themselves afterward: birds, reptiles, fish. Hence they were favored in the mass releases that were organized during the Republican period by various Buddhist groups. What more appropriate homage could there be to the compassionate Kuan-yin on her three annual festivals than to save living creatures from the dinner table? Sometimes thousands were set free. It was also done to create merit against a natural disaster. I saw this myself in 1963 when Hong Kong was in the midst of the century's worst drought. Three hundred sparrows, in addition to turtles, monkeys, and barking deer were set

63. The T'ien-t'ung Ssu comes into view across the pond for the release of living creatures.

free on March 15th. After another ten weeks passed without rain, three thousand fish were released on May 29th, followed by five hundred tortoises, as well as clams, oysters, shellfish, crabs, snakes, and eels, to a total reported cost of US $1,750.[38] Many of these animals had been obtained from local pet shops.[39] Inevitably there were stories that some resourceful pet shop proprietors had trained their birds to home, so that they could be sold to Buddhist devotees over and over again; and at least five fishing boats were seen spreading their nets in the

64. During a release of living creatures, a monk supervises as crabs and fishes are returned to the sea. Hong Kong.

65. A monk sprinkles holy water before administering the Refuges to the birds about to be released from the cages behind him. He wears a twenty-five-strip red robe, while the monk with his back to the camera wears an ordinary seven-strip robe. **Hong Kong.**

wake of the launch that was releasing the creatures of the sea. No matter: the release was still meritorious and the good karma it created offset the bad karma of a commercial city like Hong Kong, thereby removing the impediment to rain (although as it turned out, the drought did not end until a year later).

One reason it was meritorious to release the crabs and eels, even with fishnets close behind, was that all had been converted. Conversion was an essential part of *fang-sheng*. As the basket of crabs, for example, was dumped into the harbor, the monk in charge recited the Three Refuges on their behalf. Often he also recited the Five Vows, and sometimes even the twelve nidanas of cause and effect. This made the crabs "sons of the Buddha" (*fo-tzu*) and increased their chances of better rebirth—an advantage that was also bestowed on the livestock in monastery stables. But the latter had the additional advantage of spending their lives in a holy place and of acquiring wisdom and merit by listening (from their pens) to the recitation of sutras twice a day.

RELIGIOUS EXERCISES

While it was always important to earn merit through pilgrimages and good works, those devotees who were most serious about their Buddhism were not satisfied with such external methods of spiritual development. Therefore they also practiced religious cultivation (*hsiu-ch'ih*). Many of them had altars in their homes, before which they recited certain sutras at certain times of the day, most often in the early morning. Sometimes the altar had a room to itself. Sometimes it was placed to the right of the shrine that held the ancestral tablets, so that the ancestors lay to the West (where, it was hoped, they had been reborn). The devotee would offer incense to the buddha image and sit before it, often in lotus position, reciting from memory or reading a text from a lectern in front of him. The sutras recited might be the *Heart Sutra*, the *Diamond Sutra*, or the *Sutra of the August Royal Kuan-yin* (*Kao-wang Kuan-shih-yin ching*). One lay informant told me that his mother never recited the *Heart Sutra* in the evening because ghosts would come. Another said that the *Diamond Sutra* was too potent to be recited at any time. Monks have scoffed at these ideas and pointed out that if the ghosts came to hear the dharma and be fed, so much the better—an illustration of the different way in which the laity and the sangha looked upon the supernatural. A third informant, much more sophisticated than the two just mentioned, used to recite both the *Diamond* and the *Heart Sutra* every night before going to bed. He said that they helped him get to sleep.

Some devotees did not recite every day, but only on special occasions: for example, the 1st and 15th of the lunar month; the whole of the sixth month; and on the festivals of divinities. These were the same days when abstinence from meat and sexual intercourse was considered particularly meritorious.[40] Sometimes groups of devotees, particularly women in or past middle age, would hold recitations together in a convivial spirit, rather like the sewing circles of the Victorian era. The reception room of a large Chinese house would be temporarily converted into a shrine by placing an image (probably of Kuan-yin) on an altar at one end. Rosaries in hand, the women sat at a long table on which they rested the sutra or mantra they were reciting. It was often printed on one large sheet of paper, the border of which was composed of three rows of tiny circles, like lay ordination certificates. As every recitation was completed, the devotee would singe a hole through one of those circles with a stick of incense. After the entire border had been perforated, the sheet became, as it were, a personal cheque for the merit accumulated by hundreds of recitations. Some devotees burned their sheets for the sake of their deceased ancestors. Others, if they needed money, took advantage of the fact that the "cheque" was a negotiable instrument, and sold it to persons who burnt it for *their* ancestors.[41] There is the story of one old woman who left off reciting the Mantra of Great Compassion just long enough to remind her servant to kill a chicken for supper. But Chinese Buddhism surely has no monopoly on mechanical piety.

In the Republican period these recitation groups became institutionalized in the form of lay Buddhist societies, some independent, some connected with monasteries. Members often undertook to perform a set daily ritual. For example, every member of the Lien-ch'ih Hai-hui in Hangchow was obliged to do the following when he or she got out of bed in the morning:

1. Wash face and dress.
2. Salute the West with palms pressed together or kneel before the Buddha image.
3. Recite three times: "Homage to our Teacher Sakyamuni."
4. Recite once: "Homage to the great compassionate Amitabha of the Land of Bliss."
5. In one breath recite ten times: "Homage to the buddha Amitabha."
6. Recite three times each of the following:
   "Homage to Avalokitesvara."
   "Homage to Mahasthamaprapta."
   "Homage to all the bodhisattvas of the great ocean of purity."
7. Recite a gatha for the transfer of merit.[42]

Occasionally the members of such a lay Buddhist society gathered for a week of reciting buddha's name six or seven hours a day. This not only improved their prospects for rebirth in the Western Paradise, but was also considered by some to assure immunity to snakes, fire, knives, prison, and a great many other disagreeable things.[43]

It was not uncommon for devotees to recite the full liturgy of morning and evening devotions, either at home or at the headquarters of their society, especially on the 1st and the 15th of the lunar month, and to perform the appropriate rites on the festivals of the various divinities. For such occasions they wore a long Buddhist gown (*ch'ang-kua*) unless they had taken the Five Vows, in which case, as upasakas, they were entitled to wear the full-sleeved gown (*hai-ch'ing*) and the robe (*chia-sa*), so that, except for their unshaven heads, they looked undistinguishable from the sangha. In fact, however, the robe they wore was divided into five parts: it was the *wu-i* rather than the seven-part robe, or *ch'i-i,* worn by ordained monks.

Although laymen could recite the sutras, lecture on them, and perform any part of the daily ritual, there were certain things they did not have the authority to do. They could not administer the Three Refuges; they could not ordain; they could not transmit the dharma; they could not read the Vinaya. (If they read the Vinaya they might start criticizing the sangha for breaking the rules.) Finally, laymen were not supposed to perform rites for the dead. The last restriction was sometimes ignored. In Hong Kong, for example, there used to be a Tantric devotees club whose members "released the burning mouths" with a lay celebrant presiding, dressed in a red patriarch's robe and wearing a Ti-tsang hat; this became fairly common in Peking as monks and money grew scarce. But it was not generally approved of. One lay Buddhist told me that it was like a private putting on the five stars of a general. As another put it, the sangha and the laity each had its own sphere. There were certain traditions that laymen had not received and definite limits to what they could properly do. But this was not on the grounds that they were inferior to monks. Whereas in Theravada countries no layman may sit higher than a bhiksu, and no bhiksu returns a layman's salute, this is not true in the Mahayana where "everyone is equal." Not only do monks return salutes (pressing the palms together), but I have seen them return a bow and even a kowtow, though it was not quite so low as the reverence they received.

While laymen had a perfect right to join in collective Ch'an meditation, they seldom did so. Sometimes they were allowed to sit in the meditation hall of a large public monastery. The Venerable Hsü-yün encouraged this practice during the 1930's. He permitted several groups of lay supporters to come to the Nan-hua Ssu and follow part of the same schedule as the monks. Although they lived and ate in the guest quarters, they attended morning and evening devotions and after supper they sat in the meditation hall for the evening fourth period. Their places were in the east, "lower than any of the monks." The meditation patrol did not strike them over the shoulder if they dozed. In fact on one occasion a layman snored on so stertorously with the great Hsü-yün sitting there in the abbot's seat that his companions felt that they had lost face and asked him to go home. At other times Hsü-yün invited laymen to sit in the meditation hall of the Yü-fo Ssu in Shanghai[44] and the Hua-t'ing Ssu near Kunming. In the latter case he allowed John Blofeld, an English devotee, to shave his head and to lead the same life as the monks enrolled in the hall for a period of seven months—so far as I know, a unique privilege.[45]

Religious cultivation was carried furthest, perhaps, by devotees of the Tantric or Esoteric sect (Mi-tsung). During the Republican period, Tibetan lamas had almost as much of a *cachet* in China as they had in Europe—and for similar reasons. Rich laymen became their disciples to get their instruction in the exercise of paranormal powers. Others went to Japan to study Tantrism in its Japanese form of Shingon (Chen-yen). Not all Tantric masters had been ordained. Some were laymen who after studying under Tibetan or Japanese monks took disciples themselves.

One of my informants, for example, used to work for the *New York Times* in Shanghai. Although his family were Christians, he and his sister became the disciples of a Mr. Yeh Wan-chih, himself the disciple of a Tibetan lama. Mr. Yeh's paranormal powers were impressive. He could heal by laying on hands. He had developed "diamond skin" (*chin-kang p'i*), so that one could put the point of a sharp knife at his throat and then push with all one's might—indeed two or three persons could add their weight—but the knife would not penetrate the skin. His special talent, however, was telekinesis. He could shove a person who was twenty feet away from him. If he wanted to, he could knock him down. In the case of my informant, Mr. Yeh used to come to his house to give two lessons a week. During the first year he would sometimes knock him down by brushing against his body. Later he began to do so simply by a shove of the hand in his direction. It felt like a blow at the pit of his stomach and sent him reeling back ten feet. Yeh knocked him down frequently, since he said it was good for his spiritual development, particularly for learning to do the same thing to others. There were additional elements in the curriculum: conning the *Diamond Sutra* and prostration before the buddha image a hundred times a day. By the time a person had reached the ten thousandth prostration, his paranormal powers were supposed to be well developed, as the following episode reveals.

One evening my informant attended a dinner party at which a Tibetan lama sat opposite him. To try out what he had learned, my informant "shoved" him under the table with a slight move of the hand. The lama looked at him with surprise and then pronounced a few unintelligible words. Immediately he found that he had a headache so shattering that he had to leave the party. He went to another party, where he knew he could find Mr. Yeh, who, after hearing about the lama, smiled, "dissolved" his headache, and sent him back. When my informant arrived at his own dinner party again, the lama looked quite surprised to see him and appeared to shrink to a smaller size. As they said good-bye, the lama gave him a special smile, as one member of the craft to another.

Yeh Wan-chih did not insist on abstinence. In fact, if his disciples drank too much, he stood ready to "dissolve" their hangovers too. He himself smoked opium. Despite the advantages of such a teacher, after a year and a half my informant took up tennis instead. "It was more fun," he explained.

I myself was present when a lay devotee of Esoteric Buddhism demonstrated his powers of telekinesis. He had invited a large number of guests, including some U.S. Foreign Service officers in Hong Kong. He told us about his "inner work" (*nei-kung*), which sounded much the same as what has been described above, except that he had been pursuing it for many years (he was then eighty). When I expressed an interest in being "shoved," he stood at the other end of a long room, perhaps thirty feet away, and flapped his hands at me, like the ears of a hound. I felt nothing. There were different results, however, when he did the same thing to a senior Foreign Service officer, who was as skeptical as I was, but who felt a distinct draft against his cheek.

Nothing described above is beyond the powers of a skilled hypnotist, and it is mainly, perhaps, because most Chinese were unfamiliar with hypnotism as such that some of them were so impressed by the parlor tricks of the Esoteric School. It may also have been because of an interest in sexual prowess, which was another part of the curriculum. In theory, Tantric Buddhism is a complete religion, with a lofty metaphysics and a complicated psychology that uses gross symbols to purge the mind. There is no doubt that some lamas trained their Chinese disciples in this complete religion, but what one hears about most often is the least edifying part of it, and this was perhaps the part that most attracted the rich businessmen who took it up.

MOTIVATION

There is no need to discuss the motives of the "occasional Buddhists," who used Buddhism in the same way a motorist uses one of the several different brands of gasoline, without any special commitment. What interests us is the seriously religious devotee. How did he become interested in Buddhism? Why did he take the Refuges or Five Vows? What did Buddhism mean to him? The answers to these questions depend upon whom we are talking about, on sex, age, education, economic status, and (most important of all) the accidents of human life.

There are even fewer statistical data than for monks. We do learn something, however, about sex and age from ordination yearbooks. Here is a breakdown of the sexes of those taking the lay ordination according to the yearbooks[46] I have collected:

Monastery	Date	Men	Women
Nan-hua Ssu (Kwangtung)	1941	3	43
Ku Shan (Fukien)	1916	6	58
Ku Shan	1925	18	33
Ku Shan	1932	2	14
Ch'i-hsia Ssu (Kiangsu)	1929	15	52
Ch'i-hsia Ssu	1933	27	95
Ch'i-hsia Ssu	1941	2	18
Pao-hua Shan (Kiangsu)	1916	68	265
Pao-hua Shan	1930	0	17
Pao-hua Shan	1940	0	6
Lung-hua Ssu (Shanghai)	1947	18	78
		159	679

According to this small sample, at any rate, upasikas outnumbered upasakas four to one. Of those from Kiangsu only about 40 percent came from the parallelogram in the northern part of the province that produced 70 percent of the monks (see p. 255). This contrast could be interpreted in many ways. As to age distribution, there was usually a peak in the thirties and a sharp drop after the fifties. Only two received the vows at nineteen or under and both were at the Nan-hua Ssu. The picture seems to be that more women than men were attracted to Buddhism, more often in maturity than in youth or old age.

I have found only two sets of statistics that bear on the wealth and education of the Buddhist laity. A survey of one small district in Peking, conducted 1918-1919, showed an apparent correlation between Buddhism and poverty. Whereas 10 percent of the families who claimed to be Buddhist were poor, this was true for only 1 percent of Confucian families. Among all poor families, 75 percent claimed to be Buddhist, versus 25 percent among the population as a whole.[47] The crucial words here are "claimed to be." Perhaps this survey indicates not so much a correlation between Buddhism and poverty as a reluctance on the part of the upper classes to call themselves Buddhists.

If 10 percent of the Buddhists in this district were poor, did this mean that 90 percent were prosperous? A second survey was made under the Japanese occupation of north China. It showed that 11 percent of the Buddhists in the whole city of Peking were "poor" (that is, without property or wages sufficient for livelihood), and that as for the rest, 54 percent were economically middle class (that is, having either a job or property sufficient for livelihood); 28 percent were upper class (that is, having both job and property); while the status of 7 percent was unclear. The figures on education are even more interesting. 28.5 percent of the Buddhists in Peking had received higher education; 32 percent had received a middle-school education; 26 percent had received a primary education; and 13.5 percent had either received no education or their status was unclear. The 28 percent who were "upper class" match nicely the 28.5 percent who had received the higher education. Other figures in the same survey cover Hopei, Shantung, Shansi, Honan, Kiangsu, Tientsin, and Tsingtao.[48] As might be expected, the richer and better educated Buddhists were in the large cities or in the provinces around them (Shansi came out the worst, with only 12 percent of Buddhists classified as rich and only 9 percent having higher education, while no area had percentages as favorable as Peking).

Unfortunately we do not know the method by which these statistics were collected, nor do we know the size of the sample or even the criteria used for deciding who was a Buddhist. There is no breakdown as to sex. But the figures must certainly give pause to those who would portray Buddhism as the religion of the poor or the ignorant, particularly since it was less prosperous in north China than elsewhere.[49]

I have collected too few case histories to be worth tabulating. Five of them, however, illustrate the kind of motives that inspired some devotees, and I shall give them for this purpose. The first involves a Chekiangese. Although both his mother and father had been Buddhists, he took little interest in religion in the early years of his career, during which he held high office in the government. In his forties, however, when he was serving as a provincial governor, he became disgusted with politics and all it involved. He resigned his posts and took a trip around the world. In Japan, America, and Europe, he found

the same evils as at home: partisan conflict, helping friends and hurt-
ing enemies, no means to live in peace and benefit all sentient beings.
So on his return he decided to devote the rest of his life to Buddhism.
He was active in relief work both before and during the Japanese
war. He belonged, incidentally, to the Tantric School and despite his
advanced age (or perhaps because of it) one could hear sly jokes
about his relations with female disciples.

Case number two involves a devotee whose family had been such
orthodox Confucians that his father would not allow monks to enter
the house. They looked upon Buddhism as a foreign religion that was
beneath the notice of the scholar-official. Not a single ancestor had
ever been a Buddhist, he said. Yet when his eldest son died at the age
of five, he suddenly felt the need to make sense of life and "find its
real meaning." He happened to meet a member of a lay Buddhist club
in Canton who told him that he would find the meaning of life in
Buddhism. Therefore he took up the study of Buddhist texts. During
the initial phase of his studies he was a follower of Venerable Hsü-
yün. Later he became interested in the Tantric Buddhism of Japan and
built a Japanese room in his house with tatami matting and a Shingon
shrine, where he performed several hours of religious exercises every
day. His anti-Buddhist father eventually followed suit. When he fell
ill, the doctor prescribed a vegetarian diet. The old man decided that
he might as well go the whole way and become a Buddhist too.

A third lay devotee came from a family of which only one member
was a Buddhist, and that was his grandmother. When she went to
worship at the monastery, she used to take him along, and he reacted
like many other Kiangsu boys. "Our house was very small. The temple
was very large, very peaceful, and very clean. You could run around
there anywhere you liked." One monk was especially nice to him and
gave him the Refuges at an early age. When he was fourteen, he happened to get a letter of introduction to the illustrious Tsung-yang from
the cousin of an uncle by marriage—a monk who was then serving at
Chin Shan.[50] Tsung-yang liked the boy and also gave him the Refuges.
In the years that followed, while he was a student in Shanghai, he was
a devout vegetarian, but later he became a follower of Ou-yang Ching-
wu and shifted from devotional to intellectual Buddhism.

Case number four is interesting because it involves a progression
from Confucianism through Christianity to Buddhism. This infor-

mant's mother had been a worshipper of Kuan-yin and had often taken him to the monastery during his childhood in the 1890's. Although he was impressed by the sight of the monks chanting sutras, he remained in his youth an orthodox Confucian like his father. After he received his *hsiu-ts'ai* degree he went to study in Japan. There he became a friend of Sun Yat-sen and joined the T'ung-meng Hui. Fired with zeal for revolution, he decided to return to China. But how could he do underground work in safety? The answer was to become a Christian and join the YMCA. "As a Christian I would have some protection. At that time the Manchu Government was afraid of persecuting the Christians or any foreign religion. They would not dare touch me. So I had myself baptized before I went back and got the pastor to give me a baptismal certificate." When the revolution broke in 1911, he was among those present in Wuhan.

In 1917 he happened to hear T'ai-hsü lecture on the sutras in Shanghai. He did not altogether understand the lecture, but thought to himself: "This is something interesting!" He got a copy of the *Diamond Sutra* and tried to puzzle out what it meant—without success. Politics continued to preoccupy him for another ten years, but in 1928 when he was serving as a provincial official in Fukien, T'ai-hsü came to see him and invited him to attend his lectures at the Nan P'u-t'o Ssu. Again he was impressed by the depth of the Buddhist doctrine. The following year, when he transferred to Wuhan, T'ai-hsü called to welcome him and suggested that he join the local Buddhist association. Before the year was out he had taken the Five Vows. Only then, at the age of forty-seven, did he seriously begin the study of Buddhist doctrine, in which he soon became a believer. In a couple of years he was elected president of the local Buddhist association. This made his belief even stronger, he said. He realized that only by understanding the dharma could he understand life. His belief, as he put it, was correct and orthodox, "unlike the belief of ordinary worshippers." He eventually became one of the most influential Buddhists in China. When I met him, he was in his eighties and lived in a monastery, although he had still not become a monk.

The last case history involves the supernatural.[51] The devotee was a successful banker in Shanghai (one of several such among my informants). No one in his family had been Buddhist. He himself, in fact, had been baptized a Christian by a Shanghai Protestant missionary. Afterward, when he had read the Bible, he had found "nothing of significance in it." But he continued to practice the Christian virtues that seem to have made the biggest impression in China: no drinking, no gambling, no smoking. During the war he headed a government office in Chungking. He was then in his fifties. He had, he said, a bad disposition and had hurt many people. One evening on his way back from a friend's house, he thought he saw the ghost of a woman. Since he could not see her feet clearly, it was probably a ghost. He slept badly. Next morning he sent a servant to see if there was anything there. There was not: "Therefore I decided it had certainly been a ghost." He was feeling in poor health, but neither Western nor Chinese doctors could find anything wrong. A Chinese doctor suggested that he get hold of a sutra and recite it: then the ghost would not dare to come. He went to see T'ai-hsü, who was a friend of his, and received from him copies of the *Heart* and *Diamond Sutra*. He took them back and read them alone. "I was so moved with the greatness of Buddhist compassion that tears fell from my eyes. I believed in the Buddha." First he took the Refuges with Neng-hai, an advocate of the Tantric School. Though he admired Neng-hai for his asceticism, he felt no interest in the Tantrism. Ch'an attracted him more, because its doctrines were very lofty. Therefore he twice took the Refuges with Hsü-yün, who told him that he was too old to practice meditation (he was fifty-four) and that he should recite buddha's name. He did so ever after.

Unless this informant was exaggerating when he said he once had a bad disposition, Buddhism had certainly wrought a great change in him by the time we met. He was a wonderfully kind and gentle person. Indeed I have liked and admired all the laymen whose case histories have just been given. If Buddhism helped to make them what they were, I hope that it will find more converts.

All these case histories involve upasakas—devout male Buddhists who had taken the Five Vows and made a thorough study of the doctrine. Female devotees, like nuns, lie outside the scope of this book. But part of their motivation probably was due to the place of women in China. Though the Chinese woman was not in purdah, her movement was severely restricted. One of the few legitimate reasons for leaving the house was to visit a temple, and the only men with whom she could have contact outside her kin were monks. Monks were allowed to enter the women's quarters in some houses and, of course, nuns could do so even more freely. Thus religion offered an escape for the distaff side of the family. Furthermore, problems of fertility, child-bearing, children's disease, and so on fell mainly on the shoulders of women. They had more reasons than their husbands to depend on divine assistance. Few of them had received higher education. Even if they had, their temperament was more inclined to piety than to metaphysics, which was the special province of the well-educated male devotee.

THE SIZE OF THE LAITY

For the reasons given at the beginning of this chapter there are no reliable census figures on the number of Buddhists in China. Chinese Communist sources customarily quote a figure of 100 million.[52] This is probably too low if it is meant to include all the "occasional Buddhists,"[53] but too high if it is confined to serious devotees. In the 1930's, according to statistics compiled by the Chinese Buddhist Association, devotees numbered 3,890,000.[54] In 1947 the Association claimed 4,620,000 members, all of whom were theoretically supposed to have taken the Three Refuges.[55] This was equivalent to about 1 percent of the population—a reasonable figure.

But probably 90 percent of the population occasionally resorted to Buddhist rites or temples and 99 percent were affected by Buddhist contributions to Chinese thought and behavior. The gap between 1 percent and 90 percent seems unsatisfactory. Are there no criteria for distinguishing between the more and the less occasional—as, for instance, to ask whether the census respondent has kneeled in prayer before a Buddhist image at least once in the past year? Unfortunately it is too late to apply this criterion or any other, and even if we could travel back in time and space to do so, I doubt that the results would be significant. We cannot afford to be stricter in our approach to statistics than were the Chinese in their approach to religion.

CHAPTER XII

The Nature of the System

In the Christian West, division into sects has been a sign of vitality, while the conflict between sects has energized the religious sphere. In Chinese Buddhism there has been little division or conflict. New schools of Buddhist thought were introduced from India like new branches of science. Each had its translators, interpreters, and enthusiasts, but as time passed, all schools came to be regarded as mutually complementary. Dharmalaksana did not exclude Pure Land any more than physics excludes biology. A monk, on the basis of his interests and aptitudes, might want to work in one or another or perhaps in several at once. But whatever his choice, he felt no sense of rivalry or exclusiveness toward the schools that others had chosen. There was no basis for partisan struggle—any more than there is between biologists and physicists. Exceptions occurred, like the struggle within the Ch'an school during the T'ang dynasty, but they were rare and brief, and in the past century the attitude of the sangha has been that the doctrines of every school are equally valid.

One finds the same indifferentism regarding membership in sects. Chinese like English distinguishes between school of doctrine (*fa-men*) and institutionalized sect (*tsung-p'ai*). Unfortunately the same word *tsung* can mean both, just as it can mean either the doctrine on which a school is based or the lineage on which a sect is based. This is why the name given to each of the schools of doctrine in China is often translated as "such-and-such a sect," even when no sectarian institutions are involved. Thus the school of Dharmalaksana doctrines is called the "Dharmalaksana sect" (Fa-hsiang tsung). The institutionalized sect is also, of course, called "a sect." The outstanding example is the Lin-chi sect (Lin-chi tsung), which had become pure institution and no longer involved any doctrine at all. That is, if a monk's sect was Lin-chi, it meant simply that the sect of his master was Lin-chi, not that he accepted the doctrines or employed the methods of the original founder of the sect, Hui-chao I-hsüan, who lived at Mt. Lin-chi during the T'ang dynasty.

Because a monk could have several different kinds of masters, he could belong in different ways to different sects. Usually when he entered the sangha, the master who shaved his head was of the Lin-chi lineage, since it was by far the most common. That is, the generation character of his name (see p. 279) came from a gatha written by an earlier Lin-chi monk. Therefore, when he named his disciple, he used the next character in the gatha. The disciple may not have known who Lin-chi was, much less what he taught, but if someone asked him what sect he belonged to, he would reply "Lin-chi." Or if, for example, some years after his head was shaved, he had received the dharma from a master of Ts'ao-tung lineage, then he might alternatively say that his sect was Ts'ao-tung, particularly if the lineage was connected with the abbotship of a monastery. Again, this meant that his dharma name had a generation character taken from a Ts'ao-tung gatha, not that he felt special commitment to the Ts'ao-tung doctrine or practice. Even if he had received a T'ien-t'ai dharma, which was usually given in connection with study and preaching, his primary interest might still be in studying and preaching the doctrines of, let us say, the Dharmalaksana school.[1] On the other hand, if someone asked him "in respect to religious practice, what sect are you?"—the chances are that he would answer "Pure Land" or perhaps "Pure Land and Ch'an combined."

For example, one of my informants was Lin-chi by tonsure and began his career practicing meditation at a Lin-chi monastery. After a year and a half he found that this was too "lofty" (kao-shang) and hard to understand, so he tried T'ien-t'ai meditation (chih-kuan). After eight years of unsatisfactory progress in the latter, he finally shifted to the Pure Land practice of reciting buddha's name. But he still considered himself either Lin-chi on the basis of tonsure or T'ien-t'ai on the basis of the T'ien-t'ai dharma that he had received. The Venerable Tao-chieh, who acted as a witness at the ordination of T'ai-hsü in 1904, is described as following the T'ien-t'ai sect and concurrently (*chien*) the Avatamsaka and Dharmalaksana sects.[2] This was in respect to doctrine. In respect to tonsure, he was Lin-chi, and in 1924 he served as abbot of one of the leading monasteries of the Vinaya sect, the Fa-yüan Ssu in Peking. Another eminent monk, Hsü-yün, made it a point to receive the dharma not only of Lin-chi and Ts'ao-tung, but of Yün-men, Fa-yen, and Kuei-yang—sects whose lineage had terminated centuries before.[3]

Here is the way the nature of sects was summed up for me by the Venerable Ming-ch'ang, who was Lin-chi by tonsure and had received both the Lin-chi and the Ts'ao-tung dharmas in connection with the abbotship of monasteries. "Sects (*tsung-p'ai*) are merely a reflection of the number of disciples. If disciples proliferate, then the lineage tends to divide into new sects. If they dwindle, the sect may disappear. All sects have the same root, and the differences between them are not essential. They are just a question of lineage. If my disciples wanted to, they could say that they belonged to the 'Ming-ch'ang sect.'"

This has not always been understood by Western investigators accustomed to the idea that there is a connection between sect and doctrine, nor by the Buddhist specialists of Japan, where sects have remained exclusive and their doctrinal differences have been preserved. Some Japanese have taken it as evidence of decay and this may be one of the reasons why they have avoided the study of modern Chinese Buddhism.

The classification of monasteries in modern China has been almost as nominal as the classification of monks. Essentially each belonged to the sect of its founder, that is, of the ancestral master who "opened the mountain."[4] If he was Lin-chi—if his name incorporated a generation character from a Lin-chi gatha—then the monastery was Lin-chi. In its ancestors hall would be found his soul tablet and the tablets of all subsequent abbots, inscribed "The first (second, third) generation in the Lin-chi sect, Venerable So-and-so . . ." In the meditation hall the sect of the monastery would be confirmed by the shape of the board. A Lin-chi board was oblong and hung horizontally (see diagram p. 51). A Ts'ao-tung board was oblong, but hung vertically.

A Yün-men board was octagonal, a Fa-yen board was triangular, and a Kuei-yang board was semicircular.

In this technical sense there were very few monasteries in China that were not Ch'an, that is, either Lin-chi or Ts'ao-tung, except for a few Hsien-shou monasteries in north China[5] and one or two centers of the Vinaya sect, like Pao-hua Shan near Nanking (whose board was hung flat, with the surface parallel to the ground). Even the fountain-head of the T'ien-t'ai sect, the Kuo-ch'ing Ssu on T'ien-t'ai Shan, was technically Lin-chi.[6] The same was true for monasteries that gave primacy to Pure Land practice like the Fa-yü Ssu on P'u-t'o Shan.[7] The sect of the Ling-yen Ssu in Soochow is often said to have changed from Ch'an to Pure Land under the influence of the Venerable Yin-kuang,[8] but this was probably in terms of practice alone. Monasteries could only change their sect in the technical sense if they fell into complete decay and were restored by a new abbot who came in from the outside. Then he would bring in his own lineage, which would probably still be Lin-chi, although based on a different Lin-chi gatha than the lineage of his predecessor.[9]

Chinese Buddhists commonly divided their schools and sects into three main categories: "doctrinal (or teaching) schools" (chiao-men), "lineal schools" (tsung-men), and "the Vinaya school" (lü-men). The "doctrinal schools" included T'ien-t'ai, Avatamsaka, and Dharma-laksana. The "lineal schools" consisted of the five sects of Ch'an. There was only one "Vinaya school," namely the Vinaya sect (Lü-tsung). Pure Land was considered above and beyond such categories.[10] In the technical sense most Chinese monasteries belonged to one of the lineal schools; and a few of them were actively "lineal" in that they operated meditation halls. But in another sense the same monasteries belonged to the doctrinal schools since, if they held lectures, it was usually on T'ien-t'ai, Avatamsaka, or Dharmalaksana texts; while as ordination centers they belonged to the Vinaya school; and in terms of rules and system, all of them were lineal again, because they applied the pure rules of the Ch'an monk, Pai-chang.

Many monasteries carried on the joint practice of Ch'an and Pure Land (ch'an-ching shuang-hsiu). This usually meant that they had both a meditation hall and a hall for reciting the buddha's name. But there was also a special form of joint practice in one hall. This was to be found, for example, at Chiao Shan. Unfortunately the information that I have collected about it is contradictory, but it seems significant enough so that I offer a synthesis for what it may be worth. Most informants agreed that the hall at Chiao Shan could be referred to either as the "meditation hall" or as the "hall for reciting the buddha's name." There seem to have been eight periods of work a day, arranged as at Ling-yen Shan,[11] and each period was divided into circumambulation and sitting. While the inmates circumambulated, they recited buddha's name aloud. While they sat, they either worked on a Ch'an *hua-t'ou* or employed "buddha's name meditation" (*nien-fo kuan*). The latter included different techniques for people at different stages of proficiency. Beginners used the technique termed "reciting buddha's name while meditating on the buddha image" (*kuān-hsiàng nien-fo*). That is, they would fix their eyes on the image in the hall. Those further advanced would attempt to visualize the form of Amitabha with their mind's eye. This was termed "reciting buddha's name while meditating on the mental image of the buddha" (*kuān-hsiǎng nien-fo*). Those furthest advanced strove to avoid having any buddha to visualize or any ego to do the visualizing. This was termed "reciting buddha's name while meditating on the quintessence of the buddha" (*shih-hsiang nien-fo*).[12] Explanations were given of both Ch'an and Pure Land methods. Students enrolled in the seminary at this monastery took part only in three periods a day, though they participated full-time in the buddha recitation weeks held during the winter.[13]

Regardless of contradictory details, the main principles of the joint practice of Ch'an and Pure Land seem clear enough. In both sects the goal was to reduce attachment to ego. The Pure Land method of "no stirrings in the whole mind" (*i-hsin pu-luan*) did not differ essentially from the Ch'an method of "meditating to the point of perfect concentration" (*ch'an-ting*). Pure Land speaks of getting the help of another, that is, Amitabha, to reach the Western Paradise, while Ch'an asserts that one must depend on oneself to reach enlightenment. But, as the abbot of Chin Shan remarked, "Who is going to help you stop your whole mind from stirring? You have to do it yourself. In Pure Land just as much as in Ch'an, you have to depend on yourself." A lay informant said he had been told by Hsü-yün that "all the buddhas in every universe, past, present, and future, preach the same dharma. There is no real difference between the methods advocated by Saky-

amuni and Amitabha." That is why Hsü-yün used to tell some of his
disciples, who would have found Ch'an meditation too difficult, that
they should recite buddha's name instead.

The methods of the two sects are connected in many ways. For
example, the *hua-t'ou* most often used in orthodox Ch'an meditation
halls directly involved Pure Land practice, for how could one ask
"Who is this reciting buddha's name?" unless one had been reciting it?
(In the meditation hall, of course, one did not recite it *aloud*.[14]) Many
monks told me that they regarded Ch'an and Pure Land as comple-
ments essential to one another. "Pure Land without Ch'an cannot be
depended upon (*k'ao-pu-chu*). Ch'an without Pure Land has no
'principle' (*mei-yu chu*)." One of Pai-chang's Twenty Principles for
Ch'an monasteries is: "In religious practice take buddha recitation as
a sure method."[15] There was nothing new about the combination of
Ch'an and Pure Land. It goes back at least as far as Yen-shou (904-
975) and was developed, among others, by Chu-hung (1535-1615)
and Han-shan (1546-1623), both eminent Ch'an monks.[16]

SYNCRETISM

In the West, just as the division into sects has often been accompanied by a release of energy, so has the combination of sects (not
unlike chemical reactions). But once again nothing comparable has
happened in the recent history of Chinese Buddhism, perhaps because
little energy can be expected from combining things that are already
closely interlocked. The same applies to Buddhism's relationship with
Confucianism and Taoism.

While the Confucians, for example, borrowed elements of Buddhist
metaphysics, the Buddhists adopted Confucian texts and principles as
part of their common Chinese heritage. The curriculum in Buddhist
seminaries during the Republican period gave a prominent place to
the Four Books and the Five Classics, mastery of which was regarded
as the first prerequisite for spreading the dharma. On the ordination
certificates of Pao-hua Shan, the Five Buddhist Vows are identified
with the Five Cardinal Virtues of Confucius and various other equa-
tions are made between the two religions.[17] When the Venerable
Hsü-yün visited Ch'ü-fu in 1900 he paid his respects, as would any

other Chinese, at the temple and tomb of Confucius.[18] But this did not mean that the Buddhists considered themselves Buddho-Confucians nor that they had any organizational ties with Confucianism.

The same is true of Taoism. Organizationally it was a separate religion. Not even the most simple-minded peasant could make a mistake about this, for Taoist monks wore their hair in a top-knot, whereas the Buddhists were shaven. But there was a mutual borrowing of gods and rites, in which the Taoists probably owed more to the Buddhists than vice versa, particularly with regard to the monastic system. This would help to explain why Taoist monks were allowed to stay (kua-tan) in the wandering monks hall even at model Buddhist monasteries.[19] They knew how to conduct themselves when they attended devotions, when they took their meals in the refectory, and when they sat in the hall for reciting buddha's name. What they recited themselves was not necessarily the name of any buddha. One of my informants recalled that at Wo-lung Ssu, Sian, while he was chanting "Homage to the buddha Amitabha," the Taoist monks sitting nearby would be chanting "The Three Pure Ones, founders of our religion, limitlessly honored in heaven"—which they fitted into the same rhythm of chanting.[20] The Wo-lung Ssu, he recalled, had very cordial relations with the principal Taoist monastery in Sian, the Pa-hsien An. Once during a famine it sent a gift of rice to the latter, which afterwards reciprocated in kind. "But," as my informant concluded, "bhiksus were still bhiksus, and tao-shih were still tao-shih." Other informants in the sangha have expressed the view that both Buddhist and Taoist monks were "people of the Way" (tao-jen), but have voiced skepticism about the Taoist claims to be able to catch ghosts and do other magical tricks. To resume the analogy used at the beginning of this chapter, if the various sects of Buddhism were like the various branches of science, then from the Buddhist point of view Taoism was like osteopathy or parapsychology—discreditable in a degree that varied with the orthodoxy of the Buddhist in question. Some were quite "stuffy" about heterodox religions (wai-tao), but I know of one monk who made a pilgrimage to a Taoist mountain and worshipped the divinities there in order to fulfill a vow he made on behalf of his master, when the latter had fallen ill.

One rarely found specifically Taoist images in Buddhist monasteries. Wen-ch'ang and the Kitchen God were adopted by Buddhists as devas, but one did not see their images on the central altar. I can only cite one instance of unmistakable syncretism and that was at the Fu-hai Ssu, a large hereditary temple in Ju-kao, Kiangsu. Behind the great shrine-hall, which had purely Buddhist iconography, there was another hall, the Pi-hsia Tien, with three images of the Taoist goddess Pi-hsia. As my informant said, "This was a little heterodox, but ordinary people did not know any better and came to worship in great numbers." It would be natural to find syncretism further advanced at hereditary temples, since they were closer to the masses of the people, who were indifferent to religious distinctions. For most of them any image was a "bodhisattva."

Despite the rarity of such Taoist intrusions into Buddhist monasteries, there had been many transfers of temples from one religion to another, more often through organizational default than iconographic penetration. Prip-Møller mentions that the Taoists occupied 482 Buddhist monasteries in the first half of the fifteenth century and later had to return them.[21] More recently the tide seems to have been running the other way. At least three important mountains that had once been Taoist were taken over by the sangha. These mountains were: Chien-feng, near Sui-fu in Szechwan;[22] the Su-hsien Ling, Chen-hsien, in Hunan; and Nan-yüeh, also in Hunan. In the town of Nan-yüeh, which lay at the foot of the mountain of that name, there was a large temple in which the shrines on the left-hand side were Buddhist, while those on the right-hand side were Taoist.[23] Many of the Buddhist monasteries that were scattered up the slopes of the mountain had once been Taoist.[24] These instances appear to reflect a general weakening of Taoism vis-à-vis Buddhism in the course of the centuries, but more investigation is needed.

What had not weakened was the popularity of the syncretistic religions described at length by J. J. M. De Groot.[25] The Hsien-t'ien Tao, I-kuan Tao, Red Swastika Society, T'ung-shan She, T'ien-te Sheng-chiao, and other sects that purported to be a synthesis of the three religions of China—or in some cases, of these three plus Christianity and Islam—burgeoned during the Republican period, partly because they had been released from the proscription of the Ch'ing dynasty. In a Communist source we read the surprising statement that they took over 181 Buddhist monasteries out of a total of 206 in Ning-hsia province, pretending to follow the Pure Land leader, Yin-kuang, but

actually following the sectarian, Lo Wei-ch'üan.[26] The reader may recall that in 1918 when Ti-hsien was lecturing in Peking, he had a conversation through the planchette with a City God who was attending
his lectures (see p. 125). When a transcript of this seance was published, it is said to have greatly strengthened Ti-hsien's prestige and
the prestige of Buddhism. The planchette was then extremely popular
in Peking and its adherents were impressed to hear that a Buddhist
monk had been praised by several eminent spirits. It also strengthened
the faith of those who were already Buddhists. Many persons, including high officials, were said to have taken the lay ordination in consequence.[27] To those unfamiliar with the inclusiveness of religious attitudes in China, this sort of thing must seem really incomprehensible.

The fact remains, however, that contact with heterodox sects had
no organizational consequences. Sectarians seldom if ever came to
Buddhist monasteries to receive the lay ordination,[28] since they had
their own rites. Buddhist monks and devotees seldom if ever joined a
heterodox sect.

AFFILIATIONS

During the Republican period, as throughout Chinese history, there
was no single organization to which all Buddhist monks and devotees
belonged. The various Buddhist groups were localized; or if they were
national in scope, they had little effectiveness at the local level, so
that they were like a head without a body. What held Buddhists together was a series of networks of affiliation, superimposed haphazardly one upon the other.

First of all there were the networks based on religious kinship:
tonsure, dharma, and ordination. If two monks had the same tonsure
master, they felt reciprocal rights and obligations almost like those
between brothers by blood. If their common master was several generations removed, they still regarded one another as kinsmen. All those
tonsure disciples whose generation names came from the same gatha
were members, as it were, of the same clan, although the loyalties arising therefrom were weaker than those in a natural clan.

Similar rights and obligations were created by the transmission of
the dharma of a monastery (see p. 158 ff.). Monks who were ordained

together were considered "ordination brothers" (*chieh hsiung-ti*), a relation comparable to being schoolmates. They might also be like schoolmates if they had attended the same seminary or had enrolled in the same meditation hall. Monks sometimes became mutually indebted when holding office together at several monasteries in succession. This could happen because, as we shall see, monasteries too tended to be linked together in groups. It was not uncommon for monks from the same part of Kiangsu to be ordained at the same place, to enroll at the same meditation hall, and eventually to become dharma disciples of the same monastery. There were also doctrinal affinities. Those who specialized in a given text might study it together under one master and later collaborate in expounding it.

Another very important tie was loyalty to a charismatic monk. Hsü-yün, T'ai-hsü, Tan-hsü, Tz'u-chou, Ti-hsien, Yin-kuang, Ying-tz'u, Hung-i, and others had bands of faithful followers who were not necessarily their tonsure or dharma or ordination disciples, but who had studied or meditated or held office under them and, in any case, revered them. Hsü-yün, for example, had hundreds of followers in the sangha and thousands, or hundreds of thousands, in the laity. Since laymen who took the Refuges under him received the same generation names as his tonsure disciples (see p. 359), they all belonged to one great family, in which horizontal ties were tenuous, but vertical ties were often strong. That is, if two laymen had received the Refuges from Hsü-yün, it had little effect on their relationship with each other or with monks whose heads he had shaved. On the other hand, they might be both intensely devoted to him and derive a deep satisfaction from being the followers of such an eminent monk. Therefore if he wanted to restore a monastery, the money was soon forthcoming from the laity. When the time came to staff it, he had the loyal monks with which to do so.

What was particularly striking about Hsü-yün was that his leadership transcended the regionalism that characterized most other networks of affiliation. He won followers in every part of the country. A case in point is the Nan-hua Ssu. The latter had been the home of the Sixth Patriarch and many other illustrious figures in Buddhist history, and was probably the most famous monastery in Kwangtung province. It was therefore an object of pride for many Cantonese Buddhist laymen and they enthusiastically supported the decision to restore it in 1933. Because of his age and eminence they invited Hsü-yün to come down from Fukien and take over as abbot, despite the fact that he was a native of Hunan and the Cantonese are usually standoffish about anyone from outside their province who cannot speak their dialect. Under his abbotship many Cantonese went there to receive the lay ordination. When he needed money for repairs, they raised it informally among themselves. Even problems about the monasteries in the city of Canton (Nan-hua lay in the north of the province) were referred to Hsü-yün for decision.

Otherwise regionalism was a powerful force, both cohesive and divisive. In Peking many a monastery was provincial. A Hupeh abbot would be succeeded by another Hupeh abbot, and most of the senior officers would be from Hupeh too, just as in the overseas Chinese metropolis there are clubs for emigrants from this or that district of Kwangtung and Fukien, who help one another when necessary and enjoy the companionship of those who speak the same dialect. We noted in Chapter IX what a high percentage of monks from central China came from a small section of northern Kiangsu, or, as they usually called it, from "Su-pei," since the term "Chiang-pei" (northern Kiangsu) was often used contemptuously by outsiders. The northern Kiangsu accent was almost as strong as a dialect. Monks who came from there tended to appoint each other to office. They held most of the high positions in the large monasteries across the Yangtze in the southern part of the province. In one case that I know of, all the residents of the sub-temple of such a monastery came from only two *hsien* —T'ai and Ju-kao.

Naturally this caused resentment. An informant from Shantung once told me that he had stayed at some of the big Kiangsu monasteries, but had not liked the attitude toward outsiders. A small group of monks there, he said, were preoccupied with the struggle for property at the expense of the dharma. "Those great abbots who think that they embody the orthodox lineage represent the rotten elements of Buddhism in final decay," he said bitterly. I have heard a similar statement from a Hunanese monk: "The Kiangsu people are not interested in religious cultivation. What they specialize in is money and fame." Of course, Kiangsu monasteries did have money and fame, and this was one of the reasons why they were both admired and resented. Monasteries in distant parts of China, if they needed able administrators, would try to get an abbot or prior from Kiangsu. Junior officers at Chin Shan were "snapped up" by offers from Szechwan, Kwangtung, and Manchuria, especially at the end of each winter term. This was not only because they were well-trained in monastic administration, but also because they kept the Pure Rules—little paragons! No wonder that some people disliked them.

One of the causes of regionalism was the nature of the affiliation between monasteries. All the large monasteries in a region faced similar problems and their elders (*chu-shan chang-lao*) often consulted with one another, particularly in regard to the selection of abbots. Sometimes monasteries collaborated in welfare work (as did Chin Shan and Chiao Shan on an orphanage). Sometimes they assisted one another administratively (as, for example, by collecting grain rents on adjoining land in a distant area). Sometimes a rich monastery subsidized a poor one, making up any deficit of income. Dharma ties were important. The dharma lineage of one monastery could be borrowed for another, especially if the latter was newly built or restored. This meant that all subsequent abbots of the two monasteries were dharma brothers or cousins. Finally, there were affiliations based on personnel. Some monks held office together at one monastery after another. Ch'an-ting, for example, served successively as the abbot of the Kuan-tsung Ssu in Ningpo, the T'ien-t'ung Ssu nearby, and the Leng-yen Ssu in far off Yingkow. Other monks followed suit in subordinate positions. Presumably as a result of friendly ties thereby created, T'ien-t'ung subsidized Kuan-tsung, and Kuan-tsung took an active role in establishing Leng-yen.

A good example of personal ties reflected in institutional ties is provided by Chin Shan in Chen-kiang and the Wo-fo Ssu in neighboring Yangchow. Chin Shan collected the grain rents for the Wo-fo Ssu in T'ai-chou, where their lands adjoined. When necessary, it gave the Wo-fo Ssu a subsidy. The reason for this was that an earlier abbot of Chin Shan had been a tonsure heir of Wo-fo, namely Ch'an-ching, who was Chin Shan's abbot in the late Ch'ing dynasty. In deference to his memory Chin Shan was still helping the Wo-fo Ssu in the 1930's. It was also giving the same sort of help (collection of rents) to the Wanshou Ssu, another Yangchow temple, on the grounds that its former abbot, Chi-shan, was a tonsure disciple of Ch'ang-ching. In 1912, when T'ai-hsü tried to seize Chin Shan by force and change it from a meditation center into a seminary, among the monks who went to the monastery's defense was this same Chi-shan.

There was no single organization on which all the monasteries in China depended as on a central pillar. Rather they formed a geodesic dome, joined one to another in mutual support. From the nodes of this dome, so to speak, hung families of lay people, each of which might be connected with a particular monastery in any one of several ways. If my father, for example, had placed my grandfather's soul tablet in a certain monastery, then when my father died, I might well do the same for him. If rites were to be performed, I would probably turn first to his monastery (and if the monastery needed money it would turn to me). It might also be traditional for a family to make pilgrimages to some sacred mountain. If a monastery on the mountain had a sub-temple in their home town, the monk in charge of it would invite them to go up for vacations, retreats, or services. Even peasants and other occasional Buddhists might come to feel a kind of loose connection with a Buddhist place of worship. The peasant whose prayers had been granted by a certain divinity at a certain temple was likely to return when he next stood in need of divine assistance. There was also a tendency for each worshipper to go to the largest and most prosperous temple in his own area. To the simple-minded person the bigger image in the grander shrine-hall was naturally able to confer bigger favors.[29] This may explain why there were larger numbers of "occasional Buddhists" in areas like Kiangsu where Buddhism was more prosperous. Prosperity attracted devotion as devotion supplied prosperity. All these affiliations between lay people and monasteries were informal, arising and disappearing as circumstances changed. Some lay devotees were formally affiliated with clubs and study groups, but most of these, like the monasteries, were independent and not joined in any national system.

This brings to a close the present volume on Buddhist practice in modern China. We have seen a broad gamut of institutions and men, with the good and the bad—"the dragons and the snakes"—side by side. The system had room for both piety and commercialism, scholars and illiterates, vice and discipline—all making up a mixture whose components we know, although we cannot assay the proportions in which they occurred.

When modern Buddhism is discussed in almost any Western book about China, we find vivid descriptions of the commercialism, illiterates, and vice, but seldom a word about the piety, scholarship, or discipline. Here, for example, is the way the state of Chinese Buddhism in the last century has been summarized by four distinguished authorities.

H. Hackmann: "The moral level of the monks is a low one. . . . Their religious duties are purely mechanical, carried out within their own restricted circle, and their life, instead of being an example of self-conquest, becomes a life of utter idleness. . . . All intercourse with laymen is in connection with business. . . . Immorality of various kinds is but too common."[30]

Arthur H. Smith: "Buddhism . . . has long since degenerated into mere form. Its priests, like those of Taoism, are for the most part idle, ignorant, vicious parasites on the body politic. The religion, like many of its temples, is in a state of hopeless collapse."[31]

W. T. Chan: "The clergy is notoriously ignorant and corrupt. Temples are either in a poor state of preservation or saturated with an atmosphere of commercialism."[32]

Kenneth Ch'en: "Moral and spiritual decadence was universal."[33]

Anyone who has read this book would agree, I hope, that such characterizations are inadequate. They give only one side of the picture. Yet they have been echoed and re-echoed until now they are generally accepted. How and why did this happen? What were the forces cooperating to give Chinese Buddhism a black name that it does not deserve? More particularly, with regard to the so-called "Buddhist revival," inasmuch as Buddhism in China was still very much alive and what is still alive cannot properly be said to revive, was it really a revival after all? These are some of the questions that the next volume—on history rather than institutions—will attempt to answer.

Appendices

The Size of the Sangha

    The China Handbook 1937-1945, compiled by the Chinese Ministry of Information and published in New York in 1947, states on page 26: "It is estimated that at present there are in China more than 267,000 Buddhist temples and 738,000 monks and nuns." This estimate is said to have been based on "statistics compiled by branches of the Chinese Buddhist Society in 1930."[1] Fa-fang, a follower of T'ai-hsü, tells us that the branches were ordered to compile the statistics by Yüan-ying, then president of the Society. He adds, however, that because of the presence of Communist armies, no data could be collected for certain areas in Szechwan, Honan, Anhwei, and Hunan, and these areas were not included.[2]

    Although it does not allude to the exclusion of these areas, the *Shen-pao Yearbook* for 1936 appears to have published the statistics in question.[3] An introductory note states merely that they were collected in the course of an investigation by the Buddhist Society in 1930 and then worked up into statistical form and published by the Society in 1936. Perhaps by this time the missing figures had been obtained from Szechwan, Honan, Anhwei, and Hunan.

    The *Shen-pao Yearbook* is the source of the columns below that are marked with an asterisk. The other columns have been added to facilitate comparison. Some internal totals given in the *Yearbook* reveal typographical errors; the figures thereby placed in doubt have been marked with a double asterisk.

Table 1. Buddhist population of China

Area	*No. of monks in the area	No. of monks per thousand of male population[a]	*No. of nuns in the area	No. of nuns per thousand of female population[a]	*No. of male devotees in area	No. of male devotees per thousand of male population[a]	*No. of female devotees in area	No. of female devotees per thousand of female population[a]	Monks and nuns as percentage of devotees	Nuns as percentage of monks
Central										
Kiangsu	91,400[b]	5.6	80,360[c]	5.3	401,600	25	737,940	49	15	88
Chekiang	64,300	5.7	43,400	4.8	434,400	39	933,400	104	8	67
Hupeh	54,400[d]	3.8	21,640[e]	1.7	99,300	7	187,600	15	26	40
Hunan	44,600[f]	4.5	17,800[g]	1.4	44,400	3	19,700	1.5	60	40
Anhwei	22,100[h]	1.9	7,440[h]	0.7	39,800	3.3	65,500	6.4	29	34
Kiangsi	2,300[h]	0.3	340[h]	—	13,300	1.5	13,400	2.0	10	15
	279,100	3.6	170,980	2.6	1,032,800	13.2	1,957,540	30	15	61
Southeast										
Fukien	28,900	5.2	4,460	1.1	52,200	9.3	44,670	10.8	34	15
Kwangtung	15,300**	0.9	3,820**	0.3	31,150**	1.8	123,400**	8.5	12	25
	44,200	2.0	8,280	0.4	83,350	3.7	168,070	9.1	21	19

The footnotes to this table are on pages 415-416.

Table 1. (Continued)

Area	*No. of monks in the area	No. of monks per thousand of male population[a]	*No. of nuns in the area	No. of nuns per thousand of female population[a]	*No. of male devotees in area	No. of male devotees per thousand of male population[a]	*No. of female devotees in area	No. of female devotees per thousand of female population[a]	Monks and nuns as percentage of devotees	Nuns as percentage of monks
South										
Kweichow	480	0.1	240	0.1	1,780	0.5	950	0.2	26	50
Kwangsi	350	—	110	—	2,890	0.4	12,180	2.0	3	32
	830	—	350	—	4,670	0.4	13,130	1.4	13	42
West										
Szechwan	124,210	4.9	34,400	1.6	337,400	13.2	153,300	7.2	32	28
Yünnan	33,400	5.5	3,780	0.7	17,330	2.8	18,800	3.2	103	11
	157,610	5.0	38,180	1.4	354,730	11.2	172,100	6.3	37	24
North										
Shansi	15,440	2.7	1,200	0.2	3,230	0.5	2,930	0.6	260	8
Shantung	2,890	0.2	1,840	0.1	4,750	0.3	980	0.1	82	63
Honan	2,450	0.1	510	—	2,840	0.2	1,230	0.1	72	21
Hopei	1,780[h]	0.1	320	—	9,780	0.7	2,340	0.2	19	18
Shensi	780	0.1	230	—	2,840	0.5	650	0.1	29	29
Kansu	460	0.1	30	—	130	—	290	—	—	7
	23,800	0.4	4,130	0.1	23,570	0.4	8,420	0.2	86	17

The footnotes to this table are on pages 415–416.

Table 1. (Continued)

Area	*No. of monks in the area	No. of monks per thousand of male population[a]	*No. of nuns in the area	No. of nuns per thousand of female population[a]	*No. of male devotees in area	No. of male devotees per thousand of male population[a]	*No. of female devotees in area	No. of female devotees per thousand of female population[a]	Monks and nuns as percentage of devotees	Nuns as percentage of monks
Northeast[l]										
Heilungkiang	680	0.3	30	—	280	0.1	340	0.2	115	4
Liaoning	580	0.1	190	—	560	0.1	420	0.1	78	33
	1,260	0.1	220	—	840	0.1	760	0.1	90	17
Cities										
Shanghai	3,990[j]	1.9	2,210[j]	1.4	5,660	2.7	31,720	20.2	17	55
Tsingtao	1,200	1.3	290	0.5	2,390	2.5	4,900	8.1	20	24
Peking	980	2.2	360	1.3	1,850	4.2	3,060	10.7	27	37
Nanking	30	—	—	—	140	—	300	1.4	—	—
	6,200	1.6	2,860	1.1	10,040	2.6	39,980	15.0	18	46
Grand Total Given	513,000[k]	—	225,000	—	1,530,000	—	2,360,000	—	—	—
Actual Grand Total	513,000	2.3	225,200[l]	1.2	1,510,000	6.8	2,360,000	12.5	19	44

The footnotes to this table are on pages 415-416.

Table 1. (Continued)

ᵃ The population figures on which these columns are based were taken from the Chinese Year Book 1940-1941 (Chungking, 1941), pp. 46-49. The data are stated to have been gathered in the period 1928 to 1935. Cf. note i.

ᵇ According to figures compiled by the Ministry of the Interior in 1931, the number of monks in Kiangsu was 45,229. See Hai-ch'ao yin, 16.3:27 (March 1935), where a breakdown is given by hsien. Presumably these figures came from the so-called Census Report of 1931, published in that year by the Ministry of the Interior, but compiled from provincial and municipal returns of 1928. See Chinese Year Book 1935-1936 (Shanghai, 1936), p. 120. Suspicion might be aroused by the fact that the Buddhist Society reports twice as many monks in Kiangsu as the government. But its figure is not necessarily inflated. With its many local branches, it was in a better position than the government (many of whose representatives were anti-Buddhist) to count Buddhist monks. Furthermore, if it had been bent on exaggeration, it would probably not have given such low figures for provinces in the north and south and it would almost surely have given far higher figures for the number of lay devotees everywhere. In any case, by printing the totals of the Buddhist Society (in the 1937-1945 China Handbook), the government indicated that it considered the component figures to be at least as valid as its own.

ᶜ According to the figures of the Ministry of the Interior (see note b), the number of nuns in Kiangsu was 12,824.

ᵈ Interior's figure: 38,548. This is erroneously given as 28,548 in Wing-tsit Chan, Religious Trends in Modern China (New York, 1953), p. 81.

ᵉ Interior's figure: 12,028.

ᶠ Interior's figure: 42,501. C. K. Yang, on the other hand, quotes the Hunan Yearbook for 1933 to the effect that there were only 10,000 Buddhist and Taoist priests in the province: see Religion in Chinese Society (Berkeley, 1961), p. 308.

ᵍ Interior's figure: 11,517.

ʰ According to the figures of the Ministry of the Interior, Anhwei, Kiangsi, and Hopei each had 21,000 monks and nuns. Available information supports the view that for Kiangsi and Hopei this figure is a gross exaggeration, and probably no more than a casual guess.

ⁱ No figures are given for Kirin. The population figures on which column 2 is based come from the China Handbook 1937-1945, p. 2.

ʲ Monthly figures on the monastic population of Shanghai in 1934, released by the municipal Public Security Bureau, show an average of 1,034 monks and 397 nuns, not including those in the foreign concessions, where some of the largest monasteries were located. See Shang-hai-shih nien-chien (Shanghai yearbook; Shanghai, 1935), p. U7. It is not clear whether the foreign concessions were also excluded in arriving at the figures in Table 1 above.

Table 1. (*Continued*)

ᵏ Using the very different components given by the Ministry of the Interior (see notes 2-8), Hui-chu arrives at about the same estimated total, that is, 500,000 excluding lamas. See *Hai-ch'ao yin* 16.3:27 (March, 1935). Reichelt estimates a total of 1,000,000 for monks *and* nuns, with nuns amounting to "scarcely more than one-tenth." He states that the monastic population was highest in Kiangsu and Chekiang; and high also in provinces lying up the river from Kiangsu (Anhwei, Kiangsu, Hupei, Hunan, and Szechwan); and in the provinces lying down the coast from Chekiang (Fukien and Kwangtung); see *Truth and Tradition in Chinese Buddhism* (Shanghai, 1927), p. 298. He says that his figures are based on an investigation "undertaken two years ago by Professor Hodous and the author." In the unpublished personal papers of Lewis Hodous, under the heading "Religion in China, a Survey, 1920," there is the statement: "The number of monks in China has been estimated from 400,000 to over a million. The former estimate is based upon very careful observation and probably comes near the actual number." It is characteristic that Reichelt would give the more optimistic version of what appears to have been the same survey.

ˡ The difference between the total given in the *Shen-pao Yearbook* and the actual total of the component figures may not be entirely due to typographical errors. Possibly the editors of the *Yearbook* omitted the explanation when they reprinted the table, in which, oddly enough, there are blank columns with no figures for several areas (e.g., Jehol, Sinkiang, Tsinghai), but no column at all for Tibet.

Table 2. Buddhist religious institutions in China

Area	*No. of monasteries and temples having monks in residence[a]	Average no. of monks in each	*No. of nunneries having nuns in residence[a]	Average no. of nuns in each	*No of. temples with laymen in residence[b]	*No. of temples with laywomen in residence[b]
Central						
Kiangsu	24,200	3.7	54,600	1.5	349	5,400
Chekiang	14,140	4.6	38,750	1.1	390	5,630
Hupeh	7,930	6.9	8,920	2.5	120	290
Hunan	1,340[c]	33.1	1,980[c]	9.0	140	86
Anhwei	4,690	4.9	4,100	1.8	80	410
Kiangsi	870	2.7	210	1.6	40	30
	53,170	5.3	108,560	1.6	1,119	11,846
Southeast						
Fukien	7,430	3.9	3,460	1.3	380	860
Kwangtung	8,320	1.8	3,440	1.1	160	980
	15,750	2.8	6,900	1.2	540	1,840
South						
Kweichow	280	1.7	70	3.4	30	30
Kwangsi	120	2.8	60	1.8	40	70
	400	2.0	130	2.7	70	100

The footnotes to this table are on page 419.

Table 2. (Continued)

Area	*No. of monasteries and temples having monks in residence[a]	Average no. of monks in each	*No. of nunneries having nuns in residence[a]	Average no. of nuns in each	*No. of. temples with laymen in residence[b]	*No. of temples with laywomen in residence[b]
West						
Szechwan	12,429**	9.2	12,300**	2.9	870**	3,490**
Yünnan	7,340	4.7	1,520	2.5	120	940
	19,769	7.5	13,820	2.8	990	4,430
North						
Shansi	3,940	3.9	680	1.8	230	190
Shantung	790	3.7	960	1.9	140	220
Honan	850	2.9	220	2.3	120	160
Hopei	560	3.2	190	2.7	240	180
Shensi	330	2.4	120	1.9	40	—
Kansu	230	2.0	20	1.5	—	—
	6,700	3.5	2,190	2.0	770	750
Northeast						
Heilungkiang	330	2.1	20	1.5	—	—
Liaoning	350	1.7	130	1.5	—	—
	680	1.9	150	1.5	—	—

The footnotes to this table are on page 419.

Table 2. (*Continued*)

Area	*No. of monasteries and temples having monks in residence[a]	Average no. of monks in each	*No. of nunneries having nuns in residence[a]	Average no. of nuns in each	*No. of temples with laymen in residence[b]	*No. of temples with laywomen in residence[b]
Cities						
Shanghai	1,340**	3.6	2,440**	0.9	540**	840**
Peking	360[d]	3.3	180[e]	1.6	150	120
Nanking	230	4.3	130	—	30	60
Tsingtao	1	30	—	—	1	—
	1,931	3.2	2,750	1.0	721	1,020
Grand Total Given	98,400	—	144,500	—	4,210	19,980
Actual Grand Total	98,400	5.2	134,500	1.7	4,210	19,986

[a] Institutions with monks in residence and those with nuns are both termed "*ssu, miao, an, kuan.*" *Kuan* is a term normally reserved for Taoist monasteries, and may be included here because some of the latter had been taken over by Buddhists. See Chapter I, note 4. In some cases (Shanghai nunneries, for example) residence must have been part-time, since there are fewer nuns than nunneries.

[b] These are apparently institutions that had lay people, but no monks and nuns in residence. Although they are termed "*ssu, miao, kuan,*" it seems likely that the commonest variety was the "vegetarian hall" (*chai-t'ang*), to which elderly single women liked to retire for their old age.

[c] C. K. Yang cites figures from the 1933 Hunan Yearbook: 220 Buddhist monasteries and 15 Buddhist nunneries in the whole province (*Religion in Chinese Society*, p. 312).

[d] According to a police report of 1919 Peking had 296 *ssu* and 8 *ch'an-lin*, i.e., 304 institutions whose names suggest that they had monks in residence. See Sidney D. Gamble, *Peking: A Social Survey* (New York, 1921), pp. 368-369.

[e] According to the same police report Peking had 169 *an*, which were usually nunneries.

POPULATION OF LARGE MONASTERIES

Most of the figures that I have collected on the population of individual monasteries are estimates recollected by monks who lived or
stayed there, although a few figures come from documentary sources.
There is not a single monastery in China for which I have found a
physical head count on a known date. Nonetheless it is interesting how
much consistency there is in recollected estimates. One informant may
give the population of a monastery at a certain time as 150 and another
may give it as 200, but in no case have I encountered a difference in
the order of magnitude (like 200 versus 30).

I have collected figures on ninety-eight monasteries for which the
total of the estimates of population was 13,100. Among them there
were fifty-six whose size and reputation were especially well-attested
to. These fifty-six had about 9,850 monks—2 percent of the national
total. The elite within the sangha was at least this large. By "elite" is
meant those monks who were serious enough about their religion to
abide by its rules and to lead an austere life in which religious cultivation or teaching played a major role.

These figures fit in well with information on the province for which
information is the fullest—Kiangsu—where eleven monasteries alone
had about 2,600 monks or nearly 3 percent of the provincial total. As
I have indicated on p. 4, I would guess that the figure of 2 percent for
the known elite should be more than doubled to take into account
those who lived in monasteries on which I have collected no figures;
so that the total elite living in public monasteries might have been
5 percent or about 25,000 monks. Other members of the elite lived in
small temples.

APPENDIX **II**

The Forty-Eight Positions

The conventional version of the forty-eight positions (*chih-shih*) listed in twenty-four ranks (*hsü-chih*) and twenty-four offices (*lieh-chih*) may be found in the "Chin-shan kuei-yüeh" (the code of rules of Chin Shan), a manuscript copy of which has been microfilmed by the Hong Kong University Library. It is almost identical with the list in the "Chiao-shan kuei-yüeh" (the code of rules of Chiao Shan), also in manuscript; and with the data in the *Hua-pei tsung-chiao nien-chien ti-i hao* (North China yearbook of religion, No. 1; Peking, 1941), which is based on *Pai-chang ch'ing-kuei* (the Pure Rules of Pai-chuang; see p. 106). *Chüan* 6 of *Pai-chang*, however, includes some twenty-four miscellaneous positions that are in none of the other books.

Here are the forty-eight positions according to the Chin Shan code of rules:

OFFICES

West	*East*
tien-tso (chef)	*tu-chien* (provost)
t'ieh-an (taster)	*chien-yüan* (prior)
fan-t'ou (rice steward)	*fu-ssu* (subprior)
ts'ai-t'ou (vegetable steward)	*k'u-ssu* (supervisory clerk)
shui-t'ou (water steward)	*chien-shou* (rent collector)
huo-t'ou (stoker)	*yüan-chu*[1] (village agent)
ch'a-t'ou (tea steward)	*nien-t'ou* (head miller)
hsing-t'ang (waiter)	*liao-yüan* (head of the wandering monks hall)
men-t'ou (gate-keeper)	*tien-chu* (senior verger)
ching-t'ou (sanitation steward)	*chung-t'ou* (bellman)
yüan-t'ou (head gardener)	*ku-t'ou* (striker of the drum)
chao-k'o (usher)	*yeh-hsün* (night patrol)

RANKS

West	East
tso-yüan (head rector)	*wei-no* (precentor)
shou-tso (rector)	*yüeh-chung* (succentor)
hsi-t'ang (senior instructor)	*tsu-shih* (deacon)
hou-t'ang (associate instructor)	*shao-hsiang* (thurifer)
t'ang-chu (assistant instructor)	*chi-lu* (recorder)
shu-chi (secretary)	*i-po* (sacristan)
tsang-chu (librarian)	*t'ang-yao* (dispenser)
seng-chih (proctor)	*shih-che* (acolyte)
chih-tsang (canon prefect)	*ch'ing-chung* (rank and file)
chih-k'o (guest prefect)	*ch'ing-k'o* (obsolete)[2]
ts'an-t'ou (contemplative)	*hsing-che* (acolyte)
ssu-shui (water-bearer)	*hsiang-teng* (verger)

Despite the unanimity of documentary sources, living sources are equally unanimous in contradicting them. At Chin Shan and elsewhere the *wei-no* (precentor), *yüeh-chung* (succentor), *chih-k'o* (guest prefect), *seng-chih* (proctor), and *i-po* (sacristan) were *not* ranks as shown in this table, but offices. *Ch'ing-chung* (rank and file) was not a rank in itself, but a collective term that covered monks of various ranks in the east and west of the meditation hall (see Chapter I, note 42).

When I have shown this table to the abbot and high-ranking officers of Chin Shan and other monasteries, they could not explain the discrepancies between theory and practice. The abbot said that he doubted Chin Shan's code of rules was more than a century old. On the other hand, no new clauses had been added to it during his residence there. I have had no opportunity to look into its history myself. Perhaps it represents an earlier personnel system, quite different from the one in use during recent decades. Perhaps it originated as an attempt to give an ideal picture of monastic personnel, bearing the same relation to practice as the *Chou-li* bore to the administrative practice of the Chou dynasty. That is, some writer on monastic life, having decided that forty-eight was an appropriate number of positions, suppressed twenty-four that he found in *Pai-chang ch'ing-kuei*. Among those that he suppressed some were obsolete (like *tan-yün* and *hua-fan*), but some were very much in use like *k'u-t'ou* (clerk) and *hsün-shan* (grounds patrol). At the same time he added positions that did not appear to be in *Pai-chang ch'ing-kuei*, like *tso-yüan* (head rector) and *chung-t'ou* (bellman). Perhaps because he was still confronted with a smaller number of ranks than offices, he classified certain offices as ranks, which gave him the symmetry he wanted.

This is my own guess as to the origin of the discrepancies, but whatever their origin, they illustrate the danger of writing about recent Chinese Buddhist practice on the basis of documents only. This may be seen further by comparing the table of positions from the "Chinshan kuei-yüeh" given above, with the positions actually found at Chin Shan, furnished from memory by T'ai-ts'ang, who served thirty years there between 1917 and 1949, the last four as abbot. Most of the following is confirmed and none of it is contradicted by information received from other Chin Shan monks.

PERSONNEL OF THE CHIANG-T'IEN SSU, CHIN SHAN, ABOUT 1937

Section: Personnel	Number	Rank
Head (*chu-ch'ih*)		
abbot (*fang-chang*)	1	rector (*shou-tso*)
Sacristy (*i-po liao*)		
sacristans (*i-po*)	2-3	deacon (*tsu-shih*), thurifer (*shao-hsiang*)
dispensers (*t'ang-yao*)	2-3	recorder (*chi-lu*)
acolyte (*shih-che*)	1	acolyte
Meditation hall (*ch'an-t'ang*)		
rector (*shou-tso*)	1	rector
senior instructors (*hsi-t'ang*)	1-2	senior instructor
associate instructors (*hou-t'ang*)	1-2	associate instructor
assistant instructors (*t'ang-chu*)	3	assistant instructor
precentor (*wei-no*)	1	secretary
succentors (*yüeh-chung*)	6-9	deacon, thurifer, recorder
verger (*hsiang-teng*)	1	verger
water-bearer (*ssu-shui*)	1	water-bearer
rank and file (*ch'ing-chung*)	100-150	various[3]
Business office (*k'u-fang*)		
provost (*tu-chien*)	1	assistant instructor or higher
prior (*chien-yüan*)	1	assistant instructor or higher
subpriors (*fu-ssu*)	2	secretary
secretaries (*shu-chi*)	2-3	secretary

Section: Personnel	Number	Rank
functionary (*chih-shih*)[4]	1	secretary or deacon
store-keeper (*kuan-k'u*)	1	deacon or thurifer
clerks (*k'u-t'ou*)	3-5	lower than secretary[5]
village agents (*chuang-chu*)	2	secretary or librarian
Guest department (*k'o-t'ang*)		
guest prefects (*chih-k'o*)	4-10	secretary
proctor (*seng-chih*)	1	secretary
secretary (*shu-chi*)	1	secretary
Main kitchen (*ta-liao*)		
rice steward (*fan-t'ou*)	1	librarians, canon prefects,
vegetable steward (*ts'ai-t'ou*)	1	contemplatives, and a few thurifers (rank de-
tea steward (*ch'a-t'ou*)	1	pended on age and years
water steward (*shui-t'ou*)	1	in meditation hall: librar-
head stoker (*ta-huo*)	1	ian was the commonest
sanitation steward (*ching-t'ou*)	1	rank for the higher menial officers).
waiters (*hsing-t'ang*)	4-10	
Wandering monks hall (*yün-shui t'ang*)		
head (*liao-yüan*)	1	librarian
verger (*hsiang-teng*)	1	verger
wandering monks (*yün-shui seng*)	50-100	none
Great shrine-hall (*ta-tien*)		
senior verger (*tien-chu*)	1	librarian or canon prefect
verger (*hsiang-teng*)	1	verger
Buddha recitation hall (*nien-fo t'ang*)		
hall manager (*kuan-t'ang*)	1	librarian
verger (*hsiang-teng*)	1	verger
rank and file (*ch'ing-chung*)	12	various
Ordination chamber (*chieh-t'ai lou*)		
verger (*hsiang-teng*)	1	verger
Library (*tsang-ching lou*)		
librarian (*tsang-chu*)	1	librarian
verger (*hsiang-teng*)	1	verger
Pagoda (*pao-t'a*)		
verger (*hsiang-teng*)	1	verger

Section: Personnel	Number	Rank
Ch'i-feng Pavillion verger	1	verger
Ancestors hall (*tsu-t'ang*) verger	1	verger
Vegetable garden (*ts'ai-yüan*) head gardener (*yüan-t'ou*)	1	
Mill (*nien-fang*) head miller (*nien-t'ou*)		librarians, canon prefects, and contemplatives
Gate gate keeper (*men-t'ou*)	1	
Night patrol (*yeh-hsün*)	1	
Monks living in retirement (*hsien pan-shou* & *hsien shu-chi*)	20-30	various
Lay workmen	60-70	none
Total (using average figures)	375	(73 officers)

This table shows not only the differences between theory and practice in the relationship between ranks and offices, but also that certain titles listed in the Chin Shan code of rules simply did not exist at Chin Shan in recent decades; and vice versa. The following did not exist: chef; taster; supervisory clerk; rent collector; bellman; striker of the drum; *ch'ing-k'o*. The following titles not listed in the code *did* exist: functionary; clerk; store-keeper; hall manager. These discrepancies too have been pointed out to the abbot of Chin Shan, who could offer no explanation for them.

At the T'ien-ning Ssu only the lower offices were collectively known as *lieh-chih*. Offices with the rank of secretary and above were termed *ch'üan-chih*, that is, "offices with authority." The office of guest prefect, for example, was a *ch'üan-chih;* that of verger was a *lieh-chih*. This distinction was not made elsewhere so far as I know.

The Meditation Hall Schedule

The reader will find below the daily schedule of the meditation hall at Chin Shan as reported by monks who lived there during the first half of the twentieth century. The schedule varied with the season of the year. The longest period during which it remained constant was the first five months of the summer semester, that is, from the 16th of the first lunar month to the 15th of the fifth. We shall begin with these five months and then deal with later periods in the year.

The hours of activities apparently did not vary with the season. The hour of rising, for example, does not seem to have become earlier week by week toward summer as it may have at some other monasteries. According to most informants it remained 3:00 a.m. throughout the year.[1] None of my informants could remember the exact hour of every event on the schedule.

The schedule *cum* signals below is intended to convey the main features of the musical system that ordered the work of the monks in the meditation hall and their movement to and from other buildings. It is neither exhaustive nor infallible. Some details have been excluded intentionally, and, as the reader will see, the system was too complicated for my informants to remember and for me to record without omissions and errors. This caveat applies particularly to the signals given in connection with morning and afternoon devotions and with rising and retiring. For the sake of brevity I have used more or less literal translations of the original Chinese terms, a glossary of which precedes the schedule.

It should be emphasized that while the activities listed below were being carried on by the monks enrolled in the meditation hall, the majority of the residents of Chin Shan were otherwise occupied. Some were busy with their duties as officers; some were reciting buddha's name; some were living in retirement; and some were guests in the wandering monks hall. More information on the nature of activities listed below may be found in Chapter II, which should be read in conjunction with this appendix.

The schedule is perhaps bewildering in its detail. The reader may find it easier to follow if he keeps in mind the following summary

Hour	Meditation	Other Activities
4:00		devotions
6:00		breakfast congee
7:00	morning meditation fourth period	
9:00		noon rice
10:00	noon meditation fourth period sixth period	
2:00		luncheon congee
3:00		devotions
4:00		rest
6:00	evening meditation fourth period	

There were in all, then, seven cycles of meditation a day. Each consisted of one period of running and one period of sitting[2] or, in greater detail, the following phases: circumambulation; tea or Explanation; circumambulation; out to the latrine; sitting in meditation. Here as elsewhere the terms "running" and "circumambulation" are used synonymously.

GLOSSARY OF SIGNALS

All signals on the board, bell, and wooden fish in the meditation hall are struck by the duty monk (*tang-chih ti*); all signals on the hand-chime (*yin-ch'ing*) are struck by the duty succentor (*tang-chih ti yüeh-chung*). The precentor (*wei-no*) lets them know when to strike a signal by giving two taps with his fingers on the tea-table or bench, almost inaudibly; or by pointing; or by snapping his fingers (*t'an-chih*). Signals outside the meditation hall are struck by a variety of officers.

UP ONE BOARD (*ch'i[3] i-pan*), and UP TWO BOARDS (*ch'i erh-pan*)—signals given by the night patrol for the monks to retire at night.

UP THREE BOARDS (*ch'i san-pan*)—a signal for the kitchen staff to rise in the morning.

UP FOUR BOARDS (*ch'i ssu-pan*)—a signal for the rest of the monks to rise.

END FIVE BOARDS (*sha wu-pan*)—a signal that "up four boards" has been completed.

ANSWERING BELL (*ta pao-chung*)—a signal given on the bell in the meditation hall that answers some signal given outside the hall.

CONNECTING BELL (*ta chieh-chung*)—any signal struck on a bell the first two notes of which fall between the last three notes on some other instrument.

BIG FISH (*k'ai-pang*)—a signal struck on the big wooden fish image that hangs outside the refectory (Fig. 13). It informs the monastery that a meal is about to be served. It is struck by the rice steward as follows: first an accelerando, then six slow strokes.

Before and after striking it, he makes a deep bow (*wen-hsün*) to the fish image. "Accelerando" is used here for want of a better term to denote a series of strokes that get faster and faster (and therefore slightly lighter) until a limit is reached:

hereafter written

It is similar to the booming of a ruffed grouse, or the sound made by a lively rubber ball as it bounces lower and lower. Some informants give the number of strokes on the *pang* as three; or four and a half. Some place the accelerando afterwards rather than before. Some say—doubtless quite rightly—that the signal varies with the monastery and the sect.

ONE BOARD ONE BELL (*i-pan i-chung*)—a signal that a major period of meditation is beginning. "Major period" is my own term for the morning, noon, and evening meditation periods in contrast to the "minor periods," that is, the fourth and sixth periods (see summary on p. 427). Because the major periods are signalled for by "one board one bell," "hang two boards" and "three boards one bell," in Chinese they are called "board periods." For example, the morning meditation period is *tsao-pan hsiang*, whereas the fourth period, for which the board is not struck, is *ssu-chih hsiang*. "One board one bell" is given as follows. The duty succentor strikes three notes on the hand-chime, between which the duty monk strikes one stroke on the wooden fish and one on the board; then one on the bell and finally two on the wooden fish, thus:

chime | | |

fish | | |

board |

bell |

Between the notes on the chime, all the monks make two deep bows, first to the opposite side of the hall, east or west (*tui-mien wen-hsün*), and then to the north (*hsiang-shang*).[4]

HANG TWO BOARDS (*kua erh-pan*)—a signal that an Explanation is about to be given or tea served during a major period of circumambulation. Two strokes are sounded on the board followed by one on the bell above it. The disperser (*san-hsiang shih*) drops his rod (*san-hsiang*) so that it bounces an accelerando on the floor. The monks go to their seats.

THREE BOARDS ONE BELL (*san-pan i-chung*)—a signal that a major period of sitting in meditation is about to begin. Three strokes are sounded on the board followed by one on the bell above it. The duty monk then makes three prostrations before the buddha image (*li-fo*) as the succentor strikes the chime four times.[5] He strikes one final note and the period begins.

TWO FISH (*ch'iao liang-ch'ui mu-yü*)—a signal that a minor period of meditation is about to begin. Two notes are struck on the wooden fish. The hand-chime is not sounded. Some monks go to the latrine, others circumambulate informally. The precentor remains outside until everyone is back in the hall. Then he enters and circumambulation becomes formal.

THREE FISH (*ch'iao san-ch'ui mu-yü*)—a signal that a minor period of sitting in meditation is about to begin. Three notes are struck on the small wooden fish.

STOPPING BOARD (*ta chan-pan*)—a signal to stop circumambulating. One note is struck on a small board that hangs on the wall near the large bell and board (see p. 51). The disperser drops his rod so that it bounces an accelerando on the floor.

STARTING BOARD (*ta ts'ui-pan*)—a signal to start circumambulating again. Two notes are struck on the same small board.

URINATION FISH (*ta ch'ou-chieh mu-yü*)—a signal that monks may go to urinate before sitting in meditation. One note is struck on the small wooden fish. The monks stop circumambulating and stand there until they hear the disperser drop his rod three slow accelerandos on the floor outside the front door. Those who wish may then go out the main door to the latrine. When they return, they take their seats and sit cross-legged.

The precentor and disperser themselves go to the latrine. When they return, the disperser drops his rod one more accelerando outside the door before entering. Then he bows to the buddha image, uses the rod to lift the "disperser" plaque from a hook above his own seat to a hook above the monk next below him, thus passing on the duty (*chiao san-hsiang*[6]), bows to his successor, replaces the rod in its holder by the altar, and sits down, his duty over.

ONE CHIME (*ch'iao yin-ch'ing i-hsia*)—a signal that a major period of sitting is over. One note is struck on the hand-chime.

ONE FISH (*ch'iao mu-yü i-hsia*)—a signal that a minor period of sitting is over. One note is struck on the small wooden fish. The precentor strikes three strokes on the floor with the summons rod (*ta san-ch'ui chiao-hsiang*) as a signal that the monks may leave their seats. The summons rod (*chiao-hsiang pan*) is a short thick stick of wood that he keeps under the bench below him. Only after they have heard it may the monks stand up.

RAISE BOARD (*yang-pan*)—a signal that a major period and any following periods have come to an end. This is the most complicated of all the signals and involves not only the board, but the chime, bell, and refectory gong (*huo-tien*).[7] First the hand-chime is struck three times as the monks bow to the opposite side of the hall, then to the north, then leave the hall. Next a kind of counterpoint is performed on the chime and board, thus:

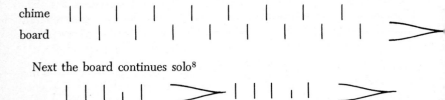

Next the board continues solo[8]

Finally it leads into three notes each on the bell in the meditation hall and the refectory gong:

board	| ||		
bell[9]		| | |	
gong		| | |	

These were the signals of immediate importance to the meditation hall, but they were not the only ones to be heard in the monastery. About fifteen minutes before each meal, for example, the rice steward made a circuit of the halls, offices, and apartments striking together two short split bamboo sticks. This was termed "calling the incense" (*chiao-hsiang*),[10] and preceded the sounding of the big wooden-fish image. Another whole realm of signals was associated with the recital of liturgy in the great shrine-hall and elsewhere. These I have excluded from my investigation since they can be easily explored in any breviary and were much less of a rarity in practice than the musical system of the model meditation hall.

CHIN SHAN MEDITATION HALL SCHEDULE 1/16-5/14

c.2:30 a.m.—UP THREE BOARDS. Carrying his small board in his hand, the night patrol makes a circuit of the apartments of those who work in the big kitchen. Outside each he strikes three notes[11]:

| ||

The kitchen staff rises. He waits until the water in the kitchen is boiling.

3:00 a.m.—UP FOUR BOARDS. The night patrol makes a circuit of the rest of the monastery, starting with the meditation hall and going to every hall, shrine-hall, office, and apartment. Outside each he strikes four notes[12]:

| | ||

The monks rise.

c.3:15—END FIVE BOARDS. The night patrol returns to the meditation hall enclosure and there, outside the ancestors hall, strikes three series of five notes to announce that he has completed his circuit. This is the signal for monks in the meditation hall to go to the latrine for both purposes and wash their hands and faces. Each series of five notes is followed by an accelerando

| | | || >

and at the end come five notes more, between the last two of which the bell in the meditation hall is struck three notes contrapuntally (*chieh-chung*)

board (night patrol) | || | |
bell (duty monk) | | |

—ANSWERING BELL. These three notes are the first of the answering bell and are followed by three series. Each series consists of 6½ rapid notes | | | | ₁ |

followed by a very, very slow[13] accelerando, the first fifteen or twenty notes of which are about four seconds apart. During the several minutes that the answering bell is being struck, the monks return to the hall, put on their gowns, robes, shoes, and stockings, prostrate themselves before the buddha image (as many at a time as space allows), and take their seats, where they are served hot water. To end this signal two more strokes are given on the bell, one on the board, and one again on the bell. These last two strokes are the "one board one bell" that signal the beginning of a major meditation period, that is, the MORNING DEVOTIONS MEDITATION PERIOD (*tsao-k'o hsiang*), which is only nominally observed. It is counted, nonetheless, as on a par with the three major periods of meditation (morning, noon, and evening) so that in one day there are considered to be four "stoppings" and four "breakings" (*ssu-chih, ssu-k'ai*), each stopping introduced by one, two, three strokes on the board and one on the bell and each breaking marked by "raise board." Except in the early morning, one major period and one or more minor periods come between each stopping and breaking, but the minor periods are not considered part of the major periods.

c.3:40—CONNECTING BELL. The large bell in the great shrine-hall is struck by the senior verger six rolls of eighteen notes each, fast alternating with slow (fast, slow, fast, slow, fast, slow).[14] These 108 notes are followed by four more that lead into the striking of the large drum in the shrine-hall and the board and bell in the meditation hall, thus:

shrine-hall bell | || | | |
shrine-hall drum | | || | | | || | | | || |
meditation hall board | |
meditation hall bell

The "two boards one bell" are the signal for the second phase in this nominal meditation period. The monks continue to sit.

—CONNECTING DRUM. The large drum in the great shrine-hall is then struck three rolls by the verger using two drumsticks, each roll with gradually increasing tempo so that at the end it is a veritable crescendo. Finally single strokes are struck that lead into the third sounding of the board and bell in the meditation hall

shrine-hall drum | || | || | ||
meditation hall board | | |
meditation hall bell |

The rest of the "three boards one bell" is then given to signal the beginning of this nominal period of sitting in meditation: while the monks continue to sit the duty monk performs three prostrations before the buddha image, and the succentor gives four strokes on hand-chime.

c.3:55—ONE CHIME. MORNING DEVOTIONS MEDITATION PERIOD ENDS. The precentor strikes three strokes on the floor with the summons rod. The monks rise.

—RAISE BOARD. They leave the hall in procession to attend morning devotions (*shang tsao-tien*) where they stand near the front. As monks stream towards the great shrine-hall from other parts of the monastery, three rolls are struck on the refectory gong (*huo-tien*),[15] each roll consisting of 6½ notes and a slow accelerando. This gives everyone time to reach his place. Then come the following signals:

After three rolls on the small drum and three strokes on the wooden fish, morning devotions begin.

Thus there has been an uninterrupted succession of signals, one leading into the next, since the night patrol struck "four boards" an hour earlier. The music has passed from hand to hand and hall to hall like an Olympic torch.

4:00—Morning devotions

c.5:15—The monks return to the meditation hall (*hui-t'ang*). When the succentor reaches his place, he strikes three notes on the hand-chime, between which he and all other monks bow first to the opposite side of the hall (east or west) and then to the north. The duty monk strikes one note on the wooden fish. He then hands over his duty (*chiao-chih*) to the monk next below him, who will hold office for the day that is beginning. The duty succentor does the same. The monks rest. In the winter time they rest sitting in silence on the meditation bench, although they do not meditate formally and it is not counted as *chih-ching*. In the summer they take off their robes and gowns and lie prone on the sleeping platform.

6:00—BIG FISH. They go to the refectory to eat morning congee (*kuo tsao-t'ang*).

c.6:40—ONE BOARD ONE BELL. They return to the meditation hall. With this signal the MORNING MEDITATION PERIOD BEGINS (*ch'i tsao-pan hsiang*). They take off their robes, gowns, stockings, and monks' shoes, and put on sandals; clean their teeth with willow twigs, go to the latrine for both purposes, and begin slow, informal circumambulation. The precentor enters and "spurs them on" (*ts'ui-hsiang*) by shouting "hurry up" (*hsing-ch'i-lai*) (see Chapter II, note 37).

—HANG TWO BOARDS. They sit down and listen to a few minutes of Explanation.[16]

—STARTING BOARD. They circumambulate again.

—URINATION FISH. They may go to the latrine. Those who do not go continue circumambulating.

7:00—THREE BOARDS ONE BELL. They sit in silence (*chih-ching*, literally "to stop and be silent"). The meditation patrol (*hsün-hsiang*) makes four circuits.

8:00—ONE CHIME. The MORNING MEDITATION PERIOD ENDS (*k'ai-ching*, literally "to break silence"). A succentor takes a stick of incense to the big kitchen (*sung-hsiang*) as a reminder that the noon rice must be ready to serve in an hour.[17] The monks in the hall wriggle their feet into their sandals while still seated. The precentor strikes three strokes on the floor with the summons rod.

—TWO FISH. With this signal the FOURTH PERIOD BEGINS (*ch'i ssu-chih hsiang*[18]). The monks circumambulate: some go to the latrine. This period is called "fourth" because its sitting is the fourth period of either running or sitting since the beginning of the morning meditation period (see Chapter II, note 23). If it is necessary to define which fourth period one is talking about, the word "morning", "noon", or "evening" (*tsao, wu, wan*) may be added: for example, *tsao ssu-chih hsiang.*

—STOPPING BOARD. They sit down and listen to a few words of Explanation; or, if no Explanation is given, they meditate for a few minutes.

—STARTING BOARD. They circumambulate for a few circuits.

—URINATION FISH. They may go to the latrine. Those who do not go continue circumambulating.

—THREE FISH. They sit in silence. The meditation patrol makes three circuits.

9:00—BIG FISH, ONE FISH. The FOURTH PERIOD ENDS. The monks dress.

—RAISE BOARD. They go to the refectory to eat noon rice, then return to the meditation hall.

c.9:30—ONE BOARD ONE BELL. With this signal the NOON MEDITATION PERIOD BEGINS (*ch'i wu-pan hsiang*). They change their clothes, clean their teeth, go to the latrine for both purposes and begin circumambulation.

—HANG TWO BOARDS. They sit down and are served the "two boards tea" (*erh-pan ch'a*). The tea mugs are collected.

—STARTING BOARD. They circumambulate again.

—URINATION FISH. They may go to the latrine.

10:00—THREE BOARDS ONE BELL. They sit in silence. The meditation patrol makes six circuits.

—ONE CHIME. The NOON MEDITATION PERIOD ENDS. They stay in their seats and are served tea. The tea mugs are collected.

c.11:30—TWO FISH. With this signal the FOURTH PERIOD BEGINS. They circumambulate.

—STOPPING BOARD. They sit down and listen to an Explanation.

—STARTING BOARD. They circumambulate again.

—URINATION FISH. They may go to the latrine.

12:00—THREE FISH. They sit in silence. The meditation patrol makes four circuits.

—ONE FISH. The FOURTH PERIOD ENDS. They put on their sandals still seated.

1:00 p.m.—TWO FISH. With this signal the SIXTH PERIOD BEGINS. They circumambulate.

—STOPPING BOARD. They sit down and listen to an Explanation.

—STARTING BOARD. They circumambulate a few circuits.

—URINATION FISH. They may go to the latrines.

—THREE FISH. They sit in silence. The meditation patrol makes perhaps three circuits.

2:00—BIG FISH, ONE FISH. The SIXTH PERIOD ENDS.

—RAISE BOARD. Without dressing in gown and robe, the monks go to the refectory to eat luncheon congee (tien-hsin chou), then return to the meditation hall. They clean their teeth, go to the latrine, dress, and prostrate themselves before the buddha image. Some go to the instructors for tutorials (ch'ing k'ai-shih).

c.2:45—The night patrol makes a circuit of the monastery, striking his board one stroke every few paces. This is the signal that afternoon devotions are about to be held. He goes last to the meditation hall and then to the Wei-t'o Tien opposite it.

c.2:55—END BOARD. There he strikes two quick strokes as a signal that he has completed his circuit. In the meditation hall the succentor strikes three strokes on his hand-chime: on the first, the monks rise and bow to the opposite side; on the second, they bow to the north; on the third, they leave the hall in procession to attend devotions.

—ANSWERING BELL. The duty monk does not go with them, but strikes three notes and then three series of notes on the meditation hall bell, each series consisting of 6½ quick notes and an accelerando, thus:

The accelerando is not so slow as in the case of the answering bell before morning devotions. It can be varied in length with the number of monks in the procession, so as to give them time to reach the great shrine-hall before the last notes are struck. These last notes lead into the first notes struck on the hand-chime and the small drum in the great shrine-hall:

meditation hall bell | || | |

shrine-hall chime | |

shrine-hall drum | | | | | ı | ⟩

The drum is followed by the large wooden fish (*mu-yü*) and the large *ch'ing* as the liturgy begins. In the meantime the duty monk has closed the door of the meditation hall and come to attend devotions himself.

3:00—Afternoon devotions.

c.4:15—The monks return to the meditation hall. They remove robes, gowns, shoes and stockings, and take a long nap on the sleeping platform (*fang yang-hsi*).

6:00—ONE BOARD ONE BELL. With this signal the EVENING MEDITATION PERIOD BEGINS (*ch'i yang-hsi hsiang*). The monks rise, dress, go to the latrine, and begin circumambulation.

——HANG TWO BOARDS. They sit down and are served the "two boards tea."

——STARTING BOARD. They circumambulate again.

——URINATION FISH. They may go to the latrine. When they have returned and all the monks are seated in their places, the proctor enters the hall, circumambulates one circuit, and takes his seat in the southwest corner. Other officers may also be present.

c.6:30—THREE BOARDS ONE BELL. They sit in silence. The meditation patrol makes three circuits.[19]

8:00—ONE CHIME. The EVENING MEDITATION PERIOD ENDS. The monks remain in their seats and are served *fang-ts'an*. This takes half to three quarters of an hour depending on the number of monks present. When they are finished they may go to the latrine for both purposes.

c.8:45—TWO FISH. With this signal the FOURTH PERIOD BEGINS. They circumambulate.

——STOPPING BOARD. They sit down and listen to an Explanation that lasts about half an hour, usually given by the abbot.

——STARTING BOARD. They circumambulate again.

——URINATION FISH. They may go to urinate.

   —THREE FISH. They sit in silence. The meditation patrol makes four circuits.

10:00—ONE FISH. The FOURTH PERIOD ENDS.

   —RAISE BOARD. The last three notes on the answering bell at the end of "raise board" lead into the striking of the large drum in the great shrine-hall:

As the three notes are struck on the hand-chime the monks make three prostrations, standing beside the sitting bench and facing north. After three long rolls are struck on the large drum, a series of strokes leads into the striking of the large bell in the great shrine-hall:

```
large drum  |  | |    |  | |    |  | |
large bell         |         |
```

Six series of 18 notes are then struck on the large bell (slow, fast, slow, fast, slow, fast—thus reversing the morning order). The sounding of the drum and bell are a signal that the end of the day has come (*k'ai ta-ching*).[20] Between the last three notes on the large bell, the night patrol, standing outside the door of the shrine-hall, strikes his hand board twice.

```
large bell   |  | |      |      |
hand board        |      |      |
```

   —UP ONE BOARD. He then makes a circuit, apparently of the main courtyard or *tan-ch'ih*, striking his board once every few paces. When he has finished this circuit, he pauses for a while.

c.10:20—UP TWO BOARDS. He makes a circuit of the whole monastery, striking his board twice every few paces as a signal that it is time for "lights out."

c.10:30—END BOARD. He returns to the great shrine-hall and strikes two quick strokes as a signal that he has completed his circuit. He goes to bed.

Variation from 5/15 through 5/29 or 5/30

c.11:30 a.m.—Instead of holding the fourth and sixth periods, the precentor asks a monk who has skill and experience in chanting liturgy to teach the others how to chant the four prayers (*ssu chu-yen*) and eight great hymns (*pa ta-tsan*).[21] The former are prayers for the peace of the nation and the latter are hymns praising the Buddha, dharma, and sangha.

Variations from 6/1 through 7/15

c.11:30 a.m.—Instead of holding the fourth and sixth periods, the monks bathe and then go to the great shrine-hall for noon devotions (*shang wu-tien*). Along with all the other monks of the monastery they chant the four prayers and the eight great hymns. They return to the meditation hall and rest until it is time to go to the refectory and eat luncheon congee. The usual schedule is then followed until 6:00 p.m.

6:00 p.m.—Instead of holding the evening meditation period, the monks go to the great shrine-hall to join all the other monks of the monastery in reciting buddha's name (*shang p'u-fo tien*). They first make three prostrations in the shrine-hall itself; then go to the main courtyard in front of it where they recite the *Amitabha Sutra* and one of the eight great hymns, standing in rows, east facing west: and finally they circumambulate in serpentine fashion, reciting the name of Amitabha (*jao-fo*).

8:45—TWO FISH. This signal begins the evening fourth meditation period, which is held as usual.

Variation from 7/16 through 9/15

In the first two months of the winter semester the schedule is the same as during the first five months of the summer semester (pp. 430-437).

Variation from 9/16 through 10/14

10:00 p.m.—Extra meditation is added (*chia-hsiang*), i.e., a sixth period with one running and one sitting. From now on every period of running throughout the day ends by shouting *ch'i*. The monks run quickly with their heads down and their attention up.

c.11:15—The monks in the meditation hall retire for the night.

Variation from 10/15 through 12/5[22]

4:00 a.m.—Instead of attending morning devotions, the monks in the meditation hall hold the "MORNING DEVOTIONS MEDITATION PERIOD" (*tsao-k'o hsiang*) with one running and one sitting. The usual schedule is then followed until 3:00 p.m.

3:00—Instead of attending afternoon devotions they hold the "AFTERNOON DEVOTIONS MEDITATION PERIOD" (*wan-k'o hsiang*) with one running and one sitting. The usual schedule is then followed until 8:00 p.m.

8:00—ONE CHIME. The EVENING MEDITATION PERIOD ENDS. Instead of eating *fang-ts'an*, the monks are each served a twelve ounce vegetable dumpling (*pao-tzu*). They go to the latrine for both purposes.

8:45—TWO FISH. With this signal the FOURTH PERIOD BEGINS. They circumambulate.

—STOPPING BOARD. Everyone stands fixed where he is and listens to an Explanation.

—STARTING BOARD. Circumambulation resumes.

—URINATION FISH. They may go to the latrine.

—THREE FISH. They sit in silence.

10:00—BIG FISH, ONE FISH. The FOURTH PERIOD ENDS.

—RAISE BOARD. The monks leave the meditation hall, go to the refectory and eat rice with vegetables cooked in sesame oil.

10:00—ANSWERING BELL. In the great shrine-hall *k'ai ta-ching* is struck as usual: three rolls on the drum leading into 108 notes on the bell.

10:30—TWO FISH. The monks return to the meditation hall. With this signal the SIXTH PERIOD BEGINS. They circumambulate.

—STOPPING BOARD. They go to their seats and drink tea.

—STARTING BOARD. They resume circumambulation.

—URINATION FISH. They may go to the latrine.

—THREE FISH. They sit in silence.

—ONE FISH. The SIXTH PERIOD ENDS.

11:30—TWO FISH. With this signal the EIGHTH PERIOD BEGINS. They circumambulate.

—STOPPING BOARD. Everyone stands fixed where he is and listens to an Explanation.

—STARTING BOARD. They resume circumambulation.

—URINATION FISH. They may go to the latrine.

—THREE FISH. They sit in silence.

—ONE FISH. The EIGHTH PERIOD ENDS. The monks remain in their seats and are served small bowls of fried dry rice (*ch'ao-mi*). The bowls are collected.

—TWO FISH. With this signal the TENTH PERIOD BEGINS. They go to the latrine. When they return, they circumambulate out of line (*pu-kuei ch-üan-tzu tsou*). At the end *ch'i* is not shouted, but spoken quickly and in a low voice.

12:15—STOPPING BOARD. Everyone stands fixed where he is and listens to a few words of Explanation given by the abbot during the time it takes him to circumambulate a half circuit walking slowly.

—STARTING BOARD. The monks circumambulate a few times.

—URINATION FISH. They may go to the latrine.

—THREE FISH. They sit in silence.

1:00 a.m.—ONE FISH. The TENTH PERIOD ENDS. The monks take a nap (*fang yang-hsi*[23]) until the day's work begins at 3:00 a.m.

Variation at New Year

For three days (the last day of the old year and the first two days of the new) there is no meditation. All the monks of the monastery divide up into three groups, each of which makes offerings at a different set of the monastery's shrines.

The following variations occur four days a month throughout the year. On the 14th and on the 29th or 30th of every lunar month, there is no work in the meditation hall from the end of breakfast congee at about 6:40 a.m. until the beginning of afternoon devotions at 4:00 p.m., a period of over nine hours. The monks use this "time off" (*fang-hsiang*) to bathe and shave,[24] wash their clothes, mend them, tidy up their belongings, and take care of personal business like writing letters. On the 8th and 23rd only the fourth and sixth period are omitted, that is, there are some two hours off from about 11:30 to 2:00, during which the monks bathe and wash their clothes, but do not shave. On all these days evening meditation is held as usual. Baths are taken not weekly, but daily from the 1st of the sixth month to the 16th of the seventh.

Chin Shan, like most other Ch'an monasteries, did not observe uposatha days by reciting the Pratimoksa rules as monks do in Theravada countries. The only special observance on these days (the 1st and 15th of every lunar month) was the addition of certain liturgy to morning and afternoon devotions, in particular a prayer for the long life of the chief of state, and offerings to tablets of the dead.

The schedule given above began as a translation of what was written out for me by the Venerable T'ai-ts'ang, the last abbot of Chin Shan, who enrolled in its meditation hall in 1917 and sat in it intermittently for thirty years thereafter (see p. 45). The signals were acted out for me by T'ai-ts'ang and a monk who had served as catechist at Pao-hua Shan (1942-1945) and who used to spend meditation weeks at the T'ien-t'ung Ssu near Ningpo. As they performed the signals, it was quite apparent that the schedule at T'ien-t'ung was almost exactly the same as at Chin Shan. Chin Shan's schedule, as given above, was corroborated by schedules independently obtained from seven other monks who enrolled there for one or more terms between 1905 and 1948. Contradictions were discussed with T'ai-ts'ang before the present version reached its final form. At no point during our conversations did any of my informants have access to a copy of Chin Shan's code of rules. What they told me was simply what they remembered having done themselves. The fact that their versions tallied closely seems to me, as suggested in Chapter II, adequate proof that the material given in this appendix represents practice not theory, not only in the case of Chin Shan, but at other model monasteries (T'ien-ning Ssu, T'ien-t'ung Ssu, Kao-min Ssu). Although I have made no special effort to record their schedules, monks from these monasteries have mentioned hours and work that closely correspond to Chin Shan's except in one respect. At both the T'ien-ning Ssu and the Kao-min Ssu there was an "evening sixth period" so that a total of eight periods were held each day, not seven as at Chin Shan. At the Kao-min Ssu, if I understood correctly, there was a morning sixth period instead of a noon sixth period, so that noon rice fell about an hour later in the day. There were four "two-board" teas rather than three as at Chin Shan with an additional one being served during the major morning period.

At monasteries that did not have meditation halls or that lay in other parts of the country, the daily schedule might differ more substantially. For example, it appears that some had three devotions a day throughout the year.

Meditation Patrols

The subject of meditation patrols bristles with complicated details. Here are a few of them, offered with no guarantee of accuracy. First, the number of *hsün-hsiang* and *chien-hsiang* varied with the lunar calendar and the work.

Dates	Work	Hsün-hsiang	Chien-hsiang
1/16-9/15	normal	1	0
9/16-10/14	*chia-hsiang*	1	1
10/15-12/5	*ch'an-ch'i*	0	2
12/6-1/15	normal	1	1

The *hsün-hsiang*, when he was serving alone, walked in alternate directions; for example, first clockwise, then counterclockwise. When two persons were on patrol they walked simultaneously in opposite directions. Between their circuits they stood on the white tiles set into the floor in front of the main altar. Two tiles were for *chien-hsiang*, one was for the *hsün-hsiang*. (These tiles are marked *chien* and *hsün* on the floor plan of the meditation hall. See p. 49.) They differed not only in where they stood, but in posture and rank. The *hsün-hsiang* always held the tip of the incense board just above his right ear as he made the circuit (see Fig. 19). The *chien-hsiang* held it vertically straight before him, as a Marine holds his sword when saluting (*ho-chang hsiang-pan*—see Fig. 20). The patrols were different persons each period. The *hsün-hsiang* served in rotation from among the rank and file of both east and west. The rotation of *chien-hsiang* was more complicated. During meditation weeks it appears to have been restricted to secretarial rank on appointment by the precentor.

The incense board carried by the *hsün-hsiang* was inscribed "*hsün-hsiang*." The one carried by the *chien-hsiang* was inscribed "*chien-hsiang*" (see Fig. 17). But every monk who had the rank of secretary was entitled to carry a *chien-hsiang* board when circumambulating.

He rested it on his right shoulder (whereas the *chien-hsiang* patrol held it vertical before him). When sitting he kept it by his seat (whereas all the patrol boards were returned to the rack by the altar). Therefore as a verb "*chien-hsiang*" can mean simply to circumambulate carrying one's incense board. All monks with the rank of secretary did this when they came to the hall in the evening and could be said to "*chien-hsiang*," although in another sense there were only two *chien-hsiang* on duty.

In the case of either *hsün-hsiang* or *chien-hsiang*, the first circuit was termed the "sandals circuit" (*ts'ao-hsieh ch'üan-tzu*), because this was when he put straight any sandals that were awry. As several informants recollected, the following number of circuits were made each period: morning period—4; fourth period—3; noon period—6; fourth and sixth periods—3; evening period—3; fourth period—3.

During a particularly long period of sitting, patrols had the right to leave their post before the altar and sit down for a few minutes.

One of the problems I have been unable to solve is the relationship between the meditation patrols and the disperser (*san-hsiang shih,* see p. 63). During the first nine months of the lunar year, the disperser *was* the patrol. The monk who stood watch before the altar during the sitting was the same person who walked outside, tapping his rod, during circumambulation. During meditation weeks there was neither *san-hsiang* nor *hsün-hsiang:* there were only *chien-hsiang*. In between these periods there were said to be separate *san-hsiang* and *hsün-hsiang*. Whatever this might have meant in practice, informants made it clear that the office of disperser, like that of patrol, was held only for a single period of meditation. The rotation of the *hsün-hsiang* had no connection with the rotation of the four duty monks, who held office for an entire day (see p. 52).

Hereditary Public Monasteries

"Hereditary public monasteries" (*tzu-sun shih-fang ts'ung-lin,* often shortened to *tzu-sun ts'ung-lin*) is a term that covers a great variety of hybrid systems of monastic administration. Monks are fond of saying that in Chinese monasticism there were "major similarities and minor differences," but this view will seem optimistic to anyone who is trying to formulate generalizations.

Generalizations about hybrids are indeed so difficult to make that it seems preferable to present three concrete examples, each from a single informant. This will at least suggest the range of possibilities.

The first informant was ordained and spent about five years at the Chin-shan Ssu, K'ai-chiang, Szechwan (which had no connection with the Chiang-t'ien Ssu, Chin Shan, Kiangsu).[1] Most of its three to four hundred monks were "outsiders" (*shih-fang jen*). Only about a hundred were "heirs" (*tzu-sun*), that is, members of the tonsure family which owned the monastery. The two leading posts of abbot and prior were reserved to heirs. All other posts, even that of rector, were open to outsiders and many were occupied by outsiders. Appointments were made as in Kiangsu by the abbot, guest prefect, and precentor.

Morning and afternoon devotions were recited daily, the Pratimoksa twice a month. During the winter, meditation weeks were held in the meditation hall. The board there was of the Lin-chi sect, which was the sect of the controlling tonsure family. There was also a buddha recitation hall and a seminary. Because of the latter the Chin-shan Ssu was considered to be a "teaching monastery" and the proctor was termed *chiu-ch'a* rather than *seng-chih* (see p. 32). Extensive land holdings provided enough income so that there was no need to perform rites for the dead. In every respect except in the reservation of leading posts to members of the tonsure family, the characteristics of this monastery were public, not hereditary.

The second example is the P'u-chi Ssu, Chen-hsien, Hunan. My informant was the abbot, who had headed it for nineteen years (1930-

1949). Although he obviously understood its operation in every detail, his Hunanese accent defeated the best efforts of the Chinese friends on whom I called for help—including even his fellow monks—and, despite his obvious intelligence and readiness to inform, he stood supreme among all the masters of confusion that I have had the pleasure of interviewing. Our interviews lasted a dozen hours. He showed better patience than I did, but I was never able to feel sure that I had gotten to the bottom of the facts.

The P'u-chi Ssu was located in the town of Chen-hsien in southeastern Hunan. Originally it had been on Su-hsien Ling, a mountain three miles away, but about two centuries ago, when the number of monks and worshippers outgrew the premises there, it subdivided: one section moved into town under the name of P'u-chi Ssu and the other section remained on the mountain under the name of Su-hsien Kuan. *Kuan* is a term for Taoist temples. Many of the temples in and around Chen-hsien had once been Taoist and had gradually been taken over by Buddhist monks. This is said to have happened "thousands of years ago," which is unlikely, but in any case, as of 1930, there were no longer Taoist monks in the temples we are discussing. The Su-hsien Kuan was an hereditary temple, staffed by its heirs. Yet the P'u-chi Ssu, which it operated as its sub-temple, was a public monastery, with office open to outsiders. Thus we have the strange anomaly of a public monastery that was a branch of an hereditary temple. The venerable head (*chu-ch'ih ta ho-shang*) of the hereditary temple usually consented to serve concurrently as the abbot (*fang-chang*) of the public monastery. He appointed an assistant (*fu fang-chang*) to manage it. During the years my informant served as head abbot, he was also president of the Chen-hsien Buddhist Association, whose headquarters were located in the P'u-chi Ssu. So when he spoke of the monastery, he often meant the association. Thus he said that all seven hundred temples in the district, including Su-hsien Kuan, "came under the jurisdiction of P'u-chi Ssu." What he meant was that they came under the jurisdiction of the Chen-hsien Buddhist Association. To add to the confusion, he always referred to the Su-hsien Kuan as the Su-hsien Ling and sometimes used "P'u-chi Ssu" to refer to both temples together.

Su-hsien Ling (the mountain, not the monastery) was four miles long and covered with temples. Three of them were sub-temples of the Su-hsien Kuan (the monastery, not the mountain). Each had a few monks and was headed by an appointee of the abbot, who would intervene himself in the administration wherever he saw fit. Usually he only did so if there had been a serious violation of the rules. The Su-hsien Kuan did not have its own code of rules, but followed *Pai-chang ch'ing-kuei* and the codes of Chin Shan and Kao-min.

Most of the sub-temples had their own land. If the income therefrom fell short of their needs, the deficiency would be made up by the Su-hsien Kuan, whose grain rents were six or seven times as much as its residents could consume.[2] Since the P'u-chi Ssu was located in the city, it specialized in performing rites for the dead, charging two Chinese dollars a day for each monk, of which he received half. This kept its seventy or eighty resident monks so busy that they had no time for religious exercises like meditation. Nor was there time for meditation at the Su-hsien Kuan, because its sixty or seventy monks were kept busy with lay visitors who came to patronize the restaurant and to consult the divination slips in the shrine-hall at two cents a throw. However, two to three buddha recitation weeks were usually held in the course of a year.

The Su-hsien Kuan had many characteristics of the large public monastery. Wandering monks could stay for as long as they liked. Permanent residence was not restricted to heirs. Only heirs could hold high office, but outsiders could fill minor posts. There was a full roster of officers, as there would be at a public monastery, and their term was by the semester. The head monk also served by terms of three to five years, not for life, and he was not chosen privately by his predecessor, but in a "selection of the worthy" at which lots were publicly drawn (see p. 155). On the other hand, only heirs could stand as candidates and the one selected had more power than he would have had at a public monastery, since no resident heir could take disciples without his permission. As a practical matter, disciples usually wanted the abbot to shave their heads himself, on the grounds that he had greater prestige. Thus, as the years passed, he came to be the tonsure master of most of the novices and many of the ordained monks under his several roofs.

This whole complex of temples was in the hands of a single tonsure family. But the scope of the family extended much farther than Chenhsien. There were, according to my informant, tens of thousands of its heirs in small temples scattered all over central and south China, as far away as Shanghai and Hong Kong. The family had grown through many successive generations. When a head was to be elected for the Su-hsien Kuan, although only heirs within fifty or a hundred miles were notified, all heirs everywhere had the right to attend the election and put up candidates. Any one of them could be a candidate if he was guaranteed by three others.

This "small temple" therefore turns out to be the largest ecclesiastical grouping that I have heard of in China. In a sense it was a nominal grouping and had no more coherence than the Lin-chi sect to which it belonged. But my informant insisted that its tens of thousands of members were all aware of their identity as heirs of the Su-hsien Kuan and looked to it as their parent monastery, despite the fact that they had not had their heads shaved there and it had no administrative control over them. This had been true for my informant. He had had his head shaved elsewhere and so had his master. Nonetheless both belonged to the Su-hsien lineage. He referred to his master, incidentally, as his *lao shih-tsun,* a term used by Taoists. His masters' temples all had Taoist names and had become Buddhist (or so he said) in the same way as the Su-hsien Kuan.

The Su-hsien Kuan in Hunan was not the only such complex of temples that I have heard of. At the foot of Omei Shan in western China there was the "Monastery of the Crouching Tiger" (Fu-hu Ssu), which had much in common with P'u-chi, including the fact that only one man seems to have escaped to tell us about it. He was a rough-and-ready individual who claimed to have had primary school education, but was unable or unwilling to write out the Chinese characters for even the simple terms that he mentioned. During the war he drove a lorry on the Burma road; then, disillusioned by the difficulties of civilian life, decided to become a monk. He was not a good source because he had never held office at the Fu-hu Ssu and hence knew how it operated only from "worm's eye" observation and hearsay; and second because he seemed prone to gross exaggeration.

According to him the Fu-hu Ssu was an hereditary temple having fifty or sixty branches within three days' journey and two hundred branches further away. During the height of the pilgrim season (May through September) about a thousand monks resided there. Morning and afternoon devotions and two meditation periods were held daily. The younger monks could not join in, since they were kept busy providing hospitality for the three to five thousand lay pilgrims who ate and slept in the monastery, as well as for the wandering monks, on whose stay there was the three-day limit usual at hereditary temples. In the winter pilgrim traffic dwindled to a handful; nearly half the monks went to live in the branches, which the parent monastery subsidized in accordance with the number of heirs and novices residing there. Some monks went farther afield to collect money pledged by pilgrims or to perform Buddhist services that the latter had requested. Those who remained at Omei Shan now had time to join the 200-300 older monks in religious practice. The latter sat in the west meditation hall while the younger monks, as well as the novices, sat in the east meditation hall. The two halls were in separate buildings and each had a full complement of ranks and offices. Participants sat for three periods a day. Although the snow might be two feet deep outside, charcoal braziers provided sufficient warmth for the motionless con-templatives.

The temple was divided into five houses (*fang*), each with a head (*fang-t'ou*). Their title was an empty one except that they alone were empowered to pass on all candidates for the post of abbot. (The role of houses is explained on pp. 166-167.) There was no limit to the abbot's term in office, but when he wished to retire (usually after at least three years) he and his predecessors nominated up to five qualified candidates. The first qualification was to be an heir of the Fu-hu Ssu. The second was to have the approval of all the house heads. Once they approved the slate, there was an open ballot in which all ordained residents signed below the names of the candidates they favored. Plurality won and the new abbot received the dharma from his predecessor.

Disciples were naturally expected to vote for their masters, so that a candidate who had shaved many of the heads present had a distinct advantage. Only officers could take disciples, and only heirs could be officers (with occasional exceptions for talent or friendship). But before an officer could take a disciple, he had to have served three years, to have reached a high position (like guest prefect), and to get the permission of the abbot or the provost. Because of these restric-tions there were usually less than fifty disciples in residence. They were divided among the five houses, each belonging to the same house as his master. They did not have their heads shaved at once (as they would in most hereditary temples). For months or years they lived in the branches, first wearing lay dress, then monastic gowns, and learned the routine of monastic life. Finally their masters took them to the parent monastery, shaved their heads, and had their names inscribed in a huge register as heirs of the Fu-hu Ssu. After this the majority of disciples returned to the branch temples from which they came, but some stayed on at the parent institution, either to study or to act as servants, depending on their talent. After six years (which is far more than the three-year novitiate considered adequate elsewhere) they could go to a public monastery, usually in Chengtu, for ordination.[3] Before the great fire in 1879, the Fu-hu Ssu had held ordinations itself, and there had been five thousand monks in residence. In the 1940's it only trained novices.

The above is all according to this one informant. What is most blatantly suspect is the figures. I have discussed them with both laymen and monks who have been to the Fu-hu Ssu and, though there was an unusually wide range in their estimates, most of them thought that in summer there were probably a few dozen monks in residence (not one thousand) and as to pilgrims, they doubted there was room for more than several hundred (not three to five thousand).[4] Exaggeration is to be expected, however, from those who have little else with which to impress their listeners. It may well be that the main features of the system, as this informant described it, are substantially correct. In that case the Fu-hu Ssu was a veritable platypus that combined every feature of the public monastery and the hereditary temple.

All this may seem too anomalous to be worth recording. But there is no way of knowing what, in fact, was statistically exceptional. The only statement that can be made with assurance is that the least anomalous institution, like Chin Shan, was the most exceptional of all. Among the many types of anomalies, we may wonder which outnumbered which. It is now too late to learn. It also may prove impossible to formulate generalizations large and loose enough so that, regardless of the peculiarities of each institution, there is still room for them.

APPENDIX VI

The Dharma of the T'ien-ning Ssu

Although it lies outside the scope of this book to discuss the historical development of the practices described, the Kiangsu system of transmitting the dharma and abbotship appears to have developed only within the last hundred years. Evidence of this may be found in the case of the T'ien-ning Ssu. A chart of its recent dharma lineage is given overleaf. Lines connect master and disciple. Names of successive abbots are given on successive lines. Names of monks who did not serve as abbot are given in brackets. The details of the history behind this chart are as follows:

In the eighteenth century two successive abbots of the T'ien-ning Ssu, Ta-hsiao Shih-ch'e (1686-1757) and his dharma disciple, T'ien-t'ao Chi-yün (1693-1767) had also served as abbots of Chin Shan.[3] They brought over its dharma, so that from that time on the T'ien-ning Ssu had the same lineage as Chin Shan.[4] Ta-hsiao was of the 35th generation of the Lin-chi lineage. His successor of the 39th generation and the only member of that generation to serve as abbot of the T'ien-ning Ssu was Hsüeh-yen Wu-chieh, who held office from 1831 to 1845. He separately transmitted the dharma to two disciples. The first, P'u-neng, headed the monastery from 1845 until the T'ai-p'ing rebels burned it to the ground in 1860, whereupon he and all the other monks fled. In 1866 he returned, and, because of age and ill health, handed over the abbotship and the task of rebuilding to his younger brother, Ting-nien. P'u-neng and Ting-nien did not transmit the dharma collectively. The former transmitted to Shan-ching, who thus represented the senior branch; while the latter transmitted to Ch'ing-kuang and Yeh-k'ai. When Ting-nien died, he was succeeded by his own disciple Ch'ing-kuang, but in 1879 Ch'ing-kuang retired in favor of P'u-neng's disciple, Shan-ching. Thus the post reverted to the senior branch. When Shan-ching died in office in 1896, he was succeeded by Yeh-k'ai (1852-1923), who was then an instructor, but belonged to the junior branch. The same thing happened in the next generation. Shan-ching transmitted to four disciples. Yeh-k'ai retired in favor of one of

Dharma lineage of the T'ien-ning Ssu[1]

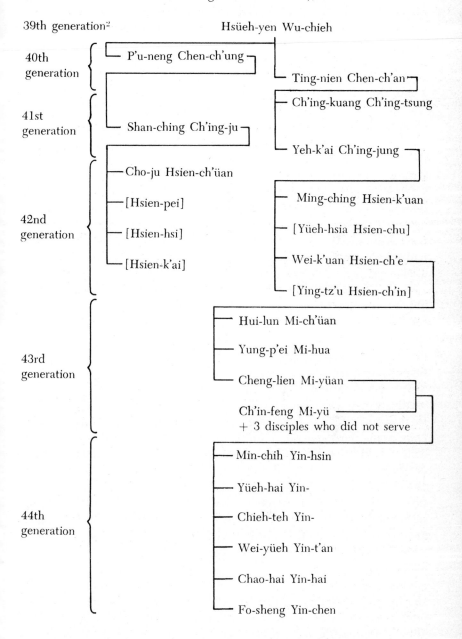

39th generation[2]   Hsüeh-yen Wu-chieh

40th generation
- P'u-neng Chen-ch'ung
- Ting-nien Chen-ch'an

41st generation
- Shan-ching Ch'ing-ju
- Ch'ing-kuang Ch'ing-tsung
- Yeh-k'ai Ch'ing-jung

42nd generation
- Cho-ju Hsien-ch'üan
- [Hsien-pei]
- [Hsien-hsi]
- [Hsien-k'ai]
- Ming-ching Hsien-k'uan
- [Yüeh-hsia Hsien-chu]
- Wei-k'uan Hsien-ch'e
- [Ying-tz'u Hsien-ch'in]

43rd generation
- Hui-lun Mi-ch'üan
- Yung-p'ei Mi-hua
- Cheng-lien Mi-yüan
- Ch'in-feng Mi-yü
  + 3 disciples who did not serve

44th generation
- Min-chih Yin-hsin
- Yüeh-hai Yin-
- Chieh-teh Yin-
- Wei-yüeh Yin-t'an
- Chao-hai Yin-hai
- Fo-sheng Yin-chen

them. Thus the post reverted to the senior branch again. But after Shan-ching's disciple had served, the junior branch took over in the person of a disciple of Yeh-k'ai. Yeh-k'ai had transmitted to four disciples in 1906. Two of them served as abbot. The other two refused to serve because they wanted to devote their time to spreading the dharma. By 1928 all abbots of this generation had died except for Wei-k'uan. He wanted to retire and therefore transmitted to seven disciples. Two followed him in quick succession, each dying in office. The third, Cheng-lien, became abbot in 1931. Because one of his younger brothers was too old to serve[5] and two of them had gone elsewhere,[6] he decided to transmit to the 44th generation in 1938. He did so jointly with his youngest brother, Ch'in-feng, who then succeeded him. This was actually the *first* collective transmission at the T'ien-ning Ssu. That does not mean that the idea of collective transmission had not been accepted there much earlier. Wei-k'uan of the 42nd generation could not have transmitted collectively in 1928 because all his elder brothers had died except for Ying-tz'u, who no longer took any interest in the T'ien-ning Ssu. Yeh-k'ai could not have transmitted collectively in 1906 for the same reason. But from the 1830's when Hsüeh-yen became abbot to the 1890's when Yeh-k'ai took office, there was separate transmission by *choice*. Two separate lines were kept going and the connection between the abbotship and the dharma was weak. The essential element—several masters sitting on a dais and transmitting to several disciples below them—was missing.

The same pattern of development appears at the Liu-yün Ssu, a relatively new monastery in Shanghai. For the first two generations the transmission was from single abbot to single abbot (*tan-ch'uan*). Only in the third generation did it become collective (*shuang-ch'uan*). This would have been about 1900. At Chin Shan transmission was "single" until the 41st generation, which probably held office about 1840.[7] But the fact that several disciples are listed in the same generation on the Chin Shan scroll at that time does not mean that they received the dharma collectively, as is shown in the case of T'ien-ning Ssu. More information is needed, but it would appear, at least, that although collective transmission has been the rule within the memory of Kiangsu abbots still living, it probably began not long before they entered the stage. In earlier times the dharma lineage seems to have shown only limited correspondence to the list of abbots. It would be interesting to learn when the custom began of picking one of the abbot's dharma disciples to succeed him, for it was this custom that probably gave rise to the Kiangsu system.

An even more interesting question is the relationship between dharma lineages and tonsure lineages. The latter are discussed on p. 279 ff., and the reader may find it helpful to have read those pages before proceeding further here. It seems likely that dharma transmission became genealogical before tonsure. The early genealogies given in the *Ch'an-men jih-sung* are stated to show who transmitted the dharma to whom, not who shaved whose head. Later, however, a name gatha written by Tsu-ting of Hsüeh-feng in Fukien, is stated to have been used both for dharma transmission and for tonsure.[8] This particular twenty-character gatha is of the greatest importance, since it came to be used not only by Chin Shan and the T'ien-ning Ssu in Kiangsu, but also by the T'ien-t'ung Ssu in Chekiang—three out of the four model monasteries of China.[9]

It was noted above (p. 449) that two abbots of Chin Shan also served as abbots of the T'ien-ning Ssu in the eighteenth century and brought over Chin Shan's lineage. The family connection between the two monasteries was maintained. At each monastery, when the character *chen* was reached (the next to last character in the gatha), the line shifted into the middle of the gatha on the opposite page of the *Ch'an-men jih-sung* (*tsung-p'ai*, 3b, 4)—a step that can only have been taken in concert. This happened about 1850 and is reflected in the table above, where the 40th generation is named with the character *chen* and the 41st with the character *ch'ing*.[10] About 1910 Chin Shan shifted to still another gatha. Therefore in the 45th generation *wei* was used as the generation character instead of *ta*, as the reader can see from p. 159.[11]

Perpetual Leaseholds

The reader may wish to know more about the "perpetual leases" mentioned on p. 222, through which the tenant retained inalienable "tillage rights" to the land he worked.

The ordinary lease, under which he did not have these rights, ran about as follows:

"[Name of tenant] accepts in lease [number] *mou* [number] *fen*, the property of the Chin Shan monastery. Each year, when the harvest is over, he will pay in rent [number] *tan* [number] *tou* of paddy and [number] *tan* [number] *tou* of wheat (or barley). In case of waterlogging or drought, he asks the owner to come to the fields and make a survey." This was written up by some literate person in the village and signed by the tenant and one or more guarantors,[1] but not by Chin Shan. It was therefore not a contract, but a unilateral pledge, kept in the business office at the monastery, bound together with other leases from the same area. Chin Shan agreed to nothing in writing, not even to letting the tenant farm the land. Legally speaking, it would appear to have had him completely at its mercy. In practice, however, it was the tenant who held the upper hand, for it was he who had the rice. He could keep the best for himself, argue that the poor crop made it impossible for him to pay rent he had pledged, then when the monastery had agreed to accept a lower rental, he could winnow it slowly so that it would contain a maximum of impurities, and protest the unfairness of a surcharge for poor quality. Under the law passed in 1930 he could not be evicted for such behavior (see p. 242), and in any case the landlord, as the abbot of Chin Shan told me with some asperity, often found it very difficult to replace him with a more satisfactory tenant.

In case of a "perpetual lease," it was not difficult, but impossible to replace him. This was because of the addition of the following apparently innocuous clause: "[I, the tenant] will myself furnish ox, plow, and outlay for fertilizer." Since these were furnished by all tenants anyway,[2] it would seem to have little importance. By custom, however, it meant that the tenants held "tillage rights (*chung-keng ch'üan*)" in perpetuity: they had "perpetual leasehold (*yung-tsu ch'üan*)." Even if they refused to pay the rent, they could not be evicted. The landlord could only sue for payment. What the landlord (*yeh-chu*) had was "ownership rights (*so-yu ch'üan*)," but these were in effect nothing more than a "right to receive the rents."[3] Under no circumstances could Chin Shan put its own plow into any of this land. It could only do so if it bought the tillage rights from the tenant. Usually if he sold them, it was to another tenant at a higher price than ownership would fetch. In I-cheng, for example, ownership rights sold for $30-40 a *mou*, but tillage rights for $50-60. This was because with tillage rights one could get two thirds of the crop, although, of course, one had to work for it; and also because the tenant owned his house, whereas under ordinary leaseholds it belonged to the landlord.[4]

The sale of tillage rights was not registered in the land office. There was no tax on the transaction. The landlord's approval was not required. The sale simply had to be attested by the "village foreman" (*chuang-t'ou*), who was the resident lay representative of the monastery. He saw to it that the buyer furnished a new rental pledge on the same terms as the old.

Perpetual leases were customary in I-cheng, Yangchow, Yang-chung, and Chen-chiang, whereas Chin Shan held both tillage and ownership rights in T'ai-chou, and Kao-yu. This is why it paid over $100 a *mou* for its land in T'ai-chou, but only $30-40 a *mou* in I-cheng. The system may sound informal compared to Western practice in leasehold and conveyancing, but it worked smoothly because, as the abbot put it, the force of custom was very strong. He was particularly lucid on the details of how it worked because of the twenty years he spent in charge of Chin Shan's leases. When I remarked that I had never heard of "tillage rights," he laughed and said that many Chinese had never heard of them either. An authority on the rice trade has told me that the system was virtually unknown outside southern Kiangsu and northern Chekiang.

Mortgage Loans

The T'ien-ning Ssu in Changchow made mortgage loans to its tenants two ways. In the Kuang-hsü period they were made and repayable in strings of cash. Interest was called *kan-tsu*[1] (quasi-rent) and paid in grain. After the founding of the Republic in 1912 mortgage loans were made and repayable in silver dollars. The land pledged to secure them was called *huo-t'ien,* a term that was also applied to the interest, which was still paid in grain. So both *kan-tsu* and *huo-t'ien* had the same characteristics: principal in money, interest in grain. The details, all given me by the former abbot of the T'ien-ning Ssu, are as follows.

KAN-TSU

Only tenants received loans on this basis. As the abbot said, "If you were not our tenant, we would not do it." Of course, the land he pledged was his own, not what he was renting from the monastery. One reason for making such a loan was to help out a tenant when he needed cash. If he had to pay for a funeral or a wedding or medical expenses or gambling debts, he would go to the monastery rather than to a money-lender, presumably because he was better treated there. The monastery, however, was unwilling to play the role of a money-lender. "It did not sound well for us in the clergy to receive interest," as the abbot put it. Therefore they asked the tenant to pay "quasi-rent" in the form of paddy rather than interest in the form of cash. Sometimes, however, the quasi-rent was inadvertently referred to as interest and we shall call it interest below for the sake of simplicity.

The rate was usually 15 to 16 percent a year. On the security of one *mou* of land the tenant paid interest of one *tan,* but could borrow varying amounts of money depending on what the *tan* was worth.

When paddy sold for $3 a *tan,* he could borrow $20.* When it sold for $4, he could borrow $25. When it sold for $5, he could borrow $30. If he was particularly trustworthy and had a particularly good relationship with the monastery, he could borrow more for less. For example, when paddy was selling for $5 a *tan,* he could borrow $30 and pay quasi-rent of only 50 or 60 catties, instead of 100.

The loans were always small, never exceeding $100. A few dozen dollars were enough to pay for a wedding. The only time that a borrower might pay interest in money rather than grain was when he had fallen three to five years behind in interest payments. Then, after selling his crop, he might pay some of the back interest in cash or the person who had guaranteed the loan might use cash to pay it off for him.

The term of these loans was usually for a full year, for example, from the tenth month to the tenth month. But if they were not paid off at the end of their term, they could be extended. Some continued for years. Interest on *kan-tsu* loans made before 1912 was still being paid in the 1930's, and the debtors knew that what they were paying was interest not rent.

The formalities were few. The tenant signed a "chit" (*t'iao-tzu*) which stated briefly how much money he was borrowing and how much quasi-rent he would have to pay. But it did not state how much land was being pledged as security. Instead, the tenant left plot certificates[2] with the monastery for an amount of land that was usually equal in value to the money he was borrowing. Unlike other lenders, who were usually only willing to loan half the value of the land pledged, the T'ien-ning Ssu did not require a margin. This was because the borrowers were its tenants, with whom it had a personal relationship. Tenants with whom the monastery was on particularly close terms were allowed to leave plot certificates for land worth even less than the amount of their loan. For example, if it were selling for $30 a *mou,* they could borrow $30 pledging only 7 to 8 *fen.* The price of land, according to the abbot, had risen steadily since the Kuang-hsü period, when it was worth about $10 a *mou.* By the 1920's it had gone up to $40, by the 1930's to $80, and by the 1940's to $100.[3] (Why then did they not pay off their original loans and borrow more on the same land? Because, the abbot said, tenants disliked shifting from the

---

* Unless otherwise specified, all figures below will be in terms of Chinese currency, that is, Chinese silver dollars (*ta-yang*). The official exchange rate, which varied widely and was not an accurate indicator of purchasing power, fluctuated between 54¢ and 22¢ (U.S. currency) in the years 1925-1934.

creditors with whom their father or grandfather had made an agreement. A former Changchow landlord explained that there were also technical difficulties. No new creditor would make a loan until he was given the *t'ien-tan* and the tenant çould not get hold of the *t'ien-tan* until he had paid off the old loan.)

About half the tenants were reliable and paid the interest when due. When tenants did not pay, the monastery would ask the guarantors to intercede. All *kan-tsu* loans were guaranteed by a *t'u-tung* or *t'u-cheng* or both.[4] Some tenants were rogues and would never pay. But the monastery had their plot certificates and so they could not sell the land. Some were poor and simply unable to pay. There was nothing to be done. If the monastery turned to the guarantors, they often had no money either. Sometimes tenants would get eight to ten years behind in interest payments and when the monastery pressed them, they would try to sell it the land they had pledged. In that case the monastery would consider whether, if it bought the land, it would be able to find a satisfactory tenant or whether it would have to rent it back to the debtor who would probably not pay rent any more regularly than he had paid interest. In that case it would tell him to sell the land to someone else. Thereby it might only recover its principal and ten catties a year of back interest, but it still preferred to take what it could get and be done with it.

HUO-T'IEN

The term *huo-t'ien* ("live fields") meant land the question of whose status was still alive since it had merely been pledged, not sold. It also meant the interest paid on the loan secured by this land.

Huo-t'ien differed from *kan-tsu* not only because the loan was in silver dollars rather than strings of cash, but also because it was secured by a "live field deed" (*huo-t'ien ch'i*), which provisionally sold the pledged land to the monastery. But because the sale was provisional, the land remained "alive"—hence its name. The borrower paid the taxes on it, harvested it, and it was still in his name on the land register.

The amount loaned was always the market value of the land pledged, neither more nor less. The term was usually for three years, but as in the case of *kan-tsu*, it could be extended indefinitely. The borrower could "plow five-year live fields or ten-year live fields," the abbot said. The interest was usually specified as one *tan* two *tou* per *mou*, but the specification varied with the quality of the land and the reliability of the borrower. It also varied with the price of paddy or land. When the price went up, interest rates would go up too, for example, from one *tan* two *tou* to one *tan* four *tou*. Although *huo-t'ien* agreements were made mostly with tenants, some were made with nontenants who had been introduced by tenants or by their own guarantors.

The "live field deed" was written up by the guarantors and, of course, signed by them. Each deed stated how many *mou* were being pledged; what the current market value was; how many *tan* of paddy per *mou* the borrower would pay each year; and it reserved his right to redeem the land if there was no default.

In case of default on interest payments, the monastery could not foreclose, since creditors did not have that right. It would ask the guarantors to investigate. If they found that the debtor was really unable to pay, they would urge him to sell and the monastery to buy the land pledged. As in the case of *kan-tsu* the monastery would consider the circumstances. If it bought the land, would it be able to find a satisfactory tenant? How far away from the monastery did it lie? Was it close to other plots? And what was the atmosphere among the peasantry in the area—were they a "bad lot"? If circumstances were favorable, the monastery might agree to buy. In that case, although it had already loaned the tenant the full value, it would have to add a little money, perhaps $20 or $30. Only then would he consent to transfer the ownership. If the monastery would not give him this extra, he would not sell. Nor did he necessarily pay the interest in arrears. As in the case of *kan-tsu*, the main concern of the monastery was to get its capital back. It did not want to have a lawsuit. If only part of the interest was paid, it was willing to forget the rest. "He was poor and had no money," the abbot said again. After a new deed had been signed and the transaction completed at the land office, the debtor might then rent the land back from the monastery.

The abbot stated that *huo-t'ien* was a more reliable arrangement than *kan-tsu*. The *huo-t'ien ch'i* was more explicit and stiffer than the "chit." I pointed out that since the monastery still could not foreclose without the debtor's consent, it sounded to me as if the "live field deed" had no great advantage. The abbot sighed: "It was not really of very much use. The landlord was not well off, but this was the local custom." Other remarks indicated that his complaint applied particularly to the years after 1927. He said, for example, that it was easy to collect in peaceful times, but hard in times of disorder. I suspect that the monastery was not so ready to write off delinquent debts before the Communists entered the countryside and the Nationalists took office with their commitment to a program of land reform.

It was difficult to get the abbot to estimate how much land was pledged to secure these loans in the early 1930's, perhaps because he had never had occasion to add it up. Finally he averred that about 4,000 *mou* was pledged in all, half on *kan-tsu* loans and half on *huo-t'ien* loans, but the income from the latter was higher because the interest rate was higher. That is, a little more than half of the interest grain was received on *huo-t'ien* and a little less than half on *kan-tsu*. After 1927 the amount of interest grain received declined faster than the grain rents on wholly owned fields (*ai-t'ien*). With so many other variables involved (varying amounts of security required and varying interest rates demanded), it is very hard to check these figures for internal consistency.

Calculations of Landed Income

The reader may wish to check the calculations that underlie the figures in Chapter VIII on the landed income of Chin Shan and the Ch'i-hsia Ssu. Since the grain they sold was what they received minus what they consumed, the first point to be established is what they consumed. Chin Shan, on the average, fed 350 persons.[1] Both here and elsewhere the rule of thumb was a catty of rice per person per day.[2] 350 × 364 days = 127,400 *chin* (catties) per year. This was polished rice. Although the loss by volume in milling and polishing rice was 50 percent or more, the loss by weight was about 30 percent.[3] These 127,400 *chin*, therefore, represented 182,000 *chin* of paddy. At Chin Shan there were about 120 *chin* in a *tan*.[4] 182,000 ÷ 120 = 1,517 *tan*. This should have been the amount of paddy consumed at Chin Shan in a year and it tallies almost exactly with the figure of 1,500 *tan* that the abbot recollected.

Chin Shan had the following holdings of farmland (all areas are approximate):

T'ai-chou	1,400 *mou*
Kao-yu	150
Yang-chung	1,350
Yangchow	300
I-cheng	1,400
Chiang-ning	100
Chen-chiang	100
	4,800

On all the land except in T'ai-chou, rent was specified and collected in *tan* by volume. When tenants came in with their grain, it was measured with a bushel container. But though the lease agreements in T'ai-chou specified so many *tan* by volume, payment there was actually by weight in *chin*. Scales were used to weigh the grain, and its weight was converted to volume at the rate of 120 *chin* to the *tan*. Curiously enough, polished rice in T'ai-chou was measured wholesale by volume as it was elsewhere.

Chin Shan usually collected rents of one *tan* to the *mou* on its properties in T'ai-chou, as specified in the leases there, but less in other areas. The lowest figure was to be found in the Yang-chung leases, where it was 8 *tou* 3 *sheng*, and even this amount the tenants were often unwilling to pay. We would probably not be far off if we assumed that except in T'ai-chou 8 *tou* was the maximum collectible in a good year. That would give the following totals:

T'ai-chou 1,400 *mou* at 1 *tan*	1,400 *tan*
Other properties 3,400 *mou* at 8 *tou*	2,720 *tan*
Total 4,800 *mou*	4,120 *tan*
Consumed at monastery	—1,500 *tan*
Available for sale	2,620 *tan*

In poor years the rents would drop to 2,000 *tan*. In good years, therefore, some would have to go into storage as a reserve. Rice had also to be supplied to sub-temples and for charity. The abbot recollected that in good years Chin Shan usually sold "about 1,500 *tan*." All in all this figure seems reasonable and it has been used in Chapter VIII.

The price fetched by this rice was, according to the abbot, about $4 a *tan*. This is the equivalent (after transportation, milling, and polishing) of the $8-9 a *tan* that polished rice was then fetching on the Shanghai rice market.[5] $4 × 1,500 *tan* = $6,000 income from the sale of rice. Barley fetched about the same price as rice, and wheat substantially more.

$4 × 700 *tan* barley = $2,800; $7 × 300 *tan* wheat = $2,100.

Rice	$ 6,000
Barley	2,800
Wheat	2,100
Total income from sale of rent grain	$10,900

As was pointed out in Chapter VIII, the value of grain consumed at the monastery should be added to this $10,900 in order to give the real income from land. 1,500 *tan* of paddy at $4, plus 150 *tan* of wheat at $7 = $7,050, giving a total real income from land of $17,950, or about $3.80 per *mou*. This compares with a national average of $4.20 per *mou* for fixed rents in 1934.[6] Part of the difference is accounted for by the fact that I have not included in real income the amount placed in storage in a good year. Rents were received immediately after each harvest, rice in the eighth or ninth lunar month, wheat and barley in the fifth or sixth. Rice and barley were stored until prices reached their annual peak in the spring, then sold, while the wheat was sold then or at any other time that prices were favorable.

CH'I-HSIA SHAN

The landed income of Ch'i-hsia Shan has been calculated on the same basis as Chin Shan's. At a rate of one *chin* per person per day, its average of 200 residents, employees, and guests consumed 72,800 catties of polished rice annually, which represented 104,000 catties of paddy. Its approximately 1,150 *mou* of farmland[7] yielded rents of about 125 *chin* per *mou* out of total production of 300 *chin* in a good year.[8] 1,150 × 125 = 143,750 *chin*. Subtracting the 104,000 consumed at the monastery leaves 39,750 *chin* that was available for sale. At a price of $4 a *tan*, it would have fetched $1,324. The sale of 100 *tan* of barley and wheat brought in $400 more. (Apparently Ch'i-hsia Shan got less for its wheat than Chin Shan.)

Notes

Bibliography

Glossary Index

Notes

CHAPTER I: THE PEOPLE OF THE MONASTERY

1. See Appendix I for a breakdown of these figures.

2. For a more detailed explanation of this estimate see Appendix I.

3. Lai-kuo, *Kao-min ssu kuei-yüeh* (Code of rules of the Kao-min Ssu; Taipei, 1960), 2:30.

4. *Ssu* was the cognomen, that is, the final character in the name of both monasteries and nunneries (though some of the latter were *an*). Because of this ambiguity as to sex, romanization of the cognomen is preferable to translation, and it also enables the reader to distinguish Buddhist from Taoist institutions. The latter were called *kung* or *kuan*. *Miao* was the generic term for all houses of worship. Generally speaking, *miao* was used as a cognomen for Taoist temples or temples of popular worship, but as a descriptive term for small Buddhist temples, even when their cognomen was *ssu*. It would be said, for example, that "the Fu-hai Ssu is a small temple (*hsiao-miao*)." The word *shan* was used to mean a mountain or mountains, island or islands, but in particular the principal monastery located thereon. Thus the Fa-yü Ssu would never be referred to as P'u-t'o Shan because it was only one of the three large monasteries on that sacred island, whereas the Lung-ch'ang Ssu (Hui-chü Ssu before 1932) was almost always called Pao-hua Shan because there were no other large monasteries in the Pao-hua range of hills. Even monks who were ordained there cannot always remember that it was the Lung-ch'ang Ssu. Similarly the Ting-hui Ssu is known as Chiao Shan; and the Ch'i-hsia Ssu is known as Ch'i-hsia Shan—although the mountain on which it stands is named She Shan. This last example testifies to the strength of the tendency to think of the monastery itself as a mountain. Yet there are limits. The main entrance of the T'ien-ning Ssu in Changchow could, in the usual way, be called the "gate of the mountain" (*shan-men*), but since it stood on level ground, the monastery as a whole was known as the T'ien-ning Ssu, never as T'ien-ning Shan. Because of the ambiguous usage of the word *shan* it is simply romanized and never translated as "mountain" in this book, whereas other geographical terms (like *ho* for "river") are translated in the usual way.

5. That is, Chinkiang. This particular spelling, although standardized by the *Postal Atlas*, is too misleading to deserve perpetuation. *Chin* Shan is in *Chen-chiang*.

6. See note 3.

7. When a large monastery was said to be in or of a large city, it might mean simply that it lay in the area dominated by that city. Pao-hua Shan, for example, lay over twenty kilometers northeast of Nanking, but it was still referred to as "Nanking Pao-hua Shan."

8. It is difficult to find appropriate translations for these and other technical terms of Chinese monastic life. There is a need to standardize: otherwise the reader will think that different writers are discussing different things when, in fact, they have merely made different translations. I have tried to select English equivalents that are native to the monastery or the university (since the Chinese monastery had characteristics of both); or sometimes terms that simply convey the function involved. My objective has been to avoid Sanskrit or Chinese romanizations as much as possible. For help in reviewing the English equivalents I am most grateful to Dom Aelred Graham, the Prior of Portsmouth Priory (Benedictine) in Rhode Island, who was kind enough to read those sections of the manuscript that dealt with monastery personnel.

9. It is difficult to achieve consistency in the capitalization of Buddhist terms. The word "buddha" is only capitalized below when it refers to *the* Buddha, Sakyamuni. The image in the guest department might be of one of the monastery's guardian deities (*ch'ieh-lan*). Hence, although it would be termed in Chinese a "buddha image" (*fo-hsiang*), there is no need for capitalization. Here and below diacritical marks, as in Śākyamuni, have been omitted on the ground that ambiguities do not necessitate them.

10. Reginald F. Johnston, *Buddhist China* (London, 1913), p. 149, asserts that pilgrim monks had their certificates endorsed and sealed at each monastery to show that they had visited it. All the informants queried have denied that this was done except in major centers of pilgrimage like P'u-t'o Shan (see p. 310). One or two informants have stated that at certain monasteries (the Chan-shan Ssu in Tsingtao, for example) all applicants were asked to produce their ordination certificates for inspection. Prip-Møller gives an instance of monks' names being recorded when they first arrived to stay at Pao-kuang Ssu. See J. Prip-Møller, *Chinese Buddhist Monasteries* (Copenhagen, 1937), p. 98. It may be that the practice there was different from in Kiangsu; or, since the date of recording was the 2nd of the seventh month, it may be that they were not newly arrived, but about to take office, at which time names were recorded (see p. 43).

11. Not all the finer details of etiquette have been described. For example, the guest prefect, when he asked where the applicant was ordained, was supposed to say "Where was your establishment of ordination (*ni-ti chieh ch'ang-chu na-erh*)?" The applicant had to reply with the formula "My hall of repentance was . . . (*ch'an-hui t'ang shih* . . .)." An amusing episode that reveals some of the etiquette will be found in *Chüeh-shih* (Awaken the world), No. 265:3. (September 21, 1964). The episode concerns a guest prefect at Yü-wang Ssu, Ningpo, who tried to bully an applicant and initially refused him admission on the grounds of "no vacancies" (*chih-tan*). As the writer says, "in the eyes of an applicant, guest prefects had a power to which nothing can be compared."

12. Lai-kuo, 2:47.

13. In 1933 when the Japanese occupied Shanhaikuan, the Nineteenth Route Army started activity in Fukien and monasteries and temples throughout the province stopped admission. "Only Ku Shan still let wandering monks stay on indefinitely, as before. The number of wandering monks reached fifteen or sixteen hundred, but despite the shortage of food, we still kept up two meals a day, one of congee and one of rice." Ts'en Hsüeh-lü, *Hsü-yün ho-shang nien-p'u* (Chronological biography of the Venerable Hsü-yün), 3rd ed. (Hong Kong, 1962), p. 94.

14. Such was the practice at the Kao-min Ssu, which in this respect as in some others (see note 26) was not so strict as Chin Shan.

15. A three-day limit is mentioned by Prip-Møller, pp. 101 and 264. Cf. J. J. M. DeGroot, *Le Code du Mahayana en Chine, son influence sur la vie monacal et sur le monde laïque* (Amsterdam, 1893), p. 129. According to my informants this was the regulation not in large public monasteries, but only in small hereditary temples, whose lesser resources made it necessary for them to place some limit on hospitality. See Chapter V.

16. Lai-kuo, 2:92b. The abbot of Chin Shan stated that such monks did not bother to apply for admission there because they knew they would be refused.

17. At Chin Shan, the T'ien-ning Ssu, and some other large Kiangsu monasteries there was no *tien-tso*. My informants did not know when the office had become obsolete. At Chin Shan its duties were assumed by the proctor.

18. The bowls were the property of the monastery. Those that monks had received at ordination were usually carried on their travels but not used except ceremonially.

19. In one respect the office of the *chien-yüan* was similar to that of the "cellarer" in a Christian monastery (alternatively entitled "procurator" or "bursar") who was in charge of the treasury, which handled money and supplies in much the same way as the *k'u-fang*. In another respect the *chien-yüan* was like the prior, who was second in command at an abbey, ranking next to the abbot, but first in command at a priory. Similarly the *chien-yüan* was, in practical matters, second in command of a monastery, and normally referred to as the *tang-chia*, that is, "manager" (see Chapter V, note 1). But *tang-chia* was the title of the head of a dependent sub-temple, who was not necessarily a *chien-yüan* of the parent institution, though he might be. The parallel with the usage of "prior" is imperfect, but suggestive enough so that the latter seems an appropriate equivalent.

20. The system of land rents will be fully discussed in Chapter VIII, pp. 218-240.

21. In some monasteries the business office included a "supervisory clerk" (*k'u-ssu*) whose special duty it was to oversee village agents and to keep a central record of all equipment loaned out to tenants. This was so at the Kao-min Ssu. See Lai-kuo, 1:69 ff. Other sources assign to the *k'u-ssu* the more general duties of the regular clerk (*k'u-t'ou*).

22. According to some sources the work of supervising the collection of rents was placed in the hands of a "rent collector" (*chien-shou*). See Prip-Møller, p. 359. I believe that in central China the office was almost obsolete, the only monastery where I have heard of it in recent years being Ku Shan.

23. See Chapter VIII, note 23.

24. Lai-kuo, 1:3b-4. I have never heard of this sort of coercion being used by other monasteries.

25. Lai-kuo, 2:38.

26. At the Kao-min Ssu, the Venerable Lai-kuo had three such acolytes, who were termed "abbatial acolytes" (*chang-shih ti shih-che*) to distinguish them from the acolytes in the meditation hall (*ch'an-t'ang ti shih-che*). They were unordained novices, which violated the rule at public monasteries. T'ai-hsü went even further afield. In 1925, according to one informant, his acolyte was not a novice but a young layman.

The number of acolytes required to serve the abbot depended on the ceremony. If he was going to preach the dharma in the dharma hall (*fa-t'ang shuo-fa*) twenty-four were needed to present the incense burner, carry the fly whisk, hold the kneeling mat, handle the texts, and so on. As many as necessary would be borrowed from the meditation hall.

27. At the Liu-yün Ssu, curiously enough, while one subprior was in charge of finances, the other was in charge of lay donors who were having rites for the dead performed there. At most monasteries they would have been looked after by a guest or visitors' prefect (see pp. 10-11). This anomaly may have been due to the fact that rites for the dead were the main source of income for the Liu-yün Ssu and therefore the principal business of its business office. This particular subprior (cf. p. 201) was often addressed as "visitors' prefect" (*chih-pin shih-fu*), and according to my informant (who held the position himself) he could be considered as a subprior serving concurrently as visitor's prefect. But officially he was the "external subprior" (*wai fu-ssu*) and on the staff of the business office rather than the guest department.

28. Prip-Møller (pp. 224, 364) states that *chiu-ch'a* was the title used in Ch'an monasteries. My informants contradict this and they are supported by the codes of rules of the two leading Ch'an monasteries, Chin Shan and the Kao-min Ssu, both of which allude to a *seng-chih*, not a *chiu-ch'a*. On the nature of the teaching or doctrinal sects or schools (*chiao-men*), see p. 398.

29. Prip-Møller, p. 240.

30. H. Hackmann, "Buddhist Monastery Life in China," *East of Asia Magazine*, 1.3:248-249 (September 1902).

31. At Chin Shan the twenty-odd "boys" (*ch'a-fang*) who worked in the guest department, business office, and abbot's quarters (*fang-chang shih*) were not paid any regular wage at all. Those who waited on the lay donors got tips. Those who did not got a share of the receipts. For example, every day that a lay donor had the monks perform rites for the dead, each of the untipped "boys" got one or two dollars depending on his age (a sum that compares favorably with what the monks received themselves). Barbers were called in to Chin Shan from the outside, particularly on the two days a month when the hundred-odd monks in the meditation hall had their heads shaved together. The resident tailors ("less than ten," according to the abbot) were fed by the monastery, but paid by individual monks on a piece work basis (40-50¢ for the making of a full-sleeved gown). Other workmen, like the carpenters and tilers who kept the buildings in repair and the ten coolies (*hsiao-kung*) who tilled the vegetable garden and adjacent rice fields, got wages of up to 20¢ a day. (All figures are in Chinese dollars and hold good for the period before 1937, when serious inflation began.)

32. This term is sometimes romanized as *hang-tan*, for example, in Prip-Møller, pp. 236, 358, 359, and sometimes as *hsing-tan*, for example, in L. S. Yang, "Buddhist Monasteries and Money Raising Institutions," *Studies in Chinese Institutional History* (Cambridge, Mass., 1961), p. 208. (Professor Yang translates the term as "itinerant monks.") All of my informants who used the term pronounced it as *heng-tan*. According to the dictionaries, *heng* is a classical or variant pronunciation of *hang* or *hsing*. It appears to have been preserved in monastic or regional patois.

33. The abbot of Chin Shan spoke with similar respect of a night patrol there.

Compare the virtuous gardener whom Hsü-yün honored by asking him to be a witness at an ordination (Ts'en Hsüeh-lü, *Hsü-yün ho-shang nien-p'u*, p. 79).

34. This title is romanized *wei-na* in most Western language accounts: for example, Prip-Møller, pp. 75, 77, 79, etc.; Jacques Gernet, *Les aspects économiques du bouddhisme dans la société chinoise du Ve siècle au Xe siècle* (Saigon, 1956), pp. 7, 36, 37, etc.; L. S. Yang, "Buddhist Monasteries and Money Raising Institutions," p. 207; DeGroot, *Le Code du Mayahana*, p. 170. J. Blofeld romanizes it *wei-na* in *The Jewel in the Lotus* (London, 1948), p. 55, but states in a letter that it was pronounced *wei-no*. K. L. Reichelt romanizes it *wei-na* in *Truth and Tradition in Chinese Buddhism* (Shanghai, 1927), pp. 237, 267, and 272. On page 278, however, he renders it *wei-lo* and on p. 268 *huei-lo*. In *Religion in Chinese Garment* (London, 1951), p. 117, he has another surprise for us: *veiloh*. Though good old Dr. Reichelt may not have been rigorous orthographically, at least he knew how the word was pronounced in modern times (around Nanking where he lived, "l" and "n" were often confused). Probably seventy or eighty of my informants used this term at some point during our interviews. Everyone of them pronounced it *wei-no*. This was true even of those who came from north China where (according to one informant) the pronunciation was sometimes *wei-na*. I suspect it has been pronounced *wei-no* from ancient times, *no* having the same reading as it has in *cha-no* (Sanskrit *ksana*: see *Tz'u-hai* [Shanghai, 1937], *wei*, p. 233). Of course it is possible that the pronunciation has changed just as the duties have. (During the Six Dynasties the *wei-no* was a monk appointed by the government to help supervise the monasteries of a certain area.)

35. One informant called it being a "nominal prior" (*ming-i chien-yüan*).

36. Lai-kuo, 2:31.

37. At some monasteries (the Liu-yün Ssu in Shanghai, for example) the 16th of the first month and the 16th of the seventh month were considered beginnings of major terms (*ta ch'i-t'ou*), while the 16th of the fourth and the 16th of the tenth month were considered beginnings of minor terms (*hsiao ch'i-t'ou*). A vacant office could be filled on these dates and monks could enter the meditation hall.

38. A "draft of the personnel register" (*hao-pu ti ts'ao ts'e*) had already been written up at the start of the semester, recording all appointments made then, and the names and personal data of the newcomers to the meditation hall (who at that time had no rank). Now the final slate of names, offices, and ranks was copied into the permanent register and the draft was thrown away. There was a new permanent register for each semester. Sometimes it was termed the *kua-hao pu* or *hu-k'ou pu* or *chih-shih pu*. Lay workmen on the staff were listed separately.

39. Ordination age (*chieh-la*) was, properly speaking, the number of summers that had passed since a monk was ordained.

40. The "ten-thousand-year book" (*wan-nien pu*) usually recorded not only all appointments, but expulsions, ordinations, acquisition of permanent property like land or images, construction or restoration of buildings, additions to the code of rules, and any noteworthy events. At Chiao Shan each department had its own. At Chin Shan there was only one, kept by the abbot. It was added to from year to year, so that it might reach five hundred pages or more and go back for decades. What a treasure house of information, and what a pity that none, so far as I know, has ever been brought out of China!

41. Lai-kuo, 1:69; 2:92b, etc.

42. The term *ch'ing-chung* meant "the main body of monks leading a pure life." Properly speaking, according to the abbot of Chin Shan, it referred to all monks whose rank was lower than secretary. Thus the sacristans (*i-po*) were *ch'ing-chung*, or, as the abbot put it, they were *ch'ing-chung* officers (*ch'ing-chung chih-shih*). But most of my informants used the term improperly (or loosely) to refer to monks who held no office at all. They would contrast the sacristans, who were office-holders, with the *ch'ing-chung*, who were not. Some informants even included among the *ch'ing-chung* all the monks who lived in the wandering monks hall—whom the abbot of Chin Shan would exclude on the grounds that they held no rank. The abbot of the T'ien-ning Ssu said that it had several hundred "rank and file without rank" (*wu-chih ti ch'ing-chung*), including the residents of the scripture chamber (see p. 103), the buddha recitation hall, and presumably the halls for the aged and infirm, as well as those who enrolled in the meditation hall after the second month of the semester in order to fill vacant places (a practice apparently not allowed at Chin Shan). In other words, *ch'ing-chung* is a very ambiguous expression. Our phrase "rank and file" has some of the same ambiguity in military usage.

43. That is, the senior succentor (*ta yüeh-chung*), who held the rank of deacon, was usually promoted to precentor (*wei-no*) with the rank of secretary, while the second succentor (*erh yüeh-chung*) was usually promoted to proctor (*seng-chih*) also with the rank of secretary. Their predecessors as precentor and proctor now became guest prefects, still with rank of secretary. This may become clearer from a diagram. Each arrow expresses promotion at the end of one or several semesters in the same office.

Monk A	Monk B
Rank and file (recorder)	Rank and file (acolyte)
↓	↓
3rd succentor (thurifer)	4th succentor (recorder)
↓	↓
Senior succentor (deacon)	2nd succentor (thurifer)
↓	↓
Precentor (secretary)	Proctor (secretary)
↓	↓
3rd guest prefect (secretary)	4th guest prefect (secretary)

Thus the rank of secretary was a kind of plateau on which officers remained until seniority or accomplishments required that they be made instructors.

44. See Appendix II, p. 422.

CHAPTER II: THE MEDITATION HALL

1. D. T. Suzuki, "Impressions of Chinese Buddhism," *Eastern Buddhist*, 5.4:327-378 (March 1935). The complete sentence reads: "Japanese Zen travellers in China deplore the fact that there is no more Zen in China as it used to prevail in T'ang and Sung." But in the context Dr. Suzuki writes as if Zen meditation no longer existed in China at all, having been replaced by the Pure Land practice of reciting Buddha's name. Many Japanese have spoken to me of the "decay" of Chinese Buddhism.

2. Like the meditation hall downstairs, the ordination chamber (*chieh-t'ai lou*) was the size of five "rooms" (*wu-chien fang-tzu*). The ordination platform (*chieh-t'ai*) stood in the center of it. There was no sleeping platform.

3. Chou Hsiang-kuang, *Dhyana Buddhism in China* (Allahabad, 1960), p. 183. Professor Chou adds that according to some sources the practice began under the Yung-cheng emperor (1723-1835) and offers the following anecdote. The emperor was looking for a monk to succeed to the title of "National Teacher" (*kuo-shih*) that his grandfather, the first Ch'ing emperor, had conferred on Yü-lin, an eminent Ch'an monk. A disciple of Yü-lin in the fifth generation, T'ien-hui, was recommended for the honor and summoned to Peking. The emperor asked him whether he understood the principles that Yü-lin had taught. T'ien-hui replied: "I have a scabby head"—perhaps thinking this would be enigmatic enough to impress his imperial interrogator. It was not. The next question was: "What will you do if I cut off your scabby head?" T'ien-hui could find no answer. The emperor concluded the interview by telling him he must produce an answer within seven days or he would certainly be decapitated. T'ien-hui retired to the meditation hall in the palace (the Yüan-ming Yüan) to work on the *hua-t'ou*: "I have a scabby head." The emperor often sent people to remind him of the passing days: "Four days are gone—only three are left," and so on. This upset T'ien-hui to the point where he could no longer sit still in meditation, and he began walking about the hall. On the seventh day he was rushing about so wildly that he hit his head against a pillar, which at once brought about his enlightenment. Yung-cheng congratulated him, conferred a purple robe, and installed him as the abbot of the first generation and founder of the Kao-min Ssu, in whose meditation hall the practice of alternating sitting with circumambulation was formally instituted. (Cf. Lai-kuo, 1:92.)

4. From the 15th of the fourth month to the 15th of the seventh.

5. See pp. 397-398.

6. There were actually four duty monks. Only the first sat by the tea-table and struck the signals on a given day. He was called the *cheng tang-chih ti* or the *chung-pan tang-chih ti*. The next day he became the *fu tang-chih ti* or "deputy duty monk"; and on the third and fourth day he became the *mo tang-chih ti* and *lao tang-chih ti*. On the last three days he had no major duties, but was supposed to help the staff of the hall with whatever work had to be done—like serving *fang-ts'an* (see p. 73).

7. Informants agreed that in general the order of precedence in processions (*p'ai-pan*) was according to rank, and within a given rank, according to seniority as a rank holder, but it appears that there were many anomalies. The place of the abbot and precentor, and possibly of the proctor, instructors and vergers varied with the sect of the monastery, the nature of the procession—and the informant I was asking. Some informants said that the abbot, if present, always walked last. One informant said that he walked last in processions to the shrine-hall, but first in those from the shrine-hall. Here is a consensus of the order in a procession to the shrine-hall at a Ch'an monastery:

> rector (*shou-tso*)
> other instructors (*pan-shou*)
> secretaries (*shu-chi*)
> librarians (*tsang-chu*)
> canon prefects (*chih-tsang*)

contemplatives (*ts'an-t'ou*)
water-bearers (*ssu-shui*)
vergers (*hsiang-teng*)
succentors (*yüeh-chung*)
deacons (*tsu-shih*)
thurifers (*shao-hsiang*)
recorders (*chi-lu*)
acolytes (*shih-che*)
monks in meditation hall still without rank
monks in buddha recitation hall of any rank
wandering monks (*yün-shui seng*)
precentor (*wei-no*) or proctor (*seng-chih*)
abbot (*fang-chang*).

If a lay donor joined in the procession, he would be accompanied by a guest prefect and walk in front of the abbot.

8. A longer version was used on the first and fifteenth of each lunar month (see Chapter IV, note 12). Other changes were made at certain monasteries, as for example, at the Ling-yen Ssu, Soochow (see Chapter III, note 9). In general, however, though some monasteries centered on Ch'an practice and others on Pure Land, their liturgy was virtually the same. Only very rarely do there appear to have been sectarian differences in terms of liturgy (for an example, see note 9).

9. Because of the exclusion of all Pure Land practice at the Kao-min Ssu, though the monks formed a serpentine procession during devotions, what they recited was "Homage to our master Sakyamuni." I do not know of any other monastery that so consciously excluded Pure Land.

10. This is what it was termed by one or two informants, but, according to the abbot of Chin Shan, it had no proper name. It was simply *hsiu-hsi* (to rest).

11. At some monasteries (for example, the Kuan-tsung Ssu in Ningpo and the Fa-yü Ssu on P'u-t'o Shan), they first used to march in serpentine procession, reciting buddha's name, from the refectory to the great shrine-hall. There they made three circumambulations, recited a mantra, and prostrated themselves thrice. Only then did they return to their quarters.

12. On monks clothing see pp. 113-115. Their footwear is of two kinds. For formal occasions (the same occasions that require a robe) they wear "monk's shoes" (*seng-hsieh*) which are made of cloth somewhat in the shape of the wooden shoe of Holland. A narrow strip of faille runs down the center of the toe and around the binding. For informal wear there is the "straw shoe" (*ts'ao-hsieh*), which is not made of straw, but of cloth. The rear part of the uppers is largely cut away, so that little more than the binding remains. It is rather like a sandal, very light and airy, and worn (in the meditation hall) without stockings. In footwear as in the rest of their attire, the Chinese monks avoid the use of animal products. To-day in Hong Kong the soles are often made of old automobile tires, both serviceable and saving.

13. In India even today people clean their teeth by chewing the twigs of *kadawa neem* (the bitter lemon). In ancient India willow twigs were employed. Another Indian custom (according to Chinese Buddhist dictionaries) was to demonstrate the sincerity of an invitation by presenting the guest with a willow twig

and scented water. Hence willow twigs were used to invite the presence of buddhas and bodhisattvas. This is said to have been the origin of the Chinese Buddhist custom of sprinkling holy water (*sa-ching*) with a leafy willow twig before
performing major rites. One Chinese source, however, traces the custom back to
T'ang Kao-tsung, who gave willow circlets to his officers as a prophylactic against
scorpion bites. Willow is also considered a powerful charm to bring rain, since
it grows near water; and finally, because of its hardiness and tender green leaves,
it is considered a symbol of vitality and hence a talisman against evil spirits. See
Tun Li-ch'en, *Annual Customs and Festivals in Peking*, tr. and annotated by Derk
Bodde (Peking, 1936), p. 27.

14. Lai-kuo, 3:39b.

15. According to informants from other monasteries the rigor of the Kao-min
Ssu was exceptional; elsewhere there was greater privacy and cleanliness—or at
any rate, fewer rules. One informant from Chin Shan said that he could recall
no limitation on washing or wiping the hands or bringing his own towel. Actually,
he said, many monks did not bother to wash their hands because China had such
excellent toilet paper—unknown in India where the rule about hand-washing had
been formulated. That may be, but Prip-Møller (p. 158) mentions a monastery
where, instead of toilet paper, the monks used strips of flat bamboo, which were
thrown into a flat box afterwards so that they could be washed and used again.
Bamboo strips are said to have been often so used in China.

The Kao-min Ssu seems also to have differed from some other monasteries in
having no partitions between the seats of each row in the latrine. The only partition was between the rows, which stood back to back. Those who were defecat-
ing in one row could see each other. The abbot alone had side partitions and a
wider seat. At Chin Shan and the T'ien-ning Ssu, on the other hand, there were
side partitions between all the seats, although they were shallow and the resulting
booth was open in front. Many small temples were even cruder than Kao-min.
The monks squatted on a long plank, perhaps sixteen inches wide, spanning a
pit. One informant said: "It was very easy to fall in." Snapping the fingers to
warn hungry ghosts was a nearly universal monastic custom.

16. "Running" is literally "running the incense" (*p'ao-hsiang*). It can also be
called "walking the incense" (*hsing-hsiang*). An older term is *ching-hsing*. Some
documentary accounts by eyewitnesses state that circumambulation increased in
tempo until towards the end it was, in fact, nearly a run. See John Blofeld, *The
Wheel of Life* (London, 1959), p. 163; Prip-Møller, p. 75; and two books by
K. L. Reichelt, *The Transformed Abbot* (London, 1954), p. 52, and *Meditation
and Piety in the Far East* (London, 1953), p. 69; but contrast Reichelt's *Truth
and Tradition*, p. 279.

Most of my informants state that the gait remained a fast walk with no increase in speed. They also say that the inner circles (with the younger monks)
moved faster than the outer circles.

17. There was no order of precedence, as there was during a procession from
hall to hall. The duty monk, however, was supposed to walk behind the precentor
so that he could get his orders to strike signals when due.

18. At Chin Shan a secretary sat in the east just below the duty succentor
whom, of course, he far outranked. Presumably this was done to fill an empty
place. Seniority was sometimes outweighed by office. Among the thurifers, for
example, a sacristan who came in for the evening period would sit higher than

monks who had held the rank of thurifer longer than he had, but did not hold any office. (This was like the proctor in the west.) One or two informants recalled that the provost, if he chose to attend, would sit to the left of the duty monk, since he (the provost) was highest in the eastern party (*tung-tan*). This is denied by informants with more experience, who say that he sat in the west in accordance with his rank. Actually there was a theoretical basis for his sitting on either side, just as the precentor (as a secretary) was entitled to sit in the west, though in fact he always sat in the east.

19. For more details on the meditation patrol, see Appendix IV.

20. John Blofeld saw the edge used on chronic dozers at the Hua-t'ing Ssu near Kunming, but it was prohibited in Kiangsu monasteries. See Blofeld, *Wheel of Life*, p. 167.

21. See note 23.

22. Here my informants appear to be in irreconcilable disagreement. Two of them were adamant in maintaining that in Chin Shan's meditation hall tea was never served. It was always hot water. Two others, including the abbot, said that it was tea but of ordinary quality. On another occasion the abbot recalled that twice a day there was tea and once a day hot water (in addition to the hot water served on rising). The abbot of the T'ien-ning Ssu, on the other hand, said that there it was tea once and hot water twice. Other informants were similarly divided. The question may not seem important, but it illustrates the exasperating difficulty encountered sometimes in establishing even the simplest facts about monastic life.

23. They are the "fourth" and "sixth" counting from beginning of the noon period: 1) running, 2) sitting, 3) running, 4) sitting, 5) running, 6) sitting. The fourth period may be considered to include the third and the sixth to include the fifth. I use the word "cycle" to mean one period of running and one of sitting. No such unambiguous usage exists in Chinese, where "one stick" can mean one or both of these periods. See Appendix III, note 2.

24. I capitalize "Explanation" to make a distinction from the ordinary usage of the word.

25. The abbot of Chin Shan denied that the contents of a *kung-an* necessarily included an instance of enlightenment.

26. Charles Luk, *Ch'an and Zen Teaching, First Series* (London, 1960), pp. 49-109; Chang Chen-chi, *The Practice of Zen* (London, 1960), pp. 61-70.

27. Monks could ask for an Explanation during any intermission in the work when the abbot or an instructor was free. It was not restricted to the period after luncheon.

28. It was not prohibited, but it seldom took place. In theory he could become the instructor's dharma disciple (see pp. 314-316).

29. *Ch'ieh-lan* is the usual abbreviation for *ch'ieh-lan shen*, the gods of the *ch'ieh-lan* (Sanskrit *sangharama*) or monastery premises. See Ting Fu-pao, *Fo-hsüeh ta tz'u-tien* (Large Buddhist dictionary; Taipei, 1956), p. 1183.

30. In the early 1930's, for example, when Hsü-yün was abbot of Ku Shan, he permitted wandering monks to sit in the meditation hall whenever they wished.

31. See p. 111.

32. The soft rice eaten now is not congee (*chou, hsi-fan*), that is, rice boiled in an excess of water, nor is it *p'ao-fan*, which is made by adding boiling water to cooked rice that has cooled. Instead, at about noon, rice is thrown into plenty

of cold water and slowly brought to the boiling point. Then the whole is placed in wooden tubs and wrapped up in wadded cotton. It retains its heat until evening, by which time it has a consistency between normal cooked rice and congee.

The serving of each bowl is done with ceremony. The verger (or one of the duty monks, who have to help out when there are many people in the hall) offers the rice bowl with his right hand and the vegetable bowl with his left to each monk in his seat, who accepts them with the opposite hands and then presses his palms together in a salute. When he has finished he leans down, without uncrossing his legs, and sets the bowls on the floor. Then, before replacing the slat, he wipes it off with a piece of toilet paper that he also keeps under the cushion. The precentor makes a circuit of the hall to make sure that all the bowls are empty. A monk who has left food uneaten must explain why (for example, illness) or risk a beating. Then the precentor shouts "pick them up!" and the bowls are collected and cleaned by the verger and his helpers with hot water, but no soap.

33. John Blofeld recollects that the meditation hall at the Hua-t'ing Ssu, Kunming, was "never without the disturbance of its whining, cruelly biting mosquitoes." (*Wheel of Life,* p. 171.) It was obviously impermissible to swat them, since that would risk taking life. Some of my informants said that it was even risky to brush them away. What if one brushed too hard? One could blow at them, of course. Sometimes a deputy duty monk might be assigned to walk around the hall waving at the mosquitoes. Or, added two informants, a coil of mosquito repellent punk was placed on the floor beside every fourth person.

34. At the Kao-min Ssu enrollment usually dropped from 70-80 in the winter to 20-30 in the summer, and there was one year when the number of rank and file dropped to five! At some monasteries (for example, the Liu-yün Ssu in Shanghai) if too few enrolled at the beginning of the term, a date would be set for late entry, and if there were still vacancies, there would be yet another such date. This was not done at Chin Shan.

35. For more information, see Appendix IV.

36. That is, by all monks with secretarial rank, plus the two meditation patrols. Instructors do not join in the shout since their boards are inscribed *ching-ts'e,* "to warn and whip on." Beside the other boards, inscribed *hsün-hsiang* and *chien-hsiang,* there are three used by the precentor. The one carried by him during circumambulation as an emblem of authority is inscribed *wei-no.* The one he uses to punish minor infractions of discipline in the hall (like talking)—always with three blows—is inscribed *t'ang-kuei* (see Fig. 17). The one he and the guest prefect use to punish major infractions of discipline (wine, women) with many blows is inscribed *ch'ing-kuei.*

One can always tell the rank of an instructor from the position in which he carries his board when circumambulating. If it is at an upward angle (about 30° above horizontal), he is an assistant instructor (*t'ang-chu*). If he holds it pointed downward (about 45° below horizontal), he is the rector (*shou-tso*). The boards of the associate and senior instructors are in between. The abbot, whose board is simply marked by three horizontal lines, holds it pointed almost vertically downward and swings it back and forth as he walks.

37. The instructors may join in beating them too. This is called *ts'ui-hsiang* or "spurring on," and according to some informants it is practiced at other times of

the year as well. There is also another kind of *ts'ui-hsiang:* at the beginning of a period of meditation, after the last monk has returned from the latrine and everyone is still circumambulating informally, the precentor comes in, shouts "get going" (*hsing-ch'i-lai*), and they begin a faster and more orderly pace.

38. It is always shouted first and last by the precentor and in between by the instructors.

39. This appears inconsistent with the usual relationship of west to east, but it is well-attested to by qualified informants.

40. Such information as I have was supplied in each case by a single informant. Here are some examples. 1) At the Liu-yün Ssu in Shanghai, which was not noted for the strictness of its rules, there were normally six cycles of meditation a day (versus seven at Chin Shan) and five meditation weeks a year (versus seven at Chin Shan), although in these weeks there were the standard twelve cycles a day. Aside from the fact that enrollment was easier, other differences from Chin Shan appear to have been slight. 2) The Chin-shan Ssu, K'ai-chiang, Szechwan, had a large meditation hall which, most of the year, was used for reciting buddha's name. Every winter, however, starting the 15th of the tenth month seven meditation weeks were held, apparently with the same rules as at Chin Shan, Kiangsu. 3) According to an unreliable informant, the Fu-hu Ssu at Omei Shan, Szechwan, had two meditation halls, each fully staffed (so that there were two precentors). Two cycles a day were held in summer, three in winter. There was at least one meditation week every winter with six cycles a day.

41. Ernst Boerschmann, *P'u-t'o Shan* (Berlin, 1911), pp. 136-137. One minor difference between this and other meditation halls was that the sitting bench was divided from the sleeping platform by a line of doors. The top half of each door was lattice-work, so that anyone inspecting could look through and see the two rows of sleeping monks.

42. Prip-Møller, pp. 70-71. It is possible that the meditation hall at the Chao-ch'ing Ssu was being used as the classroom of a seminary.

43. At some monasteries it was possible to enter after the semester began (see note 34), but even there the monks were required to stay until it ended.

44. See pp. 190-191.

45. At the Kao-min Ssu, according to one informant, even when there were "chores for everyone" (*ch'u p'u-p'o*), a skeleton force would be left to keep the work underway in the meditation hall. At Chin Shan the precentor, when called out to take part in a Buddhist service, would leave the hall in charge of an instructor.

46. Lai-kuo, 3:42, 136b. It is hard to tell what "laxity" means here.

47. Nan Huai-chin, *Ch'an-tsung ts'ung-lin chih-tu yü Chung-kuo she-hui* (The Ch'an monastic system and Chinese society; Taipei, 1962), p. 48.

48. Termed *t'aó-tān* which sounded confusingly similar to *t'aŏ-tān* "to apply for admission."

49. Lai-kuo, 2:47. This regulation was promulgated in 1936. The Yangtze bridge was not a bridge across the Yangtze River, which lay several miles away. San-ch'a Ho was a small town at the end of the waterway that came up from the Yangtze opposite Chin Shan. It had many shops and was the major settlement nearest the monastery, which was sometimes said to be located at San-ch'a Ho.

50. H. Hackmann, *Buddhism as a Religion* (London, 1910), p. 223.

51. Blofeld, *Wheel of Life,* p. 172.

52. See p. 307.

53. Ts'en Hsüeh-lü, *Hsü-yün ho-shang nien-p'u*, pp. 25-26.

54. Nowhere in this passage does he speak of *p'u-t'i* (*bodhi*) or *chüeh-wu*. He merely says that the "roots of doubts were cut" (*tuan i-ken*). According to the abbot of Chin Shan the difference between a small enlightenment and a large enlightenment was that in the latter "all doubts were settled and the truth was proven" (*tuan-huo cheng-chen*). A small enlightenment, since this was absent, "does not confer much benefit," he said. A former abbot of the Nan-hua Ssu took a similar position. From his point of view there was nothing remarkable in the fact that at the Nan-hua Ssu in 1950 "some of those who took part in meditation achieved [degrees of] enlightenment." Ts'en Hsüeh-lü, *Hsü-yün ho-shang nien-p'u*, p. 177.

55. Some paranormal powers and practices were considered to be orthodox, others heterodox. It was orthodox to recall some event from an earlier life or to see what was happening many miles away (*t'ien-yen t'ung*). Such powers were not supposed to be cultivated for their own sake, but they lay within the margin of the path towards enlightenment. On heterodox practices, see pp. 121-126.

56. Reichelt, *Truth and Tradition*, p. 281.

57. *Chüeh Yu-ch'ing* (The enlightenment), 13.2:20 (October 1950).

58. J. B. Pratt quotes monks as saying that insanity in the meditation hall was due not only to wrong methods but to evil spirits. (*The Pilgrimage of Buddhism and a Buddhist Pilgrimage*, New York, 1928, p. 344.) Although this sounds reasonable enough, the monks I have queried discount it. There is even a theory that evil spirits can be a good thing. The *Pao-wang san-mei lun* states: "When getting established in religious practices, do not seek to avoid evil spirits (*mo*). If one does not encounter them, one's resolve will not be firm. . . . Take a host of demons as comrades in the dharma" (quoted in Nan Huai-chin, p. 48).

CHAPTER III: THE BUDDHA RECITATION HALL

1. Some readers may be puzzled by the inconsistency of my usage of Sanskrit and Chinese terms. My objective is to use whichever is likelier to be familiar to the majority of readers. More are likely to recognize Amitabha than O-mi-t'o-fo, whereas more are likely to recognize Kuan Yin than Avalokitesvara. Most such equivalents are cross-referenced in the index.

2. The Chinese word *nien* which I translate as "recite" can also mean "to think of." *Nien-fo* therefore means not only to recite the words "homage to the buddha Amitabha" but also to focus the mind on Amitabha as the lord of salvation. The Sanskrit term *buddhanusmrti*, of which *nien-fo* is a translation, properly has the second meaning only. The Chinese practice of *nien-fo* has a parallel in the Christian Akoimetoi or "sleepless ones" who chanted the same phrase in endlessly alternating choirs from about 430 C.E. See *Die Religion in Geschichte und Gegenwart*, 3rd ed. (Tübingen, 1957), I, 21.

3. This account is based partly on Makita Tairyo, "Gendai chugoku bukkyo no seikatsu kihan" (The norms of Buddhist life in contemporary China), *Bukkyō daigaku kenkyū kiyō* (The memorial of records, Bukkyo University), No. 35:245 (Kyoto, 1958). This, however, shows some discrepancies with the information on Yin-kuang published in *P'u-t'i Shu*, 97:8 ff. (December 1960).

4. See p. 71. It was recited at the beginning of the fifth period. In either case chanting was accompanied on the six liturgical instruments: hand-chime (*yin-ch'ing*), wooden fish (*mu-yü*), bell and drum (*chung-ku*), cymbals (*ko-tzu*), and hand-gong (*tang-tzu*).

5. *Chuan* may here have the sense of "recite," according to one informant.

6. According to one informant they were beaten by two succentors. But when I took part in buddha recitation at a temple closely connected with Ling-yen Shan, the precentor struck the hand-chime and a succentor struck the wooden fish, whether walking or sitting. More investigation is needed.

7. My own experience leads me to believe that it is easier to get sleepy in the recitation than the meditation hall. I took part in recitation one summer day. There was not a sound but the buzzing of an occasional insect outside the window. The air was soft and warm and just right for a nap. Nothing moved. Across the hall I could see heads begin to sag. What was the point of mental effort when sleep was so sensuously inviting? What did it matter if—just for a few minutes—one had a little sleep? Sleep suddenly seemed the most beautiful thing in the world—so much so that I found it easier to understand the need for the insistent rigor of Chin Shan.

8. In the meditation hall *k'ai-ching* meant the end of an entire cycle of meditation.

9. In morning devotions there was a recitation of the *Ta-pei Chou* between the Surangama Mantra and the *Heart Sutra* (items 1 and 2, p. 56). In afternoon devotions (see p. 71) the *Amitabha Sutra* (recited daily as in most monasteries) was regularly alternated with the *Ch'an-hui wen* (which was elsewhere recited only on the 1st and 15th). The *Ch'an-hui wen* is also known as the "Eighty-eight buddhas" (*Pa-shih pa-fo*), so called because in it the monks pay homage to eighty-eight different buddhas. After the Japanese invasion of China in 1937 seven recitations of the *Ta-pei chou* were substituted for the *Amitabha Sutra* "in order to pray for an early cessation of hostilities and world peace." See *Ling-yen nien-sung i-kuei* (Liturgy and ritual of Ling-yen; Hong Kong, 1962), p. 51. In case of drought and flood, morning and afternoon devotions were each prefaced by the "Hymn to the holy water of the willow branch" (*Yang-chih ching-shui tsan*). Cf. Chapter II, note 13.

10. *Nien-fo yü-lu* or *ching-t'u yü-lu*.

11. See pp. 156-158.

12. My informant on this point, who spent three years at the Ling-yen Ssu, initially as a succentor in the buddha recitation hall, was emphatic in asserting that the first kind of transfer of merit was for the benefit of others, while the second and third were for the benefit of oneself alone. However, there is some ambiguity about this in Buddhist texts, which give many different classifications of the transfer of merit, some in two categories, some in three, and some in ten. In all cases at least part of the transfer is for the benefit of others.

13. On the first day they would make three trips upstairs. The first would be to set up the tablet (*an-wei*). The second (before lunch at 11:00) would be to offer rice and vegetable dishes (*shang-kung*). The third (in the evening) would be to transfer merit (*hui-hsiang*). But on the following six days of the seven-day service (*fo-ch'i*), they made only the latter two trips daily.

14. See Yin-shun, *T'ai-hsü ta-shih nien-p'u* (Chronological biography of the Venerable T'ai-hsü, Hong Kong, 1950), p. 46. Chou Hsiang-kuang traces the

development of the Pure Land practice at Hung-lo Shan to Ch'e-wu (1736-1805) whose *Recorded Sayings* presented "a unique idea of the harmonization between meditation and devotion." See Chou Hsiang-kuang, *A History of Chinese Buddhism* (Allahabad, 1955), pp. 216-217; *Dhyana Buddhism in China*, p. 194.

15. Boerschmann, *P'u-t'o Shan*, p. 30.

16. Boerschmann, *P'u-t'o Shan*, pp. 139-141.

17. If this was the arrangement for reciting buddha's name at other monasteries during the late Ch'ing dynasty, it may have been from the meditation hall that Yin-kuang borrowed the idea of the sitting bench, the assignment of a monk to patrol, and the alternation of sitting and circumambulating. Boerschmann says nothing about circumambulation in the buddha recitation hall at the Fa-yü Ssu, where "the old men squat for many hours through the day in the meditation position, motionless and softly murmuring . . . as they recite incessantly the name O-mi-t'o-Fo, O-mi-t'o-Fo, while the chime is constantly sounded and the wooden fish is struck" (*ibid.*, p. 140). Yet upstairs the fourteen desks "were nearly all constantly in use" by monks engaged in study. Since there were twenty-four persons enrolled, it would appear that they studied and recited in rotation. Unfortunately Boerschmann does not give their work schedule.

18. At Chin Shan it was the meditation hall that stood as close as possible to the ancestors hall and the abbot's quarters. It faced south, whereas the great shrine-hall faced east. Its residents walked and stood ahead of those enrolled in the hall for reciting buddha's name. This latter hall at Chin Shan seated just twelve persons, so that vacancies were few. But it was possible to enroll in it directly, without taking any examination and without having first spent a term in the meditation hall.

19. Not *yen-chiu*, simply *k'an*.

20. In his history of the T'ien-ning Ssu, Cheng-lien states that the "scripture-chanting hall" (*sung-ching lou*) was set up over the refectory by the then abbot, Chen-ch'an (Ting-nien), in 1870. See Cheng-lien, *Ch'ang-chou T'ien-ning ssu-chih* (History of the T'ien-ning Ssu in Changchow; Shanghai, 1948), 1:15. Presumably this is the same hall.

CHAPTER IV: OBSERVANCE OF THE RULES

1. The Chinese Pratimoksa (*Ssu-fen chieh-pen*) is translated in Samuel Beal, *A Catena of Buddhist Scriptures from the Chinese* (London, 1871), pp. 206-239. "The Sutra of Brahma's Net" (*Fan-wang ching*) is translated by DeGroot in *Le Code du Mahayana*, pp. 14-88.

2. DeGroot, *Le Code du Mahayana*, p. 2.

3. H. Hackmann, "Pai-chang Ch'ing-kuei," *T'oung pao*, 9:651-662 (1908). He offers a useful synopsis of its contents.

4. *Hua-pei tsung-chiao nien-chien* (North China yearbook of religion, No. 1; Peking, 1941), pp. 150-154.

5. My copy is a 1917 reprint by the North Kiangsu Scriptural Press. It is eight *chüan* in stitched volumes.

6. See Chapter I, note 3.

7. One of these five was for the Pure Land center at Ling-yen Shan, discussed

in the last chapter (pp. 90-100). See *Su-chou Ling-yen shan-chih* (History of Ling-yen Shan, Soochow; Shanghai, 1948), *chüan* 6. The second was for the Chan-shan Ssu in Tsingtao, a new monastery founded by T'an-hsü. Its code was based largely on the practice at the Kuan-tsung Ssu in Ningpo, where T'an-hsü had been a student. See T'an-hsü, *Ying-ch'en hui-i lu* (Reminiscences of shadows and dust; Hong Kong, 1955), II, 174-184. The third was the code compiled by Hsü-yün for the Yün-ch'i Ssu near Kunming, which he had restored. See Ts'en Hsüeh-lü, *Hsü-yün ho-shang fa-hui* (Religious writings of the Venerable Hsü-yün), 2nd ed. (Hong Kong, 1962), pp. 319-360. The fourth (largely a repetition of the third) was for another monastery restored by Hsü-yün, the Yün-men Ssu in Kwang-tung. See Ts'en Hsüeh-lü, *Yün-men shan-chih* (History of Yün-men Shan; Hong Kong, 1951), pp. 154-177. The fifth was for the Pao-lien Ssu in Hong Kong. See *Ta-yü shan-chih* (History of Ta-yü Shan; Hong Kong, 1958), pp. 68-81.

8. The release of living creatures (*fang-sheng*) is further explained on p. 378.

9. *Ch'an-men jih-sung* (Ch'an breviary; Hangchow, 1926), pp. 134-136. This compilation appears to have been first published in 1834. It is not included in any of the standard editions of the Tripitaka and is rarely found in libraries; yet no book is more of a "must" in every Chinese temple and monastery. My copy, published in Hangchow in 1926, is greasy from years of constant use. Other copies I have seen are dated 1904, 1916, and 1919—testimony to the frequency with which it was reprinted.

10. This is described in full on pp. 310-314.

11. This was termed *sung-chieh*. At some other Vinaya centers it is said to have taken place in the morning after bathing and changing clothes. But my informant from Pao-hua Shan stated quite clearly that there it took place "after the evening meal."

12. Also the Ṣhih hsiao-chou (Ten short mantras), the Ṣhih ta-yüan (Ten great resolves), and homage to the ancestral masters were usually added to morning devotions. In the evening, besides the usual Ṭa-pei chou, the monks might recite the *Ch'ieh-lan tsan*—also directed to the deities protecting the monastery (see Chapter II, note 29).

13. The Chinese term for fasting after noon is *kuo-wu pu-shih,* but it is often shortened to *kuo-wu.*

14. There were two small kitchens (*hsiao ch'u-fang*) at Chin Shan. Besides the one attached to the business office (*k'u-fang*), there was another in the abbot's quarters (*fang-chang shih*) where food was prepared not only for the abbot but for privileged lay guests.

15. Hackmann writes as if he had personally visited Pao-hua Shan, but apparently took what he was told at face value. "The evening meal is forbidden," he says. "They are only allowed tea to drink." See his *Buddhism as a Religion,* p. 241. Prip-Møller, who spent many weeks at Pao-hua Shan, explains (p. 221) that "to drink tea" meant to eat the evening meal.

16. See Holmes Welch, *Taoism: The Parting of the Way,* 2nd ed. (Boston, 1966), pp. 91, 108, 116, 119.

17. See, for example, A. J. Little, *Mount Omi and Beyond* (London, 1901), pp. 75, 81, 83. Mary A. Mullikan, "The Nine Sacred Mountains of China" (in manuscript), p. 77. In 1922 a party of foreigners visiting the Fo-ting Ssu, P'u-t'o Shan, was refused even a guest room to eat their lunch in because their menu included

fish. See Lucille Sinclair Douglass, "The Island of the 'Little White Flower,'" *China Journal of Sciences and Arts*, 1.1:153 (March 1923).

18. See Robert Fortune, *Tea Districts of China* (London, 1852), p. 235. Cf. Virgil C. Hart's account of being presented with a large piece of pork by the head of the temple he was staying at on Mount Omei. See *Western China* (Boston, 1888), p. 222.

19. In the 1930's, however, silk was permitted at some Shanghai monasteries.

20. According to one reliable informant, all the monks of Pao-hua Shan wore saffron-colored robes and gowns throughout the year. I can find no mention of this in Prip-Møller.

21. Prip-Møller, p. 372, states that the generic term is "great robe" (*tà-i*) and that *tsu-i* is used only of a patriarch's robe in a hundred and thirty sections. *Tā-i* means "to don a robe."

22. Whereas no cleaning agent of any kind was permitted when washing the hands after a visit to the latrine, the monks were allowed to use the pods of *Gleditschia sinensis* (*tsao-chüeh*) when bathing. If mixed with water, these yielded a sticky substance, good for cleansing—indeed, superior to soap, I was told, "because it did not make the water so dirty." However, according to one informant, soap came to be used half-openly, half-secretly at the Kao-min Ssu after World War II. At the T'ien-ning Ssu under its postwar abbot (who had studied under the reformer T'ai-hsü) soap was used openly.

23. Prip-Møller, p. 133, translates regulations listing differently the successive contingents of bathers at Chiao Shan. "4:00 p.m. Former abbots and important guests. 4:30 p.m. Present abbot and heads of various departments. 5:00-6:00 p.m. Inhabitants of Meditation Hall and remaining guests, etc." Since this was daily bathing in summer, two bath supervisors (*chien-yü*) were placed in charge, probably not as permanent officers.

24. Reichelt, *The Transformed Abbot*, p. 52. According to residents, spitting on the floor was forbidden there.

25. C. S. Wong, *Kek Lok Si, Temple of Paradise* (Singapore, 1963), pp. 16-17.

26. Wu Lien-teh, *Plague Fighter* (Cambridge, 1959), pp. 251-252.

27. Blofeld, *Wheel of Life*, p. 164.

28. See Chapter II, note 46.

29. The whole saying is quoted in T'an-hsü, II, 235: "Profane and saintly persons join in the work together, dragons and snakes co-mingle" (*fan-sheng chiao-ts'an, lung-she hun-tsa*).

30. Thus in 1882 he met Hsü-yün in the form of a beggar. Ts'en Hsüeh-lü, *Hsü-yün ho-shang nien-p'u*, p. 12.

31. One informant stated that vows to this effect were to be found in the *Fan-wang ching* (see Chapter IX, note 46). It is true that articles 29 and 33 prohibit certain kinds of divination (interpreting dreams, hexagrams, and the use of the planchette), but I have been unable to find any prohibitions therein of medicine or astrology. Another informant stated that it was part of the oral tradition. A third said that divination, medicine, astrology, and physiognomizing were only prohibited to Hinayana monks. A Mahayana monk could do anything to help others. A regulation of Pao-hua Shan dated 1683 strictly forbade the practice of geomancy by monks enrolled there (Prip-Møller, p. 291).

32. Ts'en Hsüeh-lü, *Hsü-yün ho-shang nien-p'u*, pp. 32-36. At the Fa-yu Ssu

Boerschmann met a monk who was expert in geomancy and physiognomizing (*P'u-t'o Shan*, p. 192).

33. This information came from T'ai-ts'ang himself, who was the most reliable of informants. He categorically denied the other curious stories that circulated about the fire, one of which is recounted by Reichelt in *The Transformed Abbot*, p. 51. Reichelt writes that during the fire (which he dates as February not April) "twenty of the older monks shut themselves inside the temple hall and continued mass until they were consumed in the flames. The abbot, who had been brought out earlier, had to be held back by force from joining the group which, through this 'purging fire,' hoped to enter Nirvana." According to T'ai-ts'ang, no one died in the fire and he himself, far from attempting self-immolation, was several miles away, oblivious of what was happening. The reader can judge from his biography whether self-immolation fits with his character (see p. 351 ff.). Another story T'ai-ts'ang denies is that Chin Shan always burned before a change of dynasty. This, he said, was a rumor put out by the Communists for their own purposes. Finally, there was a rumor that shortly before the fire all the turtles swam from the north to the south bank of the Yangtze. I have never heard T'ai-ts'ang refer to this.

34. In the nineteenth century the monks of the Hai-fu Ssu, Canton, were said to be famous for a medicine made from human excrement. Its preparation took seven years and it was considered efficacious against fever and smallpox. See John Henry Gray, *China, a History of the Laws, Manners and Customs of the People* (London, 1878), II, 124.

35. Literally "prajna tisane of all the buddhas" (*chu-fo po-jo t'ang*). The term is odd because according to the *Tz'u-hai* it is used by monks as a euphemism for wine.

36. Chu-yün, *Chin-shan huo-fo* (The living buddha of Chin Shan; Taipei, 1959), pp. 33-35.

37. *Ibid.*, pp. 29-31. Both these episodes were confirmed by T'ai-ts'ang.

38. Later I did. It is simply the Chinese version of *Om mani padme hum*.

39. Tan-hsü, I, 92-94.

40. Reichelt, *Truth and Tradition*, p. 23.

41. For example, at the Chin-shan Ssu, K'ai-chiang, Szechwan (see pp. 239-240 and p. 443), no ordinary resident was permitted to leave the monastery at all during the summer retreat, while officers on business could not go further away than 80 *li*.

42. See Chapter I, note 26 and p. 141.

CHAPTER V: HEREDITARY AND BRANCH TEMPLES

1. There were various names for the head of a Buddhist monastic institution. The title with the widest scope was *chu-ch'ih*. The abbot (*fang-chang*) of a large public monastery was often referred to as the *chu-ch'ih*. This title was also applied to the monk at the head of an hereditary temple, who could not properly be called a *fang-chang*—although at hybrid institutions (see Appendix V) he might be so called. In other words, a *fang-chang* was always a *chu-ch'ih*, but a *chu-ch'ih* was not necessarily a *fang-chang*. The alternative term for the head of an hereditary

temple was *tang-chia*. The smaller the temple, the more likely he was to be called *tang-chia* and the less likely he was to be called *chu-ch'ih*. At a branch temple he could only be called *tang-chia*, since there was already a *chu-ch'ih* at the head of the parent institution.

Tang-chia was a common term in lay life, applied to the person in charge of a household, business, organization, or a unit thereof. In monasteries it was used not only for the head of a branch temple, but also as an alternative title for the prior (*chien-yüan*) of a public monastery. He was subordinate to the *fang-chang*. Hence at a public monastery *tang-chia* could never mean the head monk while at a small temple it always meant the head monk.

Prip-Møller (p. 204) is misleading when he states that *tang-chia* was the title used by the monks while *chien-yüan* was used by lay people. In Kiangsu province *tang-chia* was used in direct address by everyone. A monk would say to the prior: "Will the *tang-chia* [that is, you] please allow us to do such-and-such . . ." Most lay people would use the same formula because they were unfamiliar with *chien-yüan*, a technical term. But if not addressing him face to face, the monk would usually say of the prior: "The *chien-yüan* has ordered us to do such-and-such . . ." In some provinces, however (for example, Anhwei), *chien-yüan* was used in direct address (see Chapter I, note 19).

As to the *fang-chang*, he might be referred to or addressed as "*ho-shang*" (a term loosely used to mean any monk, but properly meaning an important monk). "*Nin-lao*" (that is, *nin lao-ho-shang*, "you, venerable abbot") was a vocative used for the retired head of a Ch'an monastery; or (if it stood for *nin lao-fa-shih*, "you, venerable dharma master") for the retired head of some other institution; or for any elderly monk.

2. Amano cites figures for areas in Anhwei and Kiangsu showing that the average small temple there owned 100-300 *mou*. Amano Motonosuke, *Shina nōgyō keizai-ron* (The Chinese agricultural economy), 2nd ed. (Tokyo, 1942), I, 68-69. He also cites one or two examples of much higher figures, which I do not accept (see Chapter VIII, note 19).

3. *Hsien-tai fo-hsüeh* (Modern Buddhism) No. 4:27 (December 1950).

4. There had once been forty of those hermitages (*ching-she*), but most were destroyed in the T'ai-p'ing rebellion.

5. The smaller sub-temple at Ch'i-li Tien was in charge of a manager with the rank of secretary or librarian. The manager of the Shao-lung Ssu at Wu-feng Shan had the rank of instructor or secretary, since this branch was much larger. It had a hall of guardian kings, a great shrine-hall, a dharma hall, and a hall for reciting buddha's name. Together with its land it had belonged to Chin Shan since the K'ang-hsi period. This information all comes from the abbot. He did not know how the Shao-lung Ssu had been acquired. In recent decades a common reason why one monastery became the sub-temple of another was its need for repair or expansion. For example, when Yüan-ying became abbot of the Ch'ung-sheng Ssu outside Foochow in 1928, he was asked to take over as its sub-temple down in the city the Fa-hai Ssu, which was in a state of serious delapidation. Within a year he had it wholly repaired. See *Yüan-ying fa-shih chi-nien k'an* (Memorial volume for the Reverend Yüan-ying; Singapore, 1954), p. 13. Some sub-temples were originally built by the parent monastery, as, for example, those that belonged to Pao-hua Shan. See Prip-Møller, pp. 72, 284-285, 289.

6. I can think of only one exception: the Kuang-chi Mao-p'eng at Wu-t'ai Shan,

which was (and is) one of the leading large public monasteries there. See Chapter I, note 4.

7. Many of the larger and stricter hereditary temples had devotions twice a day.

8. But Prip-Møller (p. 302) errs in saying that it belonged to the Vinaya sect. It belonged to the Ts'ao-tung sub-sect of Ch'an.

9. Tokiwa Daijo, *Shina-bukkyō shiseki kinen-shū* (Buddhist monuments in China, memorial collection; Tokyo, 1931), plates 110-135. Cf. Ernst Boerschman, *Picturesque China: Architecture and Landscape* (New York, 1923), pp. 244-249.

10. Abbots were chosen by consultation among senior officers but their choice had to be ratified at a meeting of all the resident monks. Every new abbot received the Ts'ao-tung dharma unless he had it already. The election of abbots will be discussed in Chapter VI.

11. As a guest prefect told Tokiwa Daijo in 1929, it was both a *shih-fang ts'ung-lin* and a *tzu-sun ts'ung-lin*. Tokiwa Daijo, p. 216.

12. The proper name of the building was the Kuan-yin Tien. Ho-shui Yen was the place-name. The building was small and cared for by a verger, who was the only resident monk. A photograph is published in Tokiwa Daijo, plate 124.

13. The Nan P'u-t'o Ssu in Amoy also changed from hereditary to public about 1925. This happened when its head decided to enlarge its scope: the heirs approved and elected the Venerable Hui-ch'üan to come and be its first abbot. In accordance with the new public character of the monastery, he founded a Buddhist seminary there, which under T'ai-hsü became one of the most famous in China. We might note, incidentally, that the previous ancestry of the Nan P'u-t'o was not superseded. Tablets of earlier abbots were retained in the ancestors hall. But the tablets of Hui-ch'üan and his successors, according to my informant, were inscribed "the first (second, third, etc.) generation of the public monastery. . . ."

14. Ts'en Hsüeh-lü, *Hsü-yün ho-shang nien-p'u*, pp. 4-5. There is much doubt as to the reliability of the dates in this autobiography. See Chapter X, note 43.

15. *Yüan-ying fa-shih chi-nien k'an*, p. 12.

16. That is, always *"ho-shang"* never *"shih-fu."*

17. This explains the peculiar passage in Kao-min's code of rules, probably penned by Lai-kuo in the early 1930's. "As to taking disciples and privately collecting donations, because the *ts'ung-lin* is a public place of religion [lit., a place where the way is practised by persons from the ten directions], taking disciples and collecting private donations are major violations of the pure rules. At *ts'ung-lin* there is an ancient and unchanging rule that whenever there are people who come to take refuge in the Three Jewels or who wish to enter the clergy (*ch'u-chia*), the head monk alone should initiate them (*hua-tu*). No officer of the four departments may, within the monastery, take male or female refuges disciples or privately take [tonsure] disciples. If detected the matter will be treated in accordance with the pure rules. Even where it is the head of the monastery who takes disciples into the clergy, they must be over twenty years old and their hair must be shaved off outside the monastery premises in order to avoid involving a public institution (*shih-fang men-t'ing*)." Lai-kuo, 1:68. Cf. above pp. 31, 128.

CHAPTER VI: THE ABBOT

1. In later Indian Buddhism the monasteries did come to have abbots, as at Nalanda in the seventh century.

2. S. Dutt, *Early Buddhist Monachism* (London, 1924), p. 144. In a later work Dutt states that these tribes "knew nothing of personal rule: they deliberated and acted together, were 'communistic' in their property relationships, republican in the conduct of their affairs, and had the tribal council as their organ of government" (*Buddhist Monks and Monasteries of India*, London, 1962, p. 86). My statements about the monastic system in India are based mainly on Dr. Dutt's two books.

3. The sangha officers, discussed in the next paragraph, were governmental, not ecclesiastical appointees. On some sacred mountains, however, a single monk is said to have held over-all authority not as a sangha official but as a hierarch. This position at Omei Shan and Chi-tsu Shan is mentioned in Ts'en Hsüeh-lü, *Hsü-yün ho-shang nien-p'u*, pp. 34, 60; at Wu-t'ai Shan in H. Hackmann, *A German Scholar in the East* (London, 1914), pp. 119, 124; at P'u-t'o Shan in Reverend George Smith, *Narrative of an Exploratory Visit to Each of the Consular Cities of China and to the Islands of Hong Kong and Chusan in the Years 1844, 1845, 1846*, 2nd ed. (London, 1847), p. 314. But the nature of these monks' authority and the manner of their appointment are unclear.

4. The former abbot of the T'ien-ning Ssu stated that he used to receive ten times the fee that other monks received for taking part in a plenary recitation of buddha's name (*p'u-fo*). If others got 10 cash, he got 100. But this was a negligible sum, as was his unearned allowance of 4,000 cash a year. Actually, he was expected to distribute this entire allowance to the four sacristans and dispensers who served as his assistants. The only substantial sums he received were in the form of "incense gifts" (*hsiang-i*) in connection with rites for the dead, or "fruit gifts" (*kuo-i*) as a token of gratitude or respect (see Chapter X, p. 332 and note 41).

5. Two abbots of the T'ien-ning Ssu died in office between 1928 and 1931 (see Appendix VI), as did one abbot of Pao-hua Shan in the 1940's. In all cases the cause of death was said to have been exhaustion, not old age.

6. When T'ai-hsü was chosen abbot of a monastery in 1910, the reason given was that he was held in high esteem by leading officials and gentry. See Yin-shun, p. 42. Blofeld supplies two other illustrations, one of them unedifying. The abbot of a certain monastery, he states, "is reputed to be an opium smoker and to have several concubines, but though he is not respected by pious Buddhists, he serves a useful purpose on account of his friendship with several powerful persons, whose help he has enlisted in preventing any encroachments by provincial or military authorities on the temple property." *Jewel in the Lotus*, pp. 25-26.

7. This happened, for example, at the Chi-le Ssu, Harbin, when T'an-hsü wanted to retire in 1929. The lay supporters and local officials nominated (*kung-t'ui*) Ting-hsi and, when he proved reluctant to accept, persuaded him by saying that they would provide money for the monastery if he ran short. See T'an-hsü, I, 241.

8. Hackmann states that the election of the head of a large hereditary temple in Chekiang needed to be ratified by the government. See his "Buddhist Monastery Life in China," pp. 239-261. My informants denied that such things ever happened

at large institutions during the Republican period. One informant stated that the Shanghai Buddhist Association nominated an abbot for the Ching-an Ssu when its leading monks were arrested as Japanese collaborators after the Second World War. In some notes postdating 1930, Professor Lewis Hodous mentions that the Hangchow Buddhist Society, formed in 1917, brought monasteries "into relation with itself," gave financial help to two of them, and cooperated in selecting five head monks (Hodous papers, Hartford Seminary Foundation, Hartford, Conn.). But such intervention appears to have been most exceptional. Cf. Chapter XI, note 28.

9. It might be, for example, the 5th of the fifth month or the second day of the New Year. The ceremony was simple. If the new abbot was an outsider, it began with his being welcomed at the gate by all the resident monks, who made an obeisance, and escorted him in (chin-shan). The climax of every installation came when he ascended the abbot's seat and preached the dharma there for the first time, holding his emblem of authority.

10. But see Chapter VIII, note 8.

11. Holmes Welch, "Dharma Scrolls and the Succession of Abbots in Chinese Monasteries," T'oung-pao, 50.1-3:93-149 (1963).

12. Translated by D. T. Suzuki in Studies in Zen (London, 1955), p. 12. Dr. Suzuki gives the source as the Ta-tsang fan-wang shuo-wen ching (Sutra on the questions of the Mahapitaka Brahmaraja), which he calls a "spurious text." For my own translation of another version, see Welch, "Dharma Scrolls," p. 147.

13. Yin-shun, p. 49.

14. The Chinese for "tacitly cancelled" was wu-hsing ch'ü-hsiao, which, the abbot explained, meant "without any outward manifestation" (mei-yu piao-shih). This was all he would say on what was apparently a delicate subject.

15. Described by one informant as an Explanation (chiang k'ai-shih) and by another as preaching of the dharma (shuo-fa); while a third recollected that when he had received the dharma the reading of the name gathas (see p. 279) constituted the only preaching of the dharma on the occasion.

16. See Appendix VI, p. 450. On generation characters, see pp. 279 ff.

17. Wu-ming, Jen-en meng-ts'un (Kindnesses remembered; Taipei, 1963), pp. 100-101.

18. One of my informants stated that this system of balloting had been in use at least since the 1920's. A slightly different system was employed at the Nan P'u-t'o Ssu in Amoy after it was transformed from hereditary to public in 1925. At Nan P'u-t'o the franchise was both limited and indirect. Voting rights were given only to monks with the rank of secretary and above, plus six representatives of the rest: two chosen from the rank and file (ch'ing-chung), two from the wandering monks hall, and two from the seminary. A written ballot was only employed when a voice vote had failed to reveal any clear majority. At hereditary monasteries in Szechwan, where the franchise was limited to heirs, the vote in one case was always by written ballot and in another case always by a show of hands (according to single informants).

19. At some monasteries heirs who had gone elsewhere might be notified of the election and return. It was also possible for collateral as well as direct decendants to participate if they happened to be present. Wandering monks might be invited to attend as referees (chien-shih).

20. Including his own tonsure disciple, although this was not particularly

common. It should be noted that a dharma disciple could also be called the "heir" of the monastery whose dharma he held. Strictly speaking, the term "heir" (*tzu-sun*) applies only to tonsure relationships, but many monks use it loosely, so that confusion results. One monk, for example, told me: "Some hereditary temples (*tzu-sun miao*) are hereditary in respect to the dharma; some are hereditary in respect to tonsure." Strictly speaking, only the latter should be called hereditary temples.

21. There were exceptions, of course. Sometimes an•able outsider would be invited to take office if no heir or disciple of the necessary competence was available and if all the family approved. This was much more likely to happen in the case of menial officers (*heng-tan*). I did not learn whether at dharma-type monasteries in provinces other than Hunan, receiving the dharma was a prerequisite for holding a senior office. But it would not necessarily have been a restrictive prerequisite, since there too the number of disciples was often large. An informant who had received the dharma of the Ch'i-t'a Ssu, Ningpo, stated that in all it had one or two thousand disciples. Since he was only the third generation from the abbot who restored the monastery, it would seem as if every monk in the lineage must have taken an average of thirty or more disciples. Yet this informant was one of but ten brothers in his branch and generation. Perhaps the pre-restoration lineage had been preserved. Candidates for the post of abbot at the Ch'i-t'a Ssu were first nominated by the abbot from among all the dharma disciples (*fa-men chia*), who then ratified the slate. The final selection was made by drawing lots.

22. Prip-Møller, p. 146.

23. T'an-hsü, I, 201.

24. Somewhat the same thing happened at the Ch'ung-sheng Ssu, Foochow, in 1928. Ta-pen, the 82-year-old abbot, wanted to retire. He asked Yüan-ying to succeed him, but Yüan-ying persistently refused. Finally Ta-pen fell seriously ill, which made Yüan-ying give in. But as soon as he agreed to take office, Ta-pen made an unexpected recovery. See Tokiwa Daijo, pp. 200-202.

25. *Yüan-ying fa-shih chi-nien k'an*, p. 13. His term is stated to have been six years, but to have begun in 1930 and ended in 1935. Ch'an-ting evidently retired at T'ien-t'ung in 1930 and did not leave for Manchuria until the following year. In 1931 Yüan-ying concurrently headed the Lin-yang Ssu in Foochow.

26. It is not clear that he was abbot of all three at the same time. Another example of concurrent service comes from Nanking. According to one informant, there were two monasteries there, the P'u-te Ssu and the Ku-lin Ssu, which shared the same abbot for about ten years. There was no other connection between them. It happened simply because after the abbot had taken office in the first monastery, the second monastery could find no one better qualified' and persuaded him to take office there too. When he retired, separate successors were appointed.

27. T'an-hsü, II, 227-229.

28. Here and below all parentheses except those enclosing romanizations are in the original text.

29. I have not attempted to translate these two terms, which are enclosed in parentheses in the original text. *Lao ho-shang* usually means the retired abbot, but sometimes it can mean the abbot in office if he has been in office for many years. *Fa ho-shang* presumably means an abbot in a dharma-type monastery.

30. *Fang-chang ch'u* (*ch'u*). The first *ch'u* is written with the word meaning

"potential," "heir." The second *ch'u* is written with a homophonic character meaning "fledgling," "chick." Perhaps the second form of this sarcastic pun implies that the dharma disciples are not only "fledgling abbots," but also "the abbot's chicks" whom he treats with all the favoritism of a mother hen.

31. Perhaps he means tonsure master transmitting to tonsure disciple, or perhaps he means that dharma transmission has become equivalent to this.

CHAPTER VII: RITES FOR THE DEAD

1. Kaushitaki Upanishad 1.2 quoted by E. J. Thomas, *History of Buddhist Thought* (London, 1951), p. 110. Most of the material in these first five paragraphs is taken from pp. 109-110.

2. Anguttara-Nikaya, quoted by B. C. Law, *The Buddhist Conception of Spirits* (London, 1936), pp. 14-15.

3. *Ibid.*, pp. 105-109. I think that Dr. Law may be overstating his case when he says that "a hand-to-hand interchange between a *peta* and man is impossible" (p. 106). The statement by the Buddha that he quotes (see note 2) contradicts this. Today in Theravada countries people still make offerings directly to the pretas as well as to the sangha. If one form of help does not reach them, the other will.

4. *Ibid.*, p. 22. The *Petavatthu* is accepted today as an authentic part of the Pali Canon. See Thomas, *History of Buddhist Thought*, p. 272.

5. Law, *The Buddhist Conception of Spirits*, p. 15.

6. Quoted with slight changes from the Tirokudda-Sutta in *ibid.*, p. 27.

7. Because of the topographical confusion a better rendering of the Chinese *ti-yü* might be "underworld," but I use "hell" because it is customary.

8. The period of forty-nine days is mentioned in the *Abhidharmakosa* of Vasubandhu and is therefore of Indian origin (see Taisho Tripitaka, vol. 29, no. 1558, *chüan* 9). The *Abhidharmakosa* was not translated into Chinese until 567 C.E., but we hear of forty-nine-day services being conducted in the first half of the same century (see Lewis Hodous, *Buddhism and Buddhists in China*, New York, 1924, p. 34). Forty-nine-day services are mentioned in the 39th prohibition of the *Fan-wang ching* (De Groot, *Le Code du Mahayana*, pp. 10, 73). The *Fan-wang ching* has a preface that was written about 400 C.E. although much of the text may be of a later date.

9. Theoretically hungry ghosts are in no position to do harm, nor (according to one view) are orphaned souls: only *li-kuei* are dangerous. But the popular mind does not rely on such distinctions and sees all the uncared-for dead as dangerous. "If the descendants do not supply the necessities, the spirits become angry and wreak vengeance upon the living by sending misfortune" (D. H. Kulp, *Country Life in South China*, New York, 1925, p. 306). Cf. pp. 382-383.

10. Termed *Ti-tsang mao* (Ksitigarbha hats) or *P'i-lu mao* (Vairocana hats). The presiding monks were termed *cheng-tso* or *shou-tso*, while their assistants were *p'ei-tso*. At a large monastery the *cheng-tso* always had the rank of secretary or above.

11. There might only be one presiding monk and as few as four assistants sitting below. The total varied, but was always uneven.

12. For more detailed description of this and other Buddhist rites for the dead, the reader may consult Reichelt's *Truth and Tradition*, pp. 72-126; Clarence Burton Day, *Chinese Peasant Cults* (Shanghai, 1940), pp. 28-31; and J. J. M. De Groot, "Buddhist Masses for the Dead in Amoy," *Actes du Sixième Congrés Internationale des Orientalistes*, pt. 4, sec. 4, pp. 1-120 (Leiden, 1885). De Groot does not name the texts recited, so that it is difficult to identify the ceremonies he is describing, which are in any case highly syncretistic. In the *Religious System of China* (Leyden, 1892) I, 71 ff, 121 ff, 150 ff, he gives somewhat more exact information. It is a pity that De Groot never got beyond the second book of this massive work, the fifth of which was to deal with Buddhism, including the daily life of monks (see I, xiv).

13. *Tso fo-shih* ("to do Buddhist services") can mean either for monks to perform them or for laymen to have them performed. *Ching-ch'an* is an abbreviation for *sung-ching* ("to chant sutras") and *pai-ch'an* ("to recite penances"), but is used as a collective term for all kinds of services.

As a rite for the dead, sutras were usually said to be chanted (*sung*) rather then recited (*nien*). Whereas reciting might be performed without musical instruments, or with only a wooden fish, this type of chanting was always accompanied on the wooden fish, hand-chime, small drum-and-bell, hand gong, and cymbals, so that at least five monks were required to take part.

14. According to one reliable informant, the schedule of rites in Peking was rigid. On the third day after death a *fang yen-k'ou* was performed and a car was burned; on the fifth day a penance was performed (*pai-ch'an*) and a house full of paper ingots was burned; on the seventh day the coffin was sent out of the house for burial or storage. Of the seven sevenths, only the fifth was observed (by burning the paper boat). Rich and poor adhered to this program. In central and south China, according to other informants, there was variation, probably necessitated, among other things, by the different rates of decomposition in different climates.

15. The mourning period was called "three years," but was usually only a little over two. Rites could be held not only on anniversaries of the death of the deceased, but also on his birthdays.

16. In Peking, for example, a family that lived in only one room could still have a tent put up in the courtyard on which it faced; and invite the monks to perform the services there. In Shanghai no such courtyard might be available. A rich family always had the space for an altar, but they might want to have the services performed by the monks of a famous monastery, who were usually unwilling to go outside for such a purpose.

17. According to Reichelt in *Truth and Tradition* (p. 99), "at least 1,000 Chinese dollars is necessary to hold even a very modest 'sea and land mass.'" The highest figures that I have seen come from P'u-t'o Shan. In the late nineteenth century a Shanghai comprador paid £160 for a seven-day mass for his father, who had died in Canton (H. C. DuBose, *Dragon, Demon and Image*, London, 1886, p. 277). In 1907 a Ningpo widow, who was worried about her late husband's defalcations, paid 5,000 taels of silver for what was evidently a plenary mass, with 1,000 monks, drawn from all the temples on the island, taking part in the serpentine recitation of buddha's name and receiving gifts (Boerschmann, *P'u-t'o Shan*, p. 157). In the 1920's the fee was said to run from $1,000 to $5,000 (Robert F. Fitch, *Pootoo Itineraries*, Shanghai, 1929, pp. 40-42). Even a one-day

service by seven monks cost $60 in 1908 (Boerschmann, *P'u-t'o Shan*, pp. 151-156).

18. The ones in my possession are in denominations of $50,000, $100,000, and $1,000,000 (see Fig. 38). They are issued by the Bank of Hell (*ming-t'ung yin-hang*). Some bear the portrait of the bank president, the Jade Emperor, and are stated to be "for circulation in heaven and hell"—presumably indicating that heavenly officials too can be bribed.

19. The small ingots, shaped like a double axe-head were called *chin-ting, yin-ting* (gold, silver ingots) and weighed—when they were made of metal—about ten ounces. The large ingots, shaped like a hat, were called *yüan-pao* and weighed fifty ounces.

20. This penance was performed during the 1963 drought in Hong Kong and used to be performed during droughts in north China. According to De Groot, the text usually recited to bring rain was the *Ta yün-lun ch'ing-yü ching*. For a detailed description of the rites performed to change the weather and drive away locusts, see De Groot, *Le Code du Mahayana*, pp. 148-159.

21. J. Prip-Møller, *About Buddhist Temples*, p. 29. (This booklet was published by the North China Union Language School, Peiping, soon after the author had delivered it as a paper there on November 19, 1931. Elsewhere in these notes, a reference to "Prip-Møller" is a reference to his major work, *Chinese Buddhist Monasteries.*)

22. Fitch, *Pootoo Itineraries*, p. 43.

23. Lai-kuo, 1:55b. Presumably R. F. Fitch was unaware of this.

24. The term *ying-fu* was used as early as 1735 when the Ch'ien-lung emperor issued a decree ordering that *ying-fu* monks who were married (and the phrasing implies that all of them were married and that they drank wine and ate meat) be returned to lay life or live properly in a proper monastery. See J. J. M. De Groot, *Sectarianism and Religious Persecution in China* (Amsterdam, 1903) I, 123-127. I have heard of such monks in a Hakka area near Chaochow during the Republican period, but, according to my informant, they were called *ho-shang*. In the Republican period the term *ying-fu seng* appears to have been used mainly to refer to vegetarian, celibate monks who lived in the monastery, but performed Buddhist services outside it. *Ying-fu* is also used as a verb. For example, the Kao-min code of rules says that its monks "will never go out on call (*ying-fu*) to perform major or minor Buddhist services" (Lai-kuo, 1:41b). "It would be preferable for them to have nothing to eat in the refectory but hot water and to carry on their meditation with empty stomachs" (Lai-kuo, 1:55; cf. 2:69). Nan Huai-chin (pp. 14-15) states that the term *ying-men* was applied to call monks, especially in Fukien and Chekiang during the late Ch'ing and early Republic.

25. Until about 1938, when the decline in land rents under the Japanese occupation made it necessary to economize.

26. The Liu-yün Ssu had a different system of recording fees. Before each service a notice was hung up outside the guest department giving the time the services would be held and the names of all the monks assigned to it. These notices would be copied into a "services book" (*ching-ch'an pu*) by the guest prefect on duty. Another "services book" (*fo-shih pu*) was kept in parallel. When each performance was over, one strike of the character *cheng* ("orthodox") was entered next to the name of every monk who had participated. Since *cheng* had

five strokes, it was an easy matter to add up, divide by five, and compare with the figure in the other services book.

One other difference was that at the Liu-yün Ssu officers did not receive a share of the income from Buddhist services, but a fixed allowance (*tan-yin*). In 1931-1937 it was $3 a month (Chinese currency)—much more than at rural monasteries (see p. 330).

27. See Chapter I, note 27.

28. The *Yen-shou ching,* that is, the *Yao-shih hsiao-tsai yen-shou ching* (Sutra of Bhaisajyaguru for annulment of disasters and prolongation of life).

29. See pp. 90-100.

30. Fitch, *Pootoo Itineraries,* pp. 42-43. Boerschmann states: "Almost all the fishermen and boat people along the coast come [to P'u-t'o Shan] once a year and have a service performed in one of the temples." Boerschmann, *P'u-t'o Shan,* p. 151.

31. According to the Confucian tradition there was only one principal tablet, termed *shen-chu* rather than *shen-wei,* and it was usually kept in the family shrine at home. In Buddhist temples the term *shen* ("god or great spirit") was avoided. If it was the layman who ordered the carving of the tablet, it might bear the characters *shen-wei,* but as one old abbot snorted: "How could they be *shen?*" When temples ordered the tablets, the characters incised were *lien-wei,* "lotus seat." The only *chu* tablets I have seen in Buddhist temples were collective ones, representing several generations of ancestors.

32. Particularly meaning rebirth in the Western Paradise. This hall was termed a *shui-lu t'ang* at Chin Shan and other monasteries where the majority of tablets were installed at the end of a plenary mass (*shui-lu*). No tablets in the *shui-lu t'ang* came from "volunteer plenary masses," since the tablets put up for those were all made of paper and were burned at the end of the seven days. But Chin Shan's resident monks were offered a 50 percent discount if they wished to install tablets in its *shui-lu t'ang* for their masters or family. Few took advantage of the offer because few had the necessary $50 (the usual price to laymen being $100).

33. This term was also used for the quarters assigned to aged monks.

34. It was also known by euphemisms that would be the envy of American morticians, for example, "pagoda of the sea of happiness" (*fu-hai t'a*).

CHAPTER VIII: THE ECONOMY OF MONASTERIES

1. Prip-Møller, p. 372. At Pao-hua Shan a remnant of the ancient Buddhist custom was preserved in that every day monks filed over to the refectory for the noon meal holding their bowls before them. This was termed *t'o-po,* the standard term for begging with a bowl.

2. Smith, *Narrative,* p. 353; and Justus Doolittle, *Social Life of the Chinese,* rev. Paxton Hood (London, 1868), p. 185. Cf. De Groot, *Le Code du Mahayana,* pp. 196-199.

3. Prip-Møller, p. 366. Of course, this prohibition might apply only to begging by individuals.

4. T'an-hsü, I, 148.

5. Such monks had the finesse of a fund-raiser in the "Special Gifts Section."

There were probably also house-to-house solicitors, though I have heard little about them in the Republican period. A nineteenth-century missionary in Canton writes: "Mendicant friars generally travel in companies of three, two beating small gongs to announce their approach, whilst the third carries on a stand a small idol of Buddha to induce those whom they meet to contribute to the fund which they have established for the restoration of decayed monasteries. In the busy streets of Canton I once saw a Chinese shoemaker forcibly eject three such begging intruders from his shop." Gray, I, 112. De Groot describes the same thing in *Le Code du Mahayana*, p. 200.

6. John Shryock, *The Temples of Anking* (Paris, 1931), p. 74.

7. Joseph Edkins, *Chinese Buddhism* (London, 1890), p. 271. I have never heard of this practice in connection with Buddhist monasteries, though it was and is extremely common for temples of the popular religion (*shen-miao*) to have plays on the birthdays of their gods.

8. This is what I have been told by my informants and it agrees with H. Doré, *Researches into Chinese Superstitions* (Shanghai, 1917), IV, 354-355. It is contradicted by V. Burkhardt, *Chinese Creeds and Customs* (Hong Kong, 1955), II, 168; and by David Crockett Graham, *Religion in Szechwan Province, China* (Washington, 1928), vol. 80, no. 4 of Smithsonian Miscellaneous Collections, pp. 47-48. Graham mentions that in Szechwan the blocks are called *yin-yang-kua*. Doré gives their name as *pei-chiao* or *chiao-kua*. In Hong Kong I have heard them referred to as *mu-pei*. Perhaps the manner of interpreting their fall differed from place to place.

9. See, for example, F. E. Forbes, *Five Years in China* (London, 1848), p. 161, and Little, pp. 68 and 93. In the Republican period the T'an-che Ssu outside Peking is said to have offered accommodations for "a fixed tariff." See L. C. Arlington and William Lewisohn, *In Search of Old Peking* (Peking, 1935), p. 316. Compare Harry A. Franck's discovery of a five-dollar minimum at most monasteries on P'u-t'o Shan. See *Roving Through Southern China* (New York, 1925), p. 28.

10. Chinese pilgrims, including some who made the pilgrimage to Omei, have told me that none of their monastery hosts ever named the sum they should pay for eating or staying there, or objected that they had not given enough. They were surprised when I told them about the Western accounts cited because, they said, the monks were even more courteous to foreigners.

John Blofeld, who stayed at many monasteries in the 1930's, writes: "Guests are welcome at any time to stay for a meal, a night, or a year, and are expected to make a gift of money to the temple according to their means, but there are no fixed rates for such hospitality" (*Jewel In The Lotus*, p. 57). Cf. Prip-Møller, p. 139. Missionaries who used to stay in the monasteries on Omei Shan have told me the same thing. I have myself overheard the guest prefect of a mountain monastery in Hong Kong stubbornly refuse to name a figure to a party of lay visitors who kept asking "How much will it cost us to have lunch?" In the end they offered a most niggardly sum, but he still repeated "It's up to you." It is hard to reconcile this with accounts like that of A. J. Little, cited in note 9.

11. Little (see note 9) says that his donation was recorded in a *yüan-pu*. Normally a *yüan-pu* was only used for recording donations made for some special purpose, like the rebuilding of a shrine-hall. Perhaps the *yüan-pu* was brought out as a hint that Little's donation was expected to be a large one. According to one monk from Omei Shan, donations books there were usually termed *hsiao-yin pu*

and donations were usually termed *kung-te*, not *hsiang-yu* as in Hong Kong and elsewhere, where *hsiang-yu pu* is the common term for the book. See Chapter X, note 41.

12. Sometimes the stalls might be inside the monastery, and sometimes the vendor might be a menial officer who was old or sick and was therefore being permitted by the prior to earn a little money. In either case casual visitors would think that the stall was being operated by the monastery whereas, in fact, it was entirely a private enterprise. The less reputable small temples, however, might be ready to sell incense—or anything else.

13. Nan Huai-chin, pp. 31-32, 58. Farm work also violated the tenth *pacittiya* rule that a bhiksu should not dig the ground or show others how to dig it. The earliest proponent of manual labor for monks may have been Tao-hsin, the Fourth Patriarch (580-651 C.E.), who made rules requiring it of his disciples. See Heinrich Dumoulin, *A History of Zen Buddhism* (New York, 1963), pp. 102-108.

14. Prip-Møller, p. 121.

15. C. K. Yang, *Religion in Chinese Society* (Berkeley, 1961), p. 319.

16. *Ta-ch'ing lü-li hsin-tseng t'ung-tsuan chi-ch'eng* (New enlarged comprehensive edition of Ch'ing legal code; Shao-chou, 1898), 8:23.

17. It was certainly impossible if they followed the schedule given in the Ch'ing dynasty edition of Pai-chang's *Pure Rules*. See I-jun Yüan-hung, ed., *Pai-chang ts'ung-lin ch'ing-kuei cheng-i chi* (Pai-chang's pure rules for large monasteries with explanatory notes; Yangchow, 1917), 8.2:10-16.

18. Most of Ku Shan's eighty-three acres of paddy lay near Foochow and were tilled by lay laborers (*chai-kung*) under the direction of a fields overseer (*t'ien-t'ou*) who lived in a sub-temple there. Chin Shan had a few *mou* close to the monastery that were tilled by its own workmen. Ch'i-hsia Shan's workmen tilled the small area (about 100 *mou*) of nearby paddy under the supervision of a clerk.

19. According to an article by a leftist writer, the T'an-che Ssu outside Peking owned 43,000 *mou*, 2,000 of which were cultivated by hired labor and the remainder rented out for 4,000-5,000 *tan* per year—representing an average rental per *mou* so low that it seems likely that the figure of 43,000 included wasteland. (See T'ang Hu-lu, "Ku-ch'a o-seng," Hong Kong *Hsin-wan pao*, January 21, 1965.) I have been unable to find a monk who had first-hand knowledge of this monastery's finances. In the nineteenth century Edkins described it as the richest temple in the Western Hills, with an income of 12,000 silver taels, or £3,000-4,000. (See Edkins, *Chinese Buddhism*, p. 252.) About 1924, J. B. Pratt, who spent several days there, was told that it owned 365 villages with their rice fields, so that it "devoured one village a day" (Pratt, p. 325). A Chinese layman who used to go there estimated that in the early 1920's it had one or two hundred monks, who dwindled to a few dozen by 1948. According to him, the monks cultivated the land themselves, a statement supported by Arlington and Lewisohn (*In Search of Old Peking*, p. 316). This is a monastery known casually to many living persons, but about which more reliable information is needed.

Even larger landholdings are attributed to a monastery in Su-ch'ien *hsien*, northern Kiangsu. The Chi-le An is said to have owned 200,000 *mou*. It was a "feudal landowner" with its monks busy throughout the year collecting rents and making loans. The abbot had wives, concubines, and children, and lived in quarters "ten times finer than the *hsien* government." Even the monks who served as village agents had wives or concubines. The monastery was equipped with dozens of rifles, automatic pistols, knives, and spears, with which it could impose its demands on its tenants and defend its property against confiscation. See Wu Shou-p'eng, "Tou-liu yü nung-ts'un ching-chi shih-tai ti Hsü Hai ko shu" (How areas around Süchow and Haichow have lagged behind in a rural economy), *Tung-fang tsa-chih* (Eastern miscellany) 27.6:79 (March 25, 1930). Although it is neither accurate nor typical, this is one of the very few references to monastery landlords that has been translated for the Western reader (*Agrarian China*, ed. Institute of Pacific Relations, London, 1939, pp. 12-13). It has also been made available to the Japanese reader by Amano Motonosuke in *Shina nōgyō keizai-ron*, I, 67, along with figures for other monasteries that are exaggerated or hearsay (for example, the "tens of thousands of *mou*" that Amano attributes to Chin Shan). A less inflated estimate of the land owned by the Chi-le Ssu is given by Ta-hsing, *K'ou-yeh chi* (A gadfly's collected writings; Wuchang, 1934), p. 109, where, writing on October 1, 1929, he states that the Chi-le An had 50,000-60,000 *mou*. This land had just then been confiscated by the *hsien* government partly because the head monks did not keep the pure rules and were selling off monastic property.

20. Under the Ch'ing dynasty and again under the Communists, what the Nationalists call T'ai-hsien was (and is) called T'ai-chou or T'ai-chou Shih; and what the Nationalists call Chiang-yen was (and is) called T'ai-hsien. Chin Shan kept to the traditional usage, and I do the same to avoid ambiguity.

21. Prices on the Shanghai rice market usually reached their peak in May and June, but shipment in these months was prevented by the fact that nearly all available labor was engaged in planting the new crop. See William Rhoads Murphey, III, *Shanghai: Key to Modern China* (Cambridge, Mass., 1953), pp. 142-143.

22. *China Handbook 1937-1945* (New York, 1947), p. 430. Another source states that the mean size of farms in China was 21 *mou* and that the average farm had 5.6 separate plots. A. Kaiming Chiu, "Agriculture," in *China*, ed. H. F. McNair (Berkeley, 1946), pp. 477-478.

23. These village foremen (*chuang-t'ou*) were usually tenants themselves. Although it was their duty to notify the rest of the tenants and otherwise assist when rent was to be collected, they did not, like village agents, live in the village office. Another difference was that they were called on to act as middlemen and witnesses in certifying the sale of tillage rights (see Appendix VII, p. 454). For carrying out their duties, they were paid "a little something" by the monastery. There were village foremen in I-cheng, Yangchow, Chiang-ning, and Chen-chiang (see Appendix IX, p. 460 for a list of Chin Shan's land holdings). In T'ai-chou the two tenants who looked after the village agency were called neither "village agents" nor "village foremen," but simply "tenants." There *were* village foremen there, but they had no special relationship with the monastery, although they might be asked to serve as guarantors of a lease.

In contradistinction to both agents and foremen, there were also township and village headmen (*hsiang-chang* and *ts'un-chang*) who were responsible to the government rather than to the landowner. The landowner might call on them to arbitrate a dispute about rents. According to Ch'ü T'ung-tsu, who cites the *Ch'ing hui-tien* 4:3, *ts'un-chang* and *chuang-t'ou* were alternative titles for the head of a village "elected" by the villagers to take charge of local affairs (*Local Government in China under the Ch'ing*, Cambridge, Mass., 1962, p. 2).

24. Leases in some other areas are said to have run three years initially, but it is not clear whether these included fixed-rent leases like those of Chin Shan. See Morton H. Fried, *Fabric of Chinese Society* (New York, 1953), p. 108.

25. On the weight of a *tan* or picul, see Appendix IX, note 4. Here it is generally about 120 *chin* or catties, that is, about 160 pounds.

26. Neither did any other monastery I have studied. A share of about 40 percent of the crop was the commonest form of rent in Ch'u-hsien, just across the border in Anhwei, and this or a higher percentage was standard in north China. In Ch'u-hsien, even the fixed rents were the equivalent of about 40 percent of the average crop. (See Fried, pp. 102, 106.) In Kiangsu, when landlords other than monasteries received a fixed rent, it was also the equivalent of about 40 percent of the crop: see Fei Hsiao-t'ung, *Peasant Life in China* (London, 1939), p. 188; and Yen Chung-p'ing et al., *Chung-kuo chin-tai ching-chi shih, t'ung-chi tzu-liao hsüan-chi* (History of China's modern economy, selected statistical materials; Peking, 1955), pp. 303-304. Thus monasteries appear to have been satisfied with lower than average rents. Perhaps that was because they were old-fashioned in their outlook—like the gentry, who used to demand less from their tenants than the *arriviste* urban investors (Fei Hsiao-t'ung, p. 187). Perhaps another reason monasteries took less rent was their respect for the Buddhist tradition of compassion.

27. In Kiangsu during the mid-1930's the tax averaged 3.11 percent of what the owner had actually paid for his paddy land. This amount included surcharges as well as the ordinary land tax (*Chinese Year Book,* Shanghai, 1935, p. 845).

28. See p. 203 and Chapter VII, note 32.

29. This figure seems low and awaits confirmation.

30. This total fits with the $20,000 average total income recollected by the abbot, particularly since the figure on sale of paddy is conservative. For a fuller calculation of land rents, see Appendix IX.

31. Fei Hsiao-t'ung, p. 190.

32. Hence his name is listed among the supporters of the monastery. See Chu Chieh-hsien, ed., *Ch'i-hsia shan-chih* (History of Ch'i-hsia Shan; Hong Kong, 1962), p. 97.

33. There were 117 parcels, of which 39 were 2 *mou* and under and 35 were 2-5 *mou*. Thus while the average size was 12 *mou*, this was only because of a few large parcels (there were seven with 40 to 215 *mou*). A listing of all the parcels is given in Chu Chieh-hsien, pp. 123-132. While no information is available on how many of the small parcels were the sole livelihood of the tenants who rented them, the tenant who depended on a 2 *mou* parcel could not have had an easy time of it.

34. Since interest on loans to peasants in the Yangtze Valley averaged 28 percent per annum (Chiu, p. 476) this figure is hard to accept. The abbot, I believe, supplied a "round-number" illustration in which the value of land was unusually high. On a *mou* worth $30, for example, the monastery would loan $15, but still expect interest of one *tan*, worth $4 and equivalent to 27 percent a year.

35. Fei Hsiao-t'ung reports a different practice in Kaihsienkung. "After a definite period, if the borrower cannot pay back the capital as well as the interest, he is forced to transfer his title over the land, limited to the subsoil, to the lender." Fei Hsiao-t'ung, p. 183. If his title was limited to the subsoil, then he was a landlord, not a tenant, so that the cases are not comparable. Cornelius Osgood, on the

other hand, states that near Kunming "if the interest was not paid, the lender could collect his security and the borrower was helpless to intervene" (*Village Life in Old China*, New York, 1963, p. 132).

36. At P'u-t'o Shan, for example, donations reached their peak on the birthday of Kuan-yin (the 19th of the second month).

37. For example, by Hodous, p. 65. Hodous states that it had 2,000 monks, but my informants say that this figure was only reached during the ordination of 1920, shortly before Hodous was writing. The claim that T'ien-ning was the largest monastery in China could only be valid if restricted to Chinese Buddhism. The Tibetan Buddhist monastery of Kumbum, Tsinghai, had 3,000 lamas (see L. T. Wu, *China as She Is*, Shanghai, 1934, p. 298; cf. T. J. Norbu, *Tibet Is My Country*, London, 1960, p. 112).

38. Thus the monastery's customers bought not only 5,000 *tan* of rent grain and 5,000 *tan* of interest grain, but also about 1,000 *tan* of interest on grain loans and 3,300 *tan* bought by the monastery from its tenants. Assuming 40 *tan* of paddy per family per year, this means that about 360 families in Changchow could buy their rice from the T'ien-ning Ssu. This is not an improbably high figure in a city of over 100,000 population.

39. See Kenneth K. S. Ch'en, *Buddhism in China: A Historical Survey* (Princeton, 1964), p. 157.

40. For example, from 1912 on the garrison commander of Changchow, Tanyang, and Wusih, Mr. Liu Yüan-chang, had been a loyal patron and protector of the T'ien-ning Ssu. Whenever the monastery ran into trouble and the Venerable Yeh-k'ai asked him to help, "he would send some of his soldiers to put things right." (This information comes from his son.) In 1927, as a follower of Sun Ch'uan-fang who was deposed by the Nationalists in the Northern Expedition, Liu went into retirement like so many other conservative patrons of Buddhism. From a documentary source we learn that in the Wusih area before 1927 rents had been easy to collect, but after that year, "as a result of tenants' riots," the landlord's position deteriorated (*Agrarian China*, p. 7).

41. Banknotes became the sole legal tender and silver coin in banks was nationalized on November 3, 1935 (*China Year Book*, Shanghai, 1939, p. 239). Serious inflation, however, did not begin until 1937.

42. I failed to ascertain whether this was $60,000 in the currency of the time, which was rapidly becoming inflated, or the equivalent of $60,000 in pre-1937 currency.

43. In other areas of Szechwan the rents were a fixed amount equivalent to 70-80 percent of the rice crop and there was no abatement in bad years. See Vincent S. R. Brandt, "Landlord-Tenant Relations in Republican China," *Papers on China*, 17:225-226 (Harvard University, East Asian Research Center).

44. Pao-hua Shan near Nanking—3,000 *mou;* the Ling-yen Ssu in Soochow—3,000 *mou;* the Kuang-hsiao Ssu in northern Kiangsu—2,000 *mou;* the Jen-jui Ssu in Hunan—3,000 *mou;* the Chu-sheng Ssu in Hunan—2,000 *mou;* the T'ien-t'ung Ssu near Ningpo—no figures collected; Ku Shan near Foochow—apparently over 2,000 *mou.*

45. For example, according to one informant, the Shou-ning Ssu in Ying-ch'eng, Hupeh, was subsidized by the local Buddhist association.

46. See L. S. Yang, "Buddhist Monasteries and Four Money-Raising Institutions in Chinese History," *Studies in Chinese Institutional History* (Cambridge, Mass.,

1961), pp. 198-224. As to pawnbroking, Mr. Vincent S. Shui informs me that during the Japanese occupation of Peking the heirs and wives of certain old families "pawned art objects and rare editions at the Kuang-chi Ssu and Fa-yüan Ssu, Peking." I have not had the opportunity to ask an officer of these monasteries if it was a regular practice there.

47. Chiu, pp. 480-482.

CHAPTER IX: ENTERING THE SANGHA

1. Yang, p. 332.

2. M. Huc, *Journey Through the Chinese Empire* (New York, 1856), II, 193-194.

3. Hackmann, *Buddhism as a Religion,* p. 218. The cases that were "personally known" to Hackmann may all have been at the Chen-hsiang Ssu, Chekiang. Hackmann lived there from November 1, 1901 through April 1902 and states: "Adults rarely enter the monastery. It is a custom to introduce fresh blood from the very young, who are resigned as children of poor peasant families by their parents in return for payment. The little ones are brought at the age of from two to three years of age into the monastery. About twenty-five Mexican dollars are paid for such abdication of parental rights to the monastery. Now and then a family in time of sickness or death freely devotes one of their children to a monastic life . . . The children are, I have observed, well fed and carefully and kindly treated." Of the several child novices who were at this hereditary temple during Hackmann's stay, three were still two to five years old. See Hackmann, "Buddhist Monastery Life," p. 254.

4. Pratt, p. 337.

5. Blofeld, *Wheel of Life,* pp. 163-164.

6. Prip-Møller (p. 299) also states that "the average age of the ordinands varies from twenty to thirty." In this book I give ages according to Chinese reckoning, by which a person is one year old at birth and a year is added to his age each New Year's Day; so that a child born on the last day of the last lunar month would be counted as two years old on the 1st day of the first month, although by our reckoning he would be only two days old.

7. Smith, *Narrative,* p. 307.

8. Gray, I, 119.

9. This area is shown as the "cradle of monks" on the end-paper map at the back of the book.

10. The 1931 census (see Appendix I, table 1, note b) gave figures for the number of monks for each *hsien* of Kiangsu. The three highest were Tung-t'ai, Ju-kao, and T'ai *hsien,* all lying within the parallelogram. Of the ten highest, six lay within it and had 13,404 monks versus 8,045 in the other four, which included the cities of Nanking and Shanghai. Many of these 8,045 too must have been monks from the parallelogram who had moved south to staff the large monasteries there. The great majority of the high officers of Ch'i-hsia Shan and Pao-hua Shan in southern Kiangsu came from the parallelogram in the north, according to the small sample in the ordination yearbooks.

11. The explanation in terms of poverty in the north was given to me only by

persons who come from the southern part of the province. A layman from I-cheng, north of the river, said that T'ai, Tung-t'ai, and Ju-kao *hsien* were prosperous and that the farmland there was good. As to the preponderance of north Kiangsu people among some of the lower castes, he attributed it to the propinquity of Yangchow, a great center of the salt trade that was noted for the luxury and fastidiousness of its merchants, who liked bathing and massage. Even in Peking, according to this informant, the best bath stewards and masseurs came from northern Kiangsu and had been trained in the Yangchow tradition.

Despotic landlordism and tenant poverty in northern Kiangsu is depicted by some contemporary writers (see *Agrarian China,* p. 11-15). But most of the areas to which they refer lie outside the parallelogram (that is, in the northwest corner and along the coast). The relationship between poverty and monasticism in this province could best be illuminated by figures showing the economic condition of individual *hsien*—figures that, so far as I know, are not available.

12. Ch'en, pp. 33, 40-42. P'eng-ch'eng, where the earliest Buddhist community was mentioned in 65 C.E., is today's T'ung-shan in northwestern Kiangsu about 140 miles from the parallelogram under discussion.

13. It was generally supposed to be very low. Even John Blofeld, a friendly observer, states that "the standard of learning in the temples is so low that the majority of monks repeat the sutras without understanding anything of their meaning." *Jewel in the Lotus* (London, 1948) p. 27.

14. *Hsien-tai fo-hsüeh,* No. 4:33 (December 1950). The Communists would have no reason to exaggerate the literacy of the monks.

15. *Hsien-tai fo-hsüeh,* No. 33:12 (May 1953).

16. *Hsien-tai fo-hsüeh,* No. 34:12 (June 1953).

17. *China Year Book,* 1926, p. 426. The Chinese Communists sometimes give an even higher figure; 85 percent is mentioned in *Handbook of People's China* (Peking, 1957), p. 149.

18. There is one troublesome item of evidence to the contrary. J. B. Pratt writes that during his wide-ranging inspection of Buddhism in China in 1923-1924 he made it a point to ask the meaning of "Namo O-mi-t'o-f'o." He did this as "a kind of intelligence test for the monks . . . I found a good many monks that knew all about it and repeated it intelligently. But I should say that about fifty percent of the monks I asked proved to be as ignorant as the young man in the Fa Hua Ssu [in Peking]. Sometimes they had a dim notion that it had something to do with 'surrender,' frequently they only knew that they repeated it a good many times a day. The climax is reached in Annam where some of the monks take literally the Chinese characters by which the Sanskrit sound *Namas* is expressed. These characters mean *south no.* So they repeat these pious words over and over, thinking that they mean "The South has no O-mi-to Buddha! The South has no O-mi-to Buddha!'" (Pratt, pp. 331-332).

I have never met a monk whose ignorance even approached this. Those with the poorest education, who could scarcely write, were still ready at the drop of a hat to explain the doctrine of the Western Paradise and how to get there, that is, by reciting "Namo O-mi-t'o-f'o." If there is anything all monks have in common, it is this. Pratt was a reliable observer. We cannot dismiss his evidence. How can it be reconciled with the rest of what we know? He visited more temples in the outlying provinces where Buddhism was in decay than in the central provinces where it was flourishing. According to Mrs. Pratt, who accompanied him on many of his temple visits, the monk that he (like other visitors) most often talked to was the one in charge of the great shrine-hall, that is, the verger. This office was a menial one, often given to a poor brother who needed "tips" and seldom to a monk who was devoted to study or to religious cultivation. In decayed temples the quality of the vergers was doubtless even lower than in temples where Buddhism was flourishing. So if they made up the sample to whom this intelligence test was given, the score would naturally be low (just as it would be, for example, if we went from church to church in English industrial towns and asked the sexton about the meaning of the Holy Trinity).

19. These two cases are given in English-language sources. In the first a young man got into a "violent altercation" with his fiancee's father, who broke off their engagement. Although he was "of good family and prosperous," he decided to enter the monastic life which had, he said, "this advantage—that there were always superiors to order him where to go and what to do instead of leaving him to the risks of following his own will." See W. J. Clennell, *Historical Development of Religion in China* (London, 1917), pp. 99-101. The second case involved the scion of a family of rich gold and silver merchants in Tsinan. In his second year at Peking University his grandmother decided that he should marry the daughter of a magistrate, although he was actually in love with a poor relation who lived in their house, almost as a servant—a situation like that in *The Dream of the Red Chamber*. Their plans to elope were discovered. The girl was spirited away, and he searched for her without success. Running out of money far from home, he joined the army of an anti-Nationalist warlord. The next year (1926) the Nationalists were victorious and along with several other officers he had no way out but to enter a monastery. He could not forget his love and was utterly miserable as a monk—so miserable that he fell ill. A devout layman took pity on him, brought him home, treated him, and got him genuinely interested in Buddhism. Later the layman died, and when the rite of "releasing the burning mouths" was held on his behalf, his spirit spoke to the monk, who from that time on began to make progress in meditation and eventually reached a state of peace and "true happiness. . . . In the silence and stillness of my own mind I find answers to all the riddles of life." See Blofeld, *Jewel in the Lotus,* pp. 68-84.

20. It is interesting that Prip-Møller (p. 299) was told by a former monk that "at least 70% of those who enter the monkhood do so because they see no way out of their earthly difficulties."

21. Another north Kiangsu informant had an uncle and great uncle who were monks. One of the reasons he decided to enter the sangha himself was because his uncle looked so grand when he came to the house dressed in a yellow robe. "I was much impressed," he said. "I was only nine years old and knew nothing about Buddhism, but my parents approved of my decision to become a monk."

22. This was reported by several other informants, who regarded it as indicating that they had been destined from birth to become monks. One informant showed me a photograph of a disciple whose head he had shaved at the age of four. "He had been a vegetarian since birth," he said, pointing to the serious-looking four-year-old, dressed in a robe and full regalia. "What he was most opposed to was eating nonvegetarian food." The by-standers to our conversation, mostly female devotees, burbled over the picture: "Isn't he adorable! Isn't he adorable!" Would they, as *mothers,* have been less enthusiastic about his leaving the family?

23. See Chapter XI, note 6.

24. Tan-hsü, pp. 43-49.

25. Reichelt, *Truth and Tradition*, p. 232.

26. The Chinese *chieh* is equivalent to the Sanskrit *sila*. It may be translated as "prohibition," "vows," "precepts," or "ordination." To be ordained is to take the vows, that is, to accept the prohibitions.

27. His tonsure master was an officer of the Kao-min Ssu, also a model institution. Curiously enough, when Bishop Smith was at T'ien-t'ung in 1845, he was told that a child novice he saw there would have to wait until he was sixteen to be ordained (Smith, *Narrative*, p. 186). Could monasteries have become less strict about ordination age over the course of the last century? At Ku Shan in 1916 not a single ordinee was under twenty. In 1925 six were from twenty down to sixteen. The same was true in 1932, but that year two were *under* sixteen. One of my own informants was ordained in 1939 at the age of twelve, and he said there were a few other ordinees his age. All this suggests a pattern of change.

28. Besides *t'i-tu ming* (or *t'i-t'ou ming*), it was also called the tabooed name (*hui-ming*); the inside name (*nei-ming*), a term used by monks from Fukien province; and the dharma name (*fa-ming*). This last, however, was an ambiguous term, since it could refer to other religious appellations like the name given to a Refuges or dharma disciple. I generally use it to refer to the latter only.

29. The style was also termed *hao* or *fa-hao;* or "outside name" (*wai-ming*), again especially among Fukienese monks. *Tzu* or *piao-tzu,* was the official term used in ordination certificates and yearbooks.

30. T'ai-hsü, for example, used *ch'ang* for his first three disciples and *ta* for his last nine. See Yin-shun, pp. 15-16.

31. Such a second style would be termed a *hao*, not a *tzu*.

32. For example, Ming-ch'ang, of the 46th generation in the Chin Shan lineage did not alter the *ch'ang* in his style, although an ancestor of the 43rd generation, who served as abbot of Chin Shan, was Ch'ang-ching Mi-ch'uan. This may have been because *ch'ang* was merely in the latter's style. But according to one informant, any character in an ancestor's dharma name *or* style was taboo; and Min-chih Yin-hsin, the abbot of the T'ien-ning Ssu in the 44th generation, who had originally been styled Ming-chih, changed *ming* to *min* because his ancestor of the 42nd generation had been styled Ming-ching (see p. 450). Yet in the 25th and 27th generations of the Chin Shan lineage (probably sixteenth century) there was one disciple who was given a dharma name that included the same character as his "grandfather's" dharma name. They were Pao-feng Ming-hsüan and Wu-wen Ming-ts'ung (*hsüan* and *ts'ung* were the generation characters). This suggests that the modern application of the taboo had not yet begun. One informant stated that a monk would change only his style because of the taboo: he would not change his tonsure name. But Yüan-ying is said to have changed his tonsure name from Chin-wu to Hung-wu when he received the dharma of the Ch'i-t'a Ssu (Yin-shun, p. 29). Evidently the practice was elastic in many respects. About all that can be safely said is that in some provinces in recent decades there has been greater or lesser observance of name taboos, depending on the amount of respect that a monk wished to show toward his dharma forebears. The observance of name taboos among the laity is of Confucian origin and has been common in China since early times.

33. A few monks belonged to minor, little known sub-sects the name gathas of which are not listed in the *Ch'an-men jih-sung*. A monk who belonged, for example,

to the Vairocana sect (P'i-lu p'ai) told me that "it originated in the Liang dynasty before the division into sects. The ancestor of the first generation was Chih-kung." He added that this kind of lineage was particularly common in the northeast. Tokiwa mentions that the only monk left at Yün-men Shan in 1928 did not belong to the Yün-men sect, but to the P'u-t'i sect (Tokiwa Daijo, pp. 91-92).

34. More can also be found in my article "Dharma Scrolls," pp. 136-140.

35. He was the source of information on the Fu-hu Ssu given in Appendix V.

36. In a way it resembles the system practiced during the T'ang and Sung dynasties, when a stage as "postulant" preceded the stage of novice or *sramanera*. "In China a majority of the order preferred to remain as *sramanera*" and not to receive the full ordination—a very different picture from recent times. See Ch'en, pp. 245-247.

37. See note 26.

38. Prip-Møller, p. 329.

39. Prip-Møller, pp. 297-352. He returned to observe the spring ordination in 1931.

40. Reichelt, *Truth and Tradition,* pp. 234-247.

41. De Groot, *Le Code du Mahayana,* pp. 207-255.

42. Prip-Møller (p. 304) states that new arrivals came two months ahead of time, spent only three days as guests, and then moved to their separate halls. On the opening day of the course a final regrouping took place and registration was closed.

43. Prip-Møller (p. 307) states that they were usually referred to as *ta shih-fu, erh shih-fu,* and so forth.

44. See p. 363. Reichelt and Prip-Møller state that the first five vows were taken by the lay and clerical ordinands together, after which the former retired so that the latter could take the remaining five of the ten vows.

45. Prip-Møller, p. 317. Reichelt was also permitted to witness it and wrote: "A quiet solemnity, which has no parallel in the usual Buddhist worship, prevails." See his *Truth and Tradition,* p. 243.

46. The fifty-eight vows of the *Fan-wang ching* are translated by De Groot in *Le Code du Mahayana,* pp. 14-88.

47. The most striking discrepancies between the testimony of my informants and the accounts given by Prip-Møller, Reichelt, and De Groot involve the occasions on which each successive set of vows was taken. According to Prip-Møller and Reichelt, the 250 vows were taken during the sramanera ordination and the fifty-eight vows of the *Fan-wang ching* were taken during the bhiksu ordination. This is emphatically contradicted both by De Groot and all my informants. Since Reichelt was both friend and mentor for Prip-Møller, it was presumably he who misled him. It would be very easy for an observer to misunderstand what he was observing. Even if he knew Chinese, how could he catch the words of the ritual, mumbled by an aged abbot or droned in response from three hundred throats? There was no way to correlate the texts with what he saw.

But even as to what they saw, these eyewitnesses do not agree. De Groot states that the begging bowls, clothes, and other regalia were given to the ordinands during the bhiksu ordination. Reichelt, Prip-Møller and my informants say that they were given during the sramanera ordination (according to my informants, only the patriarch's robe was given during the bhiksu ordination). Reichelt puts the burning of scalps at Pao-hua Shan in the evening *after* the bodhisattva ordination. Prip-Møller puts it on the morning of the day *before* (as do De Groot and my informants).

De Groot starts his account with the extraordinary statement that leaving lay life (*ch'u-chia*) was the first part of the ordination ceremony and consisted in taking the Five Vows. This confusion of tonsure with ordination can also be found in Chinese authorities, as for example, in the *Tz'u-hai* entry on ordination certificates (*tu-tieh*—see *yen* p. 203). The Ch'ing code appears to state that certificates were given in connection with tonsure, that is, when the head was *shaved*, not burned. If tonsure was administered without an ordination certificate, the penalty was eighty blows. See *Ta-ch'ing lü-li hsin-tseng t'ung-tsuan chi-ch'eng* (New enlarged comprehensive edition of Ch'ing legal code; Shao-chou, 1898), 8:23. The only way to reconcile this with recent practice would be to assume that by "tonsure" the code meant "tonsure and ordination." This is not the current usage.

48. At P'u-t'o Shan, however, the final vows are said to have been taken on the birthday of Kuan-yin, that island's patron deity.

49. In 1925, during the autumn ordination at the Ching-tz'u Ssu, Hangchow, the opening of "ordinands' hall" fell on the 15th of the eighth month, the novices' ordination on the 1st of the ninth month, the bhiksu ordination on the 15th, and the bodhisattva ordination on the 19th, adding up to thirty-four days for the total period of ordination. Prip-Møller, p. 329.

50. From the ordination interval, it is still possible to estimate the total period of ordination, or "ordinands' hall." Assuming that preparation for the novices' vows lasted two weeks, the total period should be these two weeks plus the ordination interval. Ordination certificates show that at Pao-hua Shan in 1919, the ordination interval was twenty-four days, indicating that the total period was thirty-eight days; in 1925 the interval was again twenty-four days; in 1931, twenty-three days; in 1940, fourteen days. The last ordination, however, was exceptional, because it took place under the Japanese occupation. In recent times, then, the total period at Pao-hua Shan appears to have been close to thirty-seven or thirty-eight days, as stated by the catechist.

A longer period was often devoted to "thousand monks ordination" (*ch'ien-seng chieh*), also known as a "time of arhats" (*lo-han ch'i*). This was held to celebrate the sixtieth, seventieth, or eightieth birthday of an eminent abbot. A much larger number of ordinands than usual would flock to be ordained under his auspices, and the ordination lasted longer. In 1937 and 1948 thousand monk ordinations, said to have lasted fifty-three days, were held in honor of Yüan-ying's sixtieth and seventy-first birthdays. See *Yüan-ying fa-shih chi-nien k'an*, pp. 13-14. In 1941 the ordination at Ch'i-hsia Shan is said to have run from the 15th of the second month to the 8th of the fourth (this would have been fifty-three days if the third month had had the usual thirty days instead of twenty-nine). In 1933, however, when twelve Europeans were ordained there with exceptional solemnity, the ordination interval at Ch'i-hsia Shan was only twenty-two days (Tao-chün [Martin Steinkirk], *Buddha und China: Tsi-hia-schan*, Potsdam, 1940, p. 16).

51. The examples from Ku Shan and Hunan were supplied by my own informants; the rest are from Prip-Møller, p. 311.

52. Prip-Møller, pp. 310-312. It would appear that Hsü-yün brought the longer ordinations of central China to the monasteries he restored in other parts of the country. For example, at the Hua-t'ing Ssu in Kunming the total period of

ordination was said to have been thirty-eight days in 1948. Certificates show that the ordination interval was twenty-two days at the Nan-hua Ssu, Kwangtung, in 1944 and twenty-three days in 1949.

53. Documentary sources give the following figures:

	Spring 1916	Spring 1930	Winter 1940
Monks ordained	794	380	269
Nuns ordained	188	35	18
Novices ordained	17		7

The 1916 and 1940 figures come from the ordination yearbooks of those years, while the 1930 figures are given by Prip-Møller, p. 304. Cf. p. 1 where he states that six to eight hundred monks and nuns were ordained at Pao-hua Shan each year. He was apparently unaware that sometimes novices did not receive the bhiksu ordination, so that there may have been some "novices ordained" in 1930 who are included in his figure for "monks ordained." Six of the novices ordained in 1940 took the bodhisattva vows as well; one took the novices' vows only.

54. See Appendix I, table 1.

55. Other Kiangsu ordination centers included the Ku-lin Ssu (Nanking), Chieh-ch'uang Ssu (Soochow), (see Prip-Møller, pp. 302-304), as well as Chin Shan, Chiao Shan (Chen-chiang), Ch'ing-liang Ssu (Changchow), Kuang-hsiao Ssu (T'ai-hsien). In neighboring Chekiang there were the Ching-tz'u Ssu and Chao-ch'ing Ssu (Hangchow), and the T'ien-t'ung Ssu (Ningpo). None, so far as I know, ordained twice a year like Pao-hua Shan. For some it was annual (Ch'i-hsia, T'ien-t'ung); for others every three years (Chiao Shan and the Chieh-ch'uang Ssu); and for others irregularly. Chin Shan, for example, held ordinations in 1887, 1896, 1900, 1903, 1906, 1910, 1917, 1919, and 1924.

56. My informants did not agree on the amount of the fee. Some remembered it as $2 for monks, some as $4, and some as $5. It probably varied with inflation. In 1960 at the Pao-lien Ssu in Hong Kong it was H.K. $100, which is only a little more in real value. For those who could not afford to pay, the charge was remitted altogether.

57. On the assumption that five hundred extra persons lived at the monastery for fifty days, then to buy the extra grain alone would have cost about $1,500 in the mid-1930's. Other staples also had to be provided, as well as robes, bowls, and texts, etc. At $3 a head all these would have cost another $1,500. Yet the fees from five hundred ordinands (at $2 per bhiksu and more for the rest) might have amounted to only $2,000. If five plenary masses were held during the period of ordination, each yielding a profit of about $500, then the monastery would come out $1,500 "in the black." Otherwise it might not have been able to continue to ordain from year to year.

58. Prip-Møller, pp. 325 and 327.

59. Dr. Arthur Link has told me that he has seen no mention of it in the first series of the *Kao-seng chuan*. In 1110 c.e. the Emperor Hui-tsung, in a series of anti-Buddhist decrees, forbade burning the head, but it was evidently as a practice separate from ordination. See De Groot, *Sectarianism*, p. 80.

60. According to one informant, some monasteries in Peking (he mentioned the Nien-hua Ssu) had the same practice.

61. Pratt, p. 341.

62. Prip-Møller, pp. 318-320. A European who underwent ordination himself

gives an account that differs from Prip-Møller in only a few particulars. He states that the moxa cones were 3 cm high and 1½ cm in diameter. Lit simultaneously, their burning lasted three to four minutes "during which the pain was rather strong." The reason for avoiding sleep the following night was that "the organism had been weakened by the weeks of intensive work and, if one went to sleep, the smoke of the incense would cause an inflammation of the pulmonary system and a further weakening of the heart." See Tao-chün, p. 14.

CHAPTER X: THE MONASTIC CAREER

1. Monks in the Ch'ing dynasty were required by law to participate in ancestor worship and to observe mourning for their kin in the same way as the rest of the population, but these laws were obviously unenforceable. The important fact is that they were not on the register of households and were exempted from the corvee and military service.

2. Another translation of *ching-she* might be "retreat house." It could have a large number of residents, including laymen as well as monks. Indeed it could even be operated by laymen. The term is not confined to Buddhism.

3. Strict monasteries like Chin Shan and the T'ien-ning Ssu would not admit him, but others would. For example, I know of a master and a ten-year-old novice who were allowed to stay at the Liu-yün Ssu, Shanghai, in 1931.

4. The fifth of the 90 *pacittiya* rules (not necessarily observed). See Beal, p. 221.

5. Ts'en Hsüeh-lü, *Hsü-yün ho-shang nien-p'u,* pp. 36-37. Equanimity in the face of rebuff, as well as nine other principles to be followed by pilgrim monks, are expounded in an interesting pilgrims' manual that is summarized by Reginald F. Johnston in *Buddhist China,* pp. 158-167.

6. *Ts'an-fang* and *ts'an-hsüeh* are not in the dictionaries that I have consulted, which give only *yu-fang.* This had the same meaning as *ts'an-fang,* but was not used so often by my informants.

7. Ts'en Hsüeh-lü, *Hsü-yün ho-shang nien p'u,* pp. 14-16. The term used here for "avatar" is *hua-shen.* My informants have used the following terms more or less synonymously: *hsien-shen, hsien-sheng, hsien-ling, hsien-hsing.*

8. *An-chü* (see p. 109). De Groot states that "sermons" were also held at the beginning and in the middle of each of the four seasons; and also on certain festival days, but I think he may be speaking of *shuo-fa* rather than *chiang-ching,* the difference being that the former is not exegesis of a text, but a monk's own presentation of the doctrine. De Groot offers a detailed description of the ritual that preceded both kinds of preaching. See *Le Code du Mahayana,* pp. 133-140.

9. Note that whereas laymen are merely to "listen reverently" (*kung-wen*) monks are expected to "study" (*yen-chiu*).

10. The figures may be exaggerated, but the principle is the same: hearing lectures on the sutras led to a kind of conversion. See Ts'en Hsüeh-lü, *Hsü-yün ho-shang nien p'u,* pp. 35, 42.

11. Cheng-lien, 7:101-103. Cf. Ts'en Hsüeh-lü, *Hsü-yün ho-shang nien p'u,* p. 32, which mentions Fa-jen's lecture at the Kuei-yüan Ssu in 1901—perhaps an anachronism for 1892.

12. Yin-shun, pp. 26-31.

13. Although I have only heard the complete program discussed by the one informant mentioned above, I have been given descriptions of abbreviated *ta-tso* programs by several informants and have attended them myself.

14. See Appendix VI, p. 450.

15. See my article "Dharma scrolls," pp. 118-119.

16. There were apparently many Hua-yen (Avatamsaka) temples in Peking, however. See the list in *Hua-pei tsung-chiao nien-chien*, pp. 58-137.

17. Ts'en Hsüeh-lü, *Hsü-yün ho-shang nien-p'u*, p. 49. An account of more elaborate rites performed to secure a favourable rebirth for animals is given in De Groot, *Le Code du Mahayana*, pp. 122-126.

18. Reichelt, *Truth and Tradition*, p. 286.

19. Prip-Møller, p. 183.

20. Ts'en Hsüeh-lü, *Hsü-yün ho-shang nien-p'u*, pp. 31, 33.

21. In 1895 there were a hundred hermits living in huts on T'ien-t'ai Shan near the Hua-ting Ssu, to which they would go whenever a vegetarian feast was donated. See T. Richard, *Forty-Five Years in China* (New York, 1916), p. 280. In 1937 John Blofeld saw several thousand dollars distributed by rich Chinese pilgrims to all the monks on Wu-t'ai Shan, who received 50¢ each. Blofeld, *Wheel of Life*, p. 140.

22. This kind of ascetic's robe was termed a *na-i*. *Na* was either the character for "patch" or for "contribute." A *pai-na i* was thus a robe with a hundred patches or a robe to which patches had been contributed by a hundred devotees, one patch from each. According to one informant, it could also be called an "eight trigrams robe" (*pa-kua i*) or a "manure sweeping robe" (*fen-sao i*). It was cut like a monk's gown (*ch'ang-kua*) or a full sleeved gown (*hai-ch'ing*) rather than like a robe (*i*). It was part of the original monastic rule in India to make clothing of patches. On the cave see Prip-Møller, pp. 187-190.

23. In some cases several monks would shut themselves up together and recite in relays, day and night.

24. Hodous, p. 21. In 1933 another such monk was observed at Ch'i-hsia Shan whose vow was for three years only. See Tao-chün, p. 7. In 1908, before the Republican period began, Boerschmann photographed a monk at the Fo-ting Ssu, P'u-t'o Shan, who for "some years" had kept a vow of silence and taken no part in collective religious exercises. See Boerschmann, *P'u-t'o Shan*, pp. 173-174.

25. Joseph Edkins, *The Religious Condition of the Chinese* (London, 1859), pp. 188-189.

26. Prip-Møller, p. 323. Prip-Møller made most of his photographs between 1929 and 1933.

27. Reichelt cites a case in which the scars were made with a "spill of burning paper" and in which the branding was followed by infection and delirium. He also mentions an ascetic who "had fastened two large iron hooks into the muscles of his chest. He only wore them when pilgrims were watching." See Reichelt, *The Transformed Abbot*, pp. 56-58. I have heard of nothing like this from my informants or other sources.

28. Prip-Møller, p. 323.

29. Not all the bone was necessarily consumed. Prip-Møller mentions a monk who kept pieces of bone that were left over after burning.

30. Ts'en Hsüeh-lü, *Hsü-yün ho-shang nien-p'u*, p. 28.

31. Wing-tsit Chan, *Religious Trends in Modern China* (New York, 1953), p. 70.

32. Jacques Gernet, "Les suicides par le feu chez les bouddhistes chinois du Ve au Xe siècle." *Mélanges* (Paris: L'institut des hautes études chinoises, 1960), II, 527-558.

33. D. J. MacGowan, M.D., *Self Immolation by Fire and the Avenging Habits of the Cobra* (Shanghai, 1889), pp. 1-24. This was originally printed in the *Chinese Recorder,* 19.10:445-451, 19.11:508-521 (October and November, 1888). What is possibly an intermediate process, halfway between *normal* cremation and self-immolation, is described by Yetts: "Priests have assured me that occasionally their dying brethren are placed in the *kang* or other receptacle and the lid closed actually before death. The Reverend Wilfred Allan kindly contributes the fact that it is the custom at the Wu-ch'ang monastery to place upon the pyre moribund monks seated upon a board. Just as the final release is about to happen, the pyre is kindled and fire is then allowed to take the place of the man's spirit as it leaves the body, and also to help it on its journey to the 'Western Heaven.' " W. Perceval Yetts, "Notes on the disposal of Buddhist dead in China," *Journal of the Royal Asiatic Society* (1911), p. 700, n. 1.

34. *The Sacred Books of the East,* ed. F. Max Muller (Oxford, 1909), XXI, 378-386.

35. The first case was Lang-chao, a devout practicer of Pure Land, who immolated himself at the T'ien-ning Ssu, Changchow, on May 11, 1914 at the age of sixty-nine. He was inspired to do so by reading about Bhaisajyaraja's self-immolation in the *Lotus Sutra*. So motionless was he as he burned that, although his robe had fallen into ashes, the buckle still lay on the slope of his shoulder when they found him. See *Fo-hsüeh ts'ung-pao,* No. 12 (June 15, 1914).

The second case was Ti-chen who immolated himself at the T'ien-t'ung Ssu, Ningpo, on July 23, 1919 at the age of between thirty and forty. He was apparently prompted to do so by the spiritual progress he had made while attending lectures on the *Yüan-chüeh ching* (Sutra of complete enlightenment) given that year at the monastery. See *Hai-ch'ao yin wen-k'u* (Hai-ch'ao yin collections) sec. 3, vol. 5, pp. 119-120 (Shanghai, 1931).

On May 2, 1924 Chü-hsing, a devout menial officer at a Yünnan monastery, whom Hsü-yün had just honored by asking him to serve as witness at an ordination there, took leave part way through the ordination and returned to the subtemple where he lived. Without letting anyone know what he was doing, he piled up straw in the rear courtyard and, seating himself upon it in lotus position, facing west, set fire to the straw and died striking the wooden fish and reciting buddha's name. See Ts'en Hsüeh-lü, *Hsü-yün ho-shang nien-p'u,* p. 79.

On April 29, 1926 Chih-kang, who had spent many years in the leading meditation halls and had become such an adept in Ch'an that he was made an associate instructor at Chin Shan by the Venerable Jung-t'ung, immolated himself in a quiet spot near the Tou-shuai Ssu, Nanking, in imitation of Bhaisajyaraja. He vowed that his act was "an offering to all the buddhas of the three periods and ten directions, dedicated to saving all sentient beings in the six planes of existence." He was forty-two years old at the time. See *Hai-ch'ao yin wen-k'u,* sec. 3, vol. 5, pp. 372-374.

Prip-Møller (pp. 171, 324) mentions that the aunt of a young friend of his, who was "a Chinese lady of good and very devout Buddhist family, took the veil in her youth and entered a nunnery in central China. Not many years ago she mounted the death pyre in religious zeal, having herself made all the preparations."

The sixth case is the one described in the text.

It is interesting that three of these immolations took place at model meditation centers. (The Tou-shuai Ssu, according to some informants, became equal to Chin Shan and the Kao-min Ssu after it was taken over by a monk from Kao-min about 1919. He made it public (*shih-fang*) and operated its meditation hall as at Kao-min.)

36. My source is *To-lun ch'an-shih shih-chi* (The Activities of Reverend To-lun; Hong Kong, 1958), pp. 25-26. This is an unreliable book, but it supplies a photographic reproduction of the newspaper article mentioned, which I have not examined in the original.

37. Mrs. Alice Herz in Detroit (March 1965), Norman R. Morrison at the Pentagon, Roger A. LaPorte at the United Nations, and Mrs. Celene Jankowski in South Bend, Indiana (all in November 1965). The only case that I have heard of outside China before the Vietnamese troubles involved a Chinese monk. In 1959, according to an Associated Press dispatch from Bangkok of December 9, a Chinese Buddhist monk there was seized by the police just as he was about to immolate himself on a five-foot pile of wood, apparently because he had been defrauded of money that he collected to build a hospital.

38. If he was asked to pay a fine for the violation of certain minor rules and he did not have the money, he could be beaten instead. Still, it was pleasanter to have the money. See p. 119.

39. Prip-Møller, pp. 367, 372.

40. None of the informants queried had ever heard of another form of allowance, apparently provided in earlier dynasties to monks who were about to depart from a monastery they had been staying at. Because they would wear out their shoes in their travels, it was called "sandal money" (*ts'ao-hsieh ch'ien*). See Nan Huai-chin, p. 28.

41. The vocabulary for donation is rich. According to my informants, the verb *pu-shih* ("endow") means among other things to give money to a monastery as an institution; the verb *kung-yang* ("support") means to give money to a single monk as an individual; and *chieh-yüan* is most often used of giving money to many monks as individuals, as when for example a layman provides *chai-ch'en* at a vegetarian feast (see Chapter VIII, p. 216); but *chieh-yüan* can also be applied to "fruit gifts" (*kuo-i*) made to a single monk. If he politely refuses to accept such a gift, the donor may press him by saying: "If you do not accept this, I will be unable to make a connection with your [good karmic] causes (*chieh-pu-tao ni-ti yüan*). Please be compassionate and accept." "Incense and oil" (*hsiang-yu*) and "incense and fire" (*hsiang-huo*) are general terms for income from worshippers, including payments for Buddhist services. Whereas *hsiang-i* (see p. 331) is in the nature of a gratuity, *kuo-i* is in the nature of an offering. It is interesting how in all this terminology any reference to money is avoided.

42. There was some disagreement about this among my informants. The abbot of the Nan-hua Ssu in 1948 said that everyone ordained or re-ordained there ended up with twelve scars. But the informant who was himself re-ordained there in 1949 stated that he had his original nine scars burned over again and that no more were added; and indeed I could see with my own eyes that there were but

nine scars on his head. Although the abbot had told me that reburning old scars was dangerous, this monk reported no ill effects. Another informant who was re-ordained at Nan-hua in 1953 had additional scars burned not on his head, but on his forearm. Perhaps re-ordinees had more freedom of choice about moxa than those being ordained for the first time.

43. The dates of Hsü-yün's life are highly controversial. Since many of his followers are proud of his longevity, they resent the questions raised by Hu Shih and others. Neutral observers (that is, those who are neither anti-Buddhist like Hu Shih nor personally affiliated with Hsü-yün) sometimes assert that Hsü-yün himself never spoke of his age (an assertion that is contradicted by his followers). What has raised the gravest doubt in my own mind is the statement in his autobiography that in 1859 he was ordained at Ku Shan under the Venerable Miao-lien (Ts'en Hsüeh-lü, *Hsü-yün ho-shang nien-p'u*, p. 5). But Miao-lien himself was not ordained at Ku Shan until about 1876, and he is unlikely to have presided at an ordination until many years later. Whatever the nature of the master-disciple relationship between him and Hsü-yün, it apparently cannot have started until about twenty years later than is stated in the autobiography, and this twenty years is probably the age by which the autobiography overstates Hsü-yün's age. That would mean he was a hundred, not a hundred and twenty when he died—which is still a most venerable age. The information on Miao-lien is given in C. S. Wong, *Kek Lok Si, Temple of Paradise* (Singapore, 1963), pp. 8-9, on the basis of the monastic history *Ho-shan Chi-le ssu-chih*, 7:83-84.

44. At Chiao Shan the counterpart was said to be called the "sea-cloud hall" (*hai-yün t'ang*). The term *yen-shou t'ang* could also be applied to the hall where the tablets for the living were kept: see p. 203.

45. Also at the Liu-yün Ssu in Shanghai.

46. Prip-Møller, pp. 254-260. Hackmann describes an apartment occupied by a senior or retired officer at the Chen-hsiang Ssu, an hereditary temple in Chekiang. "The size of the floor may amount to (on an average) from twenty to twenty-five square meters. The chief article of furniture is the bed which consists of a solid brown streaked bedstead with contrivances to hang up mosquito nets, with matting and thick woolen coverlets. Besides this there are a table, several chairs, a cupboard or two, at times very pretty, a few scrolls with characters or pictures on the walls, perhaps a plant growing in the pot and a few trifles. The windows are plastered over with paper, but here and there they have a small square pane of glass in the middle, at all events not to let in much light, but so that one can glance through at what is outside. One's impression of a cell is that it is on the whole not uncomfortable. In front of those on the ground floor there is frequently a small courtyard, half garden, shut in by walls, which enhance the peaceful feeling." Hackmann, "Buddhist Monastery Life," pp. 247-248. Hackmann states that the abbot's cell was "neither more comfortable nor more beautiful," which seems not to have been true at the larger monasteries.

47. H. Hackmann, "Das Buddhisten-Kloster Tien-dong in der Chinesischen Provinz Che-kiang," *Zeitschrift für Missionskunde und Religionswissenschaft*, 17:178 (1902). Hackmann does not make it clear whether this was a hall for the aged in general or a place for retirement by ex-officers, but the former seems likely in view of the fact that entry was said to be on the basis of age rather than service. If it were not for the mention of the courtyards, this might be a description of the layout of T'ien-t'ung's eastern meditation hall (see p. 77). The hall for the

aged at the Hai-t'ung Ssu in Canton is described in less favorable terms by H. A. Giles, who saw it about 1880. He says that its three monks lived there by the abbot's "fiat" and "detested" their "enforced residence." They had individual bedchambers apparently opening onto a central hall with an altar in the center to the buddha of longevity, Bhaisajyaguru (a layout also reminiscent of T'ien-t'ung's eastern meditation hall). See H. A. Giles, *Historic China and Other Sketches* (London, 1882), p. 286.

48. At Chin Shan there were private apartments for less than 10 percent of the resident monks to live in retirement.

49. Prip-Møller (p. 163) states that corpses were dressed in their best clothes, including the robe. Yetts (p. 701) agrees. Perhaps this was done in the case of abbots.

50. Prip-Møller states that a large earthenware jar was often used and provides photographs of them. This made the ashes easier to collect.

51. Prip-Møller (p. 165) states that if ashes of the deceased were wanted by another monastery, cremation would be delayed until its representative arrived; or it might be delayed anyway for forty-nine days.

52. Some of this is based on Lai-kuo, 2:31b-32b. The rest is according to my informants. A good eye-witness account of a monk's obsequies and cremation is given by Giles, *Historic China and Other Sketches*, pp. 286-293. The deceased, who had been an ordinary resident of the hall for the aged, was paid full honors by the abbot and the other monks.

53. For a full description of different methods of cremation and burial, the reader may consult Prip-Møller, pp. 163-179.

54. H. C. DuBose, *Dragon, Image, and Demon* (London, 1886), p. 231.

55. According to my informants, they were not sold at auction, as was the earlier custom (see L. S. Yang, "Buddhist Monasteries and Four Money Raising Institutions in Chinese History," *Studies in Chinese Institutional History*, pp. 207-211). Instead, prices were set in advance by the guest department. There was no bidding and the monastery took no percentage of the proceeds, which were wholly used to pay the fees of the monks who took part in the rites and to furnish a vegetarian feast for everyone.

56. Prip-Møller, p. 163.

57. De Groot treats the holding of rites for deceased monks as if it were the usual procedure and gives some of the ritual formulae employed therein. See *Le Code du Mahayana*, pp. 144-145.

58. The names varied. De Groot mentions a "hall of the return to the West" (*hsi-kuei t'ang*), and he states that on the fifth of the seven sevenths the paper tablet was burned and the name of the deceased was inscribed there on a common tablet (*Le Code du Mahayana*, p. 145).

59. For a good discussion of this see Father Herbert Thurston, *The Physical Phenomena of Mysticism* (Chicago, 1952).

60. This is a literal translation, which I use because I find it suits the repellent nature of the object. A more sympathetic rendering would be "person in the flesh."

61. Photographs of these appear in the first edition of Hsü-yün's biography: Ts'en Hsüeh-lü, *Hsü-yün ho-shang nien-p'u* (Hong Kong, 1954), 144 pp.

62. Prip-Møller, p. 179. According to the excellent article by Yetts, meat bodies were "very common" in China. He gives six examples, all from Kiangsu and Hupeh,

and all postdating the T'ai-p'ing rebellion. His investigations showed that fat monks were usually eviscerated and washed out before preservation, whereas thin, dried-out monks were not. The body was placed in a jar on a bed of incense and packed around with charcoal and wadding. Yetts, pp. 712-713. Graham mentions a monk at the Wan-fo Ting on Omei Shan in 1925, who was planning on mummification after death so that he could join the monastery's other meat body in being worshipped as a god (Graham, p. 76).

63. Yetts, p. 721.

64. *Tz'u-hang fa-shih* (Taipei, 1963).

65. Yin-shun, p. 378.

66. They can be found in an early brochure entitled *Tz'u-hang ta-shih chuan* (Taipei, 1959), frontispiece. On the details of his exhumation, see *P'u-t'i Shu,* 7.7:42 (June 1959).

67. No mention of plans for exhumation appeared in the published account in *Hsiang-kang fo-chiao* (Buddhism in Hong Kong), 26:44 (July 1962).

68. *Hsien-tai fo-hsüeh,* No. 9: 29-30 (May 1951). Theravada Buddhists (Hinayanists) naturally find this incorrect and highly offensive.

69. Published as a series of articles in *World Buddhism,* vol. 11, no. 12 (July 1963) through vol. 14, no. 4 (November 1965).

70. For example, Prip-Møller, pp. 379 ff; Chou Hsiang-kuang, *T'ai-hsü, His Life and Teachings* (Allahabad, 1957).

71. Other dates will be given here in their Western form only, but ages will be given by Chinese reckoning.

72. For a few more details on this decision, see p. 248.

CHAPTER XI: THE LAY BUDDHIST

1. *Fo-chiao t'u* is apparently copied from Christian usage. It implies formal adherence to Buddhism just as *chi-tu t'u* implies formal membership in a Christian church, whereas the traditional phrase "to believe in the Buddha" has no such implication.

2. Sidney D. Gamble, *Peking: A Social Survey* (New York, 1921), p. 330. The religion a man claimed depended on his class and education and on who was questioning him. Many Chinese, even those professionally involved, had only a hazy idea of the distinction between religions. Once I asked a Taoist priest what sect of Taoism he belonged to. He replied that he belonged to "the Buddhist sect" (*fo-chiao p'ai*). See Holmes Welch, "The Chang T'ien Shih and Taoism in China," *Journal of Oriental Studies* 4.1-2:206 (1957-1958). Professor W. C. Smith has pointed out that even in the West, the concept of religion in our modern sense is a new one. See *The Meaning and End of Religion* (New York, 1962), ch. ii.

3. Monks and nuns.

4. It differs from the word "layman" (*tsai-chia jen*), which also means "a person living at home" but has no implication of religious affiliation. Mao Tse-tung is a layman in this sense, simply because he is not a monk.

5. In the Esoteric School (Mi-tsung) of Tantric Buddhism, a layman could administer abhiseca (*kuan-ting*) to another layman, although it was more often

done by a lama. The details of this kind of initiation were somewhat different. The disciple took refuge not only in the Three Jewels, but also in his guru.

6. Practice varied with the master. Hsü-yün, for example, gave some of his Refuges disciples both a name and a style. The generation character for the former was *k'uan* and for the latter *fo* (on generation characters, see p. 279). These were the same generation characters he used for his tonsure disciples, and so his tonsure and Refuges disciples together were sometimes referred to as "brothers" (*shih hsiung-ti*) even though the former were in the clergy and the latter in lay life. To other Refuges disciples Hsü-yün gave only a name and no style; and in at least one case he decided that the lay name, which happened to be Wu-yüan ("enlightening cause") was too good to change at all. This was unusual, but it was common to leave *half* the lay name unchanged. Mr. Chu Ching-chou, for example, became Mr. Chu K'uan-ching, that is, to the generation character *k'uan* was added the character *ching* from his lay name. Of the first hundred lay supporters listed in Chu Chieh-hsien, pp. 108-122, twenty-five have a religious name that utilizes one character from the lay name, and in five more cases there are obvious allusions (for example, *lin* "forest" and *sen* "jungle"). On the other hand, the Venerable Yin-kuang appears not to have used his tonsure gatha to name his Refuges disciples, but instead another series of characters: *fu, chih, te, hui, tsung.* When he had taken enough disciples with one, he would switch to the next. Tsung-yang, the restorer of Ch'i-hsia Shan, named his Refuges disciples with the generation character from his *dharma* gatha rather than from his tonsure gatha. One of his disciples told me that this meant that they had the right and the duty to advise and assist Tsung-yang and his dharma "descendants." In fact, Tsung-yang's dharma "grandson" had asked this lay disciple to mediate in a dispute among the monks of the dharma "family." I have heard of no other such case where the dharma gatha was so used, and I suspect that it may be a modernism arising from Tsung-yang's secular orientation.

7. There is considerable variation in the terms used for these certificates. Some were printed up with the heading "ordination certificate" (*chieh-tieh*). Some were headed "*kuei-i tieh*" or "*kuei-i cheng*," which might seem to imply that the holder had only taken the Refuges (*kuei-i*), when in fact he had also taken the Five Vows. Many certificates had borders composed of three rows of tiny circles. A circle was burned each time the holder recited a text or buddha's name. When the border was completely burned, the certificate could serve as a passport through hell and was often placed in his coffin. Cf. note 41.

8. My informant was one of the four hundred.

9. A few informants have stated that the Five Vows were taken by the novices and lay ordinees together and that the novices took the rest of the Ten Vows several days later. But on ordination certificates from Pao-hua Shan for 1931 the date of the Five Vows was the same as the date of the novice's ordination (see Prip-Møller, pp. 331 and 334). According to an upasaka who was ordained at the Nan-hua Ssu in 1935, the Five Vows were not administered until the entire ordination of monks had been completed. If so, it was exceptional.

10. Oddly enough, the abbot of Nan-hua Ssu in 1947-1948 denied that laymen made penitential prostrations until dawn, as I was informed by this informant who had done so himself. The abbot said that lay ordinees stopped their prostrations at about 11:00 p.m. and went to bed.

11. Here at Nan-hua some preferred to burn six, some nine. At Pao-hua Shan, according to one informant, the lay ordination always involved nine scars, burned on the head, not on the arm. In his description of this monastery Prip-Møller agrees that they were burned on the head, but states that in the case of women, at any rate, there were only three, burned in a small square shaved on the middle of the scalp (p. 318). An informant from Peking had only one scar burned and said that this was common there, perhaps because piety was at a lower pitch than in central China. Scars on the forearm would have the advantage of being visible evidence of the ordeal, whereas those on the head would be covered by hair. On the other hand, none of the four hundred persons who received the lay ordination from T'ai-hsü at the Right Faith Buddhist Society in Hankow had any scars burned at all. T'ai-hsü is said to have considered it "superficial."

12. For example, the 1926 ordination yearbook of Ku Shan shows that that year eight of the eighteen upasakas ordained were disciples of Ta-pen, the abbot of Ku Shan. They had taken the Refuges with him at four different small temples in four different parts of Fukien. Eight of the thirty-six upasikas had taken the Refuges with Hua-k'ai, who was one of the seven witnesses of the ordination. It was natural that a monk would bring his disciples to take the vows at an ordination where he himself was officiating. On the average, the thirty-six upasikas had taken the Refuges four years earlier. In 1949 at the Nan-hua Ssu ten of the lay ordinees had taken the Refuges with Hsü-yün ten to fifteen years before, while two had taken them with him only that year—perhaps as part of the preliminaries to the ordination.

13. The problem cannot be resolved by reference to ordination yearbooks, since they often listed persons who had received *only* the Five Vows among those who had received the Five Vows *and* Bodhisattva Vows. This failure to distinguish was "an expedient way of doing things," I was told. Sometimes the lay ordination certificates were printed up with a blank that could be filled in with the words *p'u-sa* if in fact that ordinee had received the bodhisattva ordination. Sometimes they were printed up with the words *p'u-sa yu-p'o* [blank] *chieh ti-tzu* (the blank here being for *sai* [men] or *i* [women]). With such a wording even those who had not received the bodhisattva ordination would be certified as having received it, unless the words *p'u-sa* were struck out—and they would presumably not be struck out if things were being done "the expedient way." This was how certificates were printed up at Pao-hua Shan in 1931 (see Prip-Møller, p. 334). According to the 1940 ordination yearbook of Pao-hua Shan *all* lay ordinees took both sets of vows. Yet according to monks who were ordained and officiated at Pao-hua Shan ordinations, about two-thirds took only the first set. More information is needed.

14. However, it was perfectly possible to administer the Bodhisattva Vows to laymen anywhere, either collectively or alone. Only the bhiksu ordination required an ordaining abbot, confessor, catechist, witnesses, and so on.

15. This detail is mentioned in *Village and Town Life in China*, Y. K. Leong and L. K. Tao (London, 1915), pp. 120-122.

16. J. Dyer Ball, "Tonsure," in Hasting's *Encyclopedia of Religion and Ethics* (New York, 1922), XII, 388. Ball cites this as evidence that Buddhist monks were despised in China. The same interpretation is given in Doolittle, p. 96, and echoed in Gray, I, 112.

17. See De Groot, *Sectarianism*, pp. 116-117.

18. See Appendix I, table 1, col. 6 and 8. Note that the most striking difference was not between the sexes, but between the regions. There were thirty to sixty times more devotees of both sexes in the central provinces than in the northern provinces. These regional differences will be discussed in the next volume.

19. T. Richard, *Forty-Five Years in China* (New York, 1916), pp. 281-282.

20. Day, pp. 32-36. There seems to have been little change since Nevius described the pilgrims visiting Hangchow monasteries in the spring of 1859. "The canals leading to the city were filled for miles in some directions with boats of worshippers, many of whom had come long distances to pay their homage at these sacred shrines . . ." See John L. Nevius, *China and the Chinese* (New York, 1869), pp. 96-97.

21. Reichelt, *Truth and Tradition*, pp. 293-294.

22. Graham, pp. 10-11. Graham says that they summarized these purposes as "seeking happiness"—presumably *ch'iu-fu,* a term used by Buddhists to mean seeking happiness as the reward for the meritorious acts that they are performing.

23. André Migot, "Le Bouddhisme en Chine," *Présence du Bouddhisme* (edited by René de Berval), Saigon, 1959, p. 709. Reichelt gives an even more affecting description of pilgrims, of their silence except for prayer, their pure vegetarian diet, and their swollen feet. See *Truth and Tradition*, pp. 294-295.

24. *Ch'ao-shan chin-hsiang.* According to other sources, monks and laymen alike had the names of the four elements embroidered on their bags. Reichelt states that the lay pilgrims to Chiu-hua Shan wore a sash on their chest embroidered with the character *t'u* for earth, the element corresponding to Chiu-hua Shan. See Reichelt, *The Transformed Abbot*, pp. 64-68.

25. For a photograph of one, see Prip-Møller, p. 137.

26. Hackmann, "Das Buddhisten-Kloster Tien-dong," p. 176. Boerschmann provides a really striking photograph of such a suite at the Fa-yü Ssu on P'u-t'o Shan in 1908. The furnishings, arranged in impeccable order, look fit for a palace. They had been donated by a high official in Tientsin in 1894. See Boerschmann, *P'u-t'o Shan*, p. 148 (cf. floor plan on p. 146).

27. It is a common practice for Refuges disciples in Taiwan to live permanently at a monastery and hold monastic offices, particularly those connected with housekeeping.

28. See p. 153. On the lay owners of small temples, see p. 133. Nevius states that the "superior" and "overseer" of each large monastery were "chosen by persons outside the priesthood, who act as a board of managers." See Nevius, *China and the Chinese,* p. 98. In a similar vein, J. J. M. De Groot states that "to every monastery there is attached a committee of *tung-shih,* 'managers, administrators,' composed of prominent people who organize fund-raising for the support of the institution. Their personal contributions are usually among the largest, for in China one is not prominent unless one has a lot of money and spends it on a large scale" (*Le Code du Mahayana,* p. 100). Despite repeated inquiry I have failed to discover a single large Buddhist monastery for which such a committee existed on a formal, permanent basis rather than merely as an informal, temporary association to help with some special project of reconstruction or improvement. Cf. Chapter VI, note 8. Lay committees were, on the other hand, almost always in charge of clan temples and often in charge of temples of the popular religion.

29. Mizuno Baigyo, *Shina bukkyo no genjo ni tsuite* (The present state of Chinese Buddhism; Tokyo, 1926), p. 40.

30. On the disinclination of Peking monks to lecture, see T'an-hsü, I, 91-92.

31. Pratt, p. 382. Compare Reichelt's description of the lectures by a famous monk at the Pure Karma Association in Shanghai during the early 1920's: "A number of better class Chinese, both men and women, solemnly gathered to hear the exposition of one sutra or another. All possessed copies of the sutra in question and some brought notebooks and pencils too. After a short act of devotions, the *fa-shih* mounted the rostrum and seated himself. As a rule two and a half hours elapsed before he descended. Another short hymn of devotion and they dispersed" (Reichelt, *The Transformed Abbot*, p. 48).

32. Pratt, p. 364.

33. This lay donor was a Buddhist according to my informant, who was himself a Buddhist. But the mountain involved was Miao-feng Shan, a mainly Taoist center that lay a forty miles' journey northwest of Peking. It is said to have been visited by more pilgrims than any other temple near the capital—hundreds of thousands a year, especially during the first two weeks of the fourth month—so that this lay donor, if in fact he was a Buddhist, can hardly have provided for all of them (see Tun Li-ch'en, pp. 38-39). I repeat this story because it illustrates not only the kind of action that was considered meritorious, but the indifference, perhaps, of some of the laity to the distinction between Buddhism and Taoism.

34. Mizuno Baigyo, *Shina bukkyo kinseishi no kenkyu* (Studies in the history of modern Chinese Buddhism; Tokyo, 1925), p. 86.

35. *Chiu-chi shui-tsai fa-hui. Fa-hui* is an untranslatably broad term that can mean a Buddhist occasion or organization.

36. Doolittle, p. 188; Gray, I, 127; De Groot, *Le Code du Mahayana*, pp. 111-112.

37. E. J. Eitel, *Three Lectures on Buddhism* (Hong Kong, 1871), p. 135.

38. Cf. Mizuno Baigyo, *Shina bukkyo kinseishi*, pp. 48-49.

39. According to Mizuno, lay Buddhists in mainland China during the early Republican period did not acquire their animals from dealers. They bought only those that were on their way to the slaughterhouse or soon scheduled to be. In the case of livestock they gave it not only to monasteries, but also to farmers who would feed it. See footnote 38.

40. There were several different schedules for abstinence. For example, a person fasting six days a month abstained on the 8th, 14th, 15th, 23rd, 29th, and 30th. A person fasting ten days a month added the 1st, 18th, 24th, and 28th. There was also a list of twenty-two special days throughout the year for fasting in the name of Kuan-yin.

41. Compare the practice in the Ching Lou at the T'ien-ning Ssu (p. 103). There were many similar practices. Passports through hell or drafts convertible into large sums once the payee arrived in hell were given their efficacy by the recitation of thousands of Amitabhas and then burned at death. Another meritorious practice was to recite a text, making one prostration for each character.

42. Mizuno Baigyo, *Shina bukkyo kinseishi*, pp. 48-49.

43. See Reichelt, *Truth and Tradition*, p. 169. Reichelt's source is the *Ch'üan-hsiu ching-t'u ch'ieh-yao* (The reasons for practicing Pure Land) by the Ming dynasty monk, Hsi-ming. Reichelt translated the Introduction which quotes the

Mi-le ching (Maitreya sutra) promising ten blessings to those who recite the name of Amitabha. The fifth blessing is that "you will be kept from the danger of fire, water, thieves, knives and arrows, prison, chains, accidents, and untimely death," an immunity that sounds like a Buddhist answer to competition from the Taoists, among whom such all-risk coverage had long been popular. The sixth blessing is that "all your former sins will be blotted out and the creatures you may have killed will cease to insist on revenge." The seventh promises to "invigorate your physical strength [i.e., sexual?] and make you prosperous in all your doings."

44. See Ts'en Hsüeh-lü, *Hsü-yün ho-shang nien-p'u,* pp. 215 ff. This appears to have been during meditation weeks arranged especially for laymen. The Yü-fo Ssu apparently did not have regular meditation during most of the year.

45. See p. 81. Miss Ananda Jennings, a Buddhist from California, sat briefly in the meditation hall of the Nan-hua Ssu in 1948. A monk enrolled there at the time said that she had "done quite well."

46. The figures for Pao-hua Shan in 1930 are taken from Prip-Møller, p. 304. The Ch'i-hsia Ssu yearbook for 1933 in the library of the University of California in Berkeley is the only one that I have seen in any library or bookshop.

47. Gamble, pp. 39-40, 329-330.

48. *Hua-pei tsung-chiao nien-chien,* pp. 56-57.

49. Regional differences in the prosperity of Buddhism will be discussed in the next volume.

50. This cousin was the Venerable Yin-ping; see p. 159.

51. As did the case of Dr. Ting Fu-pao, a naval surgeon. Once when he was traveling on a small overcrowded Yangtze River steamer, it began to capsize in a storm. Everyone called on Kuan-yin to save them and Dr. Ting involuntarily joined in. Just when all seemed lost, he saw a vision of Kuan-yin standing with outstretched arms on the windward side. He struggled up toward her, followed by the other passengers. The ship was saved. Dr. Ting then resigned from the navy, settled in Shanghai, and became one of the most active Buddhist editors and publishers in China. This story is told by Reichelt in *The Transformed Abbot,* pp. 45-47. The illustrious Tai Chi-t'ao, who had taken part in the anti-religious movement in the early part of 1922, tried to commit suicide in October when, on his way up the Yangtze to end the internecine fighting in Szechwan province, he read that it had broken out again. He was fished out of the river and from then on was a devout Buddhist. Ch'en T'ien-hsi, *Tai Chi-t'ao hsien-sheng pien-nien chuan-chi* (Chronological biography of Tai Chi-t'ao; Hong Kong, 1958), p. 33. I suspect that a supernatural or extraordinary experience is one of the commonest causes for conversion.

52. For example, Chao P'u-ch'u, *Buddhism in China* (Peking, 1957), p. 40.

53. In 1935 one monk estimated that three quarters of the total population of China were believers in Buddhism. *Hai-ch'ao yin,* 16.3:28 (March 1935).

54. See Appendix I.

55. *Chung-kuo fo-chiao hui wu-shih-i nien-tu nien-chien* (Yearbook of the fifty-first year of the Chinese Buddhist Association; Taipei, n.d.), p. 2.

CHAPTER XII: THE NATURE OF THE SYSTEM

1. The tenets and history of the various schools and sects of Chinese Buddhism are not essential to the argument here. The reader can find them summarized in J. Takakusu, *The Essentials of Buddhist Philosophy* (Hawaii, 1947), and Ch'en, pp. 297-364.

2. Yin-shun, p. 25.

3. Therefore he received the dharma posthumously from the last master of each sect (cf. p. 278). See Ts'en Hsüeh-lü, *Hsü-yün ho-shang fa-hui*, p. 263.

4. *K'ai-shan tsu.* If there were several monasteries on one mountain, this term might refer to the first monk who settled there. Otherwise it was used of the founder of a particular monastery.

5. See *Hua-pei tsung-chiao nien-chien*, pp. 58 ff. Hsien-shou is another designation for the Avatamsaka sect.

6. Nitchū bukkyō kenkyū-kai, eds., *Hōchū nihon bukkyō shinzen shi-dan hōkokusho* (Report of the visit to China of the Japanese Buddhist Friendship Mission), Kyoto, 1958, pp. 13-15.

7. The Fa-yü Ssu had a special shrine-hall for Bodhidharma, the first patriarch of the Ch'an sect and celebrated his anniversaries (see Boerschmann, *P'u-t'o Shan*, pp. 143-145). According to another source, all the monasteries on P'u-t'o Shan were Lin-chi (Fitch, *Pootoo Itineraries*, p. 14).

8. The monk who began the restoration of the Ling-yen Ssu in 1911 was Chen-ta. Since he served concurrently as the abbot of other monasteries (for example, the T'ai-p'ing Ssu in Shanghai and the Pao-kuo Ssu in Soochow), he left much of the administration in the hands of the prior, Miao-chen, who later became the abbot himself. Yin-kuang's role was that of pre-eminent spiritual leader, without rank or office.

9. In my article "Dharma Scrolls," pp. 103 and 113, I have described how Tsung-yang restored the Ch'i-hsia Ssu in 1919, bringing over the lineage of Chin Shan in a "dividing of the lamp" (*fen-teng*).

10. There are different versions of this categorization.

11. See pp. 92-100. Actually Ling-yen Shan only had six periods a day. One of my informants, however, said that there were also six at Chiao Shan.

12. I have still translated *nien* as "recitation" although here it has the added meaning of "to think of." This account of the three techniques comes from a former abbot of Chiao Shan whom I did not always find to be a reliable source. Professor Masatoshi Nagatomi has pointed out to me that the three techniques are mentioned in Tsung-mi's commentary on the *Avatamsaka Sutra*.

13. According to one informant the students normally did not take part in buddha recitation at all, but only during recitation weeks.

14. There was a Ch'an saying: "Recite one 'Amitabha' aloud and you must wash your mouth out for three days."

15. *Ch'an-men jih-sung*, p. 142.

16. See Ch'en, pp. 403-405, 445-447.

17. Prip-Møller, p. 333.

18. Ts'en Hsüeh-lü, *Hsü-yün ho-shang nien-p'u*, p. 30.

19. Boerschmann states that Taoist monks were only allowed to spend five days in the wandering monks hall of a Buddhist monastery and vice versa (see Boerschmann, *P'u-t'o Shan*, p. 136). My informants have said that in public monasteries there was no such limitation.

20. *Na-mo O-mi t'o-fo* is chanted as to an eight-beat rhythm, by prolonging the *t'o* and the *fo*. By avoiding such a prolongation on the last two syllables the Taoists could work in all eight syllables of *San-ch'ing chiao-chu wu-liang t'ien-tsun*.

21. Prip-Møller, p. 2.

22. Graham, pp. 61-62.

23. One of my informants referred to it as the Nan-yüeh Miao. Reichelt (*The Transformed Abbot*, pp. 85-86) gives its name as Sheng-ti Ta-miao.

24. Sekino and Tokiwa confirm that there were no Buddhists at all on Nan-yüeh before the Ch'en dynasty (557-589 C.E.). The mountain had been occupied by Taoists only. During the T'ang dynasty the Buddhist population rapidly increased. See Sekino Tei and Tokiwa Daijo, *Shina bukkyō shiseki* (Buddhist monuments in China; Tokyo, 1925-1929), IV, 48-49.

25. *Sectarianism*, pp. 149 ff.

26. *Hsien-tai fo-hsüeh*, No. 34:32 (June 1953).

27. T'an-hsü, p. 94.

28. De Groot states that a few did so. *Sectarianism*, p. 219.

29. In one area in Kiangsu "on important occasions such as 'burning incense' for newly dead relatives and fulfilling certain promises to a god after recovering from illness, people go to the big temples in the town or to the bank of the Lake where the gods are more powerful," rather than going to one of the small temples in the village. Fei Hsiao-t'ung, p. 105.

30. Hackmann, *Buddhism as a Religion*, p. 247.

31. Arthur H. Smith, *Forty Years a Missionary in China* (New York, 1912), p. 108.

32. Wing-tsit Chan, p. 54.

33. Ch'en, p. 452.

APPENDIX I: THE SIZE OF THE SANGHA

1. Tsukamoto, Zenryu, "Buddhism in China and Korea," in Kenneth W. Morgan, ed., *The Path of the Buddha* (New York, 1956), p. 224. In this appendix the term "Chinese Buddhist Society" is used for what is referred to elsewhere as the "Chinese Buddhist Association."

2. Nikka bukkyo kenkyukai, ed., *Gendai shina bukkyo kenkyu tokushugo* (Special volume on studies of modern Chinese Buddhism; Kyoto, 1936), p. 314.

3. *Shen-pao nien-chien* (Shanghai, June 1936), pp. 1278-79.

APPENDIX II: THE FORTY-EIGHT POSITIONS

1. Evidently a misprint for *chuang-chu*.

2. Prip-Møller mentions a *ch'ing-k'o* at the Pao-kuang Ssu in Szechwan. He was attached to the *i-po liao* and was in charge of the abbot's personal guests. Prip-Møller (pp. 83, 367) got this information from a "list," along with some other unusual titles. I wonder if the list reflected contemporary or ancient practice, just as I am skeptical of his statement (p. 359) that there was a *t'ieh-an* whose duty was to chop vegetables and serve at meals.

3. The abbot of Chin Shan recalled that in the west there were many canon prefects and contemplatives, but very few librarians, since most persons with

this rank were busy with menial offices. Few with the rank of secretary and above were formally attached to the hall, except for the instructors. In the east there were usually 2-3 deacons, 3-4 thurifers, 10-20 recorders, and dozens of acolytes. These figures were for the winter term. They would be much lower for summer.

4. This is homophonous with the term for an obsolete monastic office, *chih-shih*, that is, the "rooms prefect," who inspected equipment and buildings. It is similar phonetically to the regular word for any office, *chih-shih*. *The chih-shih* in the business office at Chin Shan was a kind of factotum, who took orders from the subpriors and could give orders to the clerks. According to one informant some monasteries in Szechwan had such a "functionary" who worked either in the business office or the guest department, assisting the subpriors or the guest prefects. The title was used in the Six Dynasties for a sangha official (see p. 144) and in the Ch'ing bureaucracy for the archivist or confidential clerk on the staff of a provincial judge.

5. At Chin Shan they were librarians, deacons, and thurifers. At the T'ien-ning Ssu they were canon prefects and contemplatives.

APPENDIX III: MEDITATION HALL SCHEDULE

1. This is what I was told by all but one of the informants who had lived at Chin Shan. Its code of rules, however, shows a variation in the hour of rising from 3:30 a.m. in the eleventh month to 1:45 a.m. in the sixth month; and in the hour of retiring from 11:00 p.m. in the twelfth month to 9:00 p.m. in the sixth month. There was the same discrepancy between oral and documentary accounts in the case of the Kao-min Ssu. Its code of rules has a step-by-step variation totaling one hour between the times of rising in the twelfth month and the fifth month. See Lai-kuo, 3:47. The only Kao-min monk I have queried about it denies that this variation existed in practice. The abbot of T'ien-ning Ssu denies any seasonal variation there. Because monks lived by signals, not by a clock, the truth of the matter could best be settled by interviewing the person who gave the signals, that is, the night patrol (*yeh-hsün*)—an officer I have yet to meet.

2. Hence the seven periods (*ch'i-chih hsiang*) could also be considered fourteen periods. If one asks how many periods of meditation used to be held at a certain monastery and the answer is "twelve," one cannot be sure whether it means twelve or six. "One period" (*i-chih hsiang*) can mean either one period of running (*i-chih p'ao*) or one period of sitting (*i-chih tso*) or the two together considered as one. I use "cycle" for the latter sense.

3. One informant, displaying little conviction, offered the hypothesis that this *ch'i* has the idea of starting to strike (*ch'iao-ch'i-lai*). In any case, the word is apparently reserved for the night patrol's board.

4. Bowing to the north is considered to be bowing to the buddha image, although this is in the center of the hall and hence in a different direction vis-à-vis each monk. "Anyway, the Buddha is everywhere," as one monk explained. Facing north is the traditional Chinese orientation of reverence, since the emperor faced south.

5. The duty monk stands with his back to the main door, facing north, bows, walks two paces west, three north, two east, and, at the first sound of the

chime, he prostrates himself before the buddha image and rises. At the second chime, he prostrates himself again and rises. At the third chime, he prostrates himself, at the fourth rises, bows, walks two paces east, three south, two west, and bows again. It is with this third bow that the succentor strikes the chime a fifth time and the period begins.

6. Or simply *chiaō-hsiāng*. This is confusing because it is a homophone of the *chiaō-hsiāng* struck by the rice steward, and by the precentor on his summons rod.

7. At 10:00 p.m., however, instead of the gong, the large drum in the great shrine-hall is struck.

8. The short strokes are struck lightly and hence are called "dot sounds" (*tien-sheng*). They only count as half notes, so that these two series are considered to have four and a half notes each.

9. These three strokes are termed "answering bell" (*ta pao-chung*).

10. The same term is used for the striking of the summons rod (see above under "one fish").

11. Or ||| according to one informant.

12. Or |||| according to one informant.

13. At Pao-hua Shan it was so slow that the answering bell took 30-40 minutes.

14. Each stroke represents a sentence or a word. For example, during the first stroke the bellman should recite: "May the vast sounding of this bell and the lofty intoning of this precious gatha penetrate to heaven above and reach the chambers of hell below. . . ." The text may be found in *Ch'an-men jih-sung*, p. 121. The slow strokes represent one sentence apiece; the fast strokes represent one word apiece. Different versions are given in Henri Doré, *Researches into Chinese Superstitions* (Shanghai, 1914), I, 126.

15. On which have just been struck the last notes of "raise board" (see glossary above), so that the musical chain has not been broken.

16. Some monks do not recall an Explanation being given at this point.

17. The rice steward has a clock in his apartment, but none in the kitchen itself. This custom, however, presumably dates from long before the days of clocks.

18. *Ssu-chih hsiang* could also, of course, mean "four periods of meditation." There is no distinction here between cardinal and ordinal numerals.

19. It is so few circuits for such a long period because everybody has just enjoyed a long nap and is therefore presumed to be wide awake and in little danger of nodding.

20. It is the striking of the signal, not the retiring of the monks, that is termed *k'ai ta-ching*. Thus during meditation weeks (10/15-12/5) monks do not retire until long after *k'ai ta-ching*, as the reader will see below.

21. This branch of liturgy is also referred to as *fan-pei*.

22. The end of meditation weeks (*chieh-ch'i*) is considered to come after breakfast congee on the 6th of the twelfth month.

23. The word "to sleep" (*shui-chiao*) is avoided in the terminology of the meditation hall, *fang yang-hsi* or *hsiu-hsi* being the commonest substitutes.

24. They do not shave, however, during the last three of the seven meditation weeks. At the end of the second and fourth weeks they bathe, shave, and change their clothes as usual (these days are termed *hsiao chieh-ch'i*).

APPENDIX V: HEREDITARY PUBLIC MONASTERIES

1. More information on the Szechwan monastery will be found on pp. 239-240.

2. The figure recollected by the abbot was 2,000 *tan* a year (100 *chin* to the *tan*).

3. More details on the novitiate system at the Fu-hu Ssu will be found on p. 284.

4. On the other hand, Dr. Dryden L. Phelps, translator of *Omei Illustrated Guide Book* (Chengtu, 1936), has told me that according to his recollection there might have been two hundred monks or more in residence. He knew the Fu-hu Ssu as a training center for novices with a large complex of buildings. An early Republican guidebook calls it "the largest of the numerous temples on the mountain." See *Official Guide to Eastern Asia* (Tokyo, 1915), IV, 173.

APPENDIX VI: THE DHARMA OF THE T'IEN-NING SSU

1. This chart and the information below that relates to it are partly based on statements by an abbot of the T'ien-ning Ssu and partly on the history of the monastery that he edited: Cheng-lien, *chüan* 2 and 7. The chart is not necessarily complete. The masters may have taken other disciples besides those shown here, although those shown here include all who served as abbot.

2. There is a contradiction as to the generation numbers. According to *Ch'an-men jih-sung, tsung-p'ai*, 3b, Cheng-lien 7:63, and Chu Chieh-hsien, p. 63. Shan-ching Ch'ing-ju was of the 41st generation. But according to the Cheng-lien, 8:85 and the statements of the former abbot of T'ien-ning, Wei-k'uan was of the 46th generation. I can find no means of reconciliation, not even by counting generations of service rather than of transmission. (At some temples and monasteries the abbot "of the third generation" [*san-tai*] meant the third monk to serve as abbot, who might be of a quite different generation according to tonsure or dharma lineage. This does not appear to have been an accepted way of counting at large public monasteries, where dharma brothers were considered to be abbots of the same generation.)

3. Cf. Chu Chieh-hsien, p. 62, and Cheng-lien, 2:3 and 7:27-30.

4. See pp. 159-160.

5. Seniority among dharma brothers bore no necessary relation to chronological age.

6. Cheng-lien refused to name these two, who had gone off to head monasteries in northern Kiangsu. "T'ien-ning did not recognize them," he shouted. "It [the monastery] was handed downwards, not to uncles. . . . Don't write in their names. It's all finished (*suan-le*)!" Was his vehemence because they had done something to bring discredit on the monastery or because he felt they had "let the family down" or simply because I was persisting in asking a question that he considered unimportant?

7. Although *shuang-ch'uan* strictly means dual transmission, it is applied also to multiple transmission. Before the forty-first generation the Chin Shan dharma was transmitted to several disciples in each generation, but only one of them became abbot. See Ch'iu-yai, *Chin-shan-chih hsü-chih* (Supplement to the history of Chin Shan; published by the Ya-yü T'ang in the Kuang-hsü period, n.d.), 2:37-48.

8. "This sect (*p'ai*) [i.e., this gatha] was used by meditation master Huan-yu

Cheng-ch'uan for tonsure; and by meditation masters T'ien-yin Yüan-hsiu and Mi-yün Yüan-wu for transmitting the dharma." *Ch'an-men jih-sung, tsung p'ai*, 3b. But T'ien-yin was Huan-yu's dharma disciple. They were 29th and 30th generation respectively in the Chin Shan lineage. More investigation (and perhaps a different translation) is needed.

9. It appears to be only recently that T'ien-t'ung ceased to transmit the dharma in connection with the abbotship (see p. 170). Early Republican editions of the *Ch'an-men jih-sung* state that "today" T'ien-t'ung used this gatha for dharma transmission and had even composed a continuation in twenty characters starting after the character *k'ung*, which might not have been reached until late in the nineteenth century. According to many of my informants T'ien-t'ung belonged to all sects or to no sect (Prip-Møller, p. 304, states that it "now embraces all schools indiscriminately"). The fact is, however, that its board was still Lin-chi in the 1930's and its lineage had been Lin-chi within the past century.

10. Similarly Huan-yu Cheng-ch'uan of the 29th generation incorporated in his name a shift from the original Lin-chi gatha (with the character *ch'uan*) to the gatha written by Tsu-ting (with the character *cheng*) as can be seen by comparing the third line on p. 3 with the ninth line on p. 3b of the *Ch'an-men jih-sung, tsung-p'ai*. The explanation might be that Cheng-ch'uan received the dharma from two masters—one of the original Lin-chi lineage and the second of the Tsu-ting sub-lineage—and perpetuated only the second because the gatha of the first had run out. Curiously enough, Tsu-ting is termed "the 15th generation of T'ien-t'ai," although he appears actually to have been the 11th generation under Ching-shan (see p. 3, line 12). All this bristles with problems that need investigation.

11. According to Ch'iu-yai, 2:51, Chin Shan's abbot of the fortieth generation, Kuang-tz'u Chen-chi, composed a new gatha in fifty-six characters to be used for his "descendants." (This is the gatha that was reproduced in Welch, "Dharma Scrolls," note 123. The text given there, in which two characters, *hsien* and *hua*, differ from the text in the *Chin-shan-chih hsü-chih*, was taken from a notebook kept by the abbot of the Ch'i-hsia Ssu, who was one of the descendants in this lineage.) However, the first four characters of this new gatha were identical with the eighteenth through the twenty-first characters of the hundred and twelve character gatha on p. 4 of the *tsung-p'ai* section of the *Ch'an-men jih-sung*. Two abbots of Chin Shan and the T'ien-ning Ssu informed me that these monasteries had shifted in concert about 1850 to the hundred and twelve character gatha; that T'ien-ning had continued to use it (as its lineage shows); but that about 1910 Chin Shan had shifted to an entirely new gatha composed not by Kuang-tz'u, as the history states, but by Ch'ing-ch'üan. This new gatha, however, began by utilizing as its first four characters the eighteenth through the twenty-first of the hundred and twelve character gatha in order to provide a connecting overlap. The fact that the T'ien-ning Ssu did not follow suit indicates that the "family" connection between the two monasteries had grown weaker.

Further research will be needed to determine whether the truth lies with my informants or the monastery history. In any case it is clear that I erred ("Dharma Scrolls, pp. 137-138) in stating that the first four characters of Chin Shan's new gatha "were the last four characters of the gatha that preceded it" and that the latter had "run out," as I had been told by the abbot of Ch'i-hsia Shan. Regardless of the circumstances of Chin Shan's shift or shifts, one reason appears to have been the fear that since other institutions were using its gatha, there would be duplication in naming, and monks at different monasteries might receive dharma names both characters of which were the same.

APPENDIX VII: PERPETUAL LEASEHOLDS

1. They usually signed with a cross, since most were illiterate. Sometimes a deposit would be accepted in lieu of guarantors.

2. Tenants in these areas furnished their own seed, fertilizer, tools, and labor.

3. Fei Hsiao-t'ung (pp. 174-196) reports the same tenure system in Kai-hsienkung, but what I translate as "tillage rights" he calls "surface ownership" and what I translate as "ownership rights" he calls "subsoil ownership." For neither term does he give the original Chinese. Fei points out that the price of "subsoil ownership" varied with the amount of urban capital seeking an outlet in the countryside. He states that tenants (that is, holders of surface ownership) could be expelled, according to law, if they failed to pay their rent for two years, "but the law does not apply to those places where custom is paramount" (p. 184). He does not say whether "custom was paramount" in Kaihsienkung, but my informants make it clear that it was in I-cheng, Yangchow, and so on. It is odd that we find this system along the north bank of the Yangtze and south of Lake T'ai, but not around Changchow which lay in between. At any rate, no "subsoil rights" were held by the T'ien-ning Ssu.

4. Chin Shan owned its tenants' houses in T'ai-chou and originally had to keep them in repair, a responsibility which it managed to shift to the tenants.

APPENDIX VIII: MORTGAGE LOANS

1. Elsewhere this was said to have been called *yin-tsu*. *Kan-tsu* was apparently a Changchow localism.

2. Then termed *t'ien-tan*. A plot certificate was issued on each parcel of land by the *hsien* government. When a peasant bought land, he was given a deed (*ti-ch'i*) from the former owner and took it to a *hsien* government office which handled these transactions and was popularly called the *liang-fang*. Before title could be transferred (*kuo-hu*), it had to be searched. The authorities would then stamp the deed and issue new plot certificates for all the parcels it covered. Before the deed was stamped, it was termed a "white deed" (*pai-ch'i*). Afterwards, because the stamping was done with a red seal, it was termed a "red deed" (*hung-ch'i*). Only titles covered by red deeds were guaranteed by the government (*kuan-t'ing*). Land could not be sold without giving the plot certificates to the new owner. Hence, they were often pledged as security when borrowing money. Each plot certificate had a map and a number that corresponded to the number in the land register. The term *t'ien-tan* was later replaced by *so-yu ch'üan-cheng*.

3. Published data indicate that land values in the Changchow area doubled between 1912 and 1923 and almost doubled again by 1930, but dropped back 50 percent by 1933. See John Lossing Buck, *Land Utilization in China: Statistics* (Nanking, 1937), p. 168. This may have been partly the result of the legislation for the protection of tenants that was passed in 1933 and partly the result of increasing unrest in the countryside.

4. These appear to be local terms. The abbot explained that the *t'u-tung* was a

"notary" (*kung-cheng jen-shih*) who adjudicated any matter large or small that came up in his district. The *t'u-cheng* was a kind of public land surveyor, who knew the boundaries and settled boundary disputes. He was in charge of the register of plot certificates (*t'ien-tan ti ts'e-tzu*) and knew the serial numbers of the plot certificates (*t'ien-tan ti hao-t'ou*). The register had a map of the plots, showing the number of each. Both these gentlemen worked under the head of the township or district (*hsiang-chang* or *ch'ü-chang*) as a public duty, and received no salary, nor did they receive any regular compensation from the T'ien-ning Ssu, although if they did a particularly good job, it would give them a present. The *t'u-tung* was of higher status than the *t'u-cheng*. Together they were called *tung-shih,* and to some extent played the same role as village foremen (*chuang-t'ou*) elsewhere.

APPENDIX IX: CALCULATION OF LANDED INCOME

1. The number of residents varied from a maximum of about four hundred when the meditation hall and wandering monks hall were full, as they might be in winter, to less than three hundred during the summer term. See Appendix II.

2. It was probably less in north China monasteries, where a higher proportion of the diet was wheat. I have only one figure to offer: a monk recalled that at the Chan-shan Ssu, Tsingtao, rice consumption was 12 *liang* (ounces) a day. But even in the south, wheat consumption was sometimes high. At the Ling-yin Ssu, Hangchow, according to a former subprior, the average resident ate 2.35 *tan* (piculs) of polished rice and 1.17 *tan* of wheat flour in the course of a year. The Ling-yin Ssu had a much larger per capita income from rites and devotions than the Chan-shan Ssu; they received negligible rents from farmland.

3. One *tan* (picul by volume) of the best paddy would yield five *tou* (bushels) two *sheng* (pints) of polished rice, according to the abbot of Chin Shan. However, since what they consumed at the monastery was not their best rice, they counted on getting only four *tou* from a *tan* of paddy at the mill. In other words, the loss by volume was 60 percent. This still meant a weight loss of only about 30 percent. In the rice trade the rule of thumb is that husking reduces 100 *chin* of paddy by 20 *chin*, and polishing takes off 8 *chin* more: the weight loss is 28 percent. In terms of volume, husking and polishing together result in a 50.5 percent reduction. I am indebted for this and other information on the rice trade to Mr. Yeh Hsin-ming (Hsing-min Yeh), director of the Shanghai rice market after the Second World War, and to Mr. T. Y. Tung.

4. The number of *chin* in a *tan* is a troublesome question. *Tan* may be either a unit of weight or a unit of volume. If the former, it is written with the hand radical plus the surname Chan and is normally equivalent to 100 *chin*. If it is a unit of volume, it is written with the character shih ("stone"), but pronounced *tan* in the fourth tone, exactly like the character *tan* just mentioned. Some Chinese are unaware that *tan* by weight and *tan* by volume may be written differently. Others think that the *tan* by volume should be pronounced "shih." In casual conversation it is very easy for misunderstanding to arise. The number of *chin* of paddy in a *tan* by volume varied from place to place. In the T'ai-chou *tan* there were 120 *chin* of paddy. In the Changchow *tan* there were 100. At Ch'i-hsia Shan there were 145. On the Shanghai rice market there were 110, but this was market *chin* in a market *tan*. A market *chin* was a half kilogram, equivalent to 0.8378 old

standard *chin* (*k'u-p'ing chin*). Therefore a market *tan* of paddy had 92.3 old standard *chin*. The weight of a *tan* of paddy thus varied from 92 to 145 *chin* within an area of 100 miles. The weight of the *chin* also varied. The standard *chin* contained 16 *liang*. But the T'ai-chou *chin* was equivalent to 14 *liang* 6 *ch'ien*, and the Chen-chiang *chin* was equivalent to 16 *liang* 8 *ch'ien*, in contrast to the market *chin* which was equivalent to 13 *liang* 4 *ch'ien*. Thus to say that the T'ai-chou *tan* had 120 *chin* is really to say that it had 109 *chin*. At this point I shout "save life!" to the nearest agronomist. The abbot of Chin Shan told me that the monastery kept its inventory in *tan* of 120 *chin*, but since these were presumably Chen-chiang *chin*, they were really *tan* of 124 *chin*. I wonder if the monks knew how much paddy they had any better than I do.

5. Chiu, pp. 740-741. The 1920-1936 average price for local rice on the Shanghai rice market was $12 per picul of 172 lbs., according to William Rhoads Murphey, III, *Shanghai: Key to Modern China* (Cambridge, Mass., 1953), p. 142.

6. Chiu, p. 475.

7. This as of the mid-1930's. Of its 1949 total of 1,449 *mou*, 4 were wasteland and 262 were acquired in about 1939. See Chu Chieh-hsien, pp. 123-132.

8. These were the figures recollected by its former abbot, the Venerable Ming-ch'ang. He also recollected other, contradictory figures. For example, he quoted the rule of thumb that annual production per *mou* was 3 *tan*, of which Ch'i-hsia Shan received a third. But since he insisted that there were 145 *chin* in a *tan*, this would mean per *mou* production of 435 *chin* (not 300) and rents per *mou* of 145 *chin* (not 125). I was unable to resolve these contradictions, though I am impressed by the fact that they would largely disappear if we discarded the "heavy" *tan*, about which this informant, usually so reliable, may be mistaken in what he remembers. By an odd coincidence, there are 145 *chin* in a *tan* of milled rice (old measures). I pointed this out to him, but he stuck to his figures. I have nonetheless assumed a *tan* of paddy to weigh 120 *chin* in calculating the market value of Ch'i-hsia Shan's surplus rice.

Bibliography

Agrarian China, comp. and tr. by the research staff of the Secretariat, Institute of Pacific Relations. London, 1939; 258 pp.

Amano Motonosuke 天 野 元 之 助 *Shina nogyo keizai-ron* 支 那 農 業 經 濟 論 (The Chinese agricultural economy), vol. I. 2nd ed., Tokyo, 1942; 754 pp.

Beal, Samuel. *A Catena of Buddhist Scriptures From the Chinese.* London, 1871; 436 pp.

Blofeld, John Eaton Calthorpe. *The Jewel in the Lotus.* London, 1948; 193 pp.

——*The Wheel of Life.* London, 1959; 263 pp.

Boerschmann, Ernst. *P'u-t'o Shan.* Berlin, 1911; 203 pp.

——*Picturesque China: Architecture and Landscape.* New York, 1923; 288 pp.

Chan, Wing-tsit. *Religious Trends in Modern China.* New York, 1953; 327 pp.

Ch'an-men jih-sung 禪 門 日 誦 (Ch'an breviary). Hangchow, 1926; 170 + 18 pp.

Ch'en, Kenneth K. S. *Buddhism in China, A Historical Survey.* Princeton, 1964; 560 pp.

Cheng-lien 證 蓮 *Ch'ang-chou T'ien-ning ssu-chih* 常 州 天 寧 寺 志 (History of the T'ien-ning Ssu in Changchow). Shanghai, 1948; 11 *chüan.*

Chiu, A. Kaiming. "Agriculture," in *China,* ed. H. F. McNair. Berkeley, 1946; pp. 466-491.

Ch'iu-yai 秋 崖 *Chin-shan-chih hsü-chih* 金 山 志 續 志 (Supplement to the history of Chin Shan). Published by the Ya-yü T'ang 雅 雨 堂 in the Kuang-hsü period; 2 *chüan.*

Chou Hsiang-kuang. *A History of Chinese Buddhism.* Allahabad, 1955; 264 pp.

————*Dhyana Buddhism in China.* Allahabad, 1960; 216 pp.

Chu Chieh-hsien 朱 潔 軒 ed. *Ch'i-hsia shan-chih* 棲 霞 山 志 (History of Ch'i-hsia Shan). Hong Kong, 1962; 170 pp.

Chu-yün 燕 雲 *Chin-shan huo-fo* 金 山 活 佛 (The Living Buddha of chin Shan). Taipei, 1959; 157 pp.

Chung-kuo fo-chiao hui wu-shih-i nien-tu nien-chien 中 國 佛 教 會 五 十 一 年 度 年 鑑 (Yearbook of the fifty-first year of the Chinese Buddhist Association). Taiwan, n.d.; 15 pp.

Day, Clarence Burton. *Chinese Peasant Cults.* Shanghai, 1940; 243 pp.

De Groot, J. J. M. "Buddhist Masses for the Dead in Amoy," *Actes du sixième Congrés International des Orientalistes,* pt. 4, sec. 4, pp. 1-120. Leiden, 1885.

————*Le Code du Mahayana en Chine, son influence sur la vie monacal et sur le monde laique.* Amsterdam, 1893; 271 pp.

————*Sectarianism and Religious Persecution in China.* Amsterdam; vol. I (1903), vol. II (1904); 595 pp.

Doolittle, Justus. *Social Life of the Chinese.* Rev. Paxton Hood; London, 1868; 633 pp.

Edkins, Joseph. *The Religious Condition of the Chinese.* London, 1859; 288 pp.

————*Chinese Buddhism.* London, 1890; 453 pp.

Fei Hsiao-t'ung. *Peasant Life in China.* London, 1939; 300 pp.

Fitch, Robert F. *Hangchow Itineraries.* Shanghai, 1922; 94 pp.

————*Pootoo Itineraries.* Shanghai, 1929; 90 pp.

Fried, Morton H. *Fabric of Chinese Society.* New York, 1953; 243 pp.

Gamble, Sidney D. *Peking, a Social Survey.* New York, 1921; 521 pp.

Gernet, Jacques. "Les suicides par le feu chez les bouddhistes chinois du Ve au Xe siècle," in *Mélanges.* Paris: L'institut des hautes études chinoises, 1960; II, 527-558.

Graham, David Crockett. *Religion in Szechwan Province, China.* (Washington, 1928), vol. 80, no. 4 of Smithsonian Miscellaneous Collections; 83 pp.

Gray, John Henry. *China, a History of the Laws, Manners and Customs of the People.* London, 1878; 2 vols.; vol. I, 397 pp.; vol. II, 374 pp.

Hackmann, H. "Buddhist Monastery Life in China," *East of Asia Magazine,* 1.3:239-261 (September 1902).

————"Das Buddhisten-Kloster Tien-dong in der Chinesischen Provinz Che-kiang," *Zeitschrift für Missionskunde und Religionswissenschaft,* 17:173-178 (Heidelberg, 1902).

————*Buddhism as a Religion.* London, 1910; 315 pp.

————*A German Scholar in the East.* London, 1914; 223 pp.

Hai-ch'ao yin 海 潮 音 Hangchow and elsewhere, 1920—

Hai-ch'ao yin wen-k'u 海 潮 音 文 庫 (Hai-ch'ao yin collections), sec. 3, vol. 5; Shanghai, 1931; 516 pp.

Hodous, Lewis. *Buddhism and Buddhists in China.* New York, 1924; 84 pp.

Hsien-tai fo-hsüeh 現 代 佛 學 (Modern Buddhism). Peking, 1950——

Hua-pei tsung-chiao nien-chien ti-i hao 華 北 宗 教 年 鑑 第 一 號 (North China yearbook of religion, No. 1). Peking, 1941; 712 pp.

I-jun Yüan-hung 儀 潤 源 洪 ed., *Pai-chang ts'ung-lin ch'ing-kuei cheng-i chi* 百 丈 叢 林 淸 規 證 義 記 (Pai-chang's pure rules for large monasteries with explanatory notes). Yangchow, 1917; 8 *chüan.*

Johnston, Reginald F. *Buddhist China.* London, 1913; 403 pp.

Lai-kuo 來 果 *Kao-min ssu kuei-yüeh* 高 旻 寺 規 約 (Code of rules of the Kao-min Ssu). 3 *chüan;* Taipei, 1960.

Ling-yen nien-sung i-kuei 靈 巖 念 誦 儀 規 (Liturgy and ritual of Ling-yen). Hong Kong, 1962; 202 pp.

Little, Archibald John. *Mount Omi and Beyond.* London, 1901; 272 pp.

Mizuno Baigyo 水 野 梅 曉 *Shina bukkyo kinseishi no kenkyu* 支 那 佛 敎 近 世 史 の 研 究 (Studies in the history of modern Chinese Buddhism). Tokyo, 1925; 91 pp.

Nan Huai-chin 南 懷 瑾 *Ch'an-tsung ts'ung-lin chih-tu yü chung-kuo she-hui* 禪 宗 叢 林 制 度 與 中 國 社 會 (The Ch'an monastic system and Chinese society). Taipei, 1962; 58 pp.

Osgood, Cornelius. *Village Life in Old China.* New York, 1963; 401 pp.

Pai-chang ch'ing-kuei. See I-jun Yüan-hung.

Phelps, Dryden L. *Omei Illustrated Guide Book.* Chengtu. 1936; 353 pp.

Pratt, James Bissett. *The Pilgrimage of Buddhism and a Buddhist Pilgrimage.* New York, 1928; 758 pp.

Prip-Moller, J. *Chinese Buddhist Monasteries.* Copenhagen, 1937; 369 pp.

Reichelt, Karl Ludwig. *Truth and Tradition in Chinese Buddhism.* Shanghai, 1927; 330 pp.

——*Religion in Chinese Garment.* London, 1951; 180 pp.

——*Meditation and Piety in the Far East.* London, 1953; 170 pp.

——*The Transformed Abbot.* London, 1954; 157 pp.

Sekino Tei 關 野 眞 and Tokiwa Daijo 常 盤 大 定 *Shina bukkyo shiseki* 支 那 佛 敎 史 蹟 (Buddhist monuments in China; Tokyo, 1925-1929). 5 vols.; 5 separate folios of plates, with 150 plates each.

Shryock, John. *The Temples of Anking.* Paris, 1931; 206 pp.

Smith, George. *A Narrative of an Exploratory Visit to Each of the Consular Cities of China and to the Islands of Hong Kong and Chusan in the Years 1844, 1845, 1846.* 2nd ed.; London, 1847; 467 pp.

Taisho shinshu daizokyo 大 正 新 修 大 藏 經 (Taisho Tripitaka), ed. Takakusu Junjiro 高 楠 順 次 郞 and Watanabe Kaigyoku 渡 邊 海 旭 Tokyo, 1924-1929; 55 vols.

T'an-hsü 倓 虛 *Ying-ch'en hui-i lu* 景 塵 回 憶 錄 (Reminiscences of shadows and dust). 2 vols.; Hong Kong, 1955; vol. I, 246 pp; vol. II, 304 pp.

Tao-chün [Martin Steinkirk]. *Buddha und China: Tsi-hia-schan*. Potsdam, 1940; 30 pp.

Tokiwa Daijo 常 盤 大 定 *Shina bukkyo shiseki kinen-shu* 支 那 佛 敎 史 蹟 記 念 集 (Buddhist monuments in China, memorial collection). Tokyo, 1931.

Ts'en Hsüeh-lü 岑 學 呂 *Hsü-yün ho-shang fa-hui* 虛 雲 和 尙 法 彙 (Religious writings of the Venerable Hsü-yün). 2nd ed.; Hong Kong, 1962; 442 pp.

———*Hsü-yün ho-shang nien-p'u* 虛 雲 和 尙 年 譜 (Chronological biography of the Venerable Hsü-yün). 3rd ed.; Hong Kong, 1962; 427 pp.

Tun Li-ch'en. *Annual Customs and Festivals in Peking,* tr. and annotated by Derk Bodde. Peking, 1936; 147 pp.

Welch, Holmes. "Dharma Scrolls and the Succession of Abbots in Chinese Monasteries," *T'oung Pao,* 50.1-3:93-149 (1963).

Wong, C. S. *Kek Lok Si, Temple of Paradise*. Singapore, 1963; 131 pp.

Wu-ming 悟 明 *Jen-en meng-ts'un* 仁 恩 夢 存 (Kindnesses remembered). Taipei, 1963; 271 pp.

Yang, C. K. *Religion in Chinese Society*. Berkeley, 1961; 473 pp.

Yetts, W. Perceval. "Notes on the disposal of Buddhist dead in China," *Journal of the Royal Asiatic Society* (July 1911), pp. 699-725.

Yin-shun 印 順 *T'ai-hsü ta-shih nien-p'u* 太 虛 大 師 年 譜 (Chronological biography of the Venerable T'ai-hsü). Hong Kong, 1950; 544 pp.

Yüan-ying fa-shih chi-nien k'an 圓 瑛 法 師 紀 念 刋 (Memorial volume for the Reverend Yüan-ying). Singapore, 1954; 122 pp.

Glossary Index

The ideograms for every Chinese term in this book are given in the principal entry, which is (1) the English translation if this represents an effort to standardize; or (2) the romanization if a standard translation seems unnecessary or impractical. Thus the ideograms for *chien-yüan* (prior), as well as the page numbers for all references to priors, will be found under "P", since "prior" is the translation advocated and used throughout this book; under "C" the reader will only find *"chien-yüan,* see prior." On the other hand the ideograms for *"hsin-liang hsiao,"* which might be translated a number of ways, will be found with the romanization under "H", along with the single page reference.

Common names (like Shanghai or Sun Yat-sen) are not indexed or are given without ideograms.

The location of monasteries is approximate, just as it is in Chinese usage. "T'ien-t'ung Ssu (Ningpo)" means simply that the T'ien-t'ung Ssu is in the general area of Ningpo (actually it is about twenty-two kilometers east-southeast of that city).

The names of some important persons are followed by their dates and by biographic tags, which are offered to facilitate identification, not as epitomes of their lives.

A few minor corrections of punctuation and spelling have been incorporated in the entries below.